PERSPECTIVES ON COGNITIVE CHANGE IN ADULTHOOD AND AGING

PERSPECTIVES ON COGNITIVE CHANGE IN ADULTHOOD AND AGING

Edited by

Fredda Blanchard-Fields

Georgia Institute of Technology

and

Thomas M. Hess

North Carolina State University

The McGraw-Hill Companies, Inc.
New York   St. Louis   San Francisco   Auckland   Bogotá   Caracas
Lisbon   London   Madrid   Mexico City   Milan   Montreal   New Delhi
San Juan   Singapore   Sydney   Tokyo   Toronto

McGraw-Hill

A Division of The **McGraw·Hill** *Companies*

PERSPECTIVES ON COGNITIVE CHANGE IN ADULTHOOD AND AGING

This book is printed on acid-free paper.

1 2 3 4 5 6 7 8 9 0   DOC   DOC   9 0 9 8 7 6

ISBN 0-07-028450-4

This book was set in Garamond 3 by ComCom, Inc.
The editors were Beth Kaufman and Fred H. Burns;
the production supervisor was Elizabeth J. Strange.
The cover was designed by Joan Greenfield.
R. R. Donnelley & Sons Company was printer and binder.

Library of Congress Catalog Card Number: 95-81973

Fredda Blanchard-Fields is an associate professor of developmental psychology at Georgia Institute of Technology. She received her Ph.D. in life span developmental psychology from Wayne State University in 1983, pursuing interests in social cognitive and post formal development in adulthood and aging. Since then her program of research continues to examine adaptive developmental changes in adulthood in various areas of social reasoning. She has published articles in the general area of social cognition and aging, including causal attributional processing, everyday problem solving, coping, and perceived controllability from adolescence through older adulthood. Her research on causal attributional processing and aging is funded by grants from the National Institute on Aging. She is a fellow of the American Psychological Association (APA) and serves on the editorial board of major journals in the field.

Thomas M. Hess is a professor of psychology at North Carolina State University. His interest in aging and cognition was sparked as a graduate student at Southern Illinois University and become more fully developed more fully while a postdoctoral fellow at the Duke University Center for the Study of Aging and Human Development. Since his arrival at NCSU in 1981, he has conducted extensive research (supported by the NIA) examining how people represent information in memory, with a specific focus on understanding the impact of age-related variations in both basic processing and knowledge-based mechanisms. In 1990, he edited a book, *Aging and Cognition: Knowledge Organization and Utilization,* on this topic. Currently, his research focuses on age differences in representation and decision—making in social contexts. Professor Hess serves on the editorial boards of major journals in the field. He is also a fellow in the American Psychological Association, American Psychological Society, and Gerontological Society of America.

CONTENTS

SECTION 4: COGNITION IN CONTEXT

F O R E W O R D

Our popular images of older people abound in paradox. On one hand, we associate aging with decline and disability; on the other hand, some of our most respected leaders and popular entertainers are in their 60s, 70s, and even 80s. On one hand, we characterize older adults as forgetful, slow to deliberate and act, and easily confused; on the other hand, we value their experience, achievement, and practical knowledge. On one hand, older adults are criticized for their inflexibility and rigidity; on the other hand, they are praised for their wisdom.

The irony, of course, is that each of these portrayals of older adults is accurate. The above characteristics can be observed in different people at various phases of later life, and reflect the diverse and multifaceted qualities of cognitive aging. I learned this lesson as an adolescent, when two older people were influential in my life. The first was my grandfather, a dour curmudgeon, slow to speak and act, whose commitment to routine and respect conflicted with my teenage rebelliousness. But as a retired professor of mechanical engineering, his practical skills were awe-inspiring, especially when he was repairing appliances, inventing simple tools, or when we were riding on wooden cars behind a steam locomotive that he had built from scratch during his retirement. The other older gentleman was a retired family friend who lived at a nearby nursing home, holding court when family and friends came to visit. I appreciated the thoughtful understanding he brought to our conversations even as I noticed the care with which he wrote notes to remember names, appointments, and other important reminders. Perhaps it is unsurprising that like any other period of the life course, we can see considerable variability in the kinds of cognitive changes that older adults experience with increasing age and in how they adapt to those changes.

Perspectives on Cognitive Change in Adulthood and Aging offers a fascinating portrayal of these multidimensional changes in cognition, and their origins and implications for adult life experience. The editors of this volume, Fredda Blanchard-Fields and Thomas M. Hess, are respected researchers who have studied topics such as real-world problem-solving, self-awareness of cognitive functioning, and memory in the context of everyday tasks and needs with older adults. Together they have assembled an outstanding group of contributors who are not only first-rate researchers in this field, but who also teach courses in cognitive aging for undergraduate and graduate students. The result is a resource that will be useful to teachers and students, as well as experienced researchers, interested novices, and anybody else seeking a current, comprehensive survey of theory, research, and applications of knowledge on later-life cognitive change.

One accomplishment of these contributors is that they force us to reconsider what we mean by "cognition." Rather than a single ability that waxes or wanes over time, this volume presents a dazzling array of intellectual abilities that each vary not only by age, but also by the situations to which they are applied, the kind of information that is cognitively processed, and the meaning of that information to the person. According to these authors, "cognition" includes (but is not limited to) the attentional processes by which people focus on meaningful and relevant information and ignore distractions; memory skills that can be deliberately or automatically applied to new information, and which include not only long-term retention but also the more immediate juggling of different ideas, thoughts, or directions in mind at one time; reasoning abilities (such as those evaluated on intelligence tests) that may enlist one's prior knowledge and experience, or may instead require relating new concepts and ideas; problem-solving skills that are applied to experimentally created tasks or the everyday challenges of fixing a leaky pipe, planning a vacation, or resolving a misunderstanding with a friend; adaptive thinking that confronts life problems from varying perspectives and approaches (sometimes called wisdom); and the capacity to understand and adapt to one's changing cognitive abilities in ways that maintain self-esteem and foster goal-attainment. In light of these (and other) portrayals of "cognition," it is not surprising to find that the changes that occur in later life are diverse and complex.

Likewise, these contributors also cause us to reconsider how we think about aging. Although some cognitive changes arise from the biological decline of sensory or processing capacities (consistent with everyday portrayals of aging), these are a surprisingly small part of the developmental story to be told. Another chapter in this story concerns the growth of expertise, whether concerning the professional capabilities of an experienced physician, the aesthetic sensibility of a mature poet or musician, or the practical skills of a seasoned gardener or chess-player. Other parts of the story concern the ways that older people adapt and compensate for the limitations they experience in ways that make their cognitive skills more specialized, and focused on the capabilities that are most meaningful or relevant to them. Another part of this developmental account distinguishes the intellectual resources required for abstract, hypothetical problem-solving (of the kind in which younger adults excel) from those required for practical, experience-based reflection, in which adult age differences are not so apparent. Yet another chapter in this developmental story concerns the importance of context, emphasizing that the cognitive skills that are developed or maintained in highly structured settings (like some nursing homes) are different from those fostered by the practical challenges of independent living and stimulation afforded by close friends and grandchildren who live nearby. As a consequence, how we think about the nature of development throughout the life course is challenged and richly elaborated by these portrayals of cognitive change in adulthood.

The thoughtful contributors to this volume aid our understanding of these changes in many ways. Each of these chapters provides an up-to-date, state-of-the-art presentation of current research concerning cognitive aging and brings this knowledge to the practical level by exploring its relevance to the everyday life experience of older adults, as well as examining central concerns for future research. Besides writing with obvious enthusiasm and insight for the topics they discuss, these authors also provide a list of supplementary readings to inspire further study. Each chapter is well-referenced, enabling interested students to explore in further detail the issues that interest them. Taken together, these authors make it easy to see why the study of later adulthood has inspired such interest among contemporary scholars.

The *McGraw-Hill Series in Developmental Psychology,* of which this volume is a part, has been designed to enrich and expand our common knowledge of human development by providing a forum for theorists, researchers, and practitioners to present their insights to a broad audience. As a rapidly expanding scientific field, developmental psychology has important applications to parents, educators, students, clinicians, policymakers, and others who are concerned with promoting human welfare throughout the life course. Although the fruits of scholarly research into human development can be found on the pages of research journals, and students can become acquainted with this exciting field in introductory textbooks, this series of specialized, topical books is intended to provide insightful, in-depth examinations of selected issues in the field from which undergraduates, graduate students, and academic colleagues can each benefit. As forums for highlighting important new ideas, research insights, theoretical syntheses, and applications of knowledge to practical problems, I hope that these volumes will find many uses: as books that supplement standard general textbooks in undergraduate or graduate courses, as one of several specialized texts for advanced coursework, as tutorials for scholars interested in learning about current knowledge on a topic of interest, and as sourcebooks for practitioners who wish to traverse the gap between knowledge and application. The authors who contribute to this series are committed to providing a state-of-the-art, accurate, and readable interpretation of current knowledge that will be interesting and accessible to a broad audience with many different goals and interests. We hope, too, that these volumes will inspire the efforts to improve the lives of children, adolescents, and adults through research and practice that are much needed in our world.

Whether you are reading the chapters that follow from the personal perspective of someone who is at the vanguard of adulthood or its zenith, I hope you find the study of intellectual development and adaptation that is revealed in *Perspectives on Cognitive Change in Adulthood and Aging* illuminating and provocative.

Ross A. Thompson
Consulting Editor

P R E F A C E

The field of adult development and aging is rapidly growing, owing to changes in popula-tion demographics (i.e., the graying of America) and to the realization that beyond adoles-cence, the latter half of the life span is a dynamic period of growth and change deserving of study in its own right. One result of this growth is the emergence of college courses and pro-grams of study that either incorporate or center on adult development. With the evolving sophistication of the field have also come increasingly sophisticated textbooks dealing with adulthood. For example, it used to be the case that textbooks in life span psychology were nothing more than child development texts with a few chapters dealing with adulthood and aging tacked on to the end. Now, life span books provide much greater and more coherent coverage of adulthood, another indication of the maturity of the field. Mounting research on the psychology of adulthood and aging has also led to increased specialization in course of-ferings. For example, it is not uncommon these days to find courses on cognitive change in adulthood or the social psychology of aging at the undergraduate and/or graduate level. Un-fortunately, the development of textbooks for such courses has lagged behind course devel-opment.

The creation of this book is related to this last observation and came about initially for somewhat selfish reasons. We both teach courses on cognitive change in adulthood and aging, but have been unable to find an up-to-date text that is completely to our liking. There are many excellent books on the market that deal with cognitive functioning in adulthood. They offer outstanding coverage of specific content areas on adult cognitive change (e.g., memory, information processing) and/or provide a particular conceptual orientation (e.g., focus on decrement). Often, the focus of these books is in keeping with their stated purpose as either reference volumes or treatises meant to promote a specific theoretical viewpoint. However, the strength of the focus of these books also suggests several limitations when the course to be taught demands a broader perspective on cognitive change in adulthood. First, the somewhat narrow focus of these books is inconsistent with our views of what a course on cognitive change in adulthood should be like. Thus, we wanted to develop a text that fit our needs for our courses and, at the same time, those of other people teaching similar courses. Second, many of these books also are written at a level that assumes some advanced back-ground in the study of aging and/or cognition, and thus are inappropriate for both under-graduate and graduate students who are seeking a more introductory approach.

In thinking about what we wanted this book to be like, we carefully considered our ap-proaches to teaching about aging and cognition and the goals of such a course. In our courses, we emphasize the complex nature of cognitive change in terms of both the level of analysis and the theoretical orientations guiding research. It is our belief that an emphasis on the di-versity of approaches to the study of adult development and aging, and subsequently en-couraging students to think about the implications of these different approaches is the best way to get them thinking about this complexity. This involves not only exposing students to different content areas and theories, but also having them think about basic conceptual and methodological issues associated with the study of cognitive change.

There are several ways in which this book addresses the above concerns. First, we offer broad coverage of content and associated theoretical views on cognitive change in adulthood.

We, of course, recognize that a book of this type has constraints in terms of the amount of information covered, so we selected topics that were representative of major lines of research and/or that were well-developed conceptually. For example, the area of memory has received prodigious attention in both past and present research. Accordingly, we include three chapters that deal specifically with varying perspectives on memory changes in adulthood. Our hope is that this will be an ongoing project in which future revisions will reflect changes in the field. Thus, for example, as investigations into the biological bases of cognitive change in adulthood become more sophisticated, we anticipate including a chapter that addresses this topic. Similar coverage might be afforded on topics such as creativity or wisdom.

Second, each chapter contains a discussion of basic conceptual and methodological issues and how they interrelate to provide diverse research paradigms within a content area. This approach is initiated in the first three chapters of the book, which expound upon the necessary connection between theoretical perspective, types of questions asked, and resulting methodology implemented. Third, the book is written in a manner that does not assume in-depth background in either cognition or aging. Thus, it is written more as a text than a reference book. Each chapter introduces specific issues, theories, and methodologies pertinent to the topic as well as a review of the extant literature. Finally, each chapter is written by a different author with a specific area of expertise. This approach is intended to promote a broad perspective given the diversity of viewpoints taken by these leading experts in the field.

This book is intended primarily for advanced undergraduates and beginning graduate students. At the undergraduate level, it could serve as the primary text for a course on aging and cognition or one of several texts for a broader course on the psychology of aging. At the graduate level, it could serve as the primary text around which a seminar on aging and cognition might be organized. Additional readings of primary source materials could be assigned to supplement the text. In either case, we assume that students with minimal exposure to either cognition and/or aging should benefit from use of this text. It should also serve as a convenient reference for more advanced students and researchers.

ACKNOWLEDGMENTS

Obviously, any project such as this comes about as a function of the efforts of many individuals. First of all, we would like to thank the people at McGraw-Hill for their assistance in bringing this project to fruition. In particular, we would like to thank Jane Vaicunas, whose initial enthusiasm for the project was a major impetus in motivating us to go forward. We would especially like to thank Beth Kaufman, whose subsequent encouragement, support, and advice were essential in developing the final product. Second, we would like to thank the chapter authors, whose excellent contributions to this book have helped us to realize our goal. We especially appreciate their willingness to adhere to our guidelines and put up with our organizational demands in writing their chapters. Finally, we would like to thank all those people who reviewed this book or portions thereof during its development. These people include Jane Berry, Cameron Camp, Joe Fitzgerald, Reinhold Kliegl, Ralf Krampe, Gisela Labouvie-Vief, Ulman Lindenberger, Joan McDowd, Don Mershon, David Mitchell, Jane Rankin, Robin West, and Karen Zabrucky, each of whom reviewed individual chapters. We would also like to thank several reviewers who reviewed the entire product at various stages of development: Victor Cicirelli, Purdue University; Joan Erber, Florida International University; Bert Hayslip, University of North Texas; Karen Hooker, Syracuse University; William Hoyer, Syracuse University; Susan Kotler-Cope, Department of Veterans Affairs Medical Center, Birmingham, Alabama; Margie Lachman, Brandeis University; Stuart Offenbach, Purdue University; and George Rebok, Johns Hopkins University. Their comments were invaluable in developing and fine-tuning the final product.

Fredda Blanchard-Fields
Thomas M. Hess

PERSPECTIVES ON COGNITIVE CHANGE IN ADULTHOOD AND AGING

1

FOUNDATIONS

C H A P T E R

1

INTRODUCTION TO THE STUDY OF COGNITIVE CHANGE IN ADULTHOOD

Thomas M. Hess
North Carolina State University
Fredda Blanchard-Fields
Georgia Institute of Technology

The images of aging in our culture are quite varied, both in terms of real people and in terms of societal beliefs, institutions, and symbols. Think for a moment of the manner in which we depict older adults in our society, for example, through portrayals in television shows, movies, and commercials. Often, older adults are depicted as incompetent, forgetful (but lovable) fools whose memory problems lead to comic or catastrophic outcomes. At the other extreme, the older adult may be depicted as a wise old sage whose lifetime of experience has led to a wealth of knowledge about life and whose advice is sought by those of lesser years. A good example of both of these images can be found in a recent soft drink commercial, in which a young girl asks her grandfather if he can remember when he had his first Pepsi. The grandfather proceeds to detail the circumstances surrounding each of the thousands of Pepsis he has consumed over his lifetime, only to misremember his granddaughter's name. Similar images can be seen in real life. Think for a moment of older adults whom you have known. Chances are, some of these individuals will have exhibited very real instances of problems in memory and cognitive functioning at a relatively early age (e.g., early 60s). In some cases, these problems may have been linked with aging-related health problems, such as cardiovascular disease or Alzheimer's disease. At the same time, it is also likely that you can identify individuals who have continued to exhibit high levels of competency well into their 70s and 80s. Oftentimes, these individuals are healthy, physically and socially active, and still engaged in profession-related activities. Former Supreme Court Justice William Brennan, who continued to be an energetic, articulate, and thoughtful leader until he retired at age 84, comes to mind as a clear instance of this latter case.

One thing that should be evident from these examples is that we often get mixed messages about the nature of adult development. In actuality, these mixed messages typify some of the major themes that characterize research and theory on adult development and aging. For example, there is clear evidence of individual variability in the nature and rate of change in adulthood. Although some common trends might be identified, we do not all age in the same manner. Those older adults who continue to exhibit high levels of functioning may do so partially through their ability to either adapt to changing life circumstances or compensate for normative changes in specific cognitive abilities. In addition, differential patterns of change in ability among individuals may be related to factors such as health, an individual's activities, and the context in which an individual is functioning. Similarly, the process of aging does not affect all abilities in the same way. Normative data indicate that some types of skills stay at the same level or continue to increase throughout most of adulthood, whereas others exhibit decline, sometimes beginning as early as young adulthood. In particular, older adults may continue to exhibit high levels of competency in familiar situations and in areas of expertise, where skills are well practiced and a strong knowledge base exists to support performance.

Based on these observations, it should be evident that cognitive change in adulthood is an extremely complex process. In effect, this is the basic theme of this book. In the chapters that follow, the themes introduced here will be repeatedly introduced and elaborated upon, both conceptually and empirically, within the context of specific content areas, such as memory, intelligence, and problem solving. As we note later, however, the emphasis on individual themes varies across content areas depending upon the specific theoretical and metatheoretical frameworks adopted by the researcher and the types of questions associated with these perspectives. The purpose of this chapter is to provide an introduction to the study of cognitive change in adulthood by highlighting the historical roots of the field, its current status, and some basic issues or themes that characterize research and theory. We begin by discussing societal views of aging and their relationship to science.

AGING, COGNITION, AND SOCIETY

Societal beliefs about aging become quite compelling when the rapidly changing demographic composition of the United States (the "graying" of America) is taken into consideration. In particular, the increasing number of middle-aged adults (the baby-boom generation), along with the increasing number of older adults living longer lives, has forced us to reexamine the capabilities and needs of an aging population. As an example of these changing demographics, the percentage of Americans who are 65 or older has more than tripled since 1990 (from 4.1% to 12.6%), and it is estimated that the percentage will grow to 21 percent by the year 2030 (U.S. Bureau of the Census, 1992). Such numbers highlight both the growing impact of our society's aging population and the importance of developing a realistic understanding of older adult competencies that goes beyond stereotypes.

■ Aging as a Social Issue

A number of social issues involving cognitive competence have surfaced as a result of changing population structures, including those having to do with the training and productivity of older workers, mandatory retirement, health care, housing, and older adults' place in society. Again, mixed messages about the nature of adult development and aging are reflected in controversial decision making regarding these social issues. To illustrate, one current controversy centers around the question of whether normative, aging-related deficits in cognitive skills necessarily imply a mandatory retirement age. Federal legislation in 1986 made it illegal to use age as a basis for making retirement decisions in most professions. Several professions, however, were excluded from this law, one example being commercial airline pilots. Currently, these pilots are required by law to retire by age 60 due to beliefs and data regarding the impact of normative declines in cognitive skills on performance combined with concern for public safety. For example, evidence suggests that the speed of processing auditory messages and the ability to remember text materials decline with age (see Chapter 8), which in turn has negative implications regarding the comprehension and retention of messages received from air traffic controllers. Research also shows, however, that older pilots can perform comparably to younger pilots when air traffic control messages are presented in a standard format or when voice communication is amplified by visual presentation (Morrow, Leirer, Altieri, & Fitzsimmons, 1994). In addition, there are great individual differences in memory performance in any given situation, so that some older adults actually exhibit better memory performance than some younger adults do. These types of data complicate the formulation of policies regarding mandatory retirement based solely on age. Similar issues involving mandatory retirement have surfaced in the law enforcement profession (Landy & Shankster, 1994).

Perhaps a more general workplace issue, and one that is implied in mandatory retirement policies, concerns the productivity of older workers. Given that individuals live longer, healthier lives, the average number of years spent working has increased considerably (8 years since 1900; U.S. Bureau of the Census, 1992). This trend, along with that associated with the questioning and elimination of age-based mandatory retirement policies, has naturally led to questions regarding the productivity of older workers. Concerns have been raised because productivity and job performance have been found to be associated with cognitive abilities (see, e.g., Schmidt, Hunter, Outerbridge, & Goff, 1988) and cognitive abilities have been shown to decline with age, suggesting a negative correlation between age and productivity. There is also evidence, however, that experience and job knowledge may mediate such effects in certain professions (see, e.g., Avolio, Waldman, & McDaniel, 1990). Consistent with research on older pilots, older workers may maintain a high degree of job performance due to their greater job-relevant knowledge, experience, and skills, despite normative evidence that older adults may decline in certain cognitive abilities (Salthouse & Maurer, in press). Thus, as before, the relationship between age and performance in the workplace is not a simple one.

A second issue, independence of living and everyday functioning, has also become of great concern to society given the increasing number of extremely elderly adults. However, as M. Baltes (1988) points out, dependency in older adults is at least partly a function of a social environment that operates to develop and maintain dependent behaviors and is perhaps not a reflection of the true competence level of the elderly. For example, research has shown that minor environmental manipulations to decrease dependency can result in dramatic changes in exhibited cognitive competencies (Langer & Rodin, 1976). Baltes states further that dependent behaviors can function as a means of securing control within the social domain through social contact, touch, and supportive attention (M. Baltes & Reisenzein, 1986). This latter finding relates well to research on everyday cognitive functioning in areas such as problem solving. A number of studies demonstrate that in social and emotional domains, middle-aged and older adults have a larger repertoire of experience from which to operate (Blanchard-Fields & Camp, 1990), are better at integrating emotional information (Carstensen & Turk-Charles, 1994), and use more effective strategies (Cornelius & Caspi, 1987).

Overall, these social issues and concerns emphasize the importance of research in cognition and aging. It is the mandate of such research to obtain a more complete and accurate picture of changing abilities in adulthood so that we can better evaluate and understand competencies in older adults (e.g., distinguish between deficient performance due to actual decline or deficits in the environment). Equipped with this information, we can (1) adjust our expectations and interactions with older adults and (2) better inform policy making regarding social issues on aging.

■ Social Stereotypes

As just noted, the confusion inherent in making social decisions regarding when an older adult should retire or competency decisions about the elderly placed in nursing homes highlights the need to understand the aging process better. This need for more information, as reflected in such social dilemmas, is particularly underscored by our society's history of beliefs and stereotypes of aging.

Historically, aging simply represented a time of irreversible decline and/or a necessary precursor to death (Freeman, 1979). These beliefs about aging are revealed in such folk wisdom as "You can't teach an old dog new tricks"; in derogatory stereotypes of older adults as "dirty old men" or "old geezers"; and in the biomedical view of aging solely as a physiological deteriorative process leading to death. It is interesting to note that much of the folk wisdom, views, and stereotypes about aging involve cognitive functioning. For example, Heise (1987) reports that the American stereotype entails a substantial decrease in power and activity. The older adult's mental processes are expected to return to the "shallow level of the child," unfolding at a slower rate. Studies also show that older adults are judged more negatively than are younger adults, particularly in the areas of mental competence and physical attractiveness (Kite & Johnson, 1988), absent-mindedness, forgetfulness, dependence (Heckhausen & Baltes, 1991), and cautiousness and slowing (Heckhausen, Dixon, & Baltes, 1989). In addition, social stereotypes such as decreased mental flexibility and increased dependency in the elderly may be based in cognitive stereotypes (e.g., a decrease in cognitive competence resulting in an increased reliance on others).

Recent research suggests, however, that such global negative stereotypes about older adults in our society may not reveal the entire picture of beliefs about aging. Hummert (1990) finds that, in contemporary society, individuals actually hold multiple stereotypes of the elderly which reflect both positive and negative evaluations. Similarly, Kite and Johnson (1988) conclude that individuals hold a multiplicity of attitudes toward and beliefs about older adults. They found that older adults were viewed more negatively than younger adults when they were judged as a group rather than as individuals. When individualized information was provided, the negative ratings were attenuated. For example, if more specific information about an elderly individual were provided that was inconsistent with negative stereotypes about older adults (e.g., active, achievement oriented, competent employee), judges tended to ascribe positive characteristics to the older target. Other research has suggested that stereotypic views of older adults are modified based upon experience. For example, younger adults who have had more social contact with the elderly hold more positive views about older age than those who have had little contact with them (Luszcz & Fitzgerald, 1986). Thus, when older adults are not simply viewed as an abstract group, less stereotypic views of aging emerge.

The growing diversity in people's beliefs about older adults is mirrored developmentally in an individual's evolving views of aging. For example, Heckhausen et al. (1989) found that, in contrast to younger and middle-aged adults, older adults held more differentiated expectations of changes across the latter half of the life span. The older adults not only recognized expected losses in later life but also perceived greater potential for change over adulthood. Similarly, Luszcz and Fitzgerald (1986) found that older adults have less stereotyped views of themselves growing older than they do of older people in general. In essence, it appears that the history of societal views on aging parallels individual life-course changes in how one views aging.

■ Social Issues, Stereotypes, and Behavior

Our concern in exploring stereotypes is based on the assumption that such beliefs might influence the treatment and behavior of older adults. How might social concerns and beliefs about aging impact on the behavior of the older adult? Based on her extensive research on dependency in old age, M. Baltes (1988) suggests that society's negative attitudes toward aging play an instrumental role in creating dependency in older adults. Similarly, Levy and Langer (1994) recently investigated negative stereotypes about aging and its relationship to memory loss in old age. They found that negative stereotypes of aging, such as those discussed above, were prominent in the American culture, whereas more positive views of aging were found in the Chinese culture. Furthermore, they present evidence suggesting that there is a relationship between cultural stereotypes and the extent to which aging is associated with a decline in memory performance. Although we can question the equivalence of measures used and the samples representing Chinese and American cultures in this study, the message that emerges from this research and that of M. Baltes is that psychosocial mechanisms based in negative attitudes and stereotypes of aging may contribute to memory loss, dependency, and other aspects of decline. In other words, societal beliefs about aging may in some ways result in a self-perpetuating myth regarding cognitive decline as beliefs shape our treatment of older adults, which in turn leads to outcomes that reinforce our beliefs. It becomes quite apparent that if we as a society are to deal effectively with aging-related issues, we must further develop our knowledge about cognitive change in adulthood in order to understand if stereotypes about aging have their basis in fact and, if so, how they can be explained.

AGING, COGNITION, AND SCIENCE

Approaches to the scientific study of aging and cognition have in many ways mirrored the just-described changes in societal beliefs. It has long been noted by historians of science that one must consider the social, political, and economic issues of an era to fully understand the corresponding trends, goals, and favored subject matter of scientific research of the times (the sociology of knowledge) (Marx & Hillix, 1973). In other words, sociopolitical beliefs and the current zeitgeist generally influence the manner in which science proceeds. Indeed, early scientific perspectives on the aging process reflected both societal and biomedical beliefs about aging: a portrayal of aging as an inevitable downhill path to senility. For example, William James (1890) equated inflexibility in confronting new ideas or the inability to perceive phenomena in novel ways as "old-fogeyism," which, in turn, is defined as the "inevitable terminus to which life sweeps us on." Along the same lines, G. Stanley Hall (1922) referred to child development in terms of growth and progression, whereas adulthood and aging were relegated to senescence and debilitation.

This emphasis on decline can be seen in the studies of aging that were conducted before and during the late 1940s and 1950s, at which time the scientific study of gerontology was beginning in earnest (Riegel, 1977). A substantial percentage of the empirical studies of gerontology during this time period focused on cognitive functioning, and, consistent with societal beliefs about aging, much of this early work had its basis in the biomedical model of aging, with the primary question asked being "What declines with age?" Accordingly, a prevailing research goal was aimed at discovering the nature and bases of decline in cognition. As a result, there was an abundance of research demonstrating age-related decrements in intellectual skills and memory abilities (for reviews, see Botwinick, 1977; Craik, 1977).

The dominant view in this early research was that aging was a unidimensional phenomenon reflecting irreversible and universal decline, and the prevailing theoretical frameworks were adapted to study this process. In the study of cognition, for example, associationism could be used to characterize aging as a breakdown in specific functions associated with the creation and strengthening of stimulus–response associations or the stage-analytic methods found in the verbal learning literature could be used to identify the locus of deficits in learning and memory (Kausler, 1991). With the advent of the information-processing perspective in the study of cognition during the late 1960s, powerful new conceptual and analytical techniques became available to the aging researcher and in the 1970s the study of cognition and aging began to flourish. The biomedical perspective continued to dominate such research, however, as scientists attempted to identify cognitive decrements by examining age-related variations in (1) processing resources, (2) the effectiveness and/or efficiency of individual processing components, and (3) executive functions (Salthouse, 1992).

The biomedical perspective was also exemplified in the early work on intellectual change with age. Cross-sectional studies of adult intelligence employing omnibus measures of psychometric intelligence consistently observed an overall decline in intellectual abilities (see, e.g., Jones & Conrad, 1933). Methodological and theoretical advancements in the assessment of intelligence did qualify this conclusion by demonstrating differential patterns of change across the dimensions of intelligence. Thus, for example, fluid intellectual skills (ability independent of acquired knowledge) exhibited decline at a relatively early age whereas crystallized skills (acquired knowledge) exhibited stability or continued to grow through most of the adult life span (Horn & Cattell, 1967). This pattern of results could still be interpreted, however, as one primarily reflecting regression, where a loss in complex, higher-order mental functions is associated with increasing reliance on lower-level, concrete modes of thought (Labouvie-Vief, 1985).

Early work on cognitive change in adulthood that took a developmental perspective was also consistent with an exclusively decremental model of aging. In general, developmental researchers applied youth-oriented Piagetian theory to the study of aging, measuring cognitive ability in adulthood with concrete and formal operational tasks developed for studies of child development. In turn, middle-aged and older adults demonstrated "cognitive regression" on such tasks (Hornblum & Overton, 1976; Papalia & Bielby, 1974), leading developmental researchers to adopt a linear cumulation view of development. Within this perspective, developmental change consists of the construction of more complex cognitions from more basic sensory or perceptual mechanisms. By contrast, aging is depicted as a mirror image of such growth adhering to a "first in–last out" principle, with the complex functioning achieved last in child development (e.g., formal operational thought) being the first to exhibit decline in adulthood (Coombs & Smith, 1973; Labouvie-Vief, 1980).

■ Changing Perspectives

In the 1970s and 1980s, there were several movements in the study of adult development and aging that reflected a change in the unidimensional perspective typically associated with the study of cognitive change in adulthood. First, the results of Schaie's seminal work on intellectual development (Schaie, 1979), in which the discrepancies between cross-sectional and longitudinal designs were examined, not only supported a multidimensional/multidirectional view of intelligence but also indicated the importance of understanding the historical context of development. Numerous studies demonstrated that more of the variance in test scores of both crystallized and fluid abilities could be accounted for by cohort membership than by chronological age. In concert with this research, there was also a growth in cognitive training research demonstrating that older adults could attain a higher level of functioning on fluid abilities with intervention (see, e.g., P. Baltes & Willis, 1982; Hoyer, Labouvie-Vief, & Baltes, 1973). Both lines of research highlighted the contextually determined nature of normative age trends and the plasticity in intellectual performance.

A second movement was associated with extending Piaget's work on structural reorganization of knowledge in development to adulthood. Instead of applying youth-oriented cognitive tasks to adulthood, researchers developed and examined criteria beyond formal operations (or adolescent cognitive development) that were unique to adult cognitive functioning (see Commons, Richards, & Armon, 1984). Researchers examining "postformal" development explored advances in cognitive development in middle-aged and older adults in areas such as problem finding (Arlin, 1975) and relativistic and dialectical thinking (Blanchard-Fields, 1986; Kramer & Woodruff, 1986).

This interest in examining the competencies of adults as well as cognitive decline can also be seen in several other areas. For example, alternative conceptualizations of intelligence were proposed and explored that took into account specific competencies associated with everyday problem solving that were not represented in traditional tests of intellectual ability (see, e.g., Cornelius & Caspi, 1987). Wisdom, an often-alluded-to but difficult-to-study trait associated with experience and later adulthood, began to be explored both conceptually and empirically (P. Baltes & Smith, 1990). In addition, cognitive researchers also became interested in understanding how experience moderated cognitive change in adulthood through studies of expertise (see, e.g., Charness, 1981; Salthouse, 1984), memory (Hess, 1990; West, 1986), and adaptation and compensation (Bäckman & Dixon, 1992).

Whereas these trends have not resulted in elimination of the biomedical perspective from the study of aging—and rightfully so—the current state of the field is much more diverse than it was 40 years ago in terms of the representation of theoretical frameworks and research methodologies. We view this diversity as a positive development in that it reflects the previously described differentiated picture of cognitive change in adulthood that has emerged over the years. Thus, many different aspects of adult cognition are being scrutinized from a variety of angles.

■ Questions

One way in which the diversity can be seen is in the types of questions that are emphasized as being central to the study of aging and cognition. Thus, for example, in Salthouse's (1991) recent attempt to organize knowledge in the field, he operationalized cognitive aging "in terms of the decrease in performance on various measures of cognitive functioning associated with increasing age in the adult portion of the lifespan" (pp. 1–2). This perspective is firmly grounded in the biomedical view, and the primary emphasis is on isolating the source of impaired performance (the impact of biological aging) with age. We perceive this to be a commonly held viewpoint, especially among researchers who approach the study of aging and cognition from within the information-processing perspective. In fact, in many ways the term *cognitive aging* and the study of decrements have become inextricably intertwined. Although other researchers (including several in this book) have used the term cognitive aging in a broader sense, its association with the information-processing approach plus the negative culturally based connotations typically associated with the term *aging* lead us to question its appropriateness for characterizing the more general psychology subdiscipline associated with the study of cognitive change in adulthood. Thus, we prefer to use "cognitive aging" to describe an approach to the study of aging that is consistent with Salthouse's (1991) definition with an emphasis on understanding losses.

In contrast to the cognitive aging perspective, a developmental approach to adult cognition focuses on a plurality of changes across the entire life span. The cognitive aging perspective typically specifies a unidirectional conceptualization of cognitive change that is distinctly associated with biological aging. Alternatively, the life-span developmental perspective posits that cognitive change is not bound by a single criterion of change such as biological decline. Instead, there is no single goal for development other than successful adaptation to the individual's context of living. This viewpoint depicts changes across the life span as an interplay between gains and losses and development as a multidirectional process governed by multiple factors (P. Baltes, 1987; Uttal & Perlmutter, 1989). Thus, in order to understand cognitive development in adulthood, one needs to refer to more than decline in biological structures. Both normative and nonnormative forces at the biological, psychological, and sociocultural-historical level need to be considered in explaining cognitive change. Thus, the major questions asked in this realm relate to identifying age-related gains and losses and understanding them within a broader context of development that goes beyond irreversible decline to include adaptive functioning.

From our viewpoint, we see the value of both these and other perspectives in the study of cognitive change in adulthood. The more ways in which adult cognitive change is conceptualized and examined, the greater is our potential for understanding. Indeed, research from one perspective can help inform another. Thus, for example, information about changes in physiological structures and their impact on basic information-processing structures obtained from cognitive aging research might be necessary to understanding changes in older adults' behavior as adaptations to such losses. Our belief in the value of multiple perspectives is the main reason for our creating this book with its broad spectrum of research and theory. Consistent with this belief, we would also argue for adoption of a more inclusive term to label this field, one that does not imply a specific model or set of beliefs regarding the nature of change in the way that we believe "cognitive aging" and "cognitive development" do. Thus, we prefer to use "cognitive change" as an umbrella term for research on cognitive abilities in adulthood. As you will see when you read the rest of this volume, not all chapter authors have the same concerns regarding the use of these terms as do we. Therefore, we encourage you to keep our concerns in mind as you read and to draw your own conclusions.

It is important to note at this juncture that adoption of a specific conceptual framework is not inextricably tied to a specific perspective or the specific questions one asks about adult development. For example, although the information-processing framework is closely aligned with the cognitive aging perspective, adoption of this framework to study adult cognition does not automatically lead to an exclusive focus on decrements. Studies of expertise and aging have proceeded largely from within an information-processing framework (see Chapter 13), but the emphasis in this research is on describing how experience serves to maintain skills. Interestingly, Charness and Bieman-Copland (1992) have detailed how both improvements and decrements in information processing might be explained solely in terms of experience-based changes in representational systems, further indicating that this framework does not necessarily need to be associated with the investigation of biologically based changes with age while highlighting potential alternative explanations for normative declines in performance. In addition, Hess (1994) has recently discussed how our use of the information-processing framework can be expanded to examine conceptualizations about aging that go beyond a discussion of the efficiency and effectiveness of individual processes by taking into account age-related variations in motivation, goals, and knowledge systems.

RESEARCH-BASED INSIGHTS INTO COGNITIVE CHANGE

As a result of the diverse frameworks used to formulate research, the scientific study of cognitive changes in adulthood has provided many important insights that serve to modify our culture's stereotypic notions of aging. Based on this research, the notion of a universal decline in cognitive skills can now be classified as a myth, with much research noting that there are individual differences in the rate of change throughout adulthood and that aging does not have the same impact on all cognitive abilities. For example, the work of Schaie and his colleagues (see Chapter 9) has amply demonstrated the multidimensional and multidirectional nature of intellectual change in adulthood as well as the historical embeddedness of development. Other research within a more experimental tradition has found that familiarity and expertise (see Chapters 12 and 13) modulate the type of change observed within specific realms of ability.

Importantly, research has also demonstrated that, consistent with our cultural stereotype, there do seem to be certain types of age-related changes that have a more or less universal impact on cognitive performance and that may serve to limit abilities as we get older. For example, speeded behavior is observed to slow with age, even in skills relevant to one's area of expertise (see, e.g., Salthouse, Babcock, Mitchell, Skovronek, & Palmon, 1990). In fact, cognitive slowing is often depicted as the one fact about cognition and aging on which everyone agrees. Given that time is often a constraining factor in cognitive performance, both externally (e.g., the time available to make a decision is limited) and internally (e.g., one cognitive operation must be completed before another is begun), performance in many areas may suffer as we get older and declines in speed may limit performance (see, e.g., Lindenberger, Mayr, & Kliegl, 1993). Even within this area of apparent congruence of opinion, however, there is debate among researchers regarding the nature of age-related slowing. The major debate centers around the extent to which slowing represents a generalized phenomenon characterized by one or more factors or varies as a function of the performance domain (Fisk & Fisher, 1994; Myerson, Wagstaff, & Hale, 1994). The outcome of the debate has important consequences not only for theory development but also for practical purposes. Thus, for example, the finding that age-related slowing might be more severe in some situations than in others may have implications for policies associated with the workplace and mandatory retirement.

Other research has suggested that age-related declines in sensory systems may also place limits on performance (see, e.g., Lindenberger & Baltes, 1994), as changes in visual and auditory sensory-perceptual systems (see Chapter 4) influence our ability to take in information from the outside world. An important focus of future research would be identifying the extent to which changes in intellectual performance in later adulthood might be mitigated by sensory aids and supports. The important point here is that systematic research into the aging of human abilities can influence our perceptions of the aging process and help us understand the conditions that serve to limit, maintain, or enhance performance as we get older. Our argument is that the diversity of perspectives adopted by researchers has led to a more complete picture of adult cognitive change, with the consequence that some of our stereotypical notions of aging have been reinforced whereas others have been rejected or modified.

MAJOR ISSUES IN THE STUDY OF COGNITIVE CHANGE

As you will see as you read through this book, research tends to be focused on a few major issues, though the approaches to studying these issues may vary widely depending on the area of research or the perspective of the researcher. In addition, some issues are closely aligned with specific conceptual frameworks whereas others are more general. Chapter 2 provides an in-depth discussion of some of the major themes that characterize research on cognitive change in adulthood. We briefly highlight some of these issues as well as others that will permeate the chapters in this book.

Perhaps the major issue in the field concerns the nature of cognitive change in adulthood. One aspect of this issue concerns whether, from a normative viewpoint, change is better conceptualized as an unidimensional process characterized primarily by decline or as a multidimensional process in which different processes change in different ways. Those who adhere to the former view tend to search for general determinants of cognitive decline that are operative across multiple contexts and ability systems. For those who view development in multidimensional/multidirectional terms, the concern is identifying those abilities that do change and describing the nature of change, the interrelationships between changing abilities, and the multiple causal factors underlying the different dimensions of change. Inherent within this latter viewpoint is the possibility of both gains and losses with age in adulthood. Note also that inherent in the dimensionality issue are implications regarding the determinants of change. Adoption of a unidimensional perspective implies the operation of a general mechanism governing change or, alternatively, the operation of a set of specific mechanisms with similar outcomes. In contrast, a multidimensional perspective implies the possibility of multiple mechanisms of change having different consequences.

Another aspect of this issue is that of understanding whether age-related change is quantitative or qualitative in nature. That is, is aging characterized by simple changes in the efficiency or effectiveness of individual processes or functions (see, e.g., Cerella, 1990), or are there trade-offs between skills (see, e.g., P. Baltes, Dittman-Kohli, & Dixon, 1984) or even major qualitative reorganizations in thinking (Commons et al., 1984)? In general, a unidimensional approach to the study of cognitive change will be more likely to postulate quantitative change, whereas multidimensional approaches can be associated with either quantitative or qualitative change. Thus, for example, when studying intellectual skills within the psychometric tradition (see Chapter 9), one could talk about multiple abilities that change in efficiency independently of one another (e.g., crystallized versus fluid intelligence) or that change in their relationship to one another (e.g., in terms of factor structures).

Note here that the stance taken regarding the nature of cognitive change is intimately related to the assessment procedure that is adopted by the researcher with respect to its study. For example, researchers who approach the study of adult cognitive change from the life-span development perspective and adopt the multidimensional focus argue that age-related variation in a specific skill must be interpreted within the context of both an individual's changing life circumstances and changes in other cognitive abilities (see, e.g., P. Baltes et al., 1984). Thus, for example, losses in some ability areas may be due to the selective optimization of other skills rather than to normative declines in physiological structures. Other researchers who originate from a cognitive aging tradition believe that assessment of specific skills in isolation provides reasonable information about cognitive change (Salthouse, 1992). If a decline in skill is observed relative to some standard (usually the young adult), a reasonable inference can be made that a true decrement exists and that age-related differences will occur in any situation in which the affected skill is involved. As can be inferred, the meaning assigned to change in each case may be very different.

Another major issue in the study of cognitive change concerns the uniformity or universality of change. Do we all age in the same fashion, or are there specific factors that moderate the aging process? This is an overly simplistic question since most researchers accept the idea that there are individual differences in the aging process, even in processes presumed to have strong biological foundations (e.g., speeded behavior). The issues of concern, then, are those associated with identifying the extent and nature of these individual differences. For example, are individual differences greater in some abilities than in others? In addition, are the differences that are observed primarily in the form of the function(s) (e.g., the direction or presence versus absence of change) or in the rate(s) of change (e.g., the speed of decline)? Assuming that individual differences do exist in the aging process, a related issue concerns the identity of those factors that determine the form and/or rate of change in adulthood.

Are there age-related biological factors that affect performance, such as changes in neural conductance, health, and/or sensory-perceptual skills? Do certain environmental circumstances support change or decline? Are there noncognitive factors (e.g., personality characteristics) that moderate the effects of aging, perhaps through the mediation of organism-environment interactions? And finally, are they related to primary aging factors (i.e., factors inevitably linked with the aging process, such as those having to do with genetic mechanisms) or secondary aging factors (i.e., things correlated with age but not inevitable, such as certain disease processes) (Busse, 1969)? These questions are especially important if our concern is the modification of cognitive change in adulthood.

Obviously, the issues we mention here are not the only concerns in the field, and each chapter will emphasize different issues related to the specific methods and content being discussed. These issues do, however, provide a starting point for reading and thinking about research associated with the study of cognitive change in adulthood.

ORGANIZATION OF THIS BOOK

We developed this book with one primary goal in mind: to provide a broad overview of the study of cognitive change in adulthood that is representative of the many different perspectives of researchers in the field. In some ways, our approach is consistent with what Chapter 2 refers to as the contextual/combinatory approach in that we believe that a broad perspective of the field that takes into account the diverse theoretical orientations and methodologies available is most useful in helping us to achieve a complete understanding of adult cognitive change. To this end, the chapters in this book were written by active investigators who are representative of this diversity and who are knowledgeable about the research and theory associated with the topic of their chapter. The perspectives taken in these chapters represent a wide range of worldviews and theoretical orientations, and each chapter attempts to highlight (1) the important theoretical and methodological issues, (2) representative findings, and (3) everyday implications of the research on its respective content area. As you will see, the stance taken on many of the general issues that we have discussed in this chapter is related to the content being studied.

The book is divided into four sections reflecting both pedagogical factors and our perceptions of common underlying themes or research approaches. The first section, "Foundations," provides a basic framework for studying the divergent content areas of cognitive change in adulthood. Chapters 2 and 3 elaborate on some of the basic issues that we have introduced here by discussing the dominant theoretical issues and perspectives that have been applied to the study of cognitive change in adulthood and aging. They also describe the major methodological issues and approaches employed in research, going beyond the traditional concerns associated with design, measurement, and analysis to explore specific problems associated with the study of adult development. The two chapters highlight the importance of the interface between theory/metatheory and methods.

The next chapter provides some context for interpreting change in adulthood by discussing changes in sensory-perceptual systems that undergird cognitive functioning. Chapter 4 discusses what we know about the impact of age on sensory functions with important links to cognitive functioning. The focus of the chapter is on vision and hearing, the two senses that have received the most research attention and are most often associated with cognitive performance. We assume that changes in these sensory functions with age need to be understood so that we may assess the extent to which they are important determinants of cognitive functioning in everyday life and influence our assessments of ability (e.g., are observed age differences in cognitive performance due to actual changes in cognitive skill or to the fact that the older subjects could not see the stimulus materials?). The sensory-perceptual underpinnings of cognition are discussed primarily in terms of losses, an approach that is consistent with the biomedical framework. In contrast to what might be expected with such an approach, however, there is also an emphasis on multidimensional aspects of aging in that the aging process is seen as affecting different sensory systems in different ways. In addition, there is also an emphasis on differential patterns of change. For example, although there may be strong normative trends associated with changes in certain sensory systems, such trends are moderated by environmental factors.

The second section, "Information Processing and Memory," focuses on topics that have traditionally been studied within the context of information-processing approaches to cognition, in which cognitive skill is typically viewed as a series of individual structures or processes representing parts or stages of a larger cognitive apparatus. Chapter 5 reviews the literature on attentional mechanisms. Consistent with current thought in the field, the chapter specifically emphasizes the impact of age on selective and inhibitory mechanisms associated with attention. Chapter 6 discusses changes in normal memory functioning, with an emphasis on the traditional laboratory approach to the study of retention processes. It focuses on the major research strategies used in the laboratory setting and the manner in which such research assists in the development of general theories of memory functioning in adulthood. Chapter 7 continues the discussion of memory by focusing on the important distinction between explicit and implicit memory processes. The study of implicit memory in the study of cognition has increased dramatically during the past decade, and it appears to have special relevance to the study of aging in that changes in implicit memory functioning are less severe than those in explicit functioning. The conceptual distinction between these two types of memory and the important role it may have in our understanding aging effects on cognition are also discussed. Finally, Chapter 8 reviews the extensive work on language and discourse processing, attempting to integrate current theory regarding aging and cognition with current models and theories of language comprehension in order to better understand age-related changes in language processes in adulthood.

Consistent with the cognitive aging perspective, most of the research in these chapters deals with understanding losses. For example, why do older adults have trouble focusing their attention? Why do they exhibit lower levels of memory performance in most situations? What impairments are associated with a drop in language comprehension? Although there is often a drive to identify one common factor that might underlie performance decrements across situations—for example, by relating age effects to changes in processing resources or speed—there is at least implicit acknowledgment that there are multiple dimensions of abilities in each realm that may not exhibit the same rate of decline (e.g., implicit versus explicit memory), suggesting the possibility of multiple determinants. In most cases, however, the multiple dimensions contrast skills that remain stable versus those that decline rather than examining possible avenues of growth, thus indicating more of an interest in studying determinants that are unidirectional in nature. Finally, although there are some exceptions, much of the work discussed in these chapters focuses on universal patterns of change rather than individual differences. Thus, there is an emphasis on comparing group means in order to understand normative aging effects in performance.

In contrast to the previous section, the third section, "Intelligence," previews a domain of research that emphasizes both gains and losses in cognitive functioning in adulthood and aging. Intellectual functioning in older adulthood is examined from three different theoretical and/or methodological perspectives. Chapter 9 examines one of the historically dominant approaches to the study of intellectual change in adulthood: the psychometric approach. This chapter focuses on the goals of the psychometric approach and the different ways in which psychometric test data are used to examine the structure of intelligence and the nature of change. Finally, it reviews research on psychometric ability and everyday competence as well as the reversibility of cognitive deficits occurring with age. Chapter 10 examines intellectual change in adulthood from both the psychometric and cognitive developmental perspectives in the form of practical intelligence and everyday problem solving. It begins with an examination of the impetus for studying practical problem solving in response to the limitations posed by the psychometric approach. This is followed by an examination of the relationship between traditional psychometric measures of intelligence and practical intelligence and a review and discussion of the conflicting findings on developmental differences in practical problem solving that relates them to differing theoretical perspectives on intelligence. Chapter 11 places more emphasis on a cognitive developmental approach to intelligence by examining postformal thinking. This approach has its roots in Piaget's theory of cognitive development. Of primary concern is the extent to which Piaget's basic framework for understanding cognition in childhood can be extended to understanding adult intellectual development. The chapter addresses such issues as qualitative shifts in adult thinking, the relationship among postformal thinking, personality, and emotional development, and how postformal thinking relates to an information-processing approach to cognition.

The three chapters on intelligence are prototypes of research conducted from a life-span developmental perspective. This is not surprising given that the impetus for the life-span developmental movement to understand cognition and aging began with the study of intelligence. Thus the dominant issues that characterize the nature of change from a life-span perspective are represented in these chapters. These include multidimensional components of intelligence (e.g., fluid and crystallized intelligence), gains and losses in intellectual functioning (e.g., the development of postformal thinking), and the multidirectional patterns of change in various domains of intellectual functioning (a decrease in fluid skills and an increase in crystallized and everyday problem-solving skills).

The final section of the book, "Cognition in Context," consists of four chapters that are primarily concerned with understanding the impact of aging on cognitive skills in a somewhat broader context. Chapter 12 reviews the research on memory from a functional perspective, in which attempts are made to relate age-related performance variations to various contextual factors, such as familiarity or relevance of tasks and materials to everyday life contexts. This approach, which is somewhat different from the one taken in Chapter 6, provides an equally important perspective for understanding aging and memory. Chapter 13 examines the interaction between expertise and age in determining cognitive performance in an attempt to understand how experience might affect the aging of cognitive skills, as well as the impact of age on the acquisition of new skills. Chapter 14 examines age differences in social cognitive skills. This approach to the study of adult thinking emphasizes the importance of changing roles, interpersonal contexts, motivations, goals, knowledge systems, and emotions as determinants of age-related variations in behavior. Finally, Chapter 15 explores how changes in belief systems moderate cognitive change during adulthood. Two major belief systems, metamemory and self-efficacy, are examined in terms of their conceptual and functional frameworks, how they are measured, and how they relate to changes in cognitive functioning.

Each of the chapters in this last section takes a contextualist approach to the study of cognitive change in adulthood and aging. The contextualism represented in these chapters ranges from the external to the internal context of cognitive change. For example, Chapter 12 focuses on external task factors and how they influence memory change. Chapters 14 and 15 both, in part, emphasize the internal context of the thinker, including affective processes, motivation, and schemas, while Chapter 13 emphasizes the experiential contextual factors in expertise (e.g., the amount of experience). Given this contextual approach, the chapters attempt to identify which contexts provide opportunities for and constraints on change. For example, Chapter 14 posits that reasoning in a social context allows for the study of progressive change in cognitive functioning. Chapter 13 demonstrates when gains are evident (e.g., in contexts of expertise) and when they are not. Similarly, Chapter 12 demonstrates contexts related to gains and losses in the area of memory in everyday contexts. Thus, the last section of the book presents contextual and diverse approaches, emphasizing a multiply determined and diverse picture of cognitive change in adulthood.

A CRITICAL APPROACH
TO THE STUDY OF
ADULT COGNITIVE CHANGE

Reviewing the literature in any area of study can seem a daunting and confusing exercise, and, as you read through this book, it will be evident that the field of cognitive change in adulthood is no exception. One is confronted with a variety of theoretical orientations, methodological approaches, and research findings, often presenting conflicting views or results. How do we deal with such a situation in our efforts to arrive at a reasonably complete understanding of adult cognitive functioning and change? The answer is through the adoption of a critical approach that takes into account the underpinnings of scientific investigation. How does such an approach proceed?

First, one must have a clear understanding of the goals of research and the specific assumptions and theoretical constructs on which it is based. This is true not only in the design and conduct of one's own research but also in the interpretation of investigations conducted by others. Individual research projects (or even programs) are not designed to be the be-all or end-all in our quest for knowledge. Research is an incremental process through which our knowledge is built through myriad individual projects, each of which is designed to answer a limited number of very specific questions. In one's perusal of the literature, this fact must be recognized along with the inherent pluses and minuses associated with it. On the plus side, research formulated within a specific conceptual framework or worldview can assist us in building, testing, and modifying a theory through the provision of data that relate specifically to the ideas and hypotheses derived from it. In other words, such research is consistent with the scientific method as practiced in psychology and other scientific enterprises, and the resulting data should enable us to better understand the viability of a given theory (Marx, 1976).

At the same time, however, it must be recognized that formulation of research within a specific framework also limits its scope and thus the types of questions that are asked and can be answered. For example, if an investigator was strongly influenced by biological views of aging, the problem chosen for investigation would likely be one of exploring the nature of and reasons for decline. Using traditional hypothesis-testing methods, the research itself would be designed to identify or refute the existence of decline, with little concern for examining questions that might be of importance to other orientations (e.g., individual differences in change, the extent to which decline in a specific skill might represent adaptive functioning). Assuming that the study was adequately designed, valid information about decline and relevant data could be provided within the specific theoretical context guiding the research. Questions about other aspects of aging, however, would be left unanswered since the research was not specifically designed to address them.

Given this fact, the predominance of research from one perspective over that of others can have an important impact on our perceptions regarding the nature of a specific phenomenon. Research paradigms in any scientific field undergo change, with certain views predominating at any point in history (Kuhn, 1962). This is the normal state of science and should not necessarily be seen as a negative. The dominance of a specific type of science or, in our case, a specific set of assumptions regarding aging, however, may unduly color our understanding of the field by blinding us to alternative conceptual frameworks through the bombardment of theory and data relevant to the current view. Assume for the moment that the majority of studies in the literature have their basis in the biomedical model of aging and are designed to investigate decline. (In reality, this is not an unreasonable assumption.) If you were to do a review of the literature in the field, you might come away thinking that most cognitive change in adulthood is characterized by decline, or at best stability, based simply on the number of studies examining and/or reporting decline. It is important to recognize that this conclusion may not necessarily be descriptive of all adult cognitive change but rather is a function of the zeitgeist which influences the type of research conducted in the field. A preponderance of studies examining only decline may not reflect a complete picture of cognitive change but rather the goals, assumptions, and methods of researchers sharing a common viewpoint.

Once the underlying assumptions associated with a specific research study have been identified, it is also important to critically examine these assumptions and any associated theoretical constructs in relation to the study of adult cognitive change. As often occurs when studying age-related variations in behavior, especially in adulthood, constructs and models are freely borrowed from other fields within psychology. Before we accept their utility, however, these constructs and models should be examined with regard to their appropriateness to the study of aging. For example, much initial work on aging was conducted within the experimental tradition using models and theories developed primarily with college-age adults. Implicit in their use to identify decline was the notion that the young adult represents the ideal; that is, the young adult's cognitive functioning is the standard to which individuals of all other ages are to be compared. Such a standard has certainly been used in other developmental work involving children (e.g., Piaget's theory). The question is whether the same standard can be reasonably used for the study of adult cognitive change. Put another way, we need to ask ourselves if what is adaptive (in terms of cognitive functions) for a young adult is also adaptive for middle-aged and older adults. If the answer is yes, the youth standard is a reasonable one. If the answer is no, however, our interpretation of age-related differences must be tempered accordingly.

To illustrate this point, let's take an example from the literature. Specifically, a common finding from much early research on memory and aging is that increasing age is associated with a decrease in the ability to remember lists of unrelated words (Craik, 1977). How do we interpret this result? Consistent with the youth-as-standard model inherent in much cognitive aging research, we could argue that this decrease reflects an age-related decline in functioning, perhaps due to irreversible changes in physiological structures that affect encoding and retrieval processes. Alternatively, we might search for other explanations by examining the adaptive functions associated with these skills. For example, this age difference in performance may reflect a shift in abilities associated with middle-aged and older adults' greater emphasis on application than on acquisition skills (see Chapter 12). The reality most likely lies somewhere between these two extremes.

Our point here is that adoption of the youth standard also requires acceptance of the corollary assumption that the abilities being assessed are equally important (predictive of functioning) across the entire life span. We are not necessarily suggesting that the youth-as-ideal standard is invalid; rather, we simply argue that it should not be accepted uncritically and that acceptance should be based on strong theoretical or empirical bases. At the same time, we need to adopt the same cautious approach in dismissing decline as inconsequential. Indeed, the youth standard appears to be very useful in the investigation of certain biologically based aspects of cognition. For example, a decline in the speed of information processing can have very real consequences if decision making in critical situations (e.g., air traffic controllers monitoring multiple flights) is slowed.

A critical approach to the study of adult cognitive change also requires an examination of the adequacy of the research strategies and methods being used. When reading about a specific research study, we need to understand not only the underlying assumptions and theoretical constructs but also the extent to which the methodology is consistent with the questions being asked. For example, if we are concerned with being able to identify possible progressions or adaptations in cognitive skills as well as decrements, we need to develop methodologies that enable us to acquire relevant data. A good case in point is some recent work by Adams (1991; Adams, Labouvie-Vief, Hobart, & Dorosz, 1990), who argues that the typical manner in which prose memory is examined in adulthood biases us toward finding quantitative declines in performance at the expense of qualitative progressions or adaptations. Her argument is not that the observed quantitative declines do not represent normative decrements in functioning but rather that changes in goals and adaptations to changing skills and life circumstances may also result in variations in the nature of text processing and that a focus on only quantitative change does not tell the whole story with respect to cognitive skill. Specifically, Adams argues that declines in quantitative measures of recall (e.g., the amount of prose recalled) may be accompanied by increases in attempts by older adults to meaningfully interpret the prose in terms of prior experience, which in turn may be reflected in inferences and integrative responses rather than exact reproduction of prose. In the absence of a means to assess these latter behaviors, however, this potentially positive qualitative change goes unnoticed in research reports, thereby biasing our interpretations toward those emphasizing decline.

Once we understand the importance of underlying assumptions and methods, our next step will be actually to examine the research literature and see what it has to say. Does the existing research answer the important questions? Are there gaps in the research that prevent us from understanding the phenomenon in question? What revelations have emerged from the research that are consistent or inconsistent with existing thought? Are there certain perspectives that have been either over- or underutilized? The answers to these questions can help us gain a broad perspective on the field and provide guides with respect to the direction that future research should take. We hope you will keep these questions in mind as you read this book.

CONCLUSIONS

Our intent in this chapter was to provide you with a brief introduction to the study of cognitive change in adulthood and aging. We hope that our highlighting some of the history, basic issues, and dominant perspectives in the field will assist you to organize your own thinking as you try to make sense of the vast amount of information that is contained in this book. We also hope that reading this book will not only make you knowledgeable about basic research and theory but also stimulate the generation of your own ideas and research. In this chapter, we have also repeatedly emphasized the importance of examining adult cognition from multiple perspectives and of interpreting research within the context of theoretical and metatheoretical assumptions. As you read through the chapters that follow, you should develop an appreciation of the complexity inherent in adult cognitive change. It is our hope that you will also come to see the wisdom of such an approach.

REFERENCES

Adams, C. (1991). Qualitative age differences in memory for text: A life-span developmental perspective. *Psychology and Aging, 6,* 323–336.

Adams, C., Labouvie-Vief, G., Hobart, C. J., & Dorosz, M. (1990). Adult age-group differences in story recall style. *Journal of Gerontology: Psychological Sciences, 45,* P17–P27.

Arlin, P. K. (1975). Cognitive development in adulthood: A fifth stage? *Developmental Psychology, 11,* 602–606.

Avolio, B. J., Waldman, D. A., & McDaniel, M. A. (1990). Age and work performance in nonmanagerial jobs: The effects of experience and occupational type. *Academy of Management Journal, 33,* 407–422.

Bäckman, L., & Dixon, R. A. (1992). Psychological compensation: A theoretical framework. *Psychological Bulletin, 112,* 259–283.

Baltes, M. M. (1988). The etiology and maintenance of dependency in the elderly: Three phases of operant research. *Behavior Therapy, 19,* 301–319.

Baltes, M. M., & Reisenzein, R. (1986). The social world in long-term care institutions: Psychosocial control toward dependency? In M. M. Baltes & P. B. Baltes (Eds.), *The psychology of control and aging* (pp. 315–344). Hillsdale, NJ: Erlbaum.

Baltes, P. B. (1987). Theoretical propositions of life-span development: On the dynamics between growth and decline. *Developmental Psychology, 23,* 611–626.

Baltes, P. B., Dittmann-Kohli, F., & Dixon, R. A. (1984). New perspectives on the development of intelligence in adulthood: Toward a dual-process conception and a model of selective optimization with compensation. In P. B. Baltes & O. G. Brim (Eds.), *Life-span development and behavior* (vol. 6, pp. 33–76). San Diego: Academic Press.

Baltes, P. B., & Smith, J. (1990). Toward a psychology of wisdom and its ontogenesis. In R. Sternberg (Ed.), *Wisdom: Its nature, origins, and development* (pp. 87–120). New York: Cambridge Univ. Press.

Baltes, P. B., & Willis, S. (1982). Enhancement of intellectual functioning in old age: Penn State's Adult Development and Enrichment Project. In F. I. M. Craik & S. Trehub (Eds.), *Aging and cognitive processes* (pp. 353–389). New York: Plenum.

Blanchard-Fields, F. (1986). Reasoning on social dilemmas varying in emotional saliency: An adult developmental perspective. *Psychology and Aging, 1,* 325–333.

Blanchard-Fields, F., & Camp, C. J. (1990). Affect, individual differences, and real world problem solving across the adult life span. In T. M. Hess (Ed.), *Aging and cognition: Knowledge organization and utilization* (pp. 461–497). Amsterdam: North-Holland.

Botwinick, J. (1977). Intellectual abilities. In J. E. Birren & K. W. Schaie (Eds.), *Handbook of the psychology of aging* (pp. 580–605). New York: Van Nostrand Reinhold.

Busse, E. W. (1969). Theories of aging. In E. W. Busse & E. Pfeiffer (Eds.), *Behavior and adaptation in later life* (pp. 11–32). Boston: Little, Brown.

Carstensen, L., & Turk-Charles, S. (1994). The salience of emotion across the adult life span. *Psychology and Aging, 9,* 259–264.

Cerella, J. (1990). Aging and information processing rate. In J. E. Birren & K. W. Schaie (Eds.), *Handbook of the psychology of aging* (pp. 201–221). San Diego: Academic Press.

Charness, N. (1981). Search in chess: Age and skill differences. *Journal of Experimental Psychology: Human Perception and Performance, 7,* 467–476.

Charness, N., & Bieman-Copland, S. (1992). The learning perspective: Adulthood. In R. J. Sternberg & C. A. Berg (Eds.), *Intellectual development* (pp. 301–327). New York: Cambridge Univ. Press.

Commons, M., Richards, F., & Armon, C. (1984). *Beyond formal operations.* New York: Praeger.

Coombs, C. H., & Smith, J. E. K. (1973). Detection of structure in attitudes and developmental process. *Psychological Review, 80,* 337–351.

Cornelius, S., & Caspi, A. (1987). Everyday problem solving in adulthood and old age. *Psychology and Aging, 2,* 144–153.

Craik, F. I. M. (1977). Age differences in human memory. In J. E. Birren & K. W. Schaie (Eds.), *Handbook of the psychology of aging* (pp. 384–420). New York: Van Nostrand Reinhold.

Fisk, A. D., & Fisher, D. L. (1994). Brinley plots and theories of aging: The explicit, muddled, and implicit debates. *Journal of Gerontology: Psychological Sciences, 49,* P81–P89.

Freeman, J. T. (1979). *Aging: Its history and literature.* New York: Human Sciences Press.

Hall, G. S. (1922). *Senescence: The last half of life.* New York: Appleton.

Heckhausen, J., & Baltes, P. (1991). Perceived controllability of expected psychological change across adulthood and old age. *Journal of Gerontology: Psychological Sciences, 46,* 165–173.

Heckhausen, J., Dixon, R. A., & Baltes, P. B. (1989). Gains and losses in development throughout adulthood as perceived by different age groups. *Developmental Psychology, 25,* 109–121.

Heise, D. (1987). Sociocultural determination of mental aging. In C. Schooler & K. W. Schaie (Eds.), *Cognitive functioning and social structure over the life course* (pp. 247–262). Norwood, NJ: Ablex.

Hess, T. M. (1990). Aging and schematic influences on memory. In T. M. Hess (Ed.), *Aging and cognition: Knowledge organization and utilization* (pp. 93–160). Amsterdam: North-Holland.

Hess, T. M. (1994). Social cognition in adulthood: Aging-related changes in knowledge and processing mechanisms. *Developmental Review, 14,* 373–412.

Horn, J., & Cattell, R. (1967). Age differences in fluid and crystallized intelligence. *Acta Psychologica, 26,* 107–129.

Hornblum, J. N., & Overton, W. F. (1976). Area and volume conservation among the elderly: Assessment and training. *Developmental Psychology, 12,* 68–74.

Hoyer, W. J., Labouvie-Vief, G., & Baltes, P. B. (1973). Modification of response speed deficits and intellectual performance in the elderly. *Human Development, 16,* 233–242.

Hummert, M. L. (1990). Multiple stereotypes of elderly and young adults: A comparison of structure and evaluations. *Psychology and Aging, 5,* 182–193.

James, W. (1890) *Principles of psychology.* New York: Holt.

Jones, H. E., & Conrad, H. S. (1933). The growth and decline of intelligence: A study of a homogeneous group between the ages of ten and sixty. *Genetic Psychology Monographs, 13,* 223–298.

Kausler, D. H. (1991). *Experimental psychology, cognition, and human aging* (2d ed.). New York: Springer.

Kite, M. E., & Johnson, B. T. (1988). Attitudes toward older and younger adults: A meta-analysis. *Psychology and Aging, 3,* 233–244.

Kramer, D., & Woodruff, D. (1986). Relativistic and dialectical thought in three adult age groups. *Human Development, 29,* 280–290.

Kuhn, T. S. (1962). *The structure of scientific revolutions.* Chicago: Univ. of Chicago Press.

Labouvie-Vief, G. (1980). Adaptive dimensions of adult cognition. In N. Datan & N. Lohmann (Eds.), *Transitions of aging.* New York: Academic Press.

Labouvie-Vief, G. (1985). Intelligence and cognition. In J. E. Birren & K. W. Schaie (Eds.), *Handbook of the psychology of aging* (2d ed., pp. 500–530). New York: Van Nostrand Reinhold.

Landy, F. J., & Shankster, L. J. (1994). Personnel selection and placement. *Annual Review of Psychology, 45,* 261–296.

Langer, E. J., & Rodin, J. (1976). The effects of choice and enhanced personal responsibility for the aged: A field experiment in an institutionalized setting. *Journal of Personality and Social Psychology, 34,* 191–198.

Levy, B., & Langer, E. (1994). Aging free from negative stereotypes: Successful memory in China and among the American deaf. *Journal of Personality and Social Psychology, 66,* 989–997.

Lindenberger, U., & Baltes, P. B. (1994). Sensory functioning and intelligence in old age: A strong connection. *Psychology and Aging, 9,* 339–355.

Lindenberger, U., Mayr, U., & Kliegl, R. (1993). Speed and intelligence in old age. *Psychology and Aging, 8,* 207–220.

Luszcz, M. A., & Fitzgerald, K. M. (1986). Understanding cohort differences in cross-generational, self, and peer perceptions. *Journal of Gerontology, 41,* 234–240.

Marx, M. H. (1976). Formal theory. In M. H. Marx & F. E. Goodson (Eds.), *Theories in contemporary psychology* (pp. 234–260). New York: Macmillan.

Marx, M. H., & Hillix, W. A. (1973). *Systems and theories in psychology.* New York: McGraw-Hill.

Morrow, D., Leirer, V., Altieri, P., & Fitzsimmons, C. (1994). When expertise reduces age differences in performance. *Psychology and Aging, 9,* 134–148.

Myerson, J., Wagstaff, D., & Hale, S. (1994). Brinley plots, explained variance, and the analysis of age differences in response latencies. *Journal of Gerontology: Psychological Sciences, 49,* P72–P80.

Papalia, D. E., & Bielby, D. (1974). Cognitive functioning in middle and old age adults: A review of research based on Piaget's theory. *Human Development, 17,* 424–443.

Reigel, K. F. (1977). History of psychological gerontology. In J. E. Birren & K. W. Schaie (Eds.), *Handbook of the psychology of aging* (pp. 70–102). New York: Van Nostrand Reinhold.

Salthouse, T. A. (1984). Effects of age and skill in typing. *Journal of Experimental Psychology: General, 113,* 345–371.

Salthouse, T. A. (1991). *Theoretical perspectives on cognitive aging.* Hillsdale, NJ: Erlbaum.

Salthouse, T. A. (1992). The information-processing perspective on cognitive aging. In R. J. Sternberg & C. A. Berg (Eds.), *Intellectual development* (pp. 261–277). New York: Cambridge Univ. Press.

Salthouse, T. A., Babcock, R., Mitchell, D. R., Skovronek, E., & Palmon, R. (1990). Age and experience effects in spatial visualization. *Developmental Psychology, 26,* 128–136.

Salthouse, T. A., & Maurer, T. J. (in press). Aging and work. In J. E. Birren & K. W. Schaie (Eds.), *Handbook of the psychology of aging* (4th ed.). San Diego: Academic Press.

Schaie, K. W. (1979). The primary mental abilities in adulthood: An exploration in the development of psychometric intelligence. In P. B. Baltes & O. G. Brim, Jr. (Eds.), *Life-span development and behavior* (vol. 2, pp. 67–115). San Diego: Academic Press.

Schmidt, F. L., Hunter, J. E., Outerbridge, A. N., & Goff, S. (1988). Joint relation of experience and ability with job performance: Test of three hypotheses. *Journal of Applied Psychology, 73,* 46–57.

U.S. Bureau of the Census (1992). *Statistical abstract of the United States: 1992* (112th ed.). Washington, DC: U.S. Government Printing Office.

Uttal, D., & Perlmutter, M. (1989). The dynamics of growth and decline across the life span. *Developmental Review, 9,* 101–132.

West, R. L. (1986). Everyday memory and aging. *Developmental Neuropsychology, 2,* 323–344.

C H A P T E R

2

THEORETICAL ISSUES IN COGNITION AND AGING

Roger A. Dixon
University of Victoria

Christopher Hertzog
Georgia Institute of Technology

Cognitive processes, broadly considered, are among the most theoretically fascinating, empirically challenging, and practically useful aspects of human psychological development. Throughout life we seek, process, and produce new information, acquiring and disseminating new knowledge. We solve novel problems, plan daily and future activities, resolve everyday hassles, and perform challenging tasks. We follow directions or find our way, participate in conversations, give or listen to advice, and remember past events. During our lifetimes we acquire new cognitive skills that require a prodigious investment of time and effort (e.g., a profession or a hobby such as chess) and perform complex skills with an automaticity verging on disinterest if not aplomb (e.g., driving an automobile). Rarely does a day, hour, or even minute pass without some form of cognitive activity. This is true as much for children and adolescents as it is for younger, middle-aged, and older adults.

Although cognitive activity occurs throughout life, the manner and level of any given activity may differ between individuals and may change within an individual over time. This implies that, at any particular point in life, individuals may vary in at least four important ways. First, they may vary from other individuals in the manner or strategies with which they engage in a cognitive activity. Second, they may vary from other individuals in their level of accomplishment or performance of a cognitive task. Third, they may vary from themselves (either earlier or later in life) in the manner or strategies they use while engaging in a cognitive activity. And, fourth, they may vary from themselves (either earlier or later) in their level of accomplishment or performance.

If cognitive activity is as ubiquitous—and if it can vary as much between and within individuals—as we suggest, it presents a major challenge for scientists. Not only must researchers observe and measure it accurately in its variety of manifestations, they must consider how to interpret and understand their observations. That is, however accurately we measure the manner and level of cognitive activity for a given individual or group of individuals, we must be aware that a host of other issues may have an impact at many junctures in the research process. These issues include how we as researchers: (1) determine what to observe, (2) select the methods of observing it, (3) describe our observations, (4) interpret or explain our observations, and (5) communicate our new or enhanced understanding of the phenomenon.

In brief, the role of *theory* in cognitive psychology is in part that of providing a context for planning, collecting, describing, and understanding empirical observations. As in other fields of science, theories help us organize what we know in the context of what we do not yet know. They provide a scheme for linking a set of observations and for identifying themes in the research literature. In this way, good theories are useful in pointing toward future directions of research, as well as discriminating between directions of higher and lower priority. In a certain sense, scientific theories represent our best guesses about how phenomena work. Many observers believe that theories are neither infallible nor static (Toulmin, 1972). They are and should be updated as new, unexpected, or even discordant observations accumulate. Some scientific theories may be expressed quite formally, even in precise mathematical or quantitative terms. Although specificity and comprehensiveness are valued characteristics of theories, the degree of both precision and scope possible depends in part on (1) the nature of the phenomenon of interest, (2) the pretheoretical assumptions and predilections of the pertinent scientific community, and (3) the degree to which prior theoretical arguments and empirical evidence have led to common understandings regarding a particular phenomenon. In short, theory development depends on the characteristics of the phenomenon, the science of the phenomenon, and the scientists studying the phenomenon (see, e.g., Kuhn, 1970, and Suppe, 1977, for more formal treatments of the structure and function of scientific theories).

Sometimes psychological theories may appear to be relatively informal, in that they are presented using seemingly "softer" terms such as theoretical frameworks, prototheories, tentative theories, or theoretical approaches. Such informality may be due to the complex or challenging nature of the phenomenon, the recency of the science, or the assumptions and methodological preferences of the scientists. Not all legitimate phenomena of nature lend themselves easily to precise, constrained theoretical representations—indeed, not all scientists share a goal of achieving such representations for all phenomena. In the field of cognition and aging, theories run the gamut from the relatively formal to the relatively informal. Although they differ in many respects, one underlying characteristic of theories of cognition and aging is that they address a relatively common set of theoretical issues. Theoretical issues permeate and help to define research in a given area. In this chapter we present theoretical issues as points of contention, continua along which multiple legitimate positions may be adopted and supported on the basis of both preempirical beliefs and empirical observations. In a given research area, theoretical issues help to identify underlying themes and important differences among theories, whether more informal or formal. Theoretical issues are considered in the organization of research and the determination of how to observe the phenomena, as well as the interpretation and explanation of empirical results. Theoretical issues may be implicit—if not explicit—components of theories.

Our goal in this chapter is to identify and sort some of the principal theoretical issues in the study of cognition in adulthood. More precisely, we will identify principal issues in adult cognition, and we will focus our attention on how these issues relate to cognitive change in adulthood. Increasingly, both the field that investigates cognitive change in adulthood and the complex of cognitive changes that occur throughout adulthood have become known as *cognitive aging.* As is documented in Chapter 1, some usages of this term have some unfortunate, if not sweeping, negative connotations, such as that of universal decline with advancing age. In this chapter, we use the term advisedly, so as to refer to changes and individual differences in changes in cognition that occur during adult development. In this way, then, by using the term cognitive aging, we do not prejudge the nature or trajectory of cognitive development throughout adulthood.

What are the phenomena of cognitive aging? There is a variety of psychological processes involved in human cognition that are addressed in this book. They include perception (detecting stimuli in the environment), attention (attending to particular stimuli), remembering (encoding, storing, and recalling information), and reasoning (solving problems, making decisions). It is evident that these processes are basic to a scientific understanding of human cognitive phenomena and to cognitive functioning in everyday life. Whether focusing on basic or applied scientific problems, psychologists have expended painstaking effort to develop methods of measuring these processes in laboratories or other settings. When these phenomena are measured in adults, and when developmental concerns are incorporated, the field of cognitive aging is usually implied. Cognitive aging, therefore, is a field that examines a variety of cognitive phenomena, followed across time or compared across ages.

Much of the research in the field of cognitive psychology and cognitive aging involves one (or only a few) experimental tasks administered within a single session. There are important pragmatic reasons for this approach. Perhaps the most frequent reason is that one obtains information on individuals' level of performance (and hence information about the cognitive processes involved) with a minimal investment of time and effort. There are at least two important assumptions associated with this approach, both of which are useful to consider when interpreting the results of such studies. A theoretical assumption is that cognitive attributes in adulthood are general and stable. A methodological assumption is that cognitive attributes can be validly assessed with relatively brief and simple measurement protocols. There is, however, an alternate set of assumptions that pertain to the validity of inferences drawn from such experiments. Specifically, one could assume that many important adult cognitive attributes are both complex and variable across time. The implication of this assumption is that they should be assessed with appropriately dimensionalized and change-sensitive methods. The contrast between these alternative sets of assumptions has important ramifications for the field of cognitive aging. If the nature of cognition in adulthood were relatively uncomplicated, we could, in principle, understand it thoroughly by way of relatively simple concepts and designs. The theoretical and methodological issues involved in research would be relatively straightforward. In contrast, if we assume that there is a marked, differential, and important variability in individual performance across time and domain, considerably more challenging theoretical and methodological issues emerge. In this chapter we explore a wide range of theoretical issues in cognitive development (or change) in adulthood.

THEORETICAL ISSUES IN COGNITIVE DEVELOPMENT

As the title of this chapter implies, our purpose is to present neither our own theory of cognitive aging nor a detailed explication of any of the extant theories. Instead, our goal is to offer an introduction to several prominent theoretical issues in adult cognitive development. We invite interested readers to examine the primary sources we cite in this chapter as well as other chapters in this book. for details about specific theories of cognitive aging.

There is a long history of research and theory in cognitive psychology (see, e.g., Gardner, 1985; Hearst, 1979) and an almost equally long history of scholarly interest in cognitive development.[1] In this section we identify five theoretical issues that have influenced theoretical development in this field for decades and that promise to occupy scholars for the foreseeable future. There are three reasons that they will continue to influence research and theory development. First, issues about cognitive change are consonant with theoretical issues concerning the study of change and development at all levels of analysis, from the microbiological to the evolutionary, from the psychological to the cultural, and from the historical to the philosophical (see, e.g., Harris, 1957; Nisbet, 1980; Toulmin, 1972). Second, resolving such vexing theoretical issues requires methods of analysis that are grounded in, and benefit from, careful consideration of how to conceptualize and evaluate developmental change. Because of the variety of processes and levels of analysis, the range of appropriate methods is quite broad, including traditional experiments, modeling and simulations, and techniques of philosophical analysis and historiography. Not all of these methods are evident in—or perhaps apply to—the field of cognitive aging, but the kinship among the related fields of development is well worth noting.

The third reason that some fundamental theoretical issues are enduring (and yet contemporary) requires more attention. Although prominent theoretical issues may influence the research process, they have not been completely tested, resolved, or refuted by empirical data. Indeed, one of the lessons of recent scholarship in theoretical psychology and, more specifically, theoretical developmental psychology is that there are aspects of scholarly inquiry that are pretheoretical. This implies that (1) they are closely derived from assumptions about the nature of humans or science and therefore (2) are not available for empirical testing or evaluation (see, e.g., Pepper, 1970). One may view the theoretical situation in sciences, then, as being organized hierarchically. At the "top" and containing the most assumptions and least accessible for empirical testing are theoretical systems (also known as worldviews, world hypotheses, or paradigms). There are only a few major systems, but each sponsors a hierarchically related set of theories, methods, and hypotheses (all of which are indeed available for empirical use or evaluation).

Typically, theoretical camps or schools of inquiry are associated with these worldviews, and the camps (or proponents) of one worldview are occasionally in "competition" with the camps (or proponents) of another. Each of the systems are relatively complete unto themselves and relatively incommensurable with other theoretical systems. This implies that, at

---

[1]Although no exhaustive history of cognitive aging research has been written, some useful secondary resources are available. In the series known as *Handbook of the Psychology of Aging* (see, e.g., Birren & Schaie, 1977) authors from a variety of theoretical perspectives have reviewed work in specific areas in consecutive historical periods. Intelligence and aging have been reviewed in this series by Botwinick (1977), Labouvie-Vief (1985), and Schaie (1990). Memory and aging have been reviewed by Craik (1977), Poon (1985), and Hultsch and Dixon (1990). Other cognitive functions have also been addressed (see, e.g., Cerella, 1990; McDowd & Birren, 1990; Rabbitt, 1977; Schaie, 1990). Especially lengthy reviews are available in the recent handbook on cognitive aging edited by Craik and Salthouse (1992). Kausler's (1991) review of the experimental psychology of aging contains scholarly analyses of a wide-ranging literature. Schaie's (1983) volume, in which longitudinal studies of psychometric intelligence are presented, is a useful resource, as is his chapter detailing the history of the Seattle Longitudinal Study. Historical treatments are also available in several book chapters (see, e.g., Baltes, Dittmann-Kohli, & Dixon, 1984; Dixon, Kramer, & Baltes, 1985; Salthouse, 1990). Interested readers will find primary sources cited in these reviews.

the pretheoretical level, the systems are substantially different from one another and yet internally logical and consistent. It also implies that over the years these systems have been fruitful in their promotion of research and that, although this research is pertinent to these systems, it may not bear upon alternate systems. That is, not only are the assumptions relatively inaccessible for empirical testing, but deciding firmly and finally which system—or which theoretical camp emanating from different systems—is "correct" cannot easily be accomplished.

Participants in different theoretical systems do not communicate fluently with one another, partly because the important rules and vocabulary vary from one to another system. Thus, as we saw earlier in this century, adherents of Chomsky's theory of language development clashed with proponents of Skinner's view. These clashes could not be resolved empirically, for one camp would simply not accept the rules and assumptions associated with the other. Presumably, however, such disputes are still beneficial for both camps and for scientific development in general (Campbell, 1974; Feyerabend, 1978; Popper, 1965). If nothing else, they lead to explicit statements about a system's assumptions, premises, hypotheses, criteria for testing hypotheses, and preferences for interpretation. We should note, however, that the notion that there are multiple viable systems in a given area of science is not uncontroversial. In brief, the notion that there is more than one legitimate worldview in psychology, and that each should pursue its research agenda and compete with neighboring theoretical systems, is known as pluralism. That there is—or even that there should be—only one legitimate psychological worldview is a position known as monism. Of course, all practicing scholars have a perspective and many are intellectually committed to it. Nevertheless, there is a subtle but notable difference between, on the one hand, pursuing one's own research agenda while allowing, encouraging, and occasionally even debating alternate worldviews and, on the other, pursuing one's research agenda while, in principle, discouraging or devaluing the practice or even existence of those derived from alternate systems. For this chapter we adopt the former approach, in that we attempt a relatively even-handed overview of the issues and systems.

The issues we identify cut across several theoretical systems. There are numerous ways of summarizing the present theoretical picture in cognitive aging (see, e.g., Kausler, 1991; Light, 1991; Salthouse, 1991). In a later section, we provide some details about four theoretical approaches—or, in some cases, collections of theoretical approaches—to cognitive aging. Each of the four has both shared and unique features, and each has both theoretical advantages and limitations. It is useful to name these four approaches so that they can be identified with positions on the theoretical issues. We refer to the first one as the *differential approach,* in which a principal concern is with identifying individual differences in cognitive change. We refer to the second as the *experimental approach,* in which a principal concern is with testing mechanisms and explanations for differences. We call the third collection the *contextual* (or *combinatory*) *approach* because (1) the theoretical focus is different from the first two, and (2) a principal concern is with pushing (and even merging) some of their boundaries. We label the fourth approach we discuss by its affiliation to a well-known "paradigm" of developmental psychology, that is, the *organismic approach.* A principal concern in this approach is with revealing directions of human growth—in the present case, directions of cognitive development.

Most scientific theories may be couched in higher-level theoretical systems (see, e.g., Kuhn, 1970; Pepper, 1970). The major theoretical systems relevant to developmental psychology have been identified as those relevant to most areas of scholarship, including the natural sciences, social sciences, and humanities (Pepper, 1970; Reese & Overton, 1970). One approach to identifying and partitioning the theoretical systems has been followed frequently in the developmental sciences. According to this approach, the main theoretical systems are *contextualism, mechanism,* and *organicism,* all of which have demonstrated scientific viability historically and in numerous arenas of human inquiry (see, e.g., Pepper, 1970). They fulfill the basic requirements of worldviews in that they are coherent systems containing basic assumptions that influence the nature of theoretical, empirical, and interpretive efforts. They are relatively incommensurable in that their basic assumptions are not the same, although in psychology they often share methodological tools of empirical inquiry.

Developmental psychologists have explored theoretical systems in great detail (see, e.g., Dixon & Lerner, 1992; Reese & Overton, 1970). They appear to apply equally to cognitive aging, although they have been examined less closely by this subdiscipline (see Baltes, Dittmann-Kohli, & Dixon, 1984; Salthouse, 1991, for other perspectives). Perhaps as a sign of the emerging maturity and the impressive growth of this subdiscipline, it is necessary and timely for students of cognitive aging to identify explicitly and to evaluate critically the sets of theoretical issues that may very well play a substantial role in the research process. Certainly, the notion that there is a close interplay among assumptions, theories, methods, and interpretations applies to cognitive aging. As a first approximation, we may link the theoretical approaches to the theoretical systems as follows. With some variation due to changing emphases, three may be linked fairly closely: the experimental approach derives in part from mechanism, the organismic approach derives in part from organicism, and the contextual approach derives in part from contextualism. The differential approach, as we shall see, shares features with more than one system. We turn now to an introduction to the five main theoretical issues. We present each issue as a continuum, defined by extreme positions (rarely adopted in the field), and with multiple intermediate positions.

■ Universal versus Differential

Assumptions regarding *universality* are fundamental to the concept of development in general, and to cognitive development in adulthood in particular. Given that there is change in a particular cognitive process in adulthood, universality directs attention to whether that change occurs in all normally developing individuals or only in some individuals, depending on such complex and interacting factors as contextual circumstances and genetic inheritance. At the universal end of the continuum, one assumes that there are relatively few individual differences in developmental processes. In contrast, from a differential perspective, the assumption is that there are substantial contingent and selective influences on change. The criteria for each cardinal pole of this continuum are rather stringent. Hence, most developmental processes could be viewed as falling between the two extremes. For a process to be truly universal, it must occur under all circumstances and conditions. In principle, there would be no individual differences in the timing, rate, or the direction of change. For a process to be truly differential, the change that occurs must depend on specific combinations of circumstances that coalesce differently for all individuals, resulting in massive individual differences in timing, rate, and direction of change. In aging research, Birren's (e.g., 1965; Birren, Cunningham, & Yamamato, 1982) notion of primary aging and Baltes's (e.g., Baltes, Reese, & Lipsitt, 1980) illustration of normative influences on developmental change are examples of relatively universal views. Both models, however, contain some elements that reflect more differential concerns (e.g., some notions of primary aging allow for individual differences in age of onset and rate of change).

As with most conceptual issues in the study of human development, assumptions play a role in how research is designed, data are collected, and observations are interpreted. Because one's view of this issue is steeped in one's assumptions, it is unlikely that a single experiment or set of experiments can reveal whether adult cognitive development is either universal or differential, and perhaps even whether it is more one than the other. As viewed through one theoretical lens, the universals overwhelm the relatively minor differences among individuals, which may be real but may also be a function of (for example) measurement error. As viewed through another lens, however, the variations from the rule are paramount, making the most universal rules fatally riddled with exceptions and the search for intermediate rules regarding (1) differential development and (2) contextual correlates of differential development of primary theoretical concern.

Different theoretical perspectives—associated with different approaches to science—are likely to vary in location on the universal–differential continuum. For example, theorists following an organismic perspective in developmental psychology are often more comfortable with claims regarding universality of child cognitive development than are theorists following a mechanistic perspective. Whereas the former perspective emphasizes the universal human process of maturation, the latter emphasizes the role of the environment in shaping individual change. Few theorists today argue that adult cognitive development is governed by universal maturational processes, at least relative to the degree of universality present in organismic theories focusing on child development. However, theories of adult development vary dramatically in the degree of emphasis placed on the universality of biological aging and the impact it has on adult cognitive development. Some theorists emphasize the relatively universal process of biological decline (often termed senescence) in the central nervous system and link it to postulated universal processes of decline in adult cognition. One influential case in point is Birren's (1965) arguments concerning the importance of a universal process of primary aging, the slowing of information processing, and the role aging plays in determining age changes in cognition (see, e.g., Birren, 1965; Birren, Woods, & Williams, 1980; Salthouse, 1985, 1991).

The interest in producing theories with some degree of universal implications in science is sometimes great, but not all systems of developmental psychology pursue this interest as avidly as others. Therefore, the contrary tendency to focus on individual differences is also represented in the research literature in cognitive aging (Hultsch, Hertzog, Dixon, & Small, in press). From this perspective, there are indeed important generalities about adult cognitive development, but the role of particular combinations of contextual conditions and individual differences in relevant psychological constructs act to shape patterns of cognitive development. Variables that form these combinations include, but are not limited to, (1) external environmental factors, (2) experiential factors, (3) past and current health conditions, (4) current stress, styles of coping, and effectiveness of coping, (5) individual differences in personality and affective traits, as well as concurrent affective states, and (6) individual differences in related cognitive abilities and skills.

In general, the universal–differential issue is a principal dimension that differentiates adult cognitive development. It should be noted, however, that theories with discrepant positions on this issue may share perspectives on other theoretical issues or emphasis on particular methods. Indeed, some theories with similar positions on this issue may not have similar positions on other theoretical issues or selection of research methods. For example, proponents of relatively universal primary aging decline may share little else theoretically or empirically with proponents of universal aging-related growth.

■ Directionality and Dimensionality

These two theoretical issues may be conceptually separable, but, given that their implications are inextricably intertwined, considering them together has didactic benefits. Both represent continua. We consider directionality first, for it, like universality, is associated with a continuum fundamental to the general concept of development.

Directionality

Directionality refers to the notion that developmental change may be structured so as to represent systematic progression over time or may be unstructured and lacking in identifiable systematic progression. Progressive change (building incrementally on previous levels) is related in developmental theory to goal-directed change (developing in the service of a specifiable or knowable end state). For example, Piagetian theories of child cognitive development depict a systematic set of changes in cognition from a sensorimotor stage to the stage of formal operations. Some approaches to adult cognitive development may attempt to represent such directionality. Directionality and goal-directedness represent change that is moving forward, upward, in the direction of better (if not in the pursuit of the best); both are often associated with assumptions and theoretical perspectives that emphasize inherent goal-directedness or end states to developmental processes. This sets them off from theoretical perspectives that emphasize the chance or random nature of change processes and by implication the utter absence of inherent directions to development.

As with the universality issue, a continuum of positions is implied for directionality, with relatively few adherents at either extreme. That is, most theories of cognitive development in adulthood occupy intermediate positions. Nevertheless, it is possible to contrast two clusters of positions. Some organismic theories are allied with positions close to directionality. Some organismic representations of adult ego development (including some cognitive and social aspects) (see, e.g., Erikson, 1959) seem to place a structure on developmental progression that is similar to directionality. Note that such models allow for individual differences (i.e., they are not necessarily universal) in that not all individuals achieve the final end state. They are directional, however, in that they posit a goal to adult development. In child cognitive development, Piagetian approaches portray formal operations as "goals" toward which development tends, although not without individual differences in rate of progression and level of final attainment. Such theories typically have explanatory mechanisms available, mechanisms which often reside in the social structural or biological maturational contexts of development (Chapman, 1988). Much current research in cognitive aging is, in this respect, more descriptive in nature and makes fewer assumptions about the end state of the developmental process.

Directionality may be a more fundamental theoretical concern in organismic theories of adult development in reasoning (see Chapter 11) and, interestingly, in theories of skill development (see Chapter 13). In the case of organismic theories, some adult development may be tending toward postformal operations, a form of reasoning said to be beyond formal operations in level of attainment (see Alexander & Langer, 1990, a volume devoted to investigating end points to development). Because of fairly well defined characteristics of an expertise, especially in well-structured domains, skill development can be profitably portrayed in terms of movement toward higher levels of classification with relatively few alternative directions to the goal available (see, e.g., Anderson, 1982). This directionality of skill development—as well as the constrained alternatives resulting from achieving ever higher levels of skill—obtains as well in adulthood. That is, the development of cognitive skills in late adulthood follows the same principles of progressive change as it does in earlier life (see, e.g., Charness, 1989).

The issue of directionality has a corollary concern in developmental theory, which is the issue of whether change may be portrayed as more qualitative (stagelike) or quantitative (gradual, incremental) in nature. Is development abrupt, proceeding through leaps or shifts that are qualitatively different from what has gone before? Alternatively, is development more gradual, with small, quantitative steps underlying apparently greater shifts (Wohlwill, 1973)? Some developmental theories that structure the process of development progressively portray the nature of development as stagelike. Theories of cognitive aging derived from organismic traditions have regularly offered at least weak stage models of development (see, e.g., Alexander & Langer, 1990; Erikson, 1959; Labouvie-Vief, 1982). Stage models from other traditions have occasionally been seen (see, e.g., Schaie, 1977–78). Skill development has been viewed in stagelike fashion (see, e.g., Anderson, 1982), although this is rarely the case in cognitive aging (but see Rogers, Fisk, & Hertzog, 1994). In contrast, theories of cognitive aging deemphasizing directionality in development rarely offer stage theories.

How (Multi)directionality Relates to (Multi)dimensionality

The latter term, dimensionality, refers to the nature or structure of cognition itself without, initially, any implications regarding change. The issue is whether cognition or intelligence—or any aspect thereof—represents a unitary construct or one with multiple independent but interrelated dimensions. Relatively few theories of aging, and of cognitive aging in particular, strive to cut across multiple aspects of cognition, much less other processes in the developing person. Provocative—albeit very different—attempts to develop global theories have been made by Erikson (1959), who links ego and personality theory with some cognitive aspects, and by Salthouse (1991), who explores rival explanations for aging-related cognitive decline. Some scholars have started with a limited variety of observations but with powerful methods have produced theories with potentially broad implications (see, e.g., Cerella, 1990). Most theories of cognitive aging embrace more than one dimension of cognition (within the domain of interest) and limit the range of their application such as to intelligence (see, e.g., Baltes, 1987; Horn, 1982), memory (Bäckman, 1985; Craik & Jennings, 1992), or problem solving (Hartley, 1989; Rabbitt, 1977). As seen in Chapter 9, researchers in psychometric intelligence have made a strong case for a multidimensional construct, as compared to a unidimensional view of intelligence (e.g., as represented in g).

Multidimensionality is related to the theoretical issues of directionality and universality. Specifically, with respect to universality, if there are multiple dimensions of construct domains such as memory and intelligence, then at any one point in time there may be individual differences in performance in each of the relevant dimensions. These distributions of individual differences in performance usually vary across different cognitive tasks; therefore, claims about universality may be based on different patterns of variability in performance across conceptually distinct dimensions of construct domains. To be sure, the dimensions of a construct domain are related, and, if they are uniformly and consistently highly related, individual differences in performance may not be massive. But dimensions of a construct domain may vary in their degree of relatedness, and the rank orders of individual performance may vary markedly between dimensions.

This analysis implies something theoretically important about the directionality of life-span development, in general, and cognitive development in adulthood, in particular (Baltes, 1987). First, within the same construct domain, there may be variability in the directions of change across adulthood. Put simply, while many aspects of memory may decline throughout adulthood, a select few may improve or be maintained. If memory is multidimensional, it is in principle possible that at given points in the life course, different dimensions of memory may be undergoing different rates or directions of change. Second, across cognitive processes (e.g., attention, memory, decision making), more than one rate or direction of change may occur at given points in the life course. Thus, by focusing less on a global or single indicator of cognition and more on specific dimensions (as related to other dimensions), multidimensionality provides one conceptual basis for the possibility of multidirectional change. Although multidirectionality is not intrinsically or logically antithetical to progressive change, there are few theories of development that actively embrace, much less emphasize, both.

When cognitive processes are indeed multidimensional, there can be substantial costs to reasoning about the constructs in a unidimensional fashion. Research on a given phenomenon may be designed and executed without appreciating that the theoretical construct is defined in such a way as to make it an inherently different (but related) construct from the one originally targeted. For example, a theory about the development of styles of cognition (e.g., impulsivity) could be led astray if this dimension were to be confused with related but differentiable aspects of cognitive style (e.g., behavioral inhibition). Indeed, exploring or positing the existence of multiple dimensions for a given construct can often go far to resolve apparent discrepancies in empirical data regarding developmental change. Recent research on working memory and aging (see, e.g., Babcock & Salthouse, 1990; Salthouse, 1991) has indicated that it is a complex construct and that the various operational definitions in the literature may be measuring different aspects or dimensions, each of which could be differentially related to aging or other cognitive constructs. Other examples of how positing multidimensionality has helped to resolve empirical discrepancies and advance our theoretical understanding of cognitive aging include work on metamemory (see, e.g., Hertzog & Dixon, 1994) and psychometric intelligence (see, e.g., Baltes et al., 1984; Schaie, 1990). The methodological implications of multidimensionality and multidirectionality are discussed further in Chapter 3.

■ Plasticity and Reversibility

We noted above that the issue of universality concerns the extent to which there are individual differences in patterns of change. A complementary issue is the extent to which there is an emphasis on intraindividual (within-person) change. Plasticity refers to the potential for intraindividual variability. Although it is usually used to refer to change that constitutes improvement, it is not necessarily so restricted. Indeed, it could refer to seemingly nondirectional, fluctuating variability over time (see, e.g., Nesselroade, 1991a, b). In life-span developmental theory, the implication is that (1) the potential for continued or further developmental change is present in all normally developing individuals and (2) such continuing change may be related to conditions and experiences in development (see, e.g., Lerner, 1984). A theoretically important concern is with identifying the range of possible variability for given developmental processes and populations (Baltes, 1987). Reversibility refers to whether processes that have undergone developmental change (whether positive or negative) can revert to a previous or original state. Theoretically relevant concerns include (1) the extent of potential reversibility, that is, to any previous state or just to the preceding state, and (2) whether both progressive and decremental change can be reversed. An interesting point of overlap between plasticity and reversibility is the tantalizing case of a decline being reversed through experience.

Indeed, with regard to cognitive aging, a series of theoretically challenging questions may be raised. If decline is observed in a given cognitive process—perhaps even observed universally—can that decline be reversed? If some (or all) of the individuals experiencing such decline can exhibit plasticity following enhancement of experience (such as practice or training)—and the decline can be reversed—what does that mean for theories of cognitive aging emphasizing universality, decline, or hardware-versus-software explanations? Of course, plasticity and reversibility are not dichotomous conditions—people are not either plastic or not and processes are not totally reversible or totally irreversible. Therefore, contingencies such as the following quickly become relevant for theoreticians: (1) the range of processes that can be reversed, (2) the extent of plasticity observed, (3) the duration of the reversal, as well as (4) whether aging influences any of the above. On the other hand, cognitive processes exhibiting aging-related decline that are impervious to the effects of experience-enhancing treatments (e.g., training programs) may be said to have demonstrated a robustness of decrement that should have substantial implications at the theoretical level.

If progression in a cognitive function is predicted theoretically or observed empirically, this would have implications for the theoretical issue of directionality and, in particular, the question of goal-directedness. As noted above, the relative universality of the progression has some implications for the issue of directionality. Similarly, if progress toward a developmental goal is, in everyday life, occasionally stalled or even reversed, theorists should consider relaxing or weakening theoretical claims about necessary progression. If there is no evidence that progress toward a given developmental goal is subject to natural disruptions, it might be interesting to test the robustness of that progression empirically. A progression persisting in the face of manipulations designed to depress or reverse cognitive growth would be one with noteworthy theoretical power. Conversely, a theory stipulating a goal-directed progressive process should adjust its claims accordingly if empirical evidence actually showed considerable natural or manipulated disruptions or reversals. Interestingly, this may apply as well to theories of cognitive aging in which the "progression" is presumed to be inevitable and universally decremental. If there are naturally occurring or experimentally produced limits, exceptions, or disruptions to this progressive decline, similar theoretical adjustments may be in order. In sum, considering a given process presumed to undergo inevitable decline, empirical evidence that such decline may be stalled or reversed may occasion a reconsideration of both theoretical (e.g., assumptions, explanations) and methodological (e.g., research design, measurement operations) concerns.

The cognitive aging research literature pertaining to this issue is incomplete but data are available on plasticity in such domains as intellectual aging (Baltes & Baltes, 1980; Baltes et al., 1984; Chapter 9), memory aging (Bäckman, Mäntylä, & Herlitz, 1990; Kliegl & Baltes, 1987; Chapter 6), some varieties of "practical" cognition (see Chapter 10), and cognitive skill development (Ericsson & Charness, 1994; Chapter 13). In general, normal older adults have been found to respond effectively to experience-enhancing manipulations, such as cognitive training. For psychometric intelligence, this includes training on types of tasks that typically show natural aging-related decline and that have tentatively been related to neurological decline (e.g., "fluid intelligence" tasks; see Chapter 9). The ultimate meaning of this research is, however, still controversial (see, e.g., Salthouse, 1991).

How straightforwardly can cognitive training results be incorporated into cognitive aging theories? On the one hand, showing gains where there have been losses provides a more persuasive set of evidence regarding plasticity than would have simply showing successful training on tasks on which older adults typically do well. Similarly, showing gains on tasks at which younger and older adults typically do not do exceptionally well could be supportive evidence regarding plasticity. Research showing that both younger and older adults can learn strategies to promote remembering of extensive strings of digits and words is an example of this (Kliegl, Smith, & Baltes, 1990; see also Mäntylä & Bäckman, 1992). Even on speeded tasks, in which a quantified rate of slowing is quite robust and theoretically significant, practice may shift the slowing substantially (see, e.g., Dixon, Kurzman, & Friesen, 1993; Fisk, Fisher, & Rogers, 1992). Nevertheless, the theoretical significance of this promising direction of research is still being adjudicated (see, e.g., Baltes, 1987; Hertzog, 1991; Kausler, 1990; Salthouse, 1985, 1991). As a lengthy discussion about the significance of training research in the psychometric intelligence literature revealed, there are substantial theoretical and perhaps even pretheoretical complications involved in interpreting training studies. Whereas some argued that the evidence for plasticity in intellectual aging should be regarded as theoretically significant (see, e.g., Baltes & Schaie, 1976; Schaie & Baltes, 1977), others argued that training improvements reflected simply learning how to do a particular task and not an actual change in cognitive ability (Donaldson, 1981; Horn & Donaldson, 1976). The alternative perspectives may have differed less at the empirical level than at the construct level. That is, the crux of the dispute was whether it was theoretically possible to improve actual performance on a dimension of intelligence that underwent (necessary and irreversible?) decline with aging.

The next issue we address is a product of considering all three theoretical issues we have described above. It speaks directly to the natural form of cognitive change in adulthood.

■ Gains versus Losses versus Maintenance

Since the beginning of the century numerous writers have noted the complexity of the phenomena of cognitive aging and the consequent complexity of theories to account for them (Dixon, Kramer, & Baltes, 1985). The principal alternatives for characterizing trajectories of change are gains (i.e., improvement), losses (i.e., decline), or maintenance (i.e., no fundamental change) (Baltes, 1987). It is also possible, of course, that cognitive aging could be more completely and accurately characterized as a mixture or ratio of the three alternatives. If so, a subsequent issue is whether the gains and losses are distributed differently across processes of cognition, that is, whether some processes exhibit some degree of gain with aging whereas others show decided patterns of decline. A related issue is whether the gains and losses are distributed differently across adulthood. As we show in this section, this issue is closely related to the theoretical issue of directionality in development. Indeed, it would be possible to consider the latter as a superordinate category that includes the former. We present them separately in this chapter for two reasons. First, it is possible to view the directionality issue as more closely linked to a priori expectations about the nature of developmental change, such as whether it is goal directed or stagelike. Second, the gains and losses issue resides at a level closer to the interpretation of observed patterns of actual developmental phenomena. Whereas the former is concerned with theoretical necessity, the latter pertains more to theoretical interpretation of observations.

The urge to address (and resolve) the crucial question of gains and losses has been at the heart of numerous theoretical commentaries in the fields of life-span developmental psychology, in general, and cognitive aging, in particular (see, e.g., Baltes, 1987). One perspective is that early cognitive development is incremental (growthlike) whereas adult cognitive development is decremental (declining). That is, life-span cognitive development followed a rather simple and predictable inverted U–shaped curve. Indeed, at one point in history much of the empirical research using cross-sectional designs supported such a view. If the gains-losses dynamic was as straightforward as this, theories linking this pattern to underlying physiological changes or external social-environmental shifts could easily be generated. Today we know that the situation is complicated by a host of methodological concerns (see Chapter 3) and by data that do not neatly fit the simple pattern (see Bäckman et al., 1990; Chapter 9). Complex patterns of results require attention to sophisticated methodological issues, and together these beget more complicated theories.

It is interesting to note that the gains-losses issue—and the absence of unequivocal conclusions to it—has been prominent since the early scholarship on adult cognition in the beginning of the century. Two early examples will suffice. First, Sanford (1902) associated cognitive decline with the inevitable physical decline that occurs with aging, as well as a changing social structure that restricted the active participation of older adults. He noted, however, that some maintenance of performance levels was possible if aging adults made an effort to maintain them. Second, Hollingworth (1927) argued quite early that no single curve could adequately portray the complexity of development. Aspects of development begin to grow at different times, grow at different rates, cease to grow at different times, decline at different times, and decline at different rates. The theme of coexisting gains and losses has continued to the present (see, e.g., Botwinick, 1977; Horn, 1982; Perlmutter, 1990; Schaie, 1994; Uttal & Perlmutter, 1989).

The contemporary view of the gains-losses issue has been described well by Baltes (1987), who argues that gains and losses occur at all points in the life span, not just in adulthood. What may change, according to Baltes, is that, whereas the ratio of gains to losses is quite high in early development, it is considerably lower in later life. Important points for theories of cognitive aging are that: (1) with advancing age there are growing numbers of aspects of cognition that typically decline, (2) with advancing age there are diminishing numbers of aspects that may be maintained or improved, but (3) there may be some of the latter. This view has been associated with the growth of efforts to conduct research demonstrating cognitive maintenance or even gains into late life. For example, sizable research efforts have been marshaled in examining adaptive or practical cognition (see Chapter 10) and the role of experience or skill in cognitive aging (see Chapter 13).

Some researchers have attended to a variety of areas of continued potential or performance in late life, as well as postulated growth processes such as wisdom (Perlmutter, 1990; Sternberg, 1990). In general, identifying possible domains of cognitive maintenance or growth is a useful descriptive research goal. In addition to demonstrating the existence of such patterns, however, for theoretical purposes it is crucial to examine the mechanisms involved in promoting or supporting them. After describing an example of maintenance or improvement in cognitive functioning into late life, how should an observer theoretically interpret this evidence? How and why does it occur? Two of the currently most promising interpretive categories are experience and compensation (see, e.g., Salthouse, 1987, 1990). Regarding the former, one argument would be that long-term experience (such as that resulting in expertise) in a given domain can lead to maintenance or even continued improvement in performance on tasks relevant to that domain (Ericsson & Charness, 1994). This could occur through continued practice on tasks representing aspects of cognitive abilities that would otherwise exhibit normal aging-related decline. It could occur, as well, despite normal decrements in basic cognitive abilities unrelated to the domain of experience (Charness, 1989). The fascinating possibility is raised that an observer's interpretation of cognitive gains or losses may be at least partly related to the domain(s) being assessed. Suppose an older adult is an active expert in a cognitively demanding skill (such as chess, bridge, or electronics) but is assessed for everyday competence by tasks that do not tap this expertise. Quite possibly, the evaluation of cognitive ability may not validly reflect—indeed, may underestimate—the individual's general level of adaptation to his or her everyday life, which would include a large proportion of activities related to the skill. To be sure, this does not imply that there are not vast areas of cognitive decline with aging, only that there may be some areas that are spared because they continue to be practiced by expert adults. The cognitive competence of older adults may be most accurately assessed by evaluation of performance on basic and traditional tasks, in combination with a battery tapping the individual's own domains of specialization and adaptation (Dixon, 1995; Salthouse, 1990).

Several intriguing theoretical possibilities are raised by the notion of compensation, as well. Compensation may be defined briefly as effectively counterbalancing a mismatch between environmental or task demands and accessible skills or performance levels, usually through a mechanism that substitutes for one that is declining (Bäckman & Dixon, 1992). A wide variety of compensatory mechanisms has been identified and applied to a number of research areas in which individuals may be observed overcoming deficits (see Dixon & Bäckman, 1995). For cognitive aging, some of the principal categories of mechanisms are (1) investing more effort or time, (2) shifting goals or criteria, (3) using latent (but normally inactive) skills, or (4) acquiring new skills that substitute for the declining skill (Bäckman, 1989; Brandtstädter & Wentura, 1995; Marsiske et al., 1995; Salthouse, 1990, 1995). These mechanisms could be applied to understanding (1) how growth can continue to occur in some domains despite losses in a variety of basic cognitive abilities and (2) how maintenance in cognitive functioning can occur that is not simply "zero growth and zero decline" but represents functional resilience in the face of ongoing decline in other domains. One example pertaining to cognitive development is the study by Salthouse (1984) in which expert older typists were found to have apparently experienced normal losses in some of the important components of rapid transcription typing and yet were able to maintain high levels of performance by using substitutable components (see also Bosman, 1993). There are considerable conceptual and methodological demands on researchers interested in exploring compensatory mechanisms in cognitive aging, but progress in codifying these requirements has been made (Charness, 1981, 1989; Dixon & Bäckman, 1995; Salthouse, 1987, 1995).

In sum, documenting and explaining aging-related losses is a theoretically important endeavor. Given the extensiveness of the losses, however, it is perhaps especially intriguing to document and explain the exceptions to the rule, that is, cases of maintenance and gains in cognitive functioning. These pursuits promise to be not only of theoretical value, but also of practical application. For example, if robust mechanisms of compensation can be uncovered in given domains, the possibility exists of promoting enhanced competence in some older adults.

■ Consistency versus Variability

This issue is somewhat closer to a methodological concern than the previous ones, but it has substantial theoretical implications. Furthermore, it cuts across at least two of the previous dimensions, universal–differential and plasticity–reversibility. Indeed, it was raised implicitly in both of these sections. The issue concerns whether an individual's performance on one occasion of measurement is representative of that individual's performance on the same task (or construct) at different points in time (Nesselroade, 1991a,b). That is, to what extent is there intraindividual (within-person) variability in cognitive performance versus uniformity, regularity, or constancy? If the range of intraindividual variability is small, then two related implications are that single assessments of older individuals' cognitive competence are (1) adequate methods for research, and (2) sufficient for assessment or theoretical purposes. If, on the other hand, the range of intraindividual fluctuation is large, methodological and theoretical complexities arise. Single-occasion assessments may not provide valid estimates of true competence, and much more complicated methods may be required to sample sufficient points in time to measure intraindividual variability.

The assumption of most research in life-span developmental psychology is that there is relatively little coherent intraindividual variability (Kuhn, 1995; Nesselroade, 1991b; Siegler, 1994). More specifically, measurement operations are assumed to reflect underlying traits accurately—and traits, by definition, should show temporal and cross-situational stability. Whatever variability that is observed is usually assumed to be related primarily to random influences and measurement error—that is, unreliability in the task.

What if cognitive performances are more statelike than traitlike; that is, what if performance levels may be controlled in part by (usually unmeasured) endogenous (e.g., hormonal) or exogenous (e.g., contextual) factors? Nesselroade (e.g., 1988, 1991b; Nesselroade & Ford, 1985) has argued that intraindividual variation is to be expected in a wider range of abilities than previously thought and that such fluctuation is not merely the result of imprecision of measurement. Indeed, it reflects lawful but unstable influences on cognitive performance. This implies that the assessment of a given cognitive ability may be determined by both a stable (traitlike) and a fluctuant (statelike) component. The potential complication is that one does not know—and may not be able to assume—the extent to which one's measurement reflects one or both of these components. Complicating the situation further is the possibility that other fluctuant processes (e.g., hormonal activity, anxiety, mood state, fatigue) may be influencing cognitive performance. These are potentially difficult problems for much of cognitive aging research (Hertzog, Dixon, & Hultsch, 1992; Hoyer & Rybash, 1994; Chapter 3), where some portion of the variability between individuals may be due to fluctuant intraindividual influences.

The empirical evidence for such intraindividual fluctuation in cognitive performance is small but growing and therefore of theoretical concern (for examples from child cognition, see Kuhn, 1995; Siegler, 1994). Anecdotally, clinicians expect fluctuations in the functional competence of older adults (Kaszniak, 1990), and both variability and uniformity are observed in personality assessments in older adults (Nesselroade, 1988). Adult patients with traumatic brain injury have displayed individual variability (Stuss, Pogue, Buckle, & Bondar, 1994). Normal older adults have displayed a wide range of intraindividual variability in prose memory performance across as many as ninety weekly occasions of measurement (Hertzog et al., 1992) and as few as ten (Dixon, Hertzog, Friesen, & Hultsch, 1993). Intraindividual variability has also been observed for normal young-old adults, old-old adults, and an Alzheimer's patient on a battery of neuropsychological tests (Friesen, 1993). Finally, even time-of-day effects have been observed, whereby performance levels and the magnitude of age differences vary according to whether the time of testing matches the optimal (or preferred) time of testing for younger and older adults (May, Hasher, & Stolzfus, 1993).

Thus, performance levels of older adults may indeed be affected by the time when the testing is conducted, which indicates that some portion of the variation may be due to unknown (but potentially knowable) fluctuations in statelike characteristics. Assumptions about the traitlike character of many cognitive measurement operations may be more tenuous than previously believed. It remains to be seen how extensively this affects further developments in cognitive aging theories. This theoretical issue, as compared to some of the others, is relatively available for empirical investigation.

INTERPLAY BETWEEN THEORIES AND METHODS IN COGNITIVE AGING

Just as there is no single optimal way of conceptualizing the changes associated with cognitive development in adulthood, there is no single best method of investigating such changes. Indeed, the methodological issues associated with studying change and development, in general, and cognitive aging, in particular, are as complex and intriguing as the theoretical issues (see Chapter 3). It may already be evident to many readers that the theoretical and methodological issues of psychological development overlap and even interact. Although the two sets of concerns are often treated separately in accounts of life-span development, they are not fundamentally separable (see, e.g., Baltes, Reese, & Nesselroade, 1977; Overton & Reese, 1973). The interdependence of theory and method is often inconvenient, for it demands that one attend to a number of difficult issues (e.g., can a particular question derived from a theory be addressed properly with available technology?). For many purposes it is possible to overlook or minimize this interesting inconvenience, but it is crucial to understand both that it exists and that it has some important ramifications. The purpose of this section, then, is to introduce some of the ways in which methods and theories of cognitive aging are mutually interdependent.

Theories of cognitive aging may be distributed into collectives based on similarities or family resemblances. That is, some theories, much like siblings, may vary in the expression of their particulars but are similar in some critical, underlying ways. A reason for this family resemblance is that they may derive from the same higher-order theories or models of development. Thus, those theories of cognitive aging that derive from contextualism, mechanism, or organicism should share some features with their siblings, that is, those theories derived from the same model. This suggests that families of theories will have similar profiles of positions on the fundamental theoretical issues described earlier. It does not suggest that (1) all theories in a family of theories will have precisely the same position, nor that (2) one family of theories (derived from one of the models) will take no position on (i.e., will ignore) one of the fundamental issues. However, because of different assumptions associated with the model, their interpretation of the issues and their evaluation of the pertinence of the issues may vary.

Methods of conducting empirical, experimental, developmental research may also be associated with a higher-order theoretical system or model. A simple example will illustrate. It is unlikely that an experimental psychologist would employ primarily interpretive biographical techniques (see, e.g., Bühler, 1933) for understanding the life course. Similarly, a differential psychologist is likely to prefer standardized psychometric tests of cognition that an experimental psychologist might find less appealing. Methods of research are, obviously, employed to serve a purpose; they are tools or means of answering a research question. And research questions spring from the soil of good theories, which themselves are partially derivable from theoretical systems of psychology. Therefore, methods of research are tailored in part to serve the purposes of theories and models. To be sure, this is as it should be: methods and theoretical systems in science do not have independent lives.

We have portrayed this interplay between theories and methods in the form of a flowchart (see Figure 2.1). In this figure (adapted from Dixon, Lerner, & Hultsch, 1991), we trace how a hypothetical theoretical system (system X) influences a family of theories of cognitive development. Within this family of theories there would be specific theories pertaining to attention, memory, and reasoning. The particular features and content of the theories would, of course, be different, but they would share family resemblances. They would also share an affiliation with a family of methodological preferences and tools. Although there may be multiple methods of data collection and analysis available (in the figure these are represented by methods A, B, and C), these too would be congenial to the goals of the research, which are in turn consonant with the predilections of the family of theories or even the theoretical system. Most important for theoretical advancement, the figure implies that there is also a family of interpretations. That is, it is unlikely that research conducted within the family of theories derived from system X will (1) have a direct impact on a neighboring family of theories (say, that derived from theoretical system Y) or (2) ever result in a rejection of its superordinate model.

The lessons regarding the interplay between theories and methods in cognitive aging research, as represented in this flowchart, may be summarized in four main points. First, the methods that are used are selected within the context of both system-level and theoretical

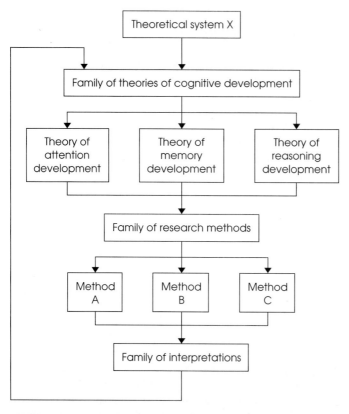

FIGURE 2.1 A schematic representation of the hierarchical relations among research activities in a hypothetical theoretical system. (*Source:* Adapted from Dixon et al., 1991.)

concerns. They are not selected from a theoretically neutral shelf on which all methods available to all cognitive aging researchers are arrayed and treated as equally accessible and useful. Not all methods may be consistent with one's theoretical system for cognitive development. There are some natural tendencies to prefer some methods over others, and this may be especially true for dramatically divergent theoretical systems. Nevertheless, there is substantial overlap in the methods that are commonly used to examine cognitive development.

Second, if the theoretical system and family of theories delimit the range and variety of methods available, they also, by implication, constrain the possibilities for potential results of research. Experimental (e.g., Craik, 1994) and differential (e.g., Schaie, 1990) cognitive aging psychologists are not likely to find evidence for structural (qualitative) change in the nature of formal reasoning. This is in part due to the fact that their research questions do not focus on such changes and that their research designs and measures are not tailored to identify this kind of change. This constitutes no criticism of either group of researchers, for parallel limitations apply to all theoretical perspectives.

Third, the interpretations of the results are engaged within the realm of explanation associated with the investigator's theoretical system. Although the results may indeed have ramifications for the investigator's theory and perhaps even for other related theories, they will not bear on alternative theoretical systems. Thus, the experimental psychologist is both unlikely to produce evidence bearing on the issue of qualitative change in cognitive structure and unlikely to perceive evidence produced by others as challenging (much less falsifying) the theoretical assumption of qualitative invariance. Similarly, the psychologist pursuing theories of qualitative structural change is unlikely to entertain (much less assimilate) experimental evidence that cognitive change is quantitative and may be reduced to underlying elements.

Fourth, the scheme in Figure 2.1 implies that critical experiments—those that test specific, fundamentally different accounts of a given phenomenon—may be performed within a family of theories but not across theoretical systems. That is, it is not possible to put to a critical test alternative organismic and mechanistic accounts of the same phenomenon. Of course, it is well known that it is not possible, either, to test a theoretical system critically, for it lives and breathes at some distance from the empirical realm (Pepper, 1970). Even within a theoretical system (but certainly from the perspective of another system) challenges are more likely to be successful on the basis of internal consistency rather than the extent to which they match the theoretical or methodological criteria of an alternative model.

Metatheories, Methods, and the Search for Why

Seeking answers to the question of *why* cognitive performance changes as it does is a crucial part of theory development (Salthouse, 1988, 1991). This search for explanations or interpretations of descriptive observations of cognitive developmental phenomena is also conducted in the context of theoretical systems or metatheories (Overton, 1984). Theoretical assumptions influence how the search for explanations is conducted, what kind of explanatory variables are considered, and how the ensuing interpretation is cast (Lakatos & Musgrave, 1970; Toulmin, 1972). There are few general principles—much less pure or universal *scientific* principles—about explanatory research. More typically, criteria for conducting explanatory research vary according to one's theoretical system and its perspective on how scientific knowledge about human behavior should be pursued. One reason theoretical systems are somewhat intrinsic and incommensurable is that the preferences for classes of explanatory variables vary to a considerable extent (Pepper, 1970). Although most scientists maintain an interest in searching for what happens (often called description) and why it happens (often called explanation), the preferred form for both phases of scientific efforts may vary considerably. In cognitive development, as in many other sciences, the search for *why* may be directed at achieving explanations of empirical phenomena (e.g., variance accounted for), or it may be directed at reaching thicker descriptions or understanding (as in *verstehen* approaches to some social and historical sciences) (Toulmin, 1972). Explanation and understanding: two goals in the search for *why,* but possibly linked to different metatheoretical and methodological approaches to science.

Earlier we introduced the three main models or metatheories of developmental psychology (i.e., mechanism, organicism, and contextualism), briefly linking them to theoretical systems in cognitive development. As has been extensively discussed in the developmental literature, these models are based in part on differing but legitimate assumptions about nature, humans, and development (e.g., Dixon & Lerner, 1992; Reese & Overton, 1970); because of these fundamental differences, they lead to programs of research differing in a variety of tendencies (Overton & Reese, 1973; Pepper, 1970). One important way in which they differ is in the goals and criteria for explanatory research. Mechanistic models tend to examine and seek explanations for cognitive change that are relatively extrinsic to the organism, clearly observable in the laboratory, and in principle manipulable through experimentation. These approaches have the advantage of well-articulated principles, such as practices and rules of inference (see, e.g., Salthouse, 1991), many of which are common to some forms and practices in the physical sciences. Organismic models tend to seek and examine developmental causes that are more intrinsic to the organism (i.e., performances represent underlying, maturing competencies), without such strict criteria of observability. Rules of inferencing allow for consideration of presumably underlying structures or competencies, without the requirement that they be directly observable or manipulable. Indeed, the presumption is often that truly developmental processes are not available to experimental manipulation. Contextual models tend to take somewhat moderate positions on how best to proceed in explanatory research. Both extrinsic and intrinsic causes may be considered, with a variety of possibly interacting internal and external variables considered. Some causal variables may be measurable, but not all are strictly observable or manipulable. Although experimental manipulation plays an important role in explanatory research, it is typically accompanied by a perspective that admits (if not seeks) distal contextual and historical explanatory variables.

CURRENT COLLECTIVES OF THEORIES OF COGNITIVE AGING

In this section, we attempt to bring together much of the foregoing in a single summary set of descriptions of families of theories of cognitive aging. The four families of theories we consider are the differential, experimental, contextual, and organismic. Constituent theories from these four families cannot always be easily differentiated. One very good reason for this inconvenience is that scientists regularly push the theoretical and methodological boundaries of their theories and paradigms. Even paradigmatic contrasts that are as sharp as that between the organismic and mechanistic models may be fuzzier when comparing specific representative theories on particular points and, perhaps most notably, methods of inquiry. The cluster we refer to as contextual borrows heavily from a variety of perspectives. Similarly, the differential and experimental perspectives often share some assumptions and methods. Our reviews of these clusters are brief, focusing only on the main theoretical characteristics, including their respective theoretical advances and limitations. We refer to original literature in each case, as well as to the chapters in this volume that cover one or more aspects of these theories in more detail.

■ Differential Approaches

The differential approach to investigating cognitive aging is best represented by the long history of research in psychometric intelligence (Botwinick, 1977; Dixon et al., 1985; Schaie, 1983). Historically, one of the foremost goals of this approach is to identify individual differences and, with respect to cognitive aging, individual differences in developmental change (Hertzog, 1985). Of the principal theoretical issues described earlier, the differential approach is intrinsically associated with positions emphasizing differential patterns of change (rather than universal patterns). This theoretical emphasis has some clear methodological implications, such as typically requiring relatively large samples and multivariate data analysis techniques (Hertzog, 1987; Nesselroade, 1970). Usually, experiments in which manipulation of one or more conditions is involved are not emphasized. Few of the other families of theories share this profile of linkages.

In the psychometric approach to cognition, intelligence is measured via a wide-ranging set of standardized items. This approach meshes neatly with an emphasis on multidimensionality and multidirectionality, precisely because theories of intelligence developed by Thurstone and others emphasized the multidimensional nature of cognitive abilities. Standardized intelligence tests—such as the Wechsler Adult Intelligence Scale (WAIS; Wechsler, 1958) or Primary Mental Abilities (PMA; Schaie, 1985)—have a shared set of characteristics. First, because such abilities were differentiated by early theorists, modern tests are wide ranging in the abilities they reflect. The comprehensiveness with which they operationally represent the construct of intelligence supports the possibility of examining multiple dimensions simultaneously. Indeed, contemporary psychometric instruments reflect this theoretical concern with multiple dimensions of intelligence. Second, as was noted earlier, if multiple dimensions of a construct are measured, the possibility of tracking them independently is promoted. This fact allows for the examination of multiple directions of developmental change within the construct of intelligence.

Third, prominent psychometric instruments were developed to have empirically determined measurement characteristics (reliability and validity). This fact supports the interest in comparing groups at one point in time, as well as, since the 1960s, differences in how groups change over time. Obviously, procedures that boast a well-measured, wide-ranging set of multiple intellectual abilities on large samples over time could produce fertile research questions and compelling empirical results. Fourth, some factorial representations of the dimensions of intelligence can be differentially linked to potentially explanatory processes. For example, in the dual-factorial model of Horn and Cattell (Horn, 1982), whereas the typically declining fluid intelligence dimension is hypothesized to be linked to declining efficiency in the neurological substrate, the typically maintained crystallized intelligence is tentatively linked to continued supportive conditions in the environment.

There is indeed an enormous body of research on cognitive aging that focuses on psychometric intelligence (see Chapter 9). Perhaps the most prominent example is Schaie's Seattle Longitudinal Study, which began in 1956 and continues at this writing (Schaie, 1983, 1994). Many results of this study have been theoretically provocative, documenting patterns or challenging assumptions about (1) the extent, degree, and timing of decline, (2) universal and individual differences in change patterns, and (3) the stability of intellectual performance in very late life (see, e.g., Schaie, 1990, 1994). The authors of a series of research reports have noted that intellectual aging follows a general pattern of gradual decline but have emphasized that (1) measurable decline begins later in the life course than often thought, (2) practically significant decline occurs even later (but not typically until after the 60s), (3) cohort differences in intellectual aging are substantial, and (4) individual differences (within a cohort) are significant. Not all psychometric studies of intellectual aging have as relatively optimistic a picture as this (see, e.g., Botwinick, 1967, 1977; Cunningham & Owens, 1983; Horn, 1982), but no study has been as exhaustive in its exploration of the issue.

As is noted in Chapter 9, the psychometric approach has also moved in the direction of examining the theoretical issue of plasticity and reversibility. The appearance of cognitive gains, losses, or even maintenance throughout adulthood could be substantially influenced by the natural life conditions of aging individuals. Changing life conditions could, in principle, modify the profile of aging-related change. As we saw above, this profound issue—the necessity of the direction(s) of cognitive aging—has been of interest since the very early contributions to cognitive aging. Although the issue is not yet resolved, researchers and theoreticians in this perspective have marshaled a considerable body of evidence pertaining to it.

In pursuing this latter effort, the psychometric approach has moved in the direction of the experimental approach. That is, more than is typical in psychometric research, well-conducted intervention research requires attention to the identification of psychological processes that are at the heart of the experimental paradigm. Thus, theoretical concerns emerging in part from descriptive psychometric research led to the adoption of additional methods of research, methods that were appropriate to test theory-based, process-oriented hypotheses. Examples of this include efforts to train older individuals to perform on fluid intelligence tests, which typically are associated with substantial and early decline with aging (see, e.g., Baltes, Dittmann-Kohli, & Kliegl, 1986; Baltes & Willis, 1982; Willis, 1985, 1990; Willis & Schaie, 1994). As we show in the next section, this effort was continued for less psychometric (and more typically cognitive) measures. In addition, other classes of explanatory variables have been explored. For example, there may be theoretically interesting aspects to the interaction between features of personality (e.g., beliefs about one's own abilities, relative rigidity or flexibility) and intellectual aging (see, e.g., Lachman, Weaver, Bandura, Elliott, & Lewkowitz, 1992; Chapter 9). At a more global level, some researchers have examined the influence of social and occupational structures (e.g., complexity of environment, availability and use of cultural resources) on the course of intellectual aging (Schooler & Schaie, 1987).

■ Experimental Approaches

Although the psychometric approach is a prominent one, the experimental approach has dominated research in cognitive aging in recent years. There is a sense in which the overlap between the two traditions is not extensive. For example, in the recent *Handbook of Aging and Cognition* (Craik & Salthouse, 1992), there is no index term for intelligence, although some coverage of psychometric-based cognitive studies is provided and issues of individual differences are occasionally noted. In the Craik and Salthouse handbook, formidable chapters review studies that have used primarily experimental methods to address questions about the cognitive mechanisms and determinants (Craik & Jennings, 1992; Light, 1992). In another sense, however, the overlap between the psychometric and experimental traditions is substantial. As noted in a thorough review by Salthouse (1991), experimental approaches often define cognition in terms of the abilities that are measured by psychometric intelligence tests. The focus in experimental approaches is on constituent processes and mechanisms thought to be involved in performance on these tests. Often stimuli in experimental tasks are used as items in ability tests and vice versa. The two traditions part company on several theoretical and methodological grounds, which we will not discuss in detail in this section (see Schaie, 1992). In brief, although the experimental tradition in cognitive aging often employs stimuli similar to those in the psychometric tradition, differences appear in both the dependent measures used and the representation of the role of age (see Chapter 3). The experimental tradition can be quick to develop new techniques and measures, which may be aggressively fielded to respond to new results and probe new, even applied, questions (see, e.g., Park, 1992). Ideally, programmatic, theory-guided, hypothesis-testing multiple-experiment research is emphasized (Kausler, 1991).

As mentioned in an earlier section, psychometric research may involve large samples, a set of measures tapping a broad range of abilities and individual difference indicators, data exploration or constrained hypothesis testing, and, ideally, multiple occasions of measurement. The experimental tradition usually focuses more on (1) a single construct, task, or set of tasks, (2) a series of experiments documenting age differences in performance, (3) hypothesis testing regarding the mechanisms and determinants of the age differences, and, typically, (4) cross-sectional designs. Nevertheless, recent efforts have probed the territory beyond each of these tendencies (see, e.g., Kliegl & Mayr, 1992; Salthouse, 1992). An example of programmatic research of this type is the series of studies by Kliegl and colleagues (Kliegl, Mayr, & Krampe, 1994; Mayr & Kliegl, 1993) in which the roles of task complexity and aging-related slowing are explored systematically. Well-designed research in both traditions can produce important information regarding cognitive aging. Indeed, some creative research programs overlap on several dimensions. The research by Salthouse (1993, 1994) examining the influence of perceptual and motor speed on cognitive aging has features of both traditions.

Given its set of characteristics, the experimental approach to cognitive aging has proven quite useful for developing theories and testing derived hypotheses about group differences and the factors that might account for them. Experimental approaches to cognitive aging have been effectively adapted to test mechanisms and explanations for age group differences (Craik & Jennings, 1992; Kausler, 1991; Salthouse, 1985, 1988, 1991; Chapter 6). Less evident for this tradition than for the psychometric tradition is the search for explanatory evidence beyond age, constituent components, and closely allied processes. For example, the fact that age is an index rather than a causal variable per se and that it may be associated with a host of other potential causal variables (such as differences in education, achievement, health, personality, sensory performance, social structure of origin, and cautiousness) is not always considered (see, e.g., Salthouse, 1991; Schaie, 1992).

The profiles of cognitive aging produced by experimental psychologists are perhaps less multidirectional and differential than those offered by some psychometric researchers. Recall that in the previous section we noted that some psychometric researchers conclude that there are multiple trajectories of cognitive change in adulthood, including the possibility that there was more maintenance of cognitive functioning later in life than previously believed (see Chapter 9). Such relatively "optimistic" interpretations of cognitive aging are rarely offered in the mainstream experimental literature. There may be several reasons for this difference. One of these is methodological: experimental researchers less frequently conduct longitudinal (and sequential) research, relying instead on cross-sectional designs, which may exacerbate the potential to infer decline. (However, longitudinal studies of cognition are infrequent, and there are limitations attendant to such designs, as well.)

A second reason is perhaps more theoretical: experimental researchers often examine processes and their components somewhat more independently than do psychometric researchers. That is, a single, hypothetically invariant "dimension" of cognition may be identified and then investigated intensively and programmatically. Some implicit, related assumptions may be manifested in this procedure, including the notions that (1) it is important and possible to "isolate" a cognitive process, (2) single tasks are effective in isolating the mechanisms, and (3) reductionism is a principal means of explanation. Associated methodological concerns—such as those raised by aggregating data across persons, trials, and variables— are occasionally addressed (see, e.g., Salthouse, 1991). Indeed, in a recent series of papers, several authors (Kliegl & Mayr, 1992; Salthouse, 1992; Schaie, 1992) agreed that multivariate methods may hold some promise for experimental research in cognitive aging.

One salient goal is to find the predictor or set of predictors that explains the age-related variance in performance on a given task (see, e.g., Light, 1991; Salthouse, 1988). Theories developed from experimental research speak with considerable authority on the micro-processes of cognitive aging and on what underlying cognitive, neurological, or physiological processes control it. Light (1991) reviews some of the principal ways of approaching theory development in experimental memory research. Her procedure was to compare four major hypotheses regarding the extent to which they accounted for observed age differences in memory performance. None of these hypotheses provided clear support for independent control of memory aging profiles, a result that may indicate (1) a lack of theoretical success by experimental memory aging researchers, (2) a need to look at a more complex explanatory matrix, (3) a need to identify more precise constituent components, (4) a need to match the processes involved in the predictor and predicted variables more closely, (5) a gap in our understanding of the role of higher-order interactions, (6) the importance of multivariate representations, or (7) several other possibilities (Kliegl & Mayr, 1992; Light, 1991; Salthouse, 1991, 1992).

Theoretical Utility of the Slowing Hypothesis

As alluded to before, one of the most powerful and frequently cited theories of cognitive aging emanating from the experimental perspective is that which accounts for age differences via the process of aging-related slowing. In this view, speed of processing provides a theoretically coherent account of many observed differences in cognitive aging (see, e.g., Birren, 1965; Brinley, 1965; Cerella, 1985, 1990, 1991; Salthouse, 1985, 1991; Welford, 1965). Certainly age differences in speed of performance (with older adults being slower than younger adults) are consistently observed for multiple cognitive and psychomotor tasks. The tasks include choice reaction time, copying, and a variety of standardized cognitive or information-processing tasks such as digit symbol substitution (see, e.g., Cerella, 1985, 1990; Salthouse, 1985, 1988, 1993). The discovery of robust age differences, with relatively little overlap and few individual differences, was a notable descriptive fact in need of a theoretical explanation. The explanation produced was that underlying and necessary resources for cognitive performance suffered inevitable diminishment with advancing age (Light, 1991; Salthouse, 1988).

A quantitative regularity relating the older to the younger adult performances was discovered and is often presented in the form of plots in which the means of older adults are plotted against the means of younger adults (see, e.g., Brinley, 1965; Cerella, 1990; Myerson, Hale, Wagstaff, Poon, & Smith, 1990). A substantial portion of adult age differences could be predicted on the basis of the response time of younger adults. For sensorimotor tasks older adults were slower than younger adults by a factor of about 1.1. For somewhat more complex but still relatively simple reaction time tasks, older adults were slower by a factor of about 1.4. For more complex cognitive tasks the slowing factor was about 1.6. In simple terms this implies that by knowing the kind of cognitive task one could multiply the mean younger adults' performance by a constant and accurately predict the mean older adults' performance. Such impressive generality and regularity are rare in psychology, and the field of cognitive aging is no exception. Relating cognitive age differences to an underlying decline in the speed of information processing (due, perhaps, to a decline in neurological efficiency) could indicate substantial theoretical progress.

The theoretical significance of this systematic relationship has continued to be explored—and debated—on both methodological and theoretical grounds (see, e.g., Cerella, 1994; Fisk & Fisher, 1994; Fisk, Fisher, & Rogers, 1992; Hartley, 1992; Hertzog, 1991; Myerson, Wagstaff, & Hale, 1994; Perfect, 1994). The debates are grounded in such issues as (1) reversibility/plasticity and the role of practice and training (see, e.g., Cerella, 1991, 1994; Dixon, Kurzman, & Friesen, 1993; Fisk & Fisher, 1994; Fisk & Rogers, 1991; Rogers, Fisk, & Hertzog, 1994), (2) the universality (individual differences) theoretical issue as it applies to theories of cognitive slowing (see, e.g., Fisk & Fisher, 1994; Hertzog, 1991), and (3) task-related issues such as difficulty, complexity, and familiarity (see, e.g., Fisk, Fisher, & Rogers, 1992; Kliegl et al., 1994; Mayr & Kliegl, 1993).

It is important in theory development to test the generality of theories—theories are as general as their accumulated complexities, dependencies, and limitations allow. It may also be important to the development of knowledge to be provocative (Salthouse, 1992). The search for one or, at most, a few general factors or mechanisms controlling aging-related changes in cognition is consonant with the experimental approach to cognitive aging and the mechanistic approach to psychological research. It has the benefit of parsimony, in that multifaceted aspects of cognitive performance are reduced to a few underlying mechanisms upon which aging has a predictable influence. For example, researchers in this model have discussed the existence of a small set of processing resources (see, e.g., Craik & Byrd, 1982; Rabinowitz, Craik, & Ackerman, 1982; Salthouse, 1991). These are described as a limited number of hypothetical resources for cognitive performance, which are relatively universal in their (1) determination of cognitive performance and (2) vulnerability to aging-related decline. Such theoretical efforts reveal the power of the experimental approach, in terms of (1) its breadth or generality, (2) its flexibility in allowing nonobservable explanatory phenomena, and (3) its ability to spark high-level theoretical debate and empirical research (see, e.g., Light, 1988, 1991; Salthouse, 1985, 1988). As the implications, strengths, and limitations of the experimental approach continue to be explored analytically and empirically, such theoretical advances will sponsor even more unique and valuable contributions.

■ Contextual Approaches

Contextual approaches is a plural term indicating that more than one approach may be involved. Indeed, contextual approaches are combinatory, in that there is a tendency of this collection of theories to borrow and combine perspectives, methods, theories, and goals from, especially, the camps of the experimental and differential collectives. This is not unique, as we have seen that both the psychometric and experimental approaches have several points of overlap. By comparison, the degree of theoretical and methodological openness—the extent to which aspects of different traditions may be adapted—of contextual approaches is perhaps somewhat greater. This openness is not an unmitigated advantage. Some researchers from the experimental approach make substantial theoretical gains by adhering to a common and specifiable set of scientific desiderata, including constraining the phenomena to be examined and programmatically pursuing ever more parsimonious explanations. Contextual approaches share few such principles, goals, or even tasks and methods, and this inevitably takes a toll on its theoretical fertility. But the openness of the contextual approach does have some advantages. More easily than the psychometric and experimental approaches—at least initially—it may accommodate new interests, research questions, methods, and applied concerns. In short, it may respond adaptively to new challenges presented by changing intellectual demands in the field of cognitive aging.

These three approaches can also be compared on other dimensions. The psychometric approach has substantial methodological strengths but perhaps some corresponding weaknesses in representing cognitive processes and developing innovative means of measuring them. The experimental approach has substantial theoretical strengths and can sponsor innovative means of assessing processes, but it is often restricted in its range of phenomena considered. Some cognitive aging theorists appear to select perceived strengths of both the differential and the experimental approaches and apply them to less frequently studied issues. Contextual approaches may, as the name implies, bring a concern for the roles of cultural, historical, or social context to the study of adult cognitive development (see, e.g., Chapter 10). It may also be associated with a set of propositions concerning a wide range of theoretical, methodological, and even substantive foci (see, e.g., Baltes, 1987). Another concern is with practical functions of cognition, or cognition as an instrumental or practical means of adapting to real-world demands (Dixon & Baltes, 1986). Scholars in this tradition may attempt to maintain a focus on cognition in context, on how aging adults adapt cognitively to changing circumstances and demands. Although this may place this research more closely at the heart of real-world development, a corresponding weakness of this approach is that conducting empirical work on complex, everyday phenomena may be considerably less precise. A lack of definitive answers to specific questions is understandably problematic to some observers from other traditions.

What are the issues addressed by contextual cognitive aging researchers? They include primarily issues that can be related to the two earlier systems and, importantly, to previous discussions in ecological cognitive psychology (see, e.g., Bruce, 1985; Neisser, 1967, 1976, 1978). In this section, we summarize briefly research in two such areas: (1) practical and social cognition and aging, and (2) the mechanisms of maintenance and skilled performance in late life. Although the purviews of both the differential and the experimental traditions are overlapping and widening, some researchers seek to extend the boundaries of these approaches even more. One interest of such theorists is in mapping the variety of contextual factors that influence cognitive performance in older adults. These factors may include internal psychological conditions (such as mood states, preexisting knowledge, and motivation) and physical and health conditions (such as aerobic capacity, health beliefs, medications, and actual health), as well as relatively external characteristics (such as culture, education, work conditions and history, and marital and social interactions). If multiple conditions play a role in determining cognitive performance, a contextually oriented aging researcher would expect that population heterogeneity in the underlying influences should produce substantial individual differences in cognitive development. The more factors that can potentially influence the trajectory(ies) of cognitive aging, the more likely it is that individuals, across life, will accumulate unique combinations of these influences. The more divergent the set of influences on individual development, the more likely it is that individuals will develop differently throughout life, and perhaps increasingly so with aging.

Obviously, this implies that researchers in this tradition are likely to be less positively disposed to embrace unidirectional models of cognitive aging. Although the range and number of aspects of cognitive development that undergo similar (and universal) directions of development may vary, contextualists are more likely to emphasize multidirectional development. Like the differential cognitive aging psychologists, contextualists easily argue for the multidimensional character of cognitive constructs. In addition, they emphasize the plasticity of cognitive functioning, even in late life. They are likely to assume that changes in the environment (including practice or training programs) can alter an older adult's performance on selected cognitive tasks. Finally, it should be evident that contextual theorists view cognitive aging as a mixture of gains, maintenance, and losses, with the balance shifting toward the latter as aging progresses (Baltes, 1987).

Practical and Social Cognition

This growing area of research includes experimental (see, e.g., Park, 1992) and psychometric (see, e.g., Willis & Schaie, 1986) methods and issues, combining them with both developmental theoretical issues and real-world applications (see, e.g., West, 1992; West & Sinnott, 1992; Chapter 10). As noted earlier in this chapter, how older adults actually perform cognitive tasks in everyday life is relevant to both basic research and fundamental theoretical issues of cognitive development. Research issues include: (1) how older adults perform when tested with materials that represent the type of tasks they perform in everyday life; (2) whether adaptation to everyday life can be better understood and promoted through intervention research; (3) the relationship between measures of practical cognition and performance on both everyday functioning tasks and standardized tests; (4) the relationship between performance on practical cognition tasks and a variety of indicators of affect and beliefs; (5) how the social context of much everyday cognitive functioning influences and moderates performance; and (6) the extent to which the environment can be modified so as to promote effective functioning (Hertzog & Dunlosky, in press; Park, 1992; Chapter 10).

Each of these research issues has theoretical implications, especially for the question of how best to represent the nature and profile of cognitive change in adulthood. For example, findings that older adults improve or maintain their level of performance for practically relevant tasks (and decline primarily on laboratory tasks) would challenge the generalization of decline models for cognitive mechanisms to cognition as manifested in real-world contexts. Thus far, such far-reaching implications have not been firmly supported, but some evidence that cognitive aging is not universally and irreversibly loss-directed has been offered (Dixon, 1992; Chapter 10). In addition, each of the issues has substantial real-world application. For example, Park's (Park & Kidder, in press; Park, 1992) research program on medication adherence applies theoretical models from cognitive psychology to a crucial practical issue for older adults and employs sophisticated methods to collect and analyze data. As Park's studies illustrate, research on practical cognition in adulthood must be well grounded in developmental theory, in developmental and experimental methods, and in problems of some consequence in everyday life.

A concern with adaptation to the environment—and with modifiable aspects of the environment to the facts of aging individuals—is typical for human factors researchers (see, e.g., Charness & Bosman, 1990). This is an important point of contact for future contextual research in cognitive aging. Similarly, research and theory in the social or interactive contexts of aging are receiving more attention. Two fronts of interest have been pursued: (1) whether social cognitive tasks produce performance that varies from that on laboratory or other practical cognition tasks (see, e.g., Chapters 12 and 14) and (2) whether adults collaborating on cognitive problems produce performance that is substantially better than they would produce as individuals. In the latter area, the products and processes of cognition performed in collaborative situations may be compared across multiple dimensions and linked to theoretically interesting concerns such as experience (or expertise in collaborating) and compensation (through the mechanism of collaborators) (Dixon, 1992, in press).

Conditions of Maintenance and Improvement

Researchers from an experimental perspective have provided evidence that some cognitive skills and competence may be maintained and even improved in late life (see, e.g., Charness, 1989; Salthouse, 1990; Chapter 13). By focusing on specific skills of individuals' professional or leisure pursuits, psychologists have been able to identify conditions under which cognitively challenging activities may be performed at high levels by older adults. Identifying the mechanisms of exceptional performance helps to address theoretical concerns about how and why such profiles should be observed (see, e.g., Kliegl & Baltes, 1987). One theoretical implication of such research is, again, that cognitive aging can indeed be multidirectional and can include, under appropriate conditions, maintenance and even select gains. Empirical observations that are relevant to these issues would be less likely to occur under the laboratory conditions of psychometric and experimental researchers.

Research and theory on expertise and aging have been associated, as well, with the examination of a related construct, compensation. The theoretical idea here is that maintenance of performance into late life may be accomplished by the same mechanisms that are involved with younger experts or, if these fail with aging, by alternative mechanisms. This latter process is one of several known as compensation (see, e.g., Bäckman, 1989; Bäckman & Dixon, 1992; Dixon & Bäckman, 1995; Salthouse, 1987). Successful cognitive aging—adapting to the cognitive requirements of daily living—could be accomplished through maximizing the match between contextual demands and accessible cognitive resources. Deficits could occur because of both aging-related decline and increases in the demands of the context. There is a variety of compensatory mechanisms through which a match might be accomplished (Bäckman & Dixon, 1992). These include: (1) investing more effort and time in the task, (2) developing substitutable mechanisms for performing the task, and (3) channeling one's effort into a tailored and select number of domains (Baltes, 1987; Charness, 1989; Dixon & Bäckman, 1993; Uttal & Perlmutter, 1989). Such possibilities impute multidimensionality, multidirectionality, and considerable plasticity to cognitive aging. In general, the research on experience and compensation in cognitive aging provides an important point of union between the approaches. It shares much methodologically with experimental techniques, and its theoretical implications—although very different—are not necessarily in complete conflict with those of experimentalists, as described before. One reason for this is that the two approaches operate at rather different levels of analysis, combining some of the methods of experimental approaches with the interests and questions of contextual approaches. There are, therefore, important points of overlap among all of these three clusters of theories.

■ Organismic Approach

The organismic approach to cognitive aging is derived at least in part from the organismic model of psychology and other sciences (see, e.g., Pepper, 1970; Reese & Overton, 1970). It is related to such movements in psychology as cognitive structuralism, Piagetian child cognitive developmental theories, and neo-Piagetian applications to adult development. According to early Piagetian models of cognitive development, little structural change was thought to occur after the attainment of formal operations in early adolescence; that is, further changes throughout the life span were quantitative (amount) rather than qualitative (kind) in nature (Flavell, 1970; Piaget, 1972). If followed literally, this would imply that (1) individual differences in cognitive aging are less important than the fact of generally universal patterns of change, (2) the direction of cognitive aging is basically set by early adulthood, at least insofar as little further qualitative change is expected, (3) the peak of cognitive development is reached fairly early and the quantitative change that does occur may be decline, and (4) reversibility and plasticity, at least with respect to basic structural change, are not a major part of the theory. In addition, given the maturational (biological) underpinnings of the model (as applied to that of child cognitive development) it might also suggest that change in adulthood is largely decremental. An interesting theoretical puzzle for scholars in this tradition is to decouple the underlying biological mechanism of early life that propels growth (maturationally and cognitively) from the biological mechanism of senescence in adulthood that would produce (biological and cognitive?) decline. If morphological growth (maturation) is largely responsible for cognitive progression in childhood, what theoretical mechanism could be responsible for cognitive growth (and also decline) in adulthood? In addressing this issue, Labouvie-Vief (1992) suggests that individualized experience assumes an ever-increasing role in directing cognitive development in adulthood. But, as she notes, this accounts only partly for cognitive growth; also responsible, perhaps, is that aging adults reorganize their structures of thought in response to biologically driven cognitive declines. The outcome of this process could be cognitive progression (Labouvie-Vief, 1992, 1994; Pascual-Leone, 1984). In this way, contemporary organismic theory has forged some links with experimental and contextual approaches.

More specifically, in research on postformal thought one expectation has been that there would be a stage of cognitive development beyond formal operations (Kitchener & King, 1981; Kramer, 1983; Labouvie-Vief, 1980, 1992). Such a stage, whether seen as problem seeking, relativistic, or dialectical in nature (see, e.g., Arlin, 1975; Kramer & Woodruff, 1986; Riegel, 1973; Sinnott, 1983), could embody further structural growth. For organismic theorists (at least in childhood) this is important, for quantitative increments in performance on a set of tasks are not as theoretically interesting as qualitative gains. Major structural or systemic changes in cognitive abilities are viewed as theoretically appealing. And these structural changes are theoretically meaningful insofar as they are normal, universal, and growthlike aspects of cognitive aging. Research with traditional Piagetian tasks, however, has not been entirely successful at indicating such a positive set of outcomes. Many life-span researchers, therefore, have moved away from standard Piagetian tasks and even Piagetian child cognitive structuralism, although still being informed by the basic tenets of organismic theory (see, e.g., Adams, 1991; Jepson & Labouvie-Vief, 1992; Kitchener & King, 1981; Labouvie-Vief, 1992; Pascual-Leone, 1984). For example, some connection with contextual approaches can be seen in the concern for the adaptive, practical features of possible adult structural progression, as well as in further examination of the interplay among affective, social, and cognitive development (see, e.g., Labouvie-Vief, 1982, 1985; Pascual-Leone, 1983; Chapter 14). Recently, Labouvie-Vief (1994) argued that there are important gender differences and age changes in the role of rationality, on the one hand, and emotion and imagination, on the other, in life-span development.

Useful reviews of these issues may be found in Alexander and Langer (1990), Labouvie-Vief (1992, 1994), and Chapter 7. These authors deal with the theoretical challenges of a life-span organismic theory, in which cognitive growth is a central expected outcome. Other theoretical issues of concern include (1) the relationships of and differences between quantitative and qualitative change processes, (2) the issue of directionality and end points to cognitive development, and (3) a specification of the mechanisms supporting directional development and structural transformations. With regard to the last, the organismic approach may be contrasted with some of the other clusters we have discussed on the issue of mechanisms of change (Rybash, Hoyer, & Roodin, 1986). Whereas the differential approach focuses on the identification of differential change patterns and the experimental approach focuses on the testing of mechanisms and explanations for aging-related changes, the organismic approach may be characterized as attempting to reveal the mechanisms of directional change.

CONCLUSION

The field of cognitive aging is fascinating, active, and theoretically rich. There are numerous issues that reach to the heart of how we view aging in general and our own aging in particular. We trust we have conveyed that there is an enormous, teeming variety in approaches, issues, and even controversies in this field. But we trust also that we have conveyed that there is some systematicity to these approaches, issues, and controversies. It is possible to identify a set of fundamental theoretical issues in cognitive aging—universality, directionality, plasticity, variability, and gains versus losses—and to compare collectives of theories on these issues. Although such issues have been puzzling scholars for decades, it is clear that definite progress has been achieved. Our understanding of cognitive aging today is far more refined than at any point in our history. The theoretical and methodological similarities and contrasts have been sharpened. Not only has a great deal of data been collected and interpreted, but organizing and fruitful theories have been proffered.

The field of cognitive aging is growing dramatically, but, like developmental psychology before it, it may risk growing into isolated theoretical camps. Our chapter has attempted to present a fair and even pluralistic treatment of some aspects of the variety of theoretical positions in the study of cognitive development in adulthood. Unlike many previous reviews of cognitive aging theory, it was not designed to explicate a single theory or approach, and it certainly has not explored the full range of ideas associated with any single issue, theoretical tradition, or metatheory. We have provided pointers to major works in most of the areas we have covered.

We believe that the sheer volume of attention being paid to this field today augers well for the prospects for continuing progress in this field. There are many new or promising avenues of scholarship for which increasing degrees of cooperation with cognitive aging are being explored. These include such emerging fields—or fields emerging as especially pertinent to cognitive aging—as cognitive neurosciences, computational approaches, social (or collective) cognition, cultural comparisons, dynamic systems approaches, developmental and evolutionary theory, and statistical methods of analyzing change (see, e.g., Cole, in press; Collins & Horn, 1991; Johnson & Rybash, 1993; Salthe, 1993; Thelen & Smith, 1994; Woodruff-Pak, 1993; Woodruff-Pak & Hanson, 1995). Clearly, there is a broad range of neighboring disciplines, with a host of research agendas, many of which concern a set of theoretical issues and research topics quite consonant with those of cognitive aging.

SUPPLEMENTAL READINGS

Baltes, P. B. (1987). Theoretical propositions of life-span developmental psychology: On the dynamics between growth and decline. *Developmental Psychology, 23,* 611–626.

Light, L. L. (1991). Memory and aging: Four hypotheses in search of data. *Annual Review of Psychology, 42,* 333–376.

Pepper, S. C. (1970). *World hypotheses.* Berkeley: Univ. of California Press.

Salthouse, T. A. (1991). *Theoretical perspectives on cognitive aging.* Hillsdale, NJ: Erlbaum.

ACKNOWLEDGMENTS

We appreciate the helpful comments of John Dunlosky, Fredda Blanchard-Fields, Tom Hess, and four anonymous reviewers. The first author acknowledges research grant support from the Natural Sciences and Engineering Research Council of Canada and the Canadian Aging Research Network.

REFERENCES

Adams, C. (1991). Qualitative age differences in memory for text: A life-span developmental perspective. *Psychology and Aging, 6,* 323–336.

Alexander, C. N., & Langer, E. J. (Eds.) (1990). *Higher stages of human development: Perspectives on adult growth.* New York: Oxford Univ. Press.

Anderson, J. R. (1982). Acquisition of cognitive skill. *Psychological Review, 89,* 369–406.

Arlin, P. K. (1975). Cognitive development in adulthood: A fifth stage? *Developmental Psychology, 11,* 602–606.

Babcock, R. L., & Salthouse, T. A. (1990). Effects of increasing processing demands on age differences in working memory. *Psychology and Aging, 5,* 421–428.

Bäckman, L. (1985). Compensation and recoding: A framework for aging and memory research. *Scandinavian Journal of Psychology, 26,* 193–207.

Bäckman, L. (1989). Varieties of memory compensation of older adults in episodic remembering. In L. W. Poon, D. C. Rubin, & B. A. Wilson (Eds.), *Everyday cognition in adulthood and late life* (pp. 509–544). Cambridge: Cambridge Univ. Press.

Bäckman, L., & Dixon, R. A. (1992). Psychological compensation: A theoretical framework. *Psychological Bulletin, 112,* 259–283.

Bäckman, L., Mäntylä, T., & Herlitz, A. (1990). The optimization of episodic remembering in old age. In P. B. Baltes & M. M. Baltes (Eds.), *Successful aging: Perspectives from the behavioral sciences* (pp. 118–163). New York: Cambridge Univ. Press.

Baltes, P. B. (1987). Theoretical propositions of life-span developmental psychology: On the dynamics between growth and decline. *Developmental Psychology, 23,* 611–626.

Baltes, P. B., & Baltes, M. M. (1980). Plasticity and variability in psychological aging: Methodological and theoretical issues. In G. Gurski (Ed.), *Determining the effects of aging on the central nervous system* (pp. 41–60). Berlin: Schering.

Baltes, P. B., Dittmann-Kohli, F., & Dixon, R. A. (1984). New perspectives on the development of intelligence in adulthood: Toward a dual-process conception and a model of selective optimization with compensation. In P. B. Baltes & O. G. Brim (Eds.), *Life-span development and behavior* (vol. 6, pp. 33–76). New York: Academic Press.

Baltes, P. B., Dittmann-Kohli, F., & Kliegl, R. (1986). Reserve capacity of the elderly in aging-sensitive tests of fluid intelligence: Replication and extension. *Psychology and Aging, 1,* 172–177.

Baltes, P. B., Reese, H. W., & Lipsitt, L. P. (1980). Life-span developmental psychology. *Annual Review of Psychology, 31,* 65–110.

Baltes, P. B., Reese, H. W., & Nesselroade, J. R. (1977). *Life-span developmental psychology: Introduction to research methods.* Monterey, CA: Brooks-Cole.

Baltes, P. B., & Schaie, K. W. (1976). On the plasticity of intelligence in adulthood and old age: Where Horn and Donaldson fail. *American Psychologist, 31,* 720–725.

Baltes, P. B., & Willis, S. L. (1982). Plasticity and enhancement of intellectual functioning in old age: Penn State's Adult Development and Enrichment Project (ADEPT). In F. I. M. Craik & S. E. Trehub (Eds.), *Aging and cognitive processes* (pp. 353–389). New York: Plenum.

Binet, A., & Simon, T. (1911). *A method of measuring the development of the intelligence of young children.* Lincoln, IL: Courier.

Birren, J. E. (1965). Age changes in speeded behavior: Its central nature and physiological correlates. In A. T. Welford & J. E. Birren (Eds.), *Behavior, aging and the nervous system* (pp. 191–216). Springfield, IL: Thomas.

Birren, J. E., Cunningham, W. R., & Yamamato, K. (1982). Psychology of adult development and aging. *Annual Review of Psychology, 34,* 543–575.

Birren, J. E., & Schaie, K. W. (eds.) (1977). *Handbook of the psychology of aging.* New York: Van Nostrand Reinhold.

Birren, J. E., Woods, A. M., & Williams, M. V. (1980). Behavioral slowing with age: Causes, organization and consequences. In L. W. Poon (Ed.), *Aging in the 1980s: Psychological issues* (pp. 293–308). Washington, DC: American Psychological Association.

Bosman, E. A. (1993). Age-related differences in the motoric aspects of transcription typing skill. *Psychology and Aging, 8,* 87–102.

Botwinick, J. (1967). *Cognitive processes in maturity and old age.* New York: Springer.

Botwinick, J. (1977). Intellectual abilities. In J. E. Birren & K. W. Schaie (Eds.), *Handbook of the psychology of aging* (pp. 580–605). New York: Van Nostrand Reinhold.

Brandtstädter, J., & Wentura, D. (1995). Adjustment of shifting possibility frontiers in later life: Complementary adaptive modes. In R. A. Dixon & L. Bäckman (Eds.), *Compensating for psychological deficits and declines: Managing losses and promoting gains* (pp. 83–106). Hillsdale, NJ: Erlbaum.

Brinley, J. F. (1965). Cognitive sets, speed and accuracy of performance in the elderly. In A. T. Welford & J. E. Birren (Eds.), *Behavior, aging and the nervous system* (pp. 114–149). Springfield, IL: Thomas.

Bruce, D. (1985). The how and why of ecological memory. *Journal of Experimental Psychology: General, 114,* 78–90.

Bühler, C. (1933). *Der menschliche Lebenslauf als psychologisches Problem* [The human life course as a topic in psychology]. Leipzig: Hirzel.

Campbell, D. T. (1974). Evolutionary epistemology. In P. Schilpp (Ed.), *The philosophy of Karl Popper* (vol. 1, pp. 413–463). La Salle, IL: Open Court.

Cerella, J. (1985). Information processing rates in the elderly. *Psychological Bulletin, 98,* 67–83.

Cerella, J. (1990). Aging and information processing rate. In J. E. Birren & K. W. Schaie (Eds.), *Handbook of the psychology of aging* (3d ed., pp. 201–221). San Diego: Academic Press.

Cerella, J. (1991). Age effects may be global, not local: Comment on Fisk and Rogers (1991). *Journal of Experimental Psychology: General, 12,* 215–223.

Cerella, J. (1994). Generalized slowing in Brinley plots. *Journal of Gerontology, 49,* P65–P71.

Chapman, M. (1988). Contextuality and directionality of cognitive development. *Human Development, 31,* 92–106.

Charness, N. (1981). Aging and skilled problem solving. *Journal of Experimental Psychology: General, 110,* 21–38.

Charness, N. (1989). Age and expertise: Responding to Talland's challenge. In L. W. Poon, D. C. Rubin, & B. A. Wilson (Eds.), *Everyday cognition in adulthood and late life* (pp. 437–456). Cambridge: Cambridge Univ. Press.

Charness, N., & Bosman, E. A. (1990). Human factors and design for older adults. In J. E. Birren & K. W. Schaie (Eds.), *Handbook of the psychology of aging* (3d ed., pp. 446–463). San Diego: Academic Press.

Cole, M. (in press). Interacting minds in a lifespan perspective: A cultural/historical approach to culture and cognitive development. In P. B. Baltes & U. M. Staudinger (Eds.), *Interactive minds: Life-span perspectives on the social foundation of cognition.* New York: Cambridge Univ. Press.

Collins, L. M., & Horn, J. L. (Eds.) (1991). *Best methods for the analysis of change.* Washington, DC: American Psychological Association.

Craik, F. I. M. (1977). Age differences in human memory. In J. E. Birren & K. W. Schaie (Eds.), *Handbook of the psychology of aging* (pp. 384–420). New York: Van Nostrand Reinhold.

Craik, F. I. M. (1994). Will cognitivism bury experimental psychology? *Canadian Psychology, 32,* 440–444.

Craik, F. I. M., & Byrd, M. (1982). Aging and cognitive deficits: The role of attentional resources. In F. I. M. Craik & S. Trehub (Eds.), *Aging and cognitive processes* (pp. 191–211). New York: Plenum.

Craik, F. I. M., & Jennings, J. M. (1992). Human memory. In F. I. M. Craik & T. A. Salthouse (Eds.), *The handbook of aging and cognition* (pp. 51–110). Hillsdale, NJ: Erlbaum.

Craik, F. I. M., & Salthouse, T. A. (Eds.) (1992). *The handbook of aging and cognition.* Hillsdale, NJ: Erlbaum.

Cunningham, W. R., & Owens, W. A. (1983). The Iowa State study of the adult development of intellectual abilities. In K. W. Schaie (Ed.), *Longitudinal studies of adult psychological development* (pp. 20–39). New York: Guilford.

Dixon, R. A. (1992). Contextual approaches to adult intellectual development. In R. J. Sternberg & C. A. Berg (Eds.), *Intellectual development* (pp. 350–380). New York: Cambridge Univ. Press.

Dixon, R. A. (1995). Promoting competence through compensation. In L. Bond, S. Cutler, & A. Gram (Eds.), *Promoting successful and productive aging.* Newbury Park, CA: Sage.

Dixon, R. A. (in press). Collaborative memory and aging. In D. J. Herrmann, M. K. Johnson, C. L. McEvoy, C. Hertzog, & P. Hertel (Eds.), *Basic and applied memory: Theory in context.* Hillsdale, NJ: Erlbaum.

Dixon, R. A., & Bäckman, L. (Eds.) (1995). *Compensating for psychological deficits and declines: Managing losses and promoting gains.* Hillsdale, NJ: Erlbaum.

Dixon, R. A., & Baltes, P. B. (1986). Toward life-span research on the functions and pragmatics of intelligence. In R. J. Sternberg & R. K. Wagner (Eds.), *Practical intelligence: Nature and origins of competence in the everyday world* (pp. 203–235). New York: Cambridge Univ. Press.

Dixon, R. A., Hertzog, C., Friesen, I. C., & Hultsch, D. F. (1993). Assessment of intraindividual change in text recall of elderly adults. In H. H. Brownell & Y. Joanette (Eds.), *Narrative discourse in neurologically impaired and normal aging adults* (pp. 77–101). San Diego: Singular.

Dixon, R. A., Kramer, D. A., & Baltes, P. B. (1985). Intelligence: A life-span perspective. In B. B. Wolman (Ed.), *Handbook of intelligence: Theories, measurements, and applications* (pp. 301–350). New York: Wiley.

Dixon, R. A., Kurzman, D., & Friesen, I. C. (1993). Handwriting performance in younger and older adults: Age, familiarity, and practice effects. *Psychology and Aging, 8,* 360–370.

Dixon, R. A., & Lerner, R. M. (1992). A history of systems in developmental psychology. In M. H. Bornstein & M. E. Lamb (Eds.), *Developmental psychology: An advanced textbook* (3d ed., pp. 3–58). Hillsdale, NJ: Erlbaum.

Dixon, R. A., Lerner, R. M., & Hultsch, D. F. (1991). The concept of development in individual and social change. In P. van Geert & L. P. Mos (eds.), *Annals of theoretical psychology, 7,* 279–323. New York: Plenum Press.

Donaldson, G. (1981). Letter to the editor. *Journal of Gerontology, 36,* 634–636.

Ericsson, K. A., & Charness, N. (1994). Expert performance: Its structure and acquisition. *American Psychologist, 49,* 725–747.

Erikson, E. H. (1959). Identity and the life cycle. *Psychological Issues Monograph 1.* New York: International Univ. Press.

Feyerabend, P. (1978). *Science in a free society.* London: NLB.

Fisk, A. D., & Fisher, D. L. (1994). Brinley plots and theories of aging: The explicit, muddled, and implicit debates. *Journal of Gerontology: Psychological Sciences, 49,* P81–P89.

Fisk, A. D., Fisher, D. L., & Rogers, W. A. (1992). General slowing alone cannot explain age-related search effects: Reply to Cerella. *Journal of Experimental Psychology: General, 121,* 73–78.

Fisk, A. D., & Rogers, W. A. (1991). Toward an understanding of age-related memory and visual search effects. *Journal of Experimental Psychology: General, 120,* 131–149.

Flavell, J. H. (1970). Cognitive changes in adulthood. In L. R. Goulet & P. B. Baltes (Eds.), *Life-span developmental psychology: Research and theory* (pp. 247–253). New York: Academic Press.

Friesen, I. C. (1993). *Intraindividual variability in the cognitive functioning of an Alzheimer patient and healthy old adults.* Unpublished master's thesis, Univ. of Victoria (British Columbia).

Gardner, H. (1985). *The mind's new science: A history of the cognitive revolution.* New York: Basic.

Harris, D. B. (Ed.) (1957). *The concept of development.* Minneapolis: Univ. of Minnesota Press.

Hartley, A. A. (1989). The cognitive ecology of problem solving. In L. W. Poon, D. C. Rubin, & B. A. Wilson (Eds.), *Everyday cognition in adulthood and late life* (pp. 300–329). New York: Cambridge Univ. Press.

Hartley, A. A. (1992). Attention. In F. I. M. Craik & T. A. Salthouse (Eds.), *The handbook of aging and cognition* (pp. 3–49). Hillsdale, NJ: Erlbaum.

Hearst, E. (Ed.) (1979). *The first century of experimental psychology.* Hillsdale, NJ: Erlbaum.

Hertzog, C. (1985). An individual differences perspective: Implications for cognitive research in gerontology. *Research on Aging, 7,* 7–45.

Hertzog, C. (1987). Applications of structural equation models in gerontological research. In K. W. Schaie (Ed.), *Annual review of gerontology and geriatrics* (vol. 7, pp. 265–293). New York: Springer.

Hertzog, C. (1991). Aging, information processing speed, and intelligence. In K. W. Schaie (Ed.), *Annual review of gerontology and geriatrics* (vol. 11, pp. 55–79). New York: Springer.

Hertzog, C., & Dixon, R. A. (1994). Metacognitive development in adulthood and old age. In J. Metcalfe & A. P. Shimamura (Eds.), *Metacognition: Knowing about knowing* (pp. 227–251). Boston: MIT Press.

Hertzog, C., Dixon, R. A., & Hultsch, D. F. (1992). Intraindividual change in text recall of the elderly. *Brain and Language, 42,* 248–269.

Hertzog, C., & Dunlosky, J. (in press). The aging of practical memory: An overview. In D. J. Herrmann, M. K. Johnson, C. L. McEvoy, C. Hertzog, & P. Hertel (Eds.), *Basic and applied memory: Theory in context.* Hillsdale, NJ: Erlbaum.

Hollingworth, H. L. (1927). *Mental growth and decline: A survey of developmental psychology.* New York: Appleton.

Horn, J. L. (1982). The theory of fluid and crystallized intelligence in relation to concepts of cognitive psychology and aging in adulthood. In F. I. M. Craik & S. Trehub (Eds.), *Aging and cognitive processes* (pp. 237–278). New York: Plenum.

Horn, J. L., & Donaldson, G. (1976). On the myth of intellectual decline in adulthood. *American Psychologist, 31,* 701–709.

Hoyer, W. J., & Rybash, J. M. (1994). Characterizing adult cognitive development. *Journal of Adult Development, 1,* 7–12.

Hultsch, D. F., & Dixon, R. A. (1990). Learning and memory in aging. In J. E. Birren & K. W. Schaie (Eds.), *Handbook of the psychology of aging* (3d ed., pp. 258–274). San Diego: Academic Press.

Hultsch, D. F., Hertzog, C., Dixon, R. A., & Small, B. (in press). *Individual differences in memory change in the aged.* Cambridge: Cambridge Univ. Press.

Jepson, K., & Labouvie-Vief, G. (1992). Symbolic processing in the elderly. In J. Sinnott & R. West (Eds.), *Everyday memory and aging: Current research and methodology* (pp. 124–137). New York: Springer.

Johnson, S. H., & Rybash, J. M. (1993). A cognitive neuroscience perspective on age-related slowing: Developmental changes in the functional architecture. In J. Cerella, J. Rybash, W. Hoyer, & M. L. Commons (Eds.), *Adult information processing: Limits on loss* (pp. 143–175). San Diego: Academic Press.

Kaszniak, A. W. (1990). Psychological assessment of the aging individual. In J. E. Birren & K. W. Schaie (Eds.), *Handbook of the psychology of aging* (3d ed., pp. 427–445). San Diego: Academic Press.

Kausler, D. H. (1991). *Experimental psychology, cognition, and human aging* (2d ed.). New York: Springer.

Kitchener, K. S., & King, P. M. (1981). Reflective judgment: Concepts of justification and their relationship to age and education. *Journal of Applied Developmental Psychology, 2,* 89–116.

Kliegl, R., & Baltes, P. B. (1987). Theory-guided analysis of development and aging mechanisms through testing-the-limits and research on expertise. In C. Schooler & K. W. Schaie (Eds.), *Cognitive functioning and social structure over the life course* (pp. 95–119). Norwood, NJ: Ablex.

Kliegl, R., & Mayr, U. (1992). Commentary. *Human Development, 35,* 343–349.

Kliegl, R., Mayr, U., & Krampe, R. T. (in press). Time-accuracy functions for determining process and person differences: An application to cognitive aging. *Cognitive Psychology.*

Kliegl, R., Smith, J., & Baltes, P. B. (1990). On the locus and process of magnification of age differences during mnemonic training. *Developmental Psychology, 26,* 894–904.

Kramer, D. A. (1983). Post-formal operations? A need for further conceptualization. *Human Development, 26,* 91–105.

Kramer, D., & Woodruff, D. (1986). Relativistic and dialectical thought in three adult age-groups. *Human Development, 29,* 280–290.

Kuhn, D. (1995). Microgenetic study of change: What has it told us? *Psychological Science, 6,* 133–139.

Kuhn, T. S. (1970). *The structure of scientific revolutions* (2d ed.). Chicago: Univ. of Chicago Press.

Labouvie-Vief, G. (1980). Beyond formal operations: Uses and limits of pure logic in life-span development. *Human Development, 23,* 141–161.

Labouvie-Vief, G. (1982). Dynamic development and mature autonomy: A theoretical prologue. *Human Development, 25,* 161–191.

Labouvie-Vief, G. (1985). Intelligence and cognition. In J. E. Birren & K. W. Schaie (Eds.), *Handbook of the psychology of aging* (2d ed., pp. 500–530). New York: Van Nostrand Reinhold.

Labouvie-Vief, G. (1992). A neo-Piagetian perspective on adult cognitive development. In R. J. Sternberg & C. A. Berg (Eds.), *Intellectual development* (pp. 197–228). Cambridge: Cambridge Univ. Press.

Labouvie-Vief, G. (1994). *Psyche and Eros: Mind and gender in the life course.* Cambridge: Cambridge Univ. Press.

Lachman, M. E., Weaver, S. L., Bandura, M., Elliott, E., & Lewkowitz, C. J. (1992). Improving memory and control beliefs through cognitive restructuring and self-generated strategies. *Journal of Gerontology: Psychological Sciences, 47,* 293–299.

Lakatos, I., & Musgrave, A. (Eds.) (1970). *Criticism and the growth of knowledge.* London: Cambridge Univ. Press.

Lerner, R. M. (1984). *On the nature of human plasticity.* Cambridge: Cambridge Univ. Press.

Light, L. L. (1988). Language and aging: Competence versus performance. In J. E. Birren & V. L. Bengtson (Eds.), *Emergent theories of aging* (pp. 177–213). New York: Springer-Verlag.

Light, L. L. (1991). Memory and aging: Four hypotheses in search of data. *Annual Review of Psychology, 42,* 333–376.

Light, L. L. (1992). The organization of memory in old age. In F. I. M. Craik & T. A. Salthouse (Eds.), *The handbook of aging and cognition* (pp. 111–165). Hillsdale, NJ: Erlbaum.

Mäntylä, T., & Bäckman, L. (1992). Aging and memory for expected and unexpected objects in real-world settings. *Journal of Experimental Psychology: Learning, Memory, and Cognition, 18,* 1298–1309.

Marsiske, M., Lang, F. R., Baltes, P. B., & Baltes, M. M. (1995). Selective optimization with compensation: Life-span perspectives on successful human development. In R. A. Dixon & L. Bäckman (Eds.), *Compensating for psychological deficits and declines: Managing losses and promoting gains* (pp. 35–79). Hillsdale, NJ: Erlbaum.

May, C. P., Hasher, L., & Stoltzfus, E. R. (1993). Optimal time of day and the magnitude of age differences in memory. *Psychological Science, 4,* 326–330.

Mayr, U., & Kliegl, R. (1993). Sequential and coordinative complexity: Age-based processing limitations in figural transformations. *Journal of Experimental Psychology: Learning, Memory, and Cognition, 19,* 1297–1320.

McDowd, J. M., & Birren, J. E. (1990). Aging and attentional processes. In J. E. Birren & K. W. Schaie (Eds.), *Handbook of the psychology of aging* (3d ed., pp. 222–233). San Diego: Academic Press.

Myerson, J., Hale, S., Wagstaff, D., Poon, L. W., & Smith, G. A. (1990). The information-loss model: A mathematical theory of age-related cognitive slowing. *Psychological Review, 97,* 475–487.

Myerson, J., Wagstaff, D., & Hale, S. (1994). Brinley plots, explained variance, and the analysis of age differences in response latencies. *Journal of Gerontology: Psychological Sciences, 49,* P72–P80.

Neisser, U. (1967). *Cognitive psychology.* New York: Appleton-Century-Crofts.

Neisser, U. (1976). *Cognition and reality: Principles and implications of cognitive psychology.* San Francisco: Freeman.

Nesselroade, J. R. (1970). Application of multivariate strategies to problems of measuring and structuring long-term change. In L. R. Goulet & P. B. Baltes (Eds.), *Life-span developmental psychology: Research and theory* (pp. 193–207). New York: Academic Press.

Nesselroade, J. R. (1988). Some implications of the trait-state distinction for the study of development over the life span: The case of personality. In P. B. Baltes, D. L. Featherman, & R. M. Lerner (Eds.), *Life-span development and behavior* (vol. 8, pp. 163–189). Hillsdale, NJ: Erlbaum.

Nesselroade, J. R. (1991a). Interindividual differences in intraindividual change. In L. M. Collins & J. L. Horn (Eds.), *Best methods for analyzing change* (pp. 92–105). Washington, DC: American Psychological Association.

Nesselroade, J. R. (1991b). The warp and woof of the developmental fabric. In R. Downs, L. Liben, & R. M. Lerner (Eds.), *Visions of aesthetics, the environment, and development: The legacy of Joachim F. Wohlwill* (pp. 213–240). Hillsdale, NJ: Erlbaum.

Nesselroade, J. R., & Ford, D. H. (1985). P-technique comes of age: Multivariate, replicated, single-subject designs for research on older adults. *Research on Aging, 7,* 46–80.

Nisbet, R. A. (1980). *History of the idea of progress.* New York: Basic.

Overton, W. F. (1984). World views and their influence on psychological theory and research: Kuhn-Lakatos-Laudan. In H. W. Reese (Ed.), *Advances in child development and behavior* (vol. 18, pp. 191–225). New York: Academic Press.

Overton, W. F., & Reese, H. W. (1973). Models of development: Methodological implications. In J. R. Nesselroade & H. W. Reese (Eds.), *Life-span developmental psychology: Methodological issues* (pp. 65–86). New York: Academic Press.

Park, D. (1992). Applied cognitive aging research. In F. I. M. Craik & T. A. Salthouse (Eds.), *The handbook of aging and cognition* (pp. 449–493). Hillsdale, NJ: Erlbaum.

Park, D. C. & Kidder, D. (in press). Prospective memory and medication adherence. In M. Brandimonte, G. Einstein, & M. McDaniel (Eds.), *Prospective memory: Theory and applications.*

Pascual-Leone, J. (1983). Growing into human maturity: Towards a metasubjective theory of adulthood stages. In P. B. Baltes & O. G. Brim, Jr. (Eds.), *Life-span development and behavior* (vol. 5, pp. 118–156). New York: Academic Press.

Pascual-Leone, J. (1984). Attentional, dialectic, and mental effort: Towards an organismic theory of life stages. In M. L. Commons, F. A. Richards, & C. Armon (Eds.), *Beyond formal operations* (pp. 182–215). New York: Praeger.

Pepper, S. C. (1970). *World hypotheses.* Berkeley: Univ. of California Press (originally published in 1942).

Perfect, T. J. (1994). What can Brinley plots tell us about cognitive aging? *Journal of Gerontology: Psychological Sciences, 49,* P60–P64.

Perlmutter, M. (Ed.) (1990). *Late life potential.* Washington, DC: Gerontological Society of America.

Piaget, J. (1972). Intellectual evolution from adolescence to adulthood. *Human Development, 15,* 1–12.

Poon, L. W. (1985). Differences in human memory with aging: Nature, causes, and clinical implications. In J. E. Birren & K. W. Schaie (Eds.), *Handbook of the psychology of aging* (2d ed., pp. 427–462). New York: Van Nostrand Reinhold.

Popper, K. R. (1965). *Conjectures and refutations: The growth of scientific knowledge.* London: Oxford Univ. Press.

Rabbitt, P. M. A. (1977). Changes in problem solving ability in old age. In J. E. Birren & K. W. Schaie (Eds.), *Handbook of the psychology of aging* (pp. 606–625). New York: Van Nostrand Reinhold.

Rabinowitz, J. C., Craik, F. I. M., & Ackerman, B. P. (1982). A processing resource account of age differences in recall. *Canadian Journal of Psychology, 36,* 325–344.

Reese, H. W., & Overton, W. F. (1970). Models of development and theories of development. In L. R. Goulet & P. B. Baltes (Eds.), *Life-span developmental psychology: Research and theory* (pp. 115–145). New York: Academic Press.

Riegel, K. F. (1973). Dialectic operations: The final period of cognitive development. *Human Development, 16,* 371–381.

Rogers, W. A., Fisk, A. D., & Hertzog, C. (1994). Do ability-performance relationships differentiate age and practice effects in visual search? *Journal of Experimental Psychology: Learning, Memory, and Cognition, 20,* 710–738.

Rybash, J. M., Hoyer, W. J., & Roodin, P. A. (1986). *Adult cognition and aging: Developmental changes in processing, knowing and thinking.* New York: Pergamon.

Salthe, S. N. (1993). *Development and evolution: Complexity and change in biology.* Cambridge, MA: MIT Press.

Salthouse, T. A. (1984). Effects of age and skill in typing. *Journal of Experimental Psychology: General, 113,* 345–371.

Salthouse, T. A. (1985). *A theory of cognitive aging.* Amsterdam: North-Holland.

Salthouse, T. A. (1987). Age, experience, and compensation. In C. Schooler & K. W. Schaie (Eds.), *Cognitive functioning and social structure over the life course* (pp. 142–157). Norwood, NJ: Ablex.

Salthouse, T. A. (1988). Initializing the formalization of theories of cognitive aging. *Psychology and Aging, 3,* 3–16.

Salthouse, T. A. (1990). Cognitive competence and expertise. In J. E. Birren & K. W. Schaie (Eds.), *Handbook of the psychology of aging* (3d ed., pp. 310–319). San Diego: Academic Press.

Salthouse, T. A. (1991). *Theoretical perspectives on cognitive aging.* Hillsdale, NJ: Erlbaum.

Salthouse, T. A. (1992). Shifting levels of analysis in the investigation of cognitive aging. *Human Development, 35,* 321–342.

Salthouse, T. A. (1993). Speed mediation of adult age differences in cognition. *Developmental Psychology, 29,* 722–738.

Salthouse, T. A. (1994). The nature of the influence of speed on adult age differences in cognition. *Developmental Psychology, 30,* 240–259.

Salthouse, T. A. (1995). Refining the concept of psychological compensation. In R. A. Dixon & L. Bäckman (Eds.), *Compensating for psychological deficits and declines: Managing losses and promoting gains* (pp. 21–34). Hillsdale, NJ: Erlbaum.

Sanford, E. C. (1902). Mental growth and decay. *American Journal of Psychology, 13,* 426–449.

Schaie, K. W. (1977–78). Toward a stage theory of adult cognitive development. *International Journal of Aging and Human Development, 8,* 129–138.

Schaie, K. W. (Ed.) (1983). *Longitudinal studies of adult psychological development.* New York: Guilford Press.

Schaie, K. W. (1985). *Manual for the Schaie-Thurstone Test of Mental Abilities (STAMAT).* Palo Alto, CA: Consulting Psychologists Press.

Schaie, K. W. (1990). Intellectual development in adulthood. In J. E. Birren & K. W. Schaie (Eds.), *Handbook of psychology and aging* (3rd ed., pp. 291–309). San Diego: Academic Press.

Schaie, K. W. (1992). Commentary. *Human Development, 35,* 350–354.

Schaie, K. W. (1994). The course of adult intellectual development. *American Psychologist, 49,* 304–313.

Schaie, K. W., & Baltes, P. B. (1977). Some faith helps to see the forest: A final comment on the Horn and Donaldson myth of the Baltes-Schaie position on adult intelligence. *American Psychologist, 32,* 1118–1120.

Siegler, R. S. (1994). Cognitive variability: A key to understanding cognitive development. *Current Directions in Psychological Science, 3,* 1–5.

Sinnott, J. D. (1983). Post-formal reasoning: The relativistic stage. In M. Commons (Ed.), *Post-formal operations.* New York: Praeger.

Sternberg, R. J. (Ed.) (1990). *Wisdom: Its nature, origins, and development.* Cambridge: Cambridge Univ. Press.

Stuss, D. T., Pogue, J., Buckle, L., & Bondar, J. (1994). Characterization of stability of performance in patients with traumatic brain injury: Variability and consistency on reaction time tests. *Neuropsychology, 8,* 316–324.

Suppe, F. (Ed.) (1977). *The structure of scientific theories* (2d ed.). Urbana: Univ. of Illinois Press.

Thelen, E., & Smith, L. B. (1994). *A dynamic systems approach to the development of cognition and action.* Cambridge, MA: MIT Press.

Thorndike, E. L., Bergman, E. O., Tilton, J. W., & Woodyard, E. (1928). *Adult learning.* New York: Macmillan.

Toulmin, S. (1972). *Human understanding.* Princeton, NJ: Princeton Univ. Press.

Uttal, D., & Perlmutter, M. (1989). The dynamics of growth and decline across the life span. *Developmental Review, 9,* 101–132.

van Geert, P. (1994). *Dynamic systems of development: Change between complexity and chaos.* New York: Harvester-Wheatsheaf.

Wechsler, D. (1952). *The range of human capacities.* Baltimore: Williams and Wilkins.

Wechsler, D. (1958). *The measurement and appraisal of adult intelligence.* Baltimore: Williams and Wilkins.

Welford, A. T. (1965). Performance, biological mechanisms and age: A theoretical sketch. In A. T. Welford & J. E. Birren (Eds.), *Behavior, aging and the nervous system* (pp. 3–20). Springfield, IL: Thomas.

West, R. L. (1992). Everyday memory and aging: A diversity of tests, tasks, and paradigms. In R. L. West & J. D. Sinnott (Eds.), *Everyday memory and aging: Current research and methodology* (pp. 3–21). New York: Springer.

West, R. L., & Sinnott, J. D. (Eds.) (1992). *Everyday memory and aging: Current research and methodology.* New York: Springer.

Willis, S. L. (1985). Towards an educational psychology of the adult learner: Cognitive and intellectual bases. In J. E. Birren & K. W. Schaie (Eds.), *Handbook of the psychology of aging* (2d ed., pp. 818–847). New York: Van Nostrand Reinhold.

Willis, S. L. (1990). Introduction to special section on cognitive training in later adulthood. *Developmental Psychology, 26,* 875–878.

Willis, S. L., & Schaie, K. W. (1986). Practical intelligence in later adulthood. In R. J. Sternberg & R. K. Wagner (Eds.), *Practical intelligence* (pp. 236–268). Cambridge: Cambridge Univ. Press.

Willis, S. L., & Schaie, K. W. (1994). Cognitive training in the normal elderly. In F. Forette, Y. Christen, & F. Boller (Eds.). *Plasticite cerebrale et stimulation cognitive* (pp. 91–113). Paris: Foundation National de Gerontologie.

Wohlwill, J. F. (1973). *The study of behavioral development.* New York: Academic Press.

Woodruff-Pak, D. S. (1993). Neural plasticity as a substrate for cognitive adaptation in adulthood and aging. In J. Cerella, J. Rybash, W. Hoyer, & M. L. Commons (Eds.), *Adult information processing: Limits on loss* (pp. 13–36). San Diego: Academic Press.

Woodruff-Pak, D. S., & Hanson, C. (1995). Plasticity and compensation in brain memory systems. In R. A. Dixon & L. Bäckman (Eds.), *Compensating for psychological deficits and declines: Managing losses and promoting gains* (pp. 191–217). Hillsdale, NJ: Erlbaum.

3

METHODOLOGICAL ISSUES IN RESEARCH ON COGNITION AND AGING

Christopher Hertzog
Georgia Institute of Technology

Roger A. Dixon
University of Victoria

INTRODUCTION

The process of conducting research on cognition and aging is simultaneously exciting, rewarding, challenging, and frustrating! Devising empirical approaches to the important questions about adult cognitive development is fraught with methodological hazards. These hazards arise because research into the cognitive changes that accompany adult development must combine (1) methods for testing and assessing cognition with (2) methods for assessing developmental change. Both aspects of our science bring with them difficult problems and have generated hosts of potential solutions.

For a student just beginning to learn about the field of adult cognitive development, the scientific methods employed by empirical research articles can seem difficult to understand and justify. As noted in Chapter 2, any mature science relies heavily on shared theoretical assumptions, prototypical questions to be investigated by empirical research, and a shared corpus of accepted empirical procedures for conducting research. A student often learns by induction and inference the system of shared principles and procedures while encountering them in research articles. All of us have experienced the confusion that can arise during this process! The concepts discussed in an article's theoretical introduction can be difficult enough to comprehend. However, by the time the student reaches the section describing the study's research methods, comprehension can be in grave danger! Without an already well established foundation of knowledge, it is often unclear what the technique being used is, let alone why it would be employed. When the article actually presents empirical results, the challenges are even more formidable. Esoteric cognitive tasks, methods of scaling the data they generate, and complex statistical procedures for analyzing that data are often introduced without fanfare or explanation. Inferences about data can seem to be far removed—even disconnected—from the concepts and hypotheses the study was supposedly designed to assess.

This problem of comprehending the primary empirical literature is, sad to say, not limited to beginning students of adult cognitive development. It is also one experienced by senior scientists with considerable research experience. One consequence of the maturing of the field of psychology, and the information explosion that has accompanied its growth, is a tremendous increase in the range and complexity of methods employed to study both cognition and development. Often the methods common to a given theoretical paradigm in the area of adult cognitive development are collectively accepted and understood without formal explication or justification. It is as though there is an implicit social contract of accepted scientific practice amongst like-minded professionals. However, methods accepted and employed in one paradigm of adult development may be poorly understood by adherents of other paradigms or even viewed with outright skepticism and suspicion. The field is also constantly evolving as new and often radically different empirical methods are invented and applied. Even within a given theoretical paradigm, experienced researchers can easily find their expertise becoming obsolete as new, unfamiliar approaches, and the technical aspects of instrumentation and analysis that accompany them, gain acceptance and widespread use. Thus students and seasoned professors alike can be sorely taxed by the difficult task of comprehending the methodological aspects of empirical research articles.

The principal goal of this chapter is to reduce the level of mystery by describing, discussing, and explaining prototypical methodological approaches in the area of adult cognitive development. No single chapter could do full justice to the complexity of the field and the methods employed by scientists working within it. We approach the problem by identifying major conceptual issues, classic methodological problems, and some common approaches to addressing them. Our goal is not to promote certain techniques over others. It is instead to provide a framework and foundation from which the practices of scientists studying cognitive aging can be understood and evaluated.

■ The Two Disciplines of Scientific Psychology

Some years ago Cronbach (1957) identified and decried the limitations on scientific psychology imposed by the existence of two rather disparate traditions: the differential and the experimental. The differential tradition seeks to describe and explain differences between persons—individual differences in such hypothetical concepts as abilities (or aptitudes), personality, and attitudes. Its chief method is passive observation of individual characteristics by means of tests, tasks, and questionnaires. Its typical means of analyzing relationships among concepts is to measure covariation of multiple, empirically defined variables. Analysis of the data generated by such studies often requires the use of complex statistical procedures (e.g., multivariate regression, factor analysis, and cluster analysis).

The experimental tradition seeks to identify regularities in human behavior through experimental manipulation of relevant environmental conditions, such as stimulus properties and behavioral contingencies. Its chief set of tools derives from the experimental method.

The goal is to isolate cause-effect relationships between psychological constructs through the systematic manipulation of independent variables of interest (sometimes defined as an experimental treatment), while controlling all other variables not specifically of interest. Its typical means of analyzing relationships is the factorial analysis of variance.

Although some research does bridge the two traditions, Cronbach's conception of these two dominant approaches of scientific psychology still seems appropriate for understanding psychological research in the mid-1990s. Graduate students interested in adult cognitive development are rarely trained in depth in both the experimental and differential traditions. Hence psychologists interested in adult cognitive development typically employ particular classes of research methods that reflect the signature of the tradition emphasized in their graduate training. The differences are reflected in a number of ways, from alternative assumptions about how aging is to be conceptualized and treated as a variable of interest to the methods used for conceptualizing and measuring the psychological constructs involved in the research (e.g., computer-controlled reaction-time studies versus structured in-home interviews).

Beyond these differences in scientific approach, however, lies a unifying truism. Research on adult cognitive development must employ (at least indirectly) certain principles of differential psychology associated with studying naturally occurring individual differences. Why? Because aging is a characteristic of persons that cannot be experimentally manipulated. It can be measured only as a characteristic of the persons being sampled in a particular research study. Standard methodological practices deriving from the experimental tradition may be optimal for operationalizing the content and process of cognition (although not all psychologists interested in cognitive development would endorse this premise). However, implementation of the standard logic and practice of the experimental method in aging research does not necessarily lead to valid scientific inferences regarding cognitive development. One must define and measure development—and this challenge must be addressed by using one or more alternative approaches for assessing individual differences. Thus an adequate methodology for adult cognitive development requires, necessarily, incorporation of principles and methods that bridge the boundaries of the two principal traditions in psychology. In brief, it requires serious consideration of the problems identified and the solutions suggested by Cronbach (1957, 1975).

The organization of this chapter reflects and acknowledges the importance of both the experimental and differential aspects of research methods for cognitive aging research. We begin by reviewing basic principles of research design, both in general and with specific reference to the study of adult development. This section identifies concepts that frame an understanding of the more complex methods and procedures that are commonly employed in research on adult cognitive development. We also discuss principles from life-span developmental perspectives on research methods that have influenced studies of psychological aging. Subsequently, we focus on the fundamental aspects of research design and statistical analysis from the differential and experimental approaches toward adult cognitive development. Each approach is described (and critiqued) separately in its own section. In doing so, we identify prototypical research questions, designs used to address these questions, and statistical methods used to treat data collected in those designs. Finally, we describe methodological features of research in which selected aspects of differential and experimental approaches are combined to study adult development.

GENERAL PRINCIPLES OF
RESEARCH DESIGN

■ Scientific Inference

Scientists seek general statements or principles that organize our understanding of the world and that enable us both to accurately characterize the present and to predict the future. Scientists seek to understand particular instances and events (e.g., the collision of the Schumacher-Levy comet with the planet Jupiter in July 1994) from a framework of theories that explain more general classes of phenomena (e.g., theories of celestial mechanics that explain the movement of objects in interstellar space). Scientists generalize from particular events to larger principles that, according to their theories, govern entire classes of events. The process of science is devoted to discovering how, when, and why such generalizations fail.

Psychological science must always come to terms with the issue of breadth of generalization. Our theories about cognition and behavior involve complex entities (typically, humans) behaving in complex environments, and our statements regarding causal relationships are necessarily probabilistic in nature (Cook & Campbell, 1979). As noted in Chapter 2, when a psychologist states, for example, that aging leads to a decline in the speed of information processing, this statement does not necessarily imply that all information is processed more slowly, that all persons experience a slowing in such processing, or that all adults experience the same rate of slowing for a particular kind of information processing. What it is taken to imply will vary, to a degree, on the world view of the scientist making the generalization. At minimum such an inference implies a lawful empirical relationship of the form that aging is associated with an increased probability of decline in information-processing speed that generalizes (fallibly) over some classes of persons, domains of cognitions, settings, and historical times. A healthy science requires both an understanding of the importance of framing and investigating general principles and, an acceptance of the necessary truth that any generalization, by aggregating over multiple complex phenomena, cannot be, strictly speaking, "true." Scientists covet general theories but cannot disregard that the heart of science lies in understanding the boundaries of a theory's generality—in effect, where a theory (necessarily) fails.

How do we identify and evaluate such generalizations, or theoretical propositions, about aging and cognition—and at the same time, do so in a way which reveals their inadequacies? The classic model of conducting science is often referred to as the hypothetico-deductive method. The scientist first stipulates a set of basic assumptions and then uses theory to formulate an assertion of fact, or hypothesis. A requirement for any scientific hypothesis is that it must be empirically testable. That is, it must predict that a particular set of observable outcomes will follow from a specific set of conditions.

In psychology, the hypothesis consists of assertions about relationships among psychological concepts, or constructs (Cronbach & Meehl, 1955), such as attitudes, beliefs, intelligence, memory, and emotions. In research on the psychology of aging, hypotheses will typically include assertions regarding relationships between aging or age-related processes and other psychological constructs. For example, one could hypothesize that aging has no effect on the likelihood of forgetting the name of someone to whom one has just been introduced.

The scientist proceeds to test this hypothesis by directly observing age-related changes in remembering and forgetting of newly learned names. Scientific logic centers on inferring that a hypothesis is false—disconfirming the hypothesis by showing that the predicted empirically observable outcomes do not conform to a structure dictated by the hypothesis. Strong scientific inference involves testing competing alternative theories by isolating their differences at the level of contradictory hypotheses and then proceeding to test these theories by evaluating the empirical evidence for and against the competing hypotheses.

■ Hypothesis Testing

The research design is the vehicle for translating a conceptual hypothesis about phenomena in the world, which we shall call the *substantive hypothesis,* into a form that is empirically testable. The hypothesis regarding aging and forgetting of newly learned names is substantive in the sense that it is a generalized statement about relationships between constructs— such as aging and forgetting—that is testable only in principle (Cronbach & Meehl, 1955). These constructs are hypothetical concepts that help to organize and explain substantive phenomena. Constructs must be clearly defined, but they are nevertheless concepts and therefore often cannot be directly observed. We can observe, indirectly, at least some manifestations of forgetting, but we cannot directly observe the forgetting process. Similarly, we can theorize about the nature of aging, debate whether it is universal, whether it differentially affects systems of the central nervous system, whether it is conceptually distinct from the concept of disease, whether it is synonymous with chronological age, and so on. We must do so in order to establish theories of aging and to determine how aging, as defined by alternative theories, will be manifested. Nevertheless, we cannot directly observe the aging process per se.

The requirement that we actually observe the phenomenon of the aging process and its effects on forgetting names requires translating the conceptual into the actual, the concept into the empirically observable manifestation. How will we measure aging? How will we measure the forgetting of names? This process of choosing a method of empirically observing, indirectly, the relationships among constructs produces an *empirical analog* to the substantive hypothesis. It is useful to label this analog as the *empirical hypothesis.* It is a statement of relationships among observable variables in a particular sample at some finite point(s) in time. As such it directly manifests the set of deducible consequences that follow from the substantive hypothesis.

How is the empirical hypothesis evaluated, given that the propositions to be tested are inherently and implicitly probabilistic in nature? Psychologists typically use statistical analyses of empirical data to evaluate empirical hypotheses. This process translates the test of an empirical hypothesis into a test of a *statistical hypothesis.* The purpose of statistics is to determine whether a particular pattern of data is robust, in the sense that it is unlikely to represent an outcome determined by chance from an uninformative set of background conditions. In common statistical practice there are two competing statistical hypotheses. One is the *null hypothesis,* which represents a quantitative model for uninformative conditions. It assumes, typically, that in the target population of interest, two (or more) variables are statistically independent of each other. For example, given two continuous variables, a typical null hypothesis is that the two variables have a Pearson product-moment correlation of zero. Statistics uses probability theory to assess the likelihood of the null hypothesis against some general alternative hypothesis (e.g., two variables have a nonzero correlation in a target population).

The important point, for our purposes, is that rejecting the null hypothesis in favor of some alternative hypothesis begins a chain of inference from the statistical hypothesis back to the empirical hypothesis and then to the substantive hypothesis. Figure 3.1 graphs this chain of inference. The most direct chain would involve falsifying a substantive hypothesis that two constructs are not related. For example, a strong biologically based perspective on age-related changes in cognition (see Chapter 2) would posit that biological aging causes an irreversible decline in cognitive function that is not materially influenced by the information-processing strategies employed by the individual. This metatheoretical perspective might lead a theorist discussing aging and the construct of episodic memory to posit that the effects of aging on memory are independent of (not affected by) age differences in another construct (e.g., strategies used to learn the to-be-remembered information; see Salt-

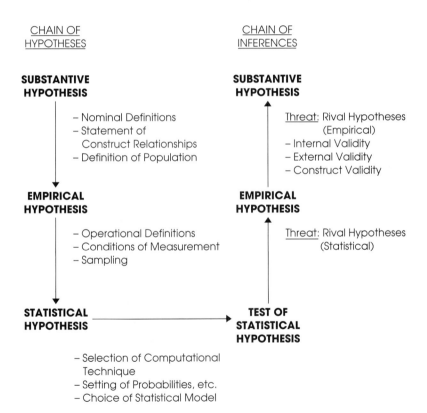

FIGURE 3.1 Chain of hypotheses and inferences in scientific research. The flow of hypothesis formation, hypothesis testing, and inference begins at the top left of the figure. A substantive hypothesis derived from theory and prior empirical data leads to a set of empirical design decisions, resulting in an empirical hypothesis. The empirical study then is evaluated in the context of one or more statistical hypotheses. The test of the statistical hypothesis then leads to a chain of inference back to the substantive hypothesis. This chain of inference must be considered in light of potential rival explanations of the empirical outcomes before substantive conclusions can be drawn. (See text for further explanation.)

house, 1991, for one such perspective). This theoretical proposition can be translated into a substantive hypothesis: Age differences in performance on episodic memory tasks do not vary as a function of age differences in strategies used to learn the information. A scientist advocating this position would, according to the logic of the hypothetico-deductive method, proceed to try to falsify it by creating an empirical test. The conceptual relationships must be translated into direct empirical observations. In this case, the researcher would observe persons of different ages and measure both their memory performance and the strategic methods they use to learn the information. The empirical test would therefore involve a series of specific choices regarding who, what, how, when, and where to observe the phenomena of interest. The scientist would define (explicitly or implicitly) a specific population and a method of sampling from that population (including a method of sampling levels of age), select a specific episodic memory task and a method of measuring learning strategies, and so on.

For example, one might formulate two linked empirical hypotheses that derive from the substantive hypothesis. First, a specific sample of 60-year-olds will not differ from a sample of 20-year-olds in the use of sorting strategies to organize related concrete nouns during a study period, prior to a free-recall test for memory of the words (see, e.g., Hultsch, 1969). Second, any age differences in organization will not affect the magnitude of age differences in recall. After the data have been gathered, a statistical test is conducted to evaluate whether it is likely that the data have been drawn from a population in which age differences in organization are unrelated to age differences in recall. How robust are any sample differences that are obtained? This issue involves computing the probability of the sample data, assuming it has been generated in a population in which the null hypothesis is true. With respect to the first of the empirical hypotheses listed above, the null hypothesis stipulates no relationship of chronological age to the amount of sorting behavior. Finding statistically reliable age differences in sorting would disconfirm the first empirical hypothesis, which would then justify testing the second empirical hypothesis. If both empirical hypotheses were disconfirmed, one would infer that the original substantive hypothesis of independence of age differences in episodic memory from age differences in organizational strategies had also been disconfirmed. The theory that generated this substantive hypothesis would then be either discarded or modified to account for the new findings.

The crucial issue for research is designing and conducting studies so as to preserve a correspondence of the three kinds of hypotheses (substantive, empirical, statistical; Hertzog, 1994). One needs to employ valid techniques of statistical analysis to ensure that acceptance of the alternative hypothesis actually allows one to make inferences about the empirical hypothesis of interest. Further, one must use sound principles of research design to ensure that the empirical hypothesis is indeed relevant to the substantive hypothesis. This level of correspondence insures valid substantive inferences from empirical results. We return to this issue in the context of discussing validity threats in the next section of the chapter.

■ The Practice of Hypothesis Testing

The different hypotheses and the chain of inference shown in Figure 3.1 merely represent the kernel process of scientific reasoning, for at least three reasons (see also Bechtel, 1988). First, scientists often do not proceed according to this logic. Often they focus primarily on the process of gathering "confirming" evidence—that is, evidence consistent with their own theory. Moreover, their theoretical perspective can motivate discounting of disconfirming evidence, often for valid reasons. Evidence that is consistent with a theory is helpful (often because it mitigates against other hypotheses). The logic of the scientific method dictates, however, that evidence that is merely consistent with a theory does not constitute a meaningful test of the validity of its premises. It must be emphasized, therefore, that science proceeds best when scientists do not cling to pet hypotheses (despite the inevitable motivations to do so) but instead treat any and all hypotheses as conjectures requiring objective efforts at refutation.

Second, scientists rarely make major substantive inferences on the basis of a single empirical test of a substantive hypothesis. An empirical hypothesis is a single, specific instantiation of a substantive hypothesis that is embedded in the specific context defined by who, what, and how one is observing. It is therefore often necessary to address rival explanations for empirical phenomena before proceeding to make substantive inferences. This phenomenon is embedded in the concept of *modus tollens*, which we develop in the next section. The important point for the moment is to understand that scientists may choose to require converging lines of empirical evidence that demonstrate correspondence of the empirical hypothesis and the substantive hypothesis before they make substantive inferences about research outcomes.

In a similar vein, the kernel process represented in Figure 3.1 is a small part of a larger process of substantive inference in scientific research. Any scientific enterprise consists of testing multiple substantive hypotheses, some of which are generated in the context of evaluating the reasons why earlier hypotheses failed. Cattell (1988) has described the repetitive sequence interrelating hypothesis generation and evaluation as the inductive/hypothetico-deductive spiral (for an illuminating introductory treatment, see Stanovich, 1992). One identifies a research question or problem, gathering information and using inductive reasoning to organize and make sense of what is already known or believed to be known. One then proceeds to formulate and test hypotheses using the hypothetico-deductive method. This process often entails the formulation of multiple hypotheses, and scientific research can thus be relatively complicated in terms of the number and interrelationships among the substantive hypotheses that are evaluated and tested.

Third, the typical scientific enterprise involves adventitious learning from empirical data, or what philosophers of science refer to as discovery. That is, it is partly a process of developing new ideas and insights from empirical data that were not necessarily anticipated prior to data collection. Anomalous (according to theory) or novel patterns of data often lead to generation of new theoretical premises and hypotheses. This is a natural and important part of the scientific process, one that is related to the inductive part of the spiral described by Cattell.

Thus the chain of deductive inference and empirical evaluation described in Figure 3.1 is by no means a complete representation of the process of scientific reasoning. It does, however, encapsulate the essential logic associated with the formulation and testing of empirical consequences of substantive hypotheses, which is at the heart of sound scientific practice.

■ Concepts of Design Validity

Campbell and Stanley (1966) introduced a taxonomy of threats to substantive inferences in empirical research that has had a profound impact upon social science research, including developmental psychology. This taxonomy, revised and updated by Cook & Campbell (1979), provides a basis for understanding several issues in aging research discussed in this chapter. It distinguishes four major threats to the validity of inferences in empirical research: construct validity, internal validity, external validity, and statistical conclusion validity. Each of these sources compromises the chain of inference from the empirical data back to the substantive hypothesis. The taxonomy represents a set of potential alternative explanations for the empirical findings other than the substantive hypothesis that is of interest to the scientist. In order to make valid substantive inferences, the scientist must design a study so as to protect against these potential alternative explanations. Although it is never possible to design a foolproof study—that is, one that strictly controls for all possible alternative interpretations—the art of research design involves identifying major sources of plausible validity threats and eliminating them through implementation of appropriate features of the research design.

Construct Validity

As noted earlier, it is important to distinguish between a hypothetical construct and a method of measuring it (an empirically observed variable). Threats to construct validity involve the extent to which the methods of measurement actually allow inferences to be made about relationships among constructs. Are the observed variables actually measures of the constructs of interest? In a traditional experiment, one identifies a hypothetical causal construct and manipulates an independent variable that represents the causal construct. The intent is to create variation in the effect (outcome) construct, as measured by the dependent variable. Construct validity refers to the assumption that the independent and dependent variables that are manipulated and observed actually are valid operational definitions (measures) of the hypothetical cause-and-effect constructs.

Construct validity is absolutely essential for linking substantive relationships to empirically observed phenomena, and yet social science is plagued by failures to adequately identify measurement assumptions, let alone to test their validity. Blalock (1982) referred to the set of assumptions as the auxiliary measurement theory, noting that this auxiliary theory is often not adequately evaluated. Apparent failures to replicate age differences in cognitive variables can often be attributed to subtle but important differences in the way in which constructs are defined and measured (see, e.g., Hertzog, Hultsch, & Dixon, 1989).

Internal Validity

Internal validity was a critical feature of Campbell and Stanley's (1966) original conception of validity threats to inference. It refers to the validity of substantive inferences given a study's research design. Typically, researchers design studies so as to systematically vary levels of an independent variable. Internal validity refers to the extent to which the manipulation of the independent variable has been confounded by simultaneous variation in other variables. The essential question for internal validity is whether there is a rival explanation for a relationship between the independent variable and the dependent variable. For example, a study which observes change in attitudes in a target population after introduction of an advertising campaign must consider all the possible causes for attitude change over the same time period other than the advertising campaign.

The problem of internal validity becomes more important in nonexperimental designs, in which classic experimental methods cannot achieve full isolation of the independent variable from other potential causes of the dependent variable (Cook & Campbell, 1979). Developmental research designs are a special case in point (see below).

External Validity

External validity refers to the generalizability of results beyond the particular units and contexts of observations—typically, generalization to other persons, settings, and times. For example, do inferences about cognitive aging based upon data collected today in the United States generalize to other cultures, or to aging in the United States in the twenty-first century? Do inferences about cognitive processes observed in an unfamiliar environmental context (e.g., a psychological laboratory) generalize to cognition in a familiar context (e.g., a person's home)?

Statistical Conclusion Validity

This type of validity is associated with the appropriate use of techniques of statistical inference (e.g., correct interpretation of failure to reject the null hypothesis, tests of hypotheses with adequate statistical power). It also includes the failure to identify and test the proper statistical hypothesis, given the empirical hypothesis of interest.

Threats to Validity and the Chain of Inference

Referring again to Figure 3.1, note that each of the validity threats can be assigned to part of the chain of inference. Statistical conclusion validity is required to make inferences about the empirical hypothesis from statistical outcomes. Internal validity, construct validity, and external validity are required to enable inferences about the substantive hypothesis from the empirical hypothesis. Construct validity ensures that the independent and dependent variable are related to the substantive phenomena of interest, internal validity ensures that rival explanations for the relationship of the two variables can be ruled out, and external validity ensures that generalization to the desired universe of persons, settings, and times is warranted.

The hazards associated with the step from empirical findings to substantive inference are well understood by philosophers of science (Bechtel, 1988). The logic of falsification of the substantive hypothesis by falsifying its consequences is conditional upon the background assumptions associated with the process of empirical observation. The falsification is predicated upon the assumption known in logic as *modus tollens*—in essence, all other things being equal. In this case, those other things being equal include assumptions of proper measurement (construct validity), appropriate observational (experimental) arrangements and design (internal validity), and appropriate observational context (external validity). Under certain conditions, the falsification of a substantive hypothesis may be attributed to special circumstances of measurement or design rather than to the inaccuracy of the substantive hypothesis itself.

The principal problem is that the opportunity to save a preferred hypothesis by invoking problems with measurement or sampling, for example, allows for some degree of subjectivity in the process, and much has been written on the extent to which scientific paradigms may lead to systematic special treatment for certain classes of favored hypotheses, despite evidence that they are inconsistent with empirical data. On the other hand, the problem of ruling out rival and uninteresting explanations for empirical findings that otherwise will be taken as evidence against a substantive hypothesis is a necessary and critically important part of the scientific enterprise. In many cases unanticipated outcomes can ultimately be traced to questionable measurement assumptions, and critical evaluation of that possibility is required before one can have confidence in substantive conclusions. In general, careful attention to the classes of validity outlined above maximizes the probability of being able to make sound substantive inferences from empirical research and helps to frame the dialogue regarding possible alternative explanations of empirical findings.

■ Life-Span Developmental Methodology

In developmental research, concern with research validity reached its apogee with the work of Schaie, Baltes, Nesselroade, and others in the life-span developmental psychology movement, which began in the 1960s (see, e.g., Baltes, Reese, & Nesselroade, 1977; Schaie, 1977; Wohlwill, 1973). A principal focus of this literature was the translation of concepts from earlier literature on research methods, most notably Campbell and Stanley (1966), into a developmental framework. Standard methods of operationally defining (and measuring) maturation and aging—for example, differences between groups of persons of different chronological ages—could actually arise because of variables that are causally unrelated to development and aging. The internal validity threats affecting developmental designs cannot be easily addressed by experimental methods given that both development and its rival explanatory variables cannot be subjected to experimental manipulation (e.g., random assignment of persons to levels of chronological age).

The literature on developmental research design has discussed these difficult and subtle issues at length. The principal issues and lessons from this literature have influenced the standard treatments of developmental methods in handbooks and textbooks. We need only highlight three issues for brief general discussion before proceeding to discuss methodological issues for research on adult cognitive development.

Selection of Observations

Campbell and Stanley (1966) treated selection as a threat to the internal validity of between-subject factors. In the context of design validity, selection is often treated as being almost exclusively the process of selecting persons to be observed in an empirical study. In that sense, selection involves creating an independent variable by assigning units of observation (in most cases, different persons or individuals) to levels of an independent variable. In a randomized experiment, the influences of unwanted variables on the dependent variable are controlled by using random assignment of units to levels of the independent variable. Random assignment ensures that there can be, in the long run, no systematic relationship of personal characteristics that are not the target of the research question to the independent variable. Random assignment, as a method of selection, is optimal for isolating the independent variable of interest from all other variables whose influences on the dependent variable could be misattributed to the variable under study.

Any method of selection other than random assignment involves a set of systematic methods for selecting and assigning units to levels. Experiments in which random assignment is not possible (quasi-experiments) often involve selecting persons or intact groups that differ intrinsically on the variable of interest (Cook & Campbell, 1979). For example, one could measure the effectiveness of teaching methods by selecting schools with differences in currently implemented educational curricula. To the extent that a research design explicitly or implicitly assigns units to levels without random assignment, the possibility arises that the process of selection (and assignment) creates differences not attributable to the variable of interest. Schools may differ in the demographic composition of students' families, the intellectual abilities of their students, the level and nature of students' prior educational experiences, the training and experience of teachers, class size, and a host of other variables besides curriculum content. These variables represent rival explanations for any group differences in educational outcomes between schools that might be attributed to differences in curricula.

Selection can and should, however, be construed more broadly in order to understand the full set of implications of selection for developmental research designs. Nesselroade (1983, 1988) has articulated this broader concept, following Cattell's (1952) treatments of research as a process of sampling of variables, persons, and occasions of measurement. Different research designs can be viewed as choices that are made regarding how widely to observe phenomena.

Standard research practices in psychology typically involve sampling of a number of persons (selecting replications across individuals) and then comparing the differences and similarities among the persons sampled. If one is sampling a number of persons and computing statistics that aggregate over persons (such as a group mean), then a sufficiently large sample of persons should be drawn for one to obtain a stable estimate of the distribution of scores (in each subgroup, if any). The emphasis in research design on the need for an adequate sample size (and such issues as statistical power that accompany the issue of sample size; see Cohen, 1988) derive from the choices about sampling embedded in the traditional research design.

In the experimental tradition, it is common for a research design to sample only one construct for the dependent variable and to create a single measure of that construct. Likewise, it is common to measure the persons on that single variable at only one point in time, in only one environmental context. The implicit assumption is that replication over persons is of paramount importance for valid inferences about relationships between independent and dependent variables but that replication across multiple measures and multiple occasions of measurement is essentially an issue of generalizability and can be deferred to subsequent research.

Sampling large numbers of persons is not a necessary condition for making valid scientific inferences, however. It is possible to design valid experiments based upon single subjects (e.g., work in the experimental analysis of behavior; see Barlow & Hersen, 1984), in which one person is observed repeatedly under different manipulations of one or more independent variables. In this case one requires sufficient density of observations on the dependent variable (i.e., a large number of occasions of measurement) so that the effects of the independent variable can be determined to be systematic in nature. The large number of occasions can be paired with systematic manipulation of the independent variable(s) in order to be sure that the effects can be attributed to the independent variable and not to other variables that might also vary across occasions and hence might be confounded with the independent variable.

In the differential research tradition, research design usually consists of extended sampling from at least two of the three dimensions (persons, variables, occasions). Research questions, and statistical methods for addressing them, involve aggregating over one dimension and analyzing relationships among levels of the dimension that is left to vary. The most common design approach in the differential tradition samples multiple persons and multiple variables. The traditional method of analyzing such data is to aggregate over persons and analyze relationships among the variables. That is, one computes measures of association among variables (e.g., Pearson product-moment correlations based upon between-person deviations from the [group] means of the measured variables). Analyses of correlations among variables, aggregated over persons, form much of the basis for theory in individual differences of constructs such as intelligence. The very same data could be treated rather differently by aggregating over variables and computing measures of association among persons (indeed, this is the basis of a statistical method termed *cluster analysis* that is used extensively in some areas of psychology; see Blashfield & Aldenderfer, 1988).

Although extensive sampling of persons and variables is the staple of the differential approach to psychology, including the major research methods extensively used in studies of adult cognitive development, it is but one possible outcome of a set of decisions regarding selection of observations. Nesselroade (1988, 1990) has emphasized the importance of extensive sampling over time or occasions of measurement. Given that developmental research questions explicitly involve the issue of change over time, attention to the issues associated with sampling occasions of measurement plays an important role in developmental research design. For instance, one can choose a particular person and then extensively sample that individual with respect to multiple variables and multiple occasions of measurement. If one aggregates over occasions, a correlation of two variables in such an analysis would reflect the extent to which both variables had similar temporal patterns of variance (across the occasions of measurement). Multivariate statistical analyses of a full matrix of such correlations can elucidate dimensions of common temporal variation (e.g., developmental change) across variables within an individual (see also Wood & Brown, 1994). Such approaches have a number of interesting potential applications in aging research (Nesselroade & Ford, 1985; Nesselroade & Jones, 1991).

There are several important points to make about the concept of selection when it is defined more broadly as carrying the full range of decisions the scientist makes regarding who and what will be observed and when the observation will occur. We list these points below and comment upon them, where appropriate, in later sections of this chapter.

1. The selection options exercised by a scientist are influenced by multiple factors, ranging from metatheoretical perspectives (see Chapter 2), to empirical dictates (practicality of sampling, availability of subpopulation segments).

2. Schools of empirical method have evolved, based upon precedents regarding selection decisions made by communities of like-minded scientists. Choices about how extensively one samples persons, variables, and occasions often reflect the benefits

and costs of such traditions. On the one hand, the scientist benefits from what has already been learned and contributes to a body of knowledge derived from shared methodological applications. Replication across different laboratories and investigators is thereby fostered. However, such traditions can also reify the blind spots of a particular discipline-bound approach to the problem. Choices may be made, implicitly, by appeal to tradition rather than by a well-reasoned process that attends to ensuring the validity of substantive inferences regarding the research questions at hand. Such an approach, taken to the extreme, could lead to a literature of well-replicated empirical findings that are not fully germane to the substantive research questions of interest.

3. Developmental research necessarily requires selection on personal attributes related to both aging and age-related change. Given this focus on age and aging, developmental designs' sampling structure must consider time as a dimension, whether by explicit selection of occasions of observation or by treating time as embedded within individual differences in the population. By comparing different age groups, a cross-sectional design does the latter (see below).

4. Multiple variables that potentially cause psychological phenomena covary with chronological age (and with the aging process) in a given population. Thus selection of observations in developmental designs attempting to assess aging-determined change must consider the internal validity of the selection plan with respect to all other age-correlated phenomena that contribute to variance in any and all dependent variables defined by the observational structure. One cannot invoke the stronger assumption enjoyed by randomized experiments—that all personal characteristics are controlled through randomized assignment—as a justification for haphazard selection of sampling frames from which to draw subjects. One must explicitly measure (or otherwise control for) background variables that could in principle correlate with both aging and the dependent variables under study. This issue requires careful attention to the issue of selection of variables. One must also have a means by which to test hypotheses about systematic relationships among sets of variables that are relevant to different developmental hypotheses about psychological constructs.

5. Sampling techniques must consider both the population composition and the nature of the hypotheses driving the research design. The issue of whether aging research requires representative samples in order to be valid is a crucial one which we address in some detail in a subsequent section of this chapter.

6. Some developmental research questions, particularly those derived from a contextual worldview on aging and cognition, will require explicit selection of multiple environmental or observational contexts (Brunswik, 1956; Dixon & Hertzog, Chapter 2).

Developmental Research Designs

The life-span developmental literature is most often identified with efforts to define how alternative research designs can either succeed or fail to capture age-related changes, particularly during adulthood. The literature focuses on the difficulties of treating age as an independent variable and identifies both the internal and external validity threats that occur, given that age effects can be only observed, not manipulated.

This methodological literature gained its impetus in large part from Schaie's (1965) perspective on time-related sampling. Aging researchers in the early twentieth century used both the cross-sectional and longitudinal methods to examine aging and age-related effects. In the cross-sectional design, persons of different ages are sampled at a single point in time and differences between persons of different ages are treated as operational definitions of the effects of aging. In a simple longitudinal design, persons of a single initial age are measured repeatedly as they grow older. Changes over time are then taken as the operational definition of the effects of aging.

Discrepancies between the results of longitudinal and cross-sectional studies in the domain of psychometric intelligence concerned gerontologists (Jones, 1959). Schaie (1965), Baltes (1968), and others synthesized the problem in terms of a conception of alternative developmental designs and the influences of three classes of variables: age, cohort, and period. These variables were also discussed in other social science literature, most notably demography. Age effects are associated with changes due to the aging process, although they are also associated with any other age-graded phenomena (e.g., retirement as an age-graded event can directly cause psychological effects that are independent of the aging process within an individual retiree). Cohort effects refer to differences between persons that arise because of membership in a particular social group. A birth cohort consists of persons born within an arbitrarily defined time period (e.g., 1 year). Birth cohorts can carry effects of common environmental circumstances (e.g., educational practices during the period in which the birth cohort attended elementary school). Period effects refer to effects that are a function of a particular historical point in time.

Despite the fact that age, cohort, and period effects are distinct and independent concepts, any developmental design relying on time-based sampling quickly confronts an unhappy problem in attempting to measure such effects empirically. At any particular point in time (T), age (A) and birth year, which defines the birth cohort (C), are perfectly confounded: in the year 2000, a person born in 1950 must, by definition, be 50 years old. Knowing any two of the numbers of the set (A, C, T) determines the remaining number; there are only two degrees of freedom among them.

It follows, then, that any developmental design focusing on age will carry with it potential confounding influences of birth cohort, time of measurement, or both. Figure 3.2 depicts the more general sampling framework developed by life-span developmental psychologists. It specifies the relationship of choices of when and who to measure (the observational design) and the issue of establishing the effects of age, cohort, and period on a dependent measure. The figure shows that the standard cross-sectional design contains an inherent confound: persons differing in chronological age at a specific point in historical time also, necessarily, differ in terms of when they were born (and, hence, are members of different birth cohorts). Indeed, cohort membership and age are completely confounded in a cross-sectional design. A traditional longitudinal study confounds age-related change with historical change (period effects). This realization led Schaie and others to argue for more complicated sampling plans, defined by Baltes (1968) as cross-sectional and longitudinal sequences. A cross-sectional sequence represents repeated cross-sectional measurement of a population at different points in time. A longitudinal sequence represents drawing repeated cross-sectional samples and following them over time. Schaie's Seattle Longitudinal Study is the best-known instance of using such sequential sampling strategies to disentangle age, cohort, and

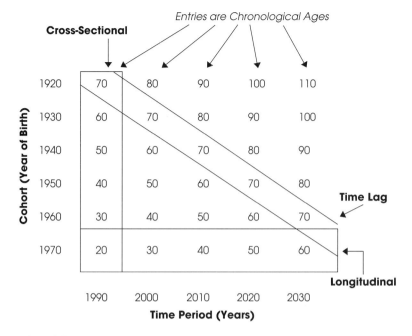

FIGURE 3.2 Illustration of basic age, cohort, and period design with traditional cross-sectional, longitudinal, and time-lag designs. Each of the designs confounds the independent variable of age with another source of variance (e.g., the cross-sectional design confounds age and cohort effects).

period effects in developmental data (see Chapter 9). Other partial sequential sampling plans have also been advocated in the literature (see, e.g., Bell, 1953). There are a number of complicated issues associated with interpretation of results from such designs (see, e.g., Donaldson & Horn, 1992; Schaie & Hertzog, 1982; Schaie, 1986).

As noted earlier, aging is fundamentally a process of within-person change. Life-span developmental psychologists extensively critiqued gerontology's traditional emphasis on the cross-sectional design on this basis (see, e.g., Baltes et al., 1977; Schaie, 1965). The cross-sectional design is unquestionably a useful time-saving device—one obtains estimates of a life span of aging changes in a very brief period of time. A longitudinal sequence covering the life span across multiple birth cohorts would require more than one scientist's lifetime to achieve. The cross-sectional design's economy is a powerful motivation for its use. However, one might be economizing on time at the expense of producing invalid estimates of true aging-related change.

The decision to operationally define aging changes in terms of between-person differences, as in the cross-sectional design, brings with it several potential confounds (Schaie, 1977). One, of course, is cohort effects, and the use of such designs to study aging requires the assumption of no cohort effects to avoid confounded inferences. Second, the decision to compare persons of different ages immediately raises the possibility of confounded effects due to differential selection of persons from different age strata in the population. Third, the population itself changes composition over time due to mortality, and hence one can legitimately wonder if today's population of, say, 70-year-old adults is comparable to today's population of persons of age 20.

At the same time, the methodological literature also identified several potential problems with longitudinal designs (Schaie, 1973). In addition to problems with period effects, the design could be adversely influenced by practice effects, experimental mortality, changes in methods of instrumentation, and other issues. The basic point is that each of these influences could operate to create (or offset) longitudinal change in a dependent variable. Indeed, recognition of these problems has led to spirited defenses of cross-sectional designs, relative to longitudinal approaches, by several reviewers in the literature on aging and cognition (see, e.g., Botwinick, 1977; Salthouse, 1991).

Measurement Assumptions

Another major focus of the life-span developmental literature has involved the problem of making quantitative comparisons either across occasions of measurement (in longitudinal studies) or between different populations of persons (in cross-sectional studies). As noted by Baltes & Nesselroade (1970), any such comparisons must invoke assumptions of *measurement equivalence* across the person, time, and context facets of variation in a sampling plan (see also Labouvie, 1980). Measurement equivalence refers to the assumption that the dependent variable(s) have equivalent measurement properties (relations of the actual observed measure to the underlying psychological construct). Without measurement equivalence, any quantitative differences (or quantitative changes) observed on a dependent variable could be a function of differences (or changes) in how persons behave on the measurement device rather than a function of differences (or changes) in the construct. Consider, for example, use of a typical reaction-time task in a cross-sectional study. Age differences in reaction times could be a function of the speed of the underlying psychological mechanisms the task was designed to measure. But they could also be influenced by age differences in the criterion for response in such tasks (see, e.g., Salthouse, 1979). The scientist studying cognitive aging generally assumes equivalent speed-versus-accuracy criteria in different age groups in order to make inferences from quantitative age differences in reaction time to age differences in the underlying phenomenon of interest.

The issue of measurement equivalence is secondary to a larger question: whether underlying developmental changes produce either pure quantitative changes or qualitative changes in the underlying psychological mechanisms (Schaie & Hertzog, 1985; Wohlwill, 1973). Development could change the underlying organization or structure of cognition (Kagan, 1980). For example, a study might find that the number of words older adults remember in intentional memory tasks decreases with increasing chronological age. This decrease might reflect decreasing efficiency of the set of mechanisms used at all ages to learn and remember the material. On the other hand, it might reflect qualitative changes in how adults intentionally learn and remember. Baltes and Nesselroade (1970) provided a useful treatment of this issue with respect to quantitative versus qualitative changes in levels of individual variables and in relationships among multiple variables. They distinguished qualitative developmental changes in the structure and organization of psychological constructs from quantitative changes (changes in level) on structurally invariant constructs and discussed some of the statistical means by which such changes could be identified (see also Hertzog, 1989; Hertzog & Nesselroade, 1987).

Schaie and Hertzog (1985) discussed the distinction between construct equivalence (or qualitative invariance at the level of psychological constructs) from measurement equivalence (qualitative changes in the measurement properties of empirical variables). One can have invariant constructs, yet have age-related changes and differences in the ways in which individuals' behavior affects empirically measured variables. Consider the example of older and younger adults responding on a personality scale measuring social extroversion. Such scales typically contain multiple items using Likert-scale responses to indicate level of agreement or disagreement with particular statements (e.g., "I often have difficulty starting a conversation with persons I have never met before"). The Likert-response format might require persons to indicate level of agreement (e.g., a 5-point scale ranging from "strongly agree" to "strongly disagree"). Typically, a scale score would be constructed by summing ratings across multiple items to produce a number hypothesized to scale individual differences in the degree of extroversion. There could be several reasons why such scores might not merely reflect quantitative differences in the underlying construct of extroversion. For instance, older adults might—for reasons having nothing to do with underlying extroversion—be more likely to concentrate responses in the middle three values on the scale, avoiding the use of either the "strongly agree" or "strongly disagree" options. Alternatively, older adults' responses might be influenced by an age-related reduction in the normative frequency with which they now converse with persons they never met before, so that instances of such situations are less accessible in memory at the time they are making the judgment. In both examples, conversational behavior with strangers may be a valid indicator of social extroversion, and it may not change qualitatively over the life span. However, in both examples, the measurement equivalence of the self-ratings is compromised by age differences in the influences of other factors on item responses.

The issue of construct equivalence for the preceding example addresses whether social extroversion is similarly organized in different age groups. The fundamental properties and manifestations of being extroverted might differ as a function of age. For example, striking up a conversation might be more associated with being extroverted in younger adults than in older adults. Extroverted behavior in older adults might be differentially manifested in the nature of communication in the conversation, the topics addressed, the degree of self-disclosure permitted, and so forth.

In general, scientists studying adult cognitive development should not necessarily assume that dependent measures identify the same psychological constructs with equivalent scaling properties at different time points or in different subpopulations.

IDENTIFYING AGE DIFFERENCES AND AGE CHANGES IN COGNITION

■ Identifying Average Age Differences

Despite the potential hazards and pitfalls, most studies of adult cognitive development use cross-sectional samples and evaluate differences between persons of different ages in average levels of cognitive task performance. The sampling design matrix of Figure 3.2 represents age and birth cohort as categorical independent variables. This schematic does not necessarily imply that cross-sectional designs *require* treatment of chronological age as a categorical independent variable. Indeed, when one thinks about chronological age as an attribute of all members of the human population, it is probably best conceptualized as a continuous random variable. If one were to draw a representative sample of the entire population at a single point in time, one would obtain a sample of adults of different ages in proportion to their representation in the population. In such cases chronological age could be treated as a continuous variable measured in years, months, or days since birth.

Most cross-sectional designs in psychological research do not create such representative samples. One reason is that a focus on the question of age-related differences motivates use of an age-stratified sampling plan. The stratified sampling plan first defines an age range of interest and a set of ordered sets of age groupings within the range. For example, the age range might span 21 to 69 years stratified into 5-year groups (21–25, 26–30, and so forth). The scientist then picks a desired number of cases at each age level and forms the sampling design. The total sample size depends upon two aspects of the sampling plan: the number of age strata and the number of persons sampled per stratum. Often the goal is to sample equal numbers of persons for each age stratum, thereby oversampling the older age ranges. Oversampling older adults is motivated by a simple principle: one must have sufficient numbers of replicated observations (in this case, different persons of the same ages) to achieve adequate statistical precision and power in any estimates of age effects.

The problem with this kind of cross-sectional design is that the sample size required to estimate age differences over a wide age span can be quite large. Given the individual differences in cognition and in the effects of aging, the number of persons sampled at each age level should be sufficient to ensure adequate statistical power. For example, one might decide to sample 5 persons for each year of chronological age from 41 to 80, yielding a total sample of 200 persons across the 40-year span. A sample of 15 persons per year would require a total sample of 600 persons. However, if the cognitive construct of interest were thought to be related to gender, one might create a gender × age stratified sampling plan. A quota of 15 men and 15 women per year would require a sample of 1,200 persons.

Two methods of reducing the expense are to restrict the age range to a period of specific developmental interest (e.g., ages 50 through 80) or to treat age as a categorical independent variable. In the latter approach, one aggregates persons over a range of chronological ages and perhaps samples only restricted age ranges. For example, one could construct an independent variable of chronological age with four levels, sampling persons of ages 20 to 25, 40 to 45, 60 to 65, and 80 to 85 years.

The most typical cross-sectional design in the literature on aging and cognition can be referred to as an extreme age groups design (see Hertzog, in press). In it a group of younger adults (typically, ages 18–21) is compared to a group of older adults (here age ranges vary more widely across studies, but typically the age range is centered around age 65). With this design, the researcher collects the minimum information needed to infer chronological age differences in cognition at two widely spaced points in the life span (onset of adulthood, late adulthood). If one is willing to assume that the cognitive variable of interest is a monotonically increasing or decreasing function of age, then an extreme age groups design provides a quick, economical, and relatively valid evaluation of whether age is related to the construct of interest.

The statistical null hypothesis in an extreme groups design is that the means of the dependent variable for the two age groups are equal. Rejecting it implies an age difference in the underlying psychological construct. From a statistical perspective, the design is efficient because with moderate to large effect sizes (e.g., mean differences of .5 or more standard deviations; see Cohen, 1988) samples of 15 to 25 persons in each age group may be sufficient to have adequate power for rejecting the null hypothesis. The practice of using extreme age groups designs can be justified as a means of exploring age differences in a field in which theories about cognitive constructs and empirical methods of measuring them are rapidly changing and evolving (as can be argued to be the case for cognitive psychology).

The relative economy of extreme age groups designs becomes especially pronounced under certain conditions. Many studies of cognitive phenomena require the simultaneous experimental manipulation of other important independent variables in order to isolate and identify the key cognitive constructs. When such designs involve between-subject factors, the number of persons required in an age × condition factorial design increases as a function of the number of experimental conditions that must be run. Simplification of the age factor to a two-level (young, old) independent variable significantly reduces the expense of running the study. Moreover, it is often the case that multiple experiments are required to identify age effects in cognitive mechanisms and to test alternative hypotheses about the substantive interpretation, based upon cognitive theory, of any obtained results. If an investigator anticipates the need for multiple experiments and at least some between-subject manipulations of experimental variables, the economy of scale provided by an extreme age groups design is very attractive indeed. Finally, scientists often need to examine more than just average age differences in dependent measures. If the research question requires tests of hypotheses about age differences in relationships among multiple measures (examination of correlational hypotheses), much larger samples must be drawn in order to get meaningful statistical analyses. Under such conditions, results from extreme age groups designs may be required before a more elaborate cross-sectional sampling design can be realistically justified.

Despite its advantages, the extreme age groups designs has a number of important limitations. First, restricting the operationalization of aging to a comparison of older and younger adults precludes an attempt to map the developmental function across the entire adult age span. Rejecting the null hypothesis of equal age group means may imply some age-related change, but one cannot address such key questions as when age-related change begins in adulthood and what shape the developmental function takes. Second, as we noted earlier, there are a number of rival explanations for any observed age differences in performance—they may not be due to aging per se. Concern for rival hypotheses may be particularly appropriate given the standard practices for implementing extreme age groups designs in research on adult cognition. The most severe internal validity threat is probably that of selection effects.

Selection Effects in Cross-sectional Designs

Selection effects represent an important internal validity threat in cross-sectional designs of development because persons who are sampled because they differ in chronological age may also differ in other characteristics besides how old they are. In order to make valid inferences about aging effects in an extreme age groups design, the cognitive psychologist must assume that the younger group represents a sample of persons who are identical in all relevant variables (i.e., those that relate to cognitive functioning) to the sample of older adults when the latter group were young adults. Otherwise, any obtained differences in cognition could be attributed to factors other than aging per se.

In cognitive aging research, subjects are rarely if ever obtained by random sampling from the population. Instead, samples of older adults are typically purposive or accidental in nature (Camp, West, & Poon, 1989). Older participants are generally volunteers recruited from organizations with high proportions of older adults, such as senior centers or church groups, or solicited through paid advertisements in newspapers and other outlets. Methodologists shudder at this kind of sampling practice because of the potential problems that arise when the representativeness of the sample to the parent population is unknown. Furthermore, it is often the case that a study will compare a relatively heterogeneous sample of older adults with a sample of undergraduate college students who participate in exchange for extra credit in a psychology class. Given this type of design, it is possible that empirically obtained age group differences in cognition are partly a function of current educational status (whether one is in school or not) or past educational attainment (R. Lachman, Lachman, & Taylor, 1982).

Why should past educational attainment matter in cognitive aging studies? Any variable which is potentially associated with cognitive ability may indirectly reflect a selection process that has skewed the age sample. One would not, for example, want to compare a group of 60-year-old former college professors with a group of 20-year-old semiskilled laborers who had not graduated from high school. Differences in background knowledge could influence age differences in cognitive tasks where such knowledge would be relevant (e.g., tests of memory for text, where reading skill and knowledge of relevant subject matter might affect original comprehension and thereby recall). However, educational attainment itself is influenced by a number of variables, including the intelligence of the individual. High-ability persons are more likely to score well on standardized tests, obtain high grades in high school, and hence be admitted to college. Thus, even if the cognitive variable of interest is not one that relies on the types of skills and knowledge obtained in a college education, it is still unwise to allow differences in educational attainment between samples, to the extent that these differences reflect differences in intelligence during adolescence and young adulthood. Forming special comparison groups that equate on years of education or occupational status may be better (R. Lachman et al., 1982), but even so there is no guarantee that controlling for such variables will achieve equivalent samples, given the historical and contextual shifts in the nature of educational and occupational contexts and practices.

Psychologists studying cognition and aging have discussed this issue. These sampling practices have often been questioned and criticized by psychologists studying cognition and aging. Salthouse, Kausler, and Saults (1988) recommended, for example, that gerontologists routinely measure older samples on standard cognitive tasks so that sample performance could be used as a means of characterizing the cognitive ability level of the sample. It is indeed routine to observe in published studies some comparison of older and younger samples on variables such as self-reported health, education, and vocabulary. However, such approaches may not suffice to establish age group comparability, for several reasons (see also Hertzog, in press). First, these variables may not provide a profile of characteristics that is actually relevant to the cognitive construct under evaluation in any given study. Second, one generally sees statistical tests of age differences in the measured background variables. Although it may be helpful to show that older adults in a particular sample are higher in vocabulary and lower in self-reported health than the sample of younger adults (given that such differences are typical in the literature), this outcome does not establish the representativeness of either group with respect to the age-stratified population distribution of these attributes. One rarely sees any comparisons of sample distributions to parent population distributions—for example, comparison to population norms for means and standard deviations. Third, the meaning of these variables with respect to the underlying conceptualization of aging is rarely made explicit. Should, for example, a sample of older persons be identified that indeed is of poorer health than a sample of younger persons? What is the conceptualization of aging, as a process, that leads to such expectations?

It is important to identify the procedures that should be instituted to maximize the validity of inferences about aging effects in cross-sectional samples. It is also important to ask the fundamental question of whether the goal of obtaining representative samples from the population is the best method of achieving validity in inferences about aging. Representativeness of the sample may ultimately be most central to the issue of generalizability of results. A study with a representative sample is broadly generalizable to the total population. However, both representativeness and the internal validity of age group comparisons must be considered, and broad generalizability—or population representativeness—is not equally important to all research questions.

Questions about population base rates and attributes, which are common in sociology, epidemiology, and demography, demand careful attention to sample representativeness. If one wishes to estimate the incidence or prevalence rates of certain age-related phenomena, one is directly asking a question about population parameters (e.g., what proportion of the population, ages 65 or older, are clinically depressed?). In such cases one must use sampling methods that obtain a probability sample—one for which the probability of representation of different population segments can be determined (see Kish, 1965). Failure to obtain a probability sample would lead to biases in the estimates of the population parameters in question. Biased samples have been shown to produce inaccurate estimates of the prevalence of clinical levels of depression in older populations (Blazer, 1989). However, questions about normative age changes in cognitive processes do not necessarily demand this kind of sampling. Indeed, it is an open question whether a representative sample of younger adults is the proper standard of comparison to older adults for inferring the effects of aging (R. Lachman et al., 1982).

Moreover, we must recognize that because the nature of cognitive research requires volunteer samples, any sample will necessarily be biased to some degree by refusals to participate. Selective refusal can indeed bias both estimates of population incidence or prevalence and assessment of the relationships between sets of variables (e.g., Thompson, Heller, & Rody, 1994). In addition, some cognitive processes of interest may involve the use of experimental tasks that cannot be administered to a substantial proportion of older persons, owing to sensory or perceptual deficits, complexity of performance requirements, and other factors. Probability-sampling techniques may make it possible to estimate the degree of bias introduced, but they cannot prevent the exclusion of subjects due to refusal or disqualification on the basis of extraneous factors.

Whether most research questions regarding aging and cognition require attention to sample representativeness is a matter which probably should be, but rarely is, debated within the community of scholars studying cognition in adulthood. Psychologists adopting a biological decrement model for aging and cognition may believe that representative samples are relatively unimportant, given their view that the research focuses on universal mechanisms of both cognition and aging. Their argument, in essence, is that anyone is representative of the parent population simply by virtue of being human, that aging is a process that affects all humans, and that the psychological mechanisms under study are also, in that sense, universal. This argument would seem to apply more to some phenomena (e.g., mechanisms of sensation and perception) than to others. With respect to cognitive mechanisms, others (e.g., Mook, 1983) argue that experimental psychologists need not worry about generalization. According to this perspective, the study of mechanisms in the sample at hand (whether it is a sample of college sophomores or older volunteers from a church social group) is of interest in its own right. Such a line of argument seems less justified for developmental research questions, but a case can be made that representativeness and diversity of a sample are not necessarily a high priority for a well-designed study. On the other hand, a theoretical perspective that argues for individual differences in patterns and rates of aging effects, as well as for contextual influences on aging, seems to lead inexorably to a view that the issue of representativeness of the sample cannot be ignored without producing at least a biased picture of aging effects.

Such considerations can lead to alternative suggestions for sampling in cross-sectional designs. Some psychologists (e.g., Schaie, 1973) have suggested that comparisons of well-defined, homogeneous, but comparable age groups might be preferable (in at least some cases) to attempting to sample broadly and representatively with little attention to historical changes in population composition. The appropriate sampling model for research on cognition and aging may be less like population demography and more like one often applied in medicine and the neurosciences (e.g., human experimental neuropsychology), where appropriate comparison groups are narrowly defined according to inclusion and exclusion criteria to maximize internal validity (Hertzog, in press). For example, university students could be compared to a high-education older group (e.g., university alumni).

There is probably no single right or wrong approach to the problem, and ultimately the answer probably lies in replication of age effects across a wider range of design alternatives than is currently common in research on aging and cognition. When such work is done, the results have often been encouraging. For example, Salthouse's (1992) extensive cross-sectional studies of large samples of adults confirm earlier extreme age groups studies in finding robust age differences in constructs such as perceptual speed and working memory.

In general, one should not assume that the type of extreme age groups design we have described necessarily and straightforwardly identifies age changes in underlying cognitive processes. Additional standards of comparison for samples, as recommended by Salthouse et al. (1988), might prove helpful if followed thoughtfully and thoroughly by more cognitive aging researchers. Findings of age differences in extreme age groups designs are probably best seen as a first step, requiring replication and extension by designs with different definitions of age groups, by studies with fuller cross-sectional sampling techniques, and by studies using alternative methods for identifying age effects. One class of alternatives involves longitudinal or sequential sampling, to which we now turn.

■ Identifying Intraindividual Change

One way to address the confounding of cohort effects in a basic cross-sectional design is to conduct sequential sampling (as in Figure 3.2). If the research goal is to identify average age changes in a population, either longitudinal sequences or cross-sectional sequences can be used. The chief advantage of such a design is that cohort and age effects are no longer perfectly confounded. Instead of identifying age differences at a single point in time, one can identify average age changes within the same birth cohort. Sequential sampling plans are extremely expensive and hence rare. Indeed, the Seattle Longitudinal Study (see Chapter 9) is unique in its use of such methods to examine age changes in intellectual abilities.

Data from longitudinal and cross-sectional sequences do not fully agree because the two types of designs are subject to different kinds of biasing influences on estimates of age changes (e.g., Schaie, 1994). Cross-sectional sequences introduce potential selection effects that vary across the occasions of sampling. Longitudinal sequences introduce potential problems with selective attrition from the longitudinal sample and practice effects. These effects would typically be expected to introduce a positive bias into the data. Hence longitudinal data may underestimate any age-related declines in cognitive functioning during adulthood. Many psychologists would therefore argue that, given well-defined and consistent definitions of population, sampling frame, and sampling methods, cross-sectional sequences provide better estimates of average age-related change. If this is true, why would one ever use longitudinal sampling methods? The answer is that average age-related change, although important, is only one aspect of change that can be measured.

■ Types of Change

Longitudinal designs repeatedly measure the same person over time and hence are the only method for measuring actual within-person (intraindividual) change (Baltes et al., 1977). The converse of change is stability, and it is meaningful to ask whether a given population of persons is relatively more stable or more changing on a given cognitive construct. It is possible to identify several different aspects of changing scores on psychological constructs (Nesselroade, 1983, 1990; Wohlwill, 1973, 1991): (1) stability or change in average intraindividual change (as already discussed); (2) consistency or stability of individual differences at different points in time (termed *covariance stability;* see Hertzog & Nesselroade, 1987); (3) individual differences in intraindividual change (termed *heterogeneity*); and (4) intraindividual variability (termed *lability*). The latter three aspects of intraindividual change (or stability) can be evaluated only when longitudinal designs are used to gather information on intraindividual change.

The three aspects of change—covariance stability, heterogeneity, and lability—are interrelated. Covariance stability refers to the extent to which individual differences are highly related at different points in time. It can be conceptualized as the correlation of a construct with itself over time. Figure 3.3 illustrates the differences between average intraindividual change and stability of individual differences in longitudinal data. The figure shows four hypothetical points of measurement. Between the first and second points there is no average age change, indicating perfect stability in individual differences. None of the persons in the sample changes at all, and scores at time 2 are perfectly predicted by the scores at time 1. There is no average change between times 2 and 3, as well, but here there are individual dif-

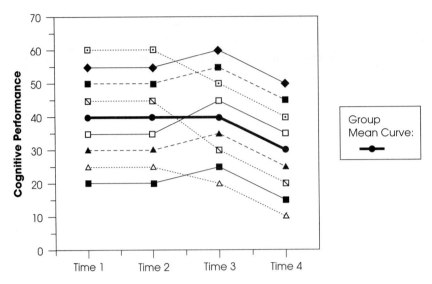

FIGURE 3.3 Hypothetical longitudinal design illustrating different combinations of mean level stability (or change) and covariance stability (or individual differences in change). Time 1 to time 2: mean stability, covariance stability; time 2 to time 3: mean stability, individual differences in change; time 3 to time 4: mean level change, covariance stability. The fourth combination (mean level change, individual differences in change) is not explicitly shown.

ferences in change. The stability of individual differences is less than perfect. There are two components of such covariance stability: (1) original or initial individual differences and (2) the heterogeneity of intraindividual change. Covariance stability will be high if the degree of heterogeneity in change is small relative to the magnitude of initial individual differences. Between time 3 and time 4 in Figure 3.3 there is substantial average age change, but again there is perfect stability of individual differences. Each person changes by the same amount.

Following Nesselroade (1990), we can distinguish between two different patterns of change that can be reflected in less-than-perfect covariance stability: *long-term intraindividual change* versus *intraindividual variability.* The former reflects trends that *may* be due to developmental processes of growth and decline. Intraindividual variability refers to the relative stability or instability of a construct within an individual person—that is, whether an individual's standing on a construct fluctuates within a short time span. One might expect that psychological states would fluctuate, whereas more enduring attributes (termed traits) would show high stability of individual differences over time (Nesselroade, 1983). Only by explicitly measuring the same persons repeatedly can the scientist differentiate long-term trends that may reflect cumulative influences of development or experience from intraindividual variability.

■ Measurement of Change

Some developmental methodologists criticize measures of covariance stability as being at best indirect indicators of what ought to be the more important aspect of change, namely, heterogeneity (Rogosa, 1988; Wohlwill, 1991). Rogosa and Willett (1985) argue that one should not analyze for covariance stability per se but should instead analyze growth (or decline) curves estimated separately for each individual in the sample. The rationale for this argument is that establishing predictors of change requires using an index of change as a variable (e.g., as the dependent variable in a multiple regression analysis).

This argument has implications for the design and statistical analysis of longitudinal data. Obtaining reliable estimates of individual patterns of growth and decline generally will require more frequent occasions of measurement than are often included in longitudinal panel studies (but see Alder, Adam, & Arenberg, 1990). Estimating each individual's change parameters requires the use of special statistical techniques, such as hierarchical linear modeling (see Bryk & Raudenbush, 1987). One major advantage of the method is that it becomes possible to estimate correlates and predictors of change in studies in which the spacing of measurement occasions may vary widely across persons, as in the Boston Normative Study. Spiro, Aldwin, Levenson, and Bosse (1990) used these methods to make generalizations about longitudinal changes across persons with very different patterns of longitudinal sampling.

If the goal of the study is to identify long-term intraindividual change, as is more frequently the case, one would typically use a longitudinal panel design. This design involves relatively fixed, equal-interval spacing of the occasions of measurement (usually separated by months or years). Examples of panel studies that involve at least some cognitive measures include the Duke Longitudinal Studies, the Victoria Longitudinal Study, and the Baltimore Longitudinal Study. Intervals of at least 2 to 4 years may be required to detect salient average intraindividual change and heterogeneity in intraindividual change. Longer retest intervals also serve to reduce the hazards of potential practice effects. The longitudinal panel design usually includes relatively large numbers of persons in the sample (numbering in the hundreds) and relatively few numbers of longitudinal occasions. It is best suited to measuring the coherent patterns of gradually accumulating long-term change that would be expected to be produced by normal aging.

If the goal of the study is to separate long-term longitudinal change from liability, one would probably use an intensive short-term longitudinal design. In this case persons are measured very frequently (daily, weekly, intermittently), generating large numbers of data points for each individual. This design involves even more frequent measurement than would be needed for the kind of individual change estimation alluded to earlier. Given the high rate of repeated measurement for each individual, studies using this kind of design typically include relatively few participants.

Such studies are rare in cognitive aging research. Hertzog, Dixon, and Hultsch (1992) used this approach to evaluate intraindividual variability and change in text recall for a small sample of elderly women. They measured text recall (and other variables) every week for up to 2 years. Figure 3.4 illustrates data for two persons, both of whom showed substantial intraindividual variability. One of the women also showed a salient longer-term decline in text recall. Dixon, Hertzog, Friesen, & Hultsch (1993) reported similar data from a shorter-term longitudinal sample, using the Wechsler Memory Scale's Logical Memory Test. The results of these studies indicate interesting lability in cognitive performance in older adults that could not have been revealed by more traditional longitudinal panel designs. Data from both these studies suggest that this kind of short-term longitudinal study could be particularly useful in identifying abnormal or pathological cognitive change associated with subclinical neurological damage in older populations.

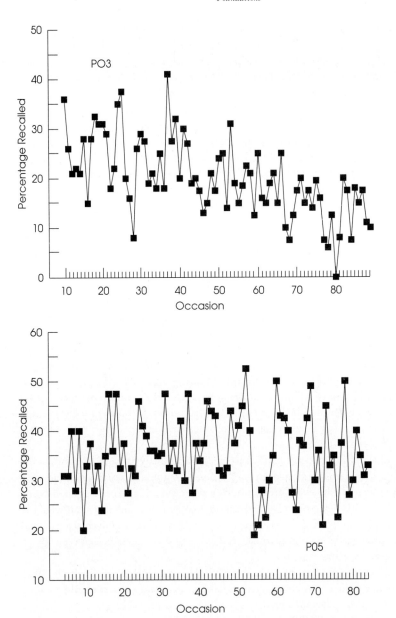

FIGURE 3.4 Data for two subjects from Hertzog, Dixon, and Hultsch (1992), in which text recall was assessed weekly for a 2-year period. Both subjects exhibit substantial intraindividual variability in text recall from week to week, despite different patterns of long-term (intraindividual) change. Subject P05 initially displayed gains in performance, followed by losses in level late in the sequence of measurement. Subject P03 displayed nearly linear decline over the assessment period. P05 clearly had a better average level of text recall. Note, however, that P03's best level of performance is at about the mean of P05's distribution of recall scores. Reprinted with permission from Academic Press.

■ Distinguishing Reliability from Stability

In discussing different types and patterns of change, it is crucial that one understands the distinction between intraindividual variability and reliability. The fluctuations that can be observed in Figure 3.4 might be attributed to random measurement error, were it not for the fact that the text-recall measures used by Hertzog et al. (1992) had been shown to have relatively high reliability. The concept of reliability, as taken from classical test score theory, implies the consistency of assignment of numbers to levels of underlying attributes for a given empirical measure. Reliability in this sense is directly tied to the measurement properties of a particular operational definition of a construct. (See Cronbach, Gleser, Nanda, & Rajaratnam, 1972, for an important, alternative treatment of inconsistency of scores across different contexts, samples, or times of measurement and methods of measuring them.)

Intraindividual variability, on the other hand, can be thought of as a property of the person and the psychological construct that one is measuring. It is in that sense a substantive phenomenon that scientists may attempt to measure empirically. High longitudinal variability suggests that a person is labile on a given construct. For example, a manic-depressive might shift mood states in a consistent fashion, producing substantial longitudinal variability in mood over time. This does not imply that any measurement of the manic-depressive's mood state is inherently unreliable. Indeed, longitudinal variability can reflect validly and reliably measured constructs that are highly organized yet fluctuating attributes.

Frequently the concepts of reliability and stability (or variability) are confused because similar correlational methods are used to index both. Both covariance stability and reliability are reflected in test–retest (longitudinal) correlations. A test–retest correlation is often used to assess a measure's reliability. This method assumes perfect stability of true underlying individual differences on the attribute being measured. If this assumption is correct, any inconsistency in the distribution of scores at test and at retest reflects inconsistent sources of influence on the empirical measure (classically termed random errors of measurement). Test–retest correlations cannot be used as estimates of reliability whenever there is true heterogenesity of change in the construct being measured (see Hertzog & Nesselroade, 1987).

By the same token, the less-than-perfect reliability of measures, which is to be expected for virtually all empirical measures of psychological constructs, dilutes the estimates of covariance stability in the underlying construct. Addressing the issue of reliability in empirical measures is therefore critically important for assessing change. An optimal estimate of longitudinal change would adjust or correct for the degree of unreliability in the empirical measures. It is therefore useful to include multiple measures of each construct of interest in longitudinal studies in that multivariate statistical methods can be used to estimate heterogeneity in change that is corrected for measurement error (Hertzog & Nesselroade, 1987; Schaie & Hertzog, 1985).

Given the time, expense, and special expertise required to use longitudinal methods to study aging, such methods are infrequently used in studies of adult cognitive development. This is both understandable and unfortunate, because questions involving individual differences in the age of onset, magnitude, and patterns of cognitive aging seem to be at the heart of the questions scientists of cognitive aging would want to study (Hertzog, 1985). Interest in aging often focuses on the question of individual differences in the effects of aging—who changes the most, and why? Such questions cannot be empirically evaluated with cross-sectional data.

EXPERIMENTAL APPROACHES TO COGNITION AND AGING

■ Prototypical Research Questions

Theories and methods from experimental psychology are prominent in research on aging and cognition today. As noted in Chapter 2, the experimental approach to cognition and aging is generally associated with a mechanistic worldview, a biologically based conceptualization of age-related decline in basic cognitive mechanisms, and a focus on compartmentalizing age-related changes in terms of specific processes and mechanisms that are responsible for more global age-related changes in cognitive performance. Although there is a variety of theoretical perspectives on how cognition should be treated, many researchers in the field adopt some kind of information-processing model of cognition and often use computer-based metaphors (e.g., cognitive architecture, cognitive hardware and software) to determine how higher-level cognitive constructs (e.g., thinking, problem solving, learning) can be decomposed into constituent processes and mechanisms. In turn, scientists interested in cognitive aging apply these models to questions of how aging influences the cognitive architecture. The underlying premise of many theories is that the hardware supporting cognition declines due to biological aging (perhaps selectively), but that changes in knowledge structures and other aspects of cognitive software remain stable or improve as a function of experience.

The modal research questions asked by scientists adopting this approach focus on identifying the extent to which normative age-related declines are relatively universal (across mechanisms) or specific to certain domains of processing. Recently, the field of cognitive neuroscience has added some impetus to the view that processing deficits may be specific to certain kinds of cognition and the discrete areas of the central nervous system (Johnson & Rybash, 1993). Some scientists in cognitive aging ask questions about specificity of aging and cognitive change that are grounded in theories and data from cognitive neuroscience, even when they do not explicitly and simultaneously measure central nervous system function (see, e.g., Hartley, 1993).

In this section we review the general rationale for methods currently used to study cognition and aging within the experimental tradition. We hasten to emphasize that there are alternative views and methods for treating cognition and cognitive change in adulthood. They may share at least some methodological commonality, but their views on age and aging can diverge quite dramatically.

■ Identifying Age Differences in Cognitive Mechanisms

Operational Definitions of Cognitive Mechanisms

Experimental approaches to cognition vary widely according to the type of cognitive mechanism under study. Nevertheless, they tend to share a common feature: manipulation of stimulus features and/or task requirements to operationally define and measure specific processing mechanisms. For example, Roger Shepard (Cooper & Shepard, 1978) and his colleagues used systematic manipulation of differences in orientation disparity between two geometric figures as a method of measuring the rate of mental rotation of the figures in two-dimensional space (Cooper & Shepard, 1978). These investigators also evaluated the ways in which the manipulations of figural orientation changed as a function of other experimental variables (e.g., type and complexity of the geometric figures, simultaneous versus sequential presentations of figures to be compared). Variations in the effects of orientation under different experimental conditions were used to test substantive claims about the nature of mental representations of objects and how these representations were manipulated to simulate spatial transformations. In aging research, such experimental manipulations are combined with an age-based sampling plan to evaluate age differences (or age changes) in the cognitive mechanisms that have been captured by the experimental task and its systematically varied task conditions. For example, age differences in the relationship of figural orientation to mental rotation task performance can help gerontologists understand the nature of age changes in spatial information processing. We illustrate these principles more concretely later in this section.

The dependent measures in such experiments are usually either the accuracy of subjects' discriminative judgments (e.g., correct or incorrect judgments that one previously studied a word in a recognition memory task or selection of alternative synonyms in a multiple-choice vocabulary test) or the response latency for making such judgments. It is also possible, although not as common, for experiments to evaluate qualitative aspects of performance (e.g., method of strategy utilization). Most studies of cognitive aging directly import standard methods and tasks from experimental research into age-comparative studies.

Operational Definitions of Aging Effects

Aging is usually defined in this research tradition by cross-sectional age differences, most often in an extreme age groups design. For instance, two levels of age (young, old) are crossed with multiple levels of one or more independent variables representing systematic variation in the influence of a hypothetical cognitive mechanism.

Analysis of variance is the typical statistical method for evaluating mean differences in dependent measures across experimental task conditions. The substantive hypothesis of interest is that aging affects the specific cognitive mechanism in question. The generic empirical hypothesis is (1) that accuracy or response time will be systematically influenced by the experimentally manipulated independent variable and that (2) the amount of influence will differ between the age groups. The predicted statistical outcome is an age × condition interaction. The statistical hypothesis tested is the null hypothesis of equivalent experimental effects in the age groups. Rejection of the null hypothesis implies differential effects, supporting the inference that the cognitive mechanism is indeed affected by aging.

Figure 3.5 provides an example set of conditions from a mental rotation task, where the subject must judge whether the two stimuli are identical ("same") or mirror images ("different") when rotated in the two-dimensional plane. Figure 3.6 graphs data collected by Hertzog and Yuasa (1988) on such a mental rotation task. In this case, three age groups were used (young, middle-aged, and old), and the relative orientation of the two figures was systematically varied as a within-subject factor. The pattern of results in Figure 3.6 shows age-related increases in response time of correct identity judgments as a function of increasing angle of rotation, suggesting age differences in the rate of mental rotation. The study also found age

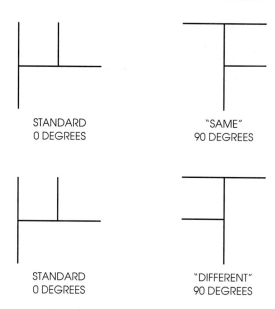

STANDARD
0 DEGREES

"SAME"
90 DEGREES

STANDARD
0 DEGREES

"DIFFERENT"
90 DEGREES

FIGURE 3.5 Example of stimuli from a mental rotation experiment. Each row corresponds to a pair of figures that are involved in a single experimental trial. In the top row, the two figures are identical, except that the comparison (right-hand) figure has been rotated 90 degrees clockwise from the standard (left-hand) figure's orientation. In the bottom row, the two figures cannot be rotated to congruence in the two-dimensional plane; the comparison figure is a mirror image of the standard figure.

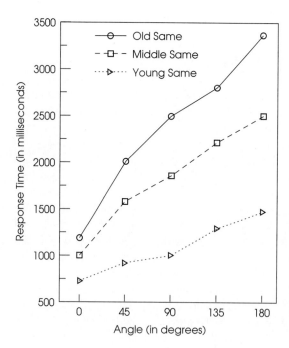

FIGURE 3.6 Results from an unpublished mental rotation study by Hertzog and Yuasa (1988). Response times for correct mental rotation discriminations (same trials only, as in the top row of Figure 3.5) are plotted as a function of (1) angle of orientation of the comparison figure, relative to the standard figure and (2) age group (young, middle-aged, old). Age is associated with increases in the intercept and slope of the linear function regressing mental rotation response times on angle of orientation. (*Source:* Reprinted from Hertzog (1994) with permission from Lawrence Erlbaum Associates.)

decreases in the relative accuracy of these judgments as the angle of rotation increased. Judgments at 180 degrees disparity were less accurate than judgments at 0 degrees (no rotation), and this difference was largest for older adults. Indeed, the statistical analysis of the data detected a significant age × angle interaction.

Why are the interaction hypotheses of special interest in a study of aging and cognition? Why not merely test the hypothesis that there are age differences in response times or accuracy across all the conditions? The answer is that the logic of the experiment is designed to isolate a process or set of processes in the experimentally varied independent variable. This isolation is not achieved in the comparison of age groups across all experimental conditions. There could be many possible age-related sources of influence that would create an age difference in response time or accuracy. Average age differences in response times are influenced by a host of processes, including slowing of perceptual processing speed, slowing of motor responses, and slowing of comparison processes (Salthouse, 1985; Welford, 1977). In principle, these influences are present in all of the experimental conditions (in the mental rotation task example, the multiple angles of rotation). However, the experimental psychologist assumes that the influence of the psychological construct under investigation (e.g., the amount of mental rotation) has in fact been specifically isolated and manipulated when the independent variable is manipulated (e.g., by varying the relative orientation of the two figures). If so, a statistically significant interaction would indicate that age differences exist in the specific mechanism isolated by the independent variable. To the extent that an experimental task can be designed to isolate cognitive processes through manipulation of the independent variable, it has the potential of showing that age differences exist for certain mechanisms but not others.

This is not to imply that age differences, in the absence of interaction, are inherently uninterpretable. The point is, however, that there are *fewer* rival explanations for an interaction effect than for a simple age difference. This is true with respect to cognitive interpretations, and of course, it is also true of rival explanations for age group differences. A selection confound could easily explain differences between two age groups formed by purposive sampling (as described above). It is often a less plausible explanation for interaction effects.

Indeed, the idea that forming a more specific prediction is beneficial for inferences about age differences in cognitive mechanisms extends beyond the case of predicting an interaction versus predicting a simple age difference. If possible, it is highly desirable to formulate an even more specific empirical prediction (empirical hypothesis) than the one reflected in the overall statistical test of an age × condition interaction. In the mental rotation task, the expectation is that the rate of mental rotation is reflected in the slope of the linear function regressing the response time on "angle." The ideal is direct reflection of this empirical hypothesis in a specifically tailored statistical test. There are two approaches to the problem. One can use a specific planned comparison—in this case, a planned comparison embodying linear trend across "angle"—and test for an age × linear angle interaction (see Hertzog, 1994). This partial interaction (Boik, 1979) tests the specific empirical hypothesis of interest. Alternatively, one can choose to directly estimate the slope of the function for each individual subject and then use these slope estimates as dependent variables. Age differences in the fitted slopes then test the substantive hypothesis of interest (see, e.g., Berg, Hertzog, & Hunt, 1982).

Threats to Validity of Inference

With respect to the general principles of research design we outlined previously, this kind of experiment is subject to several concerns regarding construct validity, internal validity, and external validity. The concerns about operationally defining age via an extreme age groups design have already been discussed. Relevant validity issues specific to this kind of experiment include (1) does the experimental manipulation truly isolate the cognitive process or mechanism of interest? and (2) are there other influences on the dependent measure that could produce the interaction effect other than age differences in the mechanism, even if it is one of the influences on the variation in the dependent measure across experimental conditions?

Issues associated with interpretations of experimental task effects are well known in cognitive psychology, and we shall say only a little more about them. In the case of the mental rotation task, there has been considerable research questioning the classic models and extensive debate about the proper interpretation of the linear function relating response time to angle of rotation. These issues are certainly relevant to issues of interpreting age differences in task performance. Early work argued that the slope was a measure of the rate of a holistic, analogue mental rotation (that is, rotation of an image of the figure "in the mind's eye"). However, subsequent work has suggested that the slope is influenced by factors other than the rotation rate (e.g., Bethell-Fox & Shepard, 1988; Just & Carpenter, 1985).

With aging research, the problem shifts to include the issue of age differences in the relative contribution of different processes to performance on an experimental task. We will highlight two issues associated with the assumption of age equivalence in measurement properties of experimental tasks.

Scaling Artifacts

The first issue has to do with artifacts of measurement scales as a possible cause of age × condition interaction effects. Note that, in Figure 3.6, the response-time functions for young and old groups on the mental rotation task barely overlap in the measurement space—the longest average response time for younger adults (at the 180-degree condition) barely exceeds the shortest average response time for older adults (at the 0-degree condition). The problem is that the functional relationship mapping the levels of true differences on the underlying attribute may not be linear and uniform across all levels of the measurement scale. The dependent variable may meaningfully separate ordinal differences but may not be a true interval scale across the entire range of possible scores. Given a nonlinear functional relationship of differences in scores to differences in cognitive mechanisms, the assumption of additivity involved in the analysis of variance may apply to the dependent measure and to tests of differences in level, but these differences may not actually reflect age differences in underlying cognitive mechanisms.

This problem has been extensively discussed in the experimental literature. Experimentally produced interactions are most unambiguously interpretable when they are what is termed crossover or disordinal interactions. When interactions are ordinal, like the ones in Figure 3.6, the possibility exists that nonlinear mapping of the underlying construct onto the measurement scale of the dependent variable *artifactually* produces a statistical interaction (see, e.g., Loftus, 1978). If the mental rotation rate to response time has a different scaling in the two age groups, the interaction may not imply age differences in underlying mental rotation rates. Given that disordinal age × condition interactions in research on cognitive mechanisms would rarely be expected, this issue is particularly problematic for experimental aging research. Unfortunately, there is usually relatively little that can be done directly to cause the performance of the two age groups to overlap on the measurement scale, given the expected age differences in the processes needed to perform on the task.

Researchers need to be sensitive to the fact that importing tasks developed on younger adult populations into aging research creates potential problems. The mean performance of younger adults may be at the middle of the measurement scale (perhaps after careful pilot work to develop the task to have just such a property). Such a task may not have optimal performance distributions when used in an older adult sample. It may indeed be difficult to develop a task that is not prone to ceiling or floor effects (performance levels close to the minimum or maximum of the measurement scale range) in one or more of the age groups. The larger point is that tinkering with the task in order to eliminate such effects is critically important and necessary for valid inference. However, it may not be sufficient to remove the issues associated with age differences in measurement properties.

A similar argument for response-time measures states that ordinal interactions are expected in the analysis of variance of age × condition data, given the age-related slowing of information processing. According to some versions of a general slowing hypothesis, an age × condition interaction can be attributed to this proportional slowing (Salthouse, 1985). This argument claims that such interactions therefore have no theoretical importance with respect to the issue of isolating age-related slowing to particular cognitive mechanisms. This issue has been hotly debated in recent literature (e.g., Perfect, 1994; see Dixon & Hertzog, Chapter 2, for additional citations). In any event, the issue regarding measurement scales raised above is more generic, and in a sense more inimical to the entire rationale of the experiment, than the problem identified by the general slowing hypothesis.

Measurement Equivalence for Experimental Tasks

The second kind of validity concern regarding such interactions is that the response behavior of the two age groups may not be determined by the same mechanism. Experimental gerontologists have often studied this issue in the context of specific tasks. For example, studies of paired associate learning (Kausler, 1994) have focused on the possible limiting effects of experimenter-paced (versus self-paced) study, and work on visual discrimination and recognition memory has considered the possibility of distorted age differences due to response bias in detection and discrimination paradigms (see, e.g., Harkins, Chapman, & Eisdorfer, 1979). For research using response times, an important issue is age equivalence in speed-versus-accuracy trade-offs. Figure 3.7 graphs a hypothetical speed-versus-accuracy trade-off. The speed-versus-accuracy curves vary according to two major influences: how long it takes to make the judgment (the horizontal axis of the graph) and how accurately the judgment can be made (the vertical axis). In theory an individual's performance in an experiment can lie anywhere on the speed-versus-accuracy function. The person can trade accuracy for speed by making a quicker discrimination or can trade speed for accuracy by delaying the discrimination until additional information about the display is processed. The function is determined by the nature of the task and the cognitive mechanisms as they operate in real time

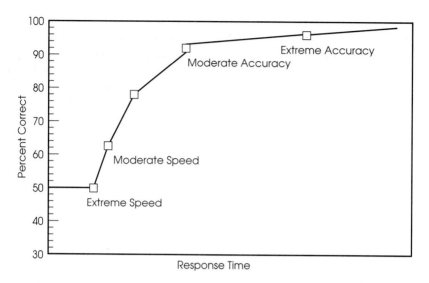

FIGURE 3.7 Hypothetical speed-versus-accuracy function plotting percentage of correct responses against response time. At very short response times, accuracy is at chance (in this case, 50%). Accuracy rises rapidly as a function of increasing response time but then asymptotes, so that large increases in response times produce relatively small gains in accuracy. The speed-versus-accuracy function characterizes the response times of a single person placing different levels of emphasis on speed or accuracy. The labeled points on the graphs correspond to different kinds of trade-offs for the two variables; an extreme speed emphasis sacrifices accuracy for fast responses, whereas an extreme accuracy emphasis sacrifices speed for accurate responses. Persons of different ages could have identical speed-versus-accuracy trade-off functions but differ in the relative degree of emphasis given to accuracy versus speed (see text). (*Source:* Reprinted from Hertzog, Vernon, & Rypma, 1993, with permission from the Gerontological Society of America.)

to provide the information needed to make the task discrimination. Different individuals might have different curves depending upon their relative efficiency in processing the information and making the required discrimination (e.g., different levels of asymptotic accuracy might reflect differences in underlying cognitive ability). However, although the *function* is determined by the task and by the individual's cognitive characteristics, as it were, the *location* of a particular individual's performance on the speed-versus-accuracy function is determined by the criterion for certainty the individual adopts prior to making the motor response.

Age differences in response criteria would result in age differences in locations on the speed-versus-accuracy curve. Therefore, such differences in criteria could result in artifactual differences in measured response time and accuracy, even when the two age groups' performance was governed by age-equivalent curves. This pattern would imply no age changes in underlying mechanisms determining performance but age differences in response criterion.

Hertzog, Vernon, and Rypma (1993) used instructions to manipulate speed-versus-accuracy criteria in a mental rotation task and observed how response times and accuracy co-varied as a function of instructions and angles of orientation. Their results suggested that older adults operate farther to the right (more conservatively) on the speed-versus-accuracy function for each angle of rotation. That is, they are less likely to trade substantial amounts of accuracy for fast decisions. To the extent that older adults intrinsically adopt response criteria that emphasize accuracy, even when told to emphasize speed, age differences in response times are contaminated by age differences in response criteria in the reaction-time task.

Systematic attention to such potential sources of variance in experimental tasks can be painfully difficult, requiring complicated designs and thousands of experimental trials (Kliegl, 1995). However, the possibility of such influences, left uncontrolled and/or unmeasured, leaves open the possibility that the substantive inferences made regarding age differences in cognitive mechanisms may not be fully valid.

DIFFERENTIAL APPROACHES TO
ADULT COGNITION

■ Psychometric Approaches to Intelligence and Cognition

As noted in Chapter 2, the differential approach, as embodied in the study of psychometric intelligence, has played a major role in studies of aging and cognition (see reviews in Botwinick, 1977; Dixon, Kramer, & Baltes, 1985; Salthouse, 1985; Chapter 9). For the purposes of this chapter, we will assume that the standard methods of psychometric testing (group or individual assessment of standardized tests consisting of multiple test items) is familiar to the reader—and say little more about it.

The standard design for differential studies of cognition and aging involves the use of multiple tests and multivariate statistical analyses to examine the correlations among the tests. The differential approach translates hypotheses of cognitive structure (assertions about how intelligence is organized into basic dimensions of content and process?) into hypotheses about the underlying dimensions of correlation in a battery of tests. The designs of differential psychologists consist of theory-driven selection of variables (tests) to assess multiple dimensions (such as Thurstone's primary mental abilities [see Chapter 9]). Statistical techniques such as factor analysis and cluster analysis are then used to determine whether the correlations of the tests contain dimensions of shared variation (individual differences) that define and differentiate the multiple dimensions.

A number of important methodological challenges arise when one is using the differential approach to assess (1) the number of dimensions of cognition (often referred to as the structure of intelligence) and whether that changes across the adult life span; and (2) the nature of age-related changes (or age differences) in dimensions that are thought to be comparable across the adult life span (Baltes & Nesselroade, 1970; Cunningham, 1978; Schaie & Hertzog, 1985). For example, it is by now clear that traditional exploratory factor-analytic methods are problematic in comparing different age groups, and there is considerable evidence that confirmatory factor analysis is the optimal way of approaching the problem (Hertzog, 1990). The literature seems to suggest that the factor structure of psychometric intelligence does not change radically as a function of aging but that aging does result in increasing correlations among dimensions of intelligence (Hertzog, 1991).

The development of advanced statistical methods, such as structural equation modeling, has enabled differential psychologists to test hypotheses about stability and change in the level and structure of intelligence while differentiating the kinds of stability and change defined earlier in the chapter. For example, Hertzog and Schaie (1986, 1988) used these kinds of modeling techniques to show that individual differences in general intelligence were highly stable (had high covariance stability) over different parts of the adult life span, even when mean levels of general intelligence showed a transition from relative stability to average decline after age 60.

■ Testing Individual Differences Hypotheses about Aging and Cognition

Methods developed within the differential tradition are, however, highly relevant to addressing questions that arise in studies using methods of measuring cognition that are derived from the experimental tradition (Hertzog, 1985). The age × condition experimental design discussed above is most often used to test hypotheses about means of dependent variables, but the general logic applies even when the hypothesis involves relationships between two (or more) variables. One could, for example, hypothesize that experimental manipulations would influence the magnitudes of correlations between two variables. In fact, this hypothesis has often played a central role in research on individual differences in cognitive psychology (see, e.g., MacLeod, Hunt, and Mathews, 1978).

Individual differences hypotheses of this kind can identify age-related phenomena that are not necessarily manifested in mean differences between experimental conditions. Hertzog, Saylor, Fleece, and Dixon (1994) recently reported one relatively simple application of this approach. They studied the accuracy of metamemory in a free-recall task. Subjects were asked to predict how many items they would recall, both before and after studying the items. They were also asked to postdict, or to estimate the number of words they had recalled immediately after they had done so. The accuracy of these predictions and postdictions is one way of gauging the ability to monitor learning and performance in memory tasks. Accuracy was operationally defined by several indices, including the correlation of predictions and postdictions with actual recall. Table 3.1 shows that prediction accuracy increased from before to after study, but more so for younger adults. Both age groups produced highly accurate postdictions. The hypothesis of increased correlation from before to after study, and of age differences in this increase in correlation, represent individual differences analogs to the age × condition interactions commonly tested by analysis of variance methods. Hertzog et al. (1994) used a covariance structures analysis to test the appropriate statistical null hypothesis of equal (dependent) correlations (Steiger, 1980).

More complicated variants of this approach involve application of multiple regression methods or structural equation models to test for these types of individual differences interactions. For example, Rogers, Fisk, and Hertzog (1994) demonstrated age differences in the relationship of intellectual ability to response time in a visual search task as a function of extensive practice. The different patterns of ability–task correlations provided critical additional evidence of age differences in the ability to develop an automatic process in the visual search task.

Perhaps the most important and interesting applications of methods from the differential tradition in research on cognition and aging involve the integration of experimental and differential approaches to examine alternative explanations of age-related cognitive change, as discussed in the next section.

	Young	Old
TABLE 3.1 Correlations of Phased Predictions and Postdictions with Free Recall across Two Recall Trials for Young and Old Adults		
Trial 1:		
Prediction 1	.15	.13
Prediction 2	.49	.30
Postdiction	.94	.92
Trial 2:		
Prediction 1	.35	.45
Prediction 2	.53	.53
Postdiction	.95	.92

Correlations are weighted averages from two experiments conducted by Hertzog, Saylor, Fleece, and Dixon (1994). Subjects were given two trials with different word lists. They made a performance prediction before studying the words (Prediction 1) and after studying the words (Prediction 2). After recalling the words they reported how many words they recalled (Postdiction). Results show that the correlations of Prediction 2 with recall are higher than the correlations of Prediction 1 with recall and that the postperformance evaluation (Postdiction) correlated highest with recall. The differences in these correlations relate to theories about aging and accuracy of memory beliefs and memory monitoring (see Hertzog et al., 1994).

EXPLANATIONS OF AGE-RELATED COGNITIVE CHANGE

Research that focuses only on determining whether there are age differences or age changes in cognitive task performance is inherently descriptive in nature. In descriptive research, one is identifying that there are associations of chronological age or change over time with cognition, but one is not providing an explanation of such age-related effects. Explanations of age-related effects in cognition can take many different forms, depending on both the level of causal explanation desired and the nature of the kinds of causal influences under consideration. Different metatheoretical perspectives will lead different scientists to consider quite disparate sets of potential explanations for aging effects (see Chapter 2). For someone who believes in aging as an immutable, ontogenetic process, a satisfactory level of explanation for the changes associated with aging might involve understanding biological theories of age change in the central nervous system and how they drive changes in cognitive functioning. In contrast, a contextualist would consider these potential explanatory variables as well as variables like habit patterns, social support networks, health, exercise, and factors under personal control.

We focus on methods associated with two classes of explanations of age-related differences and age-related changes in cognition. First *intrinsically cognitive* explanations involve accounting for changes in cognitive variables by other cognitive variables. These explanations are typically reductionistic in that they explain age effects in molar cognitive tasks by age changes in specific, perhaps basic, cognitive mechanisms and processes. Secondly, explanations that are *extrinsic to cognition* identify background characteristics of persons (e.g., health, lifestyle, education) that are associated with age-related changes. Most of the methodological issues we discuss apply to both types of explanatory mechanisms.

■ Processing Accounts of Age Differences and Age Changes in Cognition

In this section we focus on the first kind of explanation, namely, cognitive processing accounts of age changes in higher-level cognitive functioning. Our discussion is restricted to a particular kind of account, namely, processing resource theory.

Salthouse (1988, 1990, 1991) systematically investigated the hypothesis, originally advanced by Birren and colleagues (see Birren, 1974; Birren, Woods, & Williams, 1980), that age-related slowing in the speed of central nervous system processing is responsible for many of the age differences on all cognitive tasks, including complex psychometric tests of reasoning and spatial ability. Salthouse (1988, 1990) argued for a "processing resource" account of basic cognitive mechanisms, suggesting that attention, working memory, and speed of processing represent basic cognitive resources that can be allocated to the task of solving higher-level reasoning problems.

Working memory is associated with the ability to hold information in a highly accessible, limited-capacity storage mode so that it can be evaluated and used during cognition (Baddeley, 1986; Chapter 7). Holzman, Glaser, and Pellegrino (1976) showed that the empirical difficulty of series completion problems—an indicator of the ability to reason inductively by identifying patterns of relationships embedded in symbolic information—could be directly related to problems' working memory load. Series completion problems require the individual to compare the relationship among elements in a series, extract the rule governing the series, and then extrapolate that rule to determine the continuation of the series. Individual differences in working memory capacity influence the ability to identify the relationships among elements. Working memory capacity has been shown to correlate with a number of cognitive tasks (see, e.g., Carpenter & Just, 1989), and individual differences in working memory capacity are highly related to individual differences in at least some reasoning tasks (Kyllonen & Christal, 1990). Hence it is reasonable to suggest that age changes in working memory might account for age changes in performance on such tasks.

The basis of the empirical approach to testing processing resource explanations is evaluation of the extent to which age changes in complex task performance covary with age changes in basic processing resources. Investigation of this hypothesis could take one of two basic methodological avenues. One could attempt to intervene in the system experimentally. That is, one could manipulate the processing speed or working memory demands of the complex task by varying relevant independent variables and observe the effects of doing so on persons of different ages. Alternatively, one could adopt a more passive individual differences approach, measuring both resource-related constructs and more complex tasks and then determining the degree of their interrelationship with each other and with chronological age.

Cross-sectional Analyses of Resource Reduction Hypotheses

Cross-sectional age differences in a variable can be indexed by the correlation of chronological age with a cognitive measure. The similarity of cross-sectional age differences between two different variables is reflected, indirectly, in the correlations of the two variables. Salthouse (1992, 1994) emphasized the value of using correlational methods (chiefly multiple regression analysis) for determining how correlations of chronological age and complex tasks overlap with correlations of chronological age and processing resource variables. In this section we provide an introductory explanation of the logic of this approach.

One of the interesting aspects of cross-sectional data is that the correlations of different cognitive measures carry two different sources of variance: (1) relationships among constructs, as emphasized in the literature on psychometric intelligence and (2) relationships of both measures associated with chronological age. In theory the relationships among the constructs could be observed at any single point in the life span (e.g., a sample of persons all of age 20). An age-heterogeneous, cross-sectional sample adds aging-related variance to the individual differences dimensions that are determined by the structure of cognition. Consider a cross-sectional design applied to persons of different ages. The score of a 70-year-old person can be thought of as being decomposed into two parts, the same person's score at age 20 and the change from age 20 to age 70. Thus the individual differences in the entire cross-sectional sample can be thought of as being divided into individual differences in early adulthood plus individual differences in change from young adulthood to one's present age. One implication of this concept is that cognitive tasks that share common age-related influences should covary more highly in an older sample than in a younger sample (see Hertzog, 1985, 1991).

Salthouse (1992, 1994) argued that, given a developmental focus, the principal phenomenon of interest is the extent to which cross-sectional age differences in the more complex task are reduced when controlling for any and all candidate resource variables. This argument can be most easily illustrated using a Venn diagram, which is commonly used in multiple regression texts (see, e.g., Pedhazur, 1982). Figure 3.8 presents a Venn diagram of this logic (see Salthouse, 1991). The area of the circles represents the variance in each of three variables: age, working memory, and inductive reasoning. The three variables covary with one another, and the issue is the magnitude of overlap in variance of age with the other two variables. The part of the diagram labeled 5 and 7 represents the covariance of age and inductive reasoning. Note that the area labeled 7 also covaries with working memory. That is, area 7 represents covariance of age and inductive reasoning shared with working memory, whereas area 5 represents covariance of age and inductive reasoning that is statistically independent of working memory. The question is, how much of the covariance of age and inductive reasoning (area 5 + area 7) is shared in common with working memory (area 7 alone)?

Another way of representing the logic is with path diagrams that describe a system of regression equations involving age and related cognitive variables. Indeed, the case can be made that path diagrams are a better way of conceptualizing the nexus of relationships than

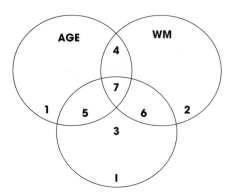

Variance partition:

1: Age alone
2: Working Memory Alone
3: Induction Alone
4: Age and Working Memory (Independent of Induction)
5: Age and Induction (Independent of Working Memory)
6: Working Memory and Induction (Independent of Age)
7: Age, Working Memory, and Induction (Shared)

FIGURE 3.8 Venn diagrams representing the concept of overlapping sources of variance in bivariate relationships among three variables, age (A), working memory (WM), and inductive reasoning (I). The shared variance is reflected in the degree of overlap of the circles; the nonoverlapping parts of the circles represent variance that is unique to each variable. Interest in aging research often focuses on shared variance with age. (See text for further explanation.)

the concepts of shared variance as depicted in Figure 3.8 (see Pedhazur, 1982). Figure 3.9 illustrates the basic concepts regarding age and processing resources. Age is conceptualized as influencing basic resource measures, which then in turn influence more complex task performance. If the basic resources fully and completely mediate the effects of aging on more complex task performance, there would be no salient path from age to the complex abilities independent of the mediated influences. In technical terms the hypothesis of complete mediation would imply zero partial covariance of age and complex skills, controlling for resources such as working memory and perceptual speed. On the other hand, if aging influences processes other than working memory and perceptual speed, there should be a residual, direct effect of age on complex performance even when the indirect route of influence mediated by the resource variables is taken into account.

Investigation of this question requires the use of some kind of multiple regression technique, including perhaps structural equation models (see Hertzog, 1991, in press, for reviews). Several studies indicate that a substantial proportion of the age-related variance in intelligence covaries with (is shared by) perceptual speed (see, e.g., Horn, Donaldson, & Engstrom, 1981; Salthouse, 1994). Salthouse (1994) has also showed that a substantial proportion of the age-related variance in working memory is associated with measures of perceptual speed. In almost all cases, however, there is a statistically significant association of age and complex task performance controlling for such resource measures.

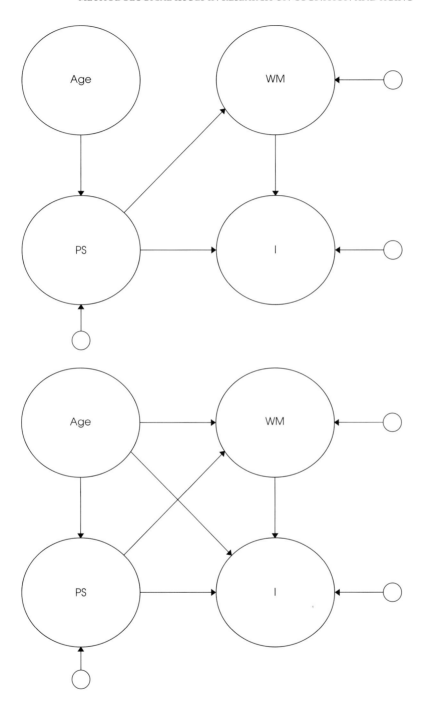

FIGURE 3.9 Two alternative path diagrams for four variables: age, working memory (WM), perceptual speed (PS), and inductive reasoning (I). In the top diagram, PS completely mediates the relationship of age to both WM and I; there is no unique relations of age to these variables. In the bottom diagram, age predicts I and WM independently of PS.

There are several limitations to using multiple regression approaches to the problem (see Hertzog, in press). Perhaps the most interesting issue is that the logic of Figures 3.8 and 3.9 indirectly invokes the assumption of additive linear effects, as opposed to more complicated interaction effects (moderated regression). For example, if resources became differentially important for older adults' performance, relative to younger adults', we might expect that the magnitude of the resource–complex task relationship would change as a function of age. This hypothesis suggests a resource × age interaction effect (Hertzog, 1985). If one existed, the logic of partitioning age-related variance embodied in the standard regression model would be invalid. One should instead proceed to characterize and decompose the interaction (Pedhazur, 1982). For examples of using regression analysis to examine these kinds of interactions in aging research, see Hertzog (1989) and Hultsch, Hertzog, & Dixon (1984, 1990).

Another important issue is that the logic of evaluating overlap of variables with chronological age using standard multiple regression techniques does not address the problem of measurement error in the resource and task variables (see Salthouse, 1991). The best way to avoid this problem is the use of structural equation models to estimate the regression relationships while correcting for measurement error (see, e.g., Lindenberger, Mayr, & Kliegl, 1993). Indeed, Kliegl and Mayr (1992) argued that the use of structural equation models is the most satisfactory general approach to the problem of identifying the relative contribution of cognitive mechanisms to age differences in complex task performance.

However, the problems associated with the application of statistical procedures per se may not be the most important issues associated with the processing resources approach. A critical set of issues do not concern the statistical methods, or statistical conclusion validity, of the regression analyses. Instead they involve whether the empirical hypothesis actually relates to the substantive hypothesis, given the nature of the experimental tasks measuring processing resources. A key assumption in this regard is that the resource measures are cognitive primitives that can be treated as basic building blocks for more complex cognitive operations. Bashore (1993) reviewed electrophysiological data suggesting that age differences in elementary response-time tasks may be primarily a function of age differences in relatively late processes associated with decision and response selection. The primitive resource of information-processing rates may not be best measured by psychometric tests or response-time tasks that require discriminative choice. Tests such as digit-symbol substitution, often used as a measure of the perceptual speed ability, are complex tasks that may reflect multiple cognitive component processes and that can be influenced by individual differences in higher-order strategies (e.g., learning and holding in memory the digit–symbol pairs, avoiding the need to scan the symbol table for each item). Multiple regression techniques can reveal whether age-related variance is shared by different variables, but it is the cognitive theory alone that stipulates how the shared variance of a Venn diagram such as Figure 3.8 is assigned to a system of potential influences in the path diagram of Figure 3.9. The problem, then, is in the substantive interpretation of the empirical results, more than it is a problem with the statistical applications themselves. Referring back to Figure 3.1, the inference from the empirical hypothesis to the substantive hypothesis may be compromised due to questionable construct validity of the measures of basic or elemental processing resources.

Other alternative interpretations of the shared age-related variance that do not treat variables like perceptual speed as indicators of prior resources are just beginning to be evaluated in the literature. For example, Lindenberger and Baltes (1994) recently demonstrated that individual differences in intelligence test performance of a very old group of adults covaried highly with auditory and visual sensory acuity. Although it is possible that this reflects a direct effect of limited perception on the quality of information processing and resulting cognition, it may also be the case that sensory acuity is merely a good marker variable for biological aging processes that influence both sensory acuity and cognitive functioning in very old adults. The same argument can be made for perceptual speed—that it is affected by aging effects on other, perhaps more primitive mechanisms.

Finally, one problem of focusing on shared and unique portions of age-related variance is the assumption that chronological age represents the best way to operationally define aging effects. There could be aging-related effects that do not perfectly covary with chronological age. Although the cross-sectional design virtually demands this operational definition of aging, that requirement can be viewed as one of its flaws. Of course, psychologists could, but typically do not, incorporate alternative indices of aging rates into a cross-sectional study. One can imagine, for example, that indices of biological aging in the central nervous system could be included in such designs.

The preceding caveats about the methods used for testing the processing resource account do not detract from the enormous significance of this approach for research on aging and cognition, both in terms of the contributions made by Salthouse to the field as a whole and in terms of the influence this perspective currently enjoys. The larger message for any student of cognition is that one must be vigilant in identifying and critically evaluating the methodological assumptions embedded in such complex approaches, so that the benefits and limits of the empirical evidence can be placed into an appropriate context.

Extensions to Longitudinal Designs

Cognitive processing resource hypotheses can be evaluated in longitudinal designs as well. Although this approach has the practical disadvantage of requiring sufficient elapsed time to measure age-related changes both in resource variables and in more complex cognitive functions, it has the virtues of allowing both direct measurement of individual differences in cognitive change and clear determination of whether these changes covary for different variables. Given the different sources of confounding influences on cross-sectional age differences and longitudinal change discussed above, it will not necessarily be the case that longitudinal data will reveal patterns of covariance in age-related changes that are consistent with the regression results from cross-sectional data.

Recent work by Hultsch and colleagues on the Victoria Longitudinal Study (VLS) illustrated this issue (Hultsch, Hertzog, Dixon, & Small, in press). As noted above, Salthouse's work indicates that perceptual speed can in some cases completely account for cross-sectional age differences in working memory. Hultsch et al. (in press) found a similar effect in the initial cross-sectional sample of the VLS. However, they also found that longitudinal changes in working memory were not completely eliminated by covarying for longitudinal changes in semantic speed. Hultsch et al. (in press) also demonstrated that aspects of episodic memory that show strong cross-sectional age differences (e.g., text recall) do not necessarily show average longitudinal decline and, conversely, that longitudinal decline can be observed in recall of world knowledge even when cross-sectional data suggest few age differences (owing in part to cohort differences in original knowledge of facts). Hultsch et al. (in press) used structural equation models to show that changes in various episodic memory tasks were only in part predictable from their initial levels and change over time in working memory and semantic information–processing speed. The VLS has a number of limitations, and it examines different sets of measures than other cross-sectional studies of resources and cognitive functioning do. Nevertheless, the major point is that one cannot be certain about shared age-related changes unless one directly measures such changes.

■ Evaluating Extrinsic Causes of Cognitive Change

The techniques just discussed for investigating relationships of cognitive mechanisms to age changes in more complex cognitive tasks can also be applied to the larger problem of understanding and explaining age effects on the basis of background characteristics such as health status, lifestyle, biological aging, and social context. The prototypical research question concerns which variables may have a role in mediating or moderating the age effects observed in cross-sectional and longitudinal studies. For example, what role do specific classes of chronic illness play in the pattern of observed decline? A terminal decline hypothesis predicts relative stability in cognitive functioning until such factors as cardiovascular disease or renal disease act to impair, directly or indirectly, central nervous system functioning (see, e.g., Riegel & Riegel, 1972). Likewise, chronic physical disability, such as that caused by extreme osteoarthritis, might limit the activity patterns of older adults, reducing social contact and creating a less enriched cognitive environment. At the other end of the life span, one could argue that individual differences in family environments determine the acquisition of intelligence and that generational shifts in the nature of such family environments are a determinant of cohort differences in intelligence (Schaie & Willis, 1994).

Note that this kind of research question begins with the metatheoretical perspective that observed age differences are not solely a function of primary biological aging but instead reflect a mixture of aging effects and other age-correlated and time-correlated phenomena. A metatheoretical perspective that age changes are essentially immutable functions of genetically programmed aging would probably be accompanied by the belief that the proper level of explanation of aging effects on cognition is in terms of the genomes that determine senescence.

Adoption of the belief in biologically mediated (ontogenetic) cognitive change can lead to three (often implicit) premises about aging, cognition, and other variables. First, one is likely to argue that any correlations of antecedent variables measuring health, social context, or other variables with age differences (or age-related changes) in cognition that could be observed are artifactual, in the sense that they do not represent "true" aging effects at all. Second, one is likely to adopt an assumption that any age differences observed in cognition *must* be due to ontogenetic influences. This assumption can be observed to operate in the vast majority of research articles on age differences in cognition, where findings of age differences are interpreted as if they were unbiased estimates of the effects of aging and not other age-correlated causal variables. Third, one is prone to accept a lack of association between candidate predictor variables (e.g., self-reported health status) and cognition as evidence against the importance of the predictor variable (as opposed to a problem in measuring the candidate construct) and as prima facie evidence for the ontogenetic determination of cognitive change. It is interesting to note that such perspectives are not necessarily shared by behavior geneticists interested in adult development and aging, who typically assume the existence of gene–environment interactions in determining the course of psychological development across the life span (Bergeman, Plomin, McClearn, Pedersen, & Friberg, 1988).

Clearly, then, the nature of one's theoretical and metatheoretical perspectives will have a major impact on the kinds of explanatory constructs one would investigate in a particular study. The position taken here is that, independent of one's perspective on the root causes of age-correlated changes, an examination of the underlying predictors of such changes is of enormous potential importance and possible explanatory value. Taking this as a starting point, we proceed to discuss generic methodological issues that apply to studies examining explanations for age differences and age-related changes in cognition.

There are three basic approaches to explaining the associations of aging and cognition: (1) passive observational approaches, (2) experimental intervention approaches, and (3) quasi-experimental comparisons of different subgroups. The techniques can be used separately or in combination. We shall describe each briefly.

■ Adding Predictor Variables to Observational Designs

The first approach is a straightforward extension of methods already discussed—namely, adding measures of variables such as health status and lifestyle to the set of measures of a study and evaluating the relationship of these variables to cross-sectional differences or longitudinal changes. There have been a number of cross-sectional studies of relationships between measures of health status and lifestyle with cognitive functioning (see, e.g., Perlmutter & Nyquist, 1990). Most longitudinal panel designs involve measurement of multiple predictors that could also be used to evaluate the degree of overlap with cognitive change (see, e.g., Field, Schaie, & Leino, 1988; Gribbin, Schaie, & Parham, 1980; Wilkie & Eisdorfer, 1971).

Clarkson-Smith and Hartley (1990) provided a useful illustration of adding antecedent variables to a cross-sectional design. They employed structural equation models to measure the constructs of health, morale, education, and physical exercise as predictors of three cognitive abilities: reaction time, working memory, and reasoning. The latent variable of health was defined by three self-report indicators: subjective health, illnesses, and number of medications. Exercise was also measured with three self-report measures: number of hours of aerobic exercise, retrospective change in exercise, and kilocalories burned per week. Self-reported health predicted exercise, and exercise predicted cognitive task performance. Age predicted cognitive performance independent of health and exercise, but health did not predict performance when controlling for exercise and age. The results suggested that there are age-related phenomena other than health status and exercise that influence cognition and that there is a relationship of exercise to cognition that is independent of health status.

Taking the Clarkson-Smith and Hartley (1990) regression analysis at face value, one can legitimately state that exercise has a relationship to cognition that cannot be explained as a spurious correlation with age or health *as measured in this study*. This conclusion implicitly acknowledges that there are limitations to what one can conclude from an analysis of some, but not all, of the relevant variables in the complex causal system associated with aging and cognition. There may be aspects of health status (generically) and physiological integrity of the central nervous system (specifically) that are not well measured by the self-report health measures employed by Clarkson-Smith and Hartley (1990). The assumption that the effects of health can be meausured by a single latent variable of this kind may be incorrect. Self-report measures of exercise may be influenced by a number of biases, from inaccurate retrospective remembering to a self-presentation bias. Furthermore, the study did not measure other candidate variables that might covary with both exercise and cognition, including control orientation, physical mobility, and so forth. Discovery of relationships that are independent of other constructs depends critically on the variables that are included in the analysis.

In such analyses one can never conclude that a direct link has been "proven." One can only test indirect consequences of direct-cause hypotheses, contingent upon a set of assumptions. Certainly a number of hypotheses regarding mechanisms that produce the exercise–cognition relationship can account for the findings. It may (or may not) be the case that aerobic exercise stimulates blood flow to the brain and that the stimulation of regular exercise has long-term benefits for central nervous system function. In order to test that hypothesis, one must simultaneously measure these hypothetical mediating mechanisms and the other variables in an empirical study.

One major concern for these kinds of studies is whether the antecedent variable should be treated as a continuous variable. With respect to health status one might want to consider types of chronic disease and the nature of the cognitive effects one might expect from them. When a latent construct such as health is defined, one must make decisions about how different kinds of illness should be scaled with respect to expected effects on cognitive functioning. Indeed, one can conceptualize health as a constellation or profile of functional status across different physiological subsystems of the body. In a sense, it is both categorical and continuous, given that one can have various types of health problems (e.g., cardiovascular disease, osteoarthritis, renal disease, cancer) and these problems can vary in functional severity (e.g., quantity and quality of toxins released in the system during renal disease, amount of blood-flow restriction in cardiovascular disease). These issues bear directly upon the kind of design and statistical analysis that should be used to evaluate relationships of these variables to cognition and vice versa. The assumption of multiple regression approaches is that individuals with different values on these variables are similar in kind, differing only in the amount of the attribute. Therefore when one examines whether self-reported health relates to changes in intelligence by regressing changes in intelligence on the independent variable of self-reported health, one assumes that there is a quantitative relationship between the two variables (presumably, good health is associated with high stability [a small amount of decremental change] in late life). An alternative possibility, however, is that self-reported health implicitly defines subpopulations of persons for whom the nature of intelligence and intellectual change varies both in kind and degree. This is, of course, the same issue we discussed earlier in the context of measurement and construct equivalence.

To the extent that the antecedent variables define different kinds of persons, who have potential qualitative differences in the nature of age-related changes, one should consider alternative statistical approaches that might capture these effects more directly. Field et al. (1988), for example, found little correlation of self-reported health with intelligence and intellectual change in a longitudinal sample. They observed, however, that poor health was associated with exceptionally bad levels of intelligence test performance and was associated with statistical outliers on their tests. This kind of effect would be consistent with the argument that there are thresholds for the effects of health on cognition. One could also argue that such effects reflect the impact of a terminal decline in both cognitive variables and physical health status—that it is a nonnormative phenomenon. Their results could also occur if it is the case that only certain kinds of poor health (not revealed, perhaps, by the self-report measure) have a negative impact on intelligence.

The methodological problem can be framed as one of identifying different types of persons who experience different patterns of age-related change in causal antecedent variables and therefore in cognitive change. One way to approach these kinds of typological questions is to use forms of cluster analysis to analyze person types with respect to change on cognition and related variables (see, e.g., Mumford & Owens, 1985). Manton, Siegler, and Woodbury (1986) provided an interesting example of this approach using data from the Duke Longitudinal Study. They used a procedure known as grade of membership to determine the degree to which individuals correspond to different profiles determined by different measures of intelligence and memory. Their results suggest that certain persons change more than others over time and that these changes may be associated with particular personal characteristics, especially multiple aspects of physical health (e.g., blood pressure, physical health rating, cause of death).

■ Comparisons of Special Subpopulations

The quasi-experimental approach requires comparing nonequivalent groups of adults (perhaps varying in chronological age) that are defined by their status on background variables such as health status, context, lifestyle, or cognitive behaviors. Indeed, this is the modal approach in neuropsychological studies, in which adults with different kinds of brain disease or trauma are compared to comparison groups of "normal" adults (Kaszniak, 1990). This approach may be most desirable when one wishes to examine the potential benefits of behaviors (or other variables) that are relatively rare in the population. For example, one might hypothesize that frequent and regular static stretching (as in hatha yoga) over the adult life span increases late-life mobility, reduces stress, and assists in maintaining higher levels of cognitive functioning. It would be virtually impossible to test this hypothesis using general probability sampling procedures, given the low probability of encountering long-term practitioners of yoga in the general population. Under such circumstances the best technique is to sample a population with the desired attributes, and compare and contrast them with other subgroups in a quasi-experimental design. (Note that introducing yoga into a randomized experiment would test a different question because one would not be identifying the long-term effects of yoga practice over the life span.)

The quasi-experimental approach differs from the passive observational approach in two ways. First, as noted, it attempts to operationally define the independent variable (e.g., physical fitness) by deliberate, purposive sampling of specific types of persons, instead of allowing these attributes to emerge as characteristics of the obtained sample. Obviously this approach is needed whenever the question focuses on small subgroups or on phenomena that are not necessarily considered normative. Second, it attempts to form valid comparison groups that are similar in all other ways to the target group (e.g., a group of physically active elders who have not had a lifetime history of yoga practice).

Achieving a matching of groups by deliberate sampling is a difficult enterprise, as is recognized in the quasi-experimental design literature (see, e.g., Cook & Campbell, 1979). Inclusion and exclusion criteria must be explicitly stated, but this is not in and of itself sufficient to guarantee equivalence of the groups with respect to all other relevant variables. For example, studies of the effects of current student status on cognitive functioning often begin by assuming that being in school may lead to certain behaviors that help to improve cognitive functioning as well as performance on cognitive tests. Comparisons of older adults who either are or are not currently enrolled in some form of educational program do not necessarily isolate the effects of being in an educational environment. Selection effects may play a role, in terms of who typically enrolls in such educational programs and the reasons why they might differ in cognitive functioning for reasons other than current educational activities. Attempts to match individuals on other variables (e.g., verbal ability) can create as many problems as it solves (see, e.g., Reichardt, 1979). Having said that, these kinds of quasi-experimental comparisons may be the only tool that is actually available. The best way to address alternative hypotheses about groups is to explicitly measure variables that might represent rival hypotheses for group differences in the dependent variables and to show that they cannot, statistically speaking, account for the differences.

■ Experimental Interventions

As discussed by Labouvie (1974), it is possible to evaluate explanatory mechanisms through experimental intervention, although the inferences are often indirect, due to the inability to manipulate aging effects directly (see Chapter 2 for a theoretical discussion of some issues associated with intervention research). For example, Schaie and Willis (1986) used cognitive training techniques to determine whether adults in the Seattle Longitudinal Study who had previous histories of longitudinal decline in spatial ability or inductive reasoning would benefit from cognitive training. They found that older adults with previous histories of decline benefited more from training than adults with previous histories of relative stability. Such evidence indirectly suggests that training may be ameliorating prior decline, although other interpretations are possible, given the inability to directly manipulate prior decline status. Others have attempted to evaluate whether changing older adults' beliefs about cognitive decline would lead to improved cognitive task performance (see, e.g., M.E. Lachman, Weaver, Bandura, & Lewcowicz, 1992) or whether exercise programs can improve cognitive functioning. These kinds of intervention studies can be controversial, because the experimental treatment may or may not be directly addressing the mechanisms that led to the age-correlated change in the first place. Individuals adopting the view that age-correlated change in cognition is inherently determined by biological aging are likely to argue that any beneficial impact of interventions cannot alter development change in the cognitive constructs under study.

CONCLUDING STATEMENTS

We hope this chapter has given the reader a sense of the subtle and complex issues that confront the psychologist doing research on aging and cognition. We have not been able to cover a number of relevant methodological issues that are specific to certain cognitive constructs (e.g., categorization or working memory capacity) or types of experimental tasks (e.g., dual tasks or divided-attention paradigms). Nevertheless, we believe that the basic principles we have discussed in this chapter generalize to understanding the problems and issues that are associated with specific measurement contexts. In the same vein, we have provided a conceptual basis from which to understand the questions, methods, and empirical approaches of this rapidly expanding field. It is our hope that this treatment will assist the reader in understanding the empirical studies described in the rest of this book and in the larger literature.

REFERENCES

Alder, A. G., Adam, J., & Arenberg, D. (1990). Individual-differences assessment of the relationship between change in and initial level of adult cognitive functioning. *Psychology and Aging, 5,* 560–568.

Baddeley, A. (1986). *Working memory.* New York: Oxford Univ. Press.

Baltes, P. B. (1968). Longitudinal and cross-sectional sequences in the study of age and generation effects. *Human Development, 11,* 145–171.

Baltes, P. B., & Nesselroade, J. R. (1970). Multivariate longitudinal and cross-sectional sequences for analyzing ontogenetic and generational change: A methodological note. *Developmental Psychology, 1,* 162–168.

Baltes, P. B., Reese, H. W., & Nesselroade, J. R. (1977). *Life-span developmental psychology: Introduction to research methods.* Monterey, CA: Brooks-Cole.

Barlow, D. H., & Hersen, M. (1984). *Single-case experimental designs: Strategies for studying behaviour change* (2d ed.). New York: Pergamon Press. (419 pages).

Bashore, T. R. (1993). Differential effects of aging on the neurocognitive functions subserving speeded mental processing. In Cerella, J., Hoyer, W. J., Rybash, J., & Commons, M. (Eds.), *Adult information processing: Limits on loss* (pp. 37–76). New York: Academic Press.

Bechtel, W. (1988). *Philosophy of science: An overview for cognitive science.* Hillsdale, NJ: Erlbaum.

Bell, R. Q. (1953). Convergence: An accelerated longitudinal approach. *Child Development, 24,* 145–152.

Berg, C., Hertzog, C., & Hunt, E. (1982). Age differences in the speed of mental rotation. *Developmental Psychology, 18,* 95–107.

Bergeman, C. S., Plomin, R., McClearn, G. E., Pedersen, N. L., & Friberg, L. T. (1988). Genotype-environment interaction in personality development: Identical twins reared apart. *Psychology and Aging, 3,* 399–406.

Bethell-Fox, C. E., & Shepard, R. N. (1988). Mental rotation: Effects of stimulus complexity & familiarity. *JEP:HPP, 14,* 12–23.

Birren, J. E. (1974). Translations in gerontology—from lab to life. Psychophysiology and the speed of response. *American Psychologist, 29,* 808–815.

Birren, J. E., Woods, A. M., & Williams, M. V. (1980). Behavioral slowing with age: Causes, organization, and consequences. In L. W. Poon (Ed.), *Aging in the 1980's: Psychological issues* (pp. 293–308). Washington, DC: American Psychological Association.

Blalock, H. M. (1982). *Conceptualization and measurement in the social sciences.* Beverly Hills, CA: Sage.

Blalock, H. M. (Ed.) (1985). *Causal models in the social sciences* (2d ed.). Chicago: Aldine.

Blashfield, R. K., & Aldenderfer, M. S. (1988). The methods and problems of cluster analysis. In J. R. Nesselroade & R. B. Cattell (Eds.), *Handbook of multivariate experimental psychology* (2d ed., pp. 447–473). New York: Plenum.

Blazer, D. (1989). The epidemiology of depression in late life. *Journal of Geriatric Psychiatry, 22,* 35–52.

Boik, R. J. (1979). Interactions, partial interactions, and interaction contrasts in the analysis of variance. *Psychological Bulletin, 86,* 1084–1089.

Botwinick, J. (1977). Intellectual abilities. In J. E. Birren & K. W. Schaie (Eds.), *Handbook of the psychology of aging* (pp. 580–605). New York: Van Nostrand Reinhold.

Brunswik, E. (1956). *The design of representative experiments.* Berkeley: Univ. of California Press.

Bryk, A. S. & Raudenbush, S. W. (1987). Application of hierarchical linear models to assessing change. *Psychological Bulletin, 101,* 147–158.

Camp, C. J., West, R. L., & Poon, L. W. (1989). Recruitment practices for psychological research in gerontology. In M. P. Lawton & A. R. Herzog (Eds.), *Special research methods for gerontology* (pp. 163–189). Amityville, NY: Baywood.

Campbell, D. T., & Stanley, J. C. (1966). *Experimental and quasi-experimental designs for research.* Chicago: Rand McNally.

Carpenter, P. A., & Just, M. A. (1989). The role of working memory in language comprehension. In D. Klahr & K. Kotovsky (Eds.), *Complex information processing: The impact of Herbert A. Simon* (pp. 31–68). Hillsdale, NJ: Erlbaum.

Cattell, R. B. (1952). The three basic factor-analytic research designs—their interrelations and derivatives. *Psychological Bulletin, 49,* 499–520.

Cattell, R. B. (1988). The data box: Its ordering of total resources in terms of possible relational systems. In J. R. Ness & R. B. Cattell (Eds.), *Handbook of multivariate experimental psychology* (2d ed., pp. 69–130). New York: Plenum.

Clarkson-Smith, L., & Hartley, A. A. (1990). Structural equation models of relationships between exercise and cognitive abilities. *Psychology and Aging, 5,* 437–446.

Cohen, J. (1988). *Statistical power analysis for the behavioral sciences* (2d ed.). Hillsdale, NJ: Erlbaum.

Cook, T. D., & Campbell, D. T. (1979). *Quasi-experimentation: Design and analysis issues for field settings.* Chicago: Rand McNally.

Cronbach, L. J. (1957). The two disciplines of scientific psychology. *American Psychologist, 12,* 671–684.

Cronbach, L. J. (1975). Beyond the two disciplines of scientific psychology. *American Psychologist, 30,* 116–127.

Cronbach, L. J., Gleser, G. C., Nanda, H., & Rajaratnam, N. (1972). *The dependability of behavioral measurements: Theory of generalizability for scores and profiles.* New York: Wiley.

Cronbach, L. J., & Meehl, P. E. (1955). Construct validity in psychological tests. *Psychological Bulletin, 52,* 281–302.

Cooper, L. A. & Shepard, R. N. (1978). Transformations on representations of objects in space. In E. C. Carterette & M. P. Friedman (Eds.), *Handbook of perception: Perceptual coding, 8,* 105–146. New York: Academic Press.

Cunningham, W. R. (1978). Principles for identifying structural differences: Some methodological issues related to comparative factor analysis. *Journal of Gerontology, 33,* 82–86.

Dixon, R. A., Hertzog, C., Friesen, I. C., & Hultsch, D. F. (1993). Assessment of intraindividual change in text recall. In H. H. Brownell & Y. Joanette (Eds.), *Narrative discourse in normal aging and neurologically impaired adults* (pp. 77–102). San Diego: Singular.

Dixon, R. A., Kramer, D. A., & Baltes, P. B. (1985). Intelligence: A life-span perspective. In B. B. Wolman (Ed.), *Handbook of intelligence: Theories, measurements, and applications* (pp. 301–350). New York: Wiley.

Donaldson, G., & Horn, J. L. (1992). Age, cohort, and time developmental muddles: Easy in practice, hard in theory. *Experimental Aging Research, 18,* 213–222.

Field, D., Schaie, K. W., & Leino, E. V. (1988). Continuity in intellectual functioning: The role of self-reported health. *Psychology and Aging, 3,* 385–392.

Gribbin, K., Schaie, K. W., & Parham, I. (1980). Complexity of life style and maintenance of intellectual abilities. *Journal of Social Issues, 36,* 47–61.

Harkins, S. W., Chapman, C. R., & Eisdorfer, C. (1979). Memory loss and response bias in senescence. *Journal of Gerontology, 34,* 66–72.

Hartley, A. A. (1993). Evidence for the selective preservation of spatial selective attention in old age. *Psychology and Aging, 8,* 371–379.

Hertzog, C. (1985). An individual differences perspective: Implications for cognitive research in gerontology. *Research on Aging, 7,* 7–45.

Hertzog, C. (1989). The influence of cognitive slowing on age differences in intelligence. *Developmental Psychology, 25,* 636–651.

Hertzog, C. (1990). On the utility of structural regression models for developmental research. In P. B. Baltes, D. L. Featherman, & R. M. Lerner (Eds.), *Life-span development and behavior* (vol. 10, pp. 257–290). Hillsdale, NJ: Erlbaum.

Hertzog, C. (1991). Aging, information processing speed, and intelligence. In K. W. Schaie (Ed.), *Annual review of gerontology and geriatrics* (vol. 11, pp. 55–79). New York: Springer.

Hertzog, C. (1994). Repeated measures analysis in developmental research: What our ANOVA text didn't tell us. In S. H. Cohen & H. W. Reese (Eds.), *Life-span developmental psychology: Methodological contributions* (pp. 187–222). Hillsdale, NJ: Erlbaum.

Hertzog, C. (in press). Research design in studies of aging and cognition. In J. E. Birren & K. W. Schaie (Eds.), *Handbook of the psychology of aging* (4th ed.). New York: Academic Press.

Hertzog, C., Dixon, R. A., & Hultsch, D. F. (1992). Intraindividual change in text recall of the elderly. *Brain and Language, 42,* 248–269.

Hertzog, C., Hultsch, D. F., & Dixon, R. A. (1989). Evidence for the convergent validity of two self-report metamemory questionnaires. *Developmental Psychology, 25,* 687–700.

Hertzog, C., & Nesselroade, J. R. (1987). Beyond autoregressive models: Some implications of the trait-state distinction for the structural modeling of developmental change. *Child Development, 58,* 93–109.

Hertzog, C., Saylor, L. L., Fleece, A. M., & Dixon, R. A. (1994). Metamemory and aging: Relations between predicted, actual, and perceived memory task performance. *Aging and Cognition, 1,* 203–237.

Hertzog, C., & Schaie, K. W. (1986). Stability and change in adult intelligence. 1: Analysis of longitudinal covariance structures. *Psychology and Aging, 1,* 159–171.

Hertzog, C., & Schaie, K. W. (1988). Stability and change in adult intelligence. 2: Simultaneous analysis of longitudinal means and covariance structures. *Psychology and Aging, 3,* 122–130.

Hertzog, C., Vernon, M. C., & Rypma, B. (1993). Age differences in mental rotation task performance: The influence of speed/accuracy tradeoffs. *Journal of Gerontology: Psychological Sciences, 48,* P150–P156.

Hertzog, C., & Yuasa, M. (1988). *Adult age differences in the speed and accuracy of mental rotation.* Paper presented at the Twenty-ninth Annual Meeting of the Psychonomic Society, Chicago.

Holzman, T. G., Glaser, R., & Pellegrino, J. W. (1976). Process training derived from a computer simulation theory. *Memory & Cognition, 4,* 349–356.

Horn, J. L., Donaldson, G., & Engstrom, R. (1981). Apprehension, memory, and fluid intelligence decline in adulthood. *Research on Aging, 3,* 33–84.

Hultsch, D. F. (1969). Adult age differences in the organization of free recall. *Developmental Psychology, 4,* 338–342.

Hultsch, D. F., Hertzog, C., & Dixon, R. A. (1984). Text processing in adulthood: The role of intellectual abilities. *Developmental Psychology, 20,* 1193–1209.

Hultsch, D. F., Hertzog, C., & Dixon, R. A. (1990). Ability correlates of memory performance in adulthood and aging. *Psychology and Aging, 5,* 356–368.

Hultsch, D. F., Hertzog, C., Dixon, R. A., & Small, B. J. (in press). *Individual differences in aging and memory: The Victoria Longitudinal Study.* New York: Cambridge Univ. Press.

Johnson, S. H. & Rybash, J. M. (1993). A cognitive neuroscience perspective on age-related slowing: Developmental changes in the functional architecture. In J. Cerella, J. M. Rybash, W. J. Hoyer, & M. L. Commons (Eds.), *Adult information processing: Limits on loss* (pp. 143–173). San Diego: Academic Press.

Jones, H. E. (1959). Intelligence and problem solving. In J. E. Birren (Ed.), *Handbook of aging and the individual* (pp. 700–738). Chicago: Univ. of Chicago Press.

Just, M. A., & Carpenter, P. A. (1985). Cognitive coordinate systems: Accounts of mental rotation and individual differences in spatial ability. *Psychological Review, 92,* 137–172.

Kagan, J. (1980). Perspectives on continuity. In O. G. Brim, Jr. & J. Kagan (Eds.), *Constancy and change in human development* (pp. 26–74). Cambridge, MA: Harvard Univ. Press.

Kaszniak, A. W. (1990). Psychological assessment of the aging individual. In J. E. Birrea & K. W. Schaie (Eds.), *Handbook of the psychology of aging* (3d ed., pp. 427–445). New York: Academic Press.

Kausler, D. H. (1994). *Learning and memory in normal aging.* New York: Academic Press.

Kish, L. (1965). *Survey sampling.* New York: Wiley.

Kliegl, R. (1995). From presentation time to processing time: A psychophysics approach to episodic memory. In W. Schneider & F. E. Weinert (Eds.), *Research on memory development: State-of-the-art and future directions.* Hillsdale, NJ: Erlbaum.

Kliegl, R., & Mayr, U. (1992). Commentary on Salthouse (1992), "Shifting levels of analysis in the investigation of cognitive aging." *Human Development, 35,* 343–349.

Kyllonen, P. C., & Christal, R. E. (1990). Reasoning ability is (little more than) working-memory capacity?! *Intelligence, 14,* 389–434.

Labouvie, E. W. (1974). Developmental causal structures for organism-environment interactions. *Human Development, 17,* 444–452.

Labouvie, E. W. (1980). Identity versus equivalence of psychological measures and constructs. In L. W. Poon (Ed.), *Aging in the 1980's: Psychological issues* (pp. 493–502). Washington, DC: American Psychological Association.

Lachman, M. E., Weaver, S. L., Bandura, E., & Lewkowicz, C. J. (1992). Improving memory and control beliefs through cognitive restructuring and self-generated strategies. *Journal of Gerontology: Psychological Sciences, 47,* P293–P299.

Lachman, R., Lachman, J. L., & Taylor, D. W. (1982). Reallocation of mental resources over the productive lifespan: Assumptions and task analyses. In F. I. M. Craik & S. Trehub (Eds.), *Aging and cognitive processes* (pp. 279–308). New York: Plenum.

Lindenberger, U., & Baltes, P. B. (1994). Sensory functioning and intelligence in old age: A strong connection. *Psychology and Aging, 9,* 339–355.

Lindenberger, U., Mayr, U., & Kliegl, R. (1993). Speed and intelligence in old age. *Psychology and Aging, 8,* 207–220.

Loftus, G. R. (1978). On interpretation of interactions. *Memory and Cognition, 6,* 312–319.

MacLeod, C. M., Hunt, E. B., & Mathews, N. N. (1978). Individual differences in the verification of sentence-picture relationships. *Journal of Verbal Learning and Verbal Behavior, 17,* 493–508.

Manton, K. G., Siegler, I., & Woodbury, M. (1986). Patterns of intellectual development in later life. *Journal of Gerontology, 41,* 486–499.

Mook, D. G. (1983). In defense of external invalidity. *American Psychologist, 38,* 379–387.

Mumford, M. D., & Owens, W. A. (1985). Individuality in a developmental context: Some empirical and theoretical considerations. *Human Development, 27,* 84–108.

Nesselroade, J. R. (1983). Temporal selection and factor invariance in the study of development and change. In P. B. Baltes & O. G. Brim, Jr. (Eds.), *Life-span development and behavior* (vol. 5, pp. 59–87). New York: Academic Press.

Nesselroade, J. R. (1988). Sampling and generalizability: Adult development and aging research issues examined with the general methodological framework of selection. In K. W. Schaie, R. T. Campbell, W. Meredith, & S. C. Rawlings (Eds.), *Methodological issues in aging research* (pp. 13–42). New York: Springer.

Nesselroade, J. R. (1990). Adult personality development: Issues in assessing constancy and change. In R. A. Zucker, A. I. Rabin, J. Aronoff, & S. Frank (Eds.), *Personality structure in the life course* (pp. 221–275). New York: Springer.

Nesselroade, J. R., & Ford, D. H. (1985). P-technique comes of age: Multivariate, replicated single-subject designs for research on older adults. *Research on Aging, 7,* 46–80.

Nesselroade, J. R., & Jones, C. J. (1991). Multi-modal selection effects in the study of adult development: A perspective on multivariate, replicated, single-subject, repeated measures designs. *Experimental Aging Research, 17,* 21–27.

Pedhazur, E. J. (1982). *Multiple regression in behavioral research: Explanation and prediction* (2d ed.). New York: Holt, Rinehart and Winston.

Perfect, T. J. (1994). What can Brinley plots tell us about cognitive aging? *Journal of Gerontology: Psychological Sciences, 49,* P60–P64.

Perlmutter, M., & Nyquist, L. (1990). Relationships between self-reported physical and mental health and intelligence performance across adulthood. *Journal of Gerontology: Psychological Sciences, 45,* P145–P155.

Reichardt, C. S. (1979). The statistical analysis of data from nonequivalent group designs. In T. D. Cook & D. T. Campbell (Eds.), *Quasi-experimentation: Design and analysis issues for field settings* (pp. 147–205). Chicago: Rand McNally.

Riegel, K. F., & Riegel, R. M. (1972). Development, drop, and death. *Developmental Psychology, 6,* 306–319.

Rogers, W. A., Fisk, A. D., & Hertzog, C. (1994). Do ability-performance relationships differentiate age and practice effects in visual search? *Journal of Experimental Psychology: Learning, Memory, and Cognition, 20,* 710–738.

Rogosa, D. (1988). Myths about longitudinal research. In K. W. Schaie, R. T. Campbell, W. Meredith, & S. C. Rawlings (Eds.), *Methodological issues in aging research* (pp. 171–209). New York: Springer.

Rogosa, D., & Willett, J. B. (1985). Understanding correlates of change by modeling individual differences in growth. *Psychometrika, 50,* 203–228.

Salthouse, T. A. (1979). Adult age and the speed–accuracy tradeoff. *Ergonomics, 22,* 811–821.

Salthouse, T. A. (1985). Speed of behavior and its implications for cognition. In J. E. Birren & K. W. Schaie (Eds.), *Handbook of the psychology of aging* (2d ed., pp. 400–426). New York: Van Nostrand Reinhold.

Salthouse, T. A. (1988). Resource-reduction interpretations of cognitive aging. *Developmental Review, 8,* 357–362.

Salthouse, T. A. (1990). Working memory as a processing resource in cognitive aging. *Developmental Review, 10,* 101–124.

Salthouse, T. A. (1991). *Theoretical perspectives on cognitive aging.* Hillsdale, NJ: Erlbaum.

Salthouse, T. A. (1992). *Mechanisms of age-cognition relations in adulthood.* Hillsdale, NJ: Erlbaum.

Salthouse, T. A. (1994). How many causes are there of aging-related decrements in cognitive functioning? *Developmental Review, 14,* 413–437.

Salthouse, T. A., Kausler, D., & Saults, J. S. (1988). Investigation of student stats, background variables, and feasibility of standard tasks in cognitive aging research. *Psychology and Aging, 3,* 29–37.

Schaie, K. W. (1965). A general model for the study of developmental problems. *Psychological Bulletin, 64,* 92–107.

Schaie, K. W. (1973). Methodological problems in descriptive developmental research on adulthood and aging. In J. R. Nesselroade & H. W. Reese (Eds.), *Life-span developmental psychology: Methodological issues* (pp. 253–280). New York: Academic Press.

Schaie, K. W. (1977). Quasi-experimental research designs in the psychology of aging. In J. E. Birren & K. W. Schaie (Eds.), *Handbook of the psychology of aging* (pp. 39–58). New York: Van Nostrand Reinhold.

Schaie, K. W. (1986). Beyond calendar definition of age, time, and cohort: The general developmental model revisited. *Developmental Review, 6,* 252–277.

Schaie, K. W., & Hertzog, C. (1982). Longitudinal methods. In B. B. Wolman (Ed.), *Handbook of developmental psychology* (pp. 91–115). Englewood Cliffs, NJ: Prentice-Hall.

Schaie, K. W., & Hertzog, C. (1985). Measurement in the psychology of adulthood and aging. In J. E. Birren & K. W. Schaie (Eds.), *Handbook of the psychology of aging* (2d ed., pp. 61–92). New York: Van Nostrand Reinhold.

Schaie, K. W., & Willis, S. L. (1986). Can intellectual decline in the elderly be reversed? *Developmental Psychology, 22,* 223–232.

Schaie, K. W., & Willis, S. L. (1994). Perceived family environments across generations. In V. L. Bengtson, K. W. Schaie, & L. M. Burton (Eds.), *Adult intergenerational relations: Effects of societal change* (pp. 174–209). New York: Springer.

Stanovich, K. E. (1992). *How to think straight about psychology* (3d ed.). New York: HarperCollins.

Steiger, J. H. (1980). Tests for comparing elements of a correlation matrix. *Psychological Bulletin, 87,* 245–251.

Thompson, M. G., Heller, K., & Rody, C. A. (1994). Recruitment challenges in studying late-life depression: Do community samples adequately represent depressed older adults? *Psychology and Aging, 9,* 121–125.

Welford, A. T. (1977). Motor performance. In J. E. Birren & K. W. Schaie (Eds.), *Handbook of the psychology of aging* (pp. 450–496). New York: Van Nostrand Reinhold.

Wilkie, F. L., & Eisdorfer, C. (1971). Intelligence and blood pressure in the aged. *Science, 172,* 959–962.

Wohlwill, J. F. (1973). *The study of behavioral development.* New York: Academic Press.

Wohlwill, J. F. (1991). The partial isomorphism between developmental theory and methods. *Annals of Theoretical Psychology, 6,* 1–43.

Wood, P., & Brown, D. (1994). The study of intraindividual differences by means of dynamic factor models: Rationale, implementation, and interpretation. *Psychological Bulletin, 116,* 166–186.

4

VISION, AUDITION, AND AGING RESEARCH

Frank Schieber and Carryl L. Baldwin
University of South Dakota

A working knowledge about the major senescent changes in sensory-perceptual systems is necessary if one is interested in isolating their effects from cognitive and/or attentional explanations of age-related changes in behavior. This chapter has been prepared as an introduction to the age-related sensory-perceptual changes that may influence the results of cognitive aging research. Since an overwhelming majority of cognitive research involves visual and/or auditory stimuli, only these domains of sensory input are considered. Those interested in age-related changes within the other sense modalities are referred to previous reviews of the literature (see, e.g., Schieber, 1992; Schieber, Fozard, Gordon-Salant, & Weiffenbach, 1991). Unlike cognitive systems, sensory-perceptual systems operate without direct recourse to knowledge and personal experience. These systems instead are informed by millions of years of evolution, which served to shape sensory and perceptual mechanisms to "fit" the informational needs of the behaving organism to the physical constraints imposed by the natural stimulus environment. Why, then, might age-related sensory-perceptual changes be of interest to cognitive aging research? The answer is quite straightforward. Age-related changes at the sensory-perceptual level can influence performance and hence be confounded with the effects of cognitive aging. This influence can be either direct or indirect. For example, Treisman and Gormican (1988) have demonstrated that reductions in target stimulus discriminability—such as those commonly experienced due to sensory aging effects—can influence the slopes of visual search time functions (i.e., display size effects). Similarly, Rabbitt (1991) has shown how higher-order resources (e.g., attention) must often be invested to compensate for sensory deficits (e.g., age-related hearing loss). The deleterious effects of deteriorations in the quality of sensory input are thought to become even more influential as information-processing rates decline in old age (Rabbitt, 1991). As such, it behooves the researcher interested in exploring the effects of cognitive aging to become familiar with the most likely sources of sense-based performance decrements in older observers as well as the techniques commonly deployed to minimize their effects.

VISION

■ Age-related Structural Changes in the Visual System

Our discussion of the structural changes in the visual system will begin with the significant optical factors which may impact performance in older individuals and will conclude with an overview of recent findings regarding age-related changes in the retina and visual areas of the brain. Light first enters the eye through the cornea (see Figure 4.1). The cornea is the principal refractive (focusing) surface of the eye, accounting for about two-thirds of its power to bend light into a focused image upon the retina. A tiny change in the curvature of the cornea will have a profound impact upon the clarity of the retinal image. Adult aging is associated with a tendency for the cornea to "flatten" somewhat, resulting in a loss of refractive power and a subsequent blurring of the retinal image (Garzia & Trick, 1992). This normative change reinforces the need to assess (and correct) refractive error among participants in cognitive research. The eyelid covering the cornea also tends to sag noticably in many older adults, a condition known as *ptosis* (Theodore, 1975). A drooping eyelid can obscure the superior aspect of the pupil of the eye and interfere with performance on some visual search tasks (e.g., radial localization). The amount of light that actually enters the eye is controlled by the pupillary aperture in the pigmented iris muscle. Through dilation and constriction, the pupil of a healthy young adult is capable of regulating the amount of light entering the eye over a 16-to-1 range (Geldard, 1972). However, as one grows older the maximum diameter attained by the pupil begins to decline, a condition known as *senile miosis*. Under conditions of dim illumination, the resting diameter of the pupil falls from approximately

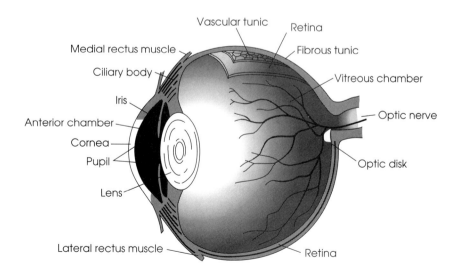

FIGURE 4.1 Anatomical structure of the eye. (*Source:* Sekuler & Blake, 1994, p. 35.

7 millimeters at age 20 to around 4 millimeters at age 80 (Lowenfeld, 1979). Senile miosis markedly reduces the amount of light which reaches the retina and can have detrimental effects upon performance, especially in low-luminance conditions. However, smaller pupil sizes may actually benefit older observers under some viewing conditions by acting to minimize the emerging optical imperfections of the aging lens (Sloane, Owsley, & Alvarez, 1988).

After passing through the pupil, light rays from the visual stimulus reach the lens. In response to the contractile force of the ciliary muscles, the lens can alter its shape and thus change its focusing power. This process, known as *accommodation,* enables the lens to dynamically increase the focusing power of the eye as required for tasks such as viewing near objects. The lens grows continuously throughout the life span, adding additional layers to its laminated structure and increasing in density and mass (Weale, 1963). As a result, the lens gradually loses its ability to change shape and the eye becomes unable to focus on near objects (a condition known as *presbyopia*). By the fifth decade of life, the prebyopic loss in accommodative ability has become so great that most persons require optical correction to read text at less than arm's length (Hofstetter, 1965). The senescent lens also yellows and becomes less transparent (Weale, 1963). This loss of transparency appears to be particularly noticeable at short wavelengths; that is, for blue light (Said & Weale, 1959). Opacification of the lens with advancing age appears to be nearly universal. The Framingham Eye Study, a large-scale epidemiological investigation, reported that more than 90 percent of those in the 75-to-85-year-old group demonstrated significant opacification of the lens (Kahn et al., 1977; Sperduto & Siegel, 1980). Due to the combined effects of lenticular opacification and senile miosis, Weale (1961) has estimated that the retina of a typical 60-year-old receives less than one-third the light of its 20-year-old counterpart. This relative reduction in retinal illuminance may be even greater under dim viewing conditions (Schieber et al., 1991). The increased optical density of the lens also contributes to intraocular scatter of light, which may reduce the effective contrast of the retinal image and contribute to age-related increases in the deleterious effects of glare (Schieber, 1988).

Age-related changes have also been noted in the visual nervous system. Ophthalmoscopic examination of the retina reveals more narrow and sclerotic blood vessels and a progressive decrease in the pigmentation and apparent thickness of the retinal pigment epithelium, which provides metabolic support for the rods and cones (Marmor, 1982). Microscopic examination of the retina reveals more profound age-related changes such as the loss of photoreceptors (Marshall, Grindle, Ansell, & Borwein, 1980; Youdelis & Hendrickson, 1986) and atrophy of retinal ganglion cells (Curcio & Drucker, 1993; Johnson, Miao, & Sadun, 1987). However, recent evidence shows that the cones which contribute to central (foveal) vision appear to remain relatively intact in older adults (Curcio, Millican, Allen, & Kalina, 1993). In contrast, the number of rods in the near periphery appears to decline significantly with advancing age. Curcio et al. (1993) reported that nearly 30 percent of the rods in the central 30 degrees of vision are lost by age 90. There is also some evidence that rods in the far periphery may succumb to the negative effects of aging (Gao & Hollyfield, 1992). Initial studies of the human visual cortex reported highly significant cell loss with advancing age. For example, Devaney and Johnson (1980) found that the number of cells in the primary visual (striate) cortex declined by approximately 25 percent as early as age 60. However, more recent studies of human striate cortex have found that there is no decrease in neuron density with aging (see, e.g., Haug, Kuhl, Mecke, Sass, & Wassner, 1984; Leuba & Garey, 1987).

Spear's (1993) recent review of the neurological basis of age differences in visual function concluded that "the available results suggest that there are no massive losses of striate neurons" in the brains of older adults (p. 2600). Given the conflicting results noted above and the critical role of these findings for generating and interpreting models of aging and human behavior, it is clear that more research is needed to accurately quantify age-related changes in human brain structure and function.

■ Age-related Changes in Visual Function

Eye Movements

The visual system's ability to resolve fine spatial detail is mediated by a relatively small region of the central retina known as the *fovea*. Optimal spatial resolution depends upon the oculomotor system's capacity to acquire, track, and image a visual target at or near the fovea. This acquisition and maintenance of visual fixation are accomplished by two separate but interacting perceptual-motor systems: the *saccadic* and *pursuit* eye movement systems. The saccadic eye movement system generates brief, high-velocity, ballistic excursions of the eye which serve to move a target image onto the fovea. The pursuit eye movement system mediates large-amplitude, continuous motions which serve to accurately track moving targets and thus enhance visual function by extending the useful range of high-resolution foveal vision.

Studies of age differences in saccadic eye movements have focused upon horizontal excursions of the eye. There is general agreement in the literature that horizontal saccades among older individuals have reduced peak velocities together with protracted onset latencies. Abel, Troost, and Dell'Osso (1983) found that the latency of saccadic eye movements that were triggered by the onset of off-fixation targets increased by an average of 45 milliseconds [msec] between the ages of 26 and 72 years (for targets in the range of 1–30 degrees). Similar results have been reported by Whitaker, Shoptaugh, and Haywood (1986), and a somewhat greater degree of slowing is evident in the data of Carter, Obler, Woodward, and Albert (1983), which is depicted in Figure 4.2. Small but significant decreases in the peak velocity achieved during saccadic eye movements also appear in late life. Pitt and Rawles (1988) found

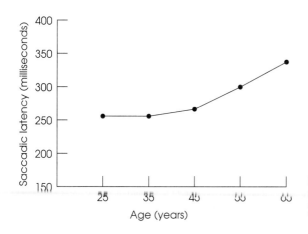

FIGURE 4.2 Saccadic eye movement latency as a function of age. (*Source:* Carter, Obler, Woodward, & Albert, 1983.)

that saccadic velocity decreased by approximately 0.25 percent per year from 20 to 68 years of age. Similar findings have been reported by Spooner, Sakala, and Baloh (1980). Despite the slowing that is apparent in the latency and peak velocity of saccadic eye movements among older observers, Hotson and Steinke (1988) found no age differences in the accuracy of saccadic eye movements. More recently, Huaman and Sharpe (1993) have extended these results to studies of vertical saccadic eye movements. Younger adults (aged 20–33) had an average latency of 180 msec for vertical saccadic excursions of 10 to 20 degrees, while older adults (aged 65–84) demonstrated significantly prolonged latencies in the range of 225 msec. The magnitude of the age difference in onset latency grew as the size of the required eye movement increased from 20 to 50 degrees.

Age-related declines in the pursuit eye movement system have also been noted. Sharpe and Sylvester (1978) reported that young subjects could accurately track targets at velocities up to 30 degrees per second, whereas the fixational accuracy of pursuit eye movements began to break down for older observers when target velocity exceeded 10 degrees per second. Similar findings have been reported by Hutton, Nagel, and Lowenson (1983). Relatedly, S. R. Kaufman and Abel (1986) have demonstrated that age differences in pursuit accuracy are exacerbated in the presence of competing or distracting stimulus backgrounds. Although the age-related oculomotor changes described above may lead to functional limitations in dynamic viewing situations, there is evidence that older adults demonstrate no loss in the ability to maintain accurate fixation while viewing a small, stationary stimulus (Kosnik, Kline, Fikre, & Sekuler, 1987).

Another aspect of oculomotor function which appears to be affected by aging is the range or extent of upward gaze (i.e., the maximum vertical extent of visual fixation which can be achieved without the benefit of head movements). The classic ophthalmology reference volumes note that the limits of voluntary upward gaze fall somewhere between 40 and 45 degrees (Adler, 1933; Duke-Elder, 1949). However, Chamberlain (1971) has reported that this value becomes markedly reduced with increasing adult age. An assessment of 367 persons aged 5 to 94 years revealed that maximum upward gaze declined linearly across the life span from 40 degrees at ages 5 to 14 to 16 degrees at ages 75 to 84. More recently, Huaman and Sharpe (1993) used improved technology (i.e., a high-resolution magnetic search coil) to assess the limits of both upward and downward gaze in young (mean = 28.3 years), middle-aged (mean = 49.8 years), and older observers (mean = 71.9 years). Maximum upward gaze was 43.1, 42.0, and 32.9 degrees for the younger, middle-aged and older groups, respectively. Similar findings were obtained for the extent of downward gaze. Although the differences between these two studies are depicted in Figure 4.3, the reasons for them remain unclear.

Spatial Resolution

Visual acuity Visual acuity is the best-known and most widely applied index of visual functioning. Acuity measures the ability of the visual system to resolve fine spatial detail. Acuity assessments are most often quantified in terms of the *minimum angle of resolution,* that is, the visual angle of the smallest spatial target which can be identified. The ability to resolve well-illuminated, high-contrast spatial features which subtend a visual angle of 1 minute of arc (minarc) represents "normal" visual acuity. The familiar *Snellen acuity fractions* for "distance" vision (20 ft or farther) are expressed in terms of the more readily interpretable min-

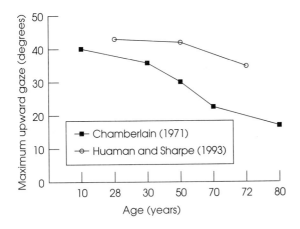

FIGURE 4.3 Maximum extent of upward gaze of the eyes as a function of age. (*Source:* Chamberlain, 1971; Huaman & Sharpe, 1993.)

imal angle of resolution in Table 4.1. Because small amounts of refractive (focusing) error in the eye yield reliable decrements in acuity, the acuity test has been widely adopted as the basis for correcting optical aberrations of the eye with spectacle lenses. However, standard tests of visual acuity may not be the best predictors of functional status for older persons in many laboratory and/or real-world settings (Schieber, 1988).

Even when screened for good ocular health and optimal refractive status, older adults, as a group, demonstrate reduced levels of visual acuity (Frisen & Frisen, 1981). Pitts (1982) reviewed the major cross-sectional studies of visual acuity as a function of increasing adult

TABLE 4.1 Snellen Acuity Levels Expressed as Minimum Angles of Resolution

Snellen Acuity	Minutes of Arc
20/10	0.5
20/20[*]	1.0
20/25	1.25
20/30	1.5
20/40[†]	2.0
20/50	2.5
20/100	5.0
20/200[§]	10.0

[*]Normal vision.

[†]Typical driver's license cutoff.

[§]Legally blind.

age. A summary of his findings is depicted in Figure 4.4. Reference to this figure reveals that mean "corrected" distance acuity remains excellent—20/20, or 1.0 minarc—to approximately age 50. Beyond age 50, however, corrected visual acuity begins to decline at an accelerated rate. Mean corrected visual acuity falls to 20/25 (i.e., a critical detail subtending 1.25 minarc can be resolved) between the ages of 65 and 74 and all the way down to 20/40 (2.0 minarc) for those over 75 years of age (Klein, Klein, & Linton, 1991; Roberts & Rowland, 1978). Longitudinal studies of age-related changes in visual acuity have yielded similar findings (see, e.g., Gittings & Fozard, 1986). However, predicting individual functional status on the basis of age-related averages can be quite misleading. For example, data from the Framingham Eye Study (Kahn et al., 1977), presented in Figure 4.5, show that the majority of older adults maintain "good" corrected vision (i.e., 20/25 [1.25 minarc] or better) through age 85, despite the fact that "average" acuity declines dramatically.

Several investigations have also revealed that age differences are exacerbated when acuity is measured under low-luminance conditions. O. W. Richards (1977) measured acuity in persons aged 16 to 90 using charts varying in luminance from 0.03 to 34 candelas per square meter (cd/m²). Although the acuity of all individuals decreased as light levels diminished, the magnitude of this effect was disproportionately stronger for those in their 70s and 80s. A more recent study by Sturr, Kline, and Taub (1990) measured acuity as lumi-

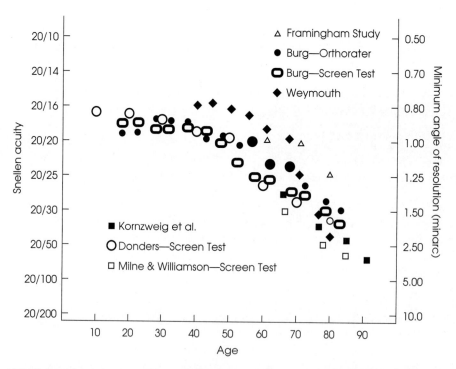

FIGURE 4.4 Average visual acuity as a function of age as reported in seven major studies. (*Source:* Adapted from Pitts, 1982, from R. Sekuler, D. W. Kline, & K. Dismukes (Eds), *Aging and human visual function.* Copyright 1982. Reprinted by permission of Wiley-Liss.)

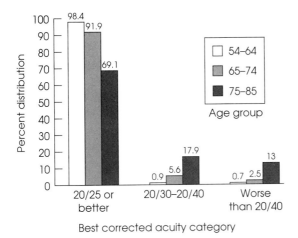

FIGURE 4.5 Acuity distributions by age groups. Based upon best eye with optical correction. (*Source:* Data from Kahn et al., 1977.)

nance was decreased from very high (245.5 cd/m^2) to very low (0.2 cd/m^2) levels in a sample of 60 younger (ages 18–25) and 91 older (ages 60–87), healthy observers. Acuity differences between the groups increased as the stimulus luminance level decreased. Sturr et al. calculated the percentage of each age group that surpassed the 20/40 acuity criterion (the typical cutoff used by state motor vehicle licensing administrations) at 2.45 cd/m^2, a very dim luminance level representative of the typical nighttime driving environment. Although 77 percent of the 60- to 64-year-olds "passed" this nighttime acuity screening, only 28 percent of the 65- to 74-year-olds and 4 percent of the 75+ group were able to demonstrate this minimal level of visual competence. Vola, Cornu, Carrvel, Gastaud, & Leid (1983) found that age differences in low luminance (0.8 cd/m^2) acuity emerge as early as 50 years of age.

Age-related differences in acuity are further exacerbated at low levels of stimulus contrast (i.e., when the ratio between the maximum luminance and minimum luminance approaches 1). Owsley and Sloane (1990) found that reductions of stimulus contrast had no demonstrable effects upon younger observers, while older persons exhibited a 10 to 25 percent decline in acuity as letter contrast was decreased from 96 percent to 4 percent. Other investigators have also demonstrated that apparently good acuity among older adults can become significantly compromised under low-contrast and low-luminance viewing conditions. Adams, Wong, Wong, and Gould (1988) examined age differences in acuity over a wide range of stimulus luminance, and contrast. All observers demonstrated 20/20 acuity (i.e., they could resolve spatial details subtending 1 minarc) under typical high-luminance/high-contrast assessment conditions. At the lowest luminance–contrast condition (10% contrast at 5.4 cd/m^2), acuity dropped to 20/50 (2.5 minarc) for the young group (<30 years old) and all the way down to 20/80 (4.0 minarc) for the older observers (50–72 years old). Similar results have been reported by Taub and Sturr (1991).

Since the crystalline lens of the eye must accommodate, or change shape, in order to focus on near targets, separate visual acuities for "near" versus "distance" (>20 ft) targets are often measured. All the work referred to above dealt with distance acuity. It is well known, however, that uncorrected visual acuity for near objects begins to decline rapidly after age 40.

Thus, a typical 55-year-old would be able to resolve a 1.0-minarc target presented at a distance of 20 feet (i.e., 20/20 acuity) yet be unable to read a newspaper held at arm's length without the help of "bifocals" or customized reading eyeglasses. Refractive correction of presbyopia (via bifocals) always represents a compromise since optimal correction depends heavily upon the viewing distance to the target of interest. Clinical practice traditionally assumes a "working distance" of 16 inches when correcting for presbyopic deficiencies in the focusing power of the eyes. Control for the effects of presbyopia is important for cognitive research since most experimental paradigms employing visual stimuli present targets within the "near" range of visual function.

Contrast sensitivity The capacity to visually detect and identify spatial form varies widely as a function of target size, contrast, and spatial orientation (Braddick, Campbell, & Atkinson, 1978; Olzak & Thomas, 1985). As a consequence, an assessment of visual acuity (the ability to resolve small, high-contrast targets) very often does not predict an individual's ability to detect objects of large size and/or diminished contrast (Ginsburg, Evans, Sekuler, & Harp, 1982; Watson, Barlow, & Robson, 1983). The *contrast sensitivity function* (CSF), however, yields information about an individual's ability to detect low-contrast targets over an extended range of target size, complementing and extending our ability to assess functional visual capacity.

The CSF is determined by calculating the minimum amount of contrast needed to detect the presence of sine-wave grating targets (see Figure 4.6). Contrast is traditionally defined by the formula (maximum luminance − minimum luminance)/(maximum luminance + minimum luminance). Sine-wave gratings possess useful mathematical properties, and re-

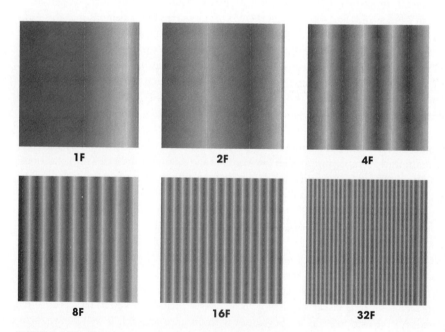

FIGURE 4.6 Sine-wave grating stimuli of varying spatial frequency (F).

searchers have discovered that early stages of visual processing are optimally sensitive to such targets (Maffei, 1978; Watson et al., 1983). Contrast thresholds are typically collected using vertically oriented gratings which vary in spatial frequency from 0.5 cycles per degree (very wide) to 32 cycles per degree (very narrow). Because high levels of visual sensitivity are associated with low-contrast thresholds, a reciprocal measure termed the *contrast sensitivity score* is computed. These sensitivity scores are plotted across the range of spatial frequencies examined during the assessment procedure and constitute an individual's CSF.

Characteristic age-related changes in the CSF are depicted in Figure 4.7, which summarizes data collected from more than 200 participants in the Baltimore Longitudinal Study of Aging (Schieber, Kline, Kline, & Fozard, 1992). Few or no age-related decrements are seen at low spatial frequencies (i.e., coarse gratings of < 2.0 cycles/degree). Small reductions in peak contrast sensitivity with a generalized loss of sensitivity spreading to high spatial frequencies emerge between ages 50 and 69. This trend becomes much more pronounced for those aged 70 and above. These results replicate and extend previous studies of age-related changes in contrast sensitivity (see, e.g., D. W. Kline, Schieber, Abusamra, & Coyne, 1983; Owsley, Sekuler, & Siemsen, 1983).

Owsley et al. (1983) found that age differences in contrast sensitivity were not eliminated when young subjects viewed the stimulus objects under conditions of simulated ocular aging (e.g., markedly reduced retinal illumination and induced refractive error). Similarly, neither the elimination of age differences in pupil size (Sloane et al., 1988) nor the replacement of cataracts with transparent intraocular lens implants (Owsley, Gardner, Sekuler, & Lieberman, 1985) succeeded in eliminating the age-related loss of contrast sensitivity for

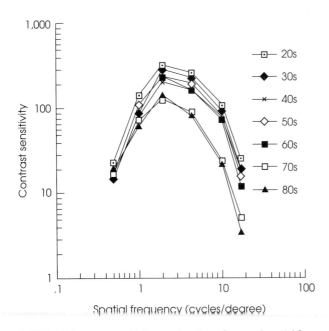

FIGURE 4.7 Contrast sensitivity as a function of age and spatial frequency.

intermediate- and high-spatial-frequency targets. These results suggest that the residual age difference in contrast sensitivity represents an age-related change in the neural, rather than optical, characteristics of the visual system. When laser imaging techniques are used to "bypass" the effects of age differences in the optics of the eye, substantial age differences in contrast sensitivity at intermediate and high spatial frequencies persist (see, e.g., Elliott, 1987; J. D. Morrison & McGrath, 1985; but see Burton, Owsley, & Sloane, 1993). Other findings also strongly indicate that much of the age-related change in contrast sensitivity results from neural differences in visual processing (Elliott, Whitaker, & MacVeigh, 1990).

The additional information provided by the CSF—over and above a simple measure of visual acuity—would be expected to yield an improved ability to predict age differences in real-world visual performance. Numerous studies have provided evidence to support this expectation. Owsley and Sloane (1987) found that age-related problems with the detection and identification of human faces—which could not be accounted for by differences in acuity—were associated with contrast sensitivity losses at intermediate spatial frequencies. Similar findings with other classes of "real-world" stimuli have been reported by other investigators (see, e.g., Evans and Ginsburg, 1985; T. J. Kline, Ghali, Kline, & Brown, 1990).

Peripheral vision Most research regarding human visual functioning deals with "foveal" vision; that is, sensitivity for fine spatial detail and color, both of which are mediated by the central region of the retina. However, mounting evidence reveals that some of the most profound age-related changes in visual functioning may involve peripheral, rather than central, visual processing. Because of its critical role in diagnosing ophthalmic disorders, *static visual perimetry* is one of the most widely studied areas of aging and visual function (Garzia & Trick, 1992). This procedure measures one's ability to detect small spots of light superimposed upon a constantly illuminated background (i.e., the increment threshold) at locations throughout the visual field. The result is a topographic map which depicts the sensitivity of the peripheral as well as central retina. Jaffe, Alvarado, and Juster (1986) found age-related decrements in sensitivity across the entire visual field. This loss appears to accrue gradually across middle age but then begins to accelerate beyond age 60 (Collin, Han, & Kohr, 1988). Both of the aforementioned studies report that age-related losses in sensitivity increase as the target location moves farther into the periphery. These age-related changes are not due to optical factors and hence appear to reflect age-related neural losses (Owsley & Sloane, 1990).

Spatial resolution has long been known to decline markedly as targets move away from the central vision into the parafoveal and far peripheral retina. Anstis (1974) has demonstrated that letter size must be incremented by a factor of 0.046 (i.e., 2.7 minutes of arc must be added to the letter height) for every degree of displacement from the center of the fovea. Recent evidence suggests that the rate of loss in visual sensitivity associated with retinal eccentricity becomes accelerated in older people. For example, Collins, Brown, and Bowman (1989) examined peripheral visual acuity in young and old subjects with 20/20 (or better) central acuity. A high-contrast-acuity target (black bars separated by a gap) with a critical detail larger than that needed to achieve 20/40 central acuity (i.e., 2.4 minarc) was moved away from the central fixation point until observers could no longer reliably determine its orientation. Younger subjects could discriminate the orientation of the critical detail up to 30.8 degrees of eccentricity, while older subjects could do so only through 22.8 degrees, representing a 23 percent age-related reduction in the "useful field of acuity." The magnitude of the observed age difference in peripheral acuity was reduced when a larger (4.8-minarc) target was employed. Similar accelerated losses in visual sensitivity with retinal eccentricity in older adults have been noted for measurements of contrast sensitivity (Crassini, Brown, & Bowman, 1988). Again, the analyses performed by these investigators suggest that age-related peripheral losses stem from neural rather than optical aging mechanisms.

Age-related losses in extrafoveal visual perception have also been noted using complex visual search paradigms. Cerella (1985) demonstrated that age differences in letter recognition times increased with the retinal eccentricity of the target. Others have found that older adults suffer from a restricted "useful field of view" in visual search tasks (Sekuler & Ball, 1986). Such age-related decrements in the ability to process parafoveal targets appear to depend heavily upon competition for "attentional resources" imposed by the concurrent presentation of "distractor" stimuli rather than upon limits imposed by the sensory-perceptual system (Ball, Beard, Roenker, Miller, & Griggs, 1988; Scialfa, Kline, & Lyman, 1987). The cognitive/attentional aspects of visual search are detailed elsewhere in this volume.

Temporal Resolution

Perhaps the most fundamental age-related change in visual function is the loss of the ability to detect and process rapid temporal changes in the visual environment. Temporally contiguous visual events that would be seen as separate and distinct by young observers often appear as "fused" or indistinguishable by older individuals (D. W. Kline & Schieber, 1982). This age-related "slowing" of the visual system not only affects higher-order events such as those revealed in sequential integration of form (see, e.g., D. W. Kline & Orme-Rogers, 1978; D. W. Kline & Schieber, 1980) and backward masking studies (see, e.g., D. W. Kline & Birren, 1975; Walsh, 1976) but can be demonstrated in the form of age-related losses in rudimentary visual functions such as flicker sensitivity, dynamic visual acuity, and motion perception.

Flicker sensitivity The *critical flicker frequency* (CFF) threshold has been the most frequently employed paradigm for assessing age differences in the temporal resolving power of the visual system. The CFF is the minimum frequency of a pulsating light source at which the light *appears* to be "fused" into a continuous, rather than flickering, stimulus. The CFF threshold is interpreted to represent the point at which the visual system can no longer track rapid temporal modulations in stimulus luminance. There is a well-documented age-related decline in the temporal resolving power of the visual system as indexed by the CFF threshold (see, e.g., Brozek & Keys, 1945; Huntington & Simonson, 1965; Misiak, 1947). Wolf and Shaffra (1964) collected CFF measures from 302 observers aged 6 to 95. CFF thresholds increased (i.e., flicker sensitivity decreased) gradually to around age 60 and then rapidly thereafter. Although a large part of the age-related loss in flicker sensitivity certainly results from a reduction in retinal illumination (due to senescent increases in the opacity of the lens and a reduction in pupillary diameter), experiments by McFarland, Warren, and Karis (1958) and Weekers and Roussel (1945) support the notion that a significant proportion of the age difference in the CFF is due to changes in the senescent visual nervous system (D. W. Kline & Schieber, 1985).

A more recently developed tool for examining the temporal resolving power of the visual system via flicker perception is the *temporal contrast sensitivity function* (TCSF). The TCSF is analogous to the spatial CSF described above. The contrast of a small illuminated target is sinusoidally modualted at a given temporal frequency. Then the minimum amplitude of contrast modulation required to detect the presence of flicker is determined for a range of temporal frequencies which typically extends from 1 to 50 cycles per second (Hz). Wright and Drasdo (1985) observed significant age-related increases in the amount of contrast needed to detect flicker. The magnitude of this age difference grew from a 1.6- to a 4.8-fold reduction in temporal sensitivity as stimulus frequency was increased from 3.3 to 30 Hz. The investigators attributed much of this loss to age differences in retinal illuminance resulting from normal senescent changes in the eye. A similar pattern of results was observed by Mayer, Kim, Svingos, and Glucs (1988). However, they observed somewhat smaller age-related declines in temporal sensitivity, consistent with the fact that they had partially controlled for age differences in retinal illumination by using a long-wavelength test stimulus and mathematically adjusting performance on the basis of each observer's pupillary diameter (see Figure 4.8).

Dynamic visual acuity Dynamic visual acuity (DVA) is a measure of one's ability to resolve spatial detail in moving targets. DVA performance declines as target velocity increases, and persons with identical static visual acuities may demonstrate markedly different dynamic acuities (T. R. Morrison, 1980). The limits placed upon DVA apparently result from errors in stimulus capture by the pursuit eye movement system which result in a "smearing" of the retinal image (Murphy, 1978). Since oculomotor accuracy appears to decline somewhat with advancing age, one would expect to observe a concomitant age-related change in DVA. Burg (1967) examined static and dynamic acuity in more than 17,000 California drivers between

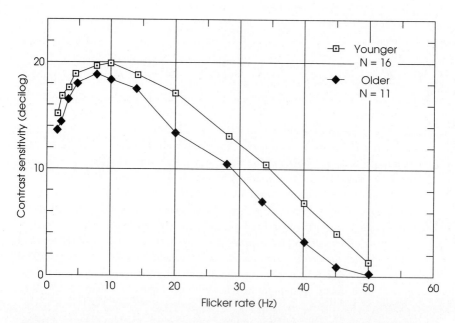

FIGURE 4.8 Temporal contrast sensitivity functions of young and older observers. (*Source:* Mayer, Kim, Svingos, & Glucs, 1988. Reprinted by permission of the Optical Society of America.)

the ages of 16 and 92. The ability to resolve fine detail in a moving target was found to decline more dramatically with age than were traditional static acuity measures. A similar pattern has been reported by other investigators (see, e.g., Farrimond, 1967; Reading, 1972; Scialfa, Garvey, Tyrell, & Leibowitz, 1989). Age-related declines in DVA performance may involve mechanisms other than oculomotor pursuit. For example, Long and Crambert (1990) recently reported large age differences in DVA even when stimulus exposure times were too brief to engage pursuit eye movements (i.e., 200 msec). Long and Crambert found that the DVA performance of their younger (aged 17–23) and old (aged 60–75) groups did not differ when the presumed age-related reduction in retinal illuminance was experimentally eliminated (see below).

Motion sensitivity Numerous studies have demonstrated age-related declines in motion sensitivity. However, both the nature and the magnitude of observed age differences in motion perception vary widely as a function of the paradigm employed to investigate them. This pattern clearly reflects the conventional belief that motion perception is a complex phenomenon mediated by several—often independent—visual mechanisms. Buckingham, Whitaker, and Banford (1987) measured threshold sensitivity for the detection of horizontal oscillatory motion as a function of age and temporal frequency (1–20 Hz). At all frequencies of oscillation, older (mean age = 69.7) observers were by about a factor of 2 less sensitive to the detection of motion than middle-aged (mean age = 48.0) subjects, who, in turn, were only slightly less sensitive than younger (mean age = 20.7) subjects. When the target grating oscillated at a frequency of 8 Hz, younger, middle-aged, and older observers required oscillation amplitudes (total spatial displacements) of approximately 39, 52, and 97 seconds of arc, respectively, to detect the occurrence of motion. Similar age-related losses in motion sensitivity have been demonstrated using a horizontally oscillating line segment (Whitaker & Elliott, 1989) and a small, vertically oscillating dot (Schieber, Hiris, Brannan, & Williams, 1990). Controls implemented by these later studies clearly revealed that the age-related deficit was independent of refractive error and retinal illumination and was hence probably of neural origin.

Several groups of investigators have recently utilized random dot motion paradigms to investigate age differences in *global motion* detection mechanisms. Observers are presented with a large number of randomly positioned dots on a computer display. These dots then take "random walks" across the screen during a brief stimulus exposure. Under these conditions, the observer can detect no principal direction of motion in the flow of the dot pattern (because there is none). The experimenter gradually adds more and more correlated directional motion to the display until the subject can reliably detect a directional trend in the flow of dots. The amount of correlated motion required to yield a percept of directional flow is the *global motion threshold*. Motion is said to be global since the dots participating in the "correlated direction of flow" vary randomly from one animation frame to the next. That is, the observer cannot detect the flow of motion by observing any given dot but must instead extract a statistical directional trend introduced into the entire population of dots moving in the aforementioned quasi-random pattern (Watamaniuk, 1992). Trick and Silverman (1991) used a random dot technique to examine age differences in global motion discrimination thresholds. They found a linear decrease in sensitivity with age such that the motion discrimination threshold doubled between the ages of 25 and 80 years. Gilmore, Wenk, Naylor, and Stuve (1992) also found an age-related deficit in global motion sensitivity; however, their observed deficits were largely the result of a differential loss of sensitivity among their elderly female participants. A similar age × gender interaction was reported by Schieber et al. (1990). Like the sensitivity to oscillatory motion described above, age differences in global motion discrimination appear to be independent of ocular factors such as reduced retinal illumination or blur due to refractive error and thus probably are mediated by age-related changes in higher-order "cooperative" visual mechanisms.

Age differences in thresholds for the detection of angular displacement over time (see, e.g., Hills, 1975) and motion in depth, or "looming" (see, e.g., Shinar, 1977), have also been reported in the literature (but see Brown & Bowman, 1987). Several studies have also demonstrated systematic age differences in the ability to judge the speed of automobiles (see, e.g., Hills, 1980; Scialfa, Kline, Lyman, & Kosnik, 1987). Older females, in particular, appear to exhibit pronounced errors in estimating the "time to arrival" of approaching vehicles (Schiff, Oldak, & Shah, 1992).

Color Vision

Human color vision is exquisitely sensitive. Normal observers are capable of distinguishing among more than 100,000 hues generated from various combinations of three "primary color" light sources (Geldard, 1972). Most investigations of age differences in color vision have employed *color confusion tests* in which the observer is required to arrange sets of "color caps" into an ordinal series extending between two anchored color exemplars (e.g., the Farnsworth-Munsell 100 Hues, or FM-100, Test). The number and type of errors exhibited via this arrangement of color samples are quantified into a color sensitivity profile. Numerous studies utilizing this technique have reported that color discrimination errors increase significantly with advancing age. These errors are primarily limited to fine discriminations within the blue-green, or short-wavelength, region of the spectrum (see, e.g., Dalderup & Fredericks, 1969; Gilbert, 1957; Knoblauch et al., 1987). Similar findings of a differential blue-green color discrimination weakness among older adults have been reported using color matching and/or production techniques (see, e.g., Eisner, Fleming, Klein, & Mauldin, 1987; Lakowski, 1958). Most of the age-related color performance shift toward the red end of the spectrum appears to result from reduced retinal illumination due to optical changes in the eye (but see Owsley & Sloane, 1990). In fact, Knoblauch et al. (1987) showed that young observers demonstrate similar blue-green weaknesses at low illumination levels and that age differences in color discrimination performance were minimized at high levels of target illumination. Although the magnitude of the age-related loss in blue-green color discrimination is small, Cody, Hurd, and Bootman (1990) demonstrated that older adults with poor FM-100 test scores were more likely to make errors in discriminating between medicine capsules with similar color-coded markings. Knoblauch et al.'s findings, however, suggest that such errors can be minimized if optimal lighting conditions are employed.

HEARING

The following sections will describe important aspects of age-related changes in audition. Age-related structural changes in the auditory system and the effects of these changes on auditory functioning will be discussed. This will be followed by a discussion of specific auditory abilities (pure-tone thresholds, frequency analysis and discrimination, and speech perception under varying listening conditions) and how they are affected by the aging process. Included in this discussion will be a brief overview of two main theories regarding the mechanisms responsible for age-related changes (i.e., peripheral versus cognitive mechanisms).

■ Age-related Structural Changes in the Auditory System

Age-related degenerative changes have been observed in nearly all peripheral and central auditory systems. The resulting age-related alterations in auditory functioning frequently observed in older individuals have important implications for cognitive research.

Outer ear In older adults the pinna of the outer ear may increase in length and breadth by several millimeters and become hard and inflexible (Corso, 1981). Atrophic changes in the outer ear noted to accompany aging include increased secretion of ear wax (cerumen) with excessive accumulation and blockage of the auditory canal (Corso, 1963) as well as a tendency for the auditory canal to collapse (Schow, Christensen, Hutchinson, & Nerbonne, 1978).

Middle ear Although not an aging phenomenon, it is common to find an accumulation of fluid in the middle ears of older individuals. This accumulation, which also is found in young children, usually occurs in conjunction with a cold and may cause a temporary hearing impairment (Corso, 1981). For this reason it may be important to screen older participants for recent illness prior to their involvement in experimental research. In the middle ear, the joints of the ossicular bone chain have been noted to show arthritic changes, becoming calcified and less elastic with advancing age (Belal, 1975; Etholm & Belal, 1974). (See Figure 4.9 for a diagram of the ear showing the ossicular bones.) However, audiometric studies indicate that arthritic changes rarely affect sound transmission in the middle ear (Corso, 1981).

Otosclerosis, a condition in which there is a formation of a new bone in the cochlear capsule forming a bridge between the footplate of the stapes and the oval window, is frequently observed in older adults (Desmond, 1970). This disease causes deafness primarily by immobilizing the footplate of the stapes in the oval window and may be treated with a surgical procedure called a stapedectomy. The stapedectomy will not restore hearing to complete normality but may return hearing to a level adequate for social purposes or for the wearing of a hearing aid (S. Richards, 1971). Otosclerosis appears to provide some protection against noise injury by blocking out noise at some frequencies. For example, in otosclerotic men who have been exposed to noise, the perceptive part of the hearing loss is lower at 4,000 Hz than in a standard exposed population; however, it is higher than in a population not exposed to noise (Gundersen, 1973).

Inner ear Antecedent factors of hearing impairment in older individuals can be divided into endogenous factors (biological changes in cells, tissue, or systems) and exogenous factors (changes in the auditory system due to environmental insult) (Willott, 1991). The term *presbycusis* is reserved for hearing impairment which is associated solely with the normal process of aging (Sanders & McCormick, 1987). The cochlea, a bean-sized, fluid-filled cavity containing specialized receptors located in the inner ear, has been identified as a site affected by presbycusis.

Schuknecht and Igarashi (1964) describe four general classes of age-related disorders in the morphological structures of the inner ear: (1) sensory presbycusis, characterized by atro-

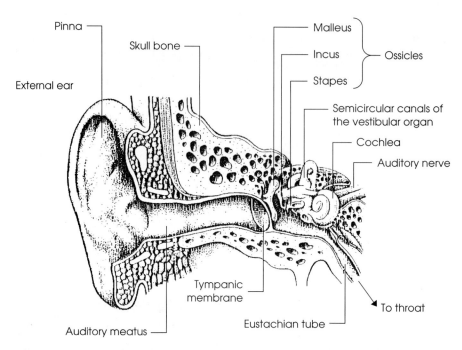

FIGURE 4.9 Structure of the ear showing the three bones of the ossicles. (*Source:* Levine & Shefner, 1991. From *Fundamentals of Sensation and Perception,* 2nd ed., by M. V. Levine & J. M. Shefner. Copyright © 1991 Brooks/Cole Publishing Company, a division of International Thomson Publishing Inc., Pacific Grove, CA 93950. By permission of the publisher.)

phy and degeneration of sensory hair cells and supporting cells in the cochlea; (2) neural presbycusis, characterized by a loss in the neuronal population of the auditory pathways; (3) strial presbycusis, characterized by atrophy of the stria vascularis (the inside layer) of the scala media, with corresponding deficiencies in the bioelectrical and biochemical properties of the endolymphatic fluids (one of the two types of fluids found in the cochlea); and (4) inner-ear conductive presbycusis, characterized by atrophic changes and stiffening of the structures associated with vibration of the cochlear membranes (Corso, 1981). Strial presbycusis is the most frequent form, occurring nearly three times as often as sensory presbycusis. Each form of presbycusis results in a characteristic pattern of hearing loss. Sensory presbycusis (occurring in about 12% of the cases) produces an abrupt high-frequency loss but does not involve speech frequencies. Neural presbycusis (occurring in about 31% of the cases) affects speech discrimination without a parallel loss in pure-tone thresholds. Strial presbycusis (occurring in about 35% of the cases) shows a nearly uniform threshold loss for all frequencies. Inner-ear conductive presbycusis (occurring in about 23% of the cases) produces increasing hearing loss values from low to high frequencies (Corso, 1981). Willott (1991) points out that the utility of distinguishing between the different classifications of presbycusis may be limited for the practicing clinician. This is due in part to the fact that the different forms often occur simultaneously. However, from the standpoint of clinical and basic scientists, the distinctions are important as they facilitate research on the mechanisms and etiology of pres-bycusis (Willott, 1991).

In addition to presbycusis, hearing loss can result from exogenous factors, such as ex-posure to occupational noise and everyday noises (sociocusis) and various common pathological conditions of the ear from other causes (nosocusis) (Kryter, 1983). In practical applications it is often difficult to disentangle the effects of presbycusis from those of sociocusis and noso-cusis. In fact, in the absence of audiometric measurement preliminary screening of partici-pants might be accomplished by determining exposure to environmental insults in past oc-cupational and recreational activities.

Central auditory pathway Information about aging neural structures is difficult to obtain. Most of the information we have comes from descriptive reports based on examination of a few specimens rather than large-scale, scientifically controlled research (Working Group on Speech Understanding and Aging, 1988). The Working Group on Speech Understanding and Aging (1988) presents a review of the pertinent literature to date and summarizes the findings by acknowledging that we can suggest, but not demonstrate, that damage to neural structures may increase with age (primarily in terms of loss of cells in such regions as the ventral cochlear nucleus, the inferior colliculus, and the cerebral cortex). However, they point out that, although this damage is thought to affect auditory functioning, actual age-based correlations between structure and functioning are not available.

■ Age-related Changes in Auditory Function

Absolute Sensitivity to Pure Tones

Numerous large-scale studies have been conducted to determine the hearing abilities of in-dividuals at various sound frequencies (Corso, 1963; Kryter, 1983; Moscicki, Elkins, Baum, & McNamara, 1985). Figure 4.10 presents mean pure-tone (single-pitch) threshold data from Corso (1963) that exemplify age-related threshold differences for females and males. Figure 4.11 presents pure-tone threshold data at higher frequencies for men and women combined. Note that the largest decrement in hearing thresholds occurs in the high frequencies (6,000 Hz and higher).

Fozard (1990) reports that changes in hearing thresholds occur continuously through-out adulthood at an average rate of 1 decibel (dB) per year at 8 kHz. Interestingly, for pri-mary speech frequencies (0.5–2.0 kHz) the change is much lower, about 0.3–0.4 dB per year through age 60 but then much greater after that, reaching a level of 1.2–1.4 dB per year in the age range 80–95 years (Brant & Fozard, 1990; Fozard, 1990).

Frequency Analysis and Discrimination

The ability to discriminate between small changes in the frequency or pitch of sounds is a significant factor in the perception of speech (Corso, 1981). Konig (1957) found that the abil-ity to discriminate among 40-dB tones of different frequencies was found to deteriorate in a linear fashion between the ages of 25 and 55 years. After 55 years this discrimination abil-ity deteriorates sharply, especially in the high (>2,000 Hz) and low (<500 Hz) frequencies. S. M. Abel, Krever, and Alberti (1990) found that aging, without concomitant hearing loss,

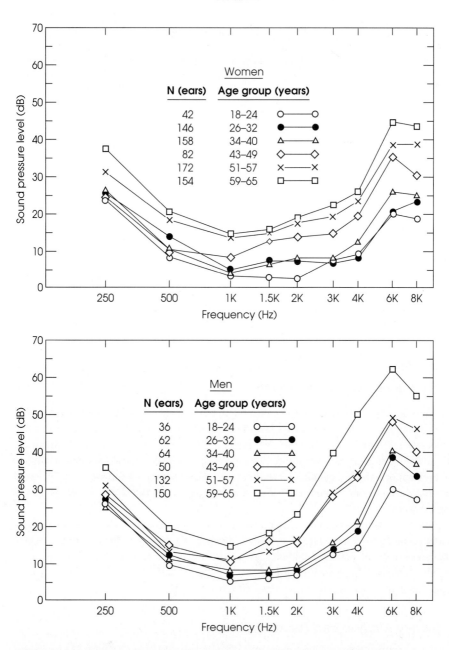

FIGURE 4.10 Mean threshold sound pressure level in dB re 0.0002 dyne/cm² for combined left and right ears for women and men screened for otological disease and selected from a quiet living environment. (*Source:* Corso, 1963. From *Archives of Environmental Health, 6,* 350–356 (1963). Reprinted with permission of the Helen Dwight Reid Educational Foundation. Published by Heldrof Publications, 1319 18th St, N. W., Washington, D. C. 20036-1802. Copyright 1963.)

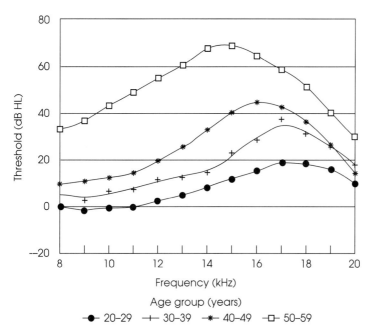

FIGURE 4.11 Pure-tone thresholds in the high-frequency range, men and women combined. (*Source:* Adapted from Stelmachowicz, Beauchaine, Kalberer, & Jesteadt, 1989.) Subjects were screened so that thresholds for 250—8,000 Hz were normal for age and sex according to Corso (1963). From *Archives of Environmental Health, 6,* 350–356 (1963). Reprinted with permission of the Helen Dwight Reid Educational Foundation. Published by Heldrof Publications, 1319 18th St, N. W., Washington, D. C. 20036-1802. Copyright 1963.)

resulted in a significantly deteriorated ability to discriminate between similar frequencies using a 500-Hz and 4,000-Hz reference tone. In addition to confirming Konig's (1957) earlier results, Abel et al. found that older subjects had greater difficulty discriminating between tones of varying durations using a 20-msec standard at both 500 Hz and 4,000 Hz. An age affect was not found for the 200-msec standard. S. M. Abel et al. point out that the 20-msec standard matched the approximate duration of a phoneme, the 200-msec standard matches the approximate duration of a syllable.

Speech Perception

Difficulties in speech recognition performance occur in older populations irrespective of pure-tone audiometric scores. Evidence suggests that age-related factors independent of pure-tone thresholds significantly influence speech recognition (Gordon-Salant, 1986). The central auditory nervous system (CANS) hypothesis assumes that the CANS ages and that this aging of the central component is responsible for the disparity between predicted and obtained speech-understanding scores. The cognitive component hypothesis assumes that the ability to process information that enters through any sensory channel is reduced in proportion to the degree of aging. The distinction between these competing alternatives is important and

warrants further investigation. If decrements are due primarily to sensory distortions, rehabilitation may involve some form of signal-processing mechanism. If decrements are primarily
cognitive in nature, rehabilitation may be aided by some form of compensatory strategy or
training method.

Jerger's (1973) classic study investigating age-related changes in speech intelligibility
suggested a disproportionate age deficit in recognition performance for monosyllabic words.
The existence of this disproportionate loss, independent of pure-tone hearing levels, provided
support for a centrally mediated mechanism of aging (Schieber, 1992). However, more recent research utilizing more intense stimuli (about ten times more intense than normal conversational levels) has failed to find this age-related deficit (Gordon-Salant, 1987). These data
are more consistent with a peripheral or pathological explanation of age-related change in
speech perception (Schieber, 1992).

Fozard (1990) points out that consonants typically require greater energy levels than
vowels for correct recognition. Gelfand, Piper, and Silman (1985) report a significant age
decline in the percentage of recognition of consonants presented at or 8 dB below normal
conversational levels. Similarly, Gordon-Salant (1986) and Guelke (1987) found that increasing the relative intensity level of consonants had the greatest effect on improving speech
recognition scores for older subjects.

Speech Perception under Degraded Listening Conditions

Conversational speech rarely takes place under ideal conditions. Background noise and reverberation are present to some degree in most situations. Numerous studies have demonstrated
exacerbated age-related performance deficits when speech is presented in less-than-ideal conditions. Additionally, various listening tests involving altered speech have been used to diagnose central disorders of hearing and to uncover deficits that are not severe enough to be revealed by speech tests under optimal conditions (Willott, 1991). In the presence of noise or
reverberation, or when the temporal rate of speech is altered (compressed speech), older adults
show speech reception decrements greater than would be predicted based on pure-tone au-
diometry (Corso, 1981; Fozard, 1990; Plomp & Mimpen, 1979). Figure 4.12 presents data showing decreases in speech intelligibility under various degraded listening conditions. Research
regarding the causal mechanisms associated with this disparity have had equivocal results.

Noise Plomp and Mimpen (1979) found little correlation between speech reception thresholds (SRTs) in quiet and SRTs in noise. That is, two subjects may have very similar hearing
thresholds for speech in quiet backgrounds but differ dramatically in their ability to understand speech in the presence of noise. Bergman (1980) notes that decrements in speech understanding in the presence of noise occur at much earlier ages than would be expected based
on pure-tone audiograms. Bergman (1980) found decrements occurring as early as age 40.
Jokinen (1973) investigated word recognition as a function of the signal-to-noise (S/N) ratio
and found a consistent decrement for each successive decade of life through the eighth for
stimuli presented for low to moderate S/N conditions. Jokinen also pointed out that the variability of performance (as demonstrated by the standard deviations) increased markedly in
each successive age group. He points out that, as the variability within each group increases,
the representativeness of the group mean score decreases. This variability increases the difficulty of interpreting the effects of aging on auditory phenomena (Working Group, 1988).

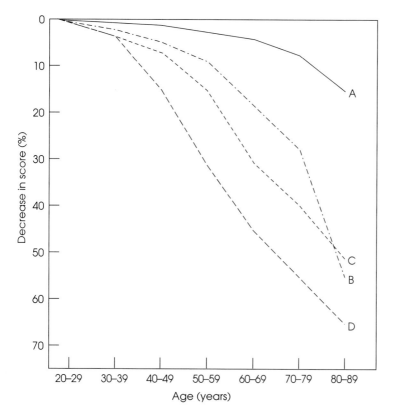

FIGURE 4.12 Curves showing the decrease in percent intelligibility for speech signal in 282 subjects, grouped according to age in years. For each curve, actual scores of the subjects in the 20-to-29-year-old age group served as zero reference. (A) unaltered speech; (B) reverberated speech; (C) overlapping speech (staggered spondaic words); (D) interrupted speech. (*Source:* Bergman, 1971. Reprinted by permission.)

Reverberation Individuals with sensorineural hearing loss and especially presbycusis appear to be disproportionately affected by the auditory distortions of echo-induced reverberation present in most listening situations (Helfer & Wilber, 1990). Nabelek and Robinson (1982) investigated reverberation times of 0.4, 0.8, and 1.2 seconds (representing echo factors for small rooms, medium-size conference rooms, and larger areas such as auditoriums and theaters). Subjects in their forties showed performance decrements as compared to younger subjects even in the shortest reverberation condition. Nabelek and Robinson (1982) suggest that the decrements grow larger with increasing age and increasing reverberation times. Helfer and Wilber (1990) confirm these results. They examined the effects of reverberation and noise on the perception of nonsense syllables in younger normal, hearing-impaired, and older (>60 years) listeners with minimal or mild to moderate sensorineural loss. A strong negative correlation between age and performance in reverberation and noise was found. Further, they found that older hearing-impaired listeners were less accurate than younger hearing-impaired listeners even though the young group had significantly greater hearing loss.

Time-compressed speech Performance on time-compressed or speeded speech has been used to diagnose problems of the central auditory system in younger and older adults (Willott, 1991). However, peripheral impairment also affects perception of time-compressed speech, and thus Willott recommends caution in attributing the poorer performance of older individuals on time-altered speech tests to the central auditory system alone. Most studies investigating the effects of speeded speech have utilized time-compressed speech in order to ensure that spectral characteristics, including fundamental frequency, remain the same throughout all the listening conditions (Working Group, 1988). Research comparing younger and older listeners' intelligibility of time-compressed speech have had equivocal results. Stricht and Gray (1969) report that the use of time-compressed speech decreases intelligibility scores for older persons. That is, the number of errors increases with increases in the words-per-minute rate of presentation. Schmitt and McCroskey (1981) report that 60 percent time compression actually increased sentence recognition. However, these results did not generalize to nursing home populations (McCroskey & Kasten, 1982) nor to measures of paragraph comprehension (Schmitt, 1983). Otto and McCandless (1982) found that young and old subjects matched for pure-tone thresholds did not differ significantly in performance on time-compressed speech intelligibility. Harris, Haines, and Myers (1960) attributed the conflicting results to differences in the frequency at which hearing loss has occurred. They report that sentence recognition for fast speech decreases for younger and older subjects with high-frequency hearing losses (3,000 Hz and above). Decrements also appear to be related to the difficulty of the material and the task (Working Group, 1988). Thus, time compression affects paragraph comprehension more than that of "stand-alone" sentences.

Synthesized speech Synthesized speech as a medium for information exchange is becoming more common in computerized interfaces. Natural speech recognition is aided by the minute variations and intonations present in human speech. The monotonic, nonprosodic tones of synthesized speech present interpretibility problems for persons of all ages, but these interpretibility problems are especially acute for older adults (Olsho, Harkins, & Lenhardt, 1985). If synthesized speech is to be presented to older adults (e.g., for automation of experimental protocol), it is recommended that a digital-to-audio peripheral be used instead of a sequential phoneme-generating device. Recent advances in technology allow high-fidelity, random-access replication of the human voice with inexpensive computer-based peripheral devices (Schieber, 1988).

COMPENSATORY RESEARCH STRATEGIES

The preceding pages have catalogued the major declines in visual and auditory function which accompany advancing age. The purpose of this exposition was to familiarize the cognitive scientist with the sensory-perceptual mechanisms which might contribute to the age-related variance observed in experimental investigations of higher-order behavioral function. Attempts to experimentally identify and explain the age differences in cognitive function must endeavor to control or eliminate sensory-perceptual contributions to group differences in performance. The pages which follow explore the techniques which have been developed to achieve this objective.

Methods of experimentally controlling age-related deficits in sensory functioning can be classified into three major categories. The first of these categories includes subject selection and screening techniques. Another approach is compensating for age-related deficits by providing older adults with some type of sensory aid. The third involves optimizing the stimulus in a manner which minimizes known age-related sensory-perceptual deficits. This approach may include paradigms such as simulating age-related deficits in younger groups or presenting stimuli to older groups at increased intensity levels. Techniques drawn from each approach will be discussed in the following sections.

■ Sensory Screening

Large group differences in visual or auditory acuity levels are capable of introducing insurmountable difficulties into the interpretation of research results. Hence, virtually all laboratory studies of cognition and aging can benefit from the use of preliminary sensory screening devices in the selection of research participants.

Vision The "corrected" visual acuity of most older adults is actually quite good. Figure 4.5 shows that screening older adults for a corrected visual acuity level of 20/25 would yield an average rejection rate of only about 8 percent for subjects in the 65-to-74-year-old group. The 20/25 acuity criterion, which is representative of good visual function, can be achieved at the cost of only modest sampling losses. Simple visual acuity tests can be devised which can be administered at the subject recruiting site, thus accomplishing even greater cost efficiencies. Unfortunately, many studies in the cognitive research literature which have accepted the necessity of visual prescreening have employed extremely loose acuity criteria. The common use of the 20/40 acuity criterion, for example, is not sufficiently stringent to rule out acuity-based explanations of age group differences in most cognitive research paradigms. Of course, standard "distance" acuity assessments do not eliminate age-related losses in the ability to focus on near objects (closer than 20 ft). Strategies for the correction and/or control of such problems stemming from the onset of presbyopia are discussed below.

It has previously been noted that age differences in acuity are exacerbated under conditions of low stimulus luminance and/or contrast. In fact, young and old observers with 20/20 acuity at high luminance levels (e.g., 85 cd/m^2 or higher) may diverge widely if assessed again at low luminance levels (e.g., 1–10 cd/m^2). This point is significant insofar as many commercially available tachistoscopes—commonly used in cognitive research—suffer from great luminance losses due to the use of multiple "beam splitters" that are required to spatially combine the stimuli from multiple channels. Under these circumstances it would appear prudent to conduct one's visual screening at luminance levels approximating those of the stimuli to be employed in the experimental protocol. A similar caveat can be offered for experimental procedures utilizing low-contrast stimuli.

Hearing Depending on the nature of the research question under investigation, a number of audiometric tests may be used for screening subjects. Audiometric tests of pure-tone sensitivity will provide a starting point but, as previously discussed, will be inadequate for predicting speech intelligibility factors. That is, a number of factors unrelated to absolute sensitivity for pure tones contribute to speech-processing problems. These factors include changes in the central auditory pathways, poor attention span, poor auditory memory, and diminished speed of processing (Gordon-Salant, 1987). At present it is difficult to differentiate the information-processing problems associated with age from those associated with the loss of hearing sensitivity alone. In an attempt to address this challenge, a number of different tests of *speech intelligibility* have been used. Typical speech intelligibility test stimuli include nonsense syllables, monosyllabic words, and isolated sentences (Working Group, 1988). Nonsense syllables are thought to reflect acoustic abilities without the influence of semantic variables. Monosyllabic words may be used to represent meaningful speech without the advantage of contextual cues, whereas isolated sentences may be used to more closely represent everyday speech. A commonly used tool for the assessment of speech intelligibility is the Speech Perception in Noise (SPIN) test. The SPIN test has several advantages as an assessment tool. First of all, it incorporates the influences of background noise on speech intelligibility. Additionally, it includes two levels of difficulty by using stimuli of both high and low predictability. The inclusion of the two difficulty levels can aid in separating peripheral hearing loss factors from cognitive influences. The Working Group on Speech Understanding and Aging (1988) points out that a subject's score on any test of speech intelligibility is not necessarily an exact predictor of that person's real-life ability to understand speech. As an adjunct to this form of assessment, a number of tests have been designed to reflect a person's perceived hearing handicap. The Hearing Handicap Inventory for the Elderly (HHIE) was developed by Ventry and Weinstein (1982) for use with noninstitutionalized older adults. Garstecki (1987) compared the results of the HHIE to those achieved with pure-tone audiograms and concluded that approximately 30 percent of aging adults who "pass" a pure-tone screening may report self-perceived hearing difficulties. Twenty to 25 percent of those who fail a hearing screening may not perceive themselves to have any hearing handicap. Given the nature of the HHIE test, it would appear to be a cost-effective means of gaining additional information about auditory information-processing status.

■ Sensory Aids

The potentially confounding influences of sensory-perceptual factors in cognitive aging research can also be minimized through the appropriate application of sensory aids. The two major forms of sensory aids are, of course, refractive eyewear and hearing aids. The majority of older adult observers will benefit from one or both of these manipulations.

Vision Distance visual acuity (i.e., for objects 20 ft or farther away) of older observers recruited for participation in laboratory research usually can be suitably controlled by having them wear their prescription eyeglasses and passing the 20/25 screening criterion described above. A few elderly observers who meet the 20/25 criterion under these conditions could probably have their distance visual acuity improved to nearly 20/20 if they were subsequently refracted in the lab, but 20/25 is acceptable for most cognitive research efforts employing well-designed stimulus materials (see below). Although ensuring adequate levels of distance acuity is a good starting point, the real problem facing most laboratory researchers is the control of near visual acuity (for objects viewed within 10 ft). Due to presbyopic changes in the senescent lens, most older observers will have insufficient accommodative reserve to sharply focus light emanating from near targets. Table 4.2 lists the amount of additional focusing

TABLE 4.2 Additional Power Needed by Normal Eye to Focus upon Near Objects	
Viewing Distance (inches)	**Optical Power Needed to Focus (diopters)**
12	3.3
18	2.2
24	1.6
30	1.3
36	1.1

power which must be applied by the lens when viewing near objects. As targets move closer, additional optical converging power is needed to achieve a focused image upon the retina. In young subjects this additional optical power is provided by accommodation of the lens. Most middle-aged and all older adults lack the ability to increase the optical power of their lenses to accommodate objects viewed within 3 feet. Instead, they must depend upon bifocals or reading glasses. By convention, bifocal lenses add focusing power suitable for reading text at the standard distance of 16 inches (i.e., approximately 0.25–2.5 diopters, depending upon age). To control for age differences in the ability to spatially resolve near visual stimuli, researchers are faced with several alternatives. In one approach, test stimuli are placed at the "standard" reading distance of 16 inches and subjects are required to view the stimuli through their reading glasses or bifocal additions to their prescription eyewear. Several problems accompany this approach. Not all bifocal "adds" to eyewear assume a reading distance of 16 inches. This can be checked by examining the prescription or by empirically measuring the eyeglasses with a lensometer (a device which is not usually available in a psychology laboratory). In addition, few commercially available tachistoscopes have a 16-inch viewing distance. Another problem is the fact that prolonged viewing of CRTs and related "head-up" devices through bifocals is noticeably uncomfortable. Another way of controlling for the effects of presbyopia is to have the subject's vision corrected for the test distance (via in-lab refraction or a special visit to an optometrist) and then implement the refractive correction via clip-on lenses over existing eyewear or using a trial lens set and frame to hold the lens corrections. This approach represents the ideal but is expensive in terms of the cost and expertise needed to implement the refraction. A third, but less effective, technique for controlling presbyopic loss of near visual acuity is to fit observers with plus spherical lenses based upon a formula determined by both viewing distance and age. Observers over the age of 60 would be given the lens powers approximating those listed in Table 4.2. However, those in the 40-to-60-year-old group would require less optical correction due to residual accommodative capacity. Finally, the effects of presbyopia can be avoided altogether by presenting test stimuli in a manner which does not require an accommodative response from the lens. These techniques involve presenting the stimuli at "optical infinity." This can be accomplished either with special optics or by using CRT projection systems to create a display large enough to be viewed at a distance approaching 20 feet.

Hearing The most common method of increasing auditory signal intensity is via a personal hearing aid. Conventional hearing aids convert sound into analog voltages via a microphone transducer located at the entrance to the auditory canal. The analog signal is then filtered and amplified. However, both the environmental noise (including reverberation) and the intended informational signal are amplified. Since the signal-to-noise ratio is typically not improved, hearing aids provide only limited assistance in improving speech intelligibility. Additionally, hearing aids can produce acoustic feedback in the form of a high-pitched squeal which can interfere with the audio recordings used in various experimental protocols. The use of *assistive listening devices* may hold more promise as a sensory remediation strategy in the research laboratory. Unlike personal hearing aids, these devices are connected directly to the target sound source either directly or via microphone. Because the target signal is not transmitted through the ambient environment, amplification of the target sound information can be achieved without concomitant increases in background noise. The result is a dramatic improvement in the signal-to-noise ratio, which often yields significant improvements in speech intelligibility.

■ Stimulus Control

In addition to careful screening of subjects and the use of sensory aids, age differences due to peripheral stimulus attenuation within the sensory-perceptual systems can be mitigated through the manipulation of physical stimulus parameters. Most stimulus optimization strategies deal with enhancing the "effective" stimulus intensity at the site of sensory transduction (i.e., the retina or inner ear) or controlling stimulus configurations which are known to exacerbate age differences in performance (e.g., poor luminance contrast, insufficient letter size and/or spacing, distracting stimulus backgrounds, poor signal-to-noise ratio).

Subjective Stimulus Equivalence

Several studies in the literature have attempted to equate the psychological level of the stimulus being delivered to different age groups by adjusting the intensity of the stimulus (e.g., brightness or loudness) according to each individual's absolute detection threshold. For example, stimulus intensity might be delivered at 2 log units above an individual's previously determined sensory threshold for a given modality. However, the assumptions behind such derived "stimulus equivalence" are difficult to justify, and interpretation of the results obtained under such conditions can become intensely problematic (Schieber et al., 1991). Improved techniques for maximizing stimulus equivalence at the peripheral sensory end organ are discussed below. Another approach assumed to yield a certain level of sensory-perceptual stimulus equivalence across adult age groups involves having experimental observers individually adjust stimulus levels (e.g., brightness, loudness, contrast, frequency spectrum) to their own perceived optimal delivery level. However, this approach is fraught with difficulty. As already noted above, observers with measurable sensory deficits may not be aware of them. In addition, research has demonstrated that observers asked to adjust stimulus intensities to their own "comfort levels" show highly idiosyncratic behavior and often select stimulus levels far removed from the known performance optima (Schieber et al., 1991). True stimulus equivalence remains the Holy Grail (if not red herring) of sensory-perceptual aging research.

Stimulus Augmentation

Potential age differences based upon sensory factors can be minimized by augmenting physical stimuli in a manner which compensates for the known age-related attenuation (or distortion) introduced by the peripheral sensory pathways. These manipulations are, by their nature, highly modality specific.

Vision The primary stimulus manipulation for minimizing the role of age-related sensory changes is the control of retinal illumination levels, that is, equating the amount of light which reaches the retinas of young versus old subjects. As noted above, the retina of the typical 60-year-old receives only about one-third of the light of its 20-year-old counterpart. This difference in retinal illumination can create significant age-related performance decrements for stimuli of low to intermediate brightness levels. Since visual performance—as a function of luminance—tends to asymptote at high luminance levels, one potential way of controlling for light loss in the senescent eye is to present stimuli at luminance intensities high enough to achieve asymptotic levels of retinal illuminance in both younger and older eyes. For example, visual acuity approaches asymptotic levels at 85 cd/m² for young observers (Schieber, 1988). Given the threefold reduction in retinal illuminance of the older eye, age differences in acuity due to light attenuation could be minimized by increasing the stimulus luminance to a level of approximately 200 cd/m² (i.e., 3 × 85 cd/m²). However, this technique is difficult to implement in the behavioral research laboratory since most CRT displays and virtually all tachistoscopes are unable to present stimuli at such high luminance levels. An alternative approach is to employ a factorial experimental design which crosses the levels of the age variable (e.g., young versus old) with two levels of stimulus luminance that are separated by a factor of three (e.g., 20 versus 60 cd/m²). This design enables the investigator to evaluate the potential interactive effects of age and target luminance upon performance. In addition, it provides the experimenter with data cells for implementing an age group comparison under conditions of experimentally equated retinal illumination (i.e., the young at 20 cd/m² versus the old at 60 cd/m²). An example of this approach is depicted in Figure 4.13, which displays the results of Long and Crambert's (1990) study of age differences in dynamic visual acuity (DVA). DVA performance was measured for two age groups (young and old) at two target luminance levels (35 and 105 cd/m², a factor-of-3 difference). Reference to the figure reveals that significant age differences in DVA existed when the age groups were compared at either the low or the high luminance level. However, this age difference in performance disappeared when the retinal illuminances of the groups were experimentally equated by tripling the luminance of stimuli presented to the older observers (i.e., the older, high-luminance versus younger, low-luminance curves). Other techniques for equating retinal illuminance of experimental subjects have recently been introduced. These approaches are based upon making individual assessments of optical density and using the results to determine the luminance intensity of the experimental stimuli (Sample, Esterson, Weinreb, & Boynton, 1988; Savage, Haegerstrom-Portnoy, Adams, & Hewlett, 1993).

Both sensory and perceptual factors combine to set the limits on letter size in textual materials used for cognitive aging research. A clear research consensus indicates that opti-

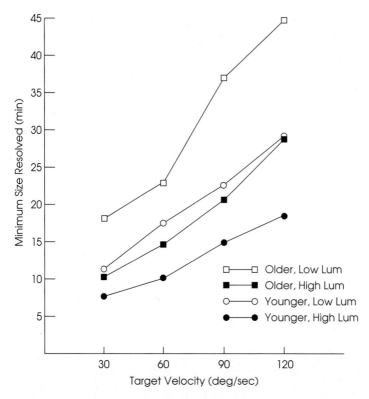

FIGURE 4.13 Dynamic visual acuity (expressed in minutes of arc) as a function of age and luninance. (*Source:* Long & Crambert, 1990. Copyright © 1990 by the American Psychological Association. Reprinted by permission.)

mal reading efficiency is achieved for text character heights of 10 to 12 points (1 point = 1/72 inch) (J. E. Kaufman & Haynes, 1981; Poulton, 1972; Tinker, 1963). A 12-point character viewed at a distance of 16 inches will subtend 0.6 degrees (36 minarc) of visual angle. This represents a seven-fold increase in size above the acuity threshold, assuming a 20/25 acuity screening criterion. Akutsu, Legge, Ross, and Schuebel (1991) found that older subjects meeting this acuity criterion can read as efficiently as young adults for text character heights ranging from 0.3 to 1.0 degree. However, age-related decrements emerged when either smaller or larger character sizes were employed. Taken together, these findings suggest that studies using older adults with acuities of 20/25 or better should employ reading materials with print no smaller than 12 points in height but no taller than 22 points, assuming a standard 16-inch viewing distance. Equivalent character sizes required for other test distances appear in Table 4.3. Investigators utilizing text stimuli must also be careful about potential "crowding" effects. That is, there is some evidence that the reading efficiency of older adults may be compromised when text materials are spaced too closely together (Cerella, 1985; Garzia & Trick, 1992). Older adults can also be systematically disadvantaged when low-contrast stimuli are employed. Fortunately, the stimulus formats and media typically

TABLE 4.3 Recommended Character Size for Text Stimuli		
Viewing Distance (inches)	Minimum Height (points)	Maximum Height (points)
12	9	16
18	14	25
24	18	33
30	22	41
36	27	49

used in cognitive aging research are characterized by high luminance contrast (i.e., 70–90%). The most common exception arises in the case of LCD display panels in laptop computer systems. The contrast of text characters on many LCD display panels (especially the "passive" matrix variety) can be low enough to introduce systematic differences in visibility across adult age groups.

Hearing Due to the concomitant hearing loss associated with increased age and increased variability in speech intelligibility scores, older people can be expected to have trouble understanding conversational speech at normal intensities. Increasing stimulus presentation levels is a very basic compensatory strategy. Listeners with presbycusis do not attain their maximum word recognition scores until the speech reaches a level of about 50 dB (rather than the usual 30–40 dB) above their sentence reception thresholds (SRTs) (Kasden, 1970). Speech understanding difficulties will be exacerbated by adverse listening conditions such as noise and reverberation. Plomp and Mimpen (1979) suggest that, if a room is to be used by older subjects, background noise should be 5 to 10 dB lower than would be necessary for normally hearing younger subjects. Soft, porous, absorptive materials (such as carpeting, curtains, and ceiling tiles) over hard surfaces help to reduce both background noise and reverberation.

Stimulus Configuration

There are several stimulus configuration dimensions which have been demonstrated to yield information-processing deficits among older adults. These configuration difficulties include factors such as the temporal presentation rate of stimuli, the potential "distracting" nature of the stimulus background, and problems regarding the spatially extended text arrays used in visual search paradigms. For example, research indicates that age differences in speech intelligibility can be reduced by the selection of optimal stimulus presentation rates or temporal expansion of consonant presentation times. Another potential stimulus-timing problem occurs in the visual domain. Brief stimulus presentation intervals are often used to eliminate the possibility of eye movements across the display. Many cases in the cognitive research literature have employed stimulus durations in the range of 200–250 msec to implement such controls. However, the findings reviewed above indicate that, while the saccadic latencies of older adults are longer than 250 msec, in many cases those of younger subjects are significantly shorter. This means that stimulus exposure times in the 200-to-250-msec range may afford young observers with an opportunity to make multiple glances across the visual scene while completely preventing older observers' doing so. This suggests that exposure durations in experiments comparing young and old should be maintained below the 200-msec level. This represents a special challenge given the assumption of a generalized age-related slowing in the rate of information processing.

Numerous studies have demonstrated that complex backgrounds appear to handicap the identification of foreground targets in older adults. The deleterious effects of such background "distractors" have been noted in both the visual (e.g., dynamic visual acuity, useful field of view) and auditory (e.g., problems with background noise) domains. Unless these effects are of specific interest to the experimenter, stimulus background conditions must be carefully selected and controlled.

Finally, many visual search tasks and related experimental paradigms utilize briefly presented text arrays which extend beyond the foveal vision into the near periphery. As noted above, there appear to be sensory-perceptual limits for peripheral stimuli which emerge in late life. In order to separate these effects from possible attentional and/or cognitive mechanisms of age-related changes in visual search performance, it may be necessary to increase the size of the letters in the text array as they diverge from the center of foveal vision. A formula for accomplishing such a scaling scheme was presented earlier (Anstis, 1974).

Simulation

A final form of experimental control involves presenting filtered or distorted stimuli to younger persons in a manner designed to simulate the predicted sensory deficit of older persons. Examples of this approach are common in the vision research literature. For example, Owsley et al. (1983) found significant age differences in contrast sensitivity. As a follow-up, they employed a special control group of young observers who viewed the experimental stimuli through a filter which reduced brightness by a factor of 3, thus mimicking the expected age-related reduction in retinal illuminance. The performance of this "simulated optical aging" group did not differ from that of the other young observers who did not experience stimulus attenuation. This pattern of results was taken as evidence that age differences in contrast sensitivity are not mediated by peripheral attenuation of light and hence appear to be due to changes in the central nervous system. Using a similar simulation strategy, Schieber et al. (1990) found that introducing refractive error (through the use of "plus" lenses) in a group of young observers failed to alter their motion sensitivity thresholds. This result supported their contention that age deficits observed using the same paradigm could not be explained on the basis of age differences in the optical properties of the eye and hence must be attributable to higher-level neural mechanisms.

Although often quite useful, the simulation method is problematic for a number of reasons. First of all, it is often quite difficult to predict the exact nature of the older group's sensory deficit, especially in the auditory domain. This difficulty is increased by the high degree of variability present in the older population. Secondly, research has shown that young adults presented with stimuli under simulated sensory deficits may show greater performance decrements than older persons with naturally occurring deficits do (Lacroix & Harris, 1979);

older adults most likely have the advantage of *compensatory strategies* developed through years of experience with a particular deficit, a phenomenon of notable research interest in its own right.

CONCLUDING REMARKS

This chapter has sounded a general warning to cognitive psychologists, namely, that they must consider the possibility that age differences in performance on complex tasks may be mediated by age-related sensory changes as well as attentional and/or cognitive mechanisms. A recent study reported by Lindenberger and Baltes (1994) appears to reinforce these concerns. They found that visual acuity and pure-tone auditory thresholds, taken together, accounted for 49.2 percent of the total and 93.1 percent of the age-related variance on a comprehensive battery of crystallized and fluid intelligence tests among 156 participants aged 70 to 103. However, closer analysis of the statistical relationship between these sensory-versus-cognitive factors revealed an intriguing possibility. Structural equation modeling provided evidence that "the assessment of visual and auditory acuity is 'transformed' into a task of cognitive functioning" in the oldest-old (p. 352). That is, cognitive/attentional capacity may become so diminished in very late adulthood that these resources (or lack of them) begin to become the limiting factor in the assessment of sensory function. Hence, our analysis has come full circle. The sensory psychologists have sounded the warning to the cognitive psychologists, who, in turn, have returned the favor regarding the emergence of top-down influences in the assessment of sensory functioning among the oldest individuals.

SUPPLEMENTAL READINGS

Schieber, F., Fozard, J. L., Gordon-Salant, S., & Weiffenbach, J. (1991). Optimizing the sensory-perceptual environment of older adults. *International Journal of Industrial Ergonomics, 7,* 133–162.

Willott, J. F. (1991). *Aging and the Auditory System: Anatomy, Physiology, and Psychophysics.* San Diego: Singular.

Working Group on Speech Understanding and Aging (1988). Speech understanding and aging. *Journal of the Acoustical Society of America, 83*(3), 859–893.

REFERENCES

Abel, L. A., Troost, B. T., & Dell'Osso, L. F. (1983). The effects of age on normal saccadic characteristics and their variability. *Vision Research, 23,* 33–37.

Abel, S. M., Krever, E. M., & Alberti, P. W. (1990). Auditory detection, discrimination and speech processing in ageing, noise-sensitive and hearing-impaired listeners. *Scandinavian Audiology, 19,* 43–54.

Adams, A. J., Wong, L. S., Wong, L., & Gould, B. (1988). Visual acuity changes with age: Some new perspectives. *American Journal of Optometry and Physiological Optics, 65,* 403–406.

Adler, F. H. (1933). *Clinical physiology of the eye.* New York: Macmillan.

Akutsu, H., Legge, G. E., Ross, J. A., & Schuebel, K. J. (1991). Psychophysics of reading. X: Effects of age-related changes in vision. *Journals of Gerontology: Psychological Sciences, 46,* P325–P331.

Anstis, S. M. (1974). A chart demonstrating variations in acuity with retinal position. *Vision Research, 14,* 589–592.

Ball, K., Beard, B. L., Roenker, D. L., Miller, R. L., & Griggs, D. S. (1988). Age and visual search: Expanding the useful field of view. *Journal of the Optical Society of America: A, 5,* 2210–2219.

Belal, A. (1975). Presbycusis: Physiological or pathological. *Journal of Laryngology, 89,* 1011–1025.

Bergman, M. (1971). Hearing and aging. *Audiology, 10,* 164–171.

Bergman, M. (1980). *Aging and the perception of speech.* Baltimore: University Park Press.

Braddick, O., Campbell, F. W., & Atkinson, J. (1978). Channels in vision: Basic aspects. In R. Held, H. W. Leibowitz, and H. Teuber (Eds.), *Perception* (pp. 3–38). Berlin: Springer.

Brandt, L. J., & Fozard, J. L. (1990). Age-changes in pure-tone hearing thresholds in a longitudinal study of normal human aging. *Journal of the Acoustical Society of America, 88,* 813–820.

Brown, B., & Bowman, K. J. (1987). Sensitivity to changes in size and velocity in young and elderly observers. *Perception, 16,* 41–47.

Brozek, J., & Keys, A. (1945). Changes in flicker-fusion frequency with age. *Journal of Consulting Psychology, 9,* 87–90.

Buckingham, T., Whitaker, D., & Banford, D. (1987). Movement in decline? Oscillatory movement displacement thresholds increase with age. *Ophthalmic and Physiological Optics, 7,* 411–413.

Burg, A. (1967). *The relationship between vision test scores and driving record: General findings.* Los Angeles: Institute of Transportation and Traffic Engineering, University of California.

Burton, K. B., Owsley, C., and Sloane, M. E. (1993). Aging and neural spatial contrast sensitivity: Photopic vision. *Vision Research, 33,* 939–946.

Carter, J. E., Obler, L., Woodward, S., & Albert, M. L. (1983). The effect of increasing age on the latency for saccadic eye movements. *Journal of Gerontology, 38,* 318–320.

Cerella, J. (1985). Age-related decline in extra-foveal letter perception. *Journal of Gerontology, 40,* 727–736.

Chamberlain, W. (1971). Restriction of upward gaze with advancing age. *American Journal of Ophthalmology, 71,* 341–346.

Cody, P. S., Hurd, P. D., & Bootman, J. L. (1990). The effects of aging and diabetes on the perception of medication color. *Journal of Geriatric Drug Therapy, 4,* 113–121.

Collin, H. B., Han, C., & Kohr, P. C. (1988). Age changes in the visual field using the Humphrey Field Analyzer. *Clinical and Experimental Optometry, 71,* 174–178.

Collins, M. J., Brown, B., & Bowman, K. J. (1989). Peripheral visual acuity and age. *Ophthalmic and Physiological Optics, 9,* 314–316.

Corso, J. F. (1963). Aging and auditory thresholds in men and women. *Archives of Environmental Health, 6,* 350–356.

Corso, J. F. (1981). *Aging, sensory systems and perception.* New York: Praeger.

Crassini, B., Brown, B., & Bowman, K. (1988). Age related changes in contrast sensitivity in central and peripheral retina. *Perception, 17,* 315–332.

Curcio, C. A., & Drucker, D. N. (1993). Retinal ganglion cells in Alzheimer's disease and aging. *Annals of Neurology, 33,* 248–257.

Curcio, C. A., Millican, C. L., Allen, K. A., & Kalina, R. E. (1993). Aging of the human photoreceptor mosaic: Evidence for selective vulnerability of rods in central vision. *Investigative Ophthalmology and Visual Science, 34,* 3278–3296.

Dalderup, L. M., & Fredericks, M. L. C. (1969). Color sensitivity in old age. *Journal of the American Geriatrics Society, 17,* 388–390.

Desmond, A. F. (1970). Otosclerosis, an analysis of 1698 operations. *Indian Journal of Otolaryngology, 22,* 11–23.

Devaney, K. O., & Johnson, H. A. (1980). Neuron loss in the aging visual cortex of man. *Journal of Gerontology, 35,* 836–841.

Duke-Elder, W. S. (1949). *Textbook of ophthalmology.* St. Louis: Mosby.

Eisner, A., Fleming, S. A., Klein, M. L., & Mauldin, M. (1987). Sensitivities in older eyes with good acuity: Cross-sectional norms. *Investigative Ophthalmology and Visual Science, 28,* 1824–1831.

Elliott, D., Whitaker, D., & MacVeigh, D. (1990). Neural contribution to spatiotemporal contrast sensitivity decline in healthy ageing eyes. *Vision Research, 30,* 541–547.

Elliott, D. B. (1987). Contrast sensitivity decline with aging: A neural or optical phenomenon? *Ophthalmic and Physiological Optics, 7,* 415–419.

Etholm, B., & Belal, A., Jr. (1974). Senile changes in the middle ear joints. *Annals of Otology, Rhinology and Laryngology, 83,* 49–64.

Evans, D. W., & Ginsburg, A. P. (1985). Contrast sensitivity predicts age differences in highway sign discriminability. *Human Factors, 23,* 59–64.

Farrimond, T. (1967). Visual and auditory performance variations with age: Some implications. *Australian Journal of Psychology, 19,* 193–201.

Fozard, J. L. (1990). Vision and hearing in aging. In J. E. Birren and K. W. Schiae (Eds.), *Handbook of the psychology of aging* (3d ed., pp. 150–170). New York: Academic Press.

Frisen, L., & Frisen, M. (1981). How good is normal acuity? A study of letter acuity threshold as a function of age. *Graefes Archives of Ophthalmology, 215,* 149–157.

Gao, H., & Hollyfield, J. G. (1992). Aging of the human retina—differential loss of neurons and retinal pigment epithelial cells. *Investigative Ophthalmology and Visual Science, 33,* 1–17.

Garstecki, D. C. (1987). Self-perceived hearing difficulty in aging adults with acquired hearing loss. *Journal of the Academy of Rehabilitative Audiology, 20,* 49–60.

Garzia, R. P., & Trick, L. R. (1992). Vision in the 90's: The aging eye. *Journal of Optometric Vision Development, 23,* 4–41.

Geldard, F. (1972). *The human senses* (2d ed.). New York: Wiley.

Gelfand, S. A., Piper, N., & Silman, S. (1985). Consonant recognition in quiet as a function of aging among normal hearing subjects. *Journal of the Acoustical Society of America, 78*(4), 1198–1206.

Gilbert, J. G. (1957). Age changes in color matching. *Journal of Gerontology, 12,* 210–215.

Gilmore, G. C., Wenk, H. E., Naylor, L. A., & Stuve, T. A. (1992). Motion perception and aging. *Psychology and Aging, 7,* 654–660.

Ginsburg, A. P., Evans, D., Sekuler, R., & Harp, S. (1982). Contrast sensitivity predicts pilots' performance in aircraft simulators. *American Journal of Optometry and Physiological Optics, 59,* 105–109.

Gittings, N. S., & Fozard, J. L. (1986). Age-related changes in visual acuity. *Experimental Gerontology, 21,* 423–433.

Gordon-Salant, S. (1986). Recognition of natural and time/intensity altered CVs by young and elderly subjects with normal hearing. *Journal of the Acoustical Society of America, 80*(6), 1599–1607.

Gordon-Salant, S. (1987). Age-related differences in speech recognition performance as a function of test format and paradigm. *Ear and Hearing, 8,* 277–282.

Guelke, R. W. (1987). Consonant burst enhancement: A possible means to improve intelligibility for the hard of hearing. *Journal of Rehabilitation Research and Development, 24*(4), 217–220.

Gundersen, T. (1973). Sensorineural hearing loss in otosclerosis. *Scandinavian Audiology, 2,* 43–51.

Harris, J. D., Haines, H. L., & Meyers, C. K. (1960). The importance of hearing at 3 kc for understanding speeded speech. *Laryngoscope, 70,* 131–146.

Haug, H., Kuhl, S., Mecke, E., Sass, N. L., & Wassner, K. (1984). The significance of morphometric procedures in the investigation of age changes in cytoarchitectonic structures of human brain. *Journal für Hirnforschung, 25,* 353–374.

Helfer, K. S., & Wilber, L. A. (1990). Hearing loss, aging, and speech perception in reverberation and noise. *Journal of Speech and Hearing Research, 33,* 149–155.

Hills, B. (1975). *Some studies of movement perception, age and accidents* (report 137). Crowethorne, U.K.: Transport and Road Research Laboratory.

Hills, B. (1980). Vision, visibility and perception in driving. *Perception, 9,* 183–216.

Hofstetter, H. W. (1965). A longitudinal study of amplitude changes in presbyopia. *American Journal of Optometry, 42,* 3–8.

Hotson, J. R., & Steinke, G. W. (1988). Vertical and horizontal saccades in aging and dementia. *Neuro-ophthalmology, 8,* 267–273.

Huaman, A. G., & Sharpe, J. A. (1993). Vertical saccades in senescence. *Investigative Ophthalmology and Visual Science, 34,* 2588–2595.

Huntington, J. M., & Simonson, E. (1965). Critical flicker fusion frequency as a function of exposure time in two different age groups. *Journal of Gerontology, 20,* 527–529.

Hutton, J. T., Nagel, J. A., & Lowenson, R. B. (1983). Variables affecting eye tracking performance. *Electroencephalography and Clinical Neurophysiology, 56,* 414–419.

Jaffe, G. J., Alvarado, J. A., & Juster, R. P. (1986). Age-related changes of the normal visual field. *Archives of Ophthalmology, 104,* 1021–1025.

Jerger, J. (1973). Audiological findings in aging. *Advances in Otorhinolaryngology, 20,* 115–124.

Johnson, B., Miao, M., & Sadun, A. A. (1987). Age-related decline of optic nerve axon populations. *Age, 10,* 5.

Jokinen, K. (1973). Presbycusis. VI: Masking of speech. *Acta Oto-laryngologica, 76,* 426–430.

Kahn, H. A., Leibowitz, H. W., Ganley, S. P., Kini, M. M., Colton, J., Nickerson, R. S., and Dawber, T. R. (1977) Framingham Eye Study. I: Outlines and major prevalences and findings. *American Journal of Epidemiology, 106,* 17–32.

Kasden, S. D. (1970). Speech discrimination in two age groups matched for hearing loss. *Journal of Audiometric Research, 10,* 210–211.

Kaufman, J. E., & Haynes, H. (Eds.) (1981). *IES lighting handbook (application volume).* New York: Illumination Engineering Society.

Kaufman, S. R., & Abel, L. A. (1986). The effects of distraction on smooth pursuit in normal subjects. *Acta Otolaryngologica, 102,* 57–64.

Klein, R., Klein, B. E. K., & Linton, K. L. P. (1991). The Beaver Dam Eye Study: Visual acuity. *Ophthalmology, 98,* 1310–1315.

Kline, D. W. & Birren, J. E. (1975). Age differences in backward dichoptic masking. *Experimental Aging Research, 1,* 17–25.

Kline, D. W., & Orme-Rogers, C. (1978). Examination of stimulus persistence as the basis for superior visual identification performance among older adults. *Journal of Gerontology, 33,* 76–81.

Kline, D. W., & Schieber, F. (1980). What are the age differences in visual sensory memory? *Journal of Gerontology, 36,* 86–89.

Kline, D. W., & Schieber, F. (1985). Vision and aging. In J. E. Birren and K. W. Schaie (Eds.), *Handbook of the psychology of aging* (pp. 296–331). New York: Van Nostrand Reinhold.

Kline, D. W., Schieber, F., Abusaura, L. C., & Coyne, A. C. (1983). Age and the visual channels: Contrast sensitivity and response speed. *Journal of Gerontology, 38,* 211–216.

Kline, T. J., Ghali, L. A., Kline, D. W., & Brown, S. (1990). Visibility distance of highway signs among young, middle-aged and older observers: Icons are better than text. *Human Factors, 32,* 609–619.

Knoblauch, K., Saunders, F., Kusuda, M., Hynes, R., Podgor, M., Higgins, K. E., & de Monasterio, F. M. (1987). Age and illuminance effects in Farnsworth-Munsell 100-Hue Test. *Applied Optics, 26,* 1441–1448.

Konig, E. (1957). Pitch discrimination and age. *Acta Oto-Laryngologica, 48,* 475–489.

Kosnik, W., Kline, D. W., Fikre, J., & Sekuler, R. (1987). Ocular fixation control as a function of age and exposure duration. *Psychology and Aging, 2,* 302–305.

Kryter, K. D. (1983). Presbycusis, sociocusis, and nosocusis. *Journal of the Acoustical Society of America, 73,* 1897–1917.

Lacroix, P. G., & Harris, J. D. (1979). Effects of high-frequency cue reduction on the comprehension of distorted speech. *Journal of Speech and Hearing Disorders, 44,* 259–269.

Lakowski, R. (1958). Age and color vision. *Advances in Science, 15,* 231–236.

Leuba, G., & Garey, L. J. (1987). Evolution of neuronal numerical density in the developing and aging human cortex. *Human Neurobiology, 6,* 11–18.

Levine, M. W., & Shefner, J. M. (1991). *Fundamentals of sensation and perception* (2d ed.). Pacific Grove, CA: Brooks-Cole.

Lindenberger, U., & Baltes, P. B. (1994). Sensory functioning and intelligence in old age: A strong connection. *Psychology and Aging, 9,* 339–355.

Long, G. M., & Crambert, R. F. (1990). The nature and basis of age-related changes in dynamic visual acuity. *Psychology and Aging, 5,* 138–143.

Lowenfeld, I. E. (1979). Pupillary changes related to age. In H. S. Thompson (Ed.), *Topics in neuro-ophthalmology* (pp. 124–150). Baltimore: Williams and Wilkins.

Maffei, L. (1978). Spatial frequency channels: Neural mechanisms. In R. Held, H. W. Leibowitz, & H. Teuber (Eds.), *Perception* (pp. 39–66). Berlin: Springer.

Marmor, M. F. (1982). Aging and the retina. In R. Sekuler, D. W. Kline, & K. Dismukes (Eds.), *Aging and human visual function* (pp. 59–78). New York: Liss.

Marshall, J., Grindle, J., Ansell, P. L., & Borwein, B. (1980). Convolution in human rods: An aging process. *British Journal of Ophthalmology, 63,* 181–187.

Mayer, M. J., Kim, C. B. Y., Svingos, A., & Glucs, A. (1988). Foveal flicker sensitivity in healthy aging eyes. I: Compensating for pupil variation. *Journal of the Optical Society of America: A, 5,* 2201–2209.

McCroskey, R. L., & Kasten, R. N. (1982). Temporal factors and the aging auditory system. *Ear and Hearing, 3,* 124–127.

McFarland, R. A., Warren, B., & Karis, C. (1958). Alterations in critical flicker frequency as a function of age and light: Dark ratio. *Journal of Experimental Psychology, 56,* 529–538.

Misiak, H. (1947). Age and sex differences in critical flicker frequency. *Journal of Experimental Psychology, 37,* 318–332.

Morrison, J. D., and McGrath, C. (1985). Assessment of optical contributions to the age-related deterioration in vision. *Quarterly Journal of Experimental Psychology, 70,* 249–269.

Morrison, T. R. (1980). *A review of dynamic visual acuity* (NAMRL monograph 28). Pensacola, FL: Naval Aerospace Medical Research Laboratory.

Moscicki, E. K., Elkins, E. F., Baum, H. F., & McNamara, P. M. (1985). Hearing loss in the elderly: An epidemiologic study of the Framingham Heart Study cohort. *Ear and Hearing, 6,* 184–190.

Murphy, B. J. (1978). Pattern thresholds for moving and stationary gratings during smooth eye movements. *Vision Research, 18,* 521–530.

Nabelek, A. K., & Robinson, P. K. (1982). Monaural and binaural speech perception in reverberation for listeners of various ages. *Journal of the Acoustical Society of America, 71,* 1242–1248.

Olsho, L. W., Harkins, S. W., & Lenhardt, M. L. (1985). Aging and the auditory system. In J. E. Birren & K. W. Schaie (Eds.), *Handbook of the psychology of aging* (2d ed., pp. 332–377). New York: Van Nostrand Reinhold.

Olzak, L. A., & Thomas, J. P. (1985). Seeing spatial patterns. In K. R. Boff, L. Kaufman, & J. P. Thomas (Eds.), *Handbook of perception and human performance* (vol. 7, pp. 1–56). New York: Wiley.

Otto, W. C., & McCandless, G. A. (1982). Aging and auditory site of lesion. *Ear and Hearing, 3,* 110–117.

Owsley, C., Gardner, T., Sekuler, R., & Lieberman, H. (1985). The role of the crystalline lens in the spatial vision loss of the elderly. *Investigative Ophthalmology and Visual Science, 26,* 1165–1170.

Owsley, C., Sekuler, R., & Siemsen, D. (1983). Contrast sensitivity throughout adulthood. *Vision Research, 23,* 689–699.

Owsley, C., & Sloane, M. E. (1987). Contrast sensitivity, acuity and the perception of real-world targets. *British Journal of Ophthalmology, 71,* 791–796.

Owsley, C., & Sloane, M. E. (1990). Vision and aging. In F. Boller and J. Grafman (Eds.), *Handbook of neuropsychology* (vol. 4, pp. 299–249). Amsterdam: Elsevier.

Pitt, M. C., & Rawles, J. M. (1988). The effect of age on saccadic latency and velocity. *Neuro-ophthalmology, 8,* 123–129.

Pitts, D. G. (1982). The effects of aging upon selected visual functions: Dark adaptation, visual acuity, stereopsis and brightness contrast. In R. Sekuler, D. W. Kline, & K. Dismukes (Eds.), *Aging and human visual function* (pp. 131–160). New York: Liss.

Plomp, R., & Mimpen, A. M. (1979). Speech reception threshold for sentences as a function of age and noise level. *Journal of the Acoustical Society of America, 66,* 1333–1342.

Poulton, E. C. (1972). Size, style, and vertical spacing in the legibility of small typefaces. *Journal of Applied Psychology, 56,* 156–161.

Rabbitt, P. (1991). Management of the working population. *Ergonomics, 34*(6), 775–790.

Reading, V. M. (1972). Visual resolution as measured by dynamic and static tests. *Pfluegers Archives, 333,* 17–26.

Richards, O. W. (1977). Effects of luminance and contrast on visual acuity, ages 16 to 90 years. *American Journal of Optometry and Physiological Optics, 54,* 178–184.

Richards, S. (1971). Deafness in the elderly. *Gerontologia Clinica, 13,* 350–358.

Roberts, J., & Rowland, M. (1978). *Refraction status and motility defects of persons 4–74 years.* Hyattsville, MD: U.S. Department of Health, Education and Welfare.

Said, F. S., & Weale, R. A. (1959). The variation with age of the spectral transmissivity of the living human crystalline lens. *Gerontologia, 3,* 213–231.

Sample, P. A., Esterson, F. D., Weinreb, R. N., & Boynton, R. M. (1988). The aging lens: *In vivo* assessment of light absorption in 84 human eyes. *Investigative Ophthalmology and Visual Science, 29,* 1306–1311.

Sanders, M. S., & McCormick, E. J. (1987). *Human factors in engineering and design.* New York: McGraw-Hill.

Savage, G. L., Haegerstrom-Portnoy, G., Adams, A. J., & Hewlett, S. E. (1993). Age changes in the optical density of human ocular media. *Clinical Vision Science, 8,* 97–108.

Schieber, F. (1988). Vision assessment technology and screening of older drivers: Past practices and emerging techniques. In National Research Council, *Transportation in an aging society: Improving mobility and safety of older persons* (special report no. 218, vol. 2, pp. 325–378). Washington, DC: Transportation Research Board.

Schieber, F. (1992). Aging and the senses. In J. E. Birren, R. B. Sloan, & G. Cohen (Eds.), *Handbook of mental health and aging* (pp. 251–306). New York: Academic Press.

Schieber, F., Fozard, J. L., Gordon-Salant, S., & Weiffenbach, J. (1991). Optimizing the sensory-perceptual environment of older adults. *International Journal of Industrial Ergonomics, 7,* 133–162.

Schieber, F., Hiris, E., Brannan, J., & Williams, M. J. (1990). Assessing age differences in motion perception using simple oscillatory displacement versus random dot cinematography. *Investigative Ophthalmology and Visual Science, 31,* 355.

Schieber, F., Kline, D. W., Kline, T. J. B., & Fozard, J. L. (1992). *Contrast sensitivity and the visual problems of older drivers* (SAE technical paper no. 920613). Warrendale, PA: Society of Automotive Engineers.

Schiff, W., Oldak, R., & Shah, V. (1992). Aging persons' estimate of vehicular motion. *Psychology and Aging, 7,* 518–525.

Schmitt, J. F. (1983). The effects of time compression and expansion on passage comprehension by elderly listeners. *Journal of Speech and Hearing Research, 26,* 373–377.

Schmitt, J. F., & McCroskey, R. L. (1981). Sentence comprehension in elderly listeners: The factor of rate. *Journal of Gerontology, 36,* 441–445.

Schow, R., Christensen, J., Hutchinson, J., & Nerbonne, M. (1978). *Communication disorders of the aged: A guide for health professions.* Baltimore: University Park Press.

Schuknecht, H. F., & Igarashi, M. (1964). Pathology of slow progressive sensori-neural deafness. *Transactions of the American Academy of Ophthalmology and Otolaryngology, 68,* 222–224.

Scialfa, C. T., Garvey, P. M., Tyrell, R. A., & Leibowitz, H. W. (1989). Age differences in dynamic contrast sensitivity. *Investigative Ophthalmology and Visual Science, 30* (suppl.), 406.

Scialfa, C. T., Kline, D. W., & Lyman, B. J. (1987). Age differences in target indentification as a function of retinal location and noise level: An examination of the useful field of view. *Psychology and Aging, 2,* 14–19.

Scialfa, C. T., Kline, D. W., Lyman, B. J., & Kosnik, W. (1987). Age differences in judgments of vehicle velocity and distance. *Proceedings of the Human Factors Society 31st Annual Meeting* (pp. 558–561).

Sekuler, R., & Ball, K. (1986). Visual localization: Age and practice. *Journal of the Optical Society of America: A, 3,* 864–867.

Sekuler, R., & Blake, R. (1994). *Perception* (3d ed.). New York: McGraw-Hill.

Sharp, J. A., & Sylvester, T. O. (1978). Effects of age on horizontal smooth pursuit. *Investigative Ophthalmology and Visual Science, 17,* 465–468.

Shinar, D. (1977). *Driver visual limitations: Diagnosis and treatment* (Department of Transportation contract DOT-HS-5-1275). Bloomington: Institute for Research in Public Safety, Indiana University.

Sloane, M. E., Owsley, C., & Alvarez, S. L. (1988). Aging, senile miosis and spatial contrast sensitivity at low luminances. *Vision Research, 28,* 1235–1246.

Spear, P. D. (1993). Neural basis of visual deficits during aging. *Vision Research, 33,* 2589–2609.

Sperduto, R. D., & Siegel, D. (1980). Senile lens and senile macular changes in a population-based sample. *American Journal of Ophthalmology, 90,* 86–91.

Spooner, J. W., Sakala, S. M., & Baloh, R. W. (1980). Effects of aging on eye tracking. *Archives of Neurology, 37,* 575–576.

Stelmachowicz, P. G., Beauchaine, K. A., Kalberer, A., & Jesteadt, W. (1989). Normative thresholds in the 8-to 20-kHz range as a function of age. *Journal of the Acoustical Society of America, 86,* 1384–1391.

Stricht, R., & Gray, B. (1969). The intelligibility of time compressed words as a function of age and hearing loss. *Journal of Speech and Hearing Research, 12,* 443–448.

Sturr, J. F., Kline, G. E., & Taub, H. A. (1990) Performance of young and older drivers on a static acuity test under photopic and mesopic luminance conditions. *Human Factors, 32,* 1–8.

Taub, H. A., & Sturr, J. F. (1991). The effects of age and ocular health on letter contrast sensitivity as a function of luminance. *Clinical Vision Science, 6,* 181–189.

Theodore, F. H. (1975). External eye problems in the elderly. *Geriatrics, 30,* 69–80.

Tinker, M. A. (1963). *Legibility of print.* Ames: Iowa State Univ. Press.

Treisman, A., & Gormican, S. (1988). Feature analysis in early vision: Evidence from search asymmetries. *Psychological Review, 95,* 15–48.

Trick, G., & Silverman, S. E. (1991). Visual sensitivity to motion: Age-related changes and deficits in senile dementia of the Alzheimer's type. *Neurology, 41,* 1437–1440.

Ventry, I., & Weinstein, B. (1982). The hearing handicap inventory for the elderly: A new tool. *Ear and Hearing, 3,* 128–134.

Vola, J. L., Cornu, L., Carruel, C., Gastaud, P., & Leid, J. (1983). L'âge et les acuités visuelles photopiques et mésopiques (High and low luminance visual acuity in relation to age). *Journal Français d'Ophtalmologie, 6,* 473–479.

Walsh, D. A. (1976). Age differences in central perceptual processing: A dichoptic backward masking investigation. *Journal of Gerontology, 31,* 178–185.

Warabi, T., Kase, M., & Kato, T. (1984). Effect of aging on the accuracy of visually guided saccadic eye movements. *Annals of Neurology, 16,* 449–454.

Watamaniuk, S. N. (1992). Temporal and spatial integration in random-dot stimuli. *Vision Research, 32,* 2341–2347.

Watson, A. B., Barlow, H. B., & Robson, J. G. (1983). What does the eye see best? *Nature, 302,* 419–422.

Weale, R. A. (1961). Retinal illumination and age. *Transactions of the Illuminating Engineering Society, 26,* 95–100.

Weale, R. A. (1963). *The ageing eye.* London: Lewis.

Weekers, R., & Roussel, F. (1945). Introduction à l'étude de la fréquence de fusion en clinique. *Ophthalmologica, 112,* 305–319.

Whitaker, D., & Elliott, D. (1989). Toward establishing a clinical displacement threshold technique to evaluate visual function behind cataract. *Clinical Vision Science, 4,* 61–69.

Whitaker, L. S., Shoptaugh, C. F., & Haywood, K. M. (1986). Effect of age on horizontal eye movement latency. *American Journal of Optometry and Physiological Optics, 63,* 152–155.

Willott, J. F. (1991). *Aging and the auditory system: Anatomy, physiology, and psychophysics.* San Diego: Singular.

Wolf, E., & Shaffra, A. M. (1964). Relationship between critical flicker frequency and age in flicker perimetry. *Archives of Ophthalmology, 72,* 832–843.

Working Group on Speech Understanding and Aging (1988). Speech understanding and aging. *Journal of the Acoustical Society of America, 83*(3), 859–893.

Wright, C. E., & Drasdo, N. (1985). The influence of age on the spatial and temporal contrast sensitivity function. *Documenta Ophthalmologica, 59,* 385–395.

Youdelis, C., & Hendrickson, A. (1986). A qualitative and quantitative analysis of the human fovea during development. *Vision Research, 26,* 847–855.

2

INFORMATION PROCESSING AND MEMORY

C H A P T E R

5

ACTIVE SELECTION AND INHIBITION IN THE AGING OF ATTENTION

Dana J. Plude, Lisa K. Schwartz, and Lisa J. Murphy
University of Maryland

INTRODUCTION

Increased distractibility is a characteristic that is often attributed to advancing age. For more than a quarter century theorists have posited an age decrement in the selectivity of the senescent information processor. For example, in 1965 Patrick Rabbitt attributed the deficit in visual search performance on the part of older adults to an age-related decrement in the ability to ignore irrelevant information. Similarly, on the basis of the extant literature available at the time, Layton (1975) proposed a "perceptual noise" hypothesis to account for the older adult's increased susceptibility to interference in a wide variety of experimental tasks. Most recently, Hasher and Zacks (1988) have argued for an inhibitory deficit on the part of the aged on the basis of age-related interference effects in perceptual processing and memory. Despite the recurrence of such hypotheses in the cognitive aging literature, however, there is also evidence that, at least in certain circumstances, older adults are *not* more prone to distraction than younger adults are. Thus, the generalizability of age–distractibility hypotheses can be questioned.

The goal of the present chapter is to review the literature pertaining to the selectivity of attention in old age and to identify themes that may inform about both facilitative and inhibitory components of selective attention. Although the attention construct is quite broad (as described below), our review focuses on the selective aspect of attention in order to limit the chapter's scope and to provide a more circumscribed domain within which to review and evaluate research findings. *Selective attention* refers to the ability to process selected information without interference from nonselected information (Johnston & Dark, 1986), and our review organizes research findings with respect to four aspects of selective attention: orienting, filtering, search, and expecting (Coren, Ward, & Enns, 1994). The themes emerging

165

from this review provide a basis for integrating seemingly discrepant findings into a unifying theory and for identifying future avenues of research.

OVERVIEW

The study of attention encompasses a wide array of theories, methods, and phenomena. In his seminal volume, *Principles of Psychology,* published more than 100 years ago, William James (1890) identified no fewer than four senses of the term (awareness of internal states, awareness of external stimuli, habit, and consciousness). With the renaissance of this construct in modern psychology, commencing with Broadbent's *Perception and Communication* (1958), there have been entire volumes (e.g., the *Attention and Performance* series) devoted to attention, with one such volume entitled *Varieties of Attention* (Parasuraman & Davies, 1984) in explicit recognition of the diversity of the attention construct. Excellent historical reviews of attention theory and research in mainstream cognitive psychology have been published elsewhere (see, e.g., Johnston & Dark, 1986; Kinchla, 1992), and the interested reader is directed to those sources. A central issue in the present chapter is the appropriateness of characterizing the older adult as being deficient in selective attention. Thus, our review focuses on one particular aspect of the attention construct, that is, selectivity, and whether or not and to what extent an age-related decrement in selective attention may be responsible for age differences in performance across a wide range of tasks.

Related to the central issue of this chapter are additional issues, some of which concern general questions about the definition of attention, others of which concern more specific questions about measurement and theory. We begin by addressing the definition of attention and then move to a brief discussion of measurement issues, theoretical concerns, and specific hypotheses about aging and attention.

■ Problems of Definition

Despite the elusiveness of a single definition of attention, many authors have argued for the heuristic value of identifying aspects of the construct. Of course, one difficulty in opting for such an approach is the potential for tautology: attention is whatever attention tasks measure. Such tautology can be circumvented, however, if converging evidence for the particular aspect(s) of attention is sought out. One way to begin to partition the attention construct is to consider the three dimensions of capacity, selectivity, and arousal, which are empirically distinguishable if not mutually exclusive of one another (Plude & Doussard-Roosevelt, 1990; Posner & Boies, 1971). The *capacity* dimension refers to the cognitive resources available to support information processing, the *selectivity* dimension refers to the specificity of allocating resources in accordance with task demands, and the *arousal* dimension refers essentially to the momentary level of excitation (alertness) in the information-processing system. These dimensions are not independent of one another because they rest on the common assumption that human information processing is limited in scope. Thus selective processing is mandated by a limited-capacity processing system that has insufficient resources or arousal to simultaneously process the plethora of stimuli (both internal and external) with which it is bombarded (Johnston & Dark, 1986).

Because it has been the focus of considerable research and theoretical efforts in the cognitive aging literature, selective attention is the focus of the present review. As noted above, we define selective attention as the ability to process selected information without interference from nonselected information.

■ Problems of Measurement

Given the diversity of the attention construct, it is of little surprise that there is disagreement over how it should be measured. In the review that follows, reaction-time (RT) studies are emphasized because they are the most common technique for inferring attentional function. This emphasis immediately gives rise to concern over the metric properties of RT and age group comparisons based upon it. Although RT studies yield valuable information regarding attention and its development, it is important to recognize explicitly three issues that qualify RT procedures in developmental investigations.

One issue centers on the considerable variability associated with older adults' RT performance when compared with the standard comparison group of young adults (see, e.g., Cerella, 1990; Salthouse, 1991). Not only does such variability complicate statistical comparisons between groups, it also gives rise to concerns about comparing the magnitude of within-subject effects between the groups (i.e., age × condition interactions). A second, related issue concerns the interpretation given to differences in RT. How is a larger difference for one age group over the other to be interpreted when the metric properties of RT differ with age? A third issue centers on the importance of coordinated RT and accuracy data. This is particularly noteworthy with respect to age-related RT comparisons because there is always the possibility that an age difference based solely on RT may be attributable to an underlying speed-versus-accuracy trade-off (see, e.g., Pachella, 1974). That is, it is possible within an RT task for an individual to "trade off" response speed for response accuracy; slower responding is usually accompanied by greater accuracy within the context of a given task. Thus, it is possible that the RT advantage exhibited by young adults may be offset by an accuracy advantage on the part of older adults. In the absence of coordinated RT and accuracy data this possibility cannot be ruled out. However, it should be noted that in most cases where speed-versus-accuracy trade-offs are examined they do not account for age differences in RT (see, e.g., Cerella, 1990; Plude & Doussard-Roosevelt, 1990).

■ Theoretical Perspectives

A variety of hypotheses about aging and attention can be identified and are considered in the next section. These hypotheses include those that implicate generalized mechanisms, such as diminished processing capacity (Craik, 1986) and generalized slowing (Cerella, 1990; Salthouse, 1991), and those that implicate more specific mechanisms, such as spatial localization (Plude & Hoyer, 1985) and nonattentional mechanisms (Scialfa, 1990). Despite the plethora of hypotheses, however, all are consistent with a human information-processing perspective on cognition (Lachman, Lachman, & Butterfield, 1979).

Although there are theorists who might disagree with us on this point, it is our contention that the information-processing perspective fits within a contextualistic worldview because of its recognition of the dynamic interplay between the individual and the environment (Pepper, 1942). This view is most appropriate for analyzing adult developmental changes in attention because it forces an explicit consideration of the context of individual performance. We note further that, in keeping with the now widely accepted view of what constitutes a *life-span* orientation (Baltes & Reese, 1984), our view of the developmental process is one of open-ended change. Thus, contrary to mechanistic biodecrement models that view the life span more narrowly in terms of growth, maturity, and decline, we adopt a perspective that is more readily influenced by context—it allows for plurality (change may occur in more than one direction at a time) and for multidimensionality (change may take place at more than one level) in the developmental process. This orientation does not deny that maturational processes may have different meanings at different points in the life span but rather recognizes that attention, like many other cognitive processes, undergoes a complex pattern of change, with some aspects exhibiting significant change and others exhibiting remarkable stability in later adulthood.

In order to accommodate these diverse patterns, any unified theory of aging and attention must provide for both continuity and change as well as stability and decline in different processing components. Moreover, the theory ought to encompass the entire life span (Plude, Enns, & Brodeur, 1994). Despite the many obstacles to such a theory, a necessary first step involves reconciling conflicting findings in the cognitive aging literature. This chapter attempts to reconcile such discrepancies by appealing to a two-process model comprising both facilitative and inhibitory attention mechanisms. Although a two-process theory may unify the divergent trends reviewed in this chapter, it is important to consider other hypotheses about aging and attention, some of which postulate general mechanisms of development and others of which postulate more specific mechanisms.

■ General Mechanisms

Three popular theories of generalized mechanisms are resource allocation, processing speed, and neural noise. In brief, the resource allocation model suggests that attentional resources that are at their peak in young adulthood wane in later life (Hoyer & Plude, 1982; Madden, 1990a; McDowd & Birren, 1990). Despite its widespread appeal in the aging literature, however, the focal deficiency with the resource allocation model is defining exactly what is meant by processing resources (see Salthouse, 1991). Nevertheless, one way to conceptualize such resources is in the form of "working memory" (Baddeley, 1986), which appears to lose efficiency during later adulthood (Salthouse, 1990).

An alternative model centers on the speed of information processing as opposed to the capacity of processing resources. According to the speed-of-processing view, age-related information-processing effects rest entirely upon the speed of elementary cognitive processes. Thus, as tasks become increasingly complex (i.e., require more processing steps), age effects will likewise increase. The central strength of this model is its parsimonious account of a wide range of age-related behavioral data (Cerella, 1990). Despite this strength, however, the speed-of-processing model is not without its limitations. First, as argued by Salthouse (1991), it is almost impossible to distinguish this account from the resource allocation model described above and is therefore prey to the same pitfalls. Second, its parsimony may be an artifact of the very RT data it intends to explicate (see, e.g., Fisk, Fisher, & Rogers, 1991). Third, it fails to incorporate coordinated consideration of error rate data (Cerella, 1990).

The third general model postulates biomaturational processes as the mechanism underlying age effects. According to the neural noise hypothesis, performance will be impaired in any situation involving the selective processing of neural signals against a background of random noise, particularly when the signal-to-noise ratio is low (see, e.g., Welford, 1965). One limitation of the biomaturational model, though, is its characterization of the aging processes as essentially destructive. Such a biodecremental view is incompatible with the divergent age trends identified in the current review as well as other psychological research (Rybash, Hoyer, & Roodin, 1986). It is noteworthy, though, that recent instantiations of the neural noise model have incorporated a brain–environment interaction component to accommodate diverse patterns of age effects (see, e.g., Allen, 1991).

■ Specific Mechanisms

Developmental models that focus on specific mechanisms theorize that age differences in selective attention are mediated by a single process or set of processes. For example, strategy-based models propose that age effects are due to the utilization of different strategies by different age groups. One candidate might be increased cautiousness, which would yield age decrements proportional to the difficulty of the decision being made. Contrary to this notion, however, the bulk of evidence indicates the existence of comparable response (and perceptual) strategies across ages, at least when forced-choice procedures eliminate the option of withholding responses (Kausler, 1992).

Another strategy-based difference is not so readily dismissed. Fisk and colleagues (Fisk & Rogers, 1991) have reported that, whereas a visual search task involving a consistent mapping of targets to responses yields automatic detection among younger adults (Schneider & Shiffrin, 1977), the same does not obtain for the elderly. Whether this age difference is the result of a deficit in differential strengthening of targets/nontargets, as suggested by Fisk, or reflects some other aspect of the task, such as the use of categorically distinct stimuli (Madden & Plude, 1993), is yet to be determined. Nonetheless, it is generally the case that, where strategy differences have been examined, there is little evidence to support the notion that age differences in strategy use fully account for age differences in selective attention.

Another specific mechanism that has been alleged to account for age differences in selective attention involves various developmental differences that can be classified as so-called data limitations (Norman & Bobrow, 1975). Data limitations comprise peripheral processing components, such as optical structures, that are suboptimal for transmitting adequate data to central processing (attentional) structures. Data limitations can mimic resource limitations and therefore constitute potential confounds for an unambiguous account of attentional effects. However, where they have been investigated, data limitations have been unable to account exclusively for age decrements in selective attention (see, e.g., Madden & Plude, 1993; Plude & Doussard-Roosevelt, 1990). Although the bulk of evidence indicates that data limitations alone cannot accommodate the diverse findings reviewed in this paper, clearly it is important to consider the role of such effects in any developmental investigation of selective attention (for further elaboration, see Chapter 4).

Another class of specific mechanisms focuses on components of information processing as the loci for age differences in selective attention. For example, Plude and Hoyer (1985) hypothesized that spatial localization underlies age decrements in visual search and age equivalence in nonsearch tasks. Specific tests of this hypothesis in the aging literature have been equivocal (Plude, 1990; Scialfa & Kline, 1988) and suggest that, although spatial location may be an important dimension in certain selective attention tasks, it is not so across all tasks (Kinchla, 1992). Nonetheless, our review indicates several trends that appear related to a specialized role for spatial localization. Thus, its ultimate status as a mediator of age-related selective attention deficits is yet to be determined.

LITERATURE REVIEW

Having outlined several extant hypotheses concerning aging and attention, we now selectively review the empirical literature to identify themes in the aging of selective attention. Our review centers around four different components of attention which, when viewed en masse, reflect diverse relationships to aging. It is noted at the outset that many different methodologies have been applied to the study of selective attention, including visual search, nonsearch (filtering), auditory shadowing, dichotic listening, divided attention, and dual-task performance. Despite their differences, the methods provide important information about facilitative and inhibitory components of selective attention and how these components change or remain stable in later adulthood.

■ Orienting

The most primitive form of attentional selection involves aligning sensory receptors with certain locations in space and orienting away from others. Reflexive visual and auditory orienting of this kind is seen whenever a sudden movement or loud noise occurs in the environment. We involuntarily move our eyes and head toward the location of a sudden sound. In addition to these location-specific responses there are changes in skin conductance, heart rate, blood flow, and breathing which signal the onset of a more general arousal response (Rohrbaugh, 1984). It is important to distinguish these overt forms of the orienting reflex from covert orienting, which has to do with an alignment of attention in the absence of a physical alignment of the sensory receptor surfaces (Posner, 1980). Orienting involves the active selection of a particular location in space and the concomitant inhibition of nonselected locations.

Reflexive Orienting

Although the orienting reflex has been studied extensively in newborns and young infants, it has not received intensive scrutiny in the adult and aging literature. Nevertheless, recent theorizing about age-related inhibitory processes (reviewed later in this chapter) has sparked an interest in this basic reflex as a measure of attentional processing. For example, McDowd and Filion (1991) used a physiological measure of skin conductance to evaluate the orienting responses of young and elderly subjects performing a selective listening task. In one condition, subjects were instructed to ignore irrelevant tones that occurred during the listening task; in the other, subjects were instructed to attend to the tones. Young adults' orienting responses habituated to the tone in the "ignore" condition but not in the "attend" condition; whereas elderly adults exhibited persistent orienting responses in both conditions. These findings were taken as support for the view that older adults have difficulty suppressing unattended information.

Electrophysiological evidence also suggests that the orienting reflex is less selective in later adulthood. Among a variety of measures that can be used as indices of underlying cortical activity, visual evoked potentials (VEPs) are commonplace in electroencephalogram (EEG) studies of attention. In brief, VEPs are measures of brain activity that are sensed via scalp electrodes and that are evoked by controlled stimulus presentation (typically on a computer video screen). By manipulating different aspects of the visual stimulus, such as comparing patterned (e.g., a checkerboard) versus unpatterned (e.g., a homogeneous color field) stimuli and measuring the latency between the onset of the visual stimulus and the corresponding brain-wave activity, investigators gain insight into various characteristics of information processing in the central nervous system (CNS). Prinz, Dustman, and Emmerson (1990) reviewed VEP studies involving younger and older adults and found evidence to suggest that young adulthood is characterized by maximally efficient excitatory and inhibitory processes in the CNS, whereas later adulthood is characterized by less selective CNS responses. For example, in research comparing VEPs for patterned and unpatterned stimuli, younger adults exhibited complete separation in the VEP profiles for the two stimulus types whereas older adults did not. Because the older adults' VEP profile differed markedly from the younger adults' profile for patterned stimuli but not unpatterned stimuli, and because patterned stimuli are thought to engage both excitatory and inhibitory responses whereas unpatterned stimuli engage only the former, the overall age effect was attributed to the older adults' deficiency in the inhibitory component of processing.

Thus, although the orienting reflex appears to be exhibited across the life span, its selectivity and specificity vary with age such that the response is maximally specific in adolescence and young adulthood and more generalized later in life. In particular, it appears that the facilitative component of orienting is preserved in aging, whereas the inhibitory component exhibits age-related decline.

Covert Orienting

Covert orienting is typically measured within a cost–benefit RT methodology developed by Posner (1980). In this task, the subject is given a very simple task—to press a key whenever a predefined target stimulus is presented. The target may be the onset of a light or a simple shape such as a circle or square. The critical experimental manipulation is the presentation of a brief stimulus called a *cue* (e.g., a flash of light, brightening of a location marker) immediately preceding the target stimulus. If the cue is presented in the same location as the subsequent target, the trial is called a valid trial; if the cue is in a different location from the target, the trial is called invalid. If no cue is presented, or if it is presented in all possible target locations, the trial is called neutral. By comparing RTs for the different types of trials, estimates of attention shifting can be obtained. When RT for valid cues is subtracted from RT for neutral cues, an estimate of orienting benefit is obtained; when RT for neutral cues is subtracted from RT for invalid cues, an estimate of orienting cost is obtained. Orienting costs and benefits provide evidence of covert shifts of attention. Several studies have investigated covert orienting in response to peripheral cues. Although these studies converge on finding roughly comparable costs and benefits across age, suggesting that attention shifting is preserved in later adulthood, there is disagreement about the time course of covert orienting.

The time course of covert orienting can be inferred by comparing the magnitude of orienting benefits and costs at different delays (i.e., stimulus onset asynchronies [SOAs]) between the cue and target events. If the target event is simultaneous with the cue, there should be no opportunity to orient attention to the cued location and thus there should be no benefits or costs. If, however, the target event follows the cue by some delay, the magnitude of benefits and costs should increase with increasing SOA. Comparisons of such time-course effects among younger and older adults have yielded inconclusive findings. For example, Hartley, Kieley, and Slabach (1990, experiment 3) found comparable costs and benefits among young and elderly adults when a bar marker indicated the likely position of a target letter on the circumference of an imaginary circle centered at fixation. Moreover, the magnitudes of age-related cuing effects were comparable across various SOAs, indicating an age-equivalent time course for cuing effects. Folk and Hoyer (1992, experiment 1) also obtained comparable costs and benefits, and at equivalent rates, among young and elderly adults when a luminance change signaled the likely position of a target at one of four positions in a display. Madden (1990b) obtained a similar outcome when targets appeared in an otherwise empty display: both young and elderly adults exhibited modest benefits at equivalent rates when an asterisk indicated the likely position of the target in a six-position array. However, when targets were accompanied by distractors (the letter *R* presented at 18 positions in the display), younger adults exhibited benefits sooner (beginning at 50 milliseconds [msec] SOA) than did older adults (whose RT benefits materialized at 150 msec SOA).

In sum, it appears that covert orienting is preserved in later life, and, at least in simple detection/recognition situations in which targets appear in otherwise blank displays, the time course of visual orienting is comparable across adult age. That benefits and costs are obtained for older adults suggests that covert orienting facilitates the processing of signals at the cued location and inhibits the processing of signals at noncued locations.

Attentional Gaze

Before moving away from the topic of covert orienting, we address the metaphor of attentional gaze (Coren et al., 1994), which offers a useful way of organizing some of the findings in visual orienting. Our use of this term is synonymous with a variety of concepts in the attention literature (e.g., zoom lens, spotlight, mind's eye) which imply the metaphor of attention behaving in a manner that is similar to that of the eye. For example, visual acuity in the attentional window is highest at the center, with a decreasing gradient in the surround; in order to move from point A to point B the attentional gaze must move through intermediate positions; and the attentional gaze cannot be centered on more than one location at a time. In the cognitive aging literature, this construct has been labeled the "perceptual window" (see, e.g., Cerella, 1985) and the "useful field of view" (see, e.g., Scialfa, 1990). There are three dimensions of the attentional gaze that are of interest in developmental comparisons: locus (where the gaze is positioned), extent (the size of the area covered), and detail (what kind of information is processed).

Research concerned with the locus of the attentional gaze was touched upon in the preceding section on covert orienting. As noted, that research suggests roughly equivalent effects of orienting cues on the locus of the attentional gaze in both younger and older adults, with some suggestion of a slower time course among the latter. Other research, involving different cuing procedures and different methodologies (reviewed below), also suggests that the control over the locus of the attentional gaze is well maintained into later adulthood.

Although control over the attentional gaze appears to be preserved in aging, there is disagreement over the age-related status of the other two dimensions, spatial extent and level of detail. The extent and detail of the attentional gaze can be measured in various ways, but the most common methodology involves a character identification task in which stimuli are presented at several different positions across a horizontal display, with the subject instructed to maintain fixation on a central point in the display. The angular separation from the target position and central fixation, called eccentricity, is manipulated, and identification speed and accuracy serve as dependent measures upon which inferences about the extent and detail of the attentional gaze are based. Employing this sort of methodology, Cerella (1985) and Scialfa, Kline, and Lyman (1987) obtained evidence to suggest that the attentional gaze is more constricted and less detailed, particularly in the peripheral visual field, for elderly compared with young adults. In these studies, subjects were required to identify characters that fell increasingly further away from central fixation, and the decrement in extrafoveal acuity occurred sooner (at smaller eccentricities) and was more precipitous for elderly compared with young adults. However, these studies do not take into account the attentional demands of performance as a mediator of the three components of the attentional gaze.

Plude and Doussard-Roosevelt (1990) have argued that, rather than viewing the useful field of view as a fixed commodity that constricts with age, it may be more appropriately viewed as a flexible commodity that can be adjusted to meet task demands. For example Ball, Roenker, and Bruni (1990) found that the spatial extent of the attentional gaze varied as a direct function of the information-processing demands of performance for both young and elderly adults. Thus, when performance required a simple detection response, the spatial extent of the gaze was much broader than when complex discriminations involving identification were involved. Moreover, the extent of the attentional gaze was comparable for younger and older adults in the simple detection task but was much smaller for older adults than for younger adults in the complex discrimination task. Thus, the extent (and detail) of the attentional gaze is susceptible to the processing demands of performance. Rather than being a consequence of the aging process per se, decrements in the attentional gaze may reflect a deficit in the cognitive resources that control its locus, extent, and detail.

The research summarized in this section indicates that attentional orienting is relatively well preserved in later life. Information that appears in a location that is oriented toward receives priority processing compared with information appearing in nonoriented locations, and this holds true for both younger and older adults. There is some evidence of diminished inhibitory processing at the physiological level as well as evidence of age-related slowing in both the facilitative and inhibitory components of covert orienting. Nonetheless, the facts that older adults exhibit costs and benefits associated with orienting and that the magnitude of these effects varies with the attentional demands of performance suggest that both the facilitative and inhibitory components of selective attention are maintained (at reduced levels, perhaps) in later life.

■ Filtering

Many attention tasks require the subject to process certain attributes of an object to the exclusion of other attributes and objects. This has often been referred to as filtering, to capture the implication that only certain perceptual attributes are permitted through a processing "gate." Note that, according to this definition, the previous attention task of orienting merely involves filtering in the spatial domain. Nonetheless, these tasks deserve separate status based on both psychophysical (Bundesen, 1990) and neurological (Mishkin, Ungerleider & Macko, 1983) evidence pointing to the unique status of an object's location versus other of its attributes such as size, color, and pitch.

Within the filtering domain, research can be partitioned into (at least) two categories of tasks: auditory selection and visual selection. The latter category might be further subdivided into tasks involving a single, fixed location for selecting visual signals and those involving the cuing of one (or more) spatial locations. Because cuing studies are reviewed in a separate section below, the present review centers on tasks involving the selection of (and focus upon) a single, fixed location.

Auditory Selection

In young adult subjects, filtering in the auditory domain has often been studied with a method based on observations at a typical cocktail party—the dichotic listening task (Cherry, 1953). In his elegant review of dichotic listening tasks involving older adult samples, Craik (1977) concluded that, when required to report the contents of two different lists presented simultaneously to both ears, older adults exhibit a greater decrement than younger adults on reporting the second list. Although this dichotic deficit may owe in part to diminished working memory capacity on the part of the elderly (Salthouse, 1991), it may also reflect diminished selective attention because older adults exhibit higher error rates than younger adults in shadowing tasks that require monitoring a target message presented on one channel while ignoring a competing message presented on the other channel. Recently, Barr and Giambra (1990) found that the shadowing deficit exhibited by older adults remains even when performance is adjusted for monaural shadowing performance, fluid intelligence, and puretone hearing loss. Thus, older adults exhibit greater susceptibility to interference than younger adults in dichotic listening situations, a finding that is consistent with an age decrement in inhibitory processing.

Visual Selection

Although it is possible to design visual filtering experiments that mirror the important aspects of the dichotic listening task (Neisser & Becklen, 1975), most of the work in the visual domain has its roots in the classic Stroop (1935) effect. The original work was conducted with words that spelled color names and used various ink colors for the words. Subjects were asked to name the ink color as rapidly as possible (central stimulus dimension) and to ignore the meaning of the words spelled out on the page (secondary or incidental stimulus dimension). The main finding was, of course, that subjects were unable to ignore the word meanings when they referred to color names (see MacLeod, 1991, for a thorough review). In one of the few life-span studies conducted, Comalli, Wapner, and Werner (1962) found that the magnitude of the Stroop effect diminished throughout childhood and into early adulthood but thereafter increased into later adulthood. Although there have been few direct follow-up studies of Stroop interference in the cognitive aging literature, other studies provide converging support for Comalli et al.'s findings of increased perceptual intrusions coupled with diminished perceptual sensitivity in the aged (Layton, 1975; Rogers & Fisk, 1991). However, we must caution that these findings are not without controversy, as described below.

Within the aging literature, filtering tasks have yielded evidence of functioning preserved well into later adulthood. Wright and Elias (1979) used a visual filtering task (Eriksen & Eriksen, 1974) to show that, if anything, young adults were more susceptible to distractors than were the elderly. Subjects were required to respond to a center (relevant) letter in a display which also contained two (irrelevant) flankers, one on each side of the center letter. When the flankers were incompatible with the response required of the target letter, young adults exhibited a larger interference effect than did the elderly. This outcome suggests that older adults are even more effective than younger adults at inhibiting irrelevant information in a filtering task.

Cerella (1985) suggested that an age-constricted "perceptual window" (see discussion of attentional gaze above) may insulate the older observer from interference associated with distractors that occupy peripheral positions in the visual field. As a result, younger adults are more prone than older adults to suffer interference effects from flankers in a filtering task. Using the same logic, Cerella argued that the same perceptual limitation that facilitates the performance of older adults in a filtering task will impair their performance in a search task because the search task typically positions targets in peripheral display positions. Consistent with this logic, Plude and Hoyer (1986) demonstrated equivalent performance between younger and older adults in a filtering (nonsearch) task and an age decrement in performance in a search task. However, contrary to the logic put forth by Cerella, Plude and Hoyer obtained the same age interaction even when data for peripheral targets were eliminated in the search task. That is, in analyzing only the data for targets that appeared at central fixation (i.e., targets that were centered on the area of maximum visual acuity, the fovea) in search against the foveal targets in nonsearch, the age decrement in search remained. Because the critical comparison involved foveal targets in both conditions, it cannot be concluded that the elderly are insulated from distractors purely on the basis of a constricted useful field of view. More recent work by D'Aloisio and Klein (1990) leads to a similar conclusion. In a filtering task involving nonfoveal targets and distractors, younger and older adults exhibited comparable distractor interference effects. Thus, different patterns of age effects are obtained in filtering tasks and search tasks: filtering tasks yield age-equivalent performance, while search tasks yield age differences in performance.

On balance, it appears that visual filtering is preserved in later life, at least in situations where the target information is spatially distinct from distractors and when the location of the target is prespecified. Note that both of these findings appear to emphasize a point raised at the outset of this section regarding the distinctive status of spatial location as a processing cue.

Another issue of long-standing interest in filtering tasks is the fate of the stimuli that are not attended while a focal stimulus is being processed. A novel method for studying this question systematically was developed by Tipper (1985) and has come to be known as the negative priming procedure. Negative priming is most easily understood as an extension of the standard Stroop task. As with the standard task, on each trial subjects are asked to report on one attribute of the display (the central task) while a secondary attribute is ignored (incidental stimulus attribute). Two different trial types are then compared—those in which the attribute to be attended in the present trial was the ignored attribute on the immediately preceding trial (ignored repetition trials) and those in which the attended attribute bears no relationship to attributes on the previous trial (control trials). Tipper's (1985) original work with young adult subjects yielded a significant increase in RT for ignored repetition trials compared to control trials, that is, the negative priming effect. This effect was attributed to the requirement of overcoming the inhibition associated with the ignored repetition condition.

In the past decade, there has been considerable research into age-related negative priming effects. This intense scrutiny has been driven in part by the search for evidence of diminished inhibitory processing on the part of the elderly (as stated at the outset of our review). If inhibitory processing is impaired in older adults, older adults should *not* exhibit negative priming effects. Indeed, several early studies obtained no evidence of negative priming effects in the elderly, coupled with evidence of age increments in interference effects (see McDowd, Oseas-Kreger, & Filion, 1995, for a review). Taken together, these findings implicated diminished inhibitory processing on the part of the elderly. For example, Hasher, Stoltzfus, Zacks, and Rypma (1991) replicated Tipper's letter-naming task and found that, compared with younger adults, older adults exhibited increased interference on control trials and no negative priming effects on ignored repetition trials. Similar findings were obtained by Tipper (1991) using a picture-naming task. In an attempt to strengthen the inhibitory requirement of the negative priming task, McDowd and Oseas-Kreger (1991) used a letter-naming task involving superimposed stimuli. Targets appeared in one color (e.g., red) and distractors in another (e.g., green) with the two letters superimposed but slightly offset to allow for target naming. Despite the inhibitory requirement of the task being strengthened, young adults exhibited negative priming whereas the elderly did not.

The early negative priming studies replicate the traditional pattern of Stroop effects by revealing larger interference effects among older adults as compared with younger adults. Perhaps not surprisingly, more recent inquiries into age-related negative priming effects have yielded less consistent findings. For example, in assessing negative priming effects within the context of a localization task—in which subjects indicate the location of a target rather than its identity—Connelly and Hasher (1993) found evidence of negative priming effects in both younger and older adults. Similarly, Sullivan and Faust (1993) demonstrated negative priming effects in older adults under certain circumstances within an identity-based task (similar in concept to the earlier studies cited above). In light of the current debate over the status of age-related negative priming effects, it appears premature to draw any firm conclusions. However, it is important to note that the magnitude of negative priming effects typically is on the order of 10 msec or so, and, as noted in the Introduction, one might question the statistical power of developmental investigations to detect such effects in light of the large RT variability that characterizes the performance of older adults.

In sum, the performance of older adults in filtering tasks suggests that both the facilitative and inhibitory components of selective attention are preserved in aging. There is some evidence from identity-based negative priming studies to suggest some age-related decline in inhibitory processing. However, the degree to which inhibitory processes may be compromised in older adults remains a topic of debate.

■ Search

Rabbitt's (1965) classic demonstration of an age decrement in visual search set the standard against which other visual search studies can be compared. In that study, young and elderly adults sorted specially prepared cards into various piles depending upon which of 2 or 8 targets appeared on the card. The targets were accompanied by 0, 1, 4, or 8 distractor letters, and older adults were slowed more dramatically than younger adults as a function of the number of distractors (i.e., display size). Although Rabbitt (1965) attributed this outcome to an age decrement in the ability to ignore irrelevant information, the studies reviewed above in the section on filtering challenge this interpretation. Hence, much research has been devoted to determining the boundary conditions of the age decrement in visual search and identifying underlying mechanisms (Madden, 1986; Plude, 1990; Plude & Hoyer, 1985). Several different mechanisms are plausible as candidates, and we address three of the more popular candidates.

Eye Movements

Eye movements may contribute to observed age differences in visual search by adding an overt motor component (i.e., shifting of the eyes) to overall processing time. Within the aging literature, few investigations have examined eye movements directly, perhaps because of the many difficulties encountered in calibrating eye movement equipment for individuals wearing bi- or trifocals and eye structures that have undergone considerable age-related changes (Kline & Schieber, 1985; Chapter 4). Nonetheless, in the few studies that have been conducted, the major age effect centers on the increased latency of eliciting saccadic movements (see, e.g., Carter, Obler, Woodward, & Albert, 1983; Rabbitt, 1982). That is, older adults exhibit longer latencies than young adults when shifting their eyes in response to an imperative command to do so. For example, Carter et al. (1983) found that the saccadic latencies of 70-year-olds averaged 300 msec whereas those of 20-year-olds averaged 150 msec. This difference in saccadic latency suggests that age differences in visual search should increase proportionally with the number of refixations required in the task, and the results of many search tasks conform to this expectation.

However, though it may be tempting to attribute visual search decrements to differences in saccadic latency, the findings reviewed below have been replicated in constrained viewing situations in which stimuli are presented too briefly for eye movements to play a role. Nonetheless, it is important to recognize that other visual changes may impose "data limits" that contribute to the obtained patterns of age effects in visual search tasks (see Scialfa, 1990; Chapter 4). It is also important to recognize that, outside the constraints of the laboratory, age decrements in saccadic latency may contribute to accidents and other difficulties experienced by the aged in everyday life (Kosnik, Winslow, Kline, Rasinski, & Sekuler, 1988).

Visual Search

One of the most popular tasks in the attention literature is that of visual search (see, e.g., Treisman, 1986; Treisman & Gormican, 1988). Subjects are asked to look for a target item that is present on a random one-half of the trials and to respond with a simple "present" or "absent" response. The primary independent variable is the number of total items in the display. Broadly speaking, two different patterns of results are often reported in such tasks. The first, typically taken as evidence of serial search, is a linear (or at least monotonic) increase in RT and/or errors as a function of display size, accompanied by a much steeper (often 2 times steeper) increase for "absent" than for "present" responses. The second pattern of results, typically taken as evidence of perceptual pop-out or parallel search, is a relatively flat or shallow increase in RT (<10 msec per item) and errors as a function of display size, with very little difference, if any, between "present" and "absent" responses. Subjects' eye movements and fixations are rarely monitored in these experiments, and when they are (Klein & Farrell, 1989), the RT and error pattern do not seem to be affected.

Visual search tasks have been a mainstay of research on aging for more than a quarter century (Plude, 1990), and, although older adults usually exhibit age decrements (in the form of increased search slopes), the magnitude of decrement can be minimized and sometimes eliminated completely by manipulating characteristics of the search task. Thus, in some respects, selective attention, as measured via visual search tasks, is selectively preserved in aging (Madden & Plude, 1993). To date, age decrements in visual search have been attenuated by a host of manipulations including target–nontarget categorization (Madden, 1990b), spatial cuing (Madden, 1984), and consistent practice (Plude & Hoyer, 1981). Although there is some debate over the specific benefits associated with extensive periods of consistent practice in visual search tasks (Fisk & Rogers, 1991), typically such practice attenuates important aspects of age-related search deficits (Madden & Plude, 1993).

Indeed, in certain instances the standard age decrement in visual search can be eliminated completely. For example, Plude and Doussard-Roosevelt (1989) required both young and elderly adults to search for a target letter in each of three conditions: feature search, conjunction search, and unconfounded conjunction search. The conditions were defined by the relationship between the target and nontarget letters that occupied displays. In the feature search condition, the target differed in both color and form from the nontargets. In the conjunction search condition, the nontargets shared either the target's color or form. And in the unconfounded conjunction search condition, the number of nontargets sharing the target's color was held constant across varying display size. Whereas the conjunction search condition yielded the standard age decrement in visual search, with search slopes for older adults nearly twice as steep compared with younger adults', the feature search condition yielded zero slopes (denoting pop-out) on the part of both young and elderly adults (see also D'Aloisio and Klein, 1990). The unconfounded conjunction search condition yielded evidence that similar search strategies, involving mixed serial and parallel components, were employed by both age groups. Within the context of feature integration theory (Treisman, 1986; Treisman & Gelade, 1980), these findings suggest age preservation of feature extraction processes coupled with age-impaired feature integration processes (Plude, 1990). In brief, feature integration theory posits two stages of visual processing: an early, automatic stage in which features are registered in parallel across the visual field (feature extraction) and a second, capacity-demanding stage in which the features registered in the first stage are conjoined to represent the objects of perception. When search can be based on a single feature, it is effortless and yields "perceptual pop-out" of a target from the background of distractors. In contrast, when search must be based upon conjunctions of features, it is effortful and instantiates a more painstaking but not necessarily serial process of integrating features across perceptual dimensions (but see Duncan & Humphreys, 1989; Bundesen, 1990, for alternative interpretations).

Evidence of age-equivalent search slopes was also obtained by Zacks and Zacks (1993) in an innovative procedure that eliminated manual RT as a dependent variable. Young and elderly adults viewed two sequentially presented displays and indicated which one contained a target. When the target was distinguishable on the basis of a single feature, the age groups exhibited equivalent search slopes; when the target was identified by a conjunction of features, however, older adults yielded search slopes that were nearly twice as steep as younger adults'. Thus, even when care is taken to eliminate motor slowing associated with manual responses, differential age effects emerge for conditions that differ in the degree of attention demand.

Regardless of the particular theoretical framework for interpreting the findings, it is clear that older adults are not always deficient with regard to visual search. Moreover, evidence accumulating suggests that within expert domains, such as skilled radiography, older experts outperform younger novices despite exhibiting normative search decrements on standard visual search tasks (Clancey & Hoyer, 1994).

The findings in the visual search literature paint a mixed picture regarding the age-related status of facilitative and inhibitory components of selective attention. In the absence of distinctive physical cues, distinct categorical differences, and expertise in the search domain, older adults appear to be less efficient than younger adults at facilitating the processing of targets and inhibiting the processing of distractors in visual search tasks. However, when distinctive cues, categorical differences, and expertise are available to the older adult, then both facilitative and inhibitory components of selective attention appear to operate efficiently. In short, the age-related integrity of facilitative and inhibitory processes in visual search is dependent on characteristics of both the physical environment and the observer.

Divided Attention

Several alternative interpretations of age effects have been obtained in visual search experiments. One possibility that has been subjected to empirical study centers on the requirement of distributed or divided attention in search tasks. Nonsearch tasks can be construed as "focused attention" situations because attention can be centered on the predetermined location of the relevant display position. Search tasks, on the other hand, require several display positions to be monitored (and compared) in order to determine whether or not they contain the target. Perhaps older adults are deficient with respect to divided-attention skills.

Although some studies have reported age-related divided-attention decrements (Salthouse, Rogan, & Prill, 1984), other studies have not (Somberg & Salthouse, 1982). In a systematic comparison of focused and divided-attention situations, McDowd and Craik (1988) found that task complexity influenced the magnitude of age effects even more than did the attention manipulation. This finding prompted the conclusion that divided-attention situations are more complex than focused attention situations and that it is the differential complexity of such tasks, rather than the requirement to divide attention per se, that mediates age decrements in divided-attention situations. Thus, it appears that age decrements in search, when they are obtained, are not due to the requirement to distribute attention across display positions in a visual search task (see also the section above on attentional gaze and Plude, 1990).

In an attempt to decompose adult age effects in search, filtering, and attentional gaze, D'Aloisio and Klein (1990) directly compared age effects in a nonsearch filtering task modeled after Eriksen and Eriksen (1974), a visual search task modeled after Treisman (1986), and an attentional gaze task modeled after LaBerge (1983). Essentially, they found that whereas the overall pattern of age effects pointed toward the preservation of the spatial dynamics of attention, the intercorrelations among the three tasks revealed an age decrement in disengaging from an attended location. One consequence of this age decrement is that the costs and benefits obtained in covert orienting should be correlated with the speed of visual search among older adults but not among younger adults. Further research is needed to determine whether or not this age effect might reflect a breakdown in the mechanism underlying the inhibition of return.

In sum, although older adults tend to perform more poorly than younger adults in most circumstances involving divided attention, it appears that it is the difficulty of the task rather than the requirement to divide attention per se that limits older adults' performance. D'Aloisio and Klein (1990) suggest that the requirement to transfer attention from one source to another may be a common mechanism underlying performance decrements on the part of the elderly in both divided-attention and visual search tasks. This implies a reduction in control over the facilitative component of selective attention.

■ Expecting

To this point our review has centered on mechanisms for orienting, which draw one's attention to conspicuous objects; operations involved in filtering, which allow one to attend to relevant stimuli; and strategies of searching, which allow one to investigate likely locations of important stimuli. However, sometimes there is specific advance information about where and when an event will occur, and such situations involve expecting. Expectancy information can come either from relatively new information we have just learned (referred to as *priming*) or from information we have already stored in long-term memory (referred to as *prompting*).

Priming

Probably the simplest demonstration of the effects of information priming involves the cost–benefit procedure that was introduced in the section on orienting. There it was used to study the nature of the reflexive orienting response generated by sudden events in the visual field. However, Posner (1980) also used it to study the voluntary (also called endogenous) orienting of attention to locations in the visual field. In many respects, the sort of endogenous orienting at issue here is distinguishable by its "cognitive" complexity relative to exogenous (or automatic) orienting, which behaves more like a lower-level reflex. Thus, instead of the orienting cue being a bright flash of light in a potential target location, the cue is an arrow appearing at fixation, pointing to either the right or left. On 80 percent of the trials involving an arrow, the target actually appeared in the location signaled by the arrow (valid trial). On the remaining 20 percent of these trials, it appeared in the noncued location (invalid trial). Neutral trials were also included in which the arrow was replaced by a plus sign and targets were equally likely to be on the left or right. Observers were not allowed to move their eyes from the fixation point for the duration of the trial; only their attention could be oriented.

Results of tests of young adult subjects in this procedure are very similar in some ways to the reflexive orienting studies: RTs reveal both a benefit on valid trials (valid RT is shorter than neutral RT) and a cost on invalid trials (invalid RT is longer than neutral RT). However, there are also some important differences, such as the fact that the time required for attention to shift in this task is much longer—the cue onset–target onset duration (the SOA) that produces maximum costs and benefits is around 300 to 500 msec rather than 50 to 100 msec (Shepard & Muller, 1989).

Several studies have addressed voluntary orienting among older adults. This research has been driven in part by the notion that voluntary orienting represents an elementary cognitive process that may provide insight into a basic component of selective attention: the control of the attentional focus. Preliminary research on voluntary orienting in response to a cue appearing at central fixation was conducted by Nissen and Corkin (1985), who presented spatial cues at SOAs of either 2 or 3 seconds prior to a target's appearance at either the left- or right-hand side of central fixation. Older adults exhibited larger costs and benefits compared with younger adults in this situation; however, the extended SOAs employed leave open the possibility that eye movements rather than attentional shifts per se mediated the effects.

Subsequent research involving central cuing has indicated comparable costs and benefits among young and elderly adults at SOAs too brief to allow eye movements. For example, Madden (1983) obtained comparable benefits for young and elderly adults when a central cue designated which two of four display positions would contain the target letter. Similarly, Hartley et al. (1990, experiment 2) obtained comparable cuing effects for young and elderly adults when a central cue indicated the likely position of a target in a circular array centered at fixation. Moreover, the time course of cuing was comparable across age groups.

Although Hoyer and Familant (1987) also obtained roughly comparable costs and benefits across age groups when a central cue indicated which one of four display positions was most likely to contain a target: the time course of the cuing effect was longer among elderly adults than young ones. Hartley (1992) has suggested that the extended time course for cuing among older adults in Hoyer and Familant's study may be a result of the particular methodology employed. Unlike other studies that involved a recognition response (Which target letter is present?), Hoyer and Familant's study required subjects to indicate which of four horizontally arrayed boxes contained a luminance increment. Another possibility is suggested by Folk and Hoyer (1992) who found no benefits of central cues among older adults (experiment 2) unless those cues were easily encoded (experiment 3) in which case approximately equal costs and benefits among young and elderly adults were obtained. Because these effects varied across cue–target SOA, Folk and Hoyer concluded that the age-related time course of cuing depends upon the symbolic processing demands (i.e., complexity) of the central cue. Thus, although the spatial dynamics of voluntary orienting are comparable for young and elderly adults, the time required to encode symbolic cues appears to increase with advancing adult age.

In summary, several investigations have established that the magnitude of costs and benefits associated with central cues is roughly comparable for younger and older adults, but there is some disagreement regarding the time course of these effects. Perhaps discrepancies regarding the age-related time course of cuing effects owe to different task demands in different studies (Hartley, 1992; Plude & Doussard-Roosevelt, 1990), or perhaps different tasks impose differential demands upon processing resources that are allocated more variably over trials by older adults compared with younger adults (Madden & Plude, 1993). The debate over the time course of cuing effects notwithstanding, there is consensus on the preservation of attention shifting in later adulthood. Comparable patterns of costs and benefits are obtained regardless of whether the cues are presented centrally (endogenous orienting) or peripherally (exogenous orienting) for both younger and older adults (Folk & Hoyer, 1992). Thus, it appears that orienting attention toward a particular location facilitates the processing of stimuli at that location and inhibits the processing of information at other locations, with the magnitude of facilitative and inhibitory effects roughly comparable across adult age.

Prompting

In order to perceive and compare stimuli efficiently, an individual must not only be able to orient to the appropriate spatial locations and register the information there but also be able to remember information from previous glances and retrieve knowledge associated with entire classes of stimuli. When this information is shown to influence visual processing, it is called *prompting*.

One way prompting has been studied in the aging literature is very similar to a standard procedure for studying priming (see previous section), except that the prompt now depends on information stored in long-term memory (Madden & Plude, 1993). For example, Hartley et al. (1990, experiments 4 and 5) prompted young and elderly adults about the type of decision required for stimuli presented in a visual display (i.e., letter or color response) and found not only equivalent costs and benefits for both age groups but also age-equivalent time courses for these effects. Madden (1984) also found comparable age-related costs and benefits with prompts that informed about the likely set of targets in a visual search task. Madden (1985) replicated the age-equivalent prompting effect in another experiment in which prompts indicated which of two targets would be *less* likely to appear in the display. However, in this study younger adults exhibited prompting effects at shorter SOAs than did the elderly, indicating age-related slowing in memory-driven selective processing.

Other approaches to prompting have also yielded evidence of age decrements in memory-driven selection. In a study involving prompts that conveyed the alphanumeric category membership of stimuli to be classified, Rabbitt (1964) found that younger adults derived benefits from the prompts relative to a no-prompt control condition. In contrast, older adults did not show this advantage. This age difference was not due to the older adults' ignoring prompts, because on invalid trials both age groups exhibited RT costs relative to the no-prompt control condition. In another approach to prompting, Rabbitt and Vyas (1980) examined stimulus–response repetition effects among young and elderly adults. Although both age groups benefited from the repetition of a physically identical target, only young adults exhibited benefits when physically different but response-compatible targets were repeated. This may indicate differential sensitivity on the part of the elderly to the processing demands of relatively late response selection stages of processing (Greenwood & Parasuraman, 1991).

In sum, it appears that among older adults memory-based expectancies that are instantiated via prompting procedures are less effective than stimulus-based expectancies that are instantiated via cuing. Comparable age-related benefits and costs are obtained when prompts are presented in a manner akin to cuing. However, when the prompts are more subtle, such as in the form of probabilistic information conveyed across trials, age differences in benefits and costs are apparent. This pattern of effects suggests that the complexity of prompting procedures plays an important role in modulating expectancy effects. Expectancies that are firmly instantiated via cues and obvious prompts facilitate the processing of expected information and inhibit the processing of unexpected information to a comparable degree in younger and older adults. Expectancy cues that place increasing demands on memory yield age reductions in the facilitative effects of such cues; their effect on inhibitory processes is not self-evident.

GENERAL DISCUSSION

Although the components of selective attention yield different patterns of age effects, two emergent themes can be identified. First, despite different patterns among the various components, there is evidence of a degree of consistency at a higher level—age effects tend to be associated with those components of selective attention that are also more effortful for young adults. That is, to the extent that a task places heavier demands on a limited-capacity or task-sharing system in college students, it also is more difficult to maintain in later life. This ubiquitous "complexity effect" has been a mainstay of cognitive aging research over the past 3 decades (see, e.g., Birren, 1965).

Another theme that pervades much of the work reviewed is that when environmental support (Craik, 1986) is available, such as in the form of distinctive target–distractor differentiation (e.g., color, size, or form) or preexisting information regarding the spatial location of targets and distractors, age differences in selectivity are greatly attenuated and sometimes eliminated altogether. Environmental support may be viewed as a means of enhancing the active selection of relevant information (by making target features more salient or by isolating the target's location apart from distractors) and/or of inhibiting the processing of nontargets (by deemphasizing their features or excluding their locations from further processing).

These themes may be brought to bear directly upon recent theorizing in developmental work as well as in the mainstream of cognitive literature that distinguishes between the active selection (facilitative) components and the strategic suppression (inhibitory) components of selective attention. Recent theorizing in cognitive psychology holds that selective attention comprises two complementary processes: facilitation of a selected signal (or channel) and suppression/inhibition of nonselected signals (or channels) (Cowan, 1988; Kinchla, 1992). In this two-process model, age decrements in selective attention may be ascribed to either or both components of attention, and a central goal of current research is to determine the relative contributions of each component to age differences in selective attention tasks (McDowd et al., 1995). Although there is some evidence that inhibitory processes may be deficient in later adulthood, there is also evidence that inhibitory processes function adequately under certain circumstances (as reviewed in the section on filtering). Thus, it may be premature to conclude that inhibitory deficits underlie the variety of age effects reported in the current review. Indeed, there is accumulating pessimism about the ability of a unitary inhibitory construct to account for the wide range of age effects identified in the cognitive aging literature (see, e.g., Kramer et al., 1994). Nonetheless, it is apparent that any successful model of the aging of attention must incorporate both facilitative and inhibitory components in order to capture the diverse age trends identified in the present review.

The two-process model of attention must incorporate the complexity and support effects summarized above. It must also leave open the possibility that the facilitative and inhibitory components operate independently of each other and moreover are likely to comprise multiple levels. Attending to a particular object or location involves the simultaneous processing of the attended information at some level(s) of analysis and inhibiting of the nonattended information, again at some level(s) of analysis. The particular foci of attention (and nonattention) and the levels at which they are engaged (or ignored) doubtless depend upon the goals of the perceiver. As such, both facilitative and inhibitory processes will vary across settings and circumstances and perhaps age as well, depending upon the particular combination of observer, task, and environmental contingencies. Situationally specific as this may sound, it is our belief that such an open-ended two-process model of attention is required to capture the complexity of the extant literature. Perhaps the goal of a unitary model of attention and aging is unrealistic (Plude et al., 1994). Nevertheless, pursuing such a goal forces consideration of its implications for other aspects of cognition.

One important implication of the two-process model of attention is that it makes different predictions about the fate of information that is facilitated versus inhibited: facilitated information is likely to be remembered, whereas inhibited information is unlikely to be remembered (Cowan, 1988, 1995). The assessment of age-related selective attention effects has for the most part been conducted quite separately from developmental work on memory, with notable exceptions involving research within the levels-of-processing framework. Although some researchers in cognitive aging have acknowledged the probable role of attentional processes in mediating age effects in memory, few studies have explicitly tested or controlled for such effects (see, e.g., Light, 1991; Madden, Pierce, & Allen, 1992). Thus an important goal for future developmental research (and theory) is to examine patterns of age differences and similarities at the interface of attention and memory, in the hope of providing a more comprehensive and integrated picture of life-span cognitive development (Plude et al., 1994). Such efforts have important implications not only for everyday memory and performance but also for the rehabilitation of age-related memory impairments. Selective attention deficits may play a key role in the memory complaints of elderly adults and, as such, deserve fuller consideration in both questionnaire-based studies and cognitive rehabilitation programs (Plude, 1992; Plude & Murphy, 1992).

CONCLUSIONS

The diversity of trends identified in the foregoing review suggest four specific avenues for future research and theory. First, longitudinal/sequential designs must be undertaken to promote a clearer picture of developmental trends in the aging of selective attention. Our entire review comprises cross-sectional studies which are appropriate for descriptive forays into developmental phenomena but are inadequate for explicating developmental (i.e., intraindividual) functions (Baltes, Reese, & Nesselroade, 1977; Wohlwill, 1973). In order to tease apart cohort, time-of-test, and age effects, sequential research designs are both desirable and necessary (e.g., Schaie, 1965).

Second, methodologies and research designs should promote age comparisons across the entire life span. Almost without exception, the studies reviewed compared young and elderly adults. With rare exceptions, middle-aged samples were not included, and rarer still were studies that encompassed the entire life span. The elucidation of suboptimal performance across the life span will be possible only when (1) researchers are able to make comparable measurements on subjects across a wide range of ages and (2) the measurements themselves distinguish the various cognitive components contributing to a given behavioral response.

Third, efforts to bring multiple levels of analysis to bear on the study of selective attention and aging should be encouraged and continued. Recent research and theory in cognitive neuroscience promises exciting new integrations between the computational and neurophysiological levels of analysis. Multidisciplinary efforts to integrate behavioral, psychophysiological, and neuroanatomical approaches in the study of attention are well under way (Kinchla, 1992; Posner & Peterson, 1990). This work began in the 1980s with efforts to study the electrophysiology of attention in various animal preparations, using single-cell electrode recording (Wurtz, Goldberg, & Robinson, 1980). More recently, this work has capitalized on technological breakthroughs which allow high-resolution neuroimaging in intact and alert human subjects (Posner & Peterson, 1990). The techniques include, but are not limited to, positron emission tomography (PET), event-related potentials (ERPs), and magnetic resonance imaging (MRI) (see Posner, 1992, for a review). The picture that is emerging from this revolutionary work is one of multiple attentional centers serving different functions and distributed widely throughout the brain. Thus, it is likely that specific mechanisms will continue to be the focus of future research.

And fourth, consistent with a life-span developmental orientation (Baltes, Reese, & Lipsitt, 1980) empirical studies and theory construction should be undertaken within a context that includes optimization and intervention as long-term goals. Evaluating patterns of age effects in the facilitative and inhibitory aspects of selective attention and establishing their connection to age-related memory function would not only provide a more comprehensive and integrative developmental theory but also promote the development of attention-based training regimes for compensating for the memory (and other cognitive) deficits commonly associated with aging. Given the emergence of attention training programs for the rehabilitation of closed-head injury (Posner & Rafal, 1987), it is likely that such programs will prove to be valuable in the rehabilitation of age-related memory deficits as well.

SUPPLEMENTAL READINGS

Hartley, A. A. (1992). Attention. In F. I. M. Craik & T. A. Salthouse (Eds.), *The handbook of aging and cognition* (pp. 3–49). Hillsdale, NJ: Erlbaum.

Madden, D. J., & Plude, D. J. (1993). Selective preservation of selective attention. In J. Cerella, W. J. Hoyer, J. Rybash, & M. L. Commons (Eds.), *Adult information processing: Limits on loss* (pp. 273–300). Orlando, FL: Academic Press.

Salthouse, T. A. (1991). *Theoretical perspectives on cognitive aging.* Hillsdale, NJ: Erlbaum.

ACKNOWLEDGMENTS

The authors wish to thank Drs. Bill Hoyer, Jim Enns, Jane Doussard-Roosevelt, Joan McDowd, and two anonymous reviewers for comments on earlier drafts.

REFERENCES

Allen, P. A. (1991). On age differences in processing variability and scanning speed. *Journal of Gerontology: Psychological Sciences, 45,* P191–201.

Baddeley, A. (1986). *Working memory.* Oxford: Clarendon.

Ball, K. K., Roenker, D. L., & Bruni, J. R. (1990). Developmental changes in attention and visual search throughout adulthood. In J. T. Enns (Ed.), *The development of attention: Research and theory* (pp. 489–508). Amsterdam: North Holland.

Baltes, P. B., & Reese, H. W. (1984). The life-span perspective in developmental psychology. In M. H. Bornstein & M. E. Lamb (Eds.), *Developmental psychology: An advanced textbook* (pp. 493–531). Hillsdale, NJ: Erlbaum.

Baltes, P. B., Reese, H. W., & Lipsitt, L. P. (1980). Life-span developmental psychology. *Annual Review of Psychology, 31,* 65–111.

Baltes, P. B., Reese, H. W., & Nesselroade, J. R. (1977). *Life-span developmental psychology: Introduction to research methods.* Belmont, CA: Wadsworth.

Barr, R. A., & Giambra, L. M. (1990). Age-related decrement in auditory selective attention. *Psychology and Aging, 5,* 597–599.

Birren, J. E. (1965). Age changes in speed of behavior: Its central nature and physiological correlates. In A. T. Welford & J. E. Birren (Eds.), *Behavior, aging and the nervous system* (pp. 191–216). Springfield, IL: Thomas.

Broadbent, D. E. (1958). *Perception and communication.* New York: Pergamon.

Bundesen, C. (1990). A theory of visual attention. *Psychological Review, 97,* 523–547.

Carter, J. C., Obler, L., Woodward, S., & Albert, M. L. (1983). The effect of increasing age on the latency for saccadic eye movements. *Journal of Gerontology, 38,* 318–320.

Cerella, J. (1985). Age-related decline in extra-foveal letter perception. *Journal of Gerontology, 40,* 727–736.

Cerella, J. (1990). Aging and information processing rate. In J. E. Birren & K. W. Schaie (Eds.), *Handbook of the psychology of aging* (3d ed., pp. 201–221). San Diego: Academic Press.

Cherry, E. C. (1953). Some experiments on the recognition of speech with one and two ears. *Journal of the Acoustical Society of America, 25,* 975–979.

Clancey, S., & Hoyer, W. J. (1994). Age and skill differences in the processing demands of visual recognition performance. *Developmental Psychology, 30,* 545–552.

Comalli, P. E., Jr., Wapner, S., & Werner, H. (1962). Interference of Stroop-Color-Word-test in childhood, adulthood, and aging. *Journal of Genetic Psychology, 100,* 47–53.

Connelly, S. L., & Hasher, L. (1993). Aging and the inhibition of spatial location. *Journal of Experimental Psychology: Human Perception and Performance, 19,* 1238–1250.

Coren, S., Ward, L. M., & Enns, J. T. (1994). *Sensation and perception* (4th ed.). New York: Harcourt Brace Jovanovich.

Cowan, N. (1988). Evolving conceptions of memory storage, selective attention, and their mutual constraints within the human information processing system. *Psychological Bulletin, 104,* 163–191.

Cowan, N. (1995). *Attention and memory: An integrated framework.* New York: Oxford Univ. Press.

Craik, F. I. M. (1977). Age differences in human memory. In J. E. Birren & K. W. Schaie (Eds.), *Handbook of the psychology of aging* (pp. 384–420). New York: Van Nostrand Reinhold.

Craik, F. I. M. (1986). A functional account of age differences in memory. In F. Klix & H. Hagendorf (Eds.), *Human memory and cognitive capabilities* (pp. 409–442). New York: Elsevier.

D'Aloisio, A., & Klein, R. M. (1990). Aging and the deployment of visual attention. In J. T. Enns (Ed.), *The development of attention: Research and theory* (pp. 447–466). Amsterdam: North Holland.

Duncan, J., & Humphreys, G. W. (1989). Visual search and stimulus similarity. *Psychological Review, 96,* 433–458.

Eriksen, B. A., & Eriksen, C. W. (1974). Effects of noise letters upon the identification of a target letter in a nonsearch task. *Perception and Psychophysics, 1,* 143–149.

Fisk, A. D., Fisher, D. L., & Rogers, W. A. (1991). General slowing alone cannot explain age-related search effects: A reply to Cerella (1992). *Journal of Experimental Psychology: General, 121,* 73–78.

Fisk, A. D., & Rogers, W. A. (1991). Toward an understanding of age-related memory and visual search effects. *Journal of Experimental Psychology: General, 120,* 131–149.

Folk, C., & Hoyer, W. J. (1992). Aging and shifts of visual spatial attention. *Psychology and Aging, 7,* 453–465.

Greenwood, P., & Parasuraman, R. (1991). Effects of aging on the speed and attentional costs of cognitive operations. *Developmental Neuropsychology, 7,* 421–434.

Hartley, A. A. (1992). Attention. In F. I. M. Craik & T. A. Salthouse (Eds.), *The handbook of aging and cognition* (pp. 3–49). Hillsdale, NJ: Erlbaum.

Hartley, A. A., Kieley, J. M., & Slabach, E. H. (1990). Age differences and similarities in the effects of cues and prompts. *Journal of Experimental Psychology: Human Perception and Performance, 16,* 523–537.

Hasher, L., Stoltzfus, E. R., Zacks, R. T., & Rypma, B. (1991). Age and inhibition. *Journal of Experimental Psychology: Learning, Memory, & Cognition, 17,* 163–169.

Hasher, L., & Zacks, R. T. (1988). Working memory, comprehension, and aging: A review and a new view. In G. H. Bower (Ed.), *The psychology of learning and motivation* (vol. 22, pp. 193–225). Orlando, FL: Academic Press.

Hoyer, W. J., & Familant, M. E. (1987). Adult age differences in the rate of processing expectancy information. *Cognitive Development, 2,* 59–70.

Hoyer, W. J., & Plude, D. J. (1982). Aging and the allocation of attentional resources in visual information processing. In R. Sekuler, D. Kline, & K. Dismukes (Eds.), *Aging and human visual function* (pp. 245–263). New York: Liss.

James, W. (1890). *Principles of psychology.* New York: Holt.

Johnston, W. A., & Dark, V. J. (1986). Selective attention. *Annual Review of Psychology, 37,* 43–75.

Kausler, D. (1992). *Experimental psychology of human aging* (2d ed.). New York: Wiley.

Kinchla, R. A. (1992). Attention. *Annual Review of Psychology, 43,* 711–742.

Klein, R. M., & Farrell, M. (1989). Search performance without eye movements. *Perception and Psychophysics, 46,* 476–482.

Kline, D. W., & Schieber, F. (1985). Vision and aging. In J. E. Birren & K. W. Schaie (Eds.), *Handbook of the psychology of aging* (2d ed., pp. 296–331). New York: Van Nostrand Reinhold.

Kosnik, W., Winslow, L., Kline, D., Rasinski, K., & Sekuler, R. (1988). Visual changes in daily life throughout adulthood. *Journal of Gerontology: Psychological Sciences, 43,* P63–P70.

Kramer, A. F., Humphrey, D. G., Larish, J. F., Logan, G. D., & Strayer, D. L. (1994). Aging and inhibition: Beyond a unitary view of inhibitory processing in attention. *Psychology and Aging, 9,* 491–512.

LaBerge, D. A. (1983). Spatial extant of attention to letters and words. *Journal of Experimental Psychology: Human Perception and Performance, 9,* 371–379.

Lachman, R., Lachman, J. L., & Butterfield, E. C. (1979). *Cognitive psychology and information processing: An introduction.* Hillsdale, NJ: Erlbaum.

Layton, B. (1975). Perceptual noise and aging. *Psychological Bulletin, 82,* 875–883.

Light, L. L. (1991). Memory and aging: Four hypotheses in search of data. *Annual Review of Psychology, 42,* 333–376.

MacLeod, C. M. (1991). Half a century of research on the Stroop effect: An integrative review. *Psychological Bulletin, 109,* 163–203.

Madden, D. J. (1983). Aging and distraction by highly familiar stimuli during visual search. *Developmental Psychology, 19,* 499–507.

Madden, D. J. (1984). Data-driven and memory-driven selective attention in visual search. *Journal of Gerontology, 39,* 72–78.

Madden, D. J. (1985). Adult age differences in memory-driven selective attention. *Developmental Psychology, 21,* 655–665.

Madden, D. J. (1986). Adult age differences in the attentional capacity demands of visual search. *Cognitive Development, 2,* 100–107.

Madden, D. J. (1990a). Adult age differences in attentional selectivity and capacity. *European Journal of Cognitive Psychology, 2,* 229–252.

Madden, D. J. (1990b). Adult age differences in the time course of visual attention. *Journal of Gerontology: Psychological Sciences, 45,* P9–P16.

Madden, D. J., Pierce, T. W., & Allen, P. A. (1992). Adult age differences in attentional allocation during memory search. *Psychology and Aging, 7,* 594–601.

Madden, D. J., & Plude, D. J. (1993). Selective preservation of selective attention. In J. Cerella, W. J. Hoyer, J. Rybash, & M. L. Commons (Eds.), *Adult information processing: Limits on loss* (pp. 273–300). Orlando, FL: Academic Press.

McDowd, J. M., & Birren, J. E. (1990). Aging and attentional processes. In J. E. Birren & K. W. Schaie (Eds.), *Handbook of the psychology of aging* (3d ed., pp. 222–233). San Diego: Academic Press.

McDowd, J. M., & Craik, F. I. M. (1988). Effects of aging and task difficulty on divided attention performance. *Journal of Experimental Psychology: Human Perception and Performance, 14*, 267–280.

McDowd, J. M., & Filion, D. L. (1991). Aging, selective attention, and inhibitory processes: A psychophysiological approach. *Psychology and Aging, 7*, 65–71.

McDowd, J. M., & Oseas-Kreger, D. M. (1991). Aging, inhibitory processes, and negative priming. *Journal of Gerontology: Psychological Sciences, 46*, P340–P345.

McDowd, J. M., Oseas-Kreger, D. M., & Filion, D. L. (1995). Inhibitory processes in cognition and aging. In F. N. Dempster & C. J. Brainerd (Eds.), *New perspectives on interference and inhibition in cognition* (pp. 363–400). San Diego: Academic Press.

Mishkin, M., Ungerleider, L. G., & Macko, K. A. (1983). Object vision and spatial vision: Two cortical pathways. *Trends in Neuroscience, 6*, 414–417.

Neisser, U., & Becklen, R. (1975). Selective looking: Attending to visually specified events. *Cognitive Psychology, 7*, 480–494.

Nissen, M. J., & Corkin, S. (1985). Effectiveness of attentional cuing in older and younger adults. *Journal of Gerontology, 41*, 181–191.

Norman, D. A., & Bobrow, D. (1975). On data-limited and resource limited processes. *Cognitive Psychology, 7*, 44–64.

Pachella, R. G. (1974). The interpretation of reaction time in information processing research. In B. H. Kantowitz (Ed.), *Human information processing: Tutorials in performance and cognition* (pp. 41–82). Hillsdale, NJ: Erlbaum.

Parasuraman, R., & Davies, D. R. (1984). *Varieties of attention.* New York: Academic Press.

Pepper, S. C. (1942). *World hypotheses.* Berkeley, CA: Univ. of California Press.

Plude, D. J. (1990). Aging, feature integration, and visual selective attention. In J. T. Enns (Ed.), *The development of attention: Research and theory* (pp. 467–487). Amsterdam: North Holland.

Plude, D. J. (1992). Attention and memory improvement. In D. Herrman, H. Weingartner, A. Searleman, & C. McEvoy (Eds.), *Memory improvement: Implications for memory theory* (pp. 150–168). New York: Springer.

Plude, D. J., & Doussard-Roosevelt, J. A. (1989). Aging, selective attention, and feature integration. *Psychology & Aging, 1*, 4–10.

Plude, D. J., & Doussard-Roosevelt, J. A. (1990). Aging and attention: Selectivity, capacity, and arousal. In E. A. Lovelace (Ed.), *Cognition and aging* (pp. 97–133). Amsterdam: Elsevier.

Plude, D. J., Enns, J. T., & Brodeur, D. (1994). The development of selective attention: A lifespan overview. *Acta Psychologica, 86*, 227–272.

Plude, D. J., & Hoyer, W. J. (1981). Adult age differences in visual search as a function of stimulus mapping and information load. *Journal of Gerontology, 36*, 598–604.

Plude, D. J., & Hoyer, W. J. (1985). Attention and performance: Identifying and localizing age deficits. In N. Charness (Ed.), *Aging and human performance* (pp. 47–99). London: Wiley.

Plude, D. J., & Hoyer, W. J. (1986). Age and the selectivity of visual information processing. *Psychology & Aging, 1*, 4–10.

Plude, D. J., & Murphy, L. J. (1992). Aging, selective attention, and everyday memory. In R. L. West & J. D. Sinnott (Eds.), *Everyday memory and aging: Current research and methodology* (pp. 235–245). New York: Springer.

Posner, M. I. (1980). Orienting of attention. *Quarterly Journal of Experimental Psychology, 32,* 3–25.

Posner, M. I. (1992). Attention as a cognitive and neural system. *Current Directions in Psychological Science, 1,* 11–14.

Posner, M. I., & Boies, S. E. (1971). Components of attention. *Psychological Review, 78,* 391–408.

Posner, M. I., & Peterson, S. E. (1990). The attention system of the human brain. *Annual Review of Neuroscience, 13,* 25–42.

Posner, M. I., & Rafal, R. D. (1987). Cognitive theories of attention and the rehabilitation of attentional deficits. In M. J. Meier, A. L. Benton, & L. Diller (Eds.), *Neuropsychological rehabilitation* (pp. 182–201). New York: Guilford.

Prinz, P. N., Dustman, R. E., & Emmerson, R. (1990). Electrophysiology and aging. In J. E. Birren & K. W. Schaie (Eds.), *Handbook of the psychology of aging* (3d ed., pp. 135–149). San Diego: Academic Press.

Rabbitt, P. M. A. (1964). Set and age in a choice-response task. *Journal of Gerontology, 19,* 301–306.

Rabbitt, P. M. A. (1965). An age decrement in the ability to ignore irrelevant information. *Journal of Gerontology, 20,* 233–238.

Rabbitt, P. M. A. (1982). Visual search. In C. R. Puff (Ed.), *Handbook of research methods in human memory and cognition* (pp. 27–62). New York: Academic Press.

Rabbitt, P. M. A., & Vyas, S. M. (1980). Selective anticipation for events in old age. *Journal of Gerontology, 35,* 913–919.

Rogers, W. A., & Fisk, A. D. (1991). Age-related differences in the maintenance and modification of automatic processes. *Human Factors, 33,* 45–56.

Rohrbaugh, J. W. (1984). The orienting reflex: Performance and central nervous system manifestations. In R. Parasuraman & D. R. Davies (Eds.), *Varieties of attention* (pp. 323–373). Orlando, FL: Academic Press.

Rybash, J., Hoyer, W. J., & Roodin, P. A. (1986). *Adult cognition and aging: Developmental changes in processing, knowing and thinking.* New York: Pergamon.

Salthouse, T. A. (1990). Working memory as a processing resource in cognitive aging. *Developmental Review, 10,* 101–124.

Salthouse, T. A. (1991). *Theoretical perspectives on cognitive aging.* Hillsdale, NJ: Erlbaum.

Salthouse, T. A., Rogan, J. D., & Prill, K. (1984). Division of attention: Age differences on a visually presented memory task. *Memory & Cognition, 12,* 613–620.

Schaie, K. W. (1965). A general model for the study of developmental problems. *Psychological Bulletin, 64,* 92–107.

Schneider, W., & Shiffrin, R. M. (1977). Controlled and automatic human information processing. I: Detection, search, and attention. *Psychological Review, 84,* 1–66.

Scialfa, C. T. (1990). Adult age differences in visual search: The role of non-attentional factors. In J. T. Enns (Ed.), *The development of attention: Research and theory* (pp. 509–526). Amsterdam: North Holland.

Scialfa, C. T., & Kline, D. W. (1988). Effects of noise type and retinal eccentricity on age differences in identification and localization. *Journal of Gerontology: Psychological Sciences, 43,* P91–P99.

Scialfa, C. T., Kline, D. W., & Lyman, B. J. (1987). Age differences in target identification as a function of retinal location and noise level: Examination of the useful field of view. *Psychology and Aging, 2,* 14–19.

Shepard, M., & Muller, H. J. (1989). Movement versus focusing of attention. *Perception and Psychophysics, 46,* 146–154.

Somberg, B. L., & Salthouse, T. A. (1982). Divided attention abilities in young and old adults. *Journal of Experimental Psychology: Human Perception and Performance, 8,* 651–663.

Stroop, J. R. (1935). Studies of interference in serial verbal reactions. *Journal of Experimental Psychology, 18,* 643–662.

Sullivan, M. P., & Faust, M. E. (1993). Evidence for identity inhibition during selective attention in old adults. *Psychology and Aging, 9,* 491–512.

Tipper, S. P. (1985). The negative priming effect: Inhibitory priming by ignored objects. *Quarterly Journal of Experimental Psychology, 37A,* 571–590.

Treisman, A. M. (1986). Properties, parts, and objects. In K. Boff, L. Kaufman, & J. Thomas (Eds.), *Handbook of perception and performance* (vol. 35, pp. 1–70). New York: Wiley.

Treisman, A. M., & Gelade, G. (1980). A feature-integration theory of attention. *Cognitive Psychology, 12,* 97–136.

Treisman, A. M., & Gormican, S. (1988). Feature analysis in early vision: Evidence from search asymmetries. *Psychological Review, 95,* 15–48.

Welford, A. T. (1965). Performance, biological mechanisms and age: A theoretical sketch. In A. T. Welford & J. E. Birren (Eds.), *Behavior, aging and the nervous system* (pp. 3–20). Springfield, IL: Thomas.

Wohlwill, J. F. (1973). *The study of behavioral development.* New York: Academic Press.

Wright, L. L., & Elias, J. W. (1979). Age differences in the effects of perceptual noise. *Journal of Gerontology, 34,* 704–708.

Wurtz, R. H., Goldberg, M. E., & Robinson, D. L. (1980). Behavioral modulation of visual responses in monkeys. *Progress in Psychobiology and Physiological Psychology, 9,* 42–83.

Zacks, J., & Zacks, R. T. (1993). Visual search times assessed without reaction times: A new method and an application to aging. *Journal of Experimental Psychology: Human Perception and Performance, 19,* 798–813.

C H A P T E R

6

MEMORY CHANGES IN NORMAL AGING

Anderson D. Smith and Julie L. K. Earles
Georgia Institute of Technology

INTRODUCTION

■ Overview

Through laboratory studies, cognitive aging researchers have validated what is a widely accepted belief about the psychology of aging, the belief that memory declines as we grow older. In a laboratory experiment, the experimenter first presents some to-be-remembered materials to the study participants (encoding). Second, some interval of time passes while typically the participants engage in some other activity (retention). Third, after the retention interval the experimenter asks the participant to remember the information presented earlier (retrieval). Laboratory studies of memory typically have the benefit of precise control so that variables being studied can be isolated and independently manipulated or measured. One criticism of laboratory studies is that they are contrived and artificial and thus do not adequately simulate everyday memory performance. There is a distinction, therefore, between studying memory in the laboratory and studying memory in the context in which memory performance occurs in everyday life. Each is important for different reasons. Studying memory in context obviously provides a description of memory use in everyday life and how memory is affected by different experiences. This research is discussed in Chapter 12. Laboratory research, on the other hand, provides the experimental control necessary to provide precise tests of theoretical hypotheses. Both bodies of literature point to the complexities involved in describing memory change and memory stability throughout the life course.

The typical result shown by laboratory experiments is poorer memory performance in older adult participants than in younger participants. For example, Salthouse (1982) examined a number of studies of paired-association learning involving different-aged adults. Paired-association learning involves presenting pairs of items and then, after the retention interval, asking for the recall of the second member of each pair when the first member is presented as a retrieval cue. As can be seen in Figure 6.1, the effect of age in all these stud-

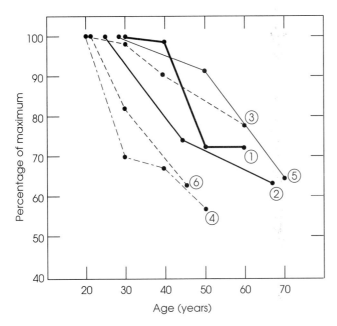

FIGURE 6.1 Paired-association scores at various ages expressed as a percentage of the maximum score across all ages. Numbers refer to different experiments: 1—adapted from Canestrari (1968); 2—adapted from Gladis & Braun (1958); 3—adapted from Hulicka (1966); 4—adapted from Monge (1971); 5—adapted from Smith (1975a); 6—adapted from Thorndike, Bregman, Tilton, & Woodyard (1928). Figure taken from Salthouse (1982). (*Source:* Reprinted with permission from Salthouse. Copyright 1982 by Springer-Verlag New York Inc.)

ies was essentially the same. Paired-associate recall becomes progressively worse with increased age (the negative slope of the lines in Figure 6.1). Each of the experiments in Figure 6.1 involved very different procedures and different to-be-remembered materials because the various experimenters were asking different questions about paired-association recall which involved different task parameters. This explains why the overall level of recall differs among the studies. The nature of the age effects, however, was very similar from one experiment to the next.

The interesting thing about laboratory studies of memory and aging, however, is that, while the finding seen with paired-associate recall is the normative finding, there are many occasions when age differences in memory performance are negligible or even nonexistent. Clearly, the relationship between age and memory is a complex one. The magnitude of age effects on memory performance can differ considerably as one manipulates the nature of the task the participant has to perform and the nature of the materials the participant has to remember.

■ Major Theories and Conceptual Frameworks

There are two major conceptual frameworks that are used to describe memory changes as a function of age. The first attempts to attribute differential age effects to one specific memory structure or memory process as opposed to others. Different memory systems (e.g., procedural, episodic, or semantic memory) or different memory structures (e.g., primary, working, or long-term memory) provide frameworks for describing age effects. By breaking memory up into its components and then showing that age differences are specific to one or another of these components, researchers of aging and memory provide a more precise analytic description of the nature of the relationship between age and memory. This conceptual framework has been very popular over the past 25 years and will be discussed in more detail throughout this chapter.

The second major conceptual framework attributes age effects in memory tasks to differences in the availability of cognitive resources, that is, the "mental energy" necessary to perform cognitive activities. Because older adults are assumed to have reduced cognitive resources, age differences will be found to the extent that the memory task requires self-initiated or deliberate processing. The cognitive resource hypothesis comes in many different forms as different cognitive mechanisms have been proposed to represent resources. Some investigators assume that perceptual speed is the underlying mechanism governing cognitive resources, accounting for the reduction in cognitive resources as we grow older (Salthouse, 1994). How fast we can perform mental operations determines the efficiency and effectiveness of the cognitive processing necessary for memory encoding, storage, and retrieval. Another possible mechanism for cognitive resources would be working memory, the ability to process information at the moment (Salthouse & Babcock, 1991). If we are less efficient at processing current information (i.e., keeping things in mind), we would not be able to engage in efficient self-initiated, deliberate processing. Another cognitive resource hypothesis attributes older persons' memory problems not to a reduction in their working memory capacity but to their inability to restrict working memory to task-relevant items. Hasher and Zacks (1988) have proposed that our ability to actively inhibit task-irrelevant thoughts interferes with effective deliberate processing. Because working memory contains task-irrelevant thoughts, there is less working memory to devote to relevant information that needs to be processed.

Other subsidiary resource hypotheses deal more with the effects of reduced resources. Craik (1986), for example, predicts that age differences will be smaller to the extent that the memory task provides "environmental support" to the participants. In other words, if the task itself provides rich and elaborate learning and retrieval cues (more environmental support), less self-initiated deliberate processing would be required and age differences would be smaller. In a similar vein, another hypothesis indicates that age differences would be larger on a memory task if the participant has to actively integrate the contextual information with the information that he or she is trying to remember (Craik & Jennings, 1992; Park, Smith, Morrell, Puglisi, & Dudley, 1990). Even though the various resource hypotheses differ in what is emphasized, they all share the assumption that older adults are less efficient in the cognitive processing required to perform memory tasks. Many of these hypotheses will be discussed throughout this chapter.

■ Major Methodological Issues

As is obvious from the above discussion, the major theoretical issue is what conceptual framework to use to best describe memory and aging. How we conceptualize memory is the major determinant of how we will best understand the effects of age on memory. It will also determine what laboratory methods are used to study aging and memory.

Given the fact that age differences are not always found on memory tasks, it becomes theoretically meaningful to determine the underlying factors that determine when age differences are found and when they are not. The way in which researchers go about this determination, however, depends on their conceptualization of memory.

Two different empirical methodologies have been used by researchers interested in determining the theoretical factors that determine age differences in memory. The first approach involves using experimental tasks to look for interactions between age and manipulated variables that are assumed to vary in some meaningful theoretical way. If significant interactions are found (i.e., larger age differences in one condition than in another condition), the assumed underlying theoretical factor is presumed to be important in determining age differences. (In this chapter we will review these interactions and the various theoretical arguments used to interpret the interactions.) There are problems with the experimental approach, however. When looking for interactions, the investigator has to be careful to avoid ceiling and floor effects that could artificially produce interactions. As can be seen in Figure 6.2, what looks like a significant memory difference in the old group and a nonexistent effect in the young group is more likely simply a ceiling effect for the young group. Because their performance in both conditions is nearly perfect, there is no room for the experimental manipulation to have an effect. The advantage of experimental techniques, however, is that the experimenter can precisely control the experimental tasks in order to make manipulations that are theoretically meaningful.

A second methodological approach to understanding age differences in memory perfor-

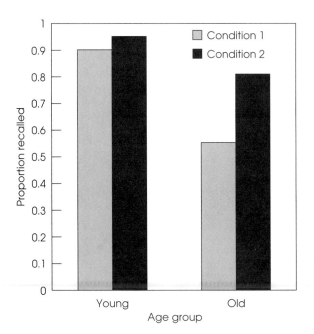

FIGURE 6.2 Illustration of interaction between age and memory task condition in which the ceiling effect compromises the interpretation of interaction.

mance utilizes statistical control techniques, rather than the analysis of interactions, as analytic procedures. If a researcher using these correlational research techniques believes that a particular factor is important in determining age differences in memory, independent measures of this factor are developed along with separate measures of memory performance. Then, with correlational techniques, the extent to which the measured factor is associated with the age-related variance in memory performance is determined. If a significant portion of the age-related variance in memory performance is associated with the measured factor, that factor is presumed to be important in understanding the age differences in memory. Studies using this technique will also be discussed in this chapter.

In summary, the experimental method is primarily used to provide a theoretical, analytic description of age effects on memory. The correlational approach is primarily used to uncover underlying mechanisms or mediators of age-related differences on memory tasks.

THEORETICAL PERSPECTIVES AND METHODOLOGICAL APPROACHES

■ Experimental Methods

Most of the research on aging and memory performance has involved using the experimental method to examine the presence or absence of age differences as task and stimulus manipulations are made. Hypotheses about the presence or absence of age effects in memory performance have been framed by the particular characteristics of one theoretical account of memory or another. For this reason, most of the theoretical debate in memory aging has dealt with advocacy of one particular theoretical view of memory or another. In this section, we will review these different theoretical views and discuss research on age-related memory differences that has been generated to address these theoretical issues. A typical study addressing memory and aging in this way would include a manipulation of some variable that is assumed to differ on some theoretical dimension and see if that variable interacts significantly with age. If some theoretical construct was responsible for age-related memory differences, manipulating this theoretical construct, by manipulating a variable assumed to differ on the construct, should determine the size of the observed age difference.

Memory Systems

One popular theoretical approach to the study of memory over the past quarter century has been a memory systems approach. Rather than conceptualizing memory as a single entity, separate memory systems are hypothesized, each with different characteristics. A summary of the memory systems approach is presented in Figure 6.3. While this particular summary certainly does not represent consensus among memory investigators (some would have fewer components and some would have more), it does at least represent the various components of memory that have been proposed to be important in understanding adult age differences. Theoretical debates about memory systems have primarily dealt with whether the various components are independent of one another (McKoon, Ratcliff, & Dell, 1986; Tulving,

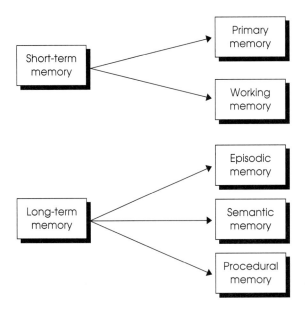

FIGURE 6.3 Hypothetical memory structures proposed by the memory systems approach.

1985) and whether the various components represent different anatomical structures in the brain (Squire, Knowlton, & Musen, 1993; Tulving, 1987). Theoretical debates about aging and memory systems have centered on what systems show age differences and what systems do not.

Short-term versus long-term memory The early version of the memory systems perspective made a distinction only between short-term memory and long-term memory (see, e.g., Atkinson & Shiffrin, 1971). Using this perspective, early cognitive aging research concluded that age differences were found in long-term memory but not short-term memory (see, e.g., Craik, 1968). One popular method for separating short-term memory performance from long-term memory performance was to examine the serial position curve seen in free recall. It was assumed that different parts of the serial position curve (differential recall of items presented at different positions in the input list) reflected the different influences of short-term memory and long-term memory. The primacy portion of the curve (better recall for the first few items presented) primarily reflects better long-term retention for the first few items in the list, probably due to differential rehearsal and distinctiveness of encoding. The recency portion (better recall for the last few items presented in the list), on the other hand, reflects recall from short-term memory. The last few items are still available in primary memory because they were the last presented and there was no retention interval or interference between them and the cue to recall. Both Craik (1968) and Smith (1975a) found that young and old adults had similar recency effects, but that older adults did worse on the primacy portion of the curve. Even though these effects have been replicated over the years by several investigators (Arenberg, 1976; Walsh & Baldwin, 1977), some investigators did find age differences on the recency portion of the curve (Parkinson, Lindholm, & Inman, 1982). Furthermore, a recent analysis of age and recency data by Salthouse (1991a) points to possible problems with the power of the comparisons as to the primacy and recency data (power represents the ability or inability of a statistical test to detect real differences when they are small). Salthouse points out that, even though individual experiments may show no significant difference in recency between young and old adults, young adults had larger recency scores in every single experiment he reviewed. In an attempt to clarify the conflicting findings about aging and short-term memory, Craik and Jennings (1992) point out that, in order for recency to be a pure measure of primary memory, the probability that recall of the recency items comes from long-term memory rather than short-term memory must be taken into account. This has not been done in most experiments. When this is done, even when there is an age difference in total recall, the age differences are limited to measures of long-term memory (Delbecq-Derouesné & Beauvois, 1989).

Primary versus working memory There is, however, another, much more fundamental, conceptual problem with the simple comparison of short-term memory and long-term memory. As can be seen in Figure 6.3, a simple dichotomy between short-term memory and long-term memory is not sufficient to capture the complexities of a systems analysis of memory. Furthermore, when a more complex conceptualization of memory is considered, age effects are not as consistent as is implied by a simple dichotomy. When different types of short-term memory and different types of long-term memory are examined, age effects in both short-term and long-term memory are either found or not found depending on which particular component is tested.

The recency effect discussed above is generally considered to represent a component of short-term memory called *primary memory* in Figure 6.3, the passive "holding in mind" of a small amount of information that was recently experienced. Often, however, short-term memory involves the processing of information as well as just storing it, such as when comprehending or producing speech, when trying to understand text while reading, or when performing a mental arithmetic task. As discussed earlier, this active, ongoing processing is referred to as "working memory" by contemporary memory researchers (see, e.g., Baddeley, 1986).

A good estimate of primary memory would be the recency effect as measured in the Delbecq-Derouesné and Beauvois (1989) study. They found no age differences in primary memory. Unlike primary memory, however, older adults seem to do consistently worse than younger adults on working memory tasks. An example of a working memory task is the computational span task developed by Salthouse and his colleagues (see, e.g., Babcock & Salthouse, 1990). A series of simple arithmetic problems is presented and the participant provides the answer to each problem (e.g., $3 + 2 = ?, 7 - 3 = ?, 4 + 5 = ?$). In addition to providing the answers as the problems are flashed on the screen ("5," "4," "9"), the participants must also remember the last digit in each problem and report the digits when a recall cue is given at the end of the problem sequence (e.g., report "2," "3," "5"). The number of digits participants can remember while performing the arithmetic task is their working memory span. Similar working memory tasks have involved listening to or reading sentences while simultaneously remembering a word from each sentence (Wingfield, Stine, Lahar, & Aberdeen, 1988).

Because age differences are nonexistent or very small on primary memory tasks and much larger on working memory tasks (see Dobbs & Rule, 1989; Wingfield et al., 1988, for direct comparisons), one hypothesis is that the processing requirement in working memory tasks rather than the storage requirement produces age differences. This hypothesis was tested directly by Salthouse and Babcock (1991), who administered component tasks specifically designed to separately measure processing efficiency, storage capacity, and coordination effectiveness, three assumed components of working memory performance. As expected, the pattern of results indicated that processing efficiency was the most important determinant of age differences in working memory. Furthermore, the speed with which elementary cognitive operations can be successfully executed proved to be the best estimate of processing efficiency.

Episodic versus semantic memory Just as the single, unitary concept of "short-term memory" was inadequate to theoretically describe age-related effects in memory, the unitary concept of "long-term memory" has had to be decomposed into several memory systems in order to describe age differences adequately. As seen in Figure 6.3, three different long-term memory components have been hypothesized: episodic memory (retrieval by reconstructing the encoded experience; the internal diary), semantic memory (retrieval as "world knowledge"; the internal encyclopedia), and procedural memory (skills). Again, whether these different systems are independent of one another is still a hotly debated issue (see, e.g., Tulving, 1985). In general, episodic memory is the one system in long-term memory most susceptible to age effects, with procedural memory and semantic memory often showing only negligible age effects.

Episodic memory involves the encoding and retrieval of specific episodes or events; until recently, it has been the memory system most studied in the laboratory. Lists of items are typically presented to the experimental participant, and later the participant is asked to remember the particular items that were presented on these lists. There is a vast literature on episodic memory and aging (Craik & Jennings, 1992; Kausler, 1991). The nature of the episodic memory deficits seen in older adults has been studied by varying the type of materials to be remembered, the instructions to the participants, the type of test used to measure episodic memory, and various other task variables to determine the conditions under which age differences are maximized and those in which they are minimized. In general, age differences are larger in episodic memory tasks that are more difficult and involve more deliberate processing, either at encoding or at retrieval (Craik, 1986; Craik & Jennings, 1992; Light, 1991).

Park, Smith, et al. (1990), for example, manipulated the degree to which deliberate processing was required to associate the stimulus cue and response item in a paired-association recall task. This was done to test the hypothesis that older adults have greater problems integrating contextual information (i.e., the stimulus cue) with to-be-remembered information (i.e., the response item). Both the stimulus cue and response items were simple line drawings of common objects. The picture pairs were (1) unrelated to each other prior to presentation of the list (e.g., cherry–ant), (2) weak semantic associates (e.g., spider–ant), or (3) presented in a perceptually interacting way (e.g., ant eating the cherry). The different types of picture pairs are illustrated in Table 6.1. As can be seen in the table, age differences were smaller when there were preexisting associations between the stimulus cues and response items. The older participants' performance was only 36 percent of the level of the younger participants' performance in the "unrelated/noninteracting" condition but 66 percent ("per-

TABLE 6.1 Mean Recall Performance as a Function of Age and Type of Association between Stimulus Cue and Response

	Cuing Condition		
Age Group	Unrelated/ Noninteracting	Perceptually Interacting	Semantically Related
Young	16.18	14.53	23.78
Old	5.79	9.6	16.59

Source: Adapted with permission from Park, Smith, Morrell, Puglisi, & Dudley (1990). *Journal of Gerontology: Psychological Sciences.* Copyright 1992, Gerontological Society of America.

ceptually interacting") and 70 percent ("semantically related") in the two associated conditions. When integration of the stimulus cue and response item already exists, less deliberate processing is necessary in order to remember the association. Because the unrelated pairs require more deliberate processing to associate them than did the weakly associated ones, age differences are larger with the unrelated pairs.

The same conclusion seems to hold at retrieval. When the nature of the test used to measure episodic memory is varied, the size of age-related differences also varies. Free recall, for example, requires more deliberate processing at retrieval than does recognition in which potential target items are presented to the participants and they only have to pick out which items were presented earlier in the presentation list. Most studies have found age differences in recognition performance to be smaller than age differences in recall tasks (see, e.g., Craik & McDowd, 1987; Schonfield & Robertson, 1966; Smith, 1975b). In their classic experiment, Schonfield and Robertson (1966) presented a list of 24 words to participants from five different adult age groups. The words were then tested first by free recall and second by recognition. There were consistent differences in free-recall performance across the age groups. No significant age differences were found at all, however, with the recognition task. While some investigators do find age differences in recognition memory, they are smaller than those found with recall tasks.

Unfortunately, because of differences in the ways in which recall and recognition are scored, as well as differences in the probability of a correct response due to guessing, it is difficult to directly compare recall and recognition performance. One clever approach, as an alternative to a direct comparison of recall and recognition, was taken by Craik and McDowd (1987). If recall requires more deliberate processing than recognition, performance on a secondary task should be more detrimentally affected while recalling than while recognizing. In other words, the greater deliberate processing required of recall tasks should interfere more with the ability of participants to perform an additional concurrent reaction-time task while trying to recall. Furthermore, while experimental participants at all ages should show losses in secondary task performance with recall, older participants should show even greater losses. Craik and McDowd (1987) had young and old participants view several different paired-association lists consisting of stimulus phrases, each followed by the response word (e.g., A body of water = POND). For half of the lists, recall was tested immediately after presentation of the list. The stimulus phrases were presented auditorially and the participant produced the response vocally. After all the lists had been presented, the other half of the lists was tested by delayed recognition. The words were presented auditorially and the participants indicated vocally, with either "yes" or "no," whether the item had been presented before. The use of delayed recognition together with immediate recall was an attempt to equate the overall performance on, and thus overall difficulty of, the two retrieval tasks. Before the lists were presented, after recall, and after recognition, baseline measures on an auditory reaction-time task was measured. Also, the auditory reaction-time task was performed during the retrieval interval at both recall and recognition. Figure 6.4 shows the performance scores at retrieval (left-hand panel) and the costs of retrieval (right-hand panel) in this experiment. The cost of retrieval (the amount of deliberate processing) was the difference between reaction time while performing the recall or recognition score minus baseline score.

Even though recall showed higher performance than recognition for both age groups (left-hand panel) because of the delayed nature of recognition, the cost of retrieval for recall was larger than in recognition (right-hand panel), and this difference was larger in the older age group. The results are consistent with the hypothesis that age differences are larger for memory tasks requiring a greater degree of deliberate processing.

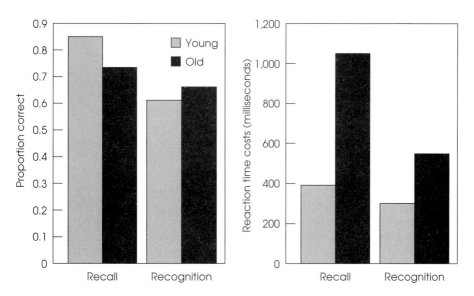

FIGURE 6.4 The left-hand panel shows age differences in percentage of correct cued recall performance and recognition performance (hits minus false alarms). The right-hand panel shows the reaction time costs in milliseconds (dual-task reaction time minus baseline reaction time) as a function of age and memory task (*Source:* Craik & McDowd, 1987. Reprinted with permission from Craik. Copyright 1987, American Psychological Association.)

As mentioned earlier, episodic memory also depends on the ability to use context to retrieve information from memory. Another hypothesis for age-related differences in episodic memory is that older adults do not pay attention to specific contextual details at encoding as well as younger adults do and therefore are deficient in their ability to use context to retrieve episodically (Burke & Light, 1981; Rabinowitz & Ackerman, 1982). If older adults do not encode as much specific contextual detail as younger adults, they should show less "encoding specificity." The encoding specificity principle holds that retrieval from episodic memory should be best when the specific context at retrieval matches the context at encoding. If older adults do not encode as much contextual detail as younger adults, their memory performance should not be as sensitive to the reinstatement of encoding context at retrieval (Kausler, 1991). There is evidence, however, with both picture recognition (Park, Puglisi, Smith, & Dudley, 1987) and with word recall (Puglisi, Park, Smith, & Dudley, 1988) that young and old adults show equivalent encoding specificity effects in most cases. In the Park et al. (1987) study, for example, a context picture that was presented with a to-be-remembered picture at encoding was either present or absent during the recognition task. Both younger and older participants showed much better recognition performance if the context picture present at encoding was also present at test (i.e., encoding specificity).

There are some findings, however, that show that, under certain conditions, older adults do have problems with context. Older adults seem to show less encoding specificity, for example, when it is difficult to integrate the context and the to-be-remembered information during learning. In a second experiment, Puglisi et al. (1988), in their word-recall task, found no encoding specificity for the older participants when they had to perform a secondary task (monitoring digits). Furthermore, Rabinowitz, Craik, and Ackerman (1982) found equal encoding specificity effects in young and old adults when the cues were strongly related to the items to be remembered but less encoding specificity in the old subjects when the cues were weak associates. Hess (1984) obtained similar results using a recognition task. Again, these examples of less encoding specificity in older adults than in younger adults may be due to the necessity of using deliberate processing to integrate the context with the information they are trying to remember, either because of difficulty in integrating context with to-be-remembered information because of the nature of the materials used or because of the secondary task's competing processing requirements, which restrict the deliberate processing one can perform. As discussed earlier, when deliberate processing is required, either at encoding or at retrieval, age differences in episodic memory seem to be larger.

So far, we have been discussing context that is a part of the memory task but not part of the to-be-remembered material (i.e., the stimulus cue in a paired-association task). Sometimes, however, the contextual information can be a characteristic of the memory stimulus, even though it is independent of the content of the information to be remembered (e.g., the color or font a word is presented in, the spatial location of the stimulus item on the screen at presentation). Early research on this "stimulus-bound" context focused on whether such contextual aspects of a memory stimulus are automatically encoded, as proposed by Hasher and Zacks (1979). Hasher and Zacks had proposed that these stimulus-bound contextual aspects were automatically encoded and thus would be insensitive to age differences. Most research on stimulus-bound context has looked at the spatial location of to-be-remembered information, and, as summarized by Smith and Park (1990), age differences are typically found in recall of spatial location. They reviewed 20 different studies looking at age and spatial memory and found that age differences were shown in 16 of the studies. Age differences have also been found with other stimulus-bound context attributes such as color (Park & Puglisi, 1985), sex of the person presenting the items (Kausler & Puckett, 1981), and source of the information (experimenter or overhead projector) (McIntyre & Craik, 1987). Clearly then, there are age differences in memory for context. Unlike the earlier context studies, in which the information was identified as a possible memory cue and thus was processed as such, the stimulus-bound context information is assumed not to be deliberately processed at encoding. Whatever information gets into memory in this case is incidental and automatic. Deliberate processing, however, would be necessary at retrieval when trying to recall stimulus-bound context, and for this reason age differences emerge when one is deliberately trying to remember the spatial information.

A new method designed to measure the age effects of deliberate processing independently of age effects on familiarity (automatic processing) within a single memory task has been developed by Jacoby (1991). For example, Jennings and Jacoby (1993, experiment 2) have shown that in a recognition memory experiment, there were significant age effects on the deliberate processing component of recognition memory but not on the familiarity component. Most theories of recognition memory assume that it involves both decisions about familiarity and judgments based on deliberate recollection (see, e.g., Mandler, 1980). In the Jennings and Jacoby (1993) study, participants first looked at a list containing words that they simply read. Then they listened to a second list that they were told they would be tested on later. Following the two lists, they were given two recognition tests. For both tests they were given pairs of words, one of which they had seen earlier, either as a word they read in the first list or as a word they heard in the second list. The second word in the pair was a new word they had not seen or heard previously. In the first memory test, they were misinformed that one word in each pair had been presented auditorially in list 2 and the other word was either new or one that was presented in list 1. They were to pick the word they had heard in list 2 (exclusion test). If they picked a word that was presented in list 1, they could do so only through familiarity, because, if they had recollected the word, they would have correctly rejected it because it was a list 1 word. In the second memory test, they were told that one word from each pair was a new item and they were to pick the one they had either seen or heard before. In this case, their judgments could be based on either familiarity or recollection (inclusion test). By subtracting the estimate of recognition due to familiarity derived from the first test (exclusion) from the score on the second test (inclusion), an estimate of recall based on recollection alone could be derived. As can be seen in Table 6.2, the results showed clearly that age effects were limited to the recollection component of recognition memory. Estimates of familiarity showed no age effects. This analytical procedure provides further support for the conclusion that age differences in episodic remembering may depend on the extent of deliberate processing required to perform the memory task.

As can be seen from the earlier discussion, even in episodic memory, where age differences are commonly found, the types of materials tested and other task variables determine the presence and size of age differences. Typically, however, age differences are seen in episodic memory but not on semantic memory tasks. While episodic memories are retrieved by contextual cues based on the original experience, semantic memories are retrieved conceptually. In fact, little or no information is typically available on when and where we learned semantic information that is available in our memories. This information is simply a part of

TABLE 6.2 Estimates of the Probability of Picking an Old Word in Recognition Memory on the Basis of Recollection and Familiarity		
Age Group	**Recollection**	**Familiarity**
Young	.19	.62
Old	.07	.58

Source: Adapted from Jennings & Jacoby (1993). Permission to use granted by Jennings. Copyright 1993, American Psychological Association.

our "world knowledge." If there were differences in the semantic memories of older adults, they would be due to differences either in the organization of semantic memory or in their ability to gain access to semantic information.

There is very little evidence that semantic knowledge is structured differently for young and old adults (Light, 1992). For example, one good measure of semantic memory is a vocabulary test in which participants provide meanings for words, such as the subtest of the Wechsler Adult Intelligence Scale (WAIS). While most of the cognitive subtests on the WAIS show age differences in favor of young adults, the WAIS vocabulary test in many cases actually shows continual improvement across the adult age span (Salthouse, 1982). Coming up with word meanings does not seem to be detrimentally affected by age.

The reverse, however, coming up with words given their meaning, does seem to be affected. Older adults seem to have problems finding words (see, e.g., Obler & Albert, 1985) and do experience more "tip-of-the-tongue" experiences (Burke, MacKay, Worthley, & Wade, 1991). Because older adults, in most cases, do eventually come up with the correct word or item, however, this suggests a problem with access rather than with underlying structure. In fact, Burke et al. (1991) concluded that tip-of-the-tongue states experienced by older adults are probably due to the problems of composing the phonological code for words rather than to problems in underlying semantic structure.

Investigators have also used a variety of other methods to determine if semantic memory structure varies according to age (Light, 1992). For example, early research on free association and aging suggested that older adults made fewer paradigmatic responses (i.e., free associations from the same class such as "dog"–"cat") on a free-association test and more syntagmatic responses (responses from a different grammatical class such as "dog"–"bark") (Riegel & Riegel, 1964). Such a finding would imply that the semantic networks of older adults are organized differently from those of younger adults in that qualitatively different responses were activated. More recent experiments, however, have failed to replicate this finding with either the free association to words (Burke & Peters, 1986; Lovelace & Cooley, 1982) or free association to pictures (Puglisi, Park, & Smith, 1987) or in providing instances for category names (Howard, 1980). Instead, it has consistently been found that there are no age differences in the type of responses given. Therefore, to the extent that free-association studies provide insight into the organization of semantic memory, there is little reliable evidence for differences.

Procedural memory represents learned cognitive and motor skills. Evidence that it is distinct from episodic memory comes from studies showing retention of skilled responses independent of any conscious recollection, even in amnesiacs who have no recollection at all that they had even learned a skill (J. Cohen and Squire, 1980). Indirect or implicit measures of memory are often used to test for procedural memory. (Because this research is discussed in Chapter 7, it is only mentioned here.) Like semantic memory, however, procedural memory seems minimally affected by age.

In summary, using the memory systems approach, for short-term memory, larger age differences have been found in working memory than in primary memory, and for long-term memory, larger age differences have been found in episodic memory than in semantic or procedural memory. Mitchell (1989) tested the different components of long-term memory—procedural memory, episodic memory, and semantic memory—in the same participants. Supporting the literature just discussed, he found large differences in episodic memory and minimal differences in procedural or semantic memory. Furthermore, he did a factor analysis on the 11 different measures of memory in his study and found 3 dominant factors that correspond to the 3 hypothesized memory systems.

In our own laboratory, we tested groups of young (18–39 years), middle-aged (40–59 years) and old (60–80 years) on measures of primary memory (digit span), working memory (reading span), episodic memory (free recall of words), and semantic memory (WAIS vocabulary) in the same testing session. As can be seen in Table 6.3, age differences were found in working memory but not in primary memory, and in episodic memory but not in semantic memory, again supporting the previous discussion.

Memory Processes

It should be noticed that, for those memory systems that show reliable and significant age differences (working memory and episodic memory), the nature of the age differences has been attributed to processing differences (i.e., processing efficiency in working memory and degree of deliberate processing in episodic memory). The nature of cognitive processes, rather than the nature of the various cognitive structures, seems to predominate in explana-

TABLE 6.3 Mean Performance on Tests of Primary Memory (Digit Span), Working Memory (Reading Span), Episodic Memory (Free Recall), and Semantic Memory (Vocabulary) as a Function of Age

Age Group	Short-Term Memory		Long-Term Memory	
	Primary	Working	Episodic	Semantic
Young	7.2	2.8	22.8	24.8
Old	7.0	1.6	14.9	27.0
	N.S.*	$p < .01$†	$p < .01$	N.S.

*N.S. = Not significant.

†p value from analysis of variance.

tions of age-related memory differences. This has been one criticism of a structural systems approach to memory aging research. Attention therefore has been focused on cognitive processing differences between age groups.

In basic memory research, the shift of attention from structure to process has primarily been influenced by the levels-of-processing conceptual framework developed by Craik and Lockhart (1972), who proposed that the durability of memory traces is determined by the level of elaborate processing at encoding. This conceptual framework was later expanded to include the level of processing required at retrieval as well as encoding. Memory would be better to the extent that elaborate semantic processing is used. The method of choice to test the levels of processing framework was the orienting task. Participants were presented lists of items with different tasks that oriented them to different aspects of the items. If the orienting task required semantic processing (e.g., "Does the word fit into this sentence?"), memory was better than if it oriented the participant to a more superficial characteristic of the item (e.g., "Does the word rhyme with this word?" "Does the word have the letter *E* in it?").

The levels-of-processing framework offered the obvious prediction that older adults had poorer memories because they engaged in less semantic processing. The prediction of an orienting task study, however, when looking at aging, was not obvious. If older participants did worse than younger participants on semantic orienting tasks, one could argue that this was evidence for a semantic processing deficit. On the other hand, if they did as well as or better than younger adults, one could argue that they had a semantic processing deficit and only when forced to do so by the orienting task did they engage in semantic processing. Unfortunately, the results of experiments looking at age differences when encoding was controlled by different orienting tasks were as inconsistent as the possible hypotheses were. Some investigators found larger age differences on semantic processing tasks (see, e.g., Eysenck, 1974; Mason, 1977), while others found smaller differences (see, e.g., Erber, Herman, & Botwinick, 1980; Perlmutter, 1978). These results may again best be interpreted by differences in the amount of deliberate processing involved in the tasks. The studies showing larger age differences typically used a recall procedure with active retrieval required. When recognition tests were used, however, as in the Erber et al. (1980) and Perlmutter (1978) studies, retrieval was less deliberate and age differences after semantic encoding were smaller. Therefore, while the results do not consistently support a semantic, or elaborative, processing deficit, they do seem to support a hypothesis that attributes age differences on laboratory memory tasks to the degree of deliberate processing involved in the tasks.

As the discussion so far has indicated, in the search for interactions involving age and memory performance, most laboratory memory researchers have studied retrospective memory (memory for events happening in the past) for verbal materials (lists of words or phrases). To-be-remembered materials, however, can also be nonverbal, and the memory requirement may call for prospective remembering (remembering to do something in the future) rather than retrospective.

Nonverbal Memory

Visuospatial memory Early research on cognition and aging had suggested that age differences in visuospatial cognition were larger than age differences in verbal cognition. Such findings were important because of the theoretical dissociation often hypothesized between verbal and visuospatial memory codes (see, e.g., Paivio, 1971) and how these codes are represented in the brain. The suggestion of greater age differences in nonverbal memory, however, was often based on psychometric test performance in which visuospatial tests tended to be timed and verbal tests tended to be untimed. The cognitive measures in type of material, therefore were confounded with the speeded nature of the tests (Smith & Park, 1990). Because older adults tend to react more slowly, they tend to do worse on timed tests.

When memory procedures like those used with verbal materials are used, age differences similar to those seen with verbal materials are typically seen with nonverbal materials. Significant age differences have been found in memory for line drawings (see, e.g., Winograd, Smith, & Simon, 1982), pictures of faces (see, e.g., Bartlett, Leslie, Tubbs, & Fulton, 1989), and spatial routes on a map (see, e.g., Lipman & Caplan, 1992). If older adults have special problems with nonverbal, visuospatial processing, there should be larger age effects when nonverbal memory items are tested than when verbal memory items are tested. When direct comparisons are made between pictures and words, the advantage of picture recall over word recall (i.e., the picture superiority effect) is equal for young and old participants, even though their recall is lower overall than that of younger adults (Winograd et al., 1982). These results do not support the hypothesis of greater age deficits with nonverbal processing than with verbal processing.

One possible exception to these findings was a study by Sharps and Gollin (1988), who found no age differences in placing objects in a spatially distinctive three-dimensional model but did find age differences in memory for nondistinctive, two-dimensional maps. They indicated that the visual distinctiveness of the three-dimensional model provided a rich visuospatial context that enhanced older adults' memory. Unfortunately, Park, Cherry, Smith, and Lafronza (1990), using an identical model, failed to replicate the Sharps and Gollin procedure and produced significant age differences with the distinctive model. Sharps (1991) has suggested that the failure to replicate their distinctiveness effect was due to the fact that the items in the Park et al. (1990) study could be categorized, thus benefiting the younger adults. Overall, however, the age differences with nonverbal, visuospatial materials seem to be very similar to the age differences seen with verbal materials.

Interestingly, there are no age differences in picture memory when complex scenes are used (Park, Puglisi, & Smith, 1986; Puglisi & Park, 1987). Unlike the age differences seen with simple line drawings, no age differences are found in recognition of complex scenes. Smith, Park, Cherry, and Berkovsky (1990) have suggested that complex scenes provide rich, distinctive linguistic and visuospatial information which supports encoding in older adults. By systematically reducing either the semantic meaning or the visuospatial detail of the pictures, Smith et al. (1990) were able to produce age differences in memory for the pictures. Complex, meaningful scenes provide environmental support and reduce the deliberate processing necessary to encode them effectively for a later memory test.

Another method of comparing the visuospatial processing of younger and older adults is comparing memory for concrete and abstract words. Dirkx and Craik (1992) found that older and younger adults were equally benefited by presenting concrete words rather than abstract words (i.e., the concreteness effect). It is assumed that concrete and abstract words differ in their ability to be imaged or visualized. If older adults have problems with nonverbal processing, they should show less of a concreteness effect. In one condition, participants had to make a difficult perceptual decision between presented words. They had to decide whether two abstract line figures were the same or different when they were presented in two different orientations (active interference condition). This condition was compared to two other conditions in which there was either no intervening visual task (control condition) or the participants passively viewed two identical, nonrotated visual figures (passive interference condition). As can be seen in Figure 6.5, the visual interference task greatly attenuated the concreteness effect, but it did so equally in both young and old participants, again providing evidence that young and old adults are equally able to use nonverbal, visuospatial processing. In Dirkx and Craik's experiments, equal concreteness effects were shown in five conditions that differed in instructions and task requirements. In only one condition, when participants were asked to actively form visual images of each word and link them together, did older participants show a smaller concreteness effect. In other words, only when deliberate image processing was required at encoding did the older adults have difficulty relative to the younger participants.

Memory for performing activities Another type of nonverbal memory that has been studied in the memory laboratory is memory for performing actions and activities. Typically, participants perform several actions and activities and are asked later to verbally describe the actions or activities they performed. There seem to be reliable age differences in memory for activities. In a classic experiment, Bromley (1958) examined the ability of participants who had completed the 11 subtests of the WAIS to describe the subtests at a later time. Younger

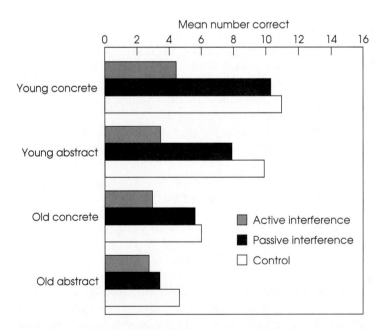

FIGURE 6.5 The mean number of words recalled as a function of age, word type (abstract versus concrete), and secondary interference task (active interference, passive interference, or control). (*Source:* Dirkx and Craik (1992). Reprinted with permission from Craik. Copyright 1992, American Psychological Association.)

participants recalled an average of 8.6 of the subtests, while older participants recalled an average of only 6.8 subtests. Kausler, Lichty, and their colleagues have replicated this finding with a variety of tasks and conditions (see, e.g., Kausler and Lichty, 1988; Kausler, Lichty, & Davis, 1985). Kausler and Lichty (1988) have suggested that encoding the activities does not involve deliberate processing; instead, the events are automatically encoded in episodic memory when performed. Evidence supporting this view comes from their studies showing no difference in the size of the age effect on activity memory under either incidental learning conditions or intentional instructions to remember their actions for later memory tests. On the other hand, while there may not be deliberate processing at encoding, there certainly would need to be deliberate processing at retrieval when trying to remember the activities. Thus, the age differences in activity recall are reliable across many studies.

Unlike complex activities, age differences in the recall of simple motor actions (e.g., blinking one's eyes, touching one's elbow) are less clear. Bäckman and his colleagues have shown no age differences in memory for actions (see, e.g., Bäckman, 1985), while others have shown age differences in remembering actions (see, e.g., R. L. Cohen, Sandler, & Schroeder, 1987; Guttentag & Hunt, 1988). Kausler and Lichty (1988) pointed out that, although there were studies showing no significant age effects in memory for actions, younger subjects typically outperformed older ones. This suggests a power problem rather than a qualitative difference between memory for actions and memory for activities.

Other researchers have looked at memory for a series of activities forming a meaningful event (e.g., putting a bicycle together). In a clay-making task, for example, Padgett & Ratner (1987) found that older adults were less able than younger adults to recall the actions involved in the task.

In summary, therefore, adult age differences are typically found in episodic memory for performed actions or activities. Even if these memories are automatically encoded and rehearsal independent, as suggested by Kausler and Lichty (1988), considerable deliberate recollection would still be necessary at retrieval to remember the actions. Because of this, age differences would be expected.

Prospective memory While most laboratory procedures of memory performance test memory for past experiences, real-life memory failure often involves the inability to remember to do something in the future (e.g., taking one's medicine, mailing the letter in one's pocket). This type of memory is called *prospective memory*. Again, age differences are typically found in prospective memory tasks, with researchers directing subjects to do such things as remembering to ask for a red pen (Dobbs & Rule, 1987), indicating when they saw a beard or pipe while looking at pictures of faces (Maylor, 1993), or making a specific computer key-press when one of several target words appeared (Einstein, Holland, McDaniel, & Guynn, 1992). When the task was simple, however, such as remembering to respond to a single target while performing another task, no age differences were found.

Making an interesting distinction, Einstein and McDaniel (1992) found age effects when participants were asked to perform an action every 10 minutes (time-based prospective memory) but no age differences when they were told to respond to a future cue (event-based prospective memory). Because event-based prospective memory would involve less deliberate recollection than time-based prospective memory due to the presence of an environmental cue, smaller age differences would have been expected.

In summary, we have reviewed laboratory research that has used experimental methods to look for interactions between adult age and both memory structures and memory processes. We have discussed not only research looking at retrospective memory for verbal materials but also research using nonverbal materials and research looking at prospective memory. While different conceptualizations of memory have guided this research, a general conclusion seems to emerge. The magnitude of the observed age differences seems to be determined by the degree of deliberate processing involved in the task. A remaining question to be answered, however, is why older adults have problems with deliberate processing. A very different research tradition has been used to answer this important question. Rather than relying solely on experimental manipulations, correlational techniques are used to identify possible mechanisms that can account for the observed age differences in memory performance.

■ Correlational Research

Much of the research that has attempted to identify the mechanisms responsible for adult age differences in memory performance has used statistical control procedures in order to examine the relationship among age, memory, and potential mechanisms or mediators of the age–memory relationship. A basic assumption of this technique is that, if a large portion of the age-related variance in memory performance is shared with another variable, this other variable is assumed to be important to the relationship between age and memory performance. The logic for these procedures, adapted from Salthouse (1992a), is presented in Figure 6.6. The circles in the Venn diagram represent the variance produced in measures of adult age, memory, and the proposed mediator or mechanism. The intersections of the circles represent the shared variances among the different measures. The proportion of the variability in

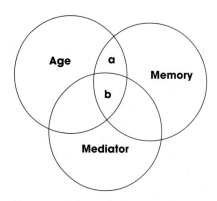

a = Proportion of variance in memory associated with age but not mediated by mediator

b = Proportion of age-related variance in memory performance mediated by mediator

FIGURE 6.6 Venn diagram showing the logic of using the correlational method to determine common variance among age, memory, and mediating construct. The overlap in circles represents shared variance. (*Source:* Adapted from Salthouse (1992a). Reprinted with permission from Salthouse. Copyright 1992, Lawrence Erlbaum Associates.)

memory performance that is accounted for by age is represented by the letters a and b. The important interaction is represented by the letter b, which is the portion of age-related variance in memory performance that is accounted for by the proposed mediator or mechanism. Any age-related variance in memory performance that is not accounted for by the proposed mediator or mechanism is represented by the letter a. Salthouse (1992a) suggests that if the shared age-related variance between memory and the potential mediator is less than 20 percent the mediator is considered to have a small influence on the age differences in memory performance, if the shared variance is between 20 percent and 40 percent the influence of the mediator may possibly be important, and if the shared variance is between 40 percent and 60 percent the mediator is probably important to the age differences in memory performance. If the shared variance is over 60 percent the mediator is assumed to be very important to the relationship between age and memory.

Several different potential mediators of the age differences in memory performance have been proposed. Some studies have tested mediators that could explain age-related memory performance but are noncognitive, such as educational or health differences. The studies have also tested possible cognitive mechanisms that could account for age-related differences such as verbal ability, working memory, or processing speed. The evidence for the importance to age differences in memory of each of these variables will be discussed below.

There is little evidence that noncognitive factors such as education can account for age differences in memory performance. Salthouse, Kausler, and Saults (1988) found that when amount of education was entered before age into a regression equation predicting memory performance, there was very little attenuation of the effects of age on memory performance. In fact, the age-related variance in both verbal memory and spatial memory was reduced by only approximately 20 percent after controlling for education. Thus 80 percent of the age-related variability in memory performance was not related to the amount of education. Earles, Brannon, and Hill (1993), using data from the 301 adults between 20 and 90 years of age from Park et al. (1994), found that the age-related variance in free recall and cued recall actually increased slightly after controlling for the amount of education. Thus, the amount of education does not seem to play a large role in the decline in memory performance with age. However, it could be that the quality of education has changed over time, and thus the same number of years of education does not mean the same thing for younger and older adults.

Age-related declines in memory and other cognitive abilities have also been suggested to be due in part to declining health among older adults (Herzog & Rodgers, 1989; Wilkie & Eisdorfer, 1971). Salthouse, Kausler, and Saults (1990), however, found little reduction in the age differences in associative memory after controlling for self-reported health status. They also found that using only healthy adults as compared to their entire sample of adults had little effect. In fact, Salthouse et al. (1988) found that only approximately 20 percent of the age-related variance in both verbal memory and spatial memory was shared with the number of prescription medications currently being taken. Earles et al. (1993) found that only 12 percent of the age-related variance in free recall was shared with self-rated health status and only 24 percent was shared with number of prescription medications. They found similar results with cued recall. In cued recall only 8 percent of the age-related variance was shared with self-rated health and 23 percent with medications. Thus health status, at least as measured by self-reported ratings, does not appear to be responsible for age-related declines in memory performance. Questions may be raised about the validity of the self-reported measures of health used in these studies. However, self-rated health has been found to be related to such things as physician assessments (see, e.g., LaRue, Bank, Jarvik, & Hetland, 1979) and number of prescription medications being taken (see, e.g., Salthouse et al., 1990) (see page 59 in Salthouse [1991a] for more relevant citations).

Unlike noncognitive factors, which seem to play only a small part in accounting for age-related differences in memory performance, cognitive mechanisms have been found to be important. As discussed earlier, age differences are found in working memory, and working memory is assumed to be a measure of the efficiency with which one can perform real-time information processing (i.e., the ability to simultaneously store and process information; Baddeley, 1986). Salthouse (1992a) summarizes the results of many studies examining the relationship among age, working memory, and cognitive ability and found that an average of about 50 percent of the age-related variance in cognition is shared with working memory capacity. Unfortunately, these studies cited by Salthouse (1992a) did not use memory tests as measures of cognition. However, Hultsch, Hertzog, and Dixon (1990) present evidence that the age differences in working memory capacity are related to age differences in memory for both text and words. Furthermore, Park et al. (1994) found that many of the effects of age on free recall and cued recall were indirect and mediated by working memory.

As discussed earlier, however, one of the most promising potential mediators of age differences in memory performance is processing efficiency, as measured by perceptual speed. Perceptual speed is the amount of time it takes to perform simple cognitive operations, and it has been found to be related to age differences in many tasks. In fact, many of the age differences in working memory are mediated by perceptual speed, so speed may actually be a more basic mechanism responsible for even the differences in working memory. Salthouse (1992b) conducted two studies to examine the effects of perceptual speed on age differences in working memory capacity. In study 1 the age-related variance in working memory was reduced from 28 percent to 8 percent by controlling for speed, and in study 2 the age-related variance in working memory was reduced from 15 percent to 1 percent by controlling for speed. Thus speed appears to be very important to the relationship between age and working memory. In fact, Salthouse and Babcock (1991) found that essentially all of the effects of age on working memory capacity were mediated by perceptual speed.

Age differences in many types of memory have been found to be associated with perceptual speed. Hultsch et al. (1990) found evidence that speed is an important mediator of age differences in memory for both text and words. Earles and Coon (1994) found that perceptual speed was associated with 70 percent of the age differences in memory for performed activities. Lindenberger, Mayr, and Kliegl (1993) found, in a sample of 70- to 100-year-old participants, no direct effect of age on memory performance. All effects of age on paired-associate recall, on memory for activities, and on text recall were mediated by speed. In a study using a larger age range, Salthouse (1993) found that age was associated with 18 percent of the variance in paired-associate memory. After controlling for speed, age was associated with only 3 percent of the variance in memory performance. In Salthouse (1994) only 1 percent of the age-related variance in associative memory was unique to age and not shared with motor or perceptual speed. Finally, Park et al. (1994) found that age differences in free recall, cued recall, and spatial memory were mediated by perceptual speed. Only for free recall was there any significant direct effect of age on memory that was not mediated by perceptual speed. Thus perceptual speed appears to be associated with most if not all of the age-related variance in memory performance.

IMPLICATIONS FOR EVERYDAY FUNCTIONING

Laboratory research on aging and memory does have implications for the everyday functioning of older adults. Through laboratory research, we are becoming closer to a clearer and more precise understanding of the nature of age differences and age invariance in memory performance, together with a clear understanding of the mechanisms responsible for such change and stability. Such description and understanding gathered from basic research are a prerequisite to applications and interventions to improve cognition in older adults. The best applied memory research is firmly grounded in good basic science. As Park (1992) indicates in her review of applied cognitive aging research, "theory-based research on cognition and aging has developed sufficiently that solutions to real-world problems are beginning to be suggested" (p. 450). In fact, Park's discussion of applied cognitive aging provides many examples of how basic, theory-based memory research can assist in designing programs that improve the lives of older adults (e.g., adherence to medication schedules; design of training programs for new skills and knowledge; design of maps, textual material, and instructions that are used by older adults). As also discussed in Chapter 7, aspects of memory that are relatively spared by aging (e.g., implicit memory, automatic skills, familiarity, semantic memory, picture memory) could be emphasized when presenting new information to older adults for them to remember later, while aspects of memory that show consistent age differences (e.g., timed tasks, episodic recall, tasks with high working memory loads) could be deemphasized. Tasks that provide a great deal of environmental support and little deliberate processing should be used.

CLOSING: WHERE DO WE STAND?
WHERE DO WE GO?

As discussed, the experimental method primarily provides an analytic description of the nature of age differences in memory. It is clear that the nature of these descriptions is theory dependent, however. Theoretical ideas have shaped both the questions asked by cognitive aging researchers and the explanations used to describe results from the experiments: Are age differences larger in one memory system rather than another? Are age differences seen with one processing requirement but not another? Are the age differences seen for retrospective memory not seen in prospective memory? The questions come from theory, so the explanations generated to deal with the results from the experiments obviously depend on the particular theoretical hypothesis the experiment was based on in the first place. Even though there are many theoretical descriptions of the data, the experimental method has in fact provided us with a large database of research findings that permit us to determine when age differences are found and when they are not, regardless of any particular theoretical conceptualization.

The correlational method is providing explanations by pointing to underlying mechanisms that account for age-related variance on specific memory tasks. As has been discussed, this methodology in a variety of studies has indicated that working memory and perceptual speed seem to be important determinants of age-related memory effects.

What is now needed is a better understanding of how these basic mechanisms, working memory and perceptual speed, specifically contribute to and control the variety of memory phenomena studied with the experimental method. We need to determine those memory tasks for which perceptual speed works through working memory and those for which perceptual speed directly determines age differences in memory. We also need to determine whether other mechanisms are also important in age-related memory effects.

To do this, we must bring the two methods (experimental research and correlational research) together in the laboratory. As an example, throughout this chapter, we have indicated that the requirement of deliberate processing seems to produce significant age effects in memory. We now need to test this idea by showing that working memory is more important for those tasks that require greater deliberate processing. Both methods are necessary to fully understand age differences in normal aging. The experimental method provides theoretical hypotheses about the memory phenomena. To the extent that adequate, reliable measures of theoretical constructs can be developed, the correlational method provides information about the underlying mechanisms that are responsible for the age-related variance with these phenomena.

Importantly, biopsychologists and neuropsychologists are now targeting in on brain mechanisms that correspond to the cognitive mechanisms discussed in this chapter. Clearly, cognitive psychologists and neuroscientists should interact more closely as the technology of studying brain mechanisms becomes more and more advanced. In their review of the literature, Moscovitch and Winocur (1992) have pointed to the two brain regions (the frontal areas of the cortex, and the hippocampus and its related areas) that are involved with memory change as we grow older. These two regions of the brain are also involved with the major categories of memory changes we have discussed in this chapter. The frontal lobes seem to be involved with cognitive resources (e.g., working memory), while the hippocampal areas are involved with deliberate recollection. New techniques of neuroimaging now provide an exciting opportunity to further refine our understanding of the relationship between age and memory, as well as the underlying biological mechanisms responsible for this relationship.

ACKNOWLEDGMENT

Julie L. K. Earles is now at Furman University. The preparation of this chapter was supported in part by an NIH grant from the National Institute on Aging (R01 AG06265-09).

SUPPLEMENTAL READINGS

Kausler, D. H. (1994). *Learning and memory in normal aging.* New York: Academic Press. A comprehensive advanced textbook that provides a thorough treatment of aging and memory.

Craik, F. I. M., & Salthouse, T. A. *The handbook of aging and cognition.* New York: Academic Press. Chapter 2, Human memory; Chapter 3, The organization of memory in old age; Chapter 7, The neuropsychology of memory and aging; Chapter 9, Applied cognitive aging research. These four advanced monograph chapters provide further discussion of many of the points made in this chapter.

Light, L. L. (1991). Memory and aging: Four hypotheses in search of data. *Annual Review of Psychology, 42,* 333–376. A thorough discussion of research from different theoretical positions in aging and memory.

Smith, A. D. (1996). Memory. In J. E. Birren & K. W. Schaie (Eds.), *The Handbook on the Psychology of Aging.* San Diego, CA: Academic Press.

REFERENCES

Arenberg, D. (1976). The effects of input condition on free recall in young and old adults. *Journal of Gerontology, 31,* 551–555.

Atkinson, R. C., & Shiffrin, R. M. (1971). The control of short-term memory. *Scientific American, 224,* 82–90.

Babcock, R. L., & Salthouse, T. A. (1990). Effects of increased processing demands on age differences in working memory. *Psychology and Aging, 5,* 421–428.

Bäckman, L. (1985). Further evidence for the lack of adult age differences on the recall of subject performed tasks: The importance of motor action. *Human Learning, 4,* 79–87.

Baddeley, A. (1986). *Working memory.* London: Oxford Univ. Press.

Bartlett, J. C., Leslie, J. E., Tubbs, A., & Fulton, A. (1989). Aging and memory of faces. *Psychology and Aging, 4,* 276–283.

Bromley, D. B. (1958). Some effects of age on short-term learning and remembering. *Journal of Gerontology, 13,* 398–406.

Burke, D. M., & Light, L. L. (1981). Memory and aging: The role of retrieval processes. *Psychological Bulletin, 90,* 513–546.

Burke, D. M., MacKay, D. G., Worthley, J. S., & Wade, E. (1991). On the tip of the tongue: What causes word-finding failures in young and older adults? *Journal of Memory and Language, 30,* 542–579.

Burke, D. M., & Peters, L. (1986). Word associations in old age: Evidence for consistency in semantic encoding during adulthood. *Psychology and Aging, 1,* 283–292.

Canestrari, R. E. (1968). Age changes in acquisition. In G. A. Talland (Ed.), *Human aging and behavior* (pp. 169–188). New York: Academic Press.

Cohen, J., & Squire, L. R. (1980). Preserved learning and retention of pattern-analyzing skill in amnesia: Dissociation of knowing how and knowing that. *Science, 210,* 207–210.

Cohen, R. L., Sandler, S. P., & Schroeder, K. (1987). Aging and memory for words and action events: The effects of item repetition and list length. *Psychology and Aging, 2,* 280–285.

Craik, F. I. M. (1968). Short-term memory and the aging process. In G. A. Talland (Ed.), *Human aging and behavior* (pp. 131–168). New York: Academic Press.

Craik, F. I. M. (1986). A functional account of age differences in memory. In F. Klix & H. Hagendorf (Eds.), *Human memory and cognitive capabilities, mechanisms, and performance.* Amsterdam: North Holland.

Craik, F. I. M., & Jennings, J. M. (1992). In F. I. M. Craik & T. A. Salthouse (Eds.), *The handbook of aging and cognition* (pp. 51–110). Hillsdale, NJ: Erlbaum.

Craik, F. I. M., & Lockhart, R. S. (1972). Levels of processing: A framework for memory research. *Journal of Verbal Learning and Verbal Behavior, 11,* 671–684.

Craik, F. I. M., & McDowd, J. M. (1987). Age differences in recall and recognition. *Journal of Experimental Psychology: Learning, Memory, and Cognition, 13,* 474–479.

Delbecq-Derouesné, J., & Beauvois, M. F. (1989). Memory processes and aging: A defect of automatic rather than controlled processes? *Archives of Gerontology and Geriatrics, 1,* 121–150.

Dirkx, E., & Craik, F. I. M. (1992). Age-related differences in memory as a function of imagery processes. *Psychology and Aging, 7,* 352–358.

Dobbs, A. R., & Rule, B. G. (1987). Prospective memory and self-reports of memory abilities in older adults. *Canadian Journal of Psychology, 41,* 209–222.

Dobbs, A. R., & Rule, B. G. (1989). Adult age differences in working memory. *Psychology and Aging, 41,* 500–503.

Earles, J. L., Brannon, K., & Hill, L. (1993). Effects of health and education on age differences in memory performance. Paper presented at the Fourth Annual Sigma Phi Omega Student Convention for Gerontology and Geriatrics, Athens, GA, March.

Earles, J. L., & Coon, V. E. (1994). Adult age differences in long-term memory for performed activities. *Journal of Gerontology: Psychological Sciences, 49,* P32–P34.

Einstein, G. O., Holland, L. J., McDaniel, M. A., & Guynn, M. J. (1992). Age-related deficits in prospective memory: The influence of task complexity. *Psychology and Aging, 7,* 471–478.

Einstein, G. O., & McDaniel, M. A. (1992). Examining the influence of self-initiated retrieval. Paper presented at the Cognitive Aging Conference, Atlanta, April.

Erber, J. T., Herman, T. G., & Botwinick, J. (1980). Age differences in memory as a function of depth of processing. *Experimental Aging Research, 6,* 341–348.

Eysenck, M. W. (1974). Age differences in incidental learning. *Developmental Psychology, 10,* 936–941.

Gladis, M., & Braun, H. W. (1958). Age differences in transfer and retroaction as a function of intertask response similarity. *Journal of Experimental Psychology, 55,* 25–30.

Guttentag, R. E., & Hunt, R. R. (1988). Adult age differences in memory for imagined and performed actions. *Journal of Gerontology: Psychological Sciences, 43,* P107–P108.

Hasher, L., & Zacks, R. T. (1979). Automatic and effortful processes in memory. *Journal of Experimental Psychology: General, 108,* 356–388.

Hasher, L., & Zacks, R. T. (1988). Working memory, comprehension, and aging: A review and a new view. In G. H. Bower (Ed.), *The psychology of learning and motivation: Advances in research and theory* (vol. 22, pp. 193–225). New York: Academic Press.

Herzog, A. R., & Rodgers, W. L. (1989). Age differences in memory performance and memory ratings as measured in a sample survey. *Psychology and Aging, 4,* 173–182.

Hess, T. M. (1984). Effects of semantically related and unrelated contexts on recognition memory of different aged adults. *Journal of Gerontology, 39,* 444–451.

Howard, D. V. (1980). Category norms: A comparison of the Batting and Montague (1969) norms with responses of adults between the ages of 20 and 80. *Journal of Gerontology, 35,* 225–231.

Hulicka, I. M. (1966). Age differences in Wechsler Memory Scale scores. *Journal of Genetic Psychology, 109,* 135–146.

Hultsch, D. F., Hertzog, C., & Dixon, R. A. (1990). Ability correlates of memory performance in adulthood and aging. *Psychology and Aging, 5,* 356–368.

Jacoby, L. L. (1991). A process dissociation framework: Separating automatic from intentional uses of memory. *Journal of Memory and Language, 30,* 513–541.

Jennings, J. M., & Jacoby, L. L. (1993). Automatic versus intentional uses of memory: Aging, attention, and control. *Psychology and Aging, 8,* 283–293.

Kausler, D. H. (1991). *Experimental psychology, cognition, and human aging* (2d ed.). New York: Springer.

Kausler, D. H., & Lichty, W. (1988). Memory for activities: Rehearsal-independence and aging. In M. L. Howe & C. J. Brainerd (Eds.), *Cognitive development in adulthood: Progress in cognitive development research* (pp. 93–101). New York: Springer.

Kausler, D. H., Lichty, W., & Davis, R. T. (1985). Adult age differences in recognition memory and frequency judgments for planned activities. *Developmental Psychology, 21,* 1132–1138.

Kausler, D. H., & Puckett, J. M. (1981). Adult age differences in memory for sex of voice. *Journal of Gerontology, 36,* 44–50.

LaRue, A., Bank, L., Jarvik, L., & Hetland, M. (1979). Health in old age: How do physicians' ratings and self-ratings compare? *Journal of Gerontology, 34,* 687–691.

Light, L. L. (1991). Memory and aging: Four hypotheses in search of data. *Annual Review of Psychology, 42,* 333–376.

Light, L. L. (1992). The organization of memory in old age. In F. I. M. Craik & T. A. Salthouse (Eds.), *The handbook of aging and cognition.* Hillsdale, NJ: Erlbaum.

Lindenberger, U., Mayr, U., & Kliegl, R. (1993). Speed and intelligence in old age. *Psychology and Aging, 8,* 207–220.

Lipman, P. D., & Caplan, L. J. (1992). Adult age differences in memory for routes: Effects of instruction and spatial diagram. *Psychology and Aging, 7,* 435–442.

Lovelace, E. A., & Cooley, S. (1982). Free association of older adults to single words and conceptually related word triads. *Journal of Gerontology, 37,* 432–437.

Mandler, G. (1980). Recognizing: The judgment of previous occurrence. *Psychological Review, 87,* 252–271.

Mason, S. E. (1977). Effects of orienting tasks on recall and recognition performance of subjects differing in age. *Developmental Psychology, 15,* 467–469.

Maylor, E. A. (1993). Aging and forgetting in prospective and retrospective memory tasks. *Psychology and Aging, 8,* 420–428.

McKoon, G., Ratcliff, R., & Dell, G. S. (1986). A critical evaluation of the semantic-episodic distinction. *Journal of Experimental Psychology: Learning, Memory, and Cognition, 12,* 295–306.

McIntyre, J. S., & Craik, F. I. M. (1987). Age differences in memory for item and source information. *Canadian Journal of Psychology, 41,* 175–192.

Mitchell, D. B. (1989). How many memory systems? Evidence from aging. *Journal of Experimental Psychology: Learning, Memory, and Cognition, 15,* 31–49.

Monge, R. H. (1971). Studies of verbal learning from the college years through middle age. *Journal of Gerontology, 26,* 324–329.

Moskovitch, M., & Winocur, G. (1992). The neuropsychology of memory and aging. In F. I. M. Craik & T. A. Salthouse (Eds.), *The handbook of aging and cognition* (pp. 315–372). Hillsdale, NJ: Erlbaum.

Obler, L. K., & Albert, M. L. (1985). Language skills across adulthood. In J. E. Birren & K. W. Schaie (Eds.), *Handbook of the psychology of aging* (2d ed.). New York: Van Nostrand Reinhold.

Padgett, R. J., & Ratner, H. H. (1987). Older and younger adults' memory for structured and unstructured events. *Experimental Aging Research, 13,* 133–139.

Paivio, A. (1971). *Imagery and verbal processing.* New York: Holt, Reinhart and Winston.

Park, D. C. (1992). Applied cognitive aging research. In F. I. M. Craik & T. A. Salthouse (Eds.), *The handbook of aging and cognition.* Hillsdale, NJ: Erlbaum.

Park, D. C., Cherry, K. E., Smith, A. D., & Lafronza, V. (1990). Effects of distinctive context on memory for objects and their locations in young and older adults. *Psychology and Aging, 5,* 250–255.

Park, D. C., & Puglisi, J. T. (1985). Older adults' memory for the color of pictures. *Journal of Gerontology, 40,* 198–204.

Park, D. C., Puglisi, J. T., & Smith, A. D. (1986). Memory for pictures: Does an age-related decline exist? *Psychology and Aging, 1,* 11–17.

Park, D. C., Puglisi, J. T., Smith, A. D., & Dudley, W. N. (1987). Cue utilization and encoding specificity in picture recognition by older adults. *Journal of Gerontology, 42,* 423–425.

Park, D. C., Smith, A. D., Lautenschlager, G., Earles, J., Frieske, D., Zwahr, M., & Gaines, C. (1994). The contributions of speed, working memory, and inhibitory function to memory performance across the life span. Paper presented at the Fifth Cognitive Aging Conference, Atlanta, April.

Park, D. C., Smith, A. D., Morrell, R. W., Puglisi, J. T., & Dudley, W. N. (1990). Effects of contextual integration on recall of pictures by older adults. *Journal of Gerontology: Psychological Sciences, 45,* P52–P57.

Parkinson, S. R., Lindholm, J. M., & Inman, V. W. (1982). An analysis of age differences in immediate recall. *Journal of Gerontology, 37,* 425–431.

Perlmutter, M. (1978). What is memory aging the aging of? *Developmental Psychology, 14,* 330–345.

Puglisi, J. T., & Park, D. C. (1987). Perceptual elaboration and memory in older adults. *Journal of Gerontology, 42,* 160–162.

Puglisi, J. T., Park, D. C., & Smith, A. D. (1987). Picture associations among old and young adults. *Experimental Aging Research, 13,* 115–116.

Puglisi, J. T., Park, D. C., Smith, A. D., & Dudley, W. N. (1988). Age differences in encoding specificity. *Journal of Gerontology: Psychological Sciences, 43,* P145–P150.

Rabinowitz, J. C., & Ackerman, B. P. (1982). General encoding of episodic events by elderly adults. In F. I. M. Craik & S. Trehub (Eds.), *Aging and cognitive processes* (pp. 145–154). New York: Plenum.

Rabinowitz, J. C., Craik, F. I. M., & Ackerman, B. P. (1982). A processing resource account of age differences in recall. *Canadian Journal of Psychology, 36,* 325–344.

Riegel, K. F., & Riegel, R. M. (1964). Changes in associative behavior during later years of life. *Vita Humana, 7,* 1–32.

Salthouse, T. A. (1982). *Adult cognition: An experimental psychology of human aging.* New York: Springer.

Salthouse, T. A. (1991a). *Theoretical perspectives on cognitive aging.* Hillsdale, NJ: Erlbaum.

Salthouse, T. A. (1992a). *Mechanisms of age-cognition relations in adulthood.* Hillsdale, NJ: Erlbaum.

Salthouse, T. A. (1992b). Influence of processing speed on adult age differences in working memory. *Acta Psychologica, 79,* 155–170.

Salthouse, T. A. (1993). Speed mediation of adult age differences in cognition. *Developmental Psychology, 29,* 722–738.

Salthouse, T. A. (1994). The nature of the influence of speed on adult age differences in cognition. *Developmental Psychology, 30,* 240–259.

Salthouse, T. A., & Babcock, R. L. (1991). Decomposing adult age differences in working memory. *Developmental Psychology, 27,* 763–776.

Salthouse, T. A., Kausler, D. H., & Saults, J. S. (1988). Investigation of student status, background variables, and feasibility of standard tasks in cognitive aging research. *Psychology and Aging, 3,* 29–37.

Salthouse, T. A., Kausler, D. H., & Saults, J. S. (1990). Age, self-assessed health status, and cognition. *Journal of Gerontology: Psychological Sciences, 45,* P156–P160.

Schonfield, D., & Robertson, B. A. (1966). Memory storage and aging. *Canadian Journal of Psychology, 20,* 228–236.

Sharps, M. J., & Gollin, E. S. (1988). Memory for object locations in young and elderly adults. *Journal of Gerontology, 42,* 336–341.

Sharp, M. J. (1991). Spatial memory in young and elderly adults: Category structure of stimulus sets. *Psychology and Aging, 6,* 309–312.

Smith, A. D. (1975a). Aging and interference with memory. *Journal of Gerontology, 30,* 319–325.

Smith, A. D. (1975b). Partial learning and recognition memory in the aged. *International Journal of Aging and Human Development, 6,* 359–365.

Smith, A. D., & Park, D. C. (1990). Adult age differences in memory for pictures and images. In E. A. Lovelace (Ed.), *Aging and cognition: Mental processes, self-awareness, and interventions* (pp. 69–96). Amsterdam: North-Holland.

Smith, A. D., Park, D. C., Cherry, K. E., & Berkovsky, K. (1990). Age differences in memory for concrete and abstract pictures. *Journal of Gerontology: Psychological Sciences, 45,* P205–P209.

Squire, L. R., Knowlton, B., & Musen, G. (1993). The structure and organization of memory. *Annual Review of Psychology, 44,* 453–495.

Thorndike, E. L., Bergman, E. O., Tilton, J. W., & Woodyard, E. (1928). *Adult learning.* New York: Macmillan.

Tulving, E. (1985). How many memory systems are there? *American Psychologist, 40,* 385–398.

Tulving, E. (1987). Multiple memory systems and consciousness. *Human Neurobiology, 6,* 67–80.

Walsh, D. A., & Baldwin, M. (1977). Age differences in integrated semantic memory. *Developmental Psychology, 13,* 509–514.

Wilkie, F., & Eisdorfer, C. (1971). Intelligence and blood pressure in the aged. *Science, 172,* 959–962.

Wingfield, A., Stine, E. A. L., Lahar, C. J., & Aberdeen, J. S. (1988). Does the capacity of working memory change with age? *Experimental Aging Research, 14,* 103–107.

Winograd, E., Smith, A. D., & Simon, E. W. (1982). Aging and the picture superiority effect in recall. *Journal of Gerontology, 37,* 70–75.

C H A P T E R

7

THE AGING OF IMPLICIT AND EXPLICIT MEMORY

Darlene V. Howard
Georgetown University

INTRODUCTION

■ A Preliminary Exercise

Please turn to Figure 7.1 and follow the instructions there before reading on.

■ Chapter Overview

What we learn about memory and its aging depends in part upon the uses to which memory is being put and the way in which memory is tested. Most of what psychologists and laypeople know about memory focuses on conscious recollection. This emphasis can be seen in this volume, for example, in Chapters 6 and 12. Yet, in everyday life, it is likely that the nonaware uses of memory are more important (albeit by their nature less noticed) than the conscious ones. Such nonaware uses of memory influence the likelihood that particular ideas will come to mind (see, e.g., Graf, Shimamura, & Squire, 1985), the meanings we assign to stimuli we encounter (see, e.g., Jacoby & Witherspoon, 1982), the ease and accuracy with which we perceive external stimuli (see, e.g., Jacoby & Dallas, 1981), and the preferences, impressions, and stereotypes we form (see, e.g., Bargh, 1992; Bornstein, 1992).

In what follows, I first draw distinctions regarding the uses to which memory is put and the ways in which memory is tested. After considering why these distinctions are important and some methodological points relevant to the study of aging, I review sample studies on aging and then consider the theoretical and practical implications of the findings. I conclude by summarizing where we are and where we need to go next.

■ Two Ways of Using Memory: As a Tool and as an Object

Consider two situations. First, a few months ago I showed a class a film on language development, a favorite of mine because it illustrates spontaneous speech of children of different

Please judge the pleasantness of each of the following words, using a scale from 1 to 5 on which 1 means extremely unpleasant and 5 extremely pleasant.

ASSASSIN
MYSTERY
PENDULUM
TWILIGHT

Now please examine each of the following figures and decide whether it is facing primarily to the right or to the left.

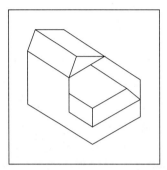 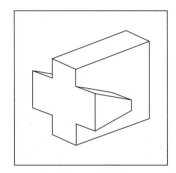

FIGURE 7.1 Objects from Figure 1 of Schacter, Cooper, and Valdiserri, 1992. (*Source:* Schacter, Cooper, & Valdiserri, 1992. Copyright 1992 by the American Psychological Association. Reprinted by permission.)

ages. The sound track had become fuzzy because the film is old and has been shown so often. But despite the fact that my middle-aged hearing is not as acute as that of my college-aged students, it was they, not I, who had trouble identifying what the children were saying. The most likely explanation is that having watched the film before (unlike my students), I have some memory for what the children said, and this memory helped me (albeit without my noticing it at the time) to hear them more clearly.

The second situation occurred in another of my classes. We had been reading *Songs of Experience: An Anthology of Literature on Growing Old* (Fowler & McCutcheon, 1991), and in this session we were recalling and discussing favorite quotations from the book. For example, I recalled May Sarton's statement "This is the best time of my life. I love being old. . . . because I am more myself than I have ever been." And then a student cited Malcolm Cowley's statement "Old age is only a costume assumed for those others; the true, the essential self is ageless."

In both of the situations just described, I was using memory, but in different ways. The first situation illustrates the use of memory *as a tool;* the second, the use of memory *as an object* (Jacoby & Kelley, 1987). That is, in the first case I was using memory unintentionally (or incidentally) and *without being aware* of doing so as a tool to help me decipher the children's speech. Here my use of memory can be considered *automatic.* My focus was not on memory itself but on listening. Rather than being my object, memory served as my unintentional means to another end. In contrast, in the second situation my students and I were engaging in conscious recollection. We were using our memories deliberately and *intentionally* to help us recollect notable quotations. In this case we were *aware* of our memories, and indeed they were the conscious objects of our attention.

As Table 7.1 shows, the italicized words in the previous paragraph have all been used to characterize the differences between these two uses of memory. And as the table illustrates, this distinction is similar to contrasts drawn by yet other authors. For example, before the turn of the century, Théodule Ribot (1882) likened memory to an iceberg. The visible tip of the iceberg he called *psychological memory,* which is memory accompanied by a conscious experience of "pastness"; this is similar to the conscious recollection involved in using memory as an object. Ribot referred to the larger, but hidden, body of the memory iceberg as *organic memory,* which is involved in using memory automatically as a tool.

In the contemporary literature, the terms used most extensively to describe this contrast are *implicit* versus *explicit* memory (Graf & Schacter, 1985). The memory processes involved in using memory without awareness as a tool are termed implicit, whereas those involved in conscious recollection are termed explicit. The terms implicit and explicit can be confusing, however, because they have been used in more than one way. Sometimes they are used as I just did, to refer to different sorts of memory processes. Other times, however, they are used to refer to a contrast between two different kinds of memory test. Before reading about those, please turn to Figure 7.2 and undertake the exercises there.

■ Two Ways of Testing Memory: Implicit and Explicit Tests

Explicit tests (also called *direct tests*) are those in which, at the time of the test, the participant is instructed to engage in conscious recollection of some earlier encounter; examples include recall and recognition tests. Most of the memory tests described in Chapters 6 and 12 are explicit tests. In contrast, *implicit tests* (also called *indirect tests*) do not include instructions to

TABLE 7.1 Related (Though Not Synonymous) Distinctions Regarding Ways of Using Memory	
Distinctions	**Sample Citations**
Memory as an object/Memory as a tool	Jacoby and Kelley (1987)
Intentional memory/Automatic memory	Jennings and Jacoby (1993)
Memory with awareness/Memory without awareness	Jacoby and Witherspoon (1982)
Psychological memory/Organic memory	Ribot (1882)
Explicit/Implicit	Graf and Schacter (1985); Schacter (1987)
Declarative/Procedural	Squire and Cohen (1984); Squire (1992)
Knowing that/Knowing how	Ryle (1949); Cohen and Squire (1980)
Memories/Habits	Mishkin and Petri (1984)
Memory system II/Memory system I	Sherry and Schacter (1987)

Please complete each of the following word stems to form the first word that comes to mind.

1. _L_MI_G_
2. TW__I__T
3. _H_O_EM
4. A__A__IN
5. G__DO_A
6. _E_D_L_M
7. _P_TU_A
8. _YS__RY

Now please judge whether each of the following items is a possible or an impossible object. You should judge it to be impossible if it has some impossible planes that would prevent it from being a coherent object in the real world.

1.
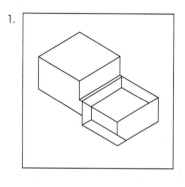

3.
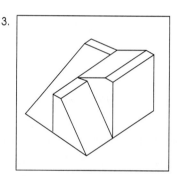

2.
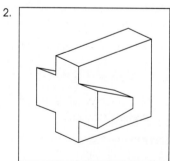

4.
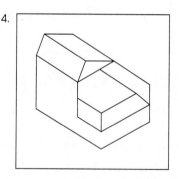

FIGURE 7.2 Objects from Figure 1 of Schacter, Cooper, and Valdiserri, 1992. (*Source:* Schacter, Cooper, & Valdiserri, 1992. Copyright 1992 by the American Psychological Association. Reprinted by permission. Word fragments taken from Tulving, Schacter, & Stark, 1982.)

recollect a specific earlier incident; instead, memory is inferred from some other aspect of performance, such as faster (or more accurate) processing of test stimuli that were presented earlier, as compared to those that were not. Facilitation of this sort is called *priming*. Thus, the critical difference between explicit and implicit tests refers to the instructions the participants are given at the time of the test.

You experienced implicit tests of memory for the items in the preliminary exercise when you did Figure 7.2. In the case of the word fragments, if you were able to complete items 2, 4, 6, and 8 more readily than items 1, 3, 5, or 7, you revealed memory for those words. The increased likelihood of producing the target words from the earlier studied list (in comparison with the new words) is an example of priming of word fragment completion.

In the case of the objects, chances are you found the object decision easier to make for possible object number 2 (which you had encountered earlier) than for possible object number 3, which you had not. If so, this again illustrates priming, but this time of object decisions.

There are many other kinds of implicit tests, some of which will be described later in this chapter. In general, in studies comparing implicit and explicit test performance, people first encounter a list of target items (usually called the study list) and are asked to perform some orienting task on the items (e.g., the pleasantness and left–right judgments you originally did). Later, memory for the target items is tested by presenting a test list, some items of which correspond to those in the study list (old test items) and some of which do not (new test items). For an explicit test, people are instructed to make their responses based on what they remember of the earlier encounter, whereas for the implicit test they are not. In either case, memory for the items in the study list is assessed by comparing performance on old items to that on new. The larger this difference, the greater the amount of memory the person is displaying for the original encounter. Notice that the new test items are serving as control items to assess the baseline level of performance that would occur without the previous encounter during the study list. Counterbalancing methods are used in such studies, so that the items (e.g., objects or words) that appear as new items for half of the participants appear as old items for the other half.

■ Dissociations between Implicit and Explicit Tests

Those of us who study the aging of memory became interested in comparing implicit and explicit tests because studies of younger adults and patients suffering from memory disorders revealed that these different tests often yielded dramatically different results. Several broad classes of such *dissociations,* as they are called, have been observed.

Clinical Cases

The first and most dramatic dissociations to be discovered were observed in patients suffering from amnesia, a condition characterized by severe impairments of memory that is often the result of Korsakoff's syndrome or certain forms of brain damage. Dissociations between implicit and explicit tests were described in such patients at least as early as the turn of the century (see, e.g., Ribot, 1882). A dramatic early example was reported in 1911 by the Swiss neuropsychiatrist Claparede. One day Claparede held a pin in his hand when he shook hands with his patient, a woman suffering severe losses in conscious recollection as the result of Korsakoff's disease. Later this patient refused to shake hands with Claparede, though she was unable to report why. The patient's behavior reveals that she had some memory for the pinprick encounter and this affected her behavior (in a very adaptive, useful way), even though she had no awareness of the earlier incident. She was able to use memory as a tool but not as an object.

In the past few decades many more dissociations have been observed between amnesics' performance on implicit as opposed to explicit tests, and these studies have revealed that amnesia patients frequently perform as well as normals on implicit tests of memory, even though they show severe deficits on explicit tests, often failing completely to remember the original encounter with the items. For example, Graf, Squire, and Mandler (1984) examined memory for a list of words using word stem–cued recall and word stem completion tests. The participants first encountered a study list of words (e.g., ACCIDENTAL). Then they were given an explicit word stem–cued recall test in which the recall cues consisted of three letters (e.g., ACC_____) and the task was to try to complete the word stems to form a word from the earlier study list. The implicit word stem completion test was identical, except that the instructions were to complete the stem to form the first word that came to mind. The amnesia patients were less likely than normals to complete the stems to form the target words (e.g., ACCIDENTAL) on the explicit recall test, but they were just as likely as the normals to do so on the implicit completion test. This dissociation is particularly impressive because the cues given at the time of the test were identical for the explicit and implicit tests; the only difference was in the instructions the subjects were given.

Similar dissociations between implicit and explicit memory skills have recently been observed in other sorts of clinical populations. These include schizophrenia patients (Schwartz, Rosse, & Deutsch, 1993), a patient with multiple personalities (Nissen, Ross, Willingham, Mackenzie, & Schacter, 1988), and people who suffered mild to moderate closed head injury following automobile accidents (Mutter, Howard, Howard, & Wiggs, 1990). All these observations suggest that implicit and explicit memory processes are affected differently by brain insult and raise the question of whether the patterns of loss and savings in normal aging are similar.

Anatomical Dissociations

There is growing evidence that explicit memory tasks call upon different areas of the brain than do implicit ones. In particular, it appears that the hippocampus (and related cortical structures, sometimes referred to collectively as the medial temporal lobe system) as well as the frontal lobes of the cerebral cortex are critical for explicit memory processes, but not for many implicit ones (see, e.g., Moscovitch & Winocur, 1992).

The importance of the hippocampus for explicit remembering has been documented in two ways. Amnesia patients who show the sorts of implicit/explicit dissociations mentioned above have often suffered damage to the hippocampus and related structures (see, e.g., Squire, 1992). In addition, brain-imaging studies have begun to provide converging evidence. For example, Squire and his colleagues (Squire, Ojemann, Miezin, Petersen, Videen, & Raichle; cited in Squire, 1992) have recorded cerebral blood-flow patterns (via PET scans) while non-memory-impaired people engaged in Graf et al.'s word stem completion and word stem–recall tasks. They found increased activation of the hippocampal region during the explicit task but not during the implicit one. In general, it has been proposed that the hippocampal system plays a role at the time of the initial encounter with some event by binding or integrating the occurrence of that event with the surrounding spatial and temporal context in such a way that these contexts can later serve as cues for conscious retrieval of the event (see, e.g., Moscovitch & Winocur, 1992; Squire, 1992).

The role of the frontal lobes is less clear, in part because they make up a large, complicated structure consisting of a number of distinct areas which likely have different functions. However, brain damage to the frontal lobes is associated with impairments in organizing, planning, and using strategies and has sometimes been characterized as a "dysexecutive syndrome" (see, e.g., Baddeley, 1986). Moscovitch and Winocur (1992) have argued that such planning and organizational functions, though not constituting memory per se, are critical for "working with memory," particularly for the sorts of strategic processes involved in encoding and retrieving memories for conscious recollection.

The evidence implicating the hippocampal region and the frontal lobes as being critical for explicit, but not for many implicit, tests is particularly interesting to those of us who study aging. This is because these two regions show particularly marked age-related declines, a conclusion derived not only from postmortem examination but also from neuroimaging studies using CT and MRI scanning (see, e.g., Jernigan, Archibald, Berhow, Sowell, Foster, & Hesselink, 1991; Terry, Deteresa, & Hansen, 1987). Studying age-related patterns of savings and loss for implicit and explicit memory tasks thus offers an opportunity to learn more about how neural changes are related to behavioral ones.

Functional Dissociations

When a given independent variable affects implicit and explicit tasks differently, this is termed a functional dissociation. One example of an independent variable that reveals such functional dissociations in non-memory-impaired people is the degree of attention devoted to the stimuli during study. Being distracted by some stimulus during the initial encounter (e.g., having to do some other task simultaneously while encountering a study list) almost always hurts memory of that stimulus on subsequent explicit tests. Strikingly, however, such distraction often has little or no effect on implicit tests (see, e.g., Jacoby, Toth, & Yonelinas, 1993).

In contrast, changes in the modality of the stimulus from study to test often have the opposite pattern of effects. Changing from a visual presentation to an auditory test, for example, usually does not hurt memory if the test is an explicit one but decreases or eliminates memory as assessed by some implicit tests (see, e.g., Rajaram & Roediger, 1993). Roediger and McDermott (1993) have published an extensive review of the many such dissociations that have been documented, but the important point here is that these functional dissociations tell us that the memory processes being tapped on implicit and explicit tests obey different sets of rules and so might well exhibit different patterns of aging.

Dissociations within Implicit and Explicit Tests

Up until now I have focused on the differences between implicit and explicit tests, but there are dissociations within each of these groups as well. Recall and recognition (both explicit tests) don't always act the same way. For example, on recall tests, high-frequency words (e.g., TREE) are recalled better than low-frequency ones (e.g., ARBOR), but the reverse is true for recognition tests (Gregg, 1976).

More relevant for present purposes is that a wide range of dissociations has been documented among implicit tests. One example important for studying aging is a contrast between implicit tests that require learning some new association (e.g., remembering a new connection between the words DRAGON and FUDGE) and those that do not (e.g., remembering that the already familiar word DRAGON occurred recently). Whether or not people form a meaningful link between the to-be-associated words during study often influences implicit memory for new associations but not implicit memory for the occurrence of familiar items (see, e.g., Graf & Schacter, 1985), demonstrating a functional dissociation. And in the domain of clinical cases, although amnesia patients almost always show implicit memory for familiar items equivalent to that of normal subjects, this is not always the case for priming of new associations (see, e.g., Bowers & Schacter, 1993).

These dissociations within the classes of implicit and explicit memory tests are particularly important for studying aging, because they tell us that people of different ages need to be compared on a wide range of implicit (and explicit) tasks if we are to get a complete picture of what is saved and what is lost with age.

■ Implications for Theories of Memory

As yet, no theory provides an adequate and detailed explanation for the dissociations that have been observed between implicit and explicit tests of memory. When the ubiquity of such dissociations first became obvious, some memory theorists argued that there are at least two distinct memory systems, one underlying performance on implicit and the other on explicit tests (see, e.g., Schacter, 1987). Based on the patterns of dissociations discussed above as well as findings from studies of other animals and of early development, it was proposed that these different memory systems evolved to serve different and mutually incompatible functions, with the implicit system having developed before the explicit one both in the evolution of the species and in the development of the individual (see, e.g., Schacter, 1987; Sherry & Schacter, 1987). However, other theorists (see, e.g., Roediger, 1990) argued that the data could be accounted for more parsimoniously by assuming that there is only one memory system, with different processes within that system being necessary for these two types of tests. As more data have been collected and as attempts have been made to specify theories in each of these camps more precisely, this early debate has subsided because the two types of theories are becoming indistinguishable from each other (see, e.g., Shimamura, 1993).

At present, most theorists agree that the priming observed on implicit tests is due to the residual effects of earlier perceptual and/or conceptual processing. The notion here is that engaging in a particular set of perceptual and/or conceptual processes (e.g., those involved in identifying the printed word TWILIGHT or the objects in Figure 7.1) automatically changes the perceptual processor so that engaging in this same set of processes again is facilitated. This facilitation can be likened to the gully left behind by water as it flows through dirt; the resulting gully makes it easier for water to flow in that same pattern again (priming). A more commonly used analogy has to do with activating a particular series of processes or a particular set of conceptual nodes; having just engaged a particular set of perceptual processes and/or having activated a particular conceptual node (e.g., the one corresponding to the meaning of the word TWILIGHT) automatically results in continuing activation (heightened accessibility) of those processes or that node, such that any subsequent stimulus calling upon those processes or nodes can be processed more readily (priming).

The patterns of dissociations observed within implicit tests themselves suggest that at least two different kinds of systems (or sets of processes) underlie implicit memory. One involves the continuing activation of presemantic perceptual representations (what Tulving and Schacter, 1990, have called a "perceptual representation system") and so occurs only when there is overlap between the perceptual processes required during initial exposure to the stimulus and those required during the time of the test (such as when a word—or at least part of a word—is presented visually both at the time of study and at the time of test). Such tasks are often called perceptual priming tasks. In contrast, priming is also observed in situations in which there is no overlap between the perceptual characteristics of the stimuli encountered during study and test, and it appears that, in such conceptual priming tasks, implicit memory reflects the continuing activation of nodes or pathways in a conceptually organized semantic memory system (e.g., continuing activation of the conceptual node for TWILIGHT). Examples of such conceptual priming tasks will occur a little later in this chapter.

What is common about both kinds of implicit memory—that due to a presemantic perceptual processing system and that due to continuing activation of a semantic memory system—is that they appear to be the automatic result of processes inherent in perceiving and understanding stimuli. In contrast, explicit memory requires controlled, strategic processes that take place when the material is studied and when it is later retrieved.

■ Methodological Matters

When examining the literature on aging, a few methodological matters need to be highlighted.

Equating Retrieval Cues

The word stem completion and cued recall tests described earlier offer an ideal example of a contrast between implicit and explicit tests in that the two types of tests differ *only* in the instructions given; the items presented at test (word stems) and the measure of memory (the difference score between target completions on old versus new items, which is termed the *prime effect,* or *priming effect*) are identical for the implicit and explicit tests. Thus any difference between them must be due to the presence versus absence of instructions to engage in conscious recollection. But in many studies comparing performance on implicit and explicit tests, the tests differ in other ways as well. For example, the experimenter might have given a word fragment completion test as the implicit measure (e.g., Make a word from this fragment: TW___I___T) and a recognition test as the explicit measure (e.g., Did you encounter the word TWILIGHT during the study list?). In such cases, when differences are observed between performance on the implicit and explicit tests, it is possible that they are due not to the presence of instructions to engage in conscious retrieval but rather to some other difference (such as the type of retrieval cue given—in this case a full word versus a word fragment). Because of this ambiguity of interpretation, researchers prefer to make comparisons in which the explicit and implicit tasks differ from each other only in instructions.

Isolating Implicit from Explicit Processes

Implicit tests are meant to tap automatic or implicit memory processes, those required for situations in which memory is used as a tool; explicit tests are meant to tap conscious recollection processes, those which reflect awareness that this stimulus was encountered earlier.

However, rarely, if ever, does a given task call upon only one of these sorts of processes. For example, in the case of implicit tests, research participants sometimes notice the connection between the words encountered in the original study list and the test items. If they do so, then during the test phase they might not respond (as instructed) with the "first item that comes to mind"; rather, they might attempt to recall and reproduce the items they encountered earlier. Thus, the participants have made the implicit test into an explicit one, so conscious recollection is being tapped in the implicit test. This is often called "explicit contamination" of the implicit test. Such contamination has received a great deal of attention in the study of aging, because it is already well established that there are age deficits in explicit memory. Thus, when age deficits are found on implicit tests, researchers must worry about whether this means that there are also age deficits in implicit memory processes or whether the age deficits on the implicit test are actually due to the operation of explicit memory.

The flip side of this problem is also important. That is, there is even more likely to be an "implicit contamination" of explicit tests. For example, if people are given the cue MYS_____ on a word stem–cued recall test but have no conscious recollection of having encountered the word MYSTERY earlier, they might still respond correctly thanks to implicit memory processes. Not recollecting the item at all, they think they are "just guessing," but they in fact are producing the target item via automatic memory processes (i.e., the continuing activation of the semantic representation of MYSTERY).

The fact that implicit and explicit tests are not pure indicators of automatic memory and conscious recollection, respectively, is often viewed as a methodological problem by researchers (witness the use of the word "contamination"), in the sense that it complicates interpretation of their results. However, the impurity of these types of tests is a feature they have in common with the everyday use of memory. In daily life, most instances in which memory is used represent some combination of these two sorts of processes, and I consider the implications of this later.

The Process Dissociation Procedure

Jacoby and his colleagues (e.g., Jacoby, Toth, & Yonelinas, 1993) have argued that, rather than attempting to find separate tests to tap automatic, implicit memory processes versus conscious recollection, we would be better off to find ways of isolating the operation of each within a given test. He proposes to do this by using a process dissociation procedure in which explicit and implicit processes are sometimes pitted against each other.

For example, imagine that you had been given the word list in Table 7.1 during some study session. In order to use the process dissociation procedure, during the test session I could present you with word stems, but I would *not* give separate implicit and explicit tests. Rather, I would tell you to try to recollect on all trials. However, on some of them I would give you *inclusion* instructions; that is, I would tell you to complete the stem to form a word from the list you just studied. On exclusion trials, however, you would be told that you should *not* complete the stem to form a word you studied earlier; instead you should be creative and complete it to form a different word. Jacoby reasons that if you produce the word TWILIGHT to the word stem TWI_____ on inclusion trials, this could be due to either implicit or explicit memory processes. However, if you produce it on exclusion trials, this means that you have implicit, but not explicit, memory for it. Had you recollected its earlier occurrence, you would have been sure *not* to report it now. Therefore, by subtracting the probability of producing the target words on inclusion minus that on exclusion trials, the process dissociation procedure provides an estimate of the degree of conscious recollection. And the level of implicit (automatic) memory can be inferred by comparing the probability of producing the word on exclusion trials with that of producing it in the absence of any earlier encounter.

One of the advantages of this procedure over comparisons of implicit and explicit tests is that it does not require that the subject be deceived into believing that the implicit test is not a test of memory. And because implicit and explicit processes are pitted against each other in the exclusion condition, age-related declines in explicit processes will not be misinterpreted as declines in implicit ones (i.e., contamination of the sort discussed earlier can be factored out). The process dissociation procedure does have limitations; see, for example, the concerns raised by Graf and Komatsu (1994). Nonetheless, it holds great promise for helping to disentangle implicit and explicit components of retrieval.

For the present, the main point of this discussion is to emphasize that when we refer to a *test* as an "implicit" or an "explicit" one, we *cannot* assume that the test is a pure measure of one sort of memory process. Rather, we are referring to the nature of the instructions given at the time of the test; separating the implicit and explicit components of retrieval is far from easy.

REVIEW OF THE LITERATURE ON AGING

■ Implicit Memory for Familiar Materials

Perceptual Priming of Words

One of the first studies of implicit memory and aging was reported by Light and Singh (1987, experiment 2). They examined memory for the recent occurrence of familiar words, using the word stem procedure of Graf et al. (1984) described earlier. During the study phase, younger adults (age range 19–33 years) and older adults (age range 62–78 years) rated the pleasantness of each of 20 target words. Then, for the memory test, half of the people of each age group were given explicit word stem–cued recall instructions in which they were told to "use the stems as cues to help them recall the words from the list." The other half of the people were given implicit word stem completion instructions which told them to "write the first word they could think of."

The results are shown in Figure 7.3. As would be expected, the likelihood of producing target words for new, baseline items (word stems not encountered during the pleasantness-rating task) is low and almost identical for both age groups and tests. In addition, when the explicit recall instructions were given, the proportion of target words produced for studied items (dark columns) was significantly larger for younger than for older adults, a finding replicating the age-related deficits usually observed on explicit tests. Of most interest, when the implicit completion instructions were given, this age difference almost disappeared and was statistically nonsignificant.

This same pattern has since been obtained in many studies using other tasks to assess implicit memory for the occurrence of familiar words (see Howard, 1991; Light, 1991; and

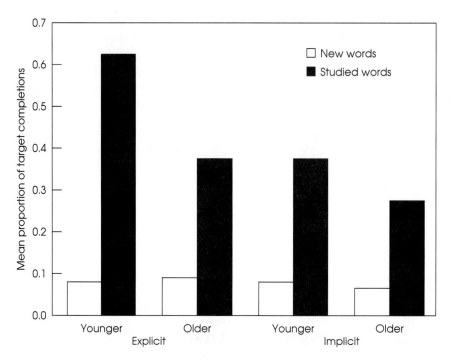

FIGURE 7.3 Mean proportion of target completions on the explicit word stem–recall and on implicit word stem completion tests for younger and older participants in Light and Singh (1987, experiment 2). (*Source:* Data from Light & Singh, 1987.)

Light & LaVoie, 1993, for reviews). In general, such studies reveal large and significant age differences favoring young people on the explicit test and much smaller, usually nonsignificant age differences on the implicit test (see, e.g., Park & Shaw, 1992).

Are the small age effects sometimes seen on the implicit tests due to an age-related decline in implicit memory processes or to explicit contamination of the sort discussed earlier? We do not know for sure, but I think the evidence points to explicit contamination. One kind of evidence comes from studies arranged so that any such explicit contamination works to *decrease* (rather than increase) memory as assessed on an implicit task. Dywan and Jacoby (1990) showed that, under such conditions, older people show a *greater* effect of prior experience than younger on the implicit test.

In their study, younger and older people first encountered a list of names they were told were nonfamous (e.g., SEBASTIAN WEISDORF). After reading these aloud, they were given a task in which they were told they should judge whether each of a series of names was famous. Some of the nonfamous names they encountered in this test were from the list they'd read aloud earlier (old nonfamous names) and some were not (new nonfamous names). Of interest was how famous the old versus new names would be judged to be. Note that here explicit and implicit memory were pitted against each other.

Imagine that you are in this study and are presented with the name "Sebastian Weisdorf." If you remember that it occurred on the list of nonfamous names read earlier, you will be sure it is nonfamous and will be very unlikely to judge it as famous. This is exactly what Dywan and Jacoby's college subjects did; they judged old nonfamous names to be famous less often than new nonfamous names (proportions of .14 and .25, respectively). However, older people did exactly the reverse; that is, they judged old nonfamous names to be famous more often than new nonfamous names (proportions of .20 and .14 respectively). So the older people had been influenced by the earlier presentation (e.g., the names had received some activation in memory), but in the absence of conscious recollection of the earlier encounter the older people ended up misattributing this feeling of familiarity to the famousness of the name. It is as if they reasoned, "That name seems familiar, so it must be famous." Young people were protected from this erroneous misattribution by their explicit recollection of why the name was familiar, that is, that it had occurred in the list of nonfamous names. It has since been shown that amnesic patients act much like older people on this task; they show a greater false-fame effect than younger people do (Squire & McKee, 1993).

Interestingly enough, younger people end up making the same misattribution as older people if they are distracted during the initial encounter with the names by having to do some other task at the same time. Under these conditions, their explicit, but not their implicit, memory is impaired, and they too judge old nonfamous names to be famous more often than new nonfamous ones (Dywan & Jacoby, 1990). This pattern fits with the functional dissociations between implicit and explicit memory mentioned above; distracting young people during study hurts explicit memory but leaves implicit memory intact.

In a more recent study using the process dissociation procedure described above, Jennings and Jacoby (1993) have derived estimates of the separate contributions of intentional (explicit) and automatic (implicit) components of memory in the false-fame task; both inclusion and exclusion instructions were given (though I will not go into the details here). They found that the estimate of conscious recollection was higher for younger than for older people but that the estimate of automatic memory was not. And, in keeping with the findings of Dywan and Jacoby (1990), when a group of younger people were distracted during the initial encounter, this did not decrease their automatic, implicit memory, but it did decrease their recollection.

In general, then, I conclude from contrasts of implicit and explicit tests and from analyses using the process dissociation procedure that, when memory for the occurrence of familiar words or names is assessed, there are large and significant age differences in explicit processes but no age differences on implicit ones. The small age differences often observed on implicit tests seem most likely due to contamination from conscious memory.

Conceptual Priming of Words

The studies just described have in common the fact that, at the time of the test, the retrieval cue (e.g., the word stem or the famous name) re-presents at least part of the cue that was processed initially. In such cases, the priming observed on implicit tests could be due to the fact that the same perceptual processing operations can be performed on the stimulus at the time of study and at the time of test. For this reason, these are often called perceptual priming tests.

Is it only such cases in which there is age constancy in implicit memory? Or would age constancy be observed on conceptual priming tasks in which no part of the original stimulus is presented at the time of the test and in which, as discussed earlier, priming must be due to continuing activation of the conceptual nodes in semantic memory? Very little research has investigated this question, but a study by Light and Albertson (1989) suggests that age constancy of priming occurs in such cases as well. Light and Albertson first asked younger and older adults to rate the pleasantness of words in a study list which contained 18 target words scattered throughout it, 3 infrequently named members of 6 different categories. For example, the target words BADGER, ELEPHANT, and DEER might have been scattered throughout the list. Then, as a test of implicit memory for the target items, people were given a category exemplar generation test in which they were asked to generate several exemplars for each of several category names (e.g., ANIMAL). Note that no mention was made of the earlier list at this point, nor had the category names themselves ever occurred during the original list. Finally, an explicit cued recall test was administered in which people were given the names of the categories again (e.g., ANIMAL) and asked to recall any words they remembered from these categories that had appeared on the study list. For both tests, Light and Albertson counted the number of target exemplars (e.g., BADGER) produced.

Their results are shown in Figure 7.4. Note that there is a large and significant age difference favoring the younger people on the explicit cued recall task but only a very small (and statistically nonsignificant) difference in their favor on the implicit exemplar generation one. And, as was the case in the perceptual priming studies described in the previous section, the nonsignificant age difference on the implicit task seems to be due to the intrusion of conscious recollection. Many people of both ages admitted that they had tried to generate list members during the implicit task; when these people were eliminated from the analyses, the hint of an age difference on the implicit task disappeared. It is of interest that such conceptual priming of category exemplars is also well preserved (when compared to cued recall) in amnesia (Graf, Shimamura, & Squire, 1985) and schizophrenia (Schwartz et al., 1993).

Pictorial Priming

The studies reviewed so far have focused on memory for words. However, language processes are known to remain relatively intact in old age, when compared to nonverbal ones, so the question arises as to whether the age constancy in implicit processes extends to pictures as well.

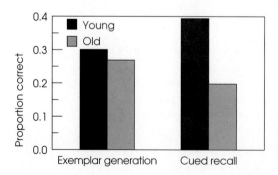

FIGURE 7.4 Mean proportion correct on the implicit exemplar generation and explicit cued recall tests for younger and older participants in Light and Albertson (1989). (*Source:* Light & Albertson, 1989. Copyright 1989 by the American Psychological Association. Reprinted by permission.)

Mitchell and his colleagues (Mitchell, 1993; Mitchell, Brown, & Murphy, 1990) have investigated this question using a picture-naming task. People first named a series of pictures (black-and-white line drawings of common objects) as quickly and accurately as possible. Then, for the implicit test, they named a second series in which some of the pictures are old, in that they also occurred in the original list, whereas others are new. The difference between the time required to name new pictures and the time to name old (repeated) ones provided the implicit measure of memory. Finally, participants were given an explicit recognition test in which they were asked to mark the pictures they encountered earlier. In order to examine the retention of implicit and explicit memory, some people did the second picture-naming session immediately, others after 1 day, 1 week, or 3 weeks.

The data Mitchell et al. (1990) obtained are shown in Figure 7.5. Looking first at the explicit recognition measure in 7.5a, it is clear that the typical age-related deficit appears at all retention intervals. In contrast, the implicit priming measure shown in Figure 5b reveals what is by now a familiar pattern, i.e., a small but nonsignificant advantage for the younger people in some of the conditions. Could this difference be due to explicit contamination? A series of studies conducted by Russo and Parkin (1993) suggest that it might. They used a different task in which, for each of a series of familiar items, people were first shown a very fragmented picture which then is replaced by a less and less fragmented version (see Figure 7.6) until the person could identify it. Two hours later an implicit memory test was given in which old sequences (from the study phase) and new sequences were shown and again subjects tried to identify them. Implicit memory was assessed by comparing the number of views needed to identify new pictures with that needed to identify old ones.

Russo and Parkin (1993) found significant age-related deficits on the implicit measure, but it was clear that the younger people had used explicit memory to help them on the implicit task; they showed more implicit memory for pictures they had recalled than for pictures they hadn't. This was not the case for older people, who showed the same amount of priming for nonrecalled as for recalled pictures. In addition, when the contributions of explicit memory processes to the implicit task were parcelled out statistically, age differences in implicit memory vanished altogether.

■ Implicit Memory for Novel Materials

In all of the cases so far, the stim   to be remembered were already well known to the person prior to the study; they cons   of familiar words or objects. Therefore, the preserved priming observed in old age cou   based upon the continuing activation of perceptual processes and/or conceptual units t   ready existed before the study began. But what happens when novel stimuli are encount   d or novel associations among previously unrelated stimuli must be learned? Given that older people are known to have particular difficulty in learning new materials (Howard & Wiggs, 1993), it is possible that they will not show spared implicit memory in such cases.

Priming of Nonverbal Visual Patterns

A few studies have examined implicit and explicit memory for novel visual patterns. One of these (Schacter, Cooper, & Valdiserri, 1992) focuses on three-dimensional objects of the sort

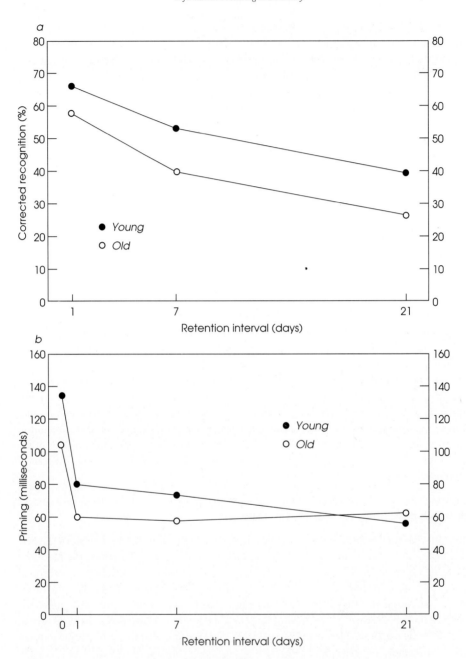

FIGURE 7.5 Performance on the explicit recognition test *(a)* and the implicit picture-naming test *(b)* for younger and older participants in Mitchell, Brown, and Murphy (1990). (*Source:* Mitchell, Brown, & Murphy, 1990. Copyright 1990 by the American Psychological Association. Reprinted by permission.)

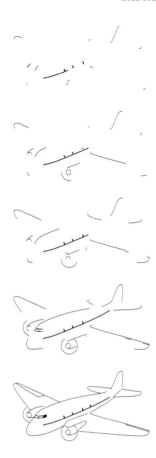

FIGURE 7.6 An example of picture sequences of the sort used by Russo and Parkin (1993). (*Source:* Reprinted with permission from Warrington & Weiskrantz, 1968.)

you encountered in the exercise shown in Figure 7.1. During the study phase, people decided (just as you did earlier) whether objects were facing primarily to the left or to the right. Later on an implicit test, they were shown a series of such objects, some presented during study and others new, and asked to decide whether the object was a possible or impossible one. For this implicit test, each object was flashed on a screen for only 100 milliseconds (msec) (100 msec = 1/10 second), and so they made many errors; thus the dependent measure was the proportion of correct judgments. The explicit test was identical except that, rather than making the possible/impossible judgment, people had to decide whether or not the object had occurred during the study phase; for this explicit test, the stimuli were presented for 6 seconds, so people had longer to make a judgment.

Schacter and his colleagues found that, as expected, the older people were poorer on the explicit recognition task than the younger ones, but the implicit measure revealed a different picture. For possible objects, both younger and older people were more accurate on previously studied than not-studied objects, and the difference was virtually identical for the two groups. The age constancy in object priming observed here is particularly interesting, because it occurred after a single presentation of complex novel stimuli. This is one case, then, in which implicit measures indicate that older people, like younger ones, are able to build up a memory representation after only a single exposure to such a stimulus.

A similar conclusion can also be drawn from a series of studies by Wiggs (1993) in which a different kind of novel visual stimulus was presented—seven-stroke Japanese *kanji* characters (ideograms)—and in which the mere exposure effect is used as an indicator of implicit memory. The mere exposure effect refers to the fact that, all other things being equal, having been exposed to an unfamiliar object increases one's preference, or liking for, that object. Such increased liking for previously presented over not-presented stimuli, then, is evidence of implicit memory for those stimuli.

Wiggs (1993, experiment 3) presented Japanese *kanji* characters 0, 1, 3, or 9 times during a study phase during which people simply observed the stimuli for 2 seconds each. On a later recognition test, older people were significantly less accurate than younger ones, indicating the expected age difference in explicit memory. Older people were also poorer than younger ones in estimating the frequency (0, 1, 3, or 9 times) with which each of the stimuli had occurred. In contrast, on the implicit task, on which people rated how much they liked each of the stimuli, Wiggs found no significant age difference. These data are depicted in Figure 7.7.

Note that, for the younger people, mean liking rating increased with the number of exposures, the usual mere exposure effect. A similar (though less systematic) pattern occurred for the older people. These findings suggest, then, that subtle changes in preferences for novel

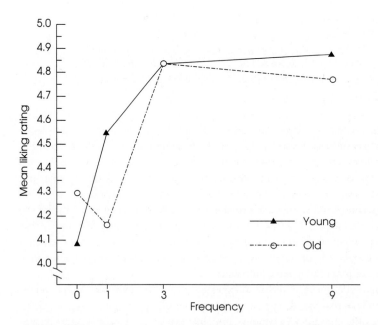

FIGURE 7.7 Mean liking ratings of *kanji* characters presented at different frequency levels for younger and older people in the implicit test used by Wiggs (1993, experiment 3). (*Source:* Wiggs, 1993. Copyright 1993 by the American Psychological Association. Reprinted by permission.)

stimuli occur in both younger and older people as the result of simply being exposed to the stimuli, and if any age-related differences in the extent of such influence exist they are small indeed. In fact, in a related study, we have found age equivalence in the mere exposure effect after three presentations of novel Turkish words (Howard & Pulido, 1994); in this study, the mere exposure effect was in the direction of being larger for the older than for the younger people.

Priming of Serial Patterned Sequences

In everyday life people also encounter repeating sequences of events, such as those required to operate devices such as a microwave oven. To what extent is there age constancy in implicit learning and memory for such repeating sequences? We have been addressing this question using a serial reaction-time task developed by Nissen and her colleagues (see, e.g., Nissen & Bullemer, 1987). People encounter a row of four squares across the bottom of a computer screen. Their task is to push the button immediately below the box in which an asterisk appears, and to do so as rapidly as possible. Their response causes that asterisk to disappear, and then an asterisk appears in another of the boxes, to which they are to respond in the same way. People encounter series of such trials, and, although they are not informed of this fact, the asterisk follows a predictable repeating sequence. Typically, people complete several such blocks in which each block consists of 10 repetitions of a 10-item-long repeating pattern. Then, to assess implicit learning and memory of the pattern, people are presented with an additional (random) block that does not contain the pattern.

The data from one such study (Howard & Howard, 1992a) are shown in Figure 7.8. Here we also included younger and older control groups who simply encountered six random blocks (i.e., for these people no predictable pattern was ever presented). As is clear, the older people were slower overall than the younger, and both control groups declined very little over blocks. So general practice at the task did not affect either group's response times very much. In contrast, consider the data indicated in the figure by circles, where the first four blocks had a repeating pattern. Here both younger and older groups got faster over trials, indicating that the presence of the repeating pattern was speeding response times. Another indication that this increase in speed was due to the presence of the pattern is that, when it was removed on block 5, response times increased dramatically (back to the block 1 performance) for both age groups. Thus, by this implicit measure of degree of disruption of response time resulting from removal of the pattern, younger and older people showed equal pattern learning.

In other studies, we have found that this same age constancy on the implicit measure of learning holds for longer, 16-element patterns and after as few as two repeating pattern blocks (Howard & Howard, 1989, 1992a). In contrast, when people are given an explicit test of pattern learning, in which they are asked to push a key to indicate which asterisk will appear next based on what they have learned about the pattern, we always find age differences favoring the younger people. We have also found age differences when people are asked to fill out a response sheet showing a typical sequence (Howard & Howard, 1992b). Thus, it is clear that older people are poorer than younger people are at recollecting the pattern but that it influences their performance nonetheless.

We are not yet sure of the limits of such age similarity in implicit pattern learning. For example, in a study by Jackson and Jackson (1992), in which a more complex hierarchical

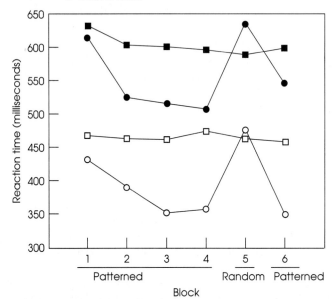

FIGURE 7.8 Mean response times by block for younger and older people in the serial reaction-time task used by Howard and Howard (1992a, experiment 2). (*Source:* Howard & Howard, 1992a. Copyright 1992 by the American Psychological Association. Reprinted by permission.)

pattern was used, an age difference in implicit learning appeared. So it is possible that older people will end up being poorer at more complex patterns, even on an implicit test. Nonetheless, it is clear that, as had been the case with the sorts of materials described earlier, implicit tests often reveal more age similarity than explicit ones do.

Priming of Verbal Associations

Several different implicit tasks have been used to study the aging of memory for new associations between words (e.g., learning to associate the words DRAGON and FUDGE with each other). Presumably, this sort of learning of paired associates is part of what is necessary for learning the vocabulary of a foreign language (e.g., learning that "dog" is *chien* in French).

One example of such research is a series in which we used Graf and Schacter's (1985) adaptation of the word stem completion method (Howard, Fry, & Brune, 1991). In this procedure, people encounter new associations during the study period. In some of our experiments, these are presented as paired associates (e.g., QUEEN–STAIRS; AUTHOR–PROJECT) and in others as sentences (e.g., THE QUEEN FELL DOWN THE STAIRS; THE AUTHOR COMPLETED THE PROJECT). During this study period, people are told to make a sentence relating the two words in the pair or (if presented with sentences) to expand on each sentence. Later, for the implicit test, memory for the new associations is assessed by presenting cues consisting of a word and word stem from the study list and asking them to complete the stem to form "the first word that comes to mind." The explicit memory test is identical, except that people are told to complete the word stem to form "a word studied earlier." Sometimes the word and word stem come from the same pair during study (e.g., QUEEN–STA_____; AUTHOR–PRO_____) whereas other times they come from different pairs (e.g., QUEEN–PRO_____; AUTHOR–STA_____). The degree of memory for the new association is inferred from the difference in target completions on same as opposed to different pairings. In a series of three studies using this method, we always found significant age differences favoring the younger group on the explicit test of associative memory. However, we found age differences on the implicit measure only when we put time constraints on the initial time allowed for studying the pairs (experiments 1 and 3); when we allowed people as much time as they wanted to produce their elaborations (experiment 2), no significant age difference in associative priming emerged.

Studies using other methods of assessing implicit associative memory have been reported, including those using speeded reading measures in which time to reread same versus different pairings is assessed (see, e.g., Balota & Duchek, 1989; Howard, Heisey, & Shaw, 1986; Moscovitch, Winocur, & McLachlan, 1986; Rabinowitz, 1986). All these studies have agreed with one another in revealing at least some conditions under which older people reveal as much implicit associative memory as younger people, despite showing deficits on explicit associative memory. The studies have differed, however, in whether or not they have found any age differences at all in implicit associative memory. The reasons for the discrepancies on this latter point are not clear. I suspect it is important, though, that many of the studies revealing age constancy in associative implicit memory allowed either unlimited study time or more than one presentation of each pair during study. In contrast, the studies showing some age differences in implicit associative memory were those using a single, fixed-time presentation of each word (see, e.g., Howard et al., 1986, experiment 2; Howard et al., 1991, experiments 1 and 3).

In summary, it is clear that when memory for new associations between familiar words is tested, age differences are often reduced or eliminated entirely compared to the age differences obtained on explicit tests. Whether older people need to have more or longer encounters with the new pairs in order to reveal such similarity to younger people remains to be established. Also unclear is the extent to which any age-related deficits observed on implicit associative priming tasks are due to explicit contamination.

■ Implications for Theories of Aging

The findings I've just reviewed offer some tentative hypotheses regarding what does and does not change in the course of normal aging.

What Is Spared?

There appears to be no decline with normal aging in the extent to which processing a stimulus automatically results in some alteration of preexisting perceptual pathways and conceptual representations; one way in which this alteration can be viewed is as a continuing activation of the relevant pathways and representations (though it is not yet clear how long any such activation continues). This hypothesis follows from the findings that, when perceptual and conceptual priming of familiar materials are examined, age differences in priming are either nonexistent or minimal.

There also appears to be age constancy in the readiness with which new perceptual pathways or representations are formed, i.e., in a system akin to Tulving and Schacter's (1990) perceptual representation system. Establishing such presemantic representations seems to be the automatic result of processing the stimuli. This hypothesis follows from the finding of age constancy in priming of novel stimuli such as three-dimensional objects, *kanji* characters, and novel Turkish words, for which no preexisting perceptual representations are likely to exist. Thus, I suggest that perceptual learning of this sort does not decline in old age.

What Declines?

In contrast, there is tentative evidence that a different kind of learning—that requiring a new conceptual link to be formed between two conceptual units—does decline in old age. This hypothesis follows from the finding that age differences sometimes emerge in the priming of new verbal associations (e.g., between DRAGON and FUDGE), particularly after minimal amounts of study. Establishing such a conceptual link between two concepts is not the automatic result of processing them next to each other; rather, it requires that some meaningful link between the two concepts be encoded at the time the pair is encountered (Graf & Schacter, 1985). Perhaps because of the reduced working memory capacity or slowing of mental processes (see, e.g., Salthouse, 1985) that occurs in old age, older people might be less likely to engage in this minimal degree of elaboration under less-than-optimal study conditions and hence less likely to form the necessary link.

All the studies reviewed above support the hypothesis that there is yet another age-related decline, a decline in conscious recollection. This decline is put into particularly sharp relief in the data shown in Figures 7.3 and 7.4 based on the results of Light and her colleagues. For both the perceptual word stem–priming study in Figure 7.3 and the conceptual exemplar generation study in Figure 7.4, when the younger people were given instructions to engage in conscious recollection (the explicit tests) they produced many more target items than they had under the implicit instructions. That is, they were able to use the instruction to recollect to engage in a strategic search of memory that enabled them to retrieve more target items. In sharp contrast, the older people either produced only slightly more items under explicit than implicit instructions (Figure 7.3) or actually produced fewer targets under explicit than implicit instructions (Figure 7.4). Thus, the older people were able to make little successful use of controlled retrieval strategies.

But what underlies this age-related deficiency in conscious recollection? We don't know. One possibility which had seemed to hold some promise is that the decline is due to a deficit in contextual processing (see, e.g., Light & LaVoie, 1993). In order to use the explicit retrieval instructions effectively, the person must be able to retrieve the information that a particular stimulus occurred in a particular time and place (e.g., on the list studied earlier). There is, in fact, a great deal of evidence that older adults are less able than younger ones to report such contextual information (see Light & LaVoie, 1993, and Chapter 6 for reviews). Perhaps, then, older adults are less likely to encode contextual detail at the initial encounter with a stimulus, and so their memories don't contain the necessary contextual detail to support conscious recollection of the initial encounter. This latter possibility is consistent with the evidence mentioned earlier that the hippocampal region is responsible for binding or integrating stimuli with their contexts and that this region declines notably in old age. Nonetheless, the fact that older people are less able to *report* the context in which they encountered a stimulus does not necessarily imply that they haven't stored that information; it only shows that they cannot consciously retrieve it. In fact, Light and her colleagues have shown that, although older people are less able than younger ones to report explicitly the modality in which a stimulus occurred, they are just as influenced as young people are when the modality is switched between study and test (Light, LaVoie, Valenica-Laver, Albertson Owens, & Mead, 1992). Thus, by the latter implicit measure they have retained as much about the modality of the stimulus as younger people have; they just can't report it.

This seemingly leads us back to where we started; it seems clear that as we age we become less skilled at conscious recollection and at engaging in strategic search and retrieval from our memories. What underlies this decline, and how it might be related to the declines in working memory capacity and the slowing that are known to occur with age, remain fascinating but unanswered questions.

■ Implications for Everyday Functioning

The fact that automatic (implicit) memory processes remain relatively intact in the course of aging while conscious recollection (explicit) processes decline has many implications for everyday functioning, some "good news" and some "bad news." Here are some examples.

Changing Negative Stereotypes and Expectations

Most people notice their own memory, and that of other people, getting worse as they age (see Chapter 12). The research discussed in that chapter indicates that this perception is likely to be accurate in the case of conscious recollection but inaccurate in the case of the automatic, implicit components of memory. Presumably, this is because people are typically not aware of the automatic aspects. If people of all ages were informed of the relative age constancy of implicit memory processes, it might help to change some of the negative, and perhaps self-fulfilling, expectations people have about cognitive decline in general.

For example, to the extent that people are convinced that they will not be able to remember some material (e.g., a new name and face), they might focus on this perceived inadequacy during the initial encounter with the new material rather than on the new material itself. They might be distracted by irrelevant, unwanted thoughts about their own inadequacies (thinking "I know I'll never remember this"), so that they fail to devote all of their attention and effort to learning the name and face. In doing this, they would have made the task into a divided-attention problem, and we know that having to do two things at once presents difficulties for older people (see, e.g., Hartley, 1992). I am speculating, then, that the intrusion of such thoughts about their own incompetence could decrease the likelihood of later conscious recollection even further than any age-related change in explicit memory processes might have. If my speculation here is correct, educating people regarding the saving of implicit memory in old age might have salutary effects on conscious recollection as well, if only because they will be less likely to focus on their own perceived memory inadequacies and more likely to focus effectively on the task at hand.

Cognitive Training and Intervention Programs

The relative age constancy of implicit memory processes is likely to be of use in designing programs for improving memory and cognition not only for people experiencing normal aging but also for those suffering from age-associated pathological conditions, such as Alzheimer's disease. Typically, such training programs have attempted to build on explicit processes, not implicit ones. For example, people are taught strategies and mnemonic techniques in which they learn to build mental images or to organize the to-be-learned material in certain ways as it is studied. These methods have met with only limited success, in that participants often fail to continue to use these strategies and to apply them in everyday life (see, e.g., Anschutz, Camp, Markley, & Kramer, 1987; Scogin & Bienias, 1988).

Furthermore, any approach based on explicit memory is unlikely to work for Alzheimer's disease patients except in the very early stages of the disease, before the catastrophic effects on explicit remembering have occurred. Remediation techniques building upon relatively spared implicit memory processes might overcome such drawbacks. For example, Glisky, Schacter, and Tulving (1986) have taught severely amnesic patients computer commands by using a method of vanishing cues which uses a training technique with tests similar to the word stem completion tasks discussed earlier.

Whether this technique, and others yet to be developed that call upon implicit memory processes, will be useful for remediating memory problems in normal aged and in Alzheimer's disease patients isn't yet known. However, there are some promising signs already. For example, Camp and McKitrick (1992) have reported success in teaching Alzheimer's disease patients the names of hospital staff members by using a technique called spaced retrieval. This technique involves progressively increasing the amount of time between successful recalls of the new material (e.g., recalling the staff member's name, given the picture). If on any test the person cannot recall the name, the correct name is given, the person must recall it immediately, and then a retest is given after a very short interval. If recall is successful, the intervals are increased again. Camp and McKitrick found that people who could not initially retain the names for more than a minute were able to recall them 5 weeks later after receiving such training. This demonstration is of interest here, because Camp and McKitrick speculate that this technique meets with such success because it calls upon implicit memory processes. For example, their patients do not seem aware of where they learned the names, correct recalls often being given with a questioning voice and sometimes followed by the patient's asking "Did you tell me that before?"

Diagnosis of Age-associated Pathological Conditions

In the early stages of Alzheimer's disease, it can be difficult to distinguish between the effects of the disease and the relatively benign declines in memory that accompany normal aging. This difficulty of diagnosis is troublesome for at least two reasons. First, if and when cures or treatments are found for the disease, it will be important to start them as soon as possible; early diagnosis will become critical. Second, because of increasing public awareness of the horrors and incidence of this dreaded disease, older adults often worry that any signs of declining memory they notice might be harbingers of it. Because the great majority of older people do not have Alzheimer's disease, much needless anxiety could be eliminated if early diagnosis could be improved.

If, as seems possible, some implicit memory processes that are spared in the course of normal aging decline early in the course of Alzheimer's disease, tests of such processes might eventually form part of a diagnostic test battery for the early detection of Alzheimer's disease. Of course, construction of such a battery is a long way off, requiring as it does collection of a great deal of longitudinal data comparing normal and early-stage Alzheimer's patients on a range of implicit and explicit memory tasks. So far, the extent to which implicit memory processes are saved in Alzheimer's disease is far from clear (see, e.g., the review by Nebes, 1992). Some studies have revealed differences between Alzheimer's patients and normal controls on implicit tests, whereas others have not. This in itself is not surprising because, as discussed earlier, there is good reason to suspect that different implicit tests call upon different underlying processes; thus, it is likely that some of these might be affected by Alzheimer's disease but others not. Much basic research needs to be done.

Change in the Subjective Nature of Recollection

The remaining implications all focus on the consequences of subtle interactions between explicit and implicit memory processes. The first has to do with the likelihood that the relative sparing of implicit as opposed to explicit processes results in changes in the subjective nature of recollection. Not all acts of conscious recollection feel the same. For example, encountering someone on the street often leads to strong feelings of familiarity, which lead you to recognize explicitly that you have encountered this person before. On some occasions, this feeling is accompanied by recollection of a specific encounter. In that case (using terminology introduced by Tulving, 1985), you can say that you *remember* encountering the person before. On other occasions, an equally strong feeling of familiarity is present, but you cannot remember a specific earlier encounter. In that case, you can be said to *know* that you encountered the person before.

Such differences in the subjective nature of recollection can be studied in the laboratory. For example, after encountering a study list of words, people are given a recognition test in which they must not only judge whether or not each test word was in the study list (a typical explicit test of memory) but also indicate for each item they recognize whether they *remember* it (i.e., have a specific recollection of what was experienced when the word appeared in the study list) or *know* that it occurred, but without recollecting anything about the original encounter. People do this readily and reliably, and research in which the participants are young adults has revealed a number of dissociations between "remember" and "know" judgments which suggest that "know" judgments are based, at least in part, on implicit memory processes.

For example, if young people are distracted during the initial encounter with the words, the number of "remember" judgments is decreased, but there is no effect on the number of "know" judgments (Gardiner & Parkin, 1990). Thus, dividing attention does not impair performance on implicit memory tests or "know" judgments, suggesting that both might rely on the same underlying process. One possible way in which this operates is that the earlier encounters have resulted in priming, so that it is easier for people to process the words encountered earlier. People might sense this increased perceptual fluency (ease of perceptual processing), resulting in a feeling of familiarity which leads them to make a "know" response. Thus, people are aware not of the implicit memory processes themselves but of their result (increased perceptual fluency), and they attribute this to having encountered the stimulus before. Implicit memory processes, then, result in a judgment of conscious recollection (i.e., I know I encountered that stimulus before) in that people attribute the current ease of processing (resulting from implicit memory processes) to some earlier encounter.

There is evidence that old age is accompanied by a change in the proportion of recollections that are judged to be "remember" as opposed to "know" experiences. In laboratory studies, the proportion of "remember" responses declines in old age, whereas the proportion of "know" responses either increases with age or remains the same. (Mäntylä, 1993; Parkin & Walter, 1992). This suggests that the subjective experience of recollecting that occurs in daily life undergoes subtle changes with age; older people seem more likely than younger ones to find themselves knowing about, but not remembering, some earlier encounter. This conclusion fits with the many studies indicating that older people are more prone than younger ones to experience source amnesia, that is, to be unable to recollect the source of information they have learned earlier. For example, older people are much poorer than younger ones at judging accurately whether they knew a fact ahead of time or were taught it in the experiment (see, e.g., McIntyre & Craik, 1987) and poorer at judging which of two people said something (Hashtroudi, Johnson, & Chrosniak, 1989). Thus, the experience of recollection seems to undergo changes with aging, changes which mean that the spared implicit memory processes have a relatively greater effect on recollection than when the person was younger.

Susceptibility to Unconscious Plagiarism and Repetition

Implicit memory processes result in stories, statements, and ideas we've encountered (or produced) before coming to mind more readily than they would have without the earlier encounter. The same is true for repetitions of our own; having told or written or thought about a story once renders it more likely to come to mind again (see, e.g., Jacoby & Kelley, 1987). How, then, do we avoid simply saying and writing the same thing over and over? And how do we avoid repeating what others have said and written? Presumably, we call upon conscious recollection, which enables us to tell that the story that has just come to mind is one we just heard Fred tell yesterday; therefore we don't repeat it to Fred (though we might decide to tell it to Jane if Fred isn't there).

The fact that implicit memory processes remain relatively intact in old age while explicit ones decline suggests that older people experience just as much priming from earlier encounters as young people but are less able to use explicit memory to help them avoid unintentional plagiarism and telling the same story more than once. I am not aware of any evidence supporting these conjectures concerning unconscious plagiarism, but both anecdotal accounts and laboratory data support the prediction that repeating oneself increases in old age. For example, two noted psychologists, Donald Hebb (1978) and B. F. Skinner (1983) lamented the fact that they found themselves engaging in more such repetition as they got older. And in a laboratory study using recall of word lists, older people were found to be more likely than younger adults to recall the same item more than once and to be unaware that they had done so (Koriat, Ben-Zur, & Sheffer, 1988). In another study, Hashtroudi et al. (1989) found that older adults were poorer than younger people at judging whether they themselves had said a word or only thought the word.

Effect on Impression Formation and Preferences

Implicit memory processes influence the impressions we form of other people, circumstances, and events. For example, in studies of impression formation, participants encounter a story (or perhaps a videotape) of a character performing a set of potentially ambiguous actions (e.g., engaging in an activity that could be viewed as being either helpful or intrusive), and they are asked to indicate their impressions of the person based on this encounter. Research with young adult participants has shown that, if these people have had earlier encounters with words relevant to one of the possible interpretations (e.g., "helpful" in this case), then, under some conditions, this increases the likelihood that participants will form that sort of impression (i.e., that the character is helpful) as opposed to the other (i.e., that the character is intrusive); see the review by Bargh (1992). Thus, the impressions formed are influenced by the earlier encounters, presumably via priming. With regard to preferences, I have already discussed the fact that mere exposure to a previously novel stimulus increases one's preference for, or liking of, that stimulus.

The fact that implicit memory processes remain relatively intact suggests that these influences are not likely to decline in old age. I am not aware of any direct evidence for such age constancy in the case of impression formation, but there is such evidence for preferences. As I described earlier, older adults' preferences for both novel Turkish words and novel *kanji* characters are influenced as much by earlier exposures as are those of younger adults (see, e.g., Howard & Pulido, 1994; Wiggs, 1993).

In fact, there is good reason to believe that older adults are likely to be *more* subject to the influences of earlier encounters on impression formation and on preferences than are younger adults. This is because research with younger people indicates that these effects are more pronounced when explicit memory for the earlier encounter is poor (e.g., because attention was divided during the initial encounter or because the earlier encounter occurred so quickly that the person was unaware of it). For example, the mere exposure effect is obtained more reliably among young people when the stimuli are presented subliminally (see, e.g., Bornstein, 1992) or while the person is engaged in some other activity (see, e.g., Howard & Pulido, 1994). In the case of impression formation studies, the effects described earlier are obtained only when the participant is not aware of the relationship between the earlier encounter with the priming words and the later impression formation task (Bargh, 1992). Presumably this occurs because, being aware of the source of the ease with which the impression or the preference judgment came to mind, people are able to discount this source. The fact that older people are less likely to remember the earlier encounters explicitly means that they will be less able to discount in this way. We saw some evidence of this in Jacoby's famous names studies described earlier.

CONCLUSIONS

■ Where Are We?

We know that age-related deficits are reduced or eliminated entirely when memory is tested via implicit, rather than explicit, means. This is true not only of memory for the occurrence of familiar stimuli but also of memory for at least some kinds of novel stimuli. Put another way, older adults are as skilled as younger adults at using memory as a tool but poorer at using memory as an object. We do not yet have an adequate theoretical explanation for why this particular pattern of savings and loss occurs. And we have only begun to explore the implications of this pattern for everyday functioning.

■ Where Do We Go Next?

A central goal should be to conduct research that will help us to construct adequate theories of why explicit and implicit tests show different patterns of aging. Such theories would clarify the mechanisms of aging in general and might illuminate how changes in behavior are related to changes in the brain. Given the dissociations that occur in explicit and implicit tests, it would be most useful to have studies in which each individual is given a battery of implicit and explicit tests, including those that tap perceptual and conceptual priming and those that examine priming of various kinds of novel materials. Each individual might also be given tasks designed to tap possible underlying mechanisms (e.g., slowing, working memory capacity, memory for context, frontal lobe functioning) so that patterns of associations and dissociations can be detected. Longitudinal data (see, e.g., Hultsch, Hertzog, Small, McDonald-Miszczak, & Dixon, 1992) and data from old-old individuals would also be helpful in constraining theory and establishing the limits of any age constancy.

All of this is, of course, a tall order of business, particularly because care must also be taken to use methods that isolate implicit (automatic) memory processes from explicit (intentional) ones. Giving a large number of implicit tests to the same individuals is often not feasible, because it is impossible to keep them from noticing the memory nature of the implicit tests. Jacoby's process dissociation procedure may be useful in this regard.

Another goal should be to explore the broader implications of research on the aging of implicit and explicit memory for such domains as social cognition (see, e.g., Hess, 1994), decision making, memory remediation, and therapy. As some of the implications discussed above suggest, it will be of particular interest to determine how the conscious and unconscious uses of memory interact in the everyday use of memory. One of the reasons that research on implicit memory has caught the fancy of so many cognitive psychologists is that it has revived interest in the role of unconscious processes in daily life (see, e.g., Jacoby & Kelley, 1987), a topic ignored during the earlier days of the cognitive revolution. And so, despite the fact that most implicit memory research is conducted in the laboratory (because the effects are so subtle that they are hard to detect outside it), it is a domain filled with promise for helping us to understand everyday functioning.

SUMMARY

Memory can be used unconsciously and implicitly as a tool or consciously and explicitly as an object. That these two ways of using memory have different properties has been revealed by the existence of various kinds of dissociations between them; they are affected differently by various independent variables, by brain damage, and by normal aging. The research sampled in this chapter shows that aging has much more dramatic effects on conscious recollection than on the unconscious use of memory and that this is true not only for memory for familiar materials but also for at least some kinds of novel material. These different patterns of the aging of implicit and explicit memory have implications for theories of aging, suggesting that, although the automatic activation that results from processing stimuli does not decline with age, the ability to engage in conscious retrieval of those stimuli does. The differential aging of implicit and explicit memory also has implications for everyday functioning, including the domains of negative stereotypes, cognitive training, diagnosis of age-associated pathological conditions, the subjective nature of recollection, susceptibility to unintentional repetition of oneself and others, and formation of impressions and preferences.

SUPPLEMENTAL READINGS

Graf, P., & Masson, M. E. J. (Eds.) (1993). *Implicit memory: New directions in cognition, development, and neuropsychology.* Hillsdale, NJ: Erlbaum.

Jacoby, L. S., Toth, J. P., Lindsay, D. S., & Debner, J. A. (1992). Lectures for a layperson: Methods for revealing unconscious processes. In R. F. Bornstein & T. S. Pittman (Eds.), *Perception without awareness* (pp. 81–120). New York: Guilford.

Moscovitch, M., & Winocur, G. (1992). The neuropsychology of memory and aging. In F. I. M. Craik & T. A. Salthouse (Eds.), *The handbook of aging and cognition* (pp. 315–372). Hillsdale, NJ: Erlbaum.

ACKNOWLEDGMENT

Preparation of this chapter and the authors' research reported herein was supported by National Institute on Aging grant R37 AG02751. I am grateful to David Mitchell for his comments on an earlier version of this manuscript.

REFERENCES

Anschutz, L., Camp, C. J., Markley, R. P., & Kramer, J. J. (1987). Remembering mnemonics: A three-year follow-up on the effects of mnemonic training in elderly adults. *Experimental Aging Research, 13,* 141–143.

Baddeley, A. (1986). *Working memory.* Oxford: Clarendon.

Balota, D. A., & Duchek, J. M. (1989). Spreading activation in episodic memory: Further evidence for age independence. *Quarterly Journal of Experimental Psychology, 41A,* 849–876.

Bargh, J. A. (1992). Does subliminality matter to social psychology? Awareness of the stimulus versus awareness of its influence. In R. F. Bornstein & T. S. Pittman (Eds.), *Perception without awareness* (pp. 236–255). New York: Guilford.

Bornstein, R. F. (1992). Subliminal mere exposure effects. In R. F. Bornstein & T. S. Pittman (Eds.), *Perception without awareness* (pp. 191–210). New York: Guilford.

Bowers, J., & Schacter, D. L. (1993). Priming of novel information in amnesic patients: Issues and data. In P. Graf & M. E. J. Masson (Eds.), *Implicit memory: New directions in cognition, development, and neuropsychology* (pp. 303–326). Hillsdale, NJ: Erlbaum.

Camp, C. J., & McKitrick, L. A. (1992). Memory interventions in Alzheimer's-type dementia populations: Methodological and theoretical issues. In R. L. West & J. D. Sinnott (Eds.), *Everyday memory and aging: Current research and methodology* (pp. 155–172). New York: Springer.

Claparede, E. (1911). Reconnaissance et moitie. *Archives de psychologie, 11,* 79–90.

Cohen, N. J., & Squire, L. R. (1980). Preserved learning and retention of pattern analyzing skill in amnesia: Dissociation of knowing how and knowing that. *Science, 210,* 207–209.

Dywan, J., & Jacoby, L. (1990). Effects of aging on source monitoring: Differences in susceptibility to false fame. *Psychology and Aging, 5,* 379–387.

Fowler, M., & McCutcheon, P. (Eds.) (1991). *Songs of experience: An anthology of literature on growing old.* New York: Ballantine.

Gardiner, J. M., & Parkin, A. J. (1990). Attention and recollective experience in recognition memory. *Memory and Cognition, 18,* 579–583.

Glisky, E. L., Schacter, D. L., & Tulving, E. (1986). Computer learning by memory-impaired patients: Acquisition and retention of complex knowledge. *Neuropsychologia, 24,* 313–328.

Graf, P., & Komatsu, S. (1994). Process dissociation procedure: Handle with caution! *European Journal of Cognitive Psychology, 6,* 113–129.

Graf, P., & Schacter, D. L. (1985). Implicit and explicit memory for new associations in normal and amnesic subjects. *Journal of Experimental Psychology: Learning, Memory, and Cognition, 11,* 501–518.

Graf, P., Shimamura, A. P., & Squire, L. R. (1985). Priming across modalities and priming across category levels: Extending the domain of preserved function in amnesia. *Journal of Experimental Psychology: Learning, Memory, and Cognition, 11,* 386–396.

Graf, P., Squire, L. R., & Mandler, G. (1984). The information that amnesic patients do not forget. *Journal of Experimental Psychology: Learning, Memory, and Cognition, 10,* 164–178.

Gregg, V. (1976). Word frequency, recognition and recall. In J. Brown (Ed.), *Recognition and recall* (pp. 183–216). Chichester, U.K.: Wiley.

Hartley, A. A. (1992). Attention. In F. I. M. Craik & T. A. Salthouse (Eds.), *The handbook of aging and cognition* (pp. 3–50). Hillsdale, NJ: Erlbaum.

Hashtroudi, S., Johnson, M. K., & Chrosniak, L. D. (1989). Aging and source monitoring. *Psychology and Aging, 4,* 106–112.

Hebb, D. O. (1978). On watching myself get old. *Psychology Today,* 15–23.

Hess, T. M. (1994). Social cognition in adulthood: Aging-related changes in knowledge and processing mechanisms. *Developmental Review, 14,* 373–412.

Howard, D. V. (1991). Implicit memory: An expanding picture of cognitive aging. In K. W. Schaie (Ed.), *Annual review of gerontology and geriatrics* (vol. 11, pp. 1–22). New York: Springer.

Howard, D. V., Fry, A., & Brune, C. (1991). Aging and memory for new associations: Direct versus indirect measures. *Journal of Experimental Psychology: Learning, Memory, and Cognition, 17,* 779–792.

Howard, D. V., Heisey, J. G., & Shaw, R. J. (1986). Aging and the priming of newly learned associations. *Developmental Psychology, 22,* 78–85.

Howard, D. V., & Howard, J. H., Jr. (1989). Age differences in learning serial patterns: Direct versus indirect measures. *Psychology and Aging, 4,* 357–364.

Howard, D. V., & Howard, J. H., Jr. (1992a). Adult age differences in the rate of learning serial patterns: Evidence from direct and indirect tests. *Psychology and Aging, 7,* 232–241.

Howard, D. V., & Howard, J. H., Jr. (1992b). *Age differences in learning to use and reproduce serial patterns.* Paper presented at the Cognitive Aging Conference, Atlanta, April.

Howard, D. V., & Pulido, A. (1994). *Differential effects of age and distraction on implicit and explicit tests: Mere exposure versus recognition of Turkish words.* Paper presented at the Cognitive Aging Conference, Atlanta, April.

Howard, D. V., & Wiggs, C. L. (1993). Aging and learning: Insights from implicit and explicit tests. In J. Cerella, J. Rybash, W. J. Hoyer, & M. L. Commons (Eds.), *Adult information processing: Limits on loss* (pp. 512–528). New York: Academic Press.

Hultsch, D. F., Hertzog, C., Small, B. J., McDonald-Miszczak, L., & Dixon, R. A. (1992). Short-term longitudinal change in cognitive performance in later life. *Psychology and Aging, 7,* 571–584.

Jackson, G. M., & Jackson, S. (1992). *Age and the acquisition of implicit and explicit knowledge.* Paper presented at the Cognitive Aging Conference, Atlanta, April.

Jacoby, L. L., & Dallas, M. (1981). On the relationship between autobiographical memory and perceptual learning. *Journal of Experimental Psychology: General, 110,* 306–340.

Jacoby, L. L., & Kelley, C. M. (1987). Unconscious influences of memory for a prior event. *Personality and Social Psychology Bulletin, 13,* 314–336.

Jacoby, L. L., Toth, J. P., & Yonelinas, A. P. (1993). Separating conscious and unconscious influences of memory: Measuring recollection. *Journal of Experimental Psychology: General, 122,* 139–154.

Jacoby, L. L., & Witherspoon, D. (1982). Remembering without awareness. *Canadian Journal of Psychology, 36,* 300–324.

Jennings, J. M., & Jacoby, L. L. (1993). Automatic versus intentional uses of memory: Aging, attention, and control. *Psychology and Aging, 8,* 283–293.

Jernigan, T. L., Archibald, S. L., Berhow, M. T., Sowell, E. R., Foster, D. S., & Hesselink, J. R. (1991). Cerebral structure on MRI. I: Localization of age-related changes. *Biological Psychiatry, 29,* 55–67.

Koriat, A., Ben-Zur, H., & Sheffer, D. (1988). Telling the same story twice: Output monitoring and age. *Journal of Memory and Language, 27,* 23–39.

Light, L. L. (1991). Memory and aging: Four hypotheses in search of data. *Annual Review of Psychology, 42,* 333–376.

Light, L. L., & Albertson, S. A. (1989). Direct and indirect tests of memory for category exemplars in young and older adults. *Psychology and Aging, 4,* 487–492.

Light, L. L., & LaVoie, D. (1993). Direct and indirect measures of memory in old age. In P. Graf & M. E. J. Masson (Eds.), *Implicit memory: New directions in cognition, development, and neuropsychology* (pp. 207–230). Hillsdale, NJ: Erlbaum.

Light, L. L., LaVoie, D., Valenica-Laver, D., Albertson Owens, S. A., & Mead, G. (1992). Direct and indirect measures of memory for modality in young and older adults. *Journal of Experimental Psychology: Learning, Memory, and Cognition, 18,* 1284–1297.

Light, L. L., & Singh, A. (1987). Implicit and explicit memory in young and older adults. *Journal of Experimental Psychology: Learning, Memory, and Cognition, 13,* 531–541.

Mäntylä, T. (1993). Knowing but not remembering: Adult age differences in recollective experience. *Memory and Cognition, 21,* 379–388.

McIntyre, J. S., & Craik, F. I. M. (1987). Age differences in memory for item and source information. *Canadian Journal of Psychology, 41,* 175–192.

Mishkin, M., & Petri, H. L. (1984). Memories and habits: Some implications for the analysis of learning and retention. In L. R. Squire & N. Butters (Eds.), *Neuropsychology of memory* (pp. 287–296). New York: Guilford.

Mitchell, D. B. (1993). Implicit and explicit memory for pictures: Multiple views across the lifespan. In P. Graf & M. E. J. Masson (Eds.), *Implicit memory: New directions in cognition, development, and neuropsychology* (pp. 171–190). Hillsdale, NJ: Erlbaum.

Mitchell, D. B., Brown, A. S., & Murphy, D. R. (1990). Dissociations between procedural and episodic memory: Effects of time and aging. *Psychology and Aging, 5,* 264–276.

Moscovitch, M., & Winocur, G. (1992). The neuropsychology of memory and aging. In F. I. M. Craik & T. A. Salthouse (Eds.), *The handbook of aging and cognition* (pp. 315–372). Hillsdale, NJ: Erlbaum.

Moscovitch, M., Winocur, G., & McLachlan, D. (1986). Memory as assessed by recognition and reading time in normal and memory-impaired people with Alzheimer's disease and other neurological disorders. *Journal of Experimental Psychology: General, 115,* 331–347.

Mutter, S. A., Howard, D. V., Howard, J. H., Jr., & Wiggs, C. L. (1990). Performance on direct and indirect tests of memory after mild closed head injury. *Cognitive Neuropsychology, 7,* 329–346.

Nebes, R. D. (1992). Cognitive dysfunction in Alzheimer's disease. In F. I. M. Craik & T. A. Salthouse (Eds.), *The handbook of aging and cognition* (pp. 373–446). Hillsdale, NJ: Erlbaum.

Nissen, M. J., & Bullemer, P. (1987). Attentional requirements of learning: Evidence from performance measures. *Cognitive Psychology, 19,* 1–32.

Nissen, M. J., Ross, J. L., Willingham, D. B., Mackenzie, T. B., & Schacter, D. L. (1988). Memory and awareness in a patient with multiple personality disorder. *Brain and Cognition, 8,* 117–134.

Park, D. C., & Shaw, R. J. (1992). Effect of environmental support on implicit and explicit memory in younger and older adults. *Psychology and Aging, 7,* 632–642.

Parkin, A. J., & Walter, B. M. (1992). Recollective experience, normal aging, and frontal dysfunction. *Psychology and Aging, 7,* 290–298.

Rabinowitz, J. C. (1986). Priming in episodic memory. *Journal of Gerontology, 41,* 204–213.

Rajaram, S., & Roediger, H. L., III (1993). Direct comparison of four implicit memory tests. *Journal of Experimental Psychology: Learning, Memory, and Cognition, 19,* 765–776.

Ribot, T. (1882). *Diseases of memory.* New York: Appleton.

Roediger, H. L. (1990). Implicit memory: Retention without remembering. *American Psychologist, 45,* 1043–1056.

Roediger, H. L., III, & McDermott, K. B. (1993). Implicit memory in normal human subjects. In H. Spinnler & F. Boller (Eds.), *Handbook of neuropsychology* (vol. 8, pp. 63–131). Amsterdam: Elsevier.

Russo, R., & Parkin, A. J. (1993). Age differences in implicit memory: More apparent than real. *Memory and Cognition, 21,* 73–80.

Ryle, G. (1949). *The concept of mind.* San Francisco: Hutchinson.

Salthouse, T. A. (1985). *Theoretical perspectives on cognitive aging.* Hillsdale, NJ: Erlbaum.

Schacter, D. L. (1987). Implicit memory: History and current status. *Journal of Experimental Psychology: Learning, Memory, and Cognition, 13,* 501–518.

Schacter, D. L., Cooper, L. A., & Valdiserri, M. (1992). Implicit and explicit memory for novel visual objects in older and younger adults. *Psychology and Aging, 7,* 299–308.

Schwartz, B. L., Rosse, R. B., & Deutsch, S. I. (1993). Limits of the processing view in accounting for dissociations among memory measures in a clinical population. *Memory and Cognition, 21,* 63–72.

Scogin, F., & Bienias, J. L. (1988). A three-year follow-up of older adult participants in a memory-skills training program. *Psychology and Aging, 3,* 334–337.

Sherry, D. F., & Schacter, D. L. (1987). The evolution of multiple memory systems. *Psychological Review, 94,* 439–454.

Shimamura, A. P. (1993). Neuropsychological analyses of implicit memory: History, methodology, and theoretical interpretations. In P. Graf & M. E. J. Masson (Eds.), *Implicit memory: New directions in cognition, development, and neuropsychology* (pp. 265–286). Hillsdale, NJ: Erlbaum.

Skinner, B. F. (1983). Intellectual self-management in old age. *American Psychologist, 38,* 239–244.

Squire, L. R. (1992). Memory and the hippocampus: A synthesis from findings with rats, monkeys, and humans. *Psychological Review, 99,* 195–231.

Squire, L. R., & Cohen, N. (1984). Human memory and amnesia. In G. Lynch, J. L. McGaugh, & N. M. Weinberger (Eds.), *Neurobiology of learning and memory* (pp. 3–64). New York: Guilford.

Squire, L. R., & McKee, R. D. (1993). Declarative and nondeclarative memory in opposition: When prior events influence amnesic patients more than normal subjects. *Memory and Cognition, 21,* 424–430.

Terry, R. D., Deteresa, R., & Hansen, L. A. (1987). Neocortical cell counts in normal human adult aging. *Annals of Neurology, 21,* 530–539.

Tulving, E. (1985). Memory and consciousness. *Canadian Journal of Psychology, 26,* 1–12.

Tulving, E., & Schacter, D. L. (1990). Priming and human memory systems. *Science, 247,* 301–306.

Wiggs, C. L. (1993). Aging and memory for frequency of occurrence of novel, visual stimuli: Direct and indirect measures. *Psychology and Aging, 8,* 400–410.

8

LANGUAGE AND DISCOURSE PROCESSING THROUGH ADULTHOOD

Elizabeth A. L. Stine, Lisa M. Soederberg, and
Daniel G. Morrow

University of New Hampshire

Effective functioning in the adult world is intimately tied to our capacity to comprehend, remember, and produce language—in effect, to participate in the "discourse world." Language gives us access to an infinite variety of knowledge domains, connects us to other people, and allows us to express our creative spirit, our needs, and the memories of our lives. Imagine what it would be like to have this conduit severed or diminished in some way. Imagine understanding the few words that you are reading right now but not knowing how they fit in with what you've read earlier in this paragraph. Imagine being unable to quite focus your attention on the meaning of a text, as though every word suggested something to you that was irrelevant to the intended meaning. Imagine trying to recount a story and not being able to immediately remember the names of objects and people you know well. Imagine what life would be like—and imagine the strategies that you might adopt to maintain your participation in the discourse world.

Certainly, we've all experienced these limitations at some time to some degree, perhaps when we're tired or stressed, but current theories of cognitive aging suggest that such experiences are more commonplace in later life. Our goals in this chapter will be to (1) consider the validity of these different notions of age deficits in language and discourse processing by examining data testing these ideas, (2) examine evidence for age differences in the use of compensatory strategies in language processing, (3) describe how deficits and compensatory strategies can interact to affect functioning in the discourse world, and (4) discuss gaps in our understanding of these processes in the hope of suggesting avenues for future research.

ISSUES, THEORIES, AND METHODS

Researchers who study the development of discourse processing over the life span are faced by the paradox of the elderly subject who has difficulty in decontextualized laboratory tasks of language memory and yet functions effectively as a reader and partner in conversation. Thus, two central questions driving research are, on the one hand, how to characterize age deficits in terms of changes in the cognitive mechanisms underlying discourse processing and, on the other, how to account for the perhaps unexpected level of performance in everyday language processing observed. It is around these two questions that we will build our discussion of language and discourse processing into late life.

■ Theories of Language and Discourse Processing

The fundamental fact that theories of discourse processing must explain is that, somehow in the face of very limited working memory capacity, we construct complex and elaborate meaning structures out of sequences of phonemes or orthographic characters. A basic assumption of most models is that we accomplish understanding by processing small segments of language, one at a time, within a limited-capacity buffer, or "working memory" (Just & Carpenter, 1992; Kintsch & van Dijk, 1978). Within each of these segments, or "input cycles" (e.g., the very clause you are reading right now), the meanings of individual words must be accessed, the interrelationships among these concepts must be established, and the constructed meaning of the current segment must be integrated with the meaning derived from earlier segments. We use the term "cycle" in this context since this kind of processing must be repeated over and over again for each successive segment of text encountered. Some words within these cycles represent relational concepts (i.e., predicates) and others represent objects to be related (i.e., arguments). This assignment of predicates and thematic roles is to some extent governed by syntactic structure; that is, the function of syntax is to provide processing instructions about *how* to construct an integrated meaning out of individual lexical items (Kintsch, 1992; Morrow, 1986). Even while readers or listeners process text in this rather piecemeal fashion, they must also construct and modify the more global representation of meaning (Sanford & Garrod, 1981). In the case of narrative comprehension, the reader must create a working model of the characters' plans, goals, and actions as well as of the setting in which they are embedded, all while integrating more microlevel text units.

According to many theorists, the basic unit of meaning is the "proposition" (Kintsch & van Dijk, 1978), which is composed of a predicate and the set of arguments which are related by the predicate. Within each input cycle, the propositional content of the text is represented and individual propositions are connected on the basis of concept overlap to form a "coherence graph" representing the meaning structure of that segment. So, for example, as you read the first sentence of this paragraph, you encoded nine idea units:

P1 (QUANTIFY THEORISTS MANY)
P2 (CLAIM THEORISTS P5)
P3 (MODIFY UNIT BASIC)
P4 (HAS UNIT MEANING)

P5 (IS P4 PROPOSITION)
P6 (COMPOSED-OF PROPOSITION P7)
P7 (AND PREDICATE ARGUMENTS)
P8 (MODIFY ARGUMENTS SET)
P9 (RELATE PREDICATE ARGUMENTS)

and detected interrelationships among them which we may represent in a coherence graph as:

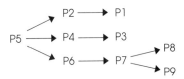

Propositions higher (further left) in the hierarchy represent the more important ideas which are modified and expanded by the elaborative detail lower (further right) in the hierarchy. As you continue to read, you hold some of these idea units in working memory to guide and provide a framework for subsequent text. Depending on your working memory capacity, you could keep all or some subset of these units active in your working memory, discarding those that are the least important and the most temporally remote. So, for example, with a capacity of four, you might retain propositions P4, P5, P6, and P7, roughly equivalent to "A proposition is a unit of meaning composed of a predicate and arguments," or with a capacity of three, you might drop P4, leaving "A proposition is composed of a predicate and arguments." An even more restricted capacity might allow for just the most topical P5 proposition, leaving a residual trace roughly equivalent to "Something about what a proposition is." Your subsequent understanding will depend on how much you were able to retain from that first sentence and how well you are able to select the most important ideas from among the barrage of idea units in your working memory.

The point here is that (1) discourse is to some extent reducible to a finite set of idea units, which must be organized to represent their interrelationships, (2) this propositional decoding and organization occurs in cycles, and (3) capacity varies across individuals such that the more information a reader or listener can process and hold in memory, the easier it is to form an integrated representation of the whole text. The evidence for this more or less generic model of discourse processing is plentiful. For example, support for the psychological reality of propositions can be found in the increase in reading time for passages that have more propositions relative to the number of words (Kintsch & Keenan, 1973). The fact that recall is greater for propositions higher in the coherence graph (those that have been processed through repeated cycles) than for propositions lower in the coherence graph provides support for the basic processing assumptions of the model (Kintsch & van Dijk, 1978). Evidence for the existence of cycling can be found in a classic study by Jarvella (1971) in which subjects listened to speech that was occasionally interrupted with a prompt to repeat as much of the text as they could. Subjects were much better at recalling the text verbatim from the current constituent than from the previous constituent, indicating that readers discard the verbatim words from past input cycles. In addition, concept verification is faster for concepts that would theoretically be held over in the buffer (Fletcher, 1981). Points of organizational processing are evident in measures of on-line reading time, indicating that more time is needed at the ends of sentences and clause boundaries as well as at the beginning of stories (cf. Aaronson & Scarborough, 1976; Haberlandt, 1984). In sum, both memory and reading time data support the notion that text is at some point represented propositionally, that this representation is conducted on a cycle-by-cycle basis in which a cycle roughly corresponds to a clause, and that the representation constructed depends upon the available capacity of working memory.

To this point, we have been describing cognitive processes associated with the text-based level, which deals with propositional coding at what has been called the "microstructural" level. Thus, we have begun our discussion of language and discourse processing in the "middle," for this text-based processing occurs in the context of both a "level below" and a "level above." At the level below, we consider how word meanings are activated and lexical access is achieved.

The "Level Below": Word Processing

Long-term memory, in which our knowledge about the meanings, sounds, and written configurations of words is stored, is conceptualized as a network of interrelated nodes, corresponding to these different aspects of word knowledge, as shown in Figure 8.1. This model rests on the metaphor "The mind is a brain," such that when information stored at these nodes is more readily available, it is said to be "activated." Just as activation spreads through a neural network, so the spread of activation is the theoretical mechanism through which information becomes available (Anderson, 1990). Thus, we can conceptualize comprehension as partly involving a spread of activation upward through the network from the surface features of language to its conceptual representation and production as a spread of activation downward from concepts to surface features. The prevailing view is that the phonemic and orthographic symbols associated with the spoken and written word, respectively, automatically and obligatorily make available to the comprehender the conceptual representation of the word (Fodor, 1983). By many accounts, this access to word meanings (which we could conceptualize as a spread of activation upward through the network) occurs "promiscuously" without respect to the constraints provided by the larger discourse context (Kintsch, 1988; Swinney, 1979). So, for example, on hearing the sentence "The townspeople were amazed to find that all the buildings had collapsed except the mint," all meanings of MINT momentarily become available (those related to MONEY and those related to CANDY); in very short order, however, context constrains the meaning to the contextually appropriate one. This selection process is enabled by an inhibition process in working memory which actively suppresses irrelevant meanings (Gernsbacher & Faust, 1991). Semantic access is promiscuous in the sense not only of making alternative meanings of a single word available but also of making available knowledge more broadly accessible.

The change in levels of activation and inhibition over time has been demonstrated in an experiment by Till, Mross, and Kintsch (1988), in which subjects read sentences containing an ambiguous priming word such as the MINT example above. After reading the sentence, subjects performed a lexical decision task in which target words were either semantically related to the priming word and appropriate to the meaning of the sentence (e.g., MONEY), se-

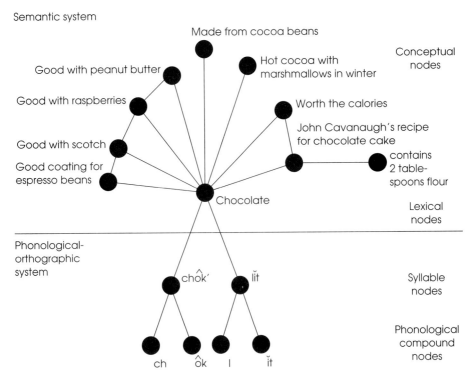

FIGURE 8.1 Hypothetical network representation for "chocolate" (with apologies to Burke, MacKay, Worthley, & Wade, 1991).

mantically related to the priming word but inappropriate to the meaning (e.g., CANDY), or inferentially related to the sentence (e.g., EARTHQUAKE). The intervals between the presentation of the prime and target varied from 200 to 1,500 milliseconds (msec). Within the first 400 msec, both contextually appropriate *and* inappropriate meanings of the priming word were facilitated, suggesting that for the briefest moment all meanings of MINT were available. At longer intervals, the contextually appropriate, but not the contextually inappropriate, meaning was facilitated, indicating that the inappropriate meaning had been suppressed. At longer intervals still (e.g., after about a second), the inference word was facilitated as well, suggesting that a more holistic representation of the sentence meaning had been achieved.

The point here is that, at this "level below," the discourse processing system appears to work by making available any concept that has the most remote chance of being useful and discarding possibilities in time only when they are unlikely. Thus, the modus operandi of working memory is that activation spreads rampantly so that nodes are pruned by the constraints of context only after some degree of indiscriminant activation. The conceptual representations derived from this level are used at the propositionally driven text-base level to construct broader units of meaning; processing at the text base level, then, is contingent upon effective activation of target meanings as well as effective suppression of inappropriate ones (cf. Gernsbacher & Faust, 1991).

Most of the cognitive aging work on language processing has addressed questions at these two levels of analysis, the text-based level and the word level. While these are important basic processes that account for many aspects of language processing, they are insufficient to explain the many facets of discourse processing. Thus, we find ourselves at that "level above." For example, the Till et al. study shows that after 1 second a representation that elaborates the text with world knowledge is created. We now turn our attention to this situational representation.

The "Level Above": Mental Models

People often go beyond word-level and propositional representations in order to understand the *situations* the speaker or writer is describing. For example, if a friend calls and complains that her old dishwasher has flooded all over the kitchen floor again, you understand her story by elaborating with several kinds of knowledge that are relevant to the account, e.g., the layout of the kitchen (location of the dishwasher, cabinets, and so forth), the unreliable history of the dishwasher, and perhaps the fact that your friend tends to panic when such mishaps occur. This process, at the "level above," is often described as building a "mental model" (Johnson-Laird, 1983) or "situation model" (van Dijk & Kintsch, 1983) that combines text information and knowledge about the described places, objects, characters, and actions. Thus, successful understanding requires that the reader or listener build a mental model that matches the one intended by the writer or speaker.

Evidence for situation models comes from several lines of research. People often remember the described situation rather than, or in addition to, the propositions conveyed by the text. For example, after reading "Three turtles sat *on* a log and a fish swam beneath *them*" readers are likely to confuse this sentence with "Three turtles sat *on* a log and a fish swam beneath *it*" during a recognition memory test. However, they do not confuse "Three turtles sat *beside* a log and a fish swam beneath *them*" with "Three turtles sat *beside* a log and a fish swam beneath *it*" (Bransford, Barclay, & Franks, 1972). While both sentence pairs differ by only one proposition ((LOC: (SIT TURTLES) ON) versus (LOC: (SIT TURTLES) BESIDE)), the pairs describe very different situations. Similarly, Garnham (1981) showed that people confuse sentence pairs that are similar in both propositional and situational content, such as the following pair: "The girl was given a complete pedicure at the podiatrist's" versus "The girl was given a complete pedicure by the podiatrist." However, they readily distinguish sentences that are propositionally similar but describe different situations: "The girl had her handbag stolen at the podiatrist's" and "The girl had her handbag stolen by the podiatrist." These examples suggest that the situational representation can take priority over the propositional representation.

The need for a situation model level of representation is perhaps most apparent in the spatial domain. In a study by Morrow, Bower, and Greenspan (1989), subjects read narratives that took place in a research center, the layout of which was familiar to all subjects. Each narrative described the main character moving from room to room in order to accomplish a goal. Thus, in a story about Wilbur the research director cleaning up the center, subjects would read critical motion sentences like "Wilbur walked from the conference room into the laboratory" (which would require Wilbur to take a path through the library, which was unmentioned). To examine how subjects create and update a situation model from the narrative, each critical sentence was followed by a probe question about objects in the research center. Probed objects could be from the goal room (in the above example, the laboratory), from the source room that the character had just left (the conference room), from the unmentioned path room (the library), or from an unmentioned room that was not relevant to the situation. Probe response times were fastest for the goal room and increased from path to source to other room, and probes about the unmentioned path were more accessible than those about the source room even though only the source was mentioned in the sentence. This pattern of response times suggests that readers inferred the character's path of motion even though the "mental completion" of the motion event was not necessary to create a propositional model. Using their knowledge of the setting, readers went beyond the propositional representation of the text in order to create a model of the situation.

The mental models created by readers are often organized around the perspective of main characters (Glenberg, Meyer, & Lindem, 1987). They are organized not only around the location and movement of the protagonist through space, but also around other facets of the characters as well. For example, situation models can be constructed around the emotional reactions of characters to events in which they participate. In a study by Gernsbacher and Robertson (1992), subjects read a story about a character who steals money from a store where a friend works and later finds out the friend has been fired. Readers are likely to draw the inference that the character feels guilt or regret. In fact, subjects in the study read target sentences more quickly when the sentences contained emotion words that were consistent with the passage (e.g., guilt) rather than inconsistent (e.g., pride). Thus, situation models are multidimensional, reflecting the rich structure of narratives, which resonates with our knowledge from many domains—spatial, causal, and emotional.

Research on expertise and text processing provides an ideal test case for distinguishing propositional and situation model representations. Experts have a well-organized knowledge base that can be readily available for interpreting domain-relevant texts. Therefore, they are likely to elaborate the text base with knowledge in order to create a situation model. Novices, on the other hand, have little choice but to create a more verbatim, propositional representation of the text because they can rely only on text information. Indeed, not only do experts recall more information from domain-relevant texts, but their protocols are more organized around domain principles (Kintsch, Welsch, Schmalhofer, & Zimny, 1990; Spilich, Vesonder, Chiesi, & Voss, 1979). In contrast to novices, experts draw on domain knowledge during comprehension in order to make elaborative inferences and create situation models. For example, Noordman and Vonk (1992) used an on-line inference verification task to show that when novice readers encounter a sentence such as "American exports have been suffering a decline in the last few months because rising inflation has produced a harmful effect on the competitive position of the USA," they do not activate the elaborative inference necessary to understand the causal relation expressed by "because" (i.e., that the deterioration of competitive position causes a decline in exports) as they read. They do so only afterward, when forced by a verification task. Economists, on the other hand, are more likely to draw such domain-specific inferences during reading. These findings suggest that readers often go beyond the text and construct a situation model when relevant knowledge is readily available. Because the functional adult is essentially an expert system in nature (who has spent many years mastering skills at work and play), we might expect the mental model level of representation to play an increasingly important role in discourse processing over the life course. As we will argue, this is a fertile area for research that so far remains substantially untilled.

Thus, insight into language processing through adulthood must take into account word-level, text-base-level, and mental model–level processing. We now turn our attention to theories of cognitive aging, considering how hypothesized age-related changes might influence language processing as we have been describing it.

■ Theories of Cognitive Aging

As we will show, the pattern of age differences in language-processing performance is complex. There are a handful of theories that have attempted to account for these data in a way that is both parsimonious and grounded in principles of development.

Resource Deficit Hypotheses

The prevailing view in cognitive aging over the last decade has been that aging brings a depletion of the processing resources needed to effectively complete cognitive operations (Salthouse, 1991). The term "processing resources" is meant to imply the existence of a unitary, limited mechanism that is required for cognitive functioning. Hypothesized change with age has been characterized alternatively as a slowing in the rate at which operations are completed, a reduction in the capacity of the work space in which mental representations are constructed, and an inability to devote attentional resources to the construction of and retrieval from the mental representation. These conceptualizations, based on metaphors of time, space, and energy, respectively, are interchangeable in terms of the empirical implications: all predict age-related deficits in comprehension and memory and the exacerbation of these problems as the text or the processing requirement becomes more difficult. Because word-level processing presumably makes slight demands on processing resources (Hasher & Zacks, 1979), this level of language processing would be expected to remain unscathed, but the construction and utilization of a coherent propositional (text-level) representation and mental model would be expected to create special problems for the elderly as the complexity required by the construction (e.g., syntactic complexity, propositional density, or spatial configuration of the mental model) is increased.

Resource Distribution Hypothesis

In contrast to the resource deficit hypothesis, which implies a deficient quantity of available processing resources, the resource distribution hypothesis posits that aging brings a decreased ability to effectively direct resources to the processing components (e.g., particular propositions or sentential constituents) that need them. In the extreme, this hypothesis does not imply that aging necessarily brings any depletion of resources but rather that the deficit lies in the "central executive" ability to manage task requirements (Baddeley, 1986). Because the effective distribution of resources would be expected to become more difficult as the number of processing components to be managed is increased, there is some predictive overlap with the resource deficit hypothesis. The distinctive empirical implication of this hypothesis, however, is that the *quality* of language comprehension and memory performance would be expected to change with age since processing resources would be allocated to the performance of *different* operations or to the processing of different contents within the work space (Stine & Wingfield, 1990; Stine, 1995). A further empirical consequence of this theory is an age difference in the effectiveness of on-line reading strategies (Stine, Cheung, & Henderson, 1995; Zabrucky & Moore, 1994).

Inhibition Hypothesis

As we noted earlier, one factor which contributes to the extraordinary flexibility of the language-processing system is that much information that is potentially relevant is activated and then suppressed only when subsequent context demonstrates its irrelevance (Gernsbacher & Faust, 1991; Till et al., 1988). A third possible explanation for age differences in discourse processing is based on the premise that aging brings a decline in the ability to effectively suppress or inhibit irrelevant information that becomes activated in the ordinary course of language comprehension (Hasher & Zacks, 1988). While explicitly not a resource deficit hypothesis (Hamm & Hasher, 1992), it can explain all the data that the resource deficit hypothesis can since activation of irrelevant information would fill the capacity needed for goal-oriented processing, thus reducing the functional capacity of the work space (Zacks & Hasher, 1994). It makes the distinctive prediction, however, that among older adults activation should be more diffuse such that they have concepts available that are not available to younger adults. Like the resource distribution hypothesis, the inhibition hypothesis predicts an age difference in the quality of the mental representation achieved in on-line processing.

Environmental Support Hypothesis

Yet another hypothesized source of age differences in cognition is that aging brings a decreased ability to initiate the allocation of processing resources in the absence of environmental support under conditions in which the learner must structure the task (Craik & Jennings, 1992). Such a position would predict that age differences in discourse processing would be most pronounced when the text is ill structured or less familiar but mitigated in the face of strong contextual constraints. The review in Chapter 12 of age differences in the benefit accrued by contextual support suggests that data relevant to this proposal are complex.

Life-Span Developmental Perspective

The final view we will consider is that the qualitative nature of cognitive processing changes over the life course in response to changes in the ecology in which intelligence and cognition occurs (Labouvie-Vief & Schell, 1982). Within this perspective, the more literal aspects of discourse are ignored in service to the understanding of the more global, personally relevant themes represented in the text; thus, the life-span perspective makes the empirical prediction that while the propositional content of the text may be substantially neglected by older adults, they would be particularly adept at uncovering the moral or metaphorical significance for broad principles of life and existential meaning.

■ Methodological Issues

A variety of methodological techniques have been adapted to test the theoretical perspectives described above.

Experimental versus Correlational Designs

These designs represent two different ways to uncover causal mechanisms underlying age-related change in discourse processing. In experimental approaches the characteristics of the language or the task conditions are manipulated in order to compare how younger and older adults respond to these changes. Differential response to the experimental manipulations can be used to make inferences about age differences in the cognitive processes underlying the task (the interpretation of such statistical interactions is well described in Chapter 6). For example, in order to test the theory that older adults have reduced processing capacity, which causes poorer memory performance, we might vary the degree to which the language memory task strains processing capacity (e.g., by increasing speech rate or syntactic or semantic complexity); if older adults' memory performance were especially affected by task difficulty such that age differences were greatest when processing capacity was strained, we could infer that a reduction in processing capacity was a contributing cause to age differences in performances (Hartley, 1993). We would have drawn this conclusion based purely on subjects' *"in vivo"* responding to natural variation in discourse.

We may contrast this approach with correlational designs in which the researcher attempts to capture the critical process in a "psychological test tube" (metaphorically, *"in vitro"*) in an effort to correlate age differences in discourse processing with age differences in that critical process. So, for example, if as before we assume that we want to test the processing capacity hypothesis, our goal now is to find some independent estimate of processing capacity and demonstrate that language memory is better among those individuals who score highly on this task and worse among those who score poorly—and that it is actually the age difference in this task that creates the age difference in language memory.

One measure that has received wide use in the aging literature is the loaded span task originally developed by Daneman and Carpenter (1980). While there are many variations on the theme, in the prototypical task, the subject reads (or listens to) a set of sentences; immediately after each sentence the subject makes a response (e.g., "true" or "false") to indicate comprehension; and then, after all of the sentences, the subject recalls the last word from each of the sentences. Thus, a high scorer on this task is a subject who can successfully comprehend language and hold information in working memory at the same time. In support of the resource deficit hypothesis, it is often found that the correlation between age and language memory performance is reduced when loaded span score is statistically controlled (Morrow, Leirer, & Altieri, 1992; Stine & Wingfield, 1987) and that younger and older adults with similar spans show similar performance levels in a discourse-processing task (Tun, Wingfield, & Stine, 1991).

A variety of other measures have been used to isolate processes outside the naturalistic language task. For example, Hartley (1988) has used speed of retrieval from short-term memory as an index of working memory functioning; word naming and category search as measures of simple verbal process; and Shipley vocabulary as a measure of word knowledge. Kemper and her colleagues (Kynette, Kemper, Norman, & Cheung, 1990) have further used repetition rate as a measure of the articulatory component of working memory. Thus, this general approach relies on the fact that there are individual differences within and between age groups in these components and attempts to ascertain the extent to which apparent age effects in global processing are explicable as changes in processing components.

The use of these techniques, including hierarchical regressions of composite indicators for numerous language processing components, has become fairly sophisticated in recent years. For example, Hultsch, Hertzog, and Dixon (1990) showed that a substantial portion of the age-related variance in text recall could be attributed to age-related differences in more basic cognitive operations like semantic and comprehension speed, working memory, and verbal fluency. More recently, this research team (Hultsch, Hertzog, Small, McDonald-Miszczak, & Dixon, 1992) has reported longitudinal declines in many of these basic processes over a period as short as 3 years, declines which were steeper for the oldest-old; interestingly, text recall did not show a reliable decline over this period even though the processes known to underlie this skill did.

Retrospective versus On-line Measures

Some studies in language processing and aging rely on the measurement of retrospective memory, in which the subject is asked to recollect (through either recall or recognition) text that was previously encoded. The most typical finding from such retrospective memory measures is that older adults show poorer retrospective memory performance than the young do (see, e.g., Dixon, Hultsch, Simon, & von Eye, 1984), though there are many subject and task variables which mitigate these differences (Hultsch & Dixon, 1984). With retrospective memory measures alone, however, specifying the locus of effects is a tenuous endeavor. For example, it may be inferred that if a manipulation at encoding—for example, scrambling the order of events (S. Smith, Rebok, Smith, Hall, & Alvin, 1983), increasing the number of new concepts introduced (Dixon et al., 1984), or increasing syntactic complexity (Kemper, 1987b)—affects subsequent recall, the cause of these differences has something to do with the degree to which these conditions tax processing capacity at encoding. While not an unreasonable position, it could always be argued that under the most difficult of these conditions, the text is understood and a representation is adequately constructed but that this representation is more fragile, or less accessible, at retrieval.

On-line methodologies, in which some aspect of behavior is measured as the text is read or listened to, allow one to better understand the response to demands during the actual comprehension process. There is a variety of such methods. As noted earlier, on-line reading time can be sensitive to many text-processing demands, for example, the difficulty of word-level decoding and organizational processing (Aaronson & Ferres, 1984), the requirement to make on-line inferences (Keenan, Potts, Golding, & Jennings, 1989), and difficulty in updating the mental model (Albrecht & O'Brien, 1993). Thus, differential variations in reading time by younger and older adults in response to such text characteristics may be used to gauge age differences in the manner in which resources are allocated during reading. In a particularly clever approach to measuring reading time, Hartley, Stojack, Mushaney, Annon, and Lee (1994) have developed a "threshold" measure based on the staircase method of detection used in psychophysics. In this technique, the reader is presented a series of sentences for a period of time controlled by the experimenter. The time per proposition is adjusted up and down to find the amount of time the reader needs to recall the sentence to a given criterion level of performance.

Another on-line technique used to assess resource allocation during comprehension is the dual-task methodology, in which subjects must respond to an extraneous probe (e.g., the presentation of a light) as quickly as possible while processing text. An increment in response time in this secondary task in response to certain text characteristics (e.g., narrative as opposed to expository text) is often taken as an indicator of the text's demand on resources (Britton, Graesser, Glynn, Hamilton, & Penland, 1983). Again, age differences in this increment provide an indicator of the effects of aging on on-line resource allocation (Tun & Wingfield, 1993).

A third on-line technique provides a window into the contents that are active in working memory as text is processed. At different points in the text, subjects are asked whether they recognize probes representing concepts from the text. A concept which is still active in working memory because it was just encountered, because it was held over from a previous input cycle due to its relative importance, or because it was a concept entailed by the mental model will be responded to more quickly than if it must be retrieved by a long-term memory search or constructed by an inference process (Fletcher, 1981).

Quantitative versus Qualitative Measures of Recall

The critical measure of the effective processing of text is very often recall performance. The recall performance of young and old may be compared with respect to quantity (i.e., do older adults recall as much as the young?) and quality (i.e., do older adults recall the same kinds of information as the young?). The quantity of recall is typically measured by dividing the to-be-remembered text into discourse units (e.g., propositions) and scoring the proportion of these units that appear in the recall protocol. Because these units represent the abstract meaning of the text rather than its verbatim content, subjects' recall can be scored for substance even when the surface features of the text are no longer available.

The issue of qualitative differences in recall revolves around whether or not older adults are as adept as the young at recalling the more important, central ideas of the text and forgetting the less important detail. One way to assess qualitative differences is to take advantage of the concept of the coherence graph that we have introduced earlier. It is typically the case that recall protocols show a *levels effect;* that is, they contain a greater proportion of idea units from higher in the hierarchy (Kintsch & van Dijk, 1978; Rubin, 1985), reflecting a penchant for recall of gist over detail. An increase in the levels effect (i.e., a relatively greater proportion of main ideas over detail) or a decrease in the levels effect (i.e., a relatively greater proportion of details over main ideas) may be interpreted as showing qualitative age differences in recall. While the levels effect itself is a robust phenomenon among both young and old, age comparisons of the levels effect have produced inconsistent findings and are fraught with interpretative difficulties (Stine & Wingfield, 1990).

An alternative way to assess qualitative age differences in recall is via *relative memorabil-*

ity (RM) (Stine & Wingfield, 1988). In an RM plot, the probability of recall for each text unit among the young is plotted as a function of the same recall probabilities for the old. Empirically, it is the case that such data are often fit by a linear function, such that the slope of such a function is interpretable in terms of the relative age differences in recall of the more and less memorable text units. Those propositions that have a higher probability of recall are, by definition, more memorable, presumably because they have been given priority in processing. A slope of unity implies that younger and older adults are remembering the same particular units. A slope greater than unity indicates an increase in discrimination among text units for the older group relative to the younger group (i.e., that they are differentially more likely to remember only the most memorable items, according to the standards of both young and old); conversely, a slope less than unity indicates a decrease in discriminability for the older group relative to the younger group.

A third way to address the issue of qualitative age differences is to classify the kinds of possible responses in recall in terms of the function they serve in the recall protocol. Thus, while much of the protocol reflects content drawn directly from the text, it may also contain elaborative inferences and commentary about the personal meaning of the text, as well as statements about one's own memory processes (Adams, 1991; Gould, Trevithick, & Dixon, 1991). Such expressions may be indicative of an individual's goals in recall; even though the experimenter's goals for the subject may be literal reproduction of the content, some individuals may respond more broadly to the task. Whether this reflects a failure to remain task oriented or a successful integration of different facets of experience is largely open to interpretation.

Brinley Plots of Response-Time (RT) Data

Plotting average response times (RTs) for the old within conditions as a function of the RTs for the young in these same conditions has been dubbed a "Brinley plot" (after the researcher who first plotted developmental data in this way; see Brinley, 1965). Such analyses serve as yet another way to address the quantitative/qualitative issue. Like relative memorability analyses, when such data can be fit by a single line, they suggest a qualitative similarity in process such that younger and older adults are performing the same set of cognitive operations to perform the task. Increase in the slope of this line from unity may be interpreted as a "slowing factor," a quantitative difference in speed rather than a qualitative difference in the kind of processes conducted (note that the interpretation of slope is quite different for Brinley and relative memorability functions). On the other hand, if such data could not be fit by a single function (e.g., if the data points for different kinds of tasks were to cluster around different functions), this would suggest that there was some qualitative age difference in the sense that different sets of processes show diverse patterns of age-related change.

■ Recapitulation

To this point, we have argued that comprehension of language is a multifaceted process, occurring at the word, text-based, and mental model levels. We have also sketched out five theories which suggest ways in which discourse processing would be expected to change with age. Finally, we have reviewed some of the methodological tools available and issues to be considered. We will now examine the empirical literature to explore what is known about how language and discourse processing change with age, with an eye toward distinguishing among the theories we have outlined.

EMPIRICAL FINDINGS

■ Age differences in the Components of Language Processing

Word-Level Processing

We consider age differences in two aspects of word-level processing: *comprehension* (or encoding), in which the conceptual representation of a word is activated as a result of processes that are initiated at the lowest level within the network (i.e., the orthographic or phonological level), and *production* processes, which are initiated at the conceptual level and require activation downward to the orthographic or phonological nodes such that the surface representation of the discourse may be generated. Because word-level comprehension processes rely on automatic processes that presumably consume few resources (LaBerge & Samuels, 1974), we would expect this level of analysis to be relatively age insensitive.

In line with this expectation, studies addressing the similarities between old and young in comprehension at the word level have revealed few or no age differences. Burke, White, and Diaz (1987) investigated the effects of both automatic and attentional priming in lexical decisions. In their experiment, category names were used to prime target words that were exemplars from the same or a different category. So, for example, a subject might see the category TREE and then the exemplar ELM and would press a button to indicate that ELM was a word. Subjects responded to ELM more quickly if it was preceded by TREE than if it was preceded by another category name (e.g., VEGETABLE), indicating that activation automatically spread from the category name to the exemplar to make it more available. Attentional priming was demonstrated by manipulating the probability of a prime being followed by a word from a given category. For example, VEGETABLE could prime ELM if, over the course of the experiment, VEGETABLE was likely to be followed by an exemplar from the tree category, but only at longer prime-target intervals (in contrast with automatic priming, which occurs very quickly). Burke et al. (1987) found that, although the older group responded more slowly than did the young group, there were no age differences in either attentional or automatic priming (see also Stern, Prather, Swinney, & Zurif, 1991).

One exception to the rule of age constancy in semantic priming is provided by Howard, Shaw, and Heisey (1986), who reported that older adults showed no priming at very short (150-msec) prime-target intervals, suggesting that spread of automatic activation may be subject to slowing. Because the Howard et al. study is unique in examining priming at such short intervals, it is impossible to know whether this represents a reliable slowing in such processes. In fact, meta-analyses of word-level processing provide mixed support for this proposal. In a meta-analysis of 15 individual semantic priming studies, Laver and Burke (1993) argue that, although older adults often show a greater prime effect than younger ones, the older subjects' prime effect plotted as a function of the younger subjects' prime effect (i.e., a Brinley plot of the prime effects) yields a slope close to unity (.96). Myerson, Ferraro, Hale, and Lima (1992), however, considering a different set of studies, did find some evidence for slowing of semantic processes with Brinley plots of both RTs and prime effects yielding slopes considerably greater than unity. The issue of speed of semantic access has also been addressed by Balota and Duchek (1988) in a naming task in which subjects read target words that were preceded by related or unrelated primes at intervals varying from 200 to 800 msec. They found that, for both young and older adults, prime effects were apparent only at longer intervals, indicating that it takes time for the spread of semantic activation to make a related word available. Although older adults were slower overall than younger adults, this pattern of priming effects was similar for the two groups, suggesting that the processes underlying spreading activation are age insensitive. Finally, analyses of word-by-word reading times have shown that, all other things being equal, older and younger adults allocate comparable amounts of time to process word-level features (Stine, 1990; Stine et al., 1995).

In sum, the overwhelming evidence is that older adults show preservation of the structure of the semantic network underlying word comprehension. Although there is some evidence that slowing may affect word-level processing, the bulk of the data support age constancy in this respect as well. This picture contrasts sharply with that of production processes. Whereas comprehension processes require upward activation that allows many possible solutions, production processes are more difficult because there are fewer paths that reach *a* specific lexical node (see Figure 8.1). Thus, we would expect age differences in word-level production processes to be more pronounced than age differences in comprehension processes. The selection and production of words have been studied using tasks that require subjects to retrieve words on cue in the laboratory (Burke, MacKay, Worthley, & Wade, 1991; Cohen, 1990) and to keep diaries of word-retrieval failures in everyday life (Burke et al., 1991). Burke et al. found that naturally occurring word-finding problems, called tip-of-the-tongue (TOT) experiences, were more pronounced for older subjects trying to recall names of acquaintances whom they had not contacted recently. Similarly, in a laboratory word-finding task, these researchers found that older subjects had particular difficulty retrieving the names of famous people.

The asymmetry in age differences between comprehension and production can be explained in terms of the transmission deficit hypothesis (Burke et al., 1991). According to this hypothesis, there is a decrease in the rate of priming due to age-weakened linkages between nodes. Movement down the network from concepts to phonological and orthographic features is more difficult than the reverse movement because there are more paths available to reach a concept than there are to produce a single word (which necessarily comprises a rigidly prescribed set of phonemes). Thus, a weakening in the links would be expected to have a more profound effect on production processes since there are no alternative paths if a needed surface feature is temporarily unavailable. For example, trying to recall the name of the object that is used to get a fire going may be difficult even though you know it has a heartlike shape and an accordianlike structure and is usually made of wood and leather. You may even be able to access a portion of the phonological representation (e.g., the word starts with the letter *b*). On the other hand, if you were reading and encountered the word "bellows," you would probably instantly comprehend the meaning of the word. There is only one name for this object, but it has many conceptual characteristics.

Further, recency and frequency of node activation contribute to activation failures. TOTs typically occur for names of acquaintances who have not been contacted recently or of famous people who have not been thought about in the near past or for words that are low in frequency. The upshot is that TOTs can be explained in terms of a degraded efficiency in the transmission of downward priming from lexical to phonological nodes (Burke et al., 1991). This principle is nicely illustrated in a recent study by Stanhope, Cohen, and Conway (1993), who measured retention of the Charles Dickens novel *Hard Times* among adult college students (aged 24–74 years). Over a retention interval of 3 years, subjects were more likely to be able to recall the roles of the characters than they were to recall the specific names of these same characters (see Figure 8.2). So even when the conceptual representations of the characters (who were richly interwoven with the plot) were available, the phonemic representations of the proper names were not.

Thus, the empirical work on word-level processing suggests remarkable preservation of the structural representation underlying word meanings. Furthermore, the bulk of the evidence suggests that the comprehension of word meanings remains unimpaired with normal aging. Production processes may show some deterioration, but this appears to be most problematic with proper names or words of infrequent usage.

Text-Base Level

At the text-base level, we consider age effects on both semantic and syntactic processes. Consistent with the resource deficit hypothesis, processes at this level tend to be more age sensitive than those at the word level. There appears to be an age difference in the effectiveness of resources that are allocated: for example, when reading time is scaled against subsequent recall, older adults have been found to recall fewer propositions per unit of time allocated in reading (Hartley et al., 1994; Stine & Hindman, 1994). In general, conditions which tax processing resources by making the text syntactically or semantically more complex increase the likelihood of age declines.

Investigations into age differences in syntactic processing have examined comprehension and production as functions of syntactic complexity. Left-branching sentences (e.g., "Because Bill left the party without his coat, John was upset") are more complex because the reader cannot fully process the subordinate clause until the completion of the main clause; this is in contrast to right-branching constructions (e.g., "John was upset because Bill left

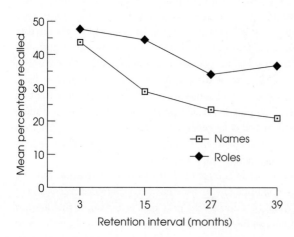

FIGURE 8.2 Relative recall of characters' names and roles over a retention interval of 3 years. (*Source:* data from Stanhope, Cohen, & Conway, 1993. Reprinted with permission of John Wiley, Inc.)

the party without his coat") in which the main clause is subsequently modified by the subordinate one. Tasks used to tap into these processes have typically included reading and auditory comprehension (Norman, Kemper, & Kynette, 1992), sentence imitation (Kemper, 1986), and keeping diaries (Kemper, 1987a). Age differences have been reported to be exaggerated when syntactic complexity is increased in every one of these cases. These results are typically interpreted to reflect an age-related decline in syntactic processing that limits the performance of simultaneous grammatical operations.

Age differences in the production of complex syntactic forms have been reported in a number of studies (see, e.g., Cheung & Kemper, 1992; Kemper, 1987a). In a longitudinal study of adults' written language, Kemper (1987a) found a significant drop in the number of embeddings and a decrease in the occurrence of subordinate and coordinate constructions indicating a drop in syntactic complexity. Similarly, Kemper (1992) found that, although the incidence of sentence fragments remains constant in later adulthood, the type and place of occurrence changes with age. Older adults aged 60 to 74 (the "young-old") produced more false starts, indicating sentence-planning problems that appeared to arise from attempts to produce syntactically complex sentences. On the other hand, older adults whose age exceeded 74 years (the "old-old") produced more filled pauses (e.g., "well," "you know," "um," "er"), which were found to be associated with noun-retrieval problems; this group produced fewer complex syntactic constructions than the young-old group who attempted these constructions. These results are consistent with the notion that an age-related decrease in working memory capacity limits the ability to comprehend and produce complex syntactic structures. This was explicitly tested by Norman, Kemper, Kynette, Cheung, and Anagnopoulos (1991). Using digit span tasks as measures of working memory capacity, they found that, in fact, smaller working memory capacity was associated with an inability to reproduce complex syntactic forms in a running memory task.

There is also evidence that the ability to create a coherent semantic representation of the text decreases as working memory capacity is taxed. The critical qualifications here are "coherent" and "working memory capacity" since the basic processes of meaning access (Burke & Harrold, 1988), propositional encoding (Stine, Wingfield, & Poon, 1986), and even integration across constituents (Zelinski, 1988) appear to remain unscathed by aging—provided propositional units and concepts can be activated and connected locally within the text. Age deficits begin to appear as the comprehension and production processes required exceed what can be accomplished within an input cycle and therefore require more global integration processes. So, for example, while older adults ordinarily have no trouble making anaphoric inferences about pronoun referents, relying on the same linguistic cues that younger adults do (Light, Capps, Singh, & Owens, 1994), they are more likely to experience difficulty as the distance between the referent and pronoun is increased (Light & Capps, 1986). Such a failure would have the consequence of creating a less coherent representation of discourse.

These principles are also illustrated by research in comprehension monitoring. In a series of experiments, Zabrucky and Moore (e.g., Moore & Zabrucky, 1992; Zabrucky, Moore, & Schultz, 1993) have shown that older adults typically have no difficulty detecting internal inconsistency (i.e., a contradiction in the propositional content of the prose), suggesting that they construct and use the representation of the semantic content of text just as the young to evaluate on-line comprehension. When the contradictory information is not adjacent in the text, however, such that integration over successive input cycles is required for detection, older readers may have difficulty (Zabrucky et al., 1994; but see Moore & Zabrucky, 1992).

A third empirical example of differential disruption of text coherence among the elderly by high processing load is research on the relative recall of gist and detail. While both younger and older adults typically show a levels effect (i.e., higher levels of recall for gist than for detail), the levels effect is likely to be decreased among the old as working memory capacity is strained (for a review, see Stine & Wingfield, 1990). Similarly, relative memorability analyses suggest that the recall protocols of older adults are more likely to contain a preponderance of less memorable idea units as text difficulty is increased by speech rate, informational density, or lack of familiarity (Hartley, 1993; Stine & Wingfield, 1988). That is, there is a high correlation between the recall probabilities of young and old, suggesting that young and old prioritize the idea units similarly in allocating resources, but conditions that strain the capacity of working memory cause the slope of this regression function to decrease, indicating that such conditions make it relatively more difficult for the old to make this discrimination.

Finally, age differences in the allocation of reading time to text also suggest that the average older adult does not usually integrate effectively across input cycles. For example, older adults appear to be less likely to spontaneously allot extra time at sentence-final words for wrap-up operations, or, when they do, they allot less time for the integration of new concepts (Stine, 1990). Figure 8.3 shows data from a study of on-line reading time of short narratives read for immediate recall (Stine et all., 1995). Regression analysis was used to pro-

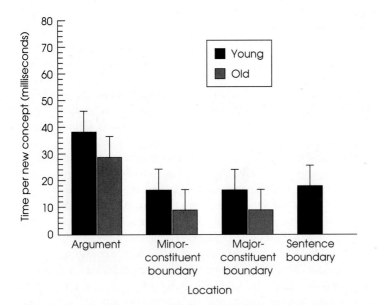

FIGURE 8.3 Time allocated to process new arguments (concepts) as soon as they are presented and at minor-constituent, major-constituent, and sentence boundaries. (*Source:* data from Stine, Cheung, & Henderson, 1995. Reprinted with permission of Swets & Zeitlinger.)

duce estimates of the reading time allocated to processing new conceptual arguments at four different points in the text: as soon as the argument noun was introduced, at minor constituent boundaries (e.g., prepositional phrases), at major constituent boundaries (e.g., noun phrases), and at sentence boundaries. While older readers did show evidence of organizational processing at constituent boundaries within sentences (though at a somewhat reduced level), they were unlike the young in failing to allocate time to integrate the new conceptual information at sentence wrap-up, the point at which the load is presumably the greatest. The point here is that, in many ways, the basic processes underlying the construction of meaning from language do not appear to show substantial change with age. Comprehension difficulties appear to arise principally out of memory difficulties when working memory limits are exceeded (cf. Light, 1990).

Consistent with the inhibition hypothesis, there is a growing body of literature suggesting that the way in which these resources are constrained in later adulthood is by the maintenance of irrelevant material in working memory—material which younger adults more easily inhibit. For example, Connelly, Hasher, and Zacks (1991) presented young and elderly readers with texts that were printed in italics but interspersed with words or short phrases printed in standard type that the subjects were instructed to ignore. This distracting material was either related or unrelated to the target text; there were also two control conditions, one in which the distraction was simply a string of x's (to control for the time it takes to simply glance over the odd type) and another in which no distraction was present. The average reading times under these different conditions for younger and older adults are shown in Figure 8.4. While both younger and older adults' reading times were slowed by the presence of the distraction, older adults experienced particular difficulty, especially when the distraction was meaningful text, suggesting that it was the activation of meaning from the extraneous material that created the difficulty for the older readers; even though reading among the young was somewhat slowed, they were able to inhibit the irrelevant information more easily. Additionally, consistent with the data on the effects of verbal ability on inhibitory processing among college students (Gernsbacher & Faust, 1991), older adults of lower verbal ability were more susceptible to distraction by irrelevant information than were those of higher verbal ability. More recent work on this phenomenon has shown, however, that older adults' susceptibility to such distraction can be greatly reduced when the distracting text is in a fixed and predictable location (Carlson, Hasher, & Connelly, in press), as would be characteristic of a newspaper or magazine layout.

Older adults also seem less facile than the young in revising their memory representations in response to new information (Zacks, Hasher, Doren, Hamm, & Attig, 1987). For example, in a study by Hamm and Hasher (1992), subjects read passages which implied an inference (e.g., the reader is led to believe that the main character is in a hospital: she was ill, called her friend who was a nurse, and subsequently entered a large building) which was inconsistent with the later text (e.g., the fact that she goes to the main desk to check out a book). By the end of the passage, younger adults, when explicitly asked, have revised their previously incorrect inference (e.g., they report that she is in a library); in contrast, older adults were equally likely to report both the first inference suggested *and* the second (e.g., she is in a library and a hospital). Such age differences lend further support to the inhibition hypothesis, in which capacity is restricted by irrelevant material which is promiscuously activated in the ordinary course of discourse understanding.

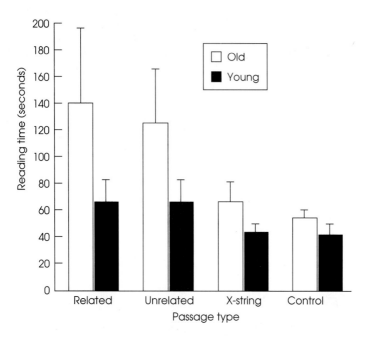

FIGURE 8.4 Reading time for texts with and without distracting material embedded; error bars are standard deviations. (*Source:* data from Connelly, Hasher, & Zacks, 1991. Reprinted with permission of the American Psychological Association.)

Capacity limits seem to have an impact on the production of semantically coherent narratives as well. Pratt, Boyes, Robins, and Manchester (1989) asked adults of varying ages to recall stories as though they were conveying them to children. Older adults made more referential errors, which would decrease the ability of the listener to construct a coherent representation. This effect was accounted for by age differences in an independent estimate of working memory capacity as well as a reduced likelihood to spontaneously use proper names. Similarly, Kemper, Rash, Kynette, and Norman (1990) found that elders' stories decreased in clausal density, syntactic complexity, and narrative cohesion with increased age (from 60 to 90 years); the stories of the oldest-old, however, were also more structurally complex, suggesting that syntax and cohesion declines may be in service to the telling of a more interesting story with a compelling plot. Thus, a decline in syntactic creativity may allow the elderly adult to exercise skills of creativity at the discourse level (Kemper & Anagnopoulos, in press).

To wrap up our discussion of text-level processing, the bulk of the data suggests that the basic processes of parsing and the construction of a propositional representation remain stable into late life. The qualitative nature of the representation may be somewhat more diffuse because of less effective inhibitory processing. The construction of this representation appears to be most clearly impaired when connections must be made distantly within the text. These conclusions, however, must necessarily remain tentative pending more thorough investigation of text-level processing in the context of a wider array of social variables.

Mental Model Level

There is scant research about age differences in the creation and use of situation models, in part because the situation model construct is still relatively new in cognitive theory. Nonetheless, research from several areas suggests that older as well as younger readers and listeners access knowledge structures and use them to create mental models while reading. As we have already seen at the text level, age differences arise primarily when comprehension taxes working memory, so that more cognitive resources are required to create the mental model. These points are made by research in memory for script-based narratives, spatial models, and expertise.

First, older as well as younger readers recall a narrative more accurately when it is organized in terms of a script or other general-knowledge structure, for example, how to order in a restaurant (Light & Anderson, 1983). Both age groups are also likely to make recognition errors consistent with the script or to distort recall in order to maintain consistency with the script (Hess, 1990). Older readers seem to be as effective as younger readers in using knowledge structures during comprehension and recall. They draw inferences that bridge sentences in order to create coherent discourse. For example, after reading "The vehicle rounded the bend," both age groups take longer to read a sentence beginning "The cart . . ." than one beginning "The bus . . . ," presumably because categorical structure and its use in inferencing is often age invariant (Zelinski, 1988). Radvansky, Gerard, Zacks, and Hasher (1990) replicated the Garnham (1981) study described earlier (the "podiatrist" example) with older readers. They found that older and younger subjects produce similar patterns of confusion for pairs of sentences that are propositionally and situationally similar, compared to pairs that describe different situations.

Second, older as well as younger readers appear to build a mental model around the narrative protagonist. Morrow, Leirer, Altieri, and Fitzsimmons (1994) examined age differences in combining layout and narrative information in order to create a spatial mental model. As in Morrow et al. (1989), subjects memorized a layout of a research center and then read narratives describing characters moving through the building. Critical sentences such as "Joe walked from the library into the laboratory" were followed by probes about objects that were in the same room as the protagonist (the laboratory in this example), in a near room, or in a far room. Both younger and older subjects in the study answered probes about objects in the same room as the protagonist more quickly and accurately than probes about objects in other rooms. Older subjects responded more slowly and less accurately than younger subjects, and age differences in response time were larger for probes relevant to locations farther away from the protagonist than for those closer to the protagonist. This might suggest that older readers have particular difficulty updating situation models with information that is not currently in working memory. Nonetheless, both groups updated the model by focusing on the protagonist, showing that they used a similar strategy to create the spatial model. Another aspect of the mental model that has been investigated in aging is the ability to track the emotions of characters. In a recent study, Soederberg and Stine (1975) showed that older adults slow down as much as as younger adults when reading information violating an implied emotional tone (cf. Gernsbacher & Robertson, 1992).

Age differences in comprehension and memory primarily occur when the process of constructing the situation model taxes the limited cognitive resources of older readers (Morrow,

Altieri, & Leirer, 1992). This is illustrated in a study by Hakala, Rizzella, Stine, and O'Brien (unpublished; cited in Stine, 1995), who showed that, while both young and older readers slowed down in response to difficulty in updating the mental model, it was only the younger adults whose subsequent recall was increased by this additional processing when the inconsistent information was not adjacent in the text. Thus, older adults show on-line evidence for an attempt at allocating resources to update the mental model. The higher levels of recall among the younger readers suggests that they were effective in this resource allocation and the consequent elaborative processing-facilitated memory (cf. Albrecht & O'Brien, 1993). Because older adults showed no increment in memory in response to these manipulations, the data suggest that older adults were not reworking the mental model sufficiently.

Third, research on age and expertise in processing domain-relevant texts shows age invariance when working memory is not highly taxed. Morrow et al. (1992) examined whether experts use domain knowledge in addition to, or rather than, text-based cues such as recency of mention in order to update their situation model. Older and younger pilots and nonpilots read and recalled narratives about aviation or general topics with two characters distinguished by narrative status (protagonist and minor character) and domain-specific roles (e.g., pilot and passenger; captain and first officer). Subjects chose referents for unambiguous target pronouns that referred to either the protagonist or minor character either mentioned in the preceding sentence or three sentences before the target. While all readers could use recency of mention and character status cues to choose referents, pilots could also use aviation knowledge cues. For example, pilots could reject the most recently mentioned character as referent if this character was unlikely to perform the action described in the target sentence. Pilots and younger readers chose referents more accurately than nonpilots and older readers for aviation narratives (only age influenced general narratives). Both older and younger pilots were more accurate than nonpilots for the distant referents. This finding suggests that experts ignore misleading text cues and rely on domain knowledge in order to update their situation model. Nonetheless, younger pilots understood and recalled the aviation narratives more accurately than the older pilots did. Thus, expertise and aging research, like the script and the spatial model studies, show that older as well as younger adults have similar knowledge structures and can access them during comprehension in order to create a situation model, with age differences arising primarily when the task of creating the model taxes cognitive resources.

We also elaborate situation models so as to encompass personally significant themes. There is some evidence that with age we become more attuned to a broadly construed representation of the text. Adams (1991; Adams, Labouvie-Vief, Hobart, & Dorosz, 1990) found that in narrative recall, younger adults tended to be reproductive in retellings, including the propositional content of the passages, but elders tended to be metaphorical, thus prompting them to argue that "aging brings the evolution of a more complex and inclusive thought structure in which outer-oriented, objective, and analytic forms of thinking are reintegrated with earlier suppressed inner-oriented, subjective, and symbolic forms" (Adams, 1991, pp. 334–335).

Thus, our generalization about the mental model level parallels that about the text-base level: the qualitative nature of processes at this level remains unscathed by aging, but working memory limits may make it more difficult to construct and update the mental model. We qualify this statement, however, by noting that the mental model is multifaceted (e.g., spatial, emotional, goal-oriented, metaphorical), with cognitive aging researchers having only barely begun to peel the onion. While some aspects of the mental model (e.g., spatial) may be subject to working memory limits, other aspects may not be. In particular, as we shall show in a moment, expertise may provide a compensatory source of mental model processing.

■ Compensatory Processing

According to Baltes and Baltes (1990), the hallmark of successful aging is selective optimization with compensation. That is, as the capacity for mental mechanics declines with normal aging, one who successfully ages is someone who is selective in nurturing a subset of the skills of which he or she is ultimately capable and who relies on this expertise to circumvent limitations in mental mechanics. In other words, successful aging involves making hard choices about the areas in which one will become an expert and those in which one will forever remain a novice and then working within the selected domain to develop strategies that mitigate the effects of declines in cognitive mechanics.

The 1993 concert tour of the Moody Blues (a rock group that got its start in the late 1960s) provides an excellent example of the complex nature of selective optimization and compensatory processing. Compensatory strategies on the part of both the band and the listeners make it difficult to be disturbed by the fact that Justin Hayward's voice does not have the dynamic range it did in the early days of the band's live performances 25 years ago. The principle of selective optimization is found in a repertoire that represents a distinctive style that has developed over the years but nevertheless presents a clear continuity. In addition, the group members create the illusion of their "younger" voices through careful ordering of the songs (such that more demanding songs occur earlier in the concert, when the group's voices will not be compromised by fatigue), accompaniment by a symphony orchestra and backup singers whose degree of involvement is adjusted to compensate for fatigue, and the inclusion of spoken poetry. (One of our parents has pointed out the use of similar strategies by Frank Sinatra.) There is also an element of compensation provided by an audience who, having listened to these songs for a number of years (as one might gauge from the average age of the audience), has developed a firm schema for the songs as originally recorded. Thus, much as one sees an aging friend or spouse whose thinning hair or fine lines around the eyes are transparent against a rich history, one is more prepared to hear the songs as intended than to find fault with inconsequential deviations.

Dixon and Bäckman (1993) have lamented the sparseness of empirical data elucidating the role of compensatory strategies in prose processing. They argue that one may infer the existence of compensation when a mismatch between available skill and environmental demand is offset by the allocation of more resources, the use of latent skills, or the acquisition of new skills.

Drawing on this perspective, we organize our discussion by distinguishing between *default* and *constructed* strategies. We assume that any cognitive activity involving language is complex and rests on the coordination of sets of both automatic and attentional processes. An age-related decline in mental mechanics would not affect all of these components in the same way. Thus, a default strategy is one which is essentially in place from very early on but takes on more importance later in the life span. For example, when a decline in the quality of sensory input increases reliance on context, the older adult defaults to context which has always been used, yet not to the same extent as when bottom-up information was more complete (cf. Wingfield, Aberdeen, & Stine, 1991). This contrasts with constructed strategies, which are adaptations over the life span, such as active strategy change or the development of expertise that can accommodate a decline in mental mechanics (Bäckman & Dixon, 1992).

Default Strategies

The use of default strategies by elderly adults is readily apparent in speech processing. Speech processing is in many ways so well preserved into late life that it is sometimes accorded a "privileged status" among cognitive abilities. Tun and Wingfield (1993) attribute this not only to the autonomy of language skills but also to the reliance of elderly listeners on contextual constraints in the language. For example, older adults appear to especially rely on prosodic contour (e.g., intonation, pauses) for comprehension and syntactic analysis (Stine & Wingfield, 1987; Wingfield, Wayland, & Stine, 1992). This is illustrated by the fact that when prosodic cues are absent, memory is disproportionately depressed for older adults (see, e.g., Stine & Wingfield, 1987).

Older adults' differential reliance on prosodic cues is also illustrated when the information provided by the lexical content of the sentence (i.e., the wording) is put into conflict with prosodic cuing. Read the following sentences aloud:

Because she wanted *romantic lighting, the candle on the table* was important.
Because she was a *romantic, lighting the candle on the table* was important.

You will notice that the lexical content of the underlined portions is identical but that when you read the two versions aloud the prosodic contour is very different. This difference reflects a difference in the underlying syntactic structure of the two sentences, so that intonational contour provides cues to the listener about how to parse this structure. In the Wingfield et al. (1992) experiment, subjects heard not only sentences like these but also variations in which each was spoken with the intonational contour of the other. So for example, in the conditions in which there was a mismatch between content and prosody, the sentences were:

Because she wanted *romantic, lighting the candle on the table* was important.
Because she was a *romantic lighting, the candle on the table* was important.

If you read these sentences aloud, you will find that the effect is very jarring. And, in fact, young and older subjects found them disturbing as well, making more recall errors under these conditions. The interesting finding from this study comes from an analysis of the qualitative nature of the errors. Older listeners were differentially likely to make recall errors in which they changed the wording of the sentences so that their reproduction matched the prosodic contour! That is, in the face of a mismatch between lexical content and prosodic contour, older adults are more likely to reconstruct the message so that it fits the intonational contour, suggesting that this level of information takes priority. Why should this be? For one thing, prosody is ordinarily redundant with syntactic structure in everyday spoken language processing, thus making available strong cues to structure and meaning and minimizing the resource-consuming analysis of lexical content. So, in ordinary language understanding (in contrast to the tricky conditions of this experiment), attention to prosodic contour is a cost-effective cue to parsing spoken language.

Similarly, older adults are particularly dependent upon sentence context for word recognition. Older adults rely more on context during reading to recognize degraded words (Madden, 1988) and during listening to recognize individual words more quickly (Wingfield et al., 1991).

It is certainly not the case that prosodic and semantic context suddenly take on importance in the cognitive system in later adulthood. Rather, top-down processing strategies are in place much earlier in the life span; as the quality of the product of bottom-up analysis is degraded (e.g., by sensory failures of the sensory system or by less effective inhibition), default strategies enable functional processing capacity to withstand (to some extent) the assaults of biological aging (Wingfield et al., 1991).

Constructed Strategies

Several researchers have pointed out that, while cognitive resources tend to gradually decline with age, knowledge structures remain stable or may even increase (Horn, 1982; Salthouse, 1988). To what extent can older adults exploit their knowledge and experience in order to compensate for declining cognitive resources? The evidence is equivocal. Some studies find no evidence for compensation: older as well as younger experts benefit from knowledge, but this knowledge does not differentially improve older expert performance so as to eliminate age differences. For example, Lindenberger, Kliegl, and Baltes (1992) found that graphic design experience was related to high spatial ability but did not reduce age differences in the ability to use the method of loci, a common imagery-based mnemonic. On the other hand, Salthouse (1984) found that the amount of typing experience is more important than age for predicting transcription typing performance, in part because older typists have a larger preview span that offsets declining motor speed. So when does compensation occur?

In language use, knowledge should compensate for age-related declines in cognitive resources when older adults are able to readily access knowledge and use it to simplify the task of understanding and remembering text. The dynamic is not unlike that for default strategies: older subjects can shift from more resource-consuming, bottom-up processing to knowledge-based, top-down processing when the strategy saves effort without degrading performance. But when is this shift most likely to occur? Morrow, Leirer, Altieri, and Fitzsimmons (1994) suggested that compensation should occur for tasks that are highly relevant to experts. Relevant tasks have materials that are compatible with expert knowledge and procedures that are familiar to experts (see also Arbuckle, Vanderleck, Harsany, & Lapidus, 1990; Chapter 13). This idea was tested by examining whether expertise reduces age differences on tasks varying in terms of how relevant they are to piloting. Older and younger pilots and nonpilots read or listened to realistic air traffic control (ATC) messages that contained commands to change aircraft heading, altitude, and speed. After each message they repeated the commands, which is a routine ATC communication procedure called "read back." Therefore, this task was highly domain relevant in terms of both messages and procedures. Subjects also performed tasks that were less relevant to piloting, such as memorizing a map of the airspace the messages described. Expertise reduced or eliminated age differences in reading back heading commands in the ATC messages but did not reduce age differences for the less relevant tasks. Similarly, Morrow, Leirer, and Altieri (1992) found that expertise did not compensate for age declines in narrative comprehension and recall tasks that were not directly related to piloting. The results suggest that expertise can compensate for age declines in processing resources when the task is highly relevant to experts. Thus, these data could explain earlier inconsistencies in the literature on the elusive age × expertise interaction. For example, Salthouse's (1984) dramatic demonstration of the complete mitigation of age deficits in the domain of typing was conducted on the very task that typists do. An additional constraint on when compensation occurs might be task difficulty. Even if a task is domain relevant, processing load can be so great as to interfere with the effective use of domain knowledge. For example, older pilots may have more difficulty responding to ATC messages that are very long or ones that are presented very rapidly.

Another way in which constructed strategies come into play is through a change in the way discourse is processed. For example, as noted earlier, the average elderly reader appears to be less likely to allocate processing resources to sentence wrap-up and integration across input cycles. There are differences, however, in the reading strategies of older adults who are above and below average in subsequent recall of the text. Specifically, good elder rememberers seem to allocate time to integrate more frequently and are more responsive to the serial position of the segments of the text (i.e., they show greater acceleration of reading speed through the text) (Stine, 1990, 1995). These data suggest that successful memory performance among the old may entail a reading strategy that involves more frequent integration as well as greater reliance on a story schema which is formed early in the text and then subsequently can facilitate processing. Thus, effective strategy must accommodate one's limits.

IMPLICATIONS OF THE LITERATURE FOR THEORIES OF COGNITIVE AGING

1. The fundamental nature of language processing appears to be preserved with nonpathological aging.
2. Functioning is somewhat compromised by a decrease in working memory capacity (i.e., the resource deficit hypothesis), but this is probably intimately tied to the ability to effectively regulate the content of working memory through inhibitory (i.e., the inhibition hypothesis) and selection (i.e., the resource distribution hypothesis) processes.
3. *However,* declines in processing resources appear to be mitigated by (a) contextual support, (b) a strong match between expertise and the discourse-processing requirements, and (c) adaptation of strategy. Thus, the environmental support hypothesis also comes into play where "environmental support" means the contextual constraints of the language as well as the skills and strategies that the elderly bring to the language-processing task. We feel that future research could be profitably directed toward a more articulate understanding of the kind of environmental support that is the most helpful.
4. There is some evidence that aging brings a more contextual approach to language and discourse processing. This is true in two ways. First, mitigation of age deficits in memory by expertise suggests that language use becomes more grounded in the particular tasks to which we have dedicated our lives. Second, more attention may be paid to the implications of the text for the more general principles governing every-

day life and social connections. These proposals are consistent with the tenets of the life-span developmental perspective. We feel that future research could be profitably directed toward a more fundamental understanding of the nature of these skills as an area of expertise, perhaps by relating it to the construct of wisdom, an expertise in the fundamental pragmatics of life (J. Smith & Baltes, 1990).

IMPLICATIONS FOR EVERYDAY FUNCTIONING

In addition to helping us understand how basic cognitive processes change across the life span, research in cognitive aging has important implications for understanding language processing in everyday life and for designing everyday tasks to fit our needs and abilities as we grow older. We will illustrate this with several real-world examples.

■ Air Traffic Control Communication

Research on compensatory strategies in the workplace informs us about how to design tasks to optimize older and younger workers' performance. For example, longer ATC messages increase the probability of communication errors for both older and younger pilots in laboratory studies (Morrow, Leirer, Fitzsimmons, & Altieri, 1994), implicating the importance of reduced message length for pilots of all ages. In addition, the older but not younger pilots in Morrow et al. (1994) had greater difficulty remembering ATC messages when they were spoken than when they were presented visually and at a slower rate. Auditory (or more rapid) presentation appeared to penalize older pilots more than younger ones, which is consistent with text-recall studies (Meyer, 1987). This finding suggests that current FAA proposals to augment ATC voice communication with visual computer presentation (Morrow & Rodvold, in press) may particularly benefit older pilots, assuming that the computer interface is well designed.

■ Assessing Performance in the Workplace

Aging and expertise research has implications for assessing job performance among older workers. Several studies (e.g., Morrow et al., 1994; Salthouse, 1984) found that expertise is most likely to reduce age differences in performance for highly domain-relevant tasks. Therefore, if level of proficiency is assessed by domain-independent tasks (e.g., standard psychometric tasks), the results may underestimate performance on the job because test performance is not supported by domain knowledge. More research is needed to explicate the role of domain knowledge in enhancing work-related communication and performance in late life.

■ Elderspeak

It has been noted that elderly adults are often spoken to in short, simple sentences with exaggerated stress patterns and intonation, a style that is often adopted when addressing children. When used with older listeners, this has been dubbed "elderspeak" (Cohen & Faulkner, 1986). Kemper (1994) assessed the spontaneous speech used by service providers and caregivers to groups of younger and older adults in a variety of settings (e.g., exercise classes, pottery classes). Speech to older adults was slower, with more pauses, shorter utterances, fewer clauses, and simpler syntax (e.g., in containing fewer left-branching constructions). Of course, while some speech accommodations when carried to an extreme with elderly listeners (e.g., implications of incompetence and patronizing forms of address) can certainly be offensive (Ryan, Bourhis, & Knops, 1991), there is evidence that some of these adjustments can facilitate communication with an elderly listener. For example, as we have seen, older adults appear to rely especially on prosodic contour to parse spoken language (Wingfield et al., 1992); in addition, older listeners are differentially more likely to remember information that is stressed in spoken language (Cohen & Faulkner, 1986). Perhaps such speech adjustments encourage sentence wrap-up and integration operations in on-line discourse understanding. Thus, these findings from the laboratory offer a potential explanation for the use of elderspeak in everyday communication.

■ Collaborative Cognition in Everyday Life

An important kind of compensatory strategy involves taking advantage of others' knowledge and expertise in order to reduce demands on physical and cognitive resources that show age-related declines (Park, 1992). For example, a natural stage in the career of many scholars is expansion of the collaborative network as one way to maintain productivity. Collaboration is an important element of many activities in everyday life, for example, the successful retrieval of past shared experiences, and there is some evidence that both younger and older adults can productively take advantage of collaborative resources to improve memory (cf. Dixon & Gould, in press).

In some ways, however, collaboration may be more difficult in later adulthood. In a recent study comparing the ability of younger and older dyads to achieve common ground in a referential communication task, Hupet, Chantraine, and Nef (1993) showed that older adults had to collaborate longer (i.e., take more and longer conversational turns) to reach agreement on how to name ambiguous figures. The authors suggest that this may in part be due to the older adults' tendency to make less use of previously agreed-upon references as well as their tendency to be more idiosyncratic in their generation of referents.

■ Real-World Problem Solving

Successful navigation through the life span requires the comprehension and resolution of problems, some relatively minor (e.g., what is the best bran cereal to buy?), some relatively more important (e.g., which is the best preschool arrangement for my child?), and some critical to survival (e.g., how do I negotiate my treatment options with my physician after I have been told I have breast cancer?). While such problem solving certainly requires skills and personal resources beyond language processing, it is typically the case that the information needed to solve these problems is available only through language, and it is often the case that effective resolutions require one to be an articulate spokesperson for one's position. The role of language processing in everyday problem solving has been investigated in recent research by Meyer, Russo, and Talbot (1995), who asked women of different ages to make treatment decisions in an unfolding breast cancer scenario. In this study, younger women showed better recall than older women of texts about breast cancer; they were also more likely to seek out additional information and to offer a more systematic rationale for the treatment options they adopted. Interestingly, there were no age differences in the ultimate decisions made, and, because older adults sought less information, they made these decisions more quickly.

CONCLUSIONS

Much research in the last decade into aging and discourse processing has been driven by two issues: how individual differences mitigate age differences and how to disentangle the various metaphors of resource decline (i.e., does aging bring decreased capacity or speed or mental energy?). It is our hope that the next decade of research will allow us to build upon these accomplishments so as to more clearly articulate how aging influences *processing mechanisms* at the level of the word, the text base, and the mental model. This latter construct is particularly complex and opens onto a horizon of cognition in everyday life. Thus, we hope that studies of individual differences (i.e., the correlational approach) will continue to inform us about skills that enhance (or diminish) our ability to process discourse, but we hope to see these expanded to more thoroughly engage individual differences in contextual processing (e.g., expertise).

In particular, questions about the interface among word, text-base, and mental model levels are the most provocative, especially since we have a very primitive understanding of how, for example, the mental model level of representation becomes instantiated at the text-base level. Because it is only through the aging process that we acquire the experience necessary to build mental models underlying expertise, aging offers us the laboratory to understand these basic principles of cognition. In addition, an understanding of how text-base (and mental model) processing supports word-level processing, and of how mental model processing supports text-base processing, may be the critical link to describing "successful aging" (Rowe & Kahn, 1987) in the discourse world.

ACKNOWLEDGMENT

This chapter was supported by Grants R29 AG08382 and R01 AG09254 from the National Institute on Aging. There are many sources of inspiration the authors could acknowledge in writing this chapter. In particular, we wish to thank the folks at the Licker Store in Durham, New Hampshire, and at the Jumpin' Java in Mountain View, California, for providing frequent stimulation in the way of both caffeine and ambiance. We also very much appreciate the comments of Bill Peterson on an earlier draft.

SUPPLEMENTAL READINGS

Kausler, D. H. (1994). *Learning and memory in normal aging.* New York: Academic Press, Chapter 8.

Kemper, S. (1992). Language and aging. In F. I. M. Craik & T. A. Salthouse (Eds.), *The handbook of aging and cognition* (pp. 213–270). Hillsdale, NJ: Erlbaum.

Light, L. L., & Burke, D. M. (Eds.) (1988). *Language, memory, and aging.* New York: Cambridge Univ. Press.

REFERENCES

Aaronson, D., & Ferres, S. (1984). The word-by-word reading paradigm: An experimental and theoretical approach. In D. E. Kieras & M. A. Just (ds.), *New methods in reading comprehension research* (pp. 31–68). Hillsdale, NJ: Erlbaum.

Aaronson, D., & Scarborough, H. S. (1976). Performance theories for sentence coding: Some qualitative evidence. *Journal of Experimental Psychology: Human Perception and Performance, 2,* 56–70.

Adams, C. (1991). Qualitative age differences in memory for text: A life-span developmental perspective. *Psychology and Aging, 6,* 323–336.

Adams, C., Labouvie-Vief, G., Hobart, C. J., & Dorosz, M. (1990). Adult age group differences in story recall style. *Journal of Gerontology: Psychological Sciences, 45,* P17–P27.

Albrecht, J. E., & O'Brien, E. J. (1993). Updating a mental model: Maintaining both local and global coherence. *Journal of Experimental Psychology: Learning, Memory, and Cognition, 19,* 1061–1070.

Anderson, J. R. (1990). *Cognitive psychology and its implications* (3d ed.). New York: Freeman.

Arbuckle, T. Y., Vanderleck, V. F., Harsany, M., & Lapidus, S. (1990). Adult age differences in memory in relation to availability and accessibility of knowledge-based schema. *Journal of Experimental Psychology: Learning, Memory, and Cognition, 16,* 305–315.

Bäckman, L., & Dixon, R. A. (1992). Psychological compensation: A theoretical framework. *Psychological Bulletin, 112,* 259–283.

Baddeley, A. D. (1986). *Working memory.* New York: Oxford Univ. Press.

Balota, D. A., & Duchek, J. M. (1988). Age-related differences in lexical access, spreading activation, and simple pronunciation. *Psychology and Aging, 3,* 84–93.

Baltes, P. B., & Baltes, M. M. (1990). Psychological perspectives on successful aging: The model of selective optimization with compensation. In P. B. Baltes & M. M. Baltes (Eds.), *Successful aging* (pp. 1–34). New York: Cambridge Univ. Press.

Bransford, J. D., Barclay, J. R., & Franks, J. J. (1972). Sentence memory: A constructive vs. interpretive approach. *Cognitive Psychology, 3,* 193–209.

Brinley, J. F. (1965). Cognitive sets, speed and accuracy of performance in the elderly. In A. T. Welford & J. E. Birren (Eds.), *Behavior, aging, and the nervous system* (pp. 114–149). Springfield, IL: Thomas.

Britton, B. K., Graesser, A. C., Glynn, S. M., Hamilton, T., & Penland, M. (1983). Use of cognitive capacity in reading: Effects of some content features of text. *Discourse Processes, 6,* 39–57.

Burke, D. M., & Harrold, R. M. (1988). Approaches to the study of memory and language in old age. In L. L. Light & D. M. Burke (Eds.), *Language, memory, and aging* (pp. 100–116). New York: Cambridge Univ. Press.

Burke, D., MacKay, D. G., Worthley, J. S., & Wade, E. (1991). On the tip of the tongue: What causes word-finding failures in young and older adults. *Journal of Memory and Language, 30,* 542–579.

Burke, D. M., White, H., & Diaz, D. L. (1987). Semantic priming in young and older adults: Evidence for age constancy in automatic and attentional priming. *Journal of Experimental Psychology: Human Perception and Performance, 13,* 79–88.

Carlson, M. C., Hasher, L., & Connelly, S. L. (in press). Aging, distraction and the benefits of predictable location. *Psychology and Aging.*

Cheung, H., & Kemper, S. (1992). Competing complexity metrics and adults' production of complex sentences. *Applied Psycholinguistics, 13,* 53–76.

Cohen, G. (1990). Recognition and retrieval or proper names: Age differences in the fan effect. *European Journal of Cognitive Psychology, 2,* 193–204.

Cohen, G., & Faulkner, D. (1986). Does "elderspeak" work? The effect of intonation and stress on comprehension and recall of spoken discourse in old age. *Language and Communication, 6,* 91–98.

Connelly, S. L., Hasher, L., & Zacks, R. T. (1991). Age and reading: The impact of distraction. *Psychology and Aging, 6,* 533–541.

Craik, F. I. M., & Jennings, J. M. (1992). Human memory. In F. I. M. Craik & T. A. Salthouse (Eds.), *The handbook of aging and cognition* (pp. 51–110). Hillsdale, NJ: Erlbaum.

Daneman, M., & Carpenter, P. A. (1980). Individual differences in working memory and reading. *Journal of Verbal Learning and Verbal Behavior, 19,* 450–466.

Dixon, R. A., & Bäckman, L. (1993). Reading and memory for prose in adulthood: Issues of expertise and compensation. In S. R. Yussen & M. C. Smith (Eds.), *Reading across the life span* (pp. 193–213). New York: Springer.

Dixon, R. A., & Gould, O. N. (in press). Adult telling and retelling stories collaboratively. In P. B. Baltes & U. M. Staudinger (Eds.), *Interactive minds: Life-span perspectives on the social foundations of cognition.* New York: Cambridge Univ. Press.

Dixon, R. A., Hultsch, D. F., Simon, E. W., & von Eye, A. (1984). Verbal ability and text structure effects on age differences in text recall. *Journal of Verbal Learning and Verbal Behavior, 37,* 358–364.

Fletcher, C. R. (1981). Short-term memory processes in text comprehension. *Journal of Verbal Learning and Verbal Behavior, 20,* 564–574.

Fodor, J. A. (1983). *The modularity of mind.* Cambridge, MA: MIT Press.

Garnham, A. (1981). Mental models as representations of text. *Memory and Cognition, 9,* 560–565.

Gernsbacher, M. A., & Faust, M. E. (1991). The mechanism of suppression: A component of general comprehension skill. *Journal of Experimental Psychology: Learning, Memory, and Cognition, 17,* 245–262.

Gernsbacher, M., & Robertson, R. (1992). Knowledge activation versus sentence mapping when representing fictional characters' emotional states. *Language and Cognition Processes, 7,* 353–371.

Glenberg, A., Meyer, M., & Lindem, K. (1987). Mental models contribute to foregrounding during text comprehension. *Journal of Memory and Language, 26,* 69–83.

Gould, O. N., Trevithick, L., & Dixon, R. A. (1991). Adult age differences in elaborations produced during prose recall. *Psychology and Aging, 6,* 93–99.

Haberlandt, K. (1984). Components of sentence and word reading times. In D. E. Kieras & M. A. Just (Eds.), *New methods in reading comprehension research* (pp. 219–251). Hillsdale, NJ: Erlbaum.

Hamm, V. P., & Hasher, L. (1992). Age and the availability of inferences. *Psychology and Aging, 7,* 56–64.

Hartley, J. T. (1988). Aging and individual differences in memory for written discourse. In L. L. Light & D. M. Burke (Eds.), *Language, memory, and aging* (pp. 36–57). New York: Cambridge Univ. Press.

Hartley, J. T. (1993). Aging and prose memory: Tests of the resource-deficit hypothesis. *Psychology and Aging, 8,* 538–551.

Hartley, J. T., Stojack, C. C., Mushaney, T. J., Annon, T. A. K., & Lee, D. W. (1994). Reading speed and prose memory in older and younger adults. *Psychology and Aging, 9,* 216–223.

Hasher, L., & Zacks, R. T. (1979). Automatic and effortful processes in memory. *Journal of Experimental Psychology: General, 108,* 356–388.

Hasher, L., & Zacks, R. T. (1988). Working memory, comprehension and aging: A review and a new view. *The Psychology of Learning and Motivation, 22,* 193–225.

Hess, T. M. (1990). Aging and schematic influences on memory. In T. M. Hess (Ed.), *Aging and cognition: Knowledge organization and utilization* (pp. 93–160). Amsterdam: North-Holland.

Horn, J. L. (1982). The aging of human abilities. In B. B. Wolman (Ed.), *Handbook of developmental psychology* (pp. 847–870). Englewood Cliffs, NJ: Prentice-Hall.

Howard, D. V., Shaw, R. J., & Heisey, J. G. (1986). Aging and the time course of semantic activation. *Journal of Gerontology, 41,* 195–203.

Hultsch, D. F., & Dixon, R. A. (1984). Memory for text materials in adulthood. In P. B. Baltes & O. G. Brim (Eds.), *Life-span development and behavior* (pp. 77–108). New York: Academic Press.

Hultsch, D. F., Hertzog, C., & Dixon, R. A. (1990). Ability correlates of memory performance in adulthood and aging. *Psychology and Aging, 5,* 356–368.

Hultsch, D. F., Hertzog, C., Small, B. J., McDonald-Miszczak, L., & Dixon, R. A. (1992). Short-term longitudinal change in cognitive performance in later life. *Psychology and Aging, 7,* 571–584.

Hupet, M., Chantraine, Y., & Nef, F. (1993). References in conversation between young and old normal adults. *Psychology and Aging, 8,* 339–346.

Jarvella, R. J. (1971). Syntactic processing of connected speech. *Journal of Verbal Learning and Verbal Behavior, 10,* 409–416.

Johnson-Laird, P. N. (1983). *Mental models.* Cambridge, MA: Harvard Univ. Press.

Just, M. A., & Carpenter, P. (1992). A capacity theory of comprehension: Individual differences in working memory. *Psychological Review, 99,* 122–149.

Keenan, J. M., Potts, G. R., Golding, J. M., & Jennings, T. M. (1989). Which elaborative inferences are drawn during reading? A question of methodologies. In D. A. Balota, G. B. F. d'Arcais, & K. Rayner (Eds.), *Comprehension processes in reading* (pp. 403–421). Hillsdale, NJ: Erlbaum.

Kemper, S. (1986). Imitation of complex syntactic constructions by elderly adults. *Applied Psycholinguistics, 7,* 277–288.

Kemper, S. (1987a). Life span changes in syntactic complexity. *Journal of Gerontology, 42,* 323–328.

Kemper, S. (1987b). Syntactic complexity and elderly adults' prose recall. *Experimental Aging Research, 13,* 47–52.

Kemper, S. (1992). Adults' sentence fragments: Who, what, when, where, and why. *Communication Research, 19,* 444–458.

Kemper, S. (1994). "Elderspeak": Speech accommodations to older adults. *Aging and Cognition, 1,* 17–28.

Kemper, S., & Anagnopoulos, C. (in press). Linguistic creativity in older adults. In C. Adams-Price (Ed.), *Creativity and aging: Theoretical and empirical perspectives.* New York: Springer.

Kemper, S., Rash, S., Kynette, D., & Norman, S. (1990). Telling stories: The structure of adults' narratives. *European Journal of Cognitive Psychology, 2,* 205–228.

Kintsch, W. (1988). The role of knowledge in discourse comprehension: A construction-integration model. *Psychological Review, 95,* 163–182.

Kintsch, W. (1992). How readers construct situation models for stories: The role of syntactic cues and causal inferences. In A. F. Healy, S. M. Kosslyn, & R. M. Shiffrin (Eds.), *From learning processes to cognitive processes: Essays in honor of William K. Estes* (vol. 2, pp. 261–278). Hillsdale, NJ: Erlbaum.

Kintsch, W., & Keenan, J. M. (1973). Reading rate and retention as a function of the number of propositions in the base structure of sentences. *Cognitive Psychology, 5,* 257–274.

Kintsch, W., & van Dijk, T. A. (1978). Toward a model of text comprehension and production. *Psychological Review, 85,* 363–394.

Kintsch, W., Welsch, D., Schmalhofer, F., & Zimny, S. (1990). Sentence memory: A theoretical analysis. *Journal of Memory and Language, 29,* 133–159.

Kynette, D., Kemper, S., Norman, S., & Cheung, H. (1990). Adults' word recall and word repetition. *Experimental Aging Research, 16,* 117–121.

LaBerge, D., & Samuels, S. J. (1974). Toward a theory of automatic information processing in reading. *Cognitive Psychology, 6,* 293–323.

Labouvie-Vief, G., & Schell, D. A. (1982). Learning and memory in later life. In B. B. Wolman (Ed.), *Handbook of developmental psychology* (pp. 828–846). Englewood Cliffs, NJ: Prentice-Hall.

Laver, G. D., & Burke, D. M. (1993). Why do semantic priming effects increase in old age? A meta-analysis. *Psychology and Aging, 8,* 34–43.

Light, L. L. (1990). Interactions between memory and language in old age. In J. E. Birren & K. W. Schaie (Eds.), *Handbook of the psychology of aging* (3d ed., pp. 275–290). New York: Academic Press.

Light, L. L., & Anderson, P. A. Memory for scripts in young and older adults. *Memory and Cognition, 11,* 435–444.

Light, L. L., & Capps, J. L. (1986). Comprehension of pronouns in younger and older adults. *Developmental Psychology, 22,* 580–585.

Light, L. L., Capps, J. L., Singh, A., & Owens, S. A. A. (1994). Comprehension and use of anaphoric devices in young and older adults. *Discourse Processes, 18,* 77–104.

Lindenberger, U., Kliegl, R., & Baltes, P. B. (1992). Professional expertise does not eliminate age differences in imagery-based memory performance during adulthood. *Psychology and Aging, 7,* 585–593.

Madden, D. J. (1988). Adult age differences in the effects of sentence context and stimulus degradation during visual word recognition. *Psychology and Aging, 3,* 167–172.

Meyer, B. J. F. (1987). Reading comprehension and aging. In W. K. Schaie (Ed.), *Annual review of gerontology and geriatrics* (pp. 93–115). New York: Springer.

Meyer, B. J. F., Russo, C., & Talbot, A. (1995). Discourse comprehension and problem solving: Decisions about the treatment of breast cancer by women across the life-span. *Psychology and Aging, 10,* 84–103.

Moore, D., & Zabrucky, K. (1992). Self-judged comprehension in adults: Effects of age and skill. *Experimental Aging Research, 18,* 3–7.

Morrow, D. G. (1986). Grammatical morphemes and conceptual structure in discourse processing. *Cognitive Science, 10,* 423–455.

Morrow, D., Altieri, P., & Leirer, V. (1992). Aging, narrative organization, presentation mode, and referent choice strategies. *Experimental Aging Research, 18,* 75–84.

Morrow, D. G., Greenspan, S. L., & Bower, G. H. (1989). Updating situation models during comprehension. *Journal of Memory and Language, 28,* 292–312.

Morrow, D. G., Leirer, V. O., & Altieri, P. A. (1992). Aging, expertise, and narrative processing. *Psychology and Aging, 7,* 376–388.

Morrow, D. G., Leirer, V. O., Altieri, P. A., & Fitzsimmons, C. (1994). Age differences in creating situation models from narratives. *Language and Cognitive Processes, 9,* 203–220.

Morrow, D. G., Leirer, V. O., Fitzsimmons, C., & Altieri, P. A. (1994). When expertise reduces age differences in performance. *Psychology and Aging, 9,* 134–148.

Morrow, D. G., & Rodvold, M. (in press). Issues in air traffic control communication. In M. Smolensky & E. Stein (Eds.), *Human factors in air traffic control.* New York: Academic Press.

Myerson, J., Ferraro, F. R., Hale, S., & Lima, S. D. (1992). General slowing in semantic priming and word recognition. *Psychology and Aging, 7,* 257–290.

Noordman, L. G. M., & Vonk, W. (1992). Readers' knowledge and control of inferences in reading. *Language and Cognitive Processes, 7,* 373–391.

Norman, S., Kemper, S., & Kynette, D. (1992). Adults' reading comprehension: Effects of syntactic complexity and working memory. *Journal of Gerontology: Psychological Sciences, 47,* P258–P265.

Norman, S., Kemper, S., Kynette, D., Cheung, H., & Anagnopoulos, C. (1991). Syntactic complexity and adults' running memory span. *Journal of Gerontology: Psychological Sciences, 46,* P346–P351.

Park, D. C. (1992). Applied cognitive aging research. In F. I. M. Craik & T. A. Salthouse (Eds.), *Handbook of cognition and aging* (pp. 449–493). Hillsdale, NJ: Erlbaum.

Pratt, M. W., Boyes, C., Robins, S., & Manchester, J. (1989). Telling tales: Aging, working memory, and the narrative cohesion of story retellings. *Developmental Psychology, 25,* 628–635.

Radvansky, G., Gerard, L., Zacks, R., & Hasher, L. (1990). Younger and older adults' use of mental models as representations for text materials. *Psychology and Aging, 5,* 209–214.

Rowe, J. W., & Kahn, R. L. (1987). Human aging: Usual and successful. *Science, 237,* 143–149.

Rubin, D. C. (1985). Memorability as a measure of processing: A unit analysis of prose and list learning. *Journal of Experimental Psychology: General, 114,* 213–238.

Ryan, E. B., Bourhis, R. Y., & Knops, U. (1991). Evaluative perceptions of patronizing speech addressed to elders. *Psychology and Aging, 6,* 442–450.

Salthouse, T. A. (1984). Effects of age and skill in typing. *Journal of Experimental Psychology: General, 113,* 345–371.

Salthouse, T. A. (1988). Initializing the formalization of theories in cognitive aging. *Psychology and Aging, 3,* 1–16.

Salthouse, T. A. (1991). *Theoretical perspectives on cognitive aging.* Hillsdale, NJ: Erlbaum.

Sanford, A. J., & Garrod, S. C. (1981). *Understanding written language.* New York: Wiley.

Smith, J., & Baltes, P. B. (1990). Wisdom-related knowledge: Age/cohort differences in response to life-planning problems. *Developmental Psychology, 26,* 494–505.

Smith, S., Rebok, G., Smith, W., Hall, S. E., & Alvin, M. (1983). Adult age differences in the use of story structure in delayed free recall. *Experimental Aging Research, 9,* 191–195.

Soederberg, L. M., & Stine, E. A. L. (1995). Activation of emotion information in text among younger and older adults. *Journal of Adult Development, 2,* 23–36.

Spilich, G., Vesonder, G., Chiesi, H., & Voss, J. (1979). Text processing of domain-related information for individuals with high and low domain knowledge. *Journal of Verbal Learning and Verbal Behavior, 18,* 275–290.

Stanhope, N., Cohen, G., & Conway, M. (1993). Very long-term retention of a novel. *Applied Cognitive Psychology, 7,* 239–256.

Stern, C., Prather, P., Swinney, D., & Zurif, E. (1991). The time course of automatic lexical access and aging. *Brain and Language, 40,* 359–372.

Stine, E. A. L. (1995). On-line processing of written text by younger and older adults. *Psychology and Aging, 5,* 68–78.

Stine, E. A. L. (1995). Aging and the distribution of resources in working memory. In P. Allen & T. Bashore (Eds.), *Age differences in word and language processing* (pp. 171–186). Amsterdam: North-Holland.

Stine, E. A. L., Cheung, H., & Henderson, D. T. (1995). Adult age differences in the on-line processing of new concepts in discourse. *Aging and Cognition, 2,* 1–18.

Stine, E. A. L., & Hindman, J. (1994). Age differences in reading time allocation for propositionally dense sentences. *Aging and Cognition, 1,* 2–16.

Stine, E. A. L., & Wingfield, A. (1987). Process and strategy in memory for speech among younger and older adults. *Psychology and Aging, 2,* 272–279.

Stine, E. A. L., & Wingfield, A. (1988). Memorability functions as an indicator of qualitative age differences in text recall. *Psychology and Aging, 3,* 179–183.

Stine, E. A. L., & Wingfield, A. (1990). The assessment of qualitative age differences in discourse processing. In T. M. Hess (Ed.), *Aging and cognition: Knowledge organization and utilization* (pp. 33–92). New York: Elsevier.

Stine, E. A. L., Wingfield, A., & Poon, L. W. (1986). How much and how fast: Rapid processing of spoken language in later adulthood. *Psychology and Aging, 1,* 303–311.

Swinney, D. A. (1979). Lexical access during sentence comprehension: (Re)consideration of context effects. *Journal of Verbal Learning and Verbal Behavior, 18,* 645–659.

Till, R., Mross, E. F., & Kintsch, W. (1988). Time course of priming for associate and inference words in discourse context. *Memory and Cognition, 16,* 283–298.

Tun, P. A., & Wingfield, A. (1993). Is speech special? Perception and recall of spoken language in complex environments. In J. Cerella, W. Hoyer, J. Rybash, & M. L. Commons (Eds.), *Adult information processing: Limits on loss* (pp. 425–457). New York: Academic Press.

Tun, P. A., Wingfield, A., & Stine, E. A. L. (1991). Speech processing capacity in younger and older adults: A dual-task study. *Psychology and Aging, 6,* 3–9.

van Dijk, T. A., & Kintsch, W. (1983). *Strategies of discourse comprehension.* New York: Academic Press.

Wingfield, A., Aberdeen, J. S., & Stine, E. A. L. (1991). Word-onset gating and linguistic context in spoken word recognition by young and elderly adults. *Journal of Gerontology: Psychological Sciences, 46,* P127–P129.

Wingfield, A., Wayland, S. C., & Stine, E. A. L. (1992). Adult age differences in the use of prosody for syntactic parsing and recall of spoken sentences. *Journal of Gerontology: Psychological Sciences, 47,* P350–P356.

Zabrucky, K., & Moore, D. (1994). Contributions of working memory and evaluation of understanding to adults' recall of texts. *Journal of Gerontology: Psychological Sciences, 49,* 201–212.

Zabrucky, K., Moore, D., & Schultz, N. R., Jr. (1993). Young and old adults' ability to use different standards to evaluate understanding. *Journal of Gerontology: Psychological Sciences, 48,* 238–244.

Zacks, R. T., & Hasher, L. (1994). Directed ignoring: Inhibitory regulation of working memory. In D. Dagenbach & T. H. Carr (Eds.), *Inhibitory mechanisms in attention, memory, and language* (pp. 241–264). New York: Academic Press.

Zacks, R. T., Hasher, L., Doren, B., Hamm, V., & Attig, M. S. (1987). Encoding and memory of explicit and implicit information. *Journal of Gerontology, 42,* 418–422.

Zelinski, E. M. (1988). Integrating information from discourse: Do older adults show deficits? In L. L. Light & D. M. Burke (Eds.), *Language, memory, and aging* (pp. 117–132). New York: Cambridge Univ. Press.

3

INTELLIGENCE

PSYCHOMETRIC INTELLIGENCE AND AGING

K. Warner Schaie and Sherry L. Willis
Pennsylvania State University

INTRODUCTION

■ Scope of Chapter

In this chapter we discuss the role of psychometric intelligence within the broader context of adult cognition. We then reflect briefly on why one should be interested in studying adult psychometric intelligence. Next we review some of the literature on the adult development of psychometric intelligence, giving due heed to the aspects of age differences, age changes, and generational shifts in ability performance. We then relate performance on measures of psychometric ability to competence in everyday living, as well as to health status and health behaviors. Finally, we review some work on the reversibility of cognitive deficit occurring across age. In providing substantive illustrations for the issues discussed we will lean heavily on our longitudinal studies within the context of the Seattle Longitudinal Study (SLS; Schaie, 1995), and the Adult Development and Enrichment Study (ADEPT; Willis, 1990, 1991). Other work has most recently been reviewed by Lindenberger (1994).

■ Hierarchical Model of Intelligence

The chapters in this volume represent several different approaches to the study of adult cognition. The section on information processing focuses on the processes by which adults process and acquire information; these processes include attention, speed, and various forms of memory (see Chapters 5, 6, and 7). The section on intelligence focuses on mental abilities as studied from a psychometric intelligence perspective and on applied cognition, including everyday intelligence and complex reasoning (see Chapters 10 and 11). Central questions addressed by each approach to the study of adult cognition include: How do adults of various ages differ in functioning? What changes in functioning occur as the adult ages? What personal and contextual factors influence functioning?

As each approach to the study of adult cognition has gained some maturity, there has been increasing interest in the *relationship* among these various approaches (Puckett & Reese, 1993; Salthouse, 1990; Sternberg, 1985; Willis & Schaie, 1993). How are information processes, mental abilities and everyday intelligence interrelated? Several theorists have proposed that intelligent behavior involves multiple forms of intelligence. Baltes and colleagues (Baltes, Dittman-Kohli, & Dixon, 1984) distinguish between the "mechanics" of intelligence, involving basic mental abilities and processes, and the "pragmatics" of intelligence concerned with everyday cognition. Similarly, in his triarchic theory Sternberg (1985) distinguishes between the contextual part of intelligence, concerned with adaptation to one's environment, and the componential part, focusing on cognitive mechanisms and processes (see Chapter 10).

While a comprehensive model of adult cognition would involve all of the various forms of intelligence, everyday intelligence is often considered to be particularly salient in middle and late adulthood (Baltes et al., 1984; Labouvie-Vief, 1985; West & Sinnott, 1992). Adults must apply their intellectual resources to the tasks of daily living, including occupations, family responsibilities, and the maintenance of an independent and productive lifestyle. A major question in adult cognition, therefore, is the relationship between the "mechanics" of intelligence and everyday functioning. In considering the interrelationship among the various approaches to adult cognition, Berg and Sternberg (1985) state: "A mechanistic theory is needed to specify the cognitive processes by which contextually appropriate behavior is carried out" (p. 348). The question then arises whether the mechanistic constructs and variables traditionally studied by cognitive psychologists (i.e., information processes and mental abilities) are relevant to the study of everyday intelligence (Park, 1992; Salthouse & Maurer, 1996; Sinnott), 1989; Sternberg & Wagner, 1986).

Our own research and that of others suggests that mental abilities and cognitive processes can be considered as "building blocks" underlying everyday intelligence (Schaie, 1978, 1987; Willis, 1991; Willis & Marsiske, 1991; Willis & Schaie, 1986, 1993). From a hierarchical perspective, basic cognitive processes and abilities are believed to be universal across cultures and contexts. When nurtured and directed by a particular context, cognitive processes and abilities develop into domain-related competencies that are manifested in daily life as cognitive performance (Berry & Irvine, 1986). This view is supported by several recent studies that have found significant relationship between everyday task performance and traditional intelligence measures. Fluid and crystallized intellectual abilities have been found to be related to everyday problem solving (Camp, Doherty, Moody-Thomas, & Denney, 1989; Crook & West, 1990; Diehl, Willis, & Schaie, 1995), interpersonal competence (Cornelius & Caspi, 1987), computer literacy (Garfein, Schaie, & Willis, 1988; Jay & Willis, 1992), and comprehension of printed materials (Willis, Jay, Diehl, & Marsiske, 1992; Willis & Marsiske, 1991; Willis & Schaie, 1986). Capon and Kuhn (1979, 1982) reported consumer behavior to be related to formal reasoning within Piagetian theory. Proficiency in leisure activities, including recalling TV shows, playing video games, and solving jigsaw and crossword puzzles, was found to be predicted by verbal ability (Cavanaugh, 1983; Tosti-Vasey, Person, Maier, & Willis, 1992), reaction time (Clark, Lanphear, & Riddick, 1987), and memory (Rice, Meyer, & Miller, 1988).

We propose that a *hierarchical relationship* exists among these various levels of cognition, such that cognitive processes and mental abilities are necessary but not sufficient antecedents for competence in tasks of everyday intelligence (Park & Kidder, 1995; Willis & Schaie, 1986, 1993). In terms of a hierarchy, information processes such as memory and speed are considered the most basic, least complex forms of cognition and are most directly associated with neuropsychological functioning (Salthouse, 1990). Mental abilities such as numerical, verbal, and reasoning abilities are viewed as the products or outcomes of information that has been acquired and processed. These abilities represent a middle level within the hierarchy. The upper, or most complex, levels of the hierarchy include everyday intelligence and postformal thought.

In constructing a complex structure, various types of building materials are used; each material makes a unique contribution to the completed structure. Somewhat analogously, tasks of daily living that require everyday intelligence are complex and multidimensional. For example, taking an over-the-counter medication requires comprehending the instructions, reasoning about the appropriateness of the drug for one's condition, and determining the correct dosage, as well as remembering to take the drug at the appropriate intervals. Several different mental abilities and cognitive processes are involved in completing such a complex task of daily living, just as a variety of materials is necessary in constructing a building (Park, 1992; Park & Mayhorn, 1994; Willis et al., 1992). Moreover, various tasks of daily living require different combinations and permutations of mental abilities and cognitive processes, just as different building materials are required for different construction projects.

Research in the building and construction industry occurs at multiple levels. At a basic level, there are the material sciences, which study the composition and durability of various types of material. This basic research has contributed much to the design and construction of complex structures. Similarly, much of the research in cognitive aging has been at the level of studying individual mental abilities (Carroll, 1993; Horn & Hofer, 1992; Lindenberger, Mayr, & Kliegel, 1993). Our knowledge of what factors influence performance on a specific ability and how a given ability changes with age has the potential to contribute much to our understanding of the more complex forms of everyday intelligence.

Given our position on the hierarchical relationship between mental abilities and everyday intelligence, we begin with a brief historical review of psychometric intelligence and then discuss in some detail the literature on the development of mental abilities in adulthood. We then present findings on the relationship between mental abilities and two domains of everyday intelligence: daily tasks required for independent living and health status and behaviors.

■ Why Should We Be Interested in the Aging of Adult Psychometric Intelligence?

Although there has been much criticism of intelligence testing, the fact remains that omnibus tests of intelligence have been quite useful in predicting people's competence in dealing with the standard educational systems in the United States and other industrialized nations. These tests have also been useful in predicting success in vocational pursuits in which job requirements depend upon educationally based knowledge or skills or involve high levels of analytic or basic problem-solving skills. Measures of specific abilities have also had utility in predicting competence in those situations where specific skills are important to successful job performance. Many have argued that motivational and other personality variables ought to have greater potency in predicting adjustment and competence in midlife than intelligence does, but little empirical evidence supports this proposition.

When dealing with the elderly, there is no question that the assessment of intellectual competence is of substantial importance. One must now ask questions such as who should be retired for cause (loss of competence) in the absence of mandatory retirement at a relatively early age (Salthouse & Maurer, 1996), whether sufficient competence remains for independent living (Fillenbaum, 1985), and whether a person remains able to conserve and dispose of his or her property (Grisso, 1986). All of these increasingly important issues essentially involve the assessment of the current level of intellectual functioning and a determination as to whether that level has sufficiently declined from a previous level to require interventions that might lead to increased dependence upon others.

Assuming that the preceding issues are of importance to our society, it becomes incumbent upon us to examine in detail the factual issues involved in the development of adult intelligence (Cattell, 1987; Horn & Hofer, 1992). Intraindividual decremental changes must be differentiated from interindividual differences that are expressed in the obsolescent behavior of older cohorts when compared with their younger peers. The ages at which developmental peaks occur must be described, and generational differences as well as within-generation age changes must be assessed. Perhaps of greatest importance is the identification of the reasons why some individuals show intellectual decline by early midlife while others maintain or increase their level of intellectual functioning well into advanced old age.

BRIEF HISTORICAL OVERVIEW

Students of the history of psychology know that applied psychology began with the investigation of psychometric intelligence. Early efforts involved procedures for the orderly tracking of mentally retarded children within the public school classroom (Binet & Simon, 1905) and the study of individual differences for the purpose of demonstrating their Darwinian characteristics (Galton, 1869). Many of the mental functions that early investigators described are still of contemporary interest. Alfred Binet provided a classic definition of intelligence: "To judge well, to comprehend well, to reason well, these are the essentials of intelligence. A person may be a moron or an imbecile if he lacks judgment; but with judgment he could not be either" (Binet & Simon, 1905, p. 106).

Early empirical studies of intelligence focused upon the question of how complex mental functions are acquired early in life (Brooks & Weintraub, 1976). Soon, however, the early applied psychologists began to trace the complexities of intellectual development beyond childhood. Some of these developments are associated with theoretical expositions of classical developmental psychologists, including G. Stanley Hall (1922), H. L. Hollingsworth (1927), and Sidney Pressey (Pressey, Janney, & Kuhlen, 1939). These authors raised questions about the age at which peak performance levels are attained and about the maintenance or transformation of intellectual structures across the life course, and they investigated the decremental changes they thought were likely to occur from late midlife into old age.

A number of empirical studies relevant to these questions soon followed. In the first standardization of the Binet tests for American use, Terman (1916) assumed that intellectual development reaches a peak at age 16 and then remains level throughout adulthood. The screening test for intellectual competence developed by army psychologists during World War I, the Army Alpha Intelligence Test (Yerkes, 1921), showed that the peak level of intellectual functioning for young adults might even be reached earlier, on average by age 13. Other empirical studies questioned these inferences. One of the first influential cross-sectional studies (Jones & Conrad, 1933) collected data on the Army Alpha on many of the inhabitants of a New England community who were between the ages of 10 and 60 years. Age differences observed in this study were quite substantial for some of the Army Alpha subtests but not for others. Wechsler's standardization studies, which led to the development of the Wechsler-Bellevue Adult Intelligence Scale, now known as the WAIS, found that the growth of intelligence does not cease in adolescence. He discovered that peak ages differed across various dimensions of intellectual functioning. Moreover, decrements at older ages were not uniform across the different measures he used to define intelligence (Wechsler, 1939).

Interest in intelligence testing reached a peak following World War II with the explosive expansion of clinical psychology and the widespread introduction into clinical practice of the WAIS and its derivatives (Matarazzo, 1972). Intelligence and/or aptitude testing became standard procedures in the public schools, and widely accepted aptitude/ability batteries such as the Differential Aptitude Test (DAT) and the General Aptitude Test Battery (GATB; cf. Anastasi, 1976; Cronbach, 1970) were introduced for purposes of employment counseling and employee selection. Disenchantment arose, however, following widespread criticism of the misapplication of intelligence tests in education (see, e.g., Kamin, 1974). Clinical psychologists began to realize that inferences drawn from profile analyses of intelligence tests were less useful than had originally been thought. Information gained on intellectual status often seemed to contribute little to the development of therapeutic interventions, which became of more central interest in clinical practice.

A resurgence of interest in the measurement of adult intelligence occurred in the 1950s and 1960s among the small group of developmental psychologists who had become interested in adult development and aging (cf. Riegel, 1977). A series of longitudinal studies of individuals followed from young adulthood into midlife on the WAIS, such as the Berkeley Growth and Guidance Study (Bayley & Oden, 1955), the New York Twin Study (Jarvik, Kallman, & Falek, 1962), and the Army Alpha follow-up of Iowa State World War I ROTC students (Owens, 1953, 1959) suggested that there was strong evidence that most intellectual abilities were maintained at least into midlife and that some abilities remained stable beyond that period of life. The senior author of this chapter reported findings from a study utilizing Thurstone's Primary Mental Abilities Test (Schaie, 1985; Thurstone & Thurstone, 1949) that peak ages of intellectual performance had shifted significantly upward by 1956 (Schaie, 1958). In a longitudinal follow-up of the original study after 7 years, he confirmed that ability declines occurred much later than previously thought (Schaie & Strother, 1968).

Norms for the recently revised form of the WAIS (through age 75) confirm the earlier finding that there is relative stability for the verbal subtests but substantial negative age differences for the performance subtests that involve perceptual speed (cf. Sattler, 1982). Evidence for the stability of this pattern into advanced old age has also been documented (Field, Schaie, & Leino, 1988; McArdle, Hamagami, Elias, & Robbins, 1991; Siegler, 1983).

The WAIS has enjoyed continuing popularity as a clinical assessment instrument (Frank, 1983). This test has also been included in several more recent longitudinal studies following older adults over time. It has been used in the Baltimore Longitudinal Study (Costa & McCrae, 1993; Shock et al., 1986), the Duke Longitudinal Studies (Busse, 1993; Palmore, Busse, Maddox, Nowlin, & Siegler, 1985), and the Berkeley Growth and Guidance Studies (Eichorn, Clausen, Haan, Honzik, & Mussen, 1981).

Although the WAIS remains popular for cognitive assessment in clinical situations, its factorial complexity makes it less attractive for assessing intellectual changes across age and time. As a consequence, most recent studies of intellectual aging in community-dwelling populations have utilized subsets of the primary mental abilities (cf. Cunningham, 1987; Johansson & Berg, 1989). The most comprehensive set of measures of primary mental abilities remains the Kit of Factor-Referenced Tests published by the Educational Testing Service (Ekstrom, French, Harman, & Derman, 1976). However, the most extensive work utilizing the primary mental abilities framework, providing information over the entire adult age range, has been done within the context of the Seattle Longitudinal Study, which has followed individuals over as long as 35 years and has studied age differences at six different points in time (cf. Schaie, 1993, 1994, 1995).

Recent attention has also been given to the confounding effects of the nature of test materials that ignore the requirements of older organisms (cf. Cornelius, 1984; Gonda, Quayhagen, & Schaie, 1981; Storandt & Futterman, 1982). These concerns have led to the development of tests with larger typefaces and other simplifications designed to make them more appropriate for work with the elderly (cf. Baltes & Willis, 1982; Schaie, 1985).

Work on psychometric intelligence has also been expanded to include measures of the more pragmatic aspects of intelligence (West & Sinott, 1992). The Educational Testing Service (1977) constructed operational definitions of everyday tasks, and more recently Willis (Willis & Marsiske, 1993) constructed a psychometrically based Everyday Problems Test (EPT), which measures performance on the Instrumental Activities of Daily Living (IADL). (For a more complete discussion, see Willis & Schaie, 1993, and the section on everyday intelligence below.)

ADULT INTELLECTUAL DEVELOPMENT

Rather different conclusions emerge when one examines cross-sectional studies that compare groups of individuals of different ages at one point in time than when one charts changes within the same individuals over time. For obvious reasons, cross-sectional data are generally not useful in predicting how individuals will change over age, because we can rarely match groups on other relevant variables than age that might produce the group differences. But cross-sectional data are indeed useful in informing us about differences in performance levels between age groups at a particular point in time. By contrast, longitudinal data are needed to chart age functions that allow the prediction of how a given individual will change across time. Since the early experiences of individuals from successive birth cohorts differ markedly due to societal changes in child-rearing practices and educational processes, we must also attend to the patterns of generational shifts to understand age differences at a particular point in time. (For discussions of the relationship between cross-sectional and longitudinal data, see Schaie & Willis, 1996, Chapter 8).

■ Cross-sectional Findings

In the Seattle Longitudinal Study (SLS) we examined age difference patterns on five basic mental abilities at six points in time 7 years apart: 1956, 1963, 1970, 1977, 1984, and 1991. The abilities we selected, which account for a large proportion of individual differences in intellectual competence, include verbal meaning (recognition vocabulary), reasoning (inferences of rules and regularities from the observation of individual instances), space (being able to mentally rotate visual objects in two-dimensional space), number (checking the addition of sets of simple sums), and word fluency (vocabulary recall according to a lexical rule, that is, recalling words beginning with a given letter of the alphabet). Examples of test items are provided in Figure 9.1.

There does not appear to be a uniform pattern of age-related changes in adulthood across all intellectual abilities. An overall index of intellectual ability (IQ) therefore does not suffice if one wishes to understand age differences (cross-sectional data) or age changes (longitudinal data). To document this fact, Figure 9.2 shows cross-sectional data over the age range from 25 to 81 years for five abilities for the 1970 and 1991 study waves. Notice the upward shift in level across the two occasions. In 1970, sharp age differences occur after age 60 for all abilities, while in 1991 these differences are much more gradual. The cross-sectional data show two different patterns: three of the abilities appear to peak in young adulthood and show linearly accelerating age differences that are steepest for spatial orientation and inductive reasoning but less pronounced for word fluency. On the other hand, verbal meaning and

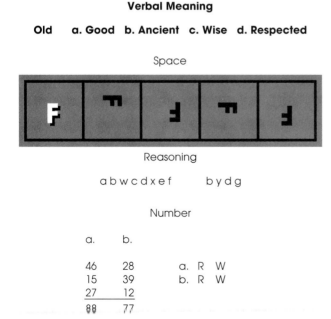

FIGURE 9.1 Examples of test items from the Primary Mental Abilities Test.

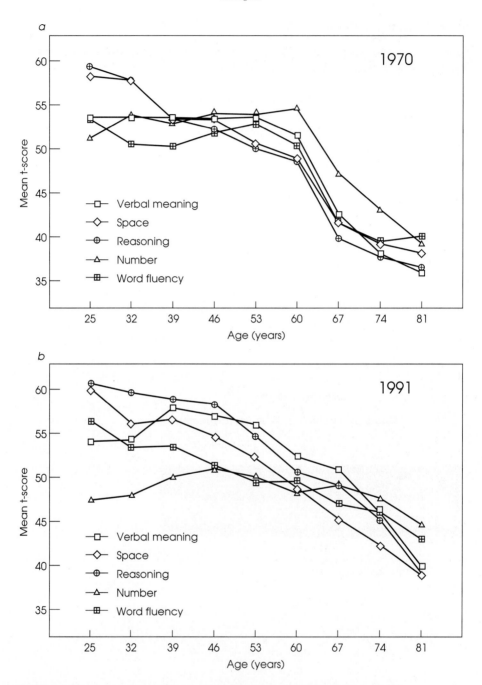

FIGURE 9.2 Cross-sectional age differences for five primary mental abilities in the Seattle Longitudinal Study in 1970 and 1991. (*Source:* Adapted from Schaie, 1995.)

number peak in midlife. However, verbal meaning, a somewhat speeded test, begins to show negative age differences by early old age. In 1970, number shows negative age differences after age 60 similar to the other abilities. However, in 1991 it has an almost level age differences profile through adulthood. Note that at each comparable age individuals were born 21 years later in the earlier than the later study wave. The differences in the shapes of the age profiles result from differences between the respective birth cohorts (see below).

■ Longitudinal Findings

Going beyond the between-group findings that confound age and differential experience, Figure 9.3 shows longitudinal gradients estimated by averaging all of the 7-year within-subject data accumulated over the entire course of our studies for a given age segment. Sufficient data are available to do this over the age range from mean age 25 to mean age 88. The longitudinal gradients are centered on the last actually observed mean for subjects aged 53.

The longitudinal gradients show at least a modest gain for all abilities from young adulthood to early middle age. But there remain differences among abilities in the attainment of peak age as well as the degree to which age changes accelerate with advancing age. There are, moreover, gender and cohort effects that differ by ability, which complicate matters. Systematic gender differences favor women on verbal meaning and inductive reasoning but men

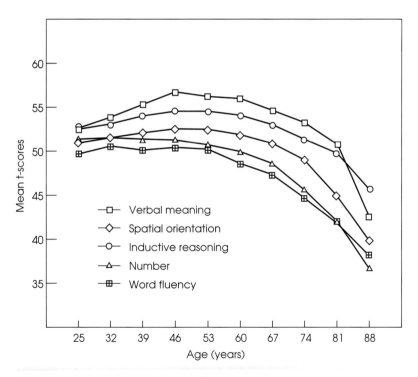

FIGURE 9.3 Longitudinal age gradients for five primary mental abilities estimated from cumulated within-subject age changes. (*Source:* Schaie, 1994.)

on spatial orientation and number. In the more recent longitudinal data, gender difference trends have emerged that suggest that women may decline earlier on fluid abilities, while men do so on crystallized abilities. Although fluid abilities begin to decline earlier, crystallized abilities show steeper decrement once the late 70s are reached (cf. Schaie, 1990, 1995; Schaie & Hertzog, 1983, 1986). (See Kaufman, Kaufman, McLean, & Reynolds, 1991 for gender differences on other tests.)

There does not seem to be a systematic sequence of which abilities decline first in a given individual. In the SLS study we have looked at the question of how many abilities decline in an individual by a certain age. We have found that by age 67 virtually everyone had declined reliably on at least one ability. But in these community-dwelling persons, even by age 88, no one had declined in all five abilities that we monitored (Schaie, 1989).

More fine-grained analyses also suggest substantial gender differences when age changes are decomposed into accuracy and speed (cf. Willis & Schaie, 1988). As men enter advanced old age, their performance loss tends to be due in greater part to speed than is true for women. One might assume that at comparable ages men are closer to death than women are; hence, the physiological infrastructure that mediates response speed has already experienced a greater reduction in efficiency.

Generational Differences

In the general population. Results from the SLS have conclusively demonstrated the prevalence of substantial generational (birth cohort) differences in psychometric abilities (Schaie, 1983, 1990; Schaie & Hertzog, 1986; Willis, 1989). These cohort trends differ in magnitude and direction by ability and can therefore not be determined from composite IQ indices. The magnitude of cohort differences for five abilities are shown in Figure 9.4. These cohort gradients are obtained by differentiating successive cohorts observed at the same age, with estimates based on cohort differences at up to five different age levels.

Almost linear positive cohort shifts were observed for inductive reasoning and verbal meaning, with a more spasmodic positive shift for spatial orientation. These cohort differences are substantial and account for differences of more than 1 population standard deviation (SD) between the earliest and latest cohorts. On the other hand, number skill peaked with the 1924 birth cohort and declined progressively thereafter by about ½ SD. More recently both cohorts are also at a disadvantage when compared with prior cohorts on the variable of word fluency. From these findings we concluded that the cross-sectional studies used to model age change overestimate age-related decline prior to the 60s for those variables that show negative cohort gradients and underestimate such declines for variables with positive cohort gradients.

Cohort-related differences in the rate and magnitude of age changes in intelligence remained fairly linear for cohorts entering old age during the first three cycles in our study (until 1970). They have since shown substantial shifts. For example, the rates of decremental age change have abated, while at the same time the earlier positive cohort trends have flattened as we began to study members of the baby-boom generation. Patterns of socialization unique to a given sex role within a specific historical period may also be major determinants for the pattern of change in abilities.

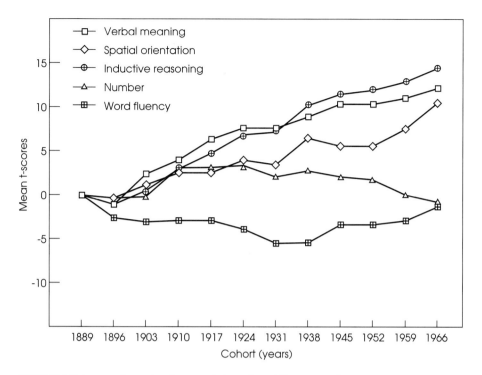

FIGURE 9.4 Cohort gradients showing cumulative cohort differences on five primary mental abilities for cohorts born in 1889 to 1966. (*Source:* Schaie, 1994.)

Within families To supplement the work on generational differences in abilities among un-related individuals, we have recently studied family members of our longitudinal study participants (Schaie, Plomin, Willis, Gruber-Baldini, & Dutta, 1992). Most work in developmental behavior genetics has been conducted by means of twin studies (Plomin & McClearn, 1990). It has only recently been recognized that, because of the unique characteristics of twins, broad generalizations from such studies will be limited and corroborative data are needed from family studies of parents/offspring and nontwin siblings. In the past, such studies employed parents and their young offspring and young siblings; our study is the first effort to explore systematic family similarity through adulthood, as well as to test for stability of such similarity over time.

An average family similarity of about .25 was observed for the mental abilities (verbal meaning, spatial orientation, inductive reasoning, number, and word fluency) and measures of flexibility (attitudinal flexibility, motor-cognitive flexibility, and psychomotor speed). Similarities were found for both parents and their offspring (adult children) and for siblings (brothers and sisters). The magnitude of parent–offspring and sibling similarly differed for specific abilities, and the overall similarity was somewhat greater for parent–offspring pairs. The size of the correlations was also comparable to those found between young adults and their children in other studies (see, e.g., DeFries et al., 1976).

Because of changes in our society, it has been argued that there ought to be a reduction in family similarity for younger as compared to older parent–offspring pairs. The possible reduction in shared environmental influence is thought to be due to increased outside influences in the more recent generation. However, this proposition could be supported only for inductive reasoning, where the older and middle generations showed somewhat greater similarity than the younger generation. For other abilities we found stability and for some abilities (verbal meaning and spatial orientation) even an increase in family similarity for more recent generations. Correlating relative performance with the longitudinal target subjects over 7, 14, and 21 years, moreover, provided strong evidence for stability of family similarity over time and age.

In summary, there do not seem to be uniform age-related patterns of change across all abilities. Cross-sectional analyses make it seem that declines occur early for those abilities where there have been positive cohort trends (e.g., inductive reasoning) but underestimate age-related change for abilities where negative or curvilinear cohort trends have occurred (e.g., number). Parents and their adult offspring show substantial correlations in ability performance.

PSYCHOMETRIC INTELLIGENCE AND EVERYDAY COMPETENCE

One of the ambiguities in studying everyday intelligence is that there is no commonly agreed-upon definition of the term (Charlesworth, 1976; Puckett & Reese, 1993; Sternberg & Wagner, 1986). However, several characteristics are frequently cited. Everyday intelligence involves an adult's ability to perform adequately those activities considered essential for living independently in our society. It involves the application of cognitive abilities and skills (Salthouse, 1990). Everyday problems are experienced in naturalistic or everyday contexts (Wagner, 1986). Finally, everyday problems are complex and multidimensional when compared with laboratory intelligence tasks.

A major issue in the study of everyday intelligence is the identification of criterion tasks for assessing intelligent behavior in real-world contexts (Crook & West, 1990; West & Sinnott, 1992). Criterion tasks will obviously vary by age or life stage. In childhood and young adulthood, there is considerable consensus regarding biologically or societally defined developmental tasks (e.g., schooling, choosing an occupation, parenting). In middle and late adulthood, there are increasing individual differences in the range of environments and experiences encountered, and there is no comparable, parsimonious set of near-universal developmental tasks that have the generality of developmental tasks in childhood. How then can the criterion tasks for assessing everyday intelligence in later adulthood be derived? One approach proceeds from the assumption that certain classes of everyday activities are critical for adaptive functioning in many life situations. A major concern in old age is the maintenance of independent living. In this approach the focus is upon tasks associated with the activities that are essential for effective independent functioning (Grisso, 1986; Lawton & Brody, 1969). Those involved in the assessment of older persons and the provision of services to the elderly have identified seven domains of daily living, known as the Instrumental Activities of Daily Living (IADLs; Fillenbaum, 1985), that are considered essential for living independently. These seven domains are: taking medications, managing finances, shopping for necessities, using the telephone, managing transportation, preparing meals, and housekeeping.

We have been conducting a program of research examining the relationship between mental abilities and older adults' competence in solving everyday problems involving printed materials (Diehl et al., 1995; Marsiske & Willis, 1995; Willis & Schaie, 1993). Tasks in each of the seven IADL domains have been examined: financial management (e.g., filling out a Medicare form), taking medications (e.g., reading a medicine bottle label), shopping (e.g., filling out a mail-order catalog form), meal preparation (e.g., reading a nutrition label), using the telephone (e.g., reading an emergency phone listing), managing transportation (e.g., reading a bus schedule), and housekeeping (e.g., reading instructions for use of a household appliance).

As we reported in earlier sections in this chapter, different mental abilities exhibit different patterns of age-related change in later adulthood. Therefore, the specific mental abilities that are related to everyday task performance are of interest. Cattell (1987) has differentiated between two broad domains of mental abilities. Crystallized abilities (e.g., verbal, numerical) are said to reflect acculturated influences, such as level of schooling; in healthy older adults, crystallized abilities remain stable on average, showing little or no decline until old-old age. In contrast, fluid abilities involve abstract reasoning and speeded responding; fluid abilities are said to be impacted by neurological assaults and to exhibit earlier patterns of decline, beginning on average in the mid-60s or earlier. Findings from the SLS support the differential rates of decline for fluid versus crystallized abilities. Thus, older adults' performance on everyday tasks would be expected to show different patterns of developmental change, depending on whether such tasks are more closely related to fluid or crystallized abilities.

In our research on the relationship between mental abilities and everyday tasks, we have found that more than half of the variance in older adults' performance on everyday tasks can be accounted for by mental ability performance (Willis & Marsiske, 1991; Willis & Schaie, 1986; Willis et al., 1992). Both fluid and crystallized abilities were found to account for everyday task performance, although a somewhat greater portion of the variance was accounted for by fluid abilities.

Causal relationships among variables cannot be determined by examining concurrent relationships. In our hierarchical model of ability–everyday intelligence relationships, basic mental abilities have been hypothesized to be salient antecedents of performance on complex tasks of daily living. To test this hypothesis, we examined whether performance on fluid and crystallized abilities at the first assessment occasion was a significant predictor of everyday task performance 7 years later. Both fluid and crystallized abilities were indeed found to be significant predictors. To further examine the reciprocal relationship between abilities and everyday task performance, a series of structural equation analyses was conducted (Willis et al., 1992). That is, the directionality of the relationship between abilities and everyday tasks was examined by contrasting models of abilities as predictors of everyday task performance versus models of everyday task performance as predictors of abilities. Findings indicated that fluid ability at the first assessment occasion predicted everyday task performance at the second assessment occasion 7 years later. Everyday task performance predicted ability at the second occasion less well. These findings provide support for our hypothesis that the level of performance on basic mental abilities is a significant antecedent of competence with every-day tasks involving printed material.

It has been suggested (Salthouse, 1990) that our findings of a relationship between mental ability performance and tasks of daily living may in part be due to the fact that both the tests of mental abilities and our everyday task measures involve printed stimuli. We therefore expanded these studies by assessing everyday problem solving through behavioral observation of the elderly performing tasks in their homes (Crook & West, 1990; Diehl et al., 1995). The elderly were observed performing prototypical everyday tasks in the three domains of telephone usage, medication intake, and meal preparation. Exemplar tasks included loading a pill reminder device, completing a patient record form, activating call forwarding on the telephone, and following instructions for use of a microwave. Sizable correlations were found between performance on the observational tasks and the mental abilities of fluid intelligence, crystallized intelligence, and psychomotor speed, with the largest correlations for fluid and crystallized intelligence. Path analyses showed that the aged's performance on measures of fluid intelligence was the strongest correlate of their practical problem-solving performance. The effects of psychomotor speed and memory span were mediated by their standing on fluid and crystallized intelligence. Age affected older adults' performance both directly and indirectly via its effect on cognitive abilities. The effect of educational level and health on practical problem solving was indirect via its impact on ability performance.

PSYCHOMETRIC INTELLIGENCE AND HEALTH

One of the first subjects that seems worthy of inquiry when one is concerned with the antecedents of individual differences in cognitive aging is the impact of health on cognition. The relationship between health and intellectual functioning is, however, not necessarily unidirectional. Recent reviews of the literature (Elias, Elias, & Elias, 1990; Siegler, 1988), suggest that this relationship may be reciprocal, that is, a healthy body facilitates intellectual competence and competent behavior facilitates the maintenance of health. Hence, we will consider the diseases that seem to affect the maintenance of cognitive functions but will also consider the role of intellectual functioning as a predictor of health status and health behaviors.

■ Relation to Health Status

The impact of disease on cognitive functioning was studied in a dissertation by Ann Gruber-Baldini (1991; also see Schaie, 1995, Chapter 10) for a sample of 845 subjects from the SLS who had been followed over at least 7 years. Prior research has suggested that ratings of poor overall health predict lowered cognitive functioning. In this study, measures of the number of chronic conditions, total number of physician visits, and number of days spent in hospital were examined. The number of chronic conditions had a negative influence on the performance level for verbal meaning, number, and word fluency and predicted a greater decline on verbal meaning and number. A greater number of physician visits predicted an increased likelihood of cognitive decline for reasoning and a later age of onset of decline for number.

Cardiovascular Disease

Research on the relation of specific diseases to cognitive functioning has focused mostly on cardiovascular disease (CVD), and in particular upon hypertension. Mixed results were found as to the direction of influence of hypertension on cognition. Earlier studies in the literature suggested that more severe CVD (atherosclerosis, cerebrovascular disease, etc.) has a negative impact on cognitive functioning (Hertzog, Schaie, & Gribben, 1978). However, much of this research was cross-sectional. Longitudinal studies in this area have often involved small samples, included a limited number of testing occasions (i.e., fewer than three points), failed to compare hypertension groups to groups with more severe CVD, and did not have information on cognitive functioning prior to disease onset.

In the analyses summarized here, multiple CVD groups were examined for the influence of the disease on cognitive functioning. Atherosclerosis was found to be associated with lower cognitive functioning and greater decline on space and number. Cerebrovascular disease was also negatively associated with cognitive level and increased the risk of and amount of cognitive decline. Hypertensives with other CVD complications performed more poorly over time than did uncomplicated hypertensives and normotensives. Noncomplicated hypertensives had higher performances and less decline than did complicated hypertensives and normotensives. The total number of hypertension episodes predicted an increased hazard of significant decline and overall level on word fluency but significantly later decline onset for spatial orientation and reasoning. Benign CVD was associated with a relatively lower rate of cognitive decline. Thus, the more serious CVD conditions (atherosclerosis and cerebrovascular disease) have generally negative influences, while benign CVD has more positive influences on cognition.

Arthritis

Only a few studies have examined the influence of arthritis on cognitive functioning, despite the high prevalence of this disease among the aged. Our results suggest that arthritics have lower functioning and greater decline on verbal meaning, spatial orientation, and inductive reasoning. Arthritis had a direct negative effect on spatial orientation level and change over 7 years. Dividing arthritics by age of onset, we found that persons who developed arthritis after age 60 had lower levels of and greater decline on verbal meaning, while persons who developed arthritis before age 60 had lower levels of and greater decline on inductive reasoning. A mixed pattern resulted for spatial orientation, with pre-60 arthritics experiencing greater decline while the post-60 group had lower overall levels of functioning by age 81.

Neoplasms (Tumors)

In prior research on neoplasms, Stone (1980) found that the presence of neoplasms had a positive effect on cognitive performance in the SLS, but she combined both benign and malignant tumors. The analysis described here distinguished between malignant and benign neoplasms and between skin (the most frequent) and other neoplasms. Results suggest that the positive effects found by Stone might be due to the high frequency of benign neoplasms. Persons with benign neoplasms (other than skin tumors) were found to have earlier onset of decline but less overall decline. Persons with malignant neoplasms and benign skin neoplasms had indirect negative influences on performance (through reduced activity). Results of the influence of neoplasms on cognition might be specific to type (malignant versus nonmalignant) as well as location (skin, bone, etc.) of the tumor.

Other Chronic Conditions

Also related to cognitive functioning were osteoporosis, hip fractures, and sensory problems. Osteoporosis and hip fractures were predictive of earlier decline on word fluency. Hearing impairment was associated with an increased risk of experiencing verbal meaning decline but with better performance and later decline on space. Vision difficulties predicted later age at onset of decline for verbal meaning and space.

In summary, because chronic diseases impose limitations on active lifestyles, they also tend to influence performance on measures of psychometric intelligence. This has been demonstrated most clearly for cardiovascular disease, arthritis, and diabetes.

■ Relation to Health Behaviors

Why are older adults with higher levels of mental functioning often in better health, and why do they suffer from fewer chronic diseases? Higher mental ability performance is associated with higher levels of education, occupational status, and income (Schaie, 1990). Adults who are advantaged in terms of education, occupation, and income often have access to better health care and have the financial resources to purchase such services. On the other hand, higher levels of mental ability may facilitate the acquisition of knowledge both about desirable health behaviors and practices (e.g., good nutrition, medical checkups, exercise) and about risk behaviors (e.g., smoking, excessive drinking, obesity) associated with certain chronic diseases (Park, 1992; Park & Kidder, 1995; Perlmutter & Nyquist, 1990; Rakowski, Julius, Hickey, & Halter, 1987). Likewise, those with higher levels of mental ability may be more likely to believe that they have control over their health and well-being (Prohaska, Leventhal, Leventhal, & Keller, 1985; Wallston & Wallston, 1982).

In a recent study within the ADEPT project, we have examined mental abilities as predictors of health behaviors and practices (Maier, McGuire, & Willis, 1994). We also examined whether internal locus of control beliefs were associated with health behaviors. Four classes of health behaviors were studied: substance abuse (e.g., smoking, alcohol consumption), positive nutrition behaviors (e.g., dietary reduction of sodium and fat), medical checkups (e.g., cholesterol, mammography/prostate, colon/rectal exams), and self-initiated health behaviors (e.g., exercise, use of seat belts, dental care). Older adults who had performed at a higher level on fluid and crystallized abilities several years previously were found to be more likely to engage in positive nutritional practices and to be more likely to engage in self-initiated health behaviors. Mental abilities were significant predictors of subsequent health practices even after age and educational level were taken into account. In contrast, mental abilities were not associated with avoiding certain risk behaviors. In addition, older adults with higher internal control beliefs also were more likely to engage regularly in health-promoting practices and behaviors.

Once again, these findings suggest a hierarchical relationship between mental abilities and everyday intelligence as reflected in health behaviors and practices. Higher ability functioning is a predictor of greater likelihood of engaging in positive health behaviors, particularly those behaviors initiated and under the control of the individual, such as good nutritional practices and health maintenance activities (e.g., exercise, dental care). Mental ability accounts for only a portion of the individual differences in health behaviors and practices. Certainly, factors in the physical and social environment (access to health care, cultural and ethnic variables), as well as the adult's personality traits and motivations, influence health behaviors, as does mental ability (Siegler & Costa, 1985). Nevertheless, the findings of mental ability as a significant predictor of practical problem solving in a variety of domains (health behaviors, nutrition, finances, transportation) argue for the importance of research to chart the course of mental functioning in old age. It would appear that decline in mental functioning in old age not only is of concern for cognition in the narrow sense but has implications for the individual's ability to engage in the everyday problem solving required in order to live independently in our society.

REVERSIBILITY OF DECLINE IN PSYCHOMETRIC INTELLIGENCE

In earlier sections of this chapter we reported findings indicating that there are wide individual differences in the rate and timing of decline in mental abilities. Contrary to ageist stereotypes suggesting that most older adults experience pervasive cognitive decline by the early 60s, the findings of longitudinal research indicate that decline in mental abilities does not begin on average until the mid-60s and that it occurs primarily for abilities involving abstract reasoning and speeded responding (i.e., fluid abilities). In contrast, decline in verbal abilities (i.e., crystallized abilities) occurs later, beginning on average in the mid-70s. Findings based on group means, however, are deceptive and mask the wide individual differences in when ability decline begins to occur for a given individual.

Age-related decline in mental abilities, even though not pathological in nature, can have serious consequences for the older adult. As we have reported, there are significant relationships between level of performance on mental abilities and a variety of tasks of daily living (e.g., managing one's finances, taking medication). Decline in the salient mental abilities can jeopardize the elderly's ability to carry out the tasks of daily living required to live independently in our society. In addition, our findings suggest that mental abilities are significant predictors of health behaviors that are important to maintaining one's health and preventing certain chronic diseases.

Even older adults who have not suffered a decline in mental abilities may be somewhat at risk for carrying out tasks involving technological advances and or new information and strategies. In previous sections, cohort differences in mental ability level have been reported. Positive cohort trends for abilities such as inductive reasoning have been shown. As a result, even older adults who have experienced no decline on inductive reasoning will be disadvantaged compared with younger cohorts, who on average perform at higher ability levels. Previous research has indicated that inductive reasoning is an important predictor of mastering new technologies, particularly those involving the computer (e.g., word processing, graphics creation; Garfein et al., 1988; Jay & Willis, 1992).

Are there behavioral interventions that could enhance older adults' mental ability functioning? While the significance of interventions that remediate ability decline appears obvious, interventions that improve the functioning of older adults with no prior ability decline are also important because of cohort differences in level of functioning. Our focus here is on interventions for community-dwelling older adults who are healthy and have no known neuropathologies. Certain chronic diseases are known to result in cognitive decline, and we are not suggesting that behavioral interventions would be successful in overcoming the impact of serious chronic diseases. Nevertheless, most older adults do not suffer from neuropathologies or multiple serious chronic diseases.

During the past two decades in cognitive aging research, there have been a number of studies that have demonstrated that behavioral interventions are effective in significantly improving the community-dwelling elderly's cognitive performance. Significant training effects have been reported for remembering names (Yesavage, Lapp, & Sheikh, 1989), episodic memory (Bäckman, Mantyla, & Herlitz, 1990), problem-solving tasks (Denney, 1982), memory span (Kliegl, Smith, & Baltes, 1990), perceptual speed (Hoyer, Labouvie, & Baltes, 1973) and fluid abilities (Baltes & Lindenberger, 1988; Willis, 1987; Willis & Schaie, 1994).

Virtually all of these training studies have focused on cognitive processes and abilities that show early normative patterns of decline. Hence, the assumption has often been made that improvement with training reflects primarily a remediation or reactivation of previous cognitive skill levels. Longitudinal research findings, however, suggest that such assumptions are too simplistic, given the wide individual differences in rate and pattern of decline. The qualitative nature of the training effects differs depending on the prior developmental history of an individual; for those suffering from prior ability decline, training effects may indeed represent remediation, while for those not suffering from prior decline, training gains reflect improvement over prior levels of functioning. In order to study these differential training effects, an intervention study would need to be conducted within an ongoing longitudinal research program so that the prior ability trajectory of the participants would be known and training results could be examined in the light of prior functioning. In the following section, we report on a program of cognitive training research within the Seattle Longitudinal Study that addresses these issues.

■ **Seattle Training Study**

Subjects in the Seattle Training Study, which began in 1984, had been participants in the SLS since 1970 or before (Schaie, 1995; Schaie & Willis, 1986; Willis, 1987; Willis & Schaie, 1994). Subjects' ability performance over the 14 years (1970–1984) prior to training was classified as having remained stable or having declined on two abilities, spatial orientation and inductive reasoning. These two abilities were chosen to be the focus of training for three reasons: (1) they exhibit a relatively early normative decline, (2) they show positive cohorts trends such that even elderly who had not experienced decline might be disadvantaged compared with more recent cohorts, and (3) they have been found to be salient predictors of everyday task performance. Only 22 percent of the subjects had declined on both reasoning and space abilities over the interval 1970–1984, 47 percent had declined on neither ability, and approximately 15 percent had declined on one of the abilities but not on the other. Subjects were assigned to training on reasoning or spatial ability on the basis of their decline status. Subjects who had decline on only one of the abilities were assigned to training on the ability on which they had declined. Subjects who had declined on both abilities or who had remained stable on both abilities were randomly assigned to training on one of the abilities.

The training study involved a pretest–training–posttest design. Following the pretest, subjects participated in five 1-hour training sessions conducted in their homes. The content of these training programs has been described in previous publications (Schaie & Willis, 1986; Willis, 1987, 1990; Willis & Schaie, 1994). A posttest to evaluate training effects was conducted within 1 week of the end of training. A follow-up study was conducted 7 years later, in 1990 (Willis & Schaie, 1994). Subjects were pretested to assess their current level of performance and to examine the question of the temporal durability of training effects. They then took part in booster training on the same ability on which they had been trained in 1983. The booster training was very similar in format to the training program used in 1983. Subjects were posttested following the booster training.

Training Effects for Stable and Decline Subjects

Figure 9.5 (top) presents the mean inductive reasoning scores for stable and decline subjects trained on reasoning on three occasions: (1) in 1970, 14 years prior to training, (2) at the 1984 pretest, immediately before training, and (3) at the 1984 posttest. Similar findings are reported for subjects trained on spatial orientation in the bottom part of the figure (Willis, 1990). In 1970, 14 years prior to training, stable and decline subjects were performing at the same level on each ability. At the 1984 pretest, decline subjects were performing at a significantly lower level. Training resulted in significant performance gain for both stable and decline subjects, as demonstrated in their 1984 posttest performance. The nature of the training effects was qualitatively different for the two groups. For the decliners, training was effective in returning (remediating) their performance close to their 1970 score level. For the stable group, on the other hand, the effect of training was to raise their performance level above that previously demonstrated.

Figure 9.5 presents information on training effects in terms of mean scores. Change or modifiability of mental ability performance is an intraindividual phenomenon, and therefore assessment of training effects at the individual level is of particular interest (Schaie & Willis, 1986; Willis, 1990). Two questions can be examined: First, what proportion of stable and decline subjects demonstrated significant training gain from pretest to posttest? Second, what proportion of decline subjects exhibited remediation to their 1970 score level? With regard to the first question, approximately 50 percent of the subjects in each training group showed significant improvement from pretest to posttest. The second question deals with the proportion of decline subjects showing complete remediation of prior age-related decline. To assess remediation of decline, we examined the proportion of decline subjects whose performance at posttest was equal to or greater than their score fourteen years previously, in 1970. Approximately 40 percent of decline subjects exhibited complete remediation. Thus, the findings indicate that training is effective both for subjects who have decline and for subjects with no prior decline.

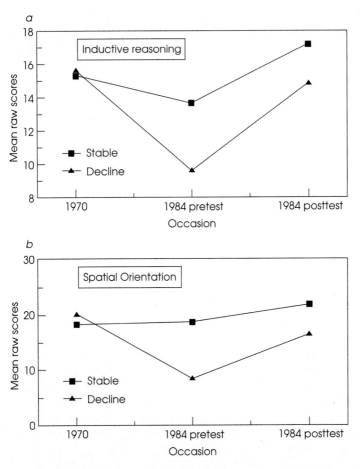

FIGURE 9.5 Mean gain from cognitive training on the abilities of inductive reasoning and spatial orientation. (*Source:* Willis and Schaie, 1994.)

Cohort Differences in Training Effects

Positive cohort trends have been reported for inductive reasoning and to a lesser extent for spatial orientation in cohort sequential research (Schaie, 1983, 1993). If there are cohort differences in level of ability scores, there is the question of whether training effects would differ by age/cohort. We examined training effects on inductive reasoning for three cohorts: the 1903 cohort, the 1910 cohort, and the 1917 cohort. At the time of training, these cohorts were 74, 67, and 60 years of age, respectively. Figure 9.6 shows the mean scores on inductive reasoning at four occasions: 1970, 1977, 1984 pretest, 1984 posttest. Significant age-related decline on inductive reasoning had occurred for the 1903 and 1910 cohorts prior to training (1970–1984 pretest). The performance of the 1917 cohort was relatively stable; they were middle-aged in the 1970–1984 interval. Note that, after training, the 1910 and 1917 cohorts were performing, on average, at a level above their 1970 base. In contrast, for the

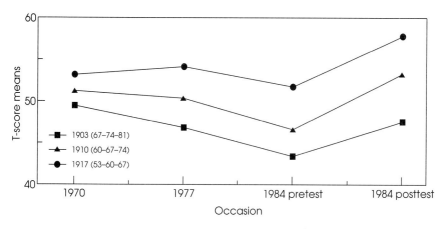

FIGURE 9.6 Cohort differences in training gains. (*Source:* Willis and Schaie, 1994.)

1903 cohort, remediation of age-related decline occurred. Note also that age/cohort differences in level of performance are present at all points of measurement. While training was effective for all three groups, the magnitude of the training effects was not sufficient to eliminate cohort differences.

Durability of Training Outcomes

It is important to consider intervention effects within a life-span context. The concern is not only that significant improvement be demonstrated immediately after training but also whether training has implications for patterns of cognitive development several years after the intervention (Willis & Nesselroade, 1990; Willis & Schaie, 1994). The longitudinal design of the Seattle study permits examination of these issues. Subjects initially trained in 1984 were reassessed in 1991; thus, the maintenance of training effects over a 7-year interval could be examined. Subsequently, subjects were administered booster training in 1991 on the same ability on which they had initially been trained in 1984.

Age-related decline would have been expected to have occurred over the 7-year interval (1984–1991) between initial and booster training, since by 1991 most of our subjects had advanced into old-old age. We were interested in comparing subjects' performance after the 1991 booster training with their performance prior to training in 1984. That is, given the increasing likelihood of age-related decline, was training effective in boosting or maintaining earlier levels of functioning?

After booster training, subjects trained on inductive reasoning were performing at a level above their 1984 pretest scores. Thus, the combined effects of initial training and booster training were sufficient to overcome whatever age-related decline had occurred during the 7-year interval. The durability of training effects was particularly evident for subjects initially classified as having decline on inductive reasoning. The durability of training effects on spatial orientation was somewhat weaker and more differentiated than that found for inductive reasoning. That is, only subjects initially classified as having declined on spatial ability were performing at a level above their 1984 pretest scores. Subjects initially classified as stable were on average functioning at the same level as they had prior to training in 1984.

Summary

Several conclusions regarding the durability of training effects and the potency of successive intervention efforts in 1984 and again in 1991 can be reached (Willis & Schaie, 1994). First, the long-term effects of training were most evident for subjects who had been classified as having declined on the target ability. That is, after booster training, decline subjects involved in each training program were performing at a level above their performance prior to training in 1984. There is suggestive evidence, therefore, that training may be particularly effective if it is begun after subjects begin to evidence decline. Second, training effects after the second training program were somewhat more potent and more durable for inductive reasoning. Both stable and decline subjects trained on inductive reasoning were performing above the level of functioning exhibited prior to training in 1983. Third, more subjects trained on a particular ability were functioning at a higher level on that ability than comparison subjects trained on another ability. That is subjects remained at an advantage on the ability trained in comparison with those not so trained.

SUMMARY AND CONCLUSIONS

This chapter began by placing psychometric intelligence into the broader context of cognitive psychology. We provided a brief historical review and then summarized major issues in the literature on psychometric intelligence by focusing on age differences and age changes in intelligence as well as on individual differences in patterns of change. We suggested that relatively little decline in psychometric abilities can be observed until the 60s are reached but that significant average decline may be observed by the 80s. Cohort (generational) differences in levels of intellectual functioning obscure these findings when attention is given only to age-comparative (cross-sectional) studies conducted at one point in time. As a consequence of the apparent plateauing of cohort effects for some abilities and negative effects for others, we can expect that age differences in adulthood may actually become more compressed over the next decade.

Although our understanding of gender differences in abilities has increased markedly, we still have almost no comparative work on intellectual aging within minority groups in the United States, nor do we have useful cross-cultural comparisons with intellectual aging in other societies. This would be an exciting topic for future research, particularly because cross-cultural research allows variation in the timing of substantial natural experiments (e.g., Great Depression, Cultural Revolution, and so on), that may affect intellectual aging; the Berlin BASE study (Baltes, Mayer, Helmchen, & Steinhagen-Thiessen, 1993) is a notable example.

We next focused on the field of practical intelligence. We described some work that has identified the dimensions of practical intelligence and examined the processes that link expressions of practical intelligence to the basic abilities, combinations and permutations of which are likely to remain the common denominators in any attempt to predict performance on everyday tasks and on the dimensions essential to independent living.

We then noted the manner in which intellectual competence is effected by health status and identified the deleterious role of chronic diseases in accelerating intellectual decline. But we also noted the importance of good intellectual competence in facilitating health behaviors which may delay the onset of chronic disease and exacerbate its severity.

Cognitive intervention efforts have been successful in showing that intellectual decline in old age is not necessarily irreversible, and it has been demonstrated that formal intervention strategies exist that may help to extend maintenance of high levels of intellectual function in community-dwelling elders. The cognitive intervention research has also shown that much of the cognitive decline observed in the elderly may be due to disuse and is at least in part reversible. The effects of cognitive training have been shown to persist for as long as 7 years. The cognitive intervention techniques must now be transferred from the laboratory into a broader social context, whether by making laboratory training paradigms more widely accessible or by taking advantage of prescribed leisure activities that are both cognitively challenging and indigenous to the daily experience of older persons.

SUPPLEMENTAL READINGS

Lindenberger, U. (1994). Intellectual aging. In R. J. Sternberg (Ed.), *Encyclopedia of intelligence* (pp. 52–56). New York: Macmillan.

Schaie, K. W. (1994). The course of adult intellectual development. *American Psychologist, 49,* 304–313.

Willis, S. L. (1990). Current issues in cognitive training research. In E. A. Lovelace (Ed.), *Aging and cognition: Mental processes, self-awareness, and interventions* (pp. 263–280). New York: North-Holland.

REFERENCES

Anastasi, A. (1976). *Psychological testing* (4th ed.). New York: Macmillan.

Bäckman, L., Mantyla, T., & Herlitz, A. (1990). The optimization of episodic remembering in old age. In P. B. Baltes & M. M. Baltes (Eds.), *Successful aging: Perspectives from the behavioral sciences* (pp. 118–163). New York: Cambridge Univ. Press.

Baltes, P. B., Dittmann-Kohli, F., & Dixon, R. A. (1984). New perspectives on the development of intelligence in adulthood: Toward a dual-process conception and a model of selective optimization and compensation. In P. B. Baltes & O. G. Brim, Jr. (Eds.), *Life-span development and behavior* (vol. 6, pp. 34–77). Orlando, FL: Academic Press.

Baltes, P. B., & Lindenberger, U. (1988). On the range of cognitive plasticity in old age as a function of experience: 15 years of intervention research. *Behavior Therapy, 19,* 283–300.

Baltes, P. B., Mayer, K. U., Helmchen, H., & Steinhagen-Thiessen, E. (1993). The Berlin Aging Study (BASE): Overview and design. *Ageing and Society, 13,* 483–533.

Baltes, P. B., & Willis, S. L. (1982). Enhancement (plasticity) of intellectual functioning: Penn State's Adult Development and Enrichment Project (ADEPT). In F. I. M. Craik & S. Trehub (Eds.), *Aging and cognitive processes* (pp. 353–389). New York: Plenum.

Bayley, N., & Oden, M. H. (1955). The maintenance of intellectual ability in gifted adults. *Journal of Gerontology, 10,* 91–107.

Berg, C. A., & Sternberg, R. J. (1985). A triarchic theory of intellectual development during adulthood. *Developmental Review, 5,* 334–370.

Berry, J., & Irvine, S. (1986). Bricolage: Savages do it daily. In R. Sternberg & R. Wagner (Eds.), *Practical intelligence* (pp. 271–306). New York: Cambridge Univ. Press.

Binet, A., & Simon, T. (1905). Méthodes nouvelles pour le diagnostic du niveau intellectuel des anormaux. *L'Année Psychologique, 11,* 191.

Brooks, J., & Weintraub, M. (1976). A history of infant intelligence testing. In M. Lewis (Ed.), *Origins of intelligence* (pp. 25–66). New York: Plenum.

Busse, E. W. (1993). Duke Longitudinal Studies of Aging. *Zeitschrift für Gerontologie, 26,* 123–128.

Camp, C., Doherty, K, Moody-Thomas, S., & Denney, N. (1989). Practical problem solving in adults: A comparison of problem types and scoring methods. In J. Sinnott (Ed.), *Everyday problem solving: Theory and applications* (pp. 211–228). New York: Praeger.

Capon, N., & Kuhn, D. (1982). Can consumers calculate best buys? *Journal of Consumer Research, 8,* 449–453.

Carroll, J. B. (1993). *Human cognitive abilities: A survey of factor-analytic studies.* New York: Cambridge Univ. Press.

Cattell, R. B. (Ed.) (1987). *Intelligence: Its structure, growth and action.* Amsterdam: North-Holland.

Cavanaugh, J. (1983). Comprehension and retention of television programs by 20- and 60-year olds. *Journal of Gerontology, 38,* 190–196.

Charlesworth, W. (1976). Intelligence as adaptation: A theological approach. In L. Resnick (Ed.), *The nature of intelligence* (pp. 147–168). Norwood, NJ: Ablex.

Clark, J., Lanphear, A., & Riddick, C. (1987). The effects of video game playing on the response selection processing of elderly adults. *Journal of Gerontology, 42,* 82–85.

Cornelius, S. W. (1984). Classic pattern of intellectual aging: Test familiarity, difficulty, and performance. *Journal of Gerontology, 39,* 201–206.

Cornelius, S. W., & Caspi, A. (1987). Everyday problem solving in adulthood and old age. *Psychology and Aging, 2,* 144–153.

Costa, P. T., Jr., & McCrae, R. R. (1993). Psychological research in the Baltimore Longitudinal Study of Aging. *Zeitschrift für Gerontologie, 26,* 138–141.

Cronbach, L. J. (1970). *Essentials of psychological testing* (3d ed.). New York: Harper and Row.

Crook, T. H., & West, R. (1990). Name recall performance across the adult life-span. *British Journal of Psychology, 81,* 335–349.

Cunningham, W. N. (1987). Intellectual abilities and age. In K. W. Schaie (Ed.), *Annual review of gerontology and geriatrics* (vol. 7, pp. 117–134). New York: Springer.

DeFries, J. C., Ashton, G. C., Johnson, R. C., Kusi, A. R., McClearn, G. E., Mi, M. P., Rashad, M. N., Vandenberg, S. G., & Wilson, J. R. (1976). Parent-offspring resemblance for specific cognitive abilities in two ethnic groups. *Nature, 261* (5556), 131–133.

Denney, N. (1982). Aging and cognitive changes. In B. B. Wolman (Ed.), *Handbook of developmental psychology* (pp. 807–827). Englewood Cliffs, NJ: Prentice-Hall.

Diehl, M., Willis, S. L., & Schaie, K. W. (1995). Older adults' everyday competence: Observational assessment and cognitive correlates. *Psychology and Aging, 10,* 478–491.

Educational Testing Service (1977). *Basic Skills Assessment Test: Reading.* Princeton, NJ: Author.

Eichorn, D. H., Clausen, J. A., Haan, N., Honzik, M. P., & Mussen, P. H. (1981). *Present and past in middle life.* New York: Academic Press.

Elias, M. F., Elias, J. W., & Elias, P. K. (1990). Biological and health influences upon behavior. In J. E. Birren & K. W. Schaie (Eds.), *Handbook of the psychology of aging* (3d ed., pp. 79–102). New York: Academic Press.

Ekstrom, R. B., French, J. W., Harman, H., & Derman, D. (1976). *Kit of factor-referenced cognitive tests* (rev. ed.). Princeton, NJ: Educational Testing Service.

Field, D., Schaie, K. W., & Leino, E. V. (1988). Continuity in intellectual functioning: The role of self-reported health. *Psychology and Aging, 3,* 385–392.

Fillenbaum, G. (1985). Screening the elderly: A brief instrumental activities of daily living measure. *Journal of the American Geriatrics Society, 33,* 698–706.

Frank, G. (1983). *The Wechsler enterprise: An assessment of the development, structure, and use of the Wechsler tests of intelligence.* Oxford: Pergamon.

Galton, F. (1869). *Hereditary genius.* London: Macmillan.

Garfein, A. J., Schaie, K. W., & Willis, S. L. (1988). Microcomputer proficiency in later-middle-aged and older adults: Teaching old dogs new tricks. *Social Behavior, 3,* 131–148.

Gonda, J., Quayhagen, M., & Schaie, K. W. (1981). Education, task meaningfulness and cognitive performance in young-old and old-old adults. *Educational Gerontology, 7,* 151–158.

Grisso, T. (1986). *Evaluating competencies: Forensic assessment and instruments.* New York: Plenum.

Gruber-Baldini, A. L. (1991). *The impact of health and disease on cognitive ability in adulthood and old age in the Seattle Longitudinal Study.* Unpublished doctoral dissertation, Pennsylvania State University, University Park.

Hall, G. S. (1922). *Senescence, the last half of life.* New York: Appleton.

Hertzog, C., Schaie, K. W., & Gribbin, K. (1978). Cardiovascular disease and changes in intellectual functioning from middle to old age. *Journal of Gerontology, 33,* 872–883.

Hollingsworth, H. L. (1927). *Mental growth and decline: A survey of developmental psychology.* New York: Appleton.

Horn, J. L., and Hofer, S. M. (1992). Major abilities and development in the adult period. In R. J. Sternberg and C. A. Berg (Eds.), *Intellectual development* (pp. 44–99). Cambridge: Cambridge Univ. Press.

Hoyer, W., Labouvie, G., & Baltes, P. B. (1973). Modification of response speed and intellectual performance in the elderly. *Human Development, 16,* 233–242.

Jarvik, L. F., Kallmann, F. J., & Falek, A. (1962). Intellectual changes in aged twins. *Journal of Gerontology, 17,* 289–294.

Jay, G. M., & Willis, S. L. (1992). Influence of direct computer experience on older adults computer attitudes. *Journal of Gerontology: Psychological Sciences, 47,* P250–P257.

Johansson, B., & Berg, S. (1989). The robustness of the terminal decline phenomenon: Longitudinal data from the digit-span test. *Journal of Gerontology: Psychological Sciences, 44,* P184–186.

Jones, H. E., & Conrad, H. S. (1933). The growth and decline of intelligence: A study of a homogenous group between the ages of ten and sixty. *Genetic Psychology Monographs, 13,* 223–298.

Kamin, L. J. (1974). *The science and politics of IQ.* Hillsdale, NJ: Erlbaum.

Kaufman, A. S., Kaufman, J. L., McLean, J. E., & Reynolds, C. R. (1991). Is the pattern of intellectual growth and decline across the adult life span different for men and women? *Journal of Clinical Psychology, 47,* 801–812.

Kliegl, R., Smith, J., & Baltes, P. B. (1990). On the locus and process of magnification of age differences during mnemonic training. *Developmental Psychology, 26,* 894–904.

Labouvie-Vief, G. (1985). Intelligence and cognition. In J. E. Birren & K. W. Schaie (Eds.), *Handbook of the psychology of aging* (2d ed., pp. 500–530). New York: Van Nostrand Reinhold.

Lawton, M. P., & Brody, E. M. (1969). Assessment of older people: Self-maintaining and instrumental activities of daily living. *Gerontologist, 9,* 179–185.

Lindenberger, U. (1994). Intellectual aging. In R. J. Sternberg (Ed.), *Encyclopedia of intelligence* (pp. 52–56). New York: Macmillan.

Lindenberger, U., Mayr, U., & Kliegl, R. (1993). Speed and intelligence in old age. *Psychology and Aging, 8,* 207–220.

Maier, H., McGuire, L. C., & Willis, S. L. (1994, April). *Everyday competence as a correlate of health behaviors in late life.* Poster presented at the Fifth Cognitive Aging Conference, Atlanta, GA.

Marsiske, M., & Willis, S. L. (1995). Dimensionality of everyday problem solving in older adults. *Psychology and Aging, 10,* 269–283.

Matarazzo, J. D. (1972). *Wechsler's measurement and appraisal of adult intelligence.* Baltimore: Williams and Wilkins.

McArdle, J. J., Hamagami, F., Elias, M. F., & Robbins, M. A. (1991). Structural modeling of mixed longitudinal and cross-sectional data. *Experimental Aging Research, 17,* 29–52.

Owens, W. A. J. (1953). Age and mental abilities: A longitudinal study. *Genetic Psychology Monographs, 48,* 3–54.

Owens, W. A. J. (1959). Is age kinder to the initially more able? *Journal of Gerontology, 14,* 334–337.

Palmore, E., Busse, E. W., Maddox, G. L., Nowlin, J. B., & Siegler, I. C. (1985). *Normal aging* (vol. 3). Durham, NC: Duke Univ. Press.

Park, D. C. (1992). Applied cognitive aging research. In F. I. M. Craik & T. A. Salthouse (Eds.), *The handbook of cognition and aging* (pp. 449–493). Hillsdale, NJ: Erlbaum.

Park, D. C., & Kidder, K. (1995). Prospective memory and medication adherence. In M. Brandimont, G. Einstein, & M. McDaniel (Eds.), *Prospective memory: Theory and applications*. Hillsdale, NJ: Erlbaum.

Park, D. C., & Mayhorn, C. B. (1994). Remembering to take medications: The importance of nonmemory variables. In D. Hermann, M. Johnson, C. McEvoy, C. Hertzog, & P. Hurtle (Eds.), *Research on practical aspects of memory* (vol. 2). Hillsdale, NJ: Erlbaum.

Perlmutter, M., & Nyquist, L. (1990). Relationships between self-reported physical and mental health and intelligence performance across adulthood. *Journal of Gerontology: Psychological Sciences, 45*, P145–P155.

Plomin, R., & McClearn, G. E. (1990). Human behavioral genetics of aging. In J. E. Birren & K. W. Schaie (Eds.), *Handbook of the psychology of aging* (3d ed., pp. 67–79). New York: Academic Press.

Puckett, J. M., & Reese, H. W. (Eds.) (1993). *Lifespan developmental psychology: Mechanisms of everyday cognition*. Hillsdale, NJ: Erlbaum.

Pressey, S. L., Janney, J. E., & Kuhlen, R. G. (1939). *Life: A psychological survey*. New York: Hayer.

Prohaska, T. R., Leventhal, E. A., Leventhal, H., & Keller, M. L. (1985). Health practices and illness cognition in young, middle-aged, and elderly adults. *Journal of Gerontology, 40*, 569–578.

Rakowski, W., Julius, M., Hickey, T., & Halter, J. B. (1987). Correlates of preventive health behavior in late life. *Research on Aging, 9*, 331–335.

Rice, G. E., Meyer, B. F., & Miller, D. (1988). Relation of everyday activities of adults to their prose recall performance. *Educational Gerontology, 14*, 147–158.

Riegel, K. F. (1977). History of psychological gerontology. In J. E. Birren & K. W. Schaie (Eds.), *Handbook of the psychology of aging* (pp. 70–102). New York: Van Nostrand Reinhold.

Salthouse, T. A. (1990). Cognitive competence and expertise in aging. In J. E. Birren & K. W. Schaie (Eds.), *Handbook of the psychology of aging* (3d ed., pp. 310–319). New York: Academic Press.

Salthouse, T., and Maurer, T. J. (1996). Aging, job performance, and career development. In J. E. Birren and K. W. Schaie (Eds.), *Handbook of the psychology of aging* (4th ed.). San Diego: Academic Press.

Sattler, J. M. (1982). Age effects on Wechsler Adult Intelligence Scale-Revised Tests. *Journal of Consulting and Clinical Psychology, 50*, 785–786.

Schaie, K. W. (1958). Rigidity-flexibility and intelligence: A cross-sectional study of the adult life-span from 20 to 70. *Psychological Monographs, 72*(462), whole no. 9.

Schaie, K. W. (1978). External validity in the assessment of intellectual performance in adulthood. *Journal of Gerontology, 33*, 695–701.

Schaie, K. W. (1983). The Seattle Longitudinal Study: A twenty-one year exploration of psychometric intelligence in adulthood. In K. W. Schaie (Eds.), *Longitudinal studies of adult psychological development* (pp. 64–135). New York: Guilford Press.

Schaie, K. W. (1985). *Manual for the Schaie-Thurstone Adult Mental Abilities Test (STAMAT)*. Palo Alto, CA: Consulting Psychologists Press.

Schaie, K. W. (1987). Application of psychometric intelligence to the prediction of everyday competence in the elderly. In C. Schooler & K. W. Schaie (Eds.), *Cognitive functioning and social structure over the life course* (pp. 50–58). New York: Ablex.

Schaie, K. W. (1989). The hazards of cognitive aging. *Gerontologist, 29,* 484–493.

Schaie, K. W. (1990). Intellectual development in adulthood. In J. E. Birren & K. W. Schaie (Eds.), *Handbook of the psychology of aging* (3d ed., pp. 291–309). New York: Academic Press.

Schaie, K. W. (1993). The Seattle Longitudinal Study: A thirty-five year inquiry of adult intellectual development. *Zeitschrift für Gerontologie, 26,* 129–137.

Schaie, K. W. (1994). The course of adult intellectual development. *American Psychologist, 49,* 304–313.

Schaie, K. W. (1995). *Intellectual development in adulthood: The Seattle Longitudinal Study.* New York: Cambridge Univ. Press.

Schaie, K. W., & Hertzog, C. (1983). Fourteen-year cohort-sequential studies of adult intellectual development. *Developmental Psychology, 19,* 531–543.

Schaie, K. W., & Hertzog, C. (1986). Toward a comprehensive model of adult intellectual development: Contributions of the Seattle Longitudinal Study. In R. J. Sternberg (Ed.), *Advances in Human Intelligence* (vol. 3, pp. 79–118). Hillsdale, NJ: Erlbaum.

Schaie, K. W., Plomin, R., Willis, S. L., Gruber-Baldini, A., & Dutta, R. (1992). Natural cohorts: Family similarity in adult cognition. In T. Sonderegger (Ed.), *Psychology and aging: Nebraska Symposium on Motivation, 1991* (pp. 205–243). Lincoln: Univ. of Nebraska Press.

Schaie, K. W., & Strother, C. R. (1968). A cross-sequential study of age changes in cognitive behavior. *Psychological Bulletin, 70,* 671–680.

Schaie, K. W., & Willis, S. L. (1986). Can intellectual decline in the elderly be reversed? *Developmental Psychology, 22,* 223–232.

Schaie, K. W., & Willis, S. L. (1996). *Adult development and aging* (4th ed.). New York: HarperCollins.

Shock, N. W., Greulick, R. C., Andres, R., Arenberg, D., Costa, P. T., Lakatta, E. G., & Tobin, J. D. (1984). *Normal human aging: The Baltimore Longitudinal Study of Aging.* Washington, DC: U.S. Government Printing Office.

Siegler, I. C. (1983). Psychological aspects of the Duke Longitudinal Studies. In K. W. Schaie (Ed.), *Longitudinal studies of adult psychological development* (pp. 136–190). New York: Guilford.

Siegler, I. E. (1988). *Developmental health psychology.* Master lecture presented as part of a series on "The adult years: Continuity and change." Annual Meeting of the American Psychological Association, August.

Siegler, I. E., & Costa, P. T., Jr. (1985). Health behavior relationships. In J. E. Birren & K. W. Schaie (Eds.), *Handbook of the psychology of aging* (2d ed., pp. 144–168). New York: Van Nostrand Reinhold.

Sinnott, J. D. (1989). *Everyday problem solving: Theory and applications.* New York: Praeger.

Sternberg, R. (1985). *Beyond IQ: A triarchic theory of human intelligence.* New York: Cambridge Univ. Press.

Sternberg, R., & Wagner, B. (Eds.) (1986). *Practical intelligence: Origins of competence in the everyday world.* London: Cambridge Univ. Press.

Stone, V. (1980). *Structural modeling of the relations among environmental variables, health status and intelligence in adulthood.* Unpubl. doctoral dissertation. University of Southern California, Los Angeles, CA.

Storandt, M., & Futterman, A. (1982). Stimulus size and performance on two subtests of the Wechsler Adult Intelligence Scale by younger and older adults. *Journal of Gerontology, 37,* 602–693.

Terman, L. M. (1916). *The measurement of intelligence.* Boston: Houghton.

Thurstone, L. L., & Thurstone, T. G. (1949). *Examiner Manual for the SRA Primary Mental Abilities Test* (Form 10-14). Chicago: Science Research Associates.

Tosti-Vsey, J. L., Person, D. C., Maier, H., & Willis, S. L. (1992, November). *The relationship of game playing to intellectual ability in old age.* Paper presented at the annual meeting of the Gerontological Society of America, Washington, D. C.

Wagner, R. (1976). The search for intraterrestrial intelligence. In R. J. Sternberg & R. K. Wagner (Eds.), *Practical intelligence: Nature and origins of competence in the everyday world* (pp. 361–378). New York: Cambridge Univ. Press.

Wallston, K. A., & Wallston, B. S. (1982). Who is responsible for your health? The construct of health locus of control. In G. S. Sanders & J. Suls (Eds.), *Social psychology of health and illness* (pp. 65–95). Hillsdale, NJ: Erlbaum.

Wechsler, D. (1939). *The measurement of adult intelligence.* Baltimore: Williams and Wilkins.

West, R., & Sinnott, J. D. (Eds.) (1992). *Everyday memory and aging: Current research and methodology.* New York: Springer.

Willis, S. L. (1987). Cognitive interventions in the elderly. In K. W. Schaie (Ed.), *Annual review of gerontology and geriatrics* (vol. 7, pp. 159–188). New York: Springer.

Willis, S. L. (1989). Cohort differences in cognitive aging: A sample case. In K. W. Schaie & C. Schooler (Eds.), *Social structure and aging: Psychological processes* (pp. 95–112). New York: Erlbaum.

Willis, S. L. (1990). Current issues in cognitive training research. In E. A. Lovelace (Ed.), *Aging and cognition: Mental processes, self-awareness, and interventions* (pp. 263–280). New York: North-Holland.

Willis, S. L. (1991). Cognition and everyday competence. In K. W. Schaie and M. P. Lawton (Eds.), *Annual review of gerontology and geriatrics* (vol. 11, pp. 80–109). New York: Springer.

Willis, S. L., Jay, G. M., Diehl, M., & Marsiske, M. (1992). Longitudinal change and the prediction of everyday task competence in the elderly. *Research on Aging, 14,* 68–91.

Willis, S. L., & Marsiske, M. (1991). Life span perspective on practical intelligence. In D. E. Tupper & K. D. Cicerone (Eds.), *The neuropsychology of everyday life: Issues in development and rehabilitation* (pp. 183–198). Boston: Kluwer.

Willis, S. L., & Marsiske, M. (1993). *Manual for the Everyday Problems Test (EPT).* University Park: Pennsylvania State Univ.

Willis, S. L., & Nesselroade, C. S. (1990). Long-term effects of fluid ability training in old-old age. *Developmental Psychology, 26,* 905–910.

Willis, S. L., & Schaie, K. W. (1986). Practical intelligence in later adulthood. In R. J. Sternberg & R. K. Wagner (Eds.), *Practical intelligence: Nature and origins of competence in the everyday world* (pp. 236–268). New York: Cambridge Univ. Press.

Willis, S. L., & Schaie, K. W. (1988). Gender differences in spatial ability in old age: Longitudinal and intervention findings. *Sex Roles, 18,* 189–203.

Willis, S. L., & Schaie, K. W. (1993). Everyday cognition: Taxonomic and methodological considerations. In J. M. Puckett & H. W. Reese (Eds.), *Mechanisms of everyday cognition* (pp. 33–54). Hillsdale, NJ: Erlbaum.

Willis, S. L., & Schaie, K. W. (1994). Cognitive training in the normal elderly. In F. Forette, Y. Christen, & F. Boller (Eds.), *Plasticité cérébrale et stimulation cognitive* [Cerebral plasticity and cognitive stimulation] (pp. 91–113). Paris: Fondation Nationale de Gérontologie.

Yerkes, R. M. (1921). Psychological examining in the United States Army. *Memoirs of the National Academy of Sciences, 15,* 1–890.

Yesavage, J. A., Lapp, D. & Sheikh, J. I. (1989). Mnemonics as modified for use by the elderly. In L. W. Poon, D. C. Rubin, & B. A. Wilson (Eds.), *Everyday cognition in adulthood and late life* (pp. 598–614). New York: Cambridge Univ. Press.

10

PRACTICAL INTELLIGENCE AND PROBLEM SOLVING: SEARCHING FOR PERSPECTIVES

Cynthia A. Berg
University of Utah

Paul A. Klaczynski
Western Carolina University

In the last 10 years, increasing attention has been given, at both the conceptual and empirical levels, to the practical origins and functions of intelligence and problem solving (see, e.g., Galotti, 1989; Poon, Rubin, & Wilson, 1989; Rogoff & Lave, 1984; Sinnott, 1989b; Sternberg & Wagner, 1986). The impetus for this new field of "practical problem solving" (also referred to as "practical intelligence," "everyday intelligence," and "everyday problem solving") has come from diverse theoretical and research directions. A common thread running throughout these literatures is a desire to understand the form and content of intellectual development during adolescence and adulthood, and skepticism toward the application of "traditional" models and measures of intelligence to adult intellectual functioning.

Numerous theorists have raised concern (see, e.g., Baltes, Dittmann-Kohli, & Dixon, 1984; Berg & Sternberg, 1985; Cavanaugh, Kramer, Sinnott, Camp, & Markley, 1985; Demming & Pressey, 1957; Labouvie-Vief, 1992) regarding the use of traditional measures of intelligence to assess the mental functioning of adults. For instance, Baltes et al. (1984) propose that "with aging . . . domains of psychological functioning other than performance on intelligence tests gain in relative significance" (p. 50). Because intelligence tests were designed to predict the academic success of children, theorists argue that these tests are inappropriate for use with adults, who are no longer in an academic environment. Rather, measures of adult intelligence should assess the skills and knowledge that adults need to function in everyday life.

Recent theories of adult intellectual development that come from divergent philosophical perspectives view practical problem solving as central to understanding intelligence. For instance, practical problem solving is integral to many postformal (Commons, Richards, & Armon, 1984; Labouvie-Vief, 1992) and contextual (Baltes, 1987; Berg & Sternberg, 1985;

Dixon, 1992) theories of adult intelligence. These views of the importance of assessing the practical skills of adults are shared by laypersons' views of what constitutes intelligence (see, e.g., Berg & Sternberg, 1992).

Given the diversity of the directions that inspired this recent interest in practical problem solving, it should not be surprising that a variety of definitions and distinctions exist regarding the properties of practical problem solving (see also Willis & Schaie, 1993). Most current definitions involve distinctions between practical problem solving and the type of intelligence required to perform well on traditional intelligence measures (i.e., "academic intelligence") (Neisser, 1976; Wagner, 1986). Some definitions of practical problem solving highlight the form of thinking required. Scribner (1986), for instance, characterizes practical thinking as "mind in action," to focus on thinking that is embedded in the functional activities of daily life. Others have emphasized the nature of the problems that are involved in solving practical problems: their interpersonal or social nature (see, e.g., Ford, 1986; Meacham & Emont, 1989), the ill-structuredness of their goals and the means of accomplishing those goals (Meacham & Emont, 1989; Sinnott, 1989a), the extent to which they represent problems that are frequently encountered in daily life (see, e.g., Camp, Doherty, Moody-Thomas, & Denney, 1989; Capon, Kuhn, & Carretero, 1989; Denney, 1989), and the extended time frame over which problem solving can take place (see, e.g., Meacham & Emont, 1989). Although the field has yet to agree on a set of criteria that defines practical problem solving, the focus has been on problem solving that occurs frequently in the lives of individuals.

Our review of the literature in this area has revealed a number of terms used to capture the concept of practical intelligence and problem solving. For example, this concept has also been called "everyday problem solving" (Sinnott, 1989a), "practical intelligence" (Sternberg & Wagner, 1986), and "everyday cognition" (Rogoff & Lave, 1984). Although the terms have somewhat different connotations, their usage in the research has been very similar and often indistinguishable. For the sake of simplicity, we will use the term "practical problem solving" throughout this paper.

In this chapter, we will review what we have learned thus far about the practical origins and functions of intelligence during adolescence and adulthood. This review will be organized around two issues that have dominated work on practical problem solving in adult development: (1) whether traditional measures of intelligence tap similar abilities as those tapped by measures of practical problem solving and (2) whether the adult developmental trajectory of practical problem-solving abilities is similar to that found for more traditional measures of intelligence. Our review of the literature will reveal that currently the empirical work is inconsistent and often contradictory on these issues.

In an attempt to impose order in the field, we will then argue that such inconsistent findings derive from both conceptual and methodological differences present in work on practical problem solving. First, we will describe three perspectives that we believe have guided work on practical problem solving. Although in most cases these perspectives have been implicit, rather than explicit, in the research, we hope that, by illuminating these perspectives, we can begin to understand the different goals and research strategies that currently exist in the practical problem-solving literature. Second, we will present methodological and design problems that make comparisons among studies difficult. These methodological shortcomings highlight the need for a closer link between perspectives on practical problem solving and the measures and criteria for specific practical problem-solving tasks. We conclude by making recommendations for future work on practical problem solving.

REVIEW OF STUDIES OF PRACTICAL PROBLEM SOLVING

As the foregoing illustrates, research on adolescent and adult practical problem solving has come from diverse methodological and theoretical directions. In general, these impetuses for the field of practical problem solving have led numerous investigators to expect that practical problem-solving tasks would tap different constructs from those tapped by traditional measures of intelligence. In the present section, we first review work examining the relation between practical problem solving and global indices of intellectual functioning. This research suggests that there is no single answer to the question of whether measures of practical problem solving assess something different than global indices of intelligence do. Second, we review research related to the developmental function of practical problem-solving skills, where again the literature is mixed as to whether practical problem solving declines, remains stable, or increases across adult development.

■ The Relationship between Measures of Practical Problem Solving and Indices of Intelligence

Research examining the relationship between performance on measures of practical problem solving and measures of intelligence has revealed three different patterns: (1) no relationship, (2) relationships that are significant, yet moderate, and (3) high relationships. The issue of whether practical problem solving is related to global indices of intelligence is important as it bears on whether practical problem solving is something different in kind than what is tapped by general intellectual measures. That is, if measures of practical problem solving are highly related to measures of intelligence, researchers' concerns, reviewed above, that a type of functioning is not being tapped by current measures of intelligence are unfounded. If, in contrast, practical problem solving is different from traditional intelligence, further examination of the processes underlying practical problem solving is clearly indicated.

No Relationship

Numerous studies have found no significant relationship between a wide assortment of practical problem-solving tasks and indices of intelligence. Several of these studies have examined the practical problem-solving skills of individuals who were particularly knowledgeable or skilled at performing specific tasks (Ceci & Liker, 1986a,b; Frederiksen, 1986). Wagner and Sternberg (1985, 1986) have examined "tacit knowledge," that is, knowledge that is not typically learned through formal instruction and is often not explicitly expressed, among psychologists and individuals in business and sales of varying levels of expertise. Tacit knowledge was measured by the extent to which individuals' ratings of strategies appropriate for solving job-relevant problems resembled those of acknowledged experts in one's field.

Tacit knowledge appears to be unrelated to measures of verbal reasoning (although in some studies these relations were moderate, approximately .30; see Wagner & Sternberg, 1986).

The finding of no relationship between measures of intelligence and measures of practical problem solving is not limited to studies that focus on the problem-solving skills of expert individuals. Meyer, Russo, and Talbot (1995) examined how women of various adult ages made decisions regarding a hypothetical scenario about breast cancer. A measure of vocabulary was not related to either the actual treatment options that women selected or to the processing characteristics of how women made those decisions (e.g., time taken to make the decision, knowledge utilized). Similar results have been found by Hartley (1989) with a different decision-making task, involving rank-ordering automobiles in terms of how well they met the needs of four buyers. Again, there were no significant relationships between a measure of goodness of fit between the car selected and the hypothetical buyer and a number of intellectual abilities.

In sum, researchers investigating a variety of practical problem-solving tasks have reported no significant relationships between performance on such tasks and performance on traditional measures of intelligence. The lack of a significant relationship between measures of practical problem solving and traditional measures of intelligence is typically interpreted as evidence that practical problem solving involves different products and processes than do those involved in solving traditional measures of intelligence.

Modest Relationships

Many of the studies examining the relationship between practical problem solving and indices of intelligence have reported significant, albeit moderate, relationships between the two types of measures. Such modest relationships are found across a rather diverse assortment of both practical problem-solving and intellectual measures and for studies involving both adolescents and adults of varying ages (see, e.g., Camp et al., 1989; Cornelius & Caspi, 1987; Frederiksen, 1986). Several of these studies have examined practical problem-solving abilities with hypothetical problem-solving instruments. For instance, Berg (1989) asked fifth-, eighth-, and eleventh-grade students to rate the efficacy of six different types of strategies for solving practical problems that could arise either in school or outside the school setting (e.g., family, club activities). The resemblance of students' ratings to teachers' ratings was used as the criterion of knowledge of strategy effectiveness. The relationship between knowledge of strategy effectiveness and intellectual performance (i.e., performance on the Iowa Test of Basic Skills) was moderate for the fifth-graders ($r = .44$ and .57 for outside-school and school problems, respectively) but nonsignificant for the eighth- and eleventh-graders, suggesting that intellectual measures may be less predictive of practical problem solving with increasing age during adolescence. Blanchard-Fields and Norris (1994) have also found a modest relationship ($r = .36$) between a measure of vocabulary and the quality of attributional reasoning in adulthood.

Several investigators have found moderate relationships between numerous decision-making tasks and measures of intelligence. For instance, Johnson, Schmitt, and Everard (1994) found that several processing variables of how individuals decided which automobile to purchase (e.g., time spent viewing information and variation in the information searched) were related to measures of vocabulary and abstraction ($r = .30$s to .40s). Similar relationships have been found by Hartley (1989) between intellectual abilities and a decision-making task involving insurance policies and performance on an advice-giving task. Capon et al. (1989) found that individuals who were classified as operating at a high level on Piagetian tests of intelligence (i.e., were categorized as reasoning formally) were more likely to utilize more sophisticated information acquisition and information integration strategies in making consumer purchasing decisions than those who scored more poorly on the tests of intelligence.

The investigators whose work is reviewed in this section typically interpret such modest relationships to mean that while practical problem solving should be considered part of the domain of intelligence, practical problem-solving measures tap something different than what is tapped by measures of intelligence. However, just exactly what is tapped by the diverse set of practical problem-solving tasks reviewed here is not always clear.

High Relationships

Willis and her colleagues have reported the strongest relationships between measures of general intellectual ability and measures of practical problem solving (see Chapter 9). For instance, Willis and Schaie (1986) measured practical problem solving by the ETS Basic Skills Test, a multiple-choice test that contains items such as reading maps and understanding technical documents and newspaper text. Test items were scored as either correct or incorrect. Older adults were given an extensive battery of intelligence tests representing fluid reasoning, crystallized knowledge, memory span, and perceptual speed. Although all correlations between measures of intellectual ability and performance on the Basic Skills Test were significant, the range in correlations was substantial (between .18 and .83), with the largest correlations being between performance on the Basic Skills Test and a relatively pure measure of fluid intelligence ($r = .83$) and a measure of vocabulary ($r = .78$).

Willis, Jay, Diehl, and Marsiske (1992) further report that measures of fluid intelligence are important predictors of longitudinal change in Basic Skills Test performance. Additionally, Diehl, Willis, and Schaie (1994) found that measures of fluid intelligence were highly related not only to a paper-and-pencil measure of understanding everyday written materials but also to observational assessments of older adults performing tasks of daily living.

Researchers such as Willis and her colleagues interpret such findings to mean that traditional intellectual abilities are an important component of practical problem solving. Such findings argue against viewing intelligence and practical problem solving as distinct theoretical constructs and instead argue that basic intellectual abilities underlie everyday functioning.

■ Developmental Trajectory of Practical Problem Solving

Numerous studies have examined developmental differences in practical problem-solving performance. As with the work reviewed above concerning the relationships between measures of practical problem solving and global indices of intelligence, there are a number of seemingly contradictory findings. For instance, some studies report that performance declines with advancing age; others show increases until middle age with decline thereafter; some show stability; and still others show improvement across adolescent and adult development. Taken as a whole, the literature seems to suggest that practical problem-solving performance does not show the marked declines that are seen on some traditional measures of intelligence (e.g., fluid intelligence), although exceptions to this general conclusion do exist.

Decline of Practical Problem-solving Performance

Hartley's (1989) work with an automobile-purchasing task has been the only work to report a linear decrease with age in practical problem-solving performance. He reported a negative correlation between age and how well adults of varying ages rank ordered automobiles in terms of their fit to hypothetical car buyers. Work by Johnson (1990), however, on a similar automobile decision task found that although older adults performed the task differently from young adults, younger and older adults did not differ in their choice of a car nor in the total time spent in making the decision.

Other studies of practical problem solving that show declines with adult age typically report increases until middle age and then declines thereafter, often with younger and older adults showing similar levels of performance. Numerous studies by Denney and her colleagues (see Denney, 1989, for a review) exemplify this pattern of findings. Adults varying in age were given hypothetical practical problems (e.g., what would you do if your refrigerator broke down?) and asked to generate solutions for each problem. In most of the studies the criterion for effective problem solving has been the number of "safe and effective" solutions that participants offered, with more solutions reflecting better problem solving. In three separate studies (Denney & Palmer, 1981; Denney & Pearce, 1989; Denney, Pearce, & Palmer, 1982) middle-aged adults outperformed younger and older adults, who did not differ from each other. Such results were obtained even when problems were designed by experimenters (Denney et al., 1982) and adults themselves (Denney & Pearce, 1989) to be problems on which older adults might be expected to outperform younger adults. Recent work by Denney, Tozier, and Schlotthauer (1992) suggests that older adults may perform less well than both younger and middle-aged adults when instructions are given that explicitly direct adults to indicate all of the different ways in which a person could solve the problem. Similar developmental trends have been obtained by Camp et al. (1989) using problems that both experimenters and participants generated with the criterion being experimenters' ratings of the probable efficacy of such solutions.

Stability in Practical Problem-solving Performance

Numerous studies have reported no significant adult age differences in practical problem-solving performance across a rather large range of practical tasks. Camp et al. (1989) found no age differences when adults were asked to rate the efficacy of their solutions on problems that both experimenters and participants generated. Berg, Klaczynski, Calderone, and Strough (1994) also found no age differences in participants' ratings of the perceived effectiveness of their solutions to their own everyday problems, even though age differences were found in the types of strategies used.

Studies investigating the types of practical decisions made by adults of varying ages have also reported no significant age differences (Capon et al., 1989; Hartley, 1989; Johnson, 1990; Meyer et al., 1995). For example, Walsh and Hershey (1993) found that younger, middle-aged, and older adults' accuracy in how much money to invest in an individual retirement account and in a 401(k) plan was no different. Similarly, Hartley (1989) found no age differences in adults' abilities to compare the information in four Medicare insurance policies to decide which policy was best.

Improvement in Practical Problem-solving Performance

Some studies have documented that, across childhood and adolescence, individuals become better at solving practical problems (Berg, 1989; Spivack & Shure, 1982). Studies examining practical problem solving across adulthood also report improvement in practical problem-solving performance. In their study of hypothetical practical problem solving, Cornelius and Caspi (1987) found that adults' performance increased with adult age in how closely they resembled the performance of a group of adult judges. Labouvie-Vief (1984a) and Diehl, Coyle, and Labouvie-Vief (1994) found that older adults interpreted problems in a more complex fashion and utilized more mature strategies of coping and defense in response to hypothetical scenarios. Perlmutter, Kaplan, and Nyquist (1990) have found that such improvement in practical problem solving across adulthood extends to work-related skills that individuals utilize in their everyday lives. Blanchard-Fields has repeatedly (1986, 1994; Blanchard-Fields & Norris, 1994) found evidence of upward progression of attributional reasoning on social dilemmas, particularly when the dilemmas involved high emotional salience.

In sum, research on practical problem solving during adulthood does not create a consistent picture regarding whether practical problem solving is something different from what is measured by more traditional measures of intelligence. In addition, this literature is rather equivocal as to whether practical problem solving evinces a particular developmental trajectory across the adult life span. Particularly troubling in this literature is the fact that inconsistent findings are often uncovered for tasks which are very similar (e.g., the inconsistent results found for some of the decision-making tasks).

As we will later illustrate, one source of these discrepancies can be found in design and methodological problems that complicate the interpretations of practical problem-solving data. The diversity in the measures used to assess practical problem solving and the criteria used to judge competent performance make it difficult to understand these discrepant findings. In the next section, we suggest that contradictory interpretations also arise from a second source—the assumptions different theorists have made regarding the development of practical problem solving, its relationship to global indices of intelligence, and the effects of environmental and social contextual forces on problem solving. Although often not stated explicitly, these assumptions, hereafter called *perspectives,* are important because they have resulted in different research paradigms and in different descriptions of adolescent and adult cognitive development. These underlying perspectives not only have dictated different goals for practical problem-solving research but also have directly influenced the way in which practical problem solving has been construed, evaluated, and investigated.

THEORETICAL PERSPECTIVES ON PRACTICAL PROBLEM SOLVING

In the present section, the perspectives that have guided practical problem-solving research are outlined. Our purpose in describing these perspectives was not to provide an exhaustive review of all of the work that has been conducted from specific perspectives. We instead will use select quotations and data from empirical research to add substance to the descriptions of each perspective and to demonstrate how these perspectives can influence data interpretation. Our intent, then, is to sample prototypical investigations from each perspective and thereby allow readers to abstract a representation of work within each perspective.

Although the influence of pretheoretical assumptions on data interpretation has long been recognized by developmental theorists (see, e.g., Lerner & Kauffman, 1985; Overton, 1984; Reese & Overton, 1970), research on practical problem solving often has appeared atheoretical. Because researchers in this field have infrequently tied data to theory, the impact of theoretical assumptions on data interpretation has gone unrecognized. The suggestion has been made that "chaotic complexity" currently characterizes the literature on practical problem solving (Sinnott, 1989b). By making these often implicit perspectives explicit, we hope to instill some order into this chaos by providing a basis for interpreting existing contradictions and by constructing a framework that could facilitate communication both within and between perspectives.

Our review of current research on practical problem solving has revealed three predominant perspectives, presented in Table 10.1. These perspectives adopt different views of development, which, in turn, have led to different characterizations of life-span changes in practical problem solving. Implicit in each perspective are underlying beliefs about the *direction* of developmental change, the *role of the environment* in explaining development, and the methods used to derive *criteria* for assessing practical problem solving. This set of beliefs, in turn, guides the development of instruments for measuring practical problem solving and the interpretations given to the data collected. Because they have not been organized into internally coherent sets of theorems, principles, and predictions, the perspectives we discuss do not represent theories. Rather, as manifestations of different world views (Altman & Rogoff, 1987; Lerner & Kauffman, 1985; Overton & Reese, 1973; Pepper, 1942), the perspectives are pretheoretical.

In the following sections, each perspective is described and illustrated with relevant quotations and research from investigators within the perspective. These sections are intended to add substance to our arguments and to more vividly demonstrate how each perspective can influence data interpretation. Consequently, we have attempted to describe research which most clearly illustrates the basic tenets of the perspectives from which it derives, although, as the reader will note, in some cases this research has not had an explicitly developmental focus.

■ The Competency Perspective

In the competency perspective, practical intellectual development is described as it occurs along trajectories associated with an underlying set of cognitive capacities. From this perspective an important goal is to determine the extent to which the underlying competencies are displayed in performance. Competency perspectives have followed from two seemingly diverse theoretical directions: (1) Revisions of psychometric theories and measures of intelligence to take into account the nonacademic demands faced by adults and (2) revisions of Piaget's theory that seek to identify unique stages of intelligence that emerge during adulthood. We call the first competency approach the *general-ability approach* and the second the *postformal operational* approach.

Perspective	View of Practical Problem Solving	View of Development
TABLE 10.1 Overview and Comparison of Predominant Practical Problem-solving Perspectives		
Competency:		
General ability	Manifestation of underlying cognitive abilities that enable practical problem solving	General developmental trends associated with underlying abilities
Postformal operational	Manifestation of an underlying reasoning structure, considered the pinnacle of adult thought	General upward progression across adult development
Knowledge-based	Outcome of familiarity and experience with problems within specific domains; knowledge driven	Becoming more expert in a particular domain
Contextualist:		
Sociohistorical	Adaptation to the demands of specific cultural contexts	Maintaining fit between changing demand of context and practical problem-solving performance
Prototype	Resemblance of problem solver to cultural prototypes of "good" practical problem solving	Maintaining fit between cultural prototypes of "good" practical problem solver and practical problem-solving performance

These two accounts of the competency perspective share the view that practical problem solving may be evaluated against a single ideal or optimal state and that development is restricted to a single trajectory or, at least, to a limited number of predetermined trajectories. Because the underlying competencies described in these approaches are seen as domain independent, practical problem solving is assessed against a generalizable standard (e.g., number of correct responses, speed of response selection, formal reasoning). Therefore, in the competency perspective, intellectual development is described in terms of optimal and nonoptimal functioning, usually by comparing an individual's problem solving against a set criterion that is used regardless of age, culture, and social background.

For competency theorists, the role of the environment in determining developmental trajectories is secondary to the role attributed to the underlying competencies. Although environmental stimulation or deprivation (e.g., culture, education) may lead to changes in the rate or speed of development (see, e.g., Basseches, 1984; Denney, 1984; Willis & Schaie, 1993), environmental forces cannot alter the *types* of competencies that emerge, improve, or decline with increasing age. In this sense, the competency perspective parallels and extends traditional theories of intellectual development, such as the theory of fluid and crystallized intelligence (Horn & Cattell, 1967) and Piaget's theory of intellectual development (Piaget, 1952). In both the general-ability and the postformal operational approach, seemingly novel intellectual abilities, developmental paths apparently specific to a culture or subculture, and cognitive skills that appear specific to a domain are interpreted as manifestations of more general abilities and trajectories that are independent of contexts and domains.

The General-Ability Approach

The general-ability approach draws much of its theory from psychometric work on intelligence. The psychometric literature on adult development (see Chapter 9) has suggested that conclusions regarding the developmental course of intelligence across the life span (i.e., increase, maintenance, or decrease) must consider the impact of historical, concurrent, and age-related variables (Schaie, 1965, 1979) and the type of ability examined (Botwinick, 1977). Those interested in practical problem solving during adulthood have further argued that because middle-aged and older adults rarely encounter the types of problems presented on intelligence tests, these tests may not tap the full intellectual potential (competence) of these age groups (Demming & Pressey, 1957; Denney, 1989). In the paragraphs that follow, specific assumptions of this position are discussed with quotations from various theorists provided to demonstrate how these tenets have been instantiated.

1. *The relationship of practical problem solving to general ability.* Researchers in the general-ability approach have typically viewed practical problem solving as stemming from a set of underlying abilities, which may be similar to those typically assessed by psychometric measures of intelligence (Schaie, 1987) or which may represent competencies unlike those measured on intelligence tests (Denney, 1984). Willis and Schaie (1986) clearly expound this approach:

> We shall use the term "intelligence" to denote those genotypic ability factors commonly identified with the psychometric approach to the study of structural intelligence. In contrast, practical intelligence will be viewed as the phenotypic expression of the combination of genotypic factors that, given minimally acceptable levels of motivation, will permit adaptive behavior within a specific situation or class of situations. (p. 240)

For Willis, Schaie, and their colleagues, a key issue involves determining the extent to which the underlying competencies (genotypes) are reflected in performance (phenotypes). Because the underlying competencies are likely to change with age (e.g., fluid and crystallized intelligence), an important enterprise involves determining whether developmental differences in practical problem solving result from these changes and whether the relative importance of specific competencies for practical problem solving shifts to compensate for declines in other competencies. This hierarchical perspective is illustrated by Schaie and Willis (this volume):

> In terms of a hierarchy, information processes such as memory and speed are considered the most basic, least complex forms of cognition. . . . The upper, or most complex, levels of the hierarchy include everyday intelligence and postformal thought.

In their research, Willis and her colleagues have found strong support for this view. For example, Marsiske, Willis, Goodwin, and Maier (1992) found that the correlations between everyday problem solving and fluid and crystallized intelligence were .73 and .66, respectively. Similarly high correlations have been reported by Willis and Schaie (1986).

An alternative account of the relationship between practical problem solving and "traditional" measures of intelligence is apparent in Denney's (1984, 1989) theory of practiced and unpracticed cognitive skills. In her theory, Denney (1984) distinguished between abilities that are relatively unpracticed and those that are trained or frequently practiced. Unexercised potential refers to the biological potential one exhibits given a normal environment in which little training or practice on the abilities in question has taken place. In contrast, optimally exercised potential refers to the maximal biological potential exhibited given a normal environment and extensive amounts of practice on a given ability. Theoretically, whereas problems on traditional intelligence tests are relatively unpracticed, especially for older persons, practical problems should be those that individuals have frequently practiced. This view, then, espouses a distinction between practical abilities and "academic," or schooled, abilities. For the study of adult intelligence, research on practical problem solving is particularly important because the quality of practical problem solving provides an index of older adults' maximum problem-solving potential.

2. *The developmental trajectory of practical problem solving.* As noted earlier, a number of parallels exist between psychometric theories of adult intelligence and the general-ability perspective on the development of practical problem solving. Specifically, like psychometric approaches, the general-ability approach posits that a limited number of developmental trajectories exist.

Because upper and lower limits on practical problem solving are determined by a set of underlying basic competencies and by the interactions among these competencies, the manner in which practical problem solving develops is restricted by the development of the basic cognitive abilities. Variations within these limits are determined by individual historical factors (education, job complexity, etc.). For example, if much practical problem solving involves utilizing and coordinating fluid intellectual skills (Willis & Schaie, 1986), because such skills diminish during later adulthood, the potential for practical problem solving cannot increase during these years. However, in a familiar environment, the practical problem-solving skills actually displayed by older individuals may equal or surpass those displayed by members of younger age groups. Like basic intellectual competencies, age changes in practical problem solving are hypothetically limited to changes in underlying ability.

Denney (1984) has been most explicit in her formulations of the developmental trajectory of adult practical problem solving. In her model, Denney proposes different trajectories for exercised and unexercised potential. Unexercised potential (i.e., biological potential) is always at a lower level than exercised potential and begins to decline after young adulthood. Exercised potential, by contrast, does not decline until after middle age. In Denney's view, everyday problems are relatively unpracticed for younger adults, because most of their lives have been spent solving "schoollike" problems. Because everyday problems become increasingly more practiced (i.e., exercised) and because exercised potential does not decline before middle age, performance on everyday problems should increase from early through middle adulthood. However, because eventually both exercised and unexercised potential decline, everyday problem solving should also decline by later adulthood. In numerous studies, Denney and her colleagues (Denny & Palmer, 1981; Denney & Pearce, 1989; Denney, Pearce, & Palmer, 1982) have found that practical problem-solving performance increased up to middle age and declined during later adulthood. These results support the notion of an underlying, generalized ability trajectory and the hypothesized inverted U-shaped curve for the development of everyday problem solving.

The Postformal Operational Approach

The postformal operational approach has in common with the general-ability approach the belief that optimal forms of intelligence exist whose properties transcend specific cultural and ecological contexts. The postformal operational approach is different from the general-ability approach, however, in that postformal operational theory has arisen as an extension of Piagetian theory (see Chapter 11). Consequently, studying development has involved the identification of unique structures of reasoning whose functioning is qualitatively superior to that of developmentally earlier structures. As Murphy and Gilligan (1980) stated, a "general upward progression . . . is required for a developmental theory" (p. 93). In this model, then, adult development is seen as progression toward a higher end state, rather than as the decline described by psychometric models (see Labouvie-Vief, 1992, for a review). An interest in practical problem solving has arisen because some postformal theorists argue that unique forms of adult reasoning are most likely to be evident on problems that have some bearing on the lives of adults (see, e.g., Blanchard-Fields & Norris, 1994).

Because postformal operational theory has its roots in Piagetian theory, the goals of postformal operational researchers have differed somewhat from those of general-ability researchers. Although the two approaches agree that optimal forms of reasoning exist whose qualities transcend context and that potential developmental trajectories are predetermined, postformal operational theorists have paid less attention to whether performance on standard tests of intelligence predicts postformal reasoning in everyday situations. Rather, the focus of postformal operational research has been on (1) demonstrating that postformal reasoning emerges during adulthood and is superior to and qualitatively different from formal operational reasoning and (2) exploring the relationship of postformal operational skills to everyday task performance.

1. *Qualitative differences between formal and postformal reasoning.* Postformal operational theories speculate that the structure of formal operations, which governs the complex thinking of late adolescents and young adults, is replaced by a more sophisticated structure during adulthood. For example, Murphy and Gilligan (1980) argued that adulthood presents moral dilemmas and conflicts that cannot be easily reconciled with the absolutist principles of right and wrong that govern adolescent thinking. As the adult grapples with decisions among contradictory alternatives, a new, relativistic stage of reasoning emerges that encourages the synthesis of moral beliefs and contextual conditions. The central idea is that postformal reasoning represents a qualitative advance over formal reasoning. Basseches (1984) argues that:

> Each of the stages . . . represents a more extended, differentiated capacity for conceptualizing the social environment than the previous stage. Each stage is also a more valid form of reasoning than its predecessor—in the sense of being less limited by structurally narrowed vision . . . each succeeding stage enables one to deal effectively with a broader range of events. (p. 106)

According to Labouvie-Vief (1984b), adult thinking also becomes more concrete and practically oriented than that of adolescents. This change represents a progression over formal operational thinking in that the adult is able to recognize that conclusions of rightness or wrongness are a function of one's initial premises. In contrast to the adolescent, whose vision of truth is linear and based solely on logic, the attainment of intersystemic reasoning allows adults to accept the existence of contradictory realities and recognize that "truth" is based not only on logic but also on the perspective of each individual (see also Arlin, 1984; Sinnott, 1984).

According to postformal operational theorists, failure to recognize the advances that occur in adult thinking can result in dramatic misinterpretations of their problem solving. For example, on many abstract formal operational tasks, older adults appear inferior to younger adults. However, on real-world problems in which both older and younger adults have a vested interest in performing well, the responses of older adults may illustrate a level of sophistication that cannot be generated by younger adults. Blanchard-Fields and Norris (1994), for example, have suggested that quantitative assessments fail to tap the richness and complexity of older adults' thought and social attributional processes (see also Sinnott, 1975). Although older adults have developed new intellectual competencies, their use of postformal operations is selective and may occur only on everyday problems that are emotionally salient and pertinent to their lives.

Several studies have examined in detail the differences in the reasoning of younger and older adults. Labouvie-Vief (1984b), for example, described adult cognitive development as a movement from the logically constrained thought of adolescence to the more autonomous thinking of older adults. In her research, participants were presented ambiguous social problems that permitted interpretations from a variety of perspectives (e.g., a woman threatening to leave her alcoholic husband). The reasoning of young adolescents indicated that they typically were unaware of the many possible interpretations of these problems and relied heavily on the information actually presented. Older adolescents and young adults, by contrast, were less likely to make decisions on the basis of the information given and instead reasoned that logic and truth are relative to the premises from which they originate and that several responses could be equally valid. Finally, the most mature reasoners, the middle-aged adults, went beyond contradictory systems of "right" and "wrong" and instead focused on the contexts of communication in which these systems were established and on the possibilities for integrating the systems and resolving their discrepancies.

More recently, Blanchard-Fields and Norris (1994) used a causal attribution paradigm to examine the tendency of adolescents and adults to engage in relativistic thinking. Participants were presented a series of vignettes in which the task was to determine whether the outcome was caused by the actor's internal dispositions, environmental factors, or the actor/environment interaction. Consistent with a dialectical perspective on adult cognition, relativistic thinking (i.e., reasoning based on both situational and dispositional factors and the synthesis of these influences into a more meaningful whole) increased through middle age, although it declined in later adulthood. Age differences in relativistic reasoning became more apparent as the causal ambiguity in the problems increased, supporting the previously mentioned speculations of Sinnott, Labouvie-Vief, and Blanchard-Fields. The observed age differences in reasoning were accounted for primarily by the level of ego development, suggesting that ego development may mediate the link between age and relativistic reasoning. Together, the results imply that both contextual variables (e.g., the ambiguity of the problems) and personality variables affect the activation and development of postformal reasoning.

2. *Relationship between postformal operational thinking and everyday problem solving.* A second goal of postformal operational research on practical problem solving has been to examine whether competence in postformal thinking underlies practical problem solving. For example, Kuhn, Pennington, and Leadbeater (1983) examined the practical thinking of experienced adult jurors to determine the relationships among formal operational thinking, postformal operational thinking, and juror decision making. Postformal operational capabilities were examined by analyzing the jurors' responses to two discrepant accounts of a historical event. The purpose of this task was to examine cognitive relativism, a hypothesized aspect of dialectical thinking.

To assess practical problem solving, a videotaped reenactment of a murder trial was presented. Participants were asked to think aloud about a verdict decision, to describe their perspective of events that had occurred during the crime and the links among these events, and to discuss whether there were alternative ways of describing the events. Formal operational ability was related to the number of links jurors observed between the events and evidence presented in the trial. Moreover, participants who did *not* display postformal operational thinking were more likely to introduce unresolved contradictions into their judicial decision making. These results suggest that both formal and postformal thinking are important determinants of adults' practical problem solving.

In general, studies conducted within the postformal approach have shown that formal and postformal operational reasoning may partially underlie the thinking required by complex practical problems. Additionally, the evidence accumulated thus far appears to support the idea that adult intellectual development is characterized by a shift away from abstract, hypothetical thought toward relativistic and dialectical thinking (see Commons, Richards, & Armon, 1984; Labouvie-Vief, 1992; and Chapter 11 for reviews). This approach has the potential for offering a theoretical explanation for developmental differences in practical thinking in terms of general structures of thought that differ qualitatively across the adult life span. However, there is not yet consensus among postformal theorists regarding the specific nature of this stage, nor is there evidence to suggest the mechanisms that bring about a transformation to this higher level.

Summary of Competency Approaches

Although the general-ability and postformal operational approaches differ in their conceptions of intellectual change during adulthood and in their reasons for exploring problem solving in practical domains, they converge on the idea that problem-solving performance can be assessed against a single set of criteria that marks optimal competency. For the general-ability position, these criteria are often determined by reference to standardized tests; for the postformal position, the criteria are determined theoretically in terms of the greater integration and generality of adult thought. There are also some similarities in the age trends that have been discerned thus far. Typically, general-ability theorists describe a trend in which practical problem-solving increases up to young or middle adulthood and then declines. Similarly, postformal operational theorists describe an increase in practical problem-solving ability up to middle adulthood, and, as in the general-ability approach, some postformal researchers (see, e.g., Blanchard-Fields & Norris, 1994) have found evidence that this type of thinking may decline in the later adult years. In each case, although their methods differ considerably, development is described as it occurs along a predetermined trajectory.

■ The Knowledge-based Perspective

In the knowledge-based perspective, practical intelligence is considered as it develops within specific knowledge domains. This perspective describes practical problem solving in terms of criteria specific to particular domains and in terms of the cognitive processes that develop with increased experience with different types of knowledge. Development is seen as the process of becoming increasingly facile and expert in solving the problems of a domain, primarily through the acquisition of new domain-specific knowledge and the reorganization of existing knowledge. Although the environment is attributed an important role in establishing the conditions for the acquisition of particular types of knowledge, knowledge is viewed as the driving force behind practical problem solving. A goal for developmental research is to examine the interplay between age and experience—for instance, by investigating the effects of knowledge while keeping age constant and vice versa. Researchers examining expertise in chess (Charness, 1981), bridge (Charness, 1983), and typing (Salthouse, 1984) have found that older adults may maintain levels of performance similar to younger adults through the use of cognitive strategies developed within a domain that compensate for losses in lower-level cognitive skills.

The knowledge-based perspective to practical problem solving is based on the belief that practical problem solving develops out of familiarity and experience with problems within specific life domains (see, e.g., Rybash, Hoyer, & Roodin, 1986). Because different domains demand different problem-solving skills, knowledge-based theorists abstain from using generalizable criteria to evaluate performance and instead focus on criteria derived from the domain of study. Perhaps due to its link with work on expertise, however, research within this area has often examined developmental processes by comparing adults at different levels of expertise, rather than by comparing individuals of different ages. Consequently, much of the research from this perspective has not explicitly dealt with age-related changes in practical intelligence.

This research has had at least three readily discernable goals: first, to determine the relationship between the acquisition of domain-specific knowledge and the complexity of domain-relevant cognitive processes; second, to understand how the mental processes operating in specific knowledge domains relate to performance on measures relevant to the domain and to performance on measures of general intellectual functioning; and third, to understand whether adult age differences in domain-relevant performance are similar to the differences observed for traditional intellectual performances. Although a number of researchers have begun employing the knowledge-based perspective to their work, as illustrations of this perspective we have selected Ceci and Liker's (1986a,b) study of horse-racing handicappers and, because of its developmental focus, Perlmutter at al.'s (1990) investigation of adult food service workers.

In their research, Ceci and Liker (1986a,b) examined the complexity of the cognitive processes involved in computing post time odds by expert and nonexpert horse racing hand-icappers. Participants were presented with hypothetical prerace forms complete with infor-mation on each horse's racing record—performance under different track conditions, on tracks of different lengths, and so on—and asked to predict the odds on each horse. Experts were better able to predict the correct odds on the horses than were nonexperts (i.e., they correctly predicted the favorite horse 91% versus 50% of the time, respectively).

The cognitive processes of experts were extraordinarily complex and often involved tak-ing into consideration as many as seven variables in a nonadditive manner, comparable to the computations performed in multiple regression analyses. Although the IQs (measured by the WAIS) of the experts ranged from 80 to 130, IQ was unrelated to the ability to pre-dict racetrack odds, suggesting that the cognitive processes involved in handicapping are not the manifestation of an underlying "genotypic" set of intellectual abilities but instead evolve within that domain, separate from intellectual development in other domains. Ceci and Liker (1986b) concluded that

> the present findings [are] supportive of a view of mental functioning that assumes there are multiple cognitive potentials . . . not all of which are measured by IQ tests. More-over, even those that are presumed to be measured by IQ tests are governed by a fairly specific set of contextual constraints. . . . Such a view runs counter to virtually all post hoc approaches to defining intelligence . . . because it implies that the limited range of abilities and contexts involved in the standardized testing situation reflects an equally limited range of practical intelligence used to cope with environmental challenges. (p. 265)

In a more developmentally focused study, Perlmutter et al. (1990) examined a variety of practical problem-solving skills (including basic physical and cognitive capacities, as well as higher cognitive and social skills) carried out by food service providers who varied in age from 19 to 60. Based on interviews and observations of food service workers, a measure of task-specific knowledge was developed that consisted of physical, technical, organizational, and social behaviors required for expert performance at service delivery. In addition, work-ers were given measures of physical dexterity and strength, cognitive abilities, and social abil-ities. Their results argued for separate developmental functions for cognitive abilities and domain-specific knowledge and performance. On each of the physical, cognitive, and social measures, performance decreased with age. However, measures of job-relevant knowledge and on-the-job ratings of performance indicated increases with age.

Summary of the Knowledge-based Perspective

These studies have found that performance within a specific knowledge domain is predicted better by problem-solving measures developed specifically for the domain than by stan-dardized tests of intelligence and basic cognitive functions. Other investigators have reported similar findings (see, e.g., Frederiksen, 1986; Sternberg & Wagner, 1989; Wagner & Stern-berg, 1985, 1986). Also, studies of young and old adult experts and novices in a variety of domains (e.g., chess, bridge playing, architectural skills, typing) suggest that separate adult developmental trajectories exist for basic and higher-level intellectual abilities and domain-relevant performance (see, e.g., Charness, 1981, 1983; Salthouse, 1984; Salthouse & Mitchell, 1990).

Explanations of these findings generally related to cognitive processes developed within specific knowledge domains (see, e.g., Ceci, 1990; Wagner & Sternberg, 1986; Chapter 13). Differences between novices and experts or between tasks which tap different degrees of expertise are explained in terms of the elaborateness of the knowledge base, which then drives and facilitates the cognitive processes required to operate on this knowledge. In the strong form of this perspective, persons with more experience and more highly elaborated domain-specific knowledge should outperform individuals with less experience and less knowledge, regardless of age. A weaker form of the knowledge-based hypothesis suggests that domain-specific knowledge can compensate for and offset age-related declines in basic general cognitive functions.

■ The Contextualist Perspective

From the contextualist perspective, practical intellectual development is described in terms of successful adaptation to specific social and cultural contexts, ultimately against criteria derived from those contexts. In this view, because contexts differ in their adaptational demands and in the types of problem-solving resources available, development is seen as a cocreation of contextual conditions and individual goals and competencies. Rather than merely providing the fuel for development, the environment is considered an active contributor not only to the rate at which practical problem-solving skills develop but also to the form those skills ultimately take.

In its orientation, the contextualist perspective differs considerably from the competency and knowledge-based perspectives; however, in both the contextualist and knowledge-based perspectives the practical problem solving of persons within specific environments is examined. The knowledge-based perspective posits that individual differences in development result from the elaboration of domain-specific knowledge. The general orientation of the contextualist perspective is to explain practical problem solving in terms of social, motivational, and cultural factors that influence adaptation to particular life contexts. Because each context has unique adaptational demands, there are neither predetermined criteria for assessing problem solving nor optimal modes of problem solving that transcend populations. In addition, because individuals of different ages across development may be situated in different contexts (see, e.g., Baltes et al., 1984; Berg & Calderone, 1994), developmental differences in problem-solving modes may be traced to the different demands present in these contexts. The contextualist perspective describes the problem-solving opportunities and demands found in particular contexts and explores how individuals, with their particular histories and goals, modify their problem solving to adapt to these contextual demands. A useful summarization of this perspective is provided by Scribner (1986):

> Unlike formal problem solving, practical problem solving cannot be understood solely in terms of problem structures and mental representations. Practical problem solving is an open system that includes components lying outside the formal problem—

objects and information in the environment and goals and interests of the problem solver. Expertise in practical thinking involves the accomplishment of a fitting relationship among these elements, an accomplishment aptly characterized as functionally adaptive. (p. 28)

Within this perspective, at least two approaches can be identified. The first is the *sociohistorical* approach. The basis of this approach is that individuals actively modify their problem solving to meet whatever demands the context presents and simultaneously modify aspects of the context to meet their personal goals. This approach has been heavily influenced by the work of Russian psychologists, particularly Vygotsky (1978) and Leont'ev (1981). The second contextualist approach we will label the *prototype* approach. In this approach, investigators have sought to discern and understand the prototypic traits of individuals who are good practical problem solvers and evaluate performance against this prototype.

The Sociohistorical Approach

Sociohistorical researchers search for social, motivational, and cultural influences that might contribute to differences in problem solving. One goal of this approach is to determine influences (e.g., social prescriptions for problem solving, cultural tasks, work conditions) evident within particular environments (e.g., school, work) that could influence practical problem solving. The development of practical problem solving is described as a process by which thinking becomes increasingly embedded in functional activities but which also changes as the individual progresses through the multiple contexts of the life course.

In a nondevelopmental exploration of contextual influences on practical problem solving, Lave, Murtaugh, and de la Rocha (1984; Lave, 1989) followed and interviewed expert adult grocery shoppers in the course of their grocery shopping to examine how they arrived at decisions between products differing on various dimensions (e.g., size and prize). The shoppers used a "gap-closing" strategy which involved reformulating the problem condition into simpler terms and weighing choices through several "rounds" of calculations, rather than algorithmic equations that would have guaranteed correct solutions. Using this strategy, the shoppers made only 4 incorrect choices (i.e., selected the more expensive choice) out of 77 total opportunities. However, these same shoppers correctly solved only 58 percent of the items on a test of "academic" arithmetic ability (i.e., skills presumably required for grocery shopping calculation, such as addition, division, etc.). Again, this research indicates that individuals often develop adaptive strategies specific to the contexts in which they face everyday problems. Scribner's (1986) research on adult dairy workers provides similar evidence for the contextually sculpted nature of adaptive everyday cognition.

In a series of developmental studies, Klaczynski and his colleagues have focused on the interplay among educational contexts, cultural developmental tasks, personal goals, and practical problem solving (Klaczynski, Laipple, & Jurden, 1992; Klaczynski & Reese, 1991). In an investigation of young adult development, Klaczynski (1994) examined the practical problem-solving strategies and ethical dilemma interpretations of students in different graduate schools. First, an ethnographic investigation of the subcultural contexts of first- and fourth-year medical students was conducted in order to discern the primary cultural developmental tasks that students in each year perceived.

Second, the practical problem solving of first- and fourth-year medical students was compared to that of first- and fourth-year graduate students. Participants were presented problems drawn from the ethnography, followed by strategies that were related to the task of first-year medical students (e.g., focusing on passing courses), the task of fourth-year medical students (e.g., preparing for residency), or the various tasks relevant to graduate students (e.g., working closely with adviser). As anticipated by the contextual perspective, results showed that participants rated as most effective those strategies that were associated with their primary cultural developmental task. Students also interpreted medical/ethical dilemmas consistent with the demands that they were faced with in their environment. Klaczynski (1994) suggested that these findings illustrate not only how individuals mold their practical problem solutions to the demands and tasks of their contexts but also how they change their underlying interpretations of and reasoning about problem situations to adjust to cultural demands.

Berg and her colleagues (Berg & Calderone, 1994; Sansone & Berg, 1993) have sought to understand the potentially changing nature of the contexts of practical problem solving across the life span and how those contexts may have consequences for the goals and strategies individuals pursue. Preadolescents, young, middle-aged, and older adults were asked to describe a recent everyday problem, first with no constraints as to the domain of the problem and then within one of six different domains (family, work, school, friends, leisure, and health). When individuals were unconstrained as to the domain, Sansone and Berg (1993) found that problem solvers reported problems that suggest that the context of everyday problem solving shifts across the life span from an emphasis on the school environment during preadolescence to contexts of work during middle adulthood and to family and health in late adulthood, with diverse contexts occupying young adulthood (school, work, romantic relationships, etc.). When examining the problems that individuals reported when they were prompted to describe a problem within a particular domain, the strategies individuals reported using to deal with these domains were impacted by the context of the problem and the age of the problem solver (Berg, Strough, Calderone, Sansone, & Weir, 1995). However, the impact of different contexts on different strategies was largely due to individuals' pursuing different goals and interpreting situations differently within each context.

As these investigations illustrate, the sociohistorical approach moves away from determining the optimality of practical problem solving toward an understanding of how these performances relate to different problem-solving contexts and to the problem solver's goals and perceptions. This research has repeatedly demonstrated that individuals across a variety of contexts adapt their thinking to the specific demands present in their environments and correspondingly shape their environments to provide a better fit with their psychological needs. Research is beginning to address how the changing context of adults' everyday lives across the life span (e.g., work, school, family) may impact practical problem solving.

The Prototype Approach

The prototype approach derives from the same tradition that sparked the current interest in people's conceptions of intelligence and involves uncovering cultural definitions of effective practical problem solving. In this approach, as in other contextualist perspectives, the criteria for optimal problem solving are not laid out a priori but are derived or discovered by an analysis of the beliefs held by individuals in specific cultural or subcultural contexts. In this sense, people's conceptions of effective practical problem solving provide an insider's perspective of the skills required for effective adaptation to specific contexts and allow the investigator to abstract a prototypical view of optimal practical problem solving that fits the perceptions of relevant subgroups. Research conducted from this approach has had two primary goals: first, to explore adults' perceptions of prototypically "good" everyday problem solvers; second, to define optimal practical problem solving in terms of the resemblance to these perceptions.

Several recent investigations have explored children's and adults' perceptions of the characteristics of prototypically "good" everyday problem solvers. For example, to tap into children's and adults' prototypical views of "good" everyday problem solvers, Berg (1990) asked participants to "describe the type of individual you think would best be able to solve" a problem that they had faced. Although few age differences were found in the frequency with which these attributes were mentioned, differences did occur with respect to certain types of problems. For instance, social skills were more frequently mentioned when the content of the problem was interpersonal, consistent with the contextual assumption that different contexts may demand different skills.

A second set of studies within this approach has, following Neisser's (1976, 1979) suggestion, operationalized optimal practical problem solving in terms of the resemblance to a cultural consensus of optimal performance. Cornelius and Caspi (1987) used this approach in assessing performance on an everyday problem-solving inventory by comparing participants' responses to the responses of a group of judges who differed in adult age. Adults from several age groups were presented problems drawn from six conceptually distinct life domains (e.g., economic/consumer, interpersonal conflicts with family, conflicts with coworkers). For problems in each domain, four response alternatives were constructed, representing problem-focused action, cognitive problem appraisal, passive-dependent behavior, and avoidant thinking/denial. Responses for each problem were rated for effectiveness by the judges, whose ratings, in turn, were used as the criteria for effective problem solving. Cornelius and Caspi found that younger adults resembled the judges' ratings less well than older adults did, although neither group differed significantly from the middle-aged group. Performance on the everyday problem-solving measure was unrelated to amount of education and was only moderately correlated with traditional measures of ability. A similar approach has been used by Berg (1989) in studying the development of adolescent everyday problem solving.

Summary of the Contextualist Perspective

As the studies in this section indicate, research from the contextualist perspective has been diverse, employing a number of different methodologies and studying a wide range of populations. The thread that ties these studies together is their uniform attention to the "fit" between the goals and characteristics of problem solvers and the demands and prescriptions of various social and developmental contexts. Each of the contextualist approaches offers a different way to understand problem solving: the sociohistorical approach examines problem solving against a cultural backdrop, looking at how individuals change their problem solving in order to meet contextually sanctioned goals, while the prototype approach provides more specific criteria for problem solving by examining what children and adults perceive to make up exceptional practical problem-solving behavior.

■ Summary of the Theoretical Perspectives

Each of the perspectives—the competency, knowledge-based, and contextualist—holds a different view of practical problem solving and its development that has influenced the research conducted within each perspective. The imposition of these perspectives onto the literature provides a basis for understanding and attempting to reconcile the inconsistent findings in the literature. Research within each perspective gives a more unified picture regarding whether practical problem solving is distinct from intelligence and the developmental trajectory of practical problem solving than work that crosscuts perspectives. For instance, work within the competency perspective reveals that traditional intellectual abilities underlie practical problem-solving performances and that the developmental trajectory of practical problem solving follows an inverted U-shaped curve. Work within the knowledge-based perspective typically finds that practical problem solving is distinct from underlying intellectual abilities and that practical problem solving improves with increases in knowledge within a domain. Research within the contextualist perspective makes no specific predictions regarding the developmental trajectory of practical problem solving or its relation to traditional measures of intelligence, as practical problem-solving skills are specific to particular cultural contexts.

METHODOLOGICAL ISSUES IN PRACTICAL PROBLEM-SOLVING RESEARCH

The imposition of the competency, knowledge-based, and contextualist perspectives onto the empirical work provides a basis for understanding and trying to reconcile these differences in results. However, even within a perspective, order is not always found. Within each perspective, studies differ as to the measures used to assess practical problem solving and the criteria used to judge optimal performance. In this final section, a further attempt is made to begin to understand the discrepant findings in this literature. This section addresses some basic methodological concerns we have regarding the research thus far conducted on practical problem solving. These problems stem, in large part, from the atheoretical manner in which problem-solving instruments have been developed and scored. Although various criticisms could be levied against this research (see also Willis & Schaie, 1993), three in particular stand out, involving (1) the diversity in the measures used to assess practical problem solving (and to a lesser extent to assess intelligence), (2) the ecological validity of practical problem-solving measures, and (3) the criteria researchers have selected to evaluate practical problem-solving performances. Below, each of these difficulties will be discussed from the position of each of the three perspectives. As this discussion illustrates, several of the seemingly contradictory and confusing findings discussed in the previous sections may be better understood when the difficulties surrounding these issues are clearly explicated.

■ Diversity in Measures of Practical Problem Solving

As reviewed above, research on practical problem solving utilizes a rather broad array of measures to assess practical problem solving, including the ETS Basic Skills Test, hypothetical dilemmas, betting at the racetrack, consumer decision making, and medication use, among others. Although all these measures have been considered indicative of practical problem solving, analytically it is unlikely that such measures represent one underlying construct. In fact, research by Marsiske and Willis (1995) indicates little commonality among different measures of everyday problem solving. A variety of problem-solving components may be represented by this diverse set of problem solving measures: reasoning, decision making, social skills, knowledge, memory, and mental flexibility. This diversity becomes problematic when trying to make sense of the relationship or lack thereof between these measures and measures of academic intelligence. The situation is further complicated in that measures used to tap intelligence also differ greatly, from digit span and vocabulary to letter series and Raven's progressive matrices.

One way in which order might be placed on the diversity of measures of practical problem solving would be to have a better sense of the mental processes or abilities involved in solving specific practical problems. Much of the work reviewed above involved presenting individuals with hypothetical problem-solving scenarios and asking them to provide a solution to the problem. Very little is known about the processes or abilities that underlie solutions to these problems. Research in this area would be improved by adopting the process approach of Ceci and Liker (1986a,b), which explicates *how* individuals mentally go about solving specific practical problems, and Willis and Schaie's (1986) work illuminating the abilities that underlie their measure of practical problem solving. This process work might eventuate in taxonomies of everyday problem solving that would facilitate further work in this area.

A process analysis might allow investigators to untangle the mixed bag of results that is found with regard to the relation between measured intelligence and practical problem solving and the developmental trajectories of practical problem solving. For instance, Denney's problems and the way in which they are scored (number of solutions offered) may involve strategies that rely on fluency, abilities that do decline with adult age (see Schaie, 1979), contributing, in part, to the age-related declines found in her studies. Cornelius and Caspi's (1987) problems, however, may involve strategies that require retrieval of a store of knowledge about socially sanctioned ways of solving problems, knowledge that accumulates with age (see Chapter 13), leading to their findings of improvement throughout adulthood.

■ Ecological Validity of Practical Problem-solving Measures

In each of the perspectives outlined above, a primary concern has been to examine mental processes that are used in everyday life and that are thus ecologically valid. Despite the promise of ecologically valid problems for research on intelligence across adulthood, a review of the research reveals that this promise has only partially been fulfilled.

Within the competency perspective, concerns for ecological validity have been key as the performance decrements typically observed in the elderly on intelligence tests were thought to be due, in part, to factors such as lack of familiarity with the problems or the testing situation, or low motivation to solve the problems (Cornelius, 1984; Reese & Rodeheaver, 1985). The general-competency approach has had mixed results in achieving ecological validity. Recent work by Denney and Pearce (1989) and Diehl et al. (1994) has tried to ensure that the tasks presented to adults were familiar to them and were viewed by them as important to daily living. Other studies, however, have yet to examine the ecological validity of their instruments (see, e.g., Hartley, 1989; Labouvie-Vief, 1984b; Sinnott, 1984) and seem to rely nearly exclusively on face validity for the test of ecological validity.

As the focus of the knowledge-based perspective is on contrasting the cognitive processes that differentiate the problem solving of persons highly experienced versus less experienced in a domain, the practical problems individuals are tested on must be drawn from the domain in question. Each of the studies reviewed earlier (i.e., Ceci & Liker, 1986a,b; Frederiksen, 1986; Perlmutter et al., 1990; Wagner & Sternberg, 1986) employed problems that were both relevant to and frequent in the everyday lives of participants in their studies.

Contextualists are interested in practical problem solving as a way to determine how persons use cognitive operations to facilitate their adaptation to particular contexts (see, e.g., Berg, 1989; Klaczynski & Reese, 1991; Scribner, 1986). Somewhat surprisingly, work originating from the contextualist perspective has been mixed in the extent to which the problems participants have been presented are ecologically valid. Researchers such as Scribner (1986), Lave et al. (1984), Klaczynski (1994), and Berg et al. (1995) did examine problem solving as it unfolds in the everyday contexts where individuals actually solve such problems. However, several other studies (Berg, 1989; Cornelius & Caspi, 1987; Klaczynski & Reese, 1991; Klaczynski et al., 1992) developed problem situations on the basis of relevant literatures for adolescent or adult problem solving rather than on the direct experiences of their participants. In fact, Berg (1989) and Cornelius and Caspi (1987) found that the problems used in their studies were experienced fairly infrequently in the lives of their research participants.

Future research, particularly within the competency and contextual approaches, should be directed toward determining the ecological validity of the instruments used to assess practical problem solving. Virtually nothing is known about the ecological validity of the numerous paper-and-pencil instruments used to assess practical problem solving. In addition, most of the existing measures, reviewed above, assessed what adults *perceive* they would do in *hypothetical* situations, not what they *actually* do when solving their *own* everyday problems. Very little is known about the correspondence between problem solvers' actual behavior versus their perceptions of how they might behave in a problem situation. Research from the child development literature on solving interpersonal problems indicates that the correspondence between behavior and perceptions of behavior may be modest, at best (see Kendall & Fischler, 1984). Such validation work will be necessary before statements can be made that such instruments tap mental abilities that are relevant to real-life problem-solving situations.

■ Criteria for Assessing Practical Problem-solving Performance

Unlike in traditional laboratory problems, where a single correct score (e.g., based on formal logic) often is easily agreed upon, the criteria for scoring everyday problems are more ambiguous. Throughout our review, we have noted that research conducted within the three perspectives to practical problem solving differs in the type of criteria developed to assess practical problem solving and the generality of such criteria across tasks and across developmental levels. However, researchers have not always made explicit their rationales for scoring specific problem-solving performances. As a result, it is difficult to envision why certain problem solutions are considered good and others are considered poor.

Competency Scoring Systems

Within the competency perspective, the same criteria are applied to problem-solving performances regardless of participants' age, social class, culture, and so on. In the work of Willis and her colleagues with the ETS Basic Skills Test, criteria are straightforward as there is one correct solution to each problem presented (which may explain the high relationship that is found with measures of intelligence, as both are instances of well-structured tasks). However, many competency researchers must resolve *why* particular solutions are universally better or worse than others in terms of theoretically defined criteria that presumably reflect underlying general competencies.

The need for explicit justification becomes more evident when the research within this perspective is closely examined. Consider the following examples: Denney and Palmer (1981) and Denney et al. (1982) used the number of solutions participants proposed that involved "self-actions" as the criterion for effective problem solving. Why self-actions are considered more complex or effective than actions involving reliance on others, however, is unclear. Equally unclear is how this measure of problem solving relates to cognitive competence. Certainly, it is possible to envision situations in everyday life in which reliance on others not only produces effective solutions but may be necessary for effective problem solving. Berg and colleagues (Berg et al., 1995; Sansone & Berg, 1993) found that one of the most frequent strategies individuals reported using to deal with their own everyday problems involved reliance on others. Unless these issues are addressed, drawing conclusions regarding the cognitive differences among younger, middle-aged, and older adults is difficult.

Postformal operational theorists have been much more consistent in the extent to which the theoretical rationales for their scoring systems have been explicitly defined and justified. Because the postformal operational approach is an extension of general Piagetian theory, an important argument for postformal operational theorists involves explicating precisely how postformal thought is an advancement over formal operational thought. Despite this difficulty, individual theorists have nonetheless gone to considerable lengths to define specific criteria that mark postformal thought as superior to formal thought (Labouvie-Vief, 1992; Sinnott, 1984). The issue remains, however, of demonstrating, possibly against external criteria (Adams, Labouvie-Vief, Hobart, & Dorosz, 1989), the superiority of postformal operational thinking over other forms of thinking (e.g., over formal operational thinking).

Knowledge-based Scoring Systems

Within the knowledge-based perspective, although the specific criteria for practical problem solving generally differ between domains, overall these criteria seem to reflect the complex processing or knowledge that characterizes the problem solving of experienced or expert problem solvers in the domain. In most cases, knowledge-based theorists have provided either empirical demonstrations or indirect evidence along with theoretical justifications that the practical problem solving of more experienced or more expert persons in a domain is more cognitively complex than that of other individuals (see, e.g., Ceci & Liker, 1986a,b; Wagner & Sternberg, 1985, 1986).

Contextualist Scoring Systems

The contextualist perspective generally does not place as much emphasis on criteria of performance, although, when relevant, the criteria are often derived from what individuals who occupy the context perceive is effective in solving problems. The contextualist perspective dictates that criteria for practical problem solving should revolve around whether adaptation to the contexts in which problems are embedded is achieved, either by increasing the "fit" between the individual and the problem context (see, e.g., Berg, 1989) or by facilitating the attainment of personal and cultural goals within the conditions established by the context (see, e.g., Klaczynski & Reese, 1991; Scribner, 1986). This relativistic view suggests that problem solving in different contexts should be evaluated along different lines.

Examination of contextualist research reveals that what characterizes adaptation has varied from study to study: Lave et al. (1984) found strategies that utilized the smallest amount of effort necessary for adapting to the demands of grocery shopping, while Klaczynski (1994; Klaczynski & Reese, 1991; Klaczynski et al., 1992) used the extent to which the participants' problem-solving strategies reflected the cultural developmental tasks and goals of their contexts as the criterion for effective problem solving. Other contextualist studies, however, have been less clear in delineating the rationales underlying their scoring criteria. For example, both Berg (1989) and Cornelius and Caspi (1987) compared individuals' ratings of strategy effectiveness to the ratings provided by some criterion group (e.g., teachers or adult judges) to assess their fit to the group standard. It is not always evident from these studies why the "criterion group" should represent the most or only suitable standard for fit between the problem solver and the environment.

The above critique of the various scoring criteria that have thus far been utilized in practical problem-solving research illustrates that different perspectives—with their different assumptions regarding the nature of change and different views of optimal intellectual functioning—have different imperatives for problem-scoring systems. The issue of defining acceptable criteria for practical problem solving is clearly an important one, particularly if one is to make sense of the developmental trends in practical problem solving that have been unearthed. For example, the different developmental trajectories found in the same study by Camp et al. (1989) for ratings of effectiveness by participants (no age differences) and by experimenters (older adults performing worse than younger and middle-aged adults) points out how theoretical rationales are needed for scoring schemes to determine whether older adults are less efficient in practical problem solving.

In sum, these methodological limitations of the practical problem-solving research will most directly be addressed by a closer link between perspectives and specific models of problem solving and the particular measures and scoring schemes used to assess practical problem solving. Such theoretical perspectives would provide better rationalizations for selecting both appropriate practical problem-solving tasks and appropriate ability measures.

SUMMARY AND RECOMMENDATIONS FOR FUTURE RESEARCH

In this chapter we have reviewed work examining practical problem solving across adolescence and the adult life span. This review was organized around two issues that have dominated this field: (1) whether practical problem solving measures something different than is assessed by more traditional measures of intelligence and (2) whether the developmental trajectory of practical problem solving is similar to that found for measures of intelligence. Our review of the literature found that research can be found to support nearly any position one wishes to take on these two issues.

In order to make sense of these conflictual findings, we proposed that three different perspectives currently underlie work on practical problem solving: the competency, knowledge-based, and contextualist perspectives. We showed that these perspectives hold different assumptions with respect to the developmental trajectory of practical problem solving and the relationship between practical problem solving and traditional measures of intelligence, assumptions that contribute to many of the inconsistent findings in this literature. Research emanating within a perspective portrays a much more consistent view of the nature of practical problem solving than research crossing different perspectives. In addition, we discussed how some of the inconsistent findings found in the literature can be addressed through an examination of methodological differences among studies, many of which derive from the differences in the perspectives guiding the research.

Knowledge of the multiple perspectives underlying practical problem-solving research, along with an appreciation for the various methodological difficulties that have surfaced in this research, may provide grounds for debating, sorting out, and potentially resolving many of the contradictory findings reported in this literature. As these perspectives are derived from different worldviews (see Altman & Rogoff, 1987; Lerner & Kauffman, 1985; Pepper, 1942), which make different assumptions about the nature of development, an understanding of these perspectives may clarify for researchers the goals of other investigators whose basic assumptions differ from their own. Thus, in many respects one would anticipate that the research emanating from these different perspectives might also produce inconsistent findings. However, within perspectives, one would expect that the research would portray a more consistent picture of the development of practical problem solving, which is indeed the case. A knowledge of these perspectives may assist researchers to identify those theorists with whom they share underlying assumptions and thus forge a path for better communication. In addition, knowledge of these perspectives may help address many of the methodological problems identified in this literature, as these problems often derive from the atheoretical manner in which problem tasks and task criteria have been developed.

In closing, we would like to make specific recommendations for future research that we feel would lead the literature beyond its current state and address some of the limitations of previous work. Previously we discussed how the field is in need of work addressing (1) the ecological validity of hypothetical practical problem-solving instruments, (2) the relationship between hypothetical instruments and what adults actually do when they solve their own problems, and (3) what constitutes "optimal" practical problem-solving performance that is theoretically based. In the following section we outline two other areas of research that we feel will be vital to a further understanding of practical problem solving: an examination of the actual contexts in which practical problem solving takes place and an examination of the larger process through which individuals approach their practical problems.

■ Contexts in Which Practical Problem Solving Occurs

Throughout our review, we have noted that much of the assessment of practical problem solving has occurred with tasks and in contexts that are somewhat removed from the actual contexts in which practical problem solving occurs, although clearly such tasks are thought to reflect these everyday contexts. It will be important for future research to be informed by the "real-life" problem-solving capabilities of individuals who are actively engaged in solving their own everyday problems. From an examination of problem solving as it occurs within the practical contexts of everyday life, we may find facets of practical problem solving that have gone unexamined and acquire a better sense of what constitutes the construct of "practical" problem solving.

From our own work with a life-span investigation of everyday problem solving, where problem solvers report on the everyday problems they have actually experienced, we are beginning to understand new aspects of practical problem solving (see Sansone & Berg, 1993). For example, across a wide variety of indicators (including goals, strategies, and problem representations) we have found that everyday problem solving occurs within a social context, in which problem solvers have numerous goals not only for themselves but for others and utilize strategies that involve regulating and relying on others (see Berg et al., in press; Sansone & Berg, 1993; Strough, Berg, & Sansone, in press). We have also found that many of the practical problems that individuals face across the life span are those that involve a long-term strategy plan and are not solved on a onetime basis (e.g., dealing with an alcoholic husband, fighting with siblings, dealing with teachers at school, solving financial matters). Individuals regularly devise and revise strategies according to the outcomes of previous problem-solving attempts (see Berg, Calderone, Strough, & Williams, 1993; Meyer et al., 1995).

■ Process through Which Individuals Approach Practical Problems

As discussed above, much of the confusion in the literature created by diverse measures and models of practical problem solving may be resolved by understanding the process by which individuals solve their everyday problems. Future research should include a better understanding of the mental processes involved in solving practical problems. To this end, incorporation of other models in cognitive psychology, may prove useful; these include script models (see, e.g., Ross & Berg, 1992; Schank & Abelson, 1977), decision-making models (see, e.g., Kahneman, Slovic, & Tversky, 1982), reasoning models (Galotti, 1989; Kunda, 1990), planning models (Friedman, Scholnick, & Cocking, 1987), and information-processing models of problem solving (Sternberg, 1985).

Our recent work on practical problem solving is informed by a model that begins to describe some of the cognitive, experiential, and motivational processes involved in practical problem solving. The model emphasizes the problem representations or interpretations that individuals hold in an attempt to understand the developmental differences in the plans and strategies that individuals use to deal with their everyday problems (Berg & Calderone, 1994;

Berg et al., in press; Klaczynski, 1994; Klaczynski & Berg, 1992; Klaczynski et al., 1992; Sansone & Berg, 1993; Strough et al., in press). In numerous studies, we have found that individuals of different ages interpret the same problem in systematically different ways, and these interpretations hold consequences for the strategies they perceive as effective in dealing with their problems (see also Laipple, 1991; Sinnott, 1989a). In addition, we have found that individual difference factors, other than age, are important for understanding practical problem-solving performance. In several studies (Berg & Calderone, 1994; Blanchard-Fields & Norris, 1994; Strough et al., in press), gender has served as an important variable in understanding how individuals represent and deal with practical problems. In addition, Klaczynski and colleagues (Klaczynski, 1994; Klaczynski & Reese, 1991; Klaczynski et al., 1992) have found that educational trajectory serves as an important variable in understanding problem interpretations, goals, and strategies for dealing with practical problems.

Such process work may illuminate components of the problem-solving process that we have yet to uncover. For instance, Berg et al. (in press) have found not only that individuals plan to deal with problems once they have occurred but that many individuals plan to prevent everyday problems from occurring. Such process work will benefit from an understanding of what other related fields know about how individuals adapt to their everyday contexts, such as models of stress and coping (Lazarus & Folkman, 1984), models of control (see, e.g., Heckhausen & Schulz, 1993; Skinner & Connell, 1986), and interpersonal problem solving (Dodge, Pettit, McClaskey, & Brown, 1986; Rubin & Rose-Krasnor, 1992).

In sum, these new directions for research and models for practical problem solving will take the field beyond the questions that have dominated it for the last couple of decades. It may no longer be fruitful to try to address whether practical problem solving is related to "intelligence" or map out the developmental trajectory of practical problem solving, before we take into account that multiple models, which may be at odds with how practical problem solving is conceived and measured, are guiding research. The field of practical problem solving is at a crucial point in needing a framework such as that provided in the present chapter that could serve as a basis for better communication among researchers.

In closing, in the last two decades a great deal has been learned about the practical origins and functions of practical problem solving, although a great deal yet has to be uncovered. The field of practical problem solving need not be chaotically complex, although all would agree that the construct itself is complex. The challenge for the field is to begin to understand the phenomenon of intelligence as it occurs in real-world settings without adding chaos to the already complex phenomenon of practical problem solving.

SUPPLEMENTAL READINGS

Klaczynski, P. A., Laipple, J. J., & Jurden, F. H. (1992). Educational context differences in practical problem-solving during adolescence. *Merrill-Palmer Quarterly, 38,* 417–438.

Marsiske, M., & Willis, S. L. (1995). Dimensionality of everyday problem solving in older adults. *Psychology and Aging, 10,* 269–283.

Perlmutter, M., Kaplan, M., & Nyquist, L. (1990). Development of adaptive competence in adulthood. *Human Development, 33,* 185–197.

Sansone, C., & Berg, C. A. (1993). Adapting to the environment across the life span: Different process or different inputs? *International Journal of Behavioral Development, 16,* 215–241.

ACKNOWLEDGMENTS

Much of Cynthia A. Berg's research reviewed in this chapter was supported by grant HD 25728 from the National Institute of Child and Human Development and the National Institute of Aging, awarded to Cynthia A. Berg and Carol Sansone. This chapter was prepared while Cynthia A. Berg was a Spencer Foundation Fellow awarded from the National Academy of Education.

REFERENCES

Adams, C., Labouvie-Vief, G., Hobart, C. J., & Dorosz, M. (1990). Adult age group differences in story recall style. *Journal of Gerontology, 45,* 17–27.

Altman, I., & Rogoff, B. (1987). World views in psychology: Trait, interactional, organismic, and transactional perspectives. In D. Stokols & I. Altman (Eds.), *Handbook of environmental psychology* (vol. 1, pp. 7–40). New York: Wiley.

Arlin, P. K. (1984). Adolescent and adult thought: A structural interpretation. In M. L. Commons, F. A. Richards, & C. Armon (Eds.), *Beyond formal operations: Late adolescent and adult cognitive development* (pp. 258–271). New York: Praeger.

Baltes, P. B. (1987). Theoretical propositions of life-span developmental psychology: On the dynamics between growth and decline. *Developmental Psychology, 23,* 611–626.

Baltes, P. B., Dittmann-Kohli, F., & Dixon, R. A. (1984). New perspectives on the development of intelligence in adulthood: Toward a dual-process conception and a model of selective optimization with compensation. In P. B. Baltes & O. G. Brim, Jr. (Eds.), *Life-span development and behavior* (vol. 6, pp. 33–76). New York: Academic Press.

Basseches, M. (1984). *Dialectical thinking and adult development.* Norwood, NJ: Ablex.

Berg, C. A. (1989). Knowledge of strategies for dealing with everyday problems from childhood through adolescence. *Developmental Psychology, 25,* 607–618.

Berg, C. (1990). What is intellectual efficacy over the life course?: Using adults' conceptions to address the question. In J. A. Rodin, C. Schooler, & K. W. Schaie (Eds.), *Self-directedness: Causes and effects throughout the life course* (pp. 155–181). Hillsdale, NJ: Erlbaum.

Berg, C. A., & Calderone, K. S. (1994). The role of problem interpretations in understanding the development of everyday problem solving. In R. J. Sternberg & R. K. Wagner (Eds.), *Mind in context: Interactionist perspectives on human intelligence* (pp. 105–132). New York: Cambridge Univ. Press.

Berg, C. A., Calderone, K. S., Strough, J., & Williams, J. (1993). Everyday problem solving: Strategy use and revision across the life span. Paper presented at the meeting of the Society for Research in Child Development, New Orleans, April.

Berg, C. A., Klaczynski, P., Calderone, K. S., & Strough, J. (1994). Adult age differences in cognitive strategies: Adaptive or deficient. In J. Sinnott (Ed.), *Interdisciplinary handbook of adult lifespan learning* (pp. 371–388). Westport, CT: Greenwood.

Berg, C. A., & Sternberg, R. J. (1985). A triarchic theory of intellectual development during adulthood. *Developmental Review, 5,* 334–370.

Berg, C. A., & Sternberg, R. J. (1992). Adults' conception of intelligence across the life span. *Psychology and Aging, 7,* 221–231.

Berg, C. A., Strough, J., Calderone, K. S., Meegan, S. P., & Sansone, C. (in press). Planning to prevent everyday problems from occurring. In S. L. Friedman & E. K. Scholnick (Eds.), *Why, how, and when do we plan? The developmental psychology of planning.* Hillsdale, NJ: Erlbaum.

Berg, C. A., Strough, J., Calderone, K. S., Sansone, C., & Weir, C. (1995). *The role of goals in understanding age and context effects on strategies for solving everyday problems.* Unpublished manuscript, Univ. of Utah, Salt Lake City.

Blanchard-Fields, F. (1986). Reasoning on social dilemmas varying in emotional saliency: An adult developmental perspective. *Psychology and Aging, 1,* 325–333.

Blanchard-Fields, F. (1994). Age differences in causal attributions from an adult developmental perspective. *Journal of Gerontology: Psychological Sciences, 49,* P43–P51.

Blanchard-Fields, F., & Norris, L. (1994). Causal attributions from adolescence through adulthood: Age differences, ego level, and generalized response style. *Aging and Cognition, 1,* 67–86.

Botwinick, J. (1977). Intellectual abilities. In J. E. Birren & K. W. Schaie (Eds.), *Handbook of the psychology of aging* (pp. 580–605). New York: Van Nostrand Reinhold.

Camp, C. J., Doherty, K., Moody-Thomas, S., & Denney, N. W. (1989). Practical problem solving in adults: A comparison of problem types and scoring methods. In J. D. Sinnott (Ed.), *Everyday problem solving: Theory and applications* (pp. 211–228). New York: Praeger.

Capon, N., Kuhn, D., & Carretero, M. (1989). Consumer reasoning. In J. D. Sinnott (Ed.), *Everyday problem solving: Theory and applications* (pp. 153–174). New York: Praeger.

Cavanaugh, J., Kramer, D. A., Sinnott, J. D., Camp, C. J., & Markley, R. P. (1985). On missing links and such: Interfaces between cognitive research and everyday problem solving. *Human Development, 28,* 146–168.

Ceci, S. J. (1990). *On intelligence . . . more or less: A bio-ecological treatise on intellectual development.* Englewood Cliffs, NJ: Prentice Hall.

Ceci, S. J., & Liker, J. (1986a). Academic and nonacademic intelligence: An experimental separation. In R. J. Sternberg & R. K. Wagner (Eds.), *Practical intelligence: Nature and origins of competence in the everyday world* (pp. 119–142). New York: Cambridge Univ. Press.

Ceci, S. J., & Liker, J. K. (1986b). A day at the races: A study of IQ, expertise, and cognitive complexity. *Journal of Experimental Psychology: General, 115,* 255–266.

Charness, N. (1981). Aging and skilled problem solving. *Journal of Experimental Psychology: General, 110,* 21–38.

Charness, N. (1983). Age, skill, and bridge bidding: A chronometric analysis. *Journal of Verbal Learning and Verbal Behavior, 22,* 406–416.

Commons, M. L., Richards, F. A., & Armon, C. (Eds.) (1984). *Beyond formal operations: Late adolescent and adult cognitive development.* New York: Praeger.

Cornelius, S. W. (1984). Classic pattern of intellectual aging: Test familiarity, difficulty, and performance. *Journal of Gerontology, 39,* 201–206.

Cornelius, S. W., & Caspi, A. (1987). Everyday problem solving in adulthood and old age. *Psychology and Aging, 2,* 144–153.

Demming, J. A., & Pressey, S. L. (1957). Tests "indigenous" to adult and older years. *Journal of Counseling Psychology, 4,* 144–148.

Denney, N. W. (1984). A model of cognitive development across the life span. *Development Review, 4,* 171–191.

Denney, N. W. (1989). Everyday problem solving: Methodological issues, research findings, and a model. In L. W. Poon, D. C. Rubin, & B. A. Wilson (Eds.), *Everyday cognition in adulthood and late life* (pp. 330–351). New York: Cambridge Univ. Press.

Denney, N. W., & Palmer, A. M. (1981). Adult age differences on traditional and practical problem-solving measures. *Journal of Gerontology, 36,* 323–328.

Denney, N. W., & Pearce, K. A. (1989). A developmental study of practical problem solving in adults. *Psychology and Aging, 4,* 438–442.

Denney, N. W., Pearce, K. A., & Palmer, A. M. (1982). A developmental study of adults' performance on traditional and practical problem-solving tasks. *Experimental Aging Research, 8,* 115–118.

Denney, N. W., Tozier, T. L., & Schlotthauer, C. A. (1992). The effect of instructions on age differences in practical problem solving. *Journal of Gerontology: Psychological Sciences, 47,* P142–P145.

Diehl, M., Coyle, N., & Labouvie-Vief, G. (1994). Age and gender differences in strategies of coping and defense across the life span. Unpublished manuscript, Wayne State University, Detroit.

Diehl, M., Willis, S. L., & Schaie, K. W. (1994). Practical problem solving in older adults: Observational assessment and cognitive correlates. Unpublished manuscript, Wayne State University, Detroit.

Dixon, R. (1992). Contextual approaches to adult intellectual development. In R. J. Sternberg & C. A. Berg (Eds.), *Intellectual development* (pp. 350–380). New York: Cambridge Univ. Press.

Dodge, K. A., Pettit, G. S., McClaskey, C. L., & Brown, M. M. (1986). Social competence in children. *Monographs of the Society for Research in Child Development, 51,* 1–83.

Ford, M. E. (1986). For all practical purposes: Criteria for defining and evaluating practical intelligence. In R. J. Sternberg & R. K. Wagner (Eds.), *Practical intelligence: Nature and origins of competence in the everyday world* (pp. 183–202). New York: Cambridge Univ. Press.

Frederiksen, N. (1986). Toward a broader conception of human intelligence. *American Psychologist, 41,* 445–452.

Friedman, S. L., Scholnick, E. K., & Cocking, R. R. (Eds.) (1987). *Blueprints for thinking.* New York: Cambridge Univ. Press.

Galotti, K. M. (1989). Approaches to studying formal and everyday reasoning. *Psychological Bulletin, 105,* 331–351.

Hartley, A. A. (1989). The cognitive ecology of problem solving. In L. W. Poon, D. C. Rubin & B. A. Wilson (Eds.), *Everyday cognition in adulthood and late life* (pp. 300–329). New York: Cambridge Univ. Press.

Heckhausen, J., & Schulz, R. (1993). Optimisation by selection and compensation: Balancing primary and secondary control in life span development. *International Journal of Behavioral Development, 16,* 287–303.

Horn, J. L., & Cattell, R. B. (1967). Age differences in fluid and crystallized intelligence. *Acta Psychologica, 26,* 107–129.

Johnson, M. M. S. (1990). Age differences in decision making: A process methodology for examining strategic information processing. *Journal of Gerontology, 45,* 75–78.

Johnson, M. M. S., Schmitt, F. A., & Everard, K. (1994). Task driven strategies: The impact of age and information on decision-making performance. Unpublished manuscript, University of Kentucky, Lexington.

Kahneman, D., Slovic, P., & Tversky, A. (1982). *Judgment under uncertainty: Heuristics and biases.* New York: Cambridge Univ. Press.

Kendall, P. C., & Fischler, G. L. (1984). Behavioral and adjustment correlates of problem solving: Validational analyses of interpersonal cognitive problem-solving measures. *Child Development, 55,* 879–892.

Klaczynski, P. A. (1994). Cognitive development in context: An investigation of practical problem solving and developmental tasks. *Journal of Youth and Adolescence, 23,* 141–168.

Klaczynski, P. A., & Berg, C. A. (1992). What's the real problem? Age, perceived control and perceived difficulty as predictors of everyday problem definitions. Paper presented at Cognitive Aging Conference, Atlanta, April.

Klaczynski, P. A., Laipple, J. J., & Jurden, F. H. (1992). Educational context differences in practical problem-solving during adolescence. *Merrill-Palmer Quarterly, 38,* 417–438.

Klaczynski, P. A., & Reese, H. W. (1991). Educational trajectory and "action orientation": Grade and track differences. *Journal of Youth and Adolescence, 18,* 441–462.

Kuhn, D., Pennington, N., & Leadbeater, B. (1983). Adult thinking in developmental perspective. In P. B. Baltes & O. G. Brim (Eds.), *Life-span development and behavior* (vol. 5, pp. 157–195). New York: Academic Press.

Kunda, Z. (1990). The case for motivated reasoning. *Psychological Bulletin, 108,* 480–498.

Labouvie-Vief, G. (1982). Dynamic development and mature autonomy: A theoretical prologue. *Human Development, 25,* 161–191.

Labouvie-Vief, G. (1984a). Logic and self-regulation from youth to maturity: A model. In M. L. Commons, F. A. Richards, & C. Armon (Eds.), *Beyond formal operations.* New York: Praeger.

Labouvie-Vief, G. (1984b). Culture, language, and mature rationality. In K. A. McCluskey & H. W. Reese (Eds.), *Life-span developmental psychology: Historical and generational effects* (pp. 109–128). New York: Academic Press.

Labouvie-Vief, G. (1992). A neo-Piagetian perspective on adult cognitive development. In R. J. Sternberg & C. A. Berg (Eds.), *Intellectual development* (pp. 197–228). New York: Cambridge Univ. Press.

Laipple, J. S. (1991). *Problem solving in young and old adulthood: The role of task interpretation.* Unpublished doctoral dissertation, West Virginia University, Morgantown.

Lave, J. (1989). *Cognition in practice.* New York: Cambridge Univ. Press.

Lave, J., Murtaugh, M., & de la Rocha, O. (1984). The dialectic of arithmetic in grocery shopping. In B. Rogoff & J. Lave (Eds.), *Everyday cognition: Its development in social context* (pp. 67–94). Cambridge, MA: Harvard Univ. Press.

Lazarus, R. S., & Folkman, S. (1984). *Stress, appraisal, and coping.* New York: Springer.

Leont'ev, A. N. (1981). A contribution to the theory of the development of the child's psyche. In A. N. Leont'ev (Ed.), *Problems of the development of the mind* (pp. 391–416). Moscow: Progress.

Lerner, R. M., & Kauffman, M. B. (1985). The concept of development in contextualism. *Developmental Review, 5,* 309–333.

Marsiske, M., & Willis, S. L. (1995). Dimensionality of everyday problem solving in older adults. *Psychology and Aging, 10,* 269–283.

Marsiske, M., Willis, S. L., Goodwin, P. E., & Maier, H. (1992). Relationships among cognitive processes, intellectual abilities, and everyday task performance. Paper presented at Cognitive Aging Conference, Atlanta, April.

Meacham, J. A., & Emont, N. C. (1989). The interpersonal basis of everyday problem solving. In J. D. Sinnott (Ed.), *Everyday problem solving: Theory and applications* (pp. 7–23). New York: Praeger.

Meyer, B. J. F., Russo, C., & Talbot, A. (1995). Discourse comprehension and problem solving: Decisions about the treatment of breast cancer by women across the life-span. *Psychology in Aging, 10,* 84–103.

Murphy, J. M., & Gilligan, C. (1980). Moral development in late adolescence and adulthood: A critique and reconstruction of Kohlberg's theory. *Human Development, 23,* 77–104.

Neisser, U. (1976). General, academic, and artificial intelligence. In L. B. Resnick (Ed.), *The nature of intelligence* (pp. 135–144). Hillsdale, NJ: Erlbaum.

Neisser, U. (1979). The concept of intelligence. In R. J. Sternberg & D. K. Detterman (Eds.), *Human intelligence: Perspectives on its theory and measurement* (pp. 179–189). Norwood, NJ: Ablex.

Overton, W. F. (1984). World views and their influence on psychological theory and research: Kuhn-Lakatos-Laudan. In H. W. Reese (Ed.), *Advances in child development and behavior* (vol. 18, pp. 191–226). New York: Academic Press.

Overton, W. F., & Reese, H. W. (1973). Models of development: Methodological implications. In J. R. Nesselroade & H. W. Reese (Eds.), *Life-span developmental psychology: Methodological issues* (pp. 65–86). New York: Academic Press.

Pepper, S. C. (1942). *World hypotheses.* Berkeley: Univ. of California Press.

Perlmutter, M., Kaplan, M., & Nyquist, L. (1990). Development of adaptive competence in adulthood. *Human Development, 33,* 185–197.

Piaget, J. (1952). *The origins of intelligence in children* (M. Cook, trans.). New York: International Univ. Press.

Poon, L. W., Rubin, D. C., & Wilson, B. A. (Eds.) (1989). *Everyday cognition in adulthood and late life.* New York: Cambridge Univ. Press.

Reese, H. W., & Overton, W. F. (1970). Models and development and theories of development. In L. R. Goulet & P. B. Baltes (Eds.), *Life-span developmental psychology: Research and theory* (pp. 115–145). New York: Academic Press.

Reese, H. W., & Rodeheaver, D. (1985). Problem solving and complex decision making. In J. E. Birren & K. W. Schaie (Eds.), *Handbook of the psychology of aging* (2d ed., pp. 474–499). New York: Van Nostrand Reinhold.

Rogoff, B., & Lave, J. (Eds.) (1984). *Everyday cognition: Its development in social context.* Cambridge, MA: Harvard Univ. Press.

Ross, B. L., & Berg, C. A. (1992). Examining idiosyncracies in script reports across the life span: Distortions or derivations of experience. In R. West & J. Sinnott (Eds.), *Everyday memory and aging* (pp. 39–53). New York: Springer.

Rubin, K. H., & Rose-Krasnor, L. (1992). Interpersonal problem solving and social competence in children. In V. B. Van Hasselt & M. Hersen (Eds.) *Handbook of social development: A lifespan perspective* (pp. 283–323). New York: Plenum.

Rybash, J. M., Hoyer, W. J., & Roodin, P. A. (1986). *Adult cognition and aging: Developmental changes in processing, knowing, and thinking.* New York: Pergamon.

Salthouse, T. A. (1984). Effects of age and skill in typing. *Journal of Experimental Psychology: General, 113,* 345–371.

Salthouse, T. A., & Mitchell, D. R. D. (1990). Effects of age and naturally occurring experience on spatial visualization performance. *Developmental Psychology, 26,* 845–854.

Sansone, C., & Berg, C. A. (1993). Adapting to the environment across the life span: Different process or different inputs? *International Journal of Behavioral Development, 16,* 215–241.

Schaie, K. W. (1965). A general model for the study of developmental problems. *Psychological Bulletin, 64,* 92–107.

Schaie, K. W. (1978). External validity in the assessment of intellectual development in adulthood. *Journal of Gerontology, 33,* 695–701.

Schaie, K. W. (1979). The primary mental abilities in adulthood: An exploration in the development of psychometric intelligence. In P. B. Baltes & O. G. Brim, Jr. (Eds.), *Life-span development and behavior* (vol. 2, pp. 67–115). New York: Academic Press.

Schaie, K. W. (1987). Application of psychometric intelligence to the prediction of everyday competence in the elderly. In K. W. Schaie (Ed.), *Cognitive functioning and social structure of the life course* (pp. 50–58). Norwood, NJ: Ablex.

Schank, R. C., & Abelson, R. (1977). *Scripts, plans, goals, and understanding.* Hillsdale, NJ: Erlbaum.

Scribner, S. (1986). Thinking in action: Some characteristics of practical thought. In R. J. Sternberg & R. Wagner (Eds.), *Practical intelligence: Nature and origins of competence in the everyday world* (pp. 143–162). New York: Cambridge Univ. Press.

Sinnott, J. D. (1975). Everyday thinking and Piagetian operativity in older adults. *Human Development, 18,* 430–443.

Sinnott, J. D. (1984). Postformal reasoning: The relativistic stage. In M. L. Commons, R. A. Richards, & C. Armon (Eds.), *Beyond formal operations: Late adolescent and adult cognitive development* (pp. 298–325). New York: Praeger.

Sinnott, J. D. (1989a). A model for solution of ill-structured problems: Implications for everyday and abstract problem solving. In J. D. Sinnott (Ed.), *Everyday problem solving: Theory and applications* (pp. 72–99). New York: Praeger.

Sinnott, J. D. (Ed.) (1989b). *Everyday problem solving: Theory and applications.* New York: Praeger.

Skinner, E. A., & Connell, J. P. (1986). Control understanding: Suggestions for a developmental framework. In M. M. Baltes & P. B. Baltes (Eds.), *The psychology of control and aging* (pp. 35–69). Hillsdale, NJ: Erlbaum.

Spivack, G., & Shure, M. B. (1982). The cognition of social adjustment: Interpersonal cognitive problem-solving thinking. In B. Lahey & A. E. Kazdin (Eds.), *Advances in clinical child psychology* (vol. 5, pp. 323–372). New York: Plenum.

Sternberg, R. J. (1985). *Beyond IQ: A triarchic theory of human intelligence.* New York: Cambridge Univ. Press.

Sternberg, R. J., & Wagner, R. K. (Eds.) (1986). *Practical intelligence.* New York: Cambridge Univ. Press.

Sternberg, R. J., & Wagner, R. K. (1989). Individual differences in practical knowledge and its acquisition. In P. L. Ackerman, R. J. Sternberg, & R. Glaser (Eds.), *Learning and individual differences* (pp. 255–278). New York: Freeman.

Strough, J., Berg, C. A., & Sansone, C. (in press). Goals for everyday problem solving across the life span: Age and gender differences in the salience of interpersonal concerns. Developmental Psychology.

Vygotsky, L. S. (1978). *Mind in society* (M. Cole, V. John-Steiner, S. Scribner, & E. Souberman, Eds.). Cambridge, MA: Harvard Univ. Press.

Wagner, R. K. (1986). The search for intraterrestrial intelligence. In R. J. Sternberg & R. K. Wagner (Eds.), *Practical intelligence: Nature and origins of competence in the everyday world* (pp. 361–378). New York: Cambridge Univ. Press.

Wagner, R. K., & Sternberg, R. J. (1985). Practical intelligence in real-world pursuits: The role of tacit knowledge. *Journal of Personality and Social Psychology, 48,* 436–458.

Wagner, R. K., & Sternberg, R. J. (1986). Tacit knowledge and intelligence in the everyday world. In R. J. Sternberg & R. K. Wagner (Eds.), *Practical intelligence: Nature and origins of competence in the everyday world* (pp. 51–83). New York: Cambridge Univ. Press.

Walsh, D. A., & Hershey, D. A. (1993). Mental models and the maintenance of complex problem solving skills into old age. In J. Cerella & W. Hoyer (Eds.), *Adult information processing: Limits on loss* (pp. 553–584). New York: Academic Press.

Willis, S. L., Jay, G. M., Diehl, M., & Marsiske, M. (1992). Longitudinal change and the prediction of everyday task competence in the elderly. *Research on Aging, 14,* 68–91.

Willis, S. L., & Schaie, K. W. (1986). Practical intelligence in later adulthood. In R. J. Sternberg & R. K. Wagner (Eds.), *Practical intelligence: Nature and origins of competence in the everyday world* (pp. 236–268). New York: Cambridge Univ. Press.

Willis, S. L., & Schaie, K. W. (1993). Everyday cognition: Taxonomic and methodological considerations. In J. M. Puckett & H. W. Reese (Eds.), *Life-span developmental psychology: Mechanisms of everyday cognition* (pp. 33–54). Hillsdale, NJ: Erlbaum.

11

THE DEVELOPMENTAL APPROACH: POSTFORMAL THOUGHT AS ADAPTIVE INTELLIGENCE

Jan Sinnott

Towson State University

FOUNDATIONS OF THE FIELD

■ Evolution of the Field

Developmentalists tend to study changes over time in the living organism as an adaptive system in a context. The developmental approach examines qualitative and quantitative changes in behavior over a lifetime. The *postformal* perspective, the subject of this chapter, which is based on the developmental perspective on cognitive change in adulthood and aging (the subject of this book) includes different, synthesis-based questions that set the approach apart from others in subtle ways. This approach includes emphasis on both laboratory and naturalistic studies. The developmental approach also complements psychometric and information-processing approaches to intelligence and cognition by opening study to elements of emotion, life-stage tasks, and personal meaning. Thus the developmental approach leads us across the boundaries of the "objective" and the "subjective," the experimental and the phenomenological, the clinical and the research domains.

In the study of adult intelligence, the subject of this section of the book, we can approach our topic differently if we use a developmental approach in its current, modern sense. Earlier chapters examined psychometric and practical intelligence; here we address adaptive intelligence. Without a modern developmental emphasis we have been accustomed to asking questions about "average," "above-average," and "below-average" performance, about comparing performance among a wide assortment of persons ("nomothetic studies"). We have been accustomed to labeling kinds of intelligence or factors in it and to discovering kinds of settings or processes that raise performance to some desired norm or presumed underlying competence. In other words, we have been enacting a particularly American sort of approach where one tries to find out what is normal and "level the field" to get those other-than-normal individuals closer to (or above!) the norm. The value "We're all created equal" sometimes gets translated into "We should all be the same in every way." Sometimes the developmental approach serves that important value too, addressing questions such as "How do individuals achieve higher levels of intelligence as they mature?"

The developmental approach can also be used to study other questions. These include individual differences, adaptive style, meaning, choice, process and interactions *over time,* and the parameters of expert performance. This side of the developmental approach feels less comfortable for most of us as scientists since it threatens the nomothetic, positivistic, mechanistic view of the world in which we are trained. It also feels dangerous to us as participants in a democracy to talk about basic differences, since such talk sometimes leads (politically) to discrimination in favor of or against certain persons with certain traits. But this side of the modern developmental approach often feels very important to the study of human behavior both to us and to those who make use of our studies. As many scientists reach their own mature years, this approach seems to them to be in line with their experience of human existence. It does offer a bridge between the experiences of life expressed by science, by medicine, and by the humanities. This side of the developmental approach is grounded in the exploratory strategies of "hard" sciences, such as quantum physics, evolutionary biology, chaos, complexity theory, and other theories of open systems (see the supplemental readings). So such *idiographic* inquiries may provide a useful alternative view of our phenomena of interest. Figure 11.1 is an attempt to graphically illustrate where life-span cognitive development studies overlap with other historically important approaches to the study of cognitive changes in adulthood and aging. The other approaches sometimes overlap with one another, too, as seen in the figure. Recently, each of these areas has begun to explore questions in the other areas, using its preferred methods and tests. So, to reflect *today's* reality, not historical reality, overlap *all* areas on the figure.

Figure 11.1 is included to give an idea of why developmental approaches give fresh insights into adult cognitive changes. Notice that our field of adult cognition has rested on the very useful contributions of sciences that can be described as reductionistic in nature, oriented to pathology, focused on a norm of *young* adult performance in Western middle-class cultures, and not oriented to change over time or to process. Some philosophical and scientific models of reality influencing the study of cognition in middle and old age in all these fields are discussed in Chapters 2 and 3.

Finally, early investigations were done by younger investigators, who studied children or young adults, for the most part. These investigators based their hypotheses and theories on their own views of the world (as younger persons) and on the tools and paradigms they created for testing younger persons. Yet, while all older adults have experienced being young, no younger adults have experienced being old. We can use more research drawn from the developmental perspective of adaptive mature adults. (If this seems like an unimportant concern, imagine your elementary school–age or teenage sibling or child devising a test of *your* intelligence or cognitive ability, based on what they think is intelligent. How would you perform?)

This chapter is devoted to a review of postformal thought. Due to space limitations, it cannot include a fair discussion of the literatures on complex reasoning or wisdom (see, e.g.,

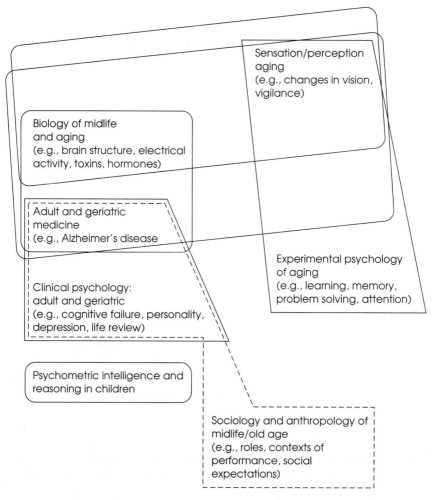

FIGURE 11.1 Traditions influencing the study of cognitive development in middle and old age, and their historical overlap with one another.

Sternberg, 1990). Each of these topics is worthy of an additional separate chapter. Postformal thought descended from the traditions of biology and the Piagetian study of the development of reasoning in children. The emphasis in Piaget's original theory was on adaptive biology, epistemology, and child development. In Piagetian theory reality is constructed by the knower through *assimilation* of new information to current structures and by gradual *accommodation* of those knowing structures to the new information. Piaget and early Piagetians spent their time examining qualities of *reasoning,* in *children and adolescents,* culminating in a list of *stages* having qualitative differences: the sensorimotor stage, the preoperational transition period, the concrete operational stage, and the formal operational stage.

In the formal stage the knower uses propositional reasoning and hypothetico-deductive reasoning, as a scientist would, to test logical derivatives of one consistent system of truths. The term "stage" has been problematic. A stage of reasoning has been defined as a qualitatively different way of organizing reality. But this can be a matter of degree as transitions between stages or different contexts for stage development lead to overlaps in an individual's stage repertoire. Operations from one stage sometimes appear (in a fresh way) in other stages. It was clear when one heard Piaget speak that this focus on reasoning and young persons was meant to be a *first* step (you have to start somewhere . . .) and that stages were meant to show the order in which styles of thinking developed. Of course, the next thing that happened was the imposition of a different model for interpreting what Piaget was doing, with subsequent attempts to give norms for the development of each stage. The final state of Piagetian theory formation was the attack against straw men: investigators tried to discredit statements that had never even been a part of Piaget's theory, namely, "Everything important happens in childhood," "All behavior is based on reasoning," and "Age norms exist for the development of reason."

Based as it is on Piagetian inquiries into the development of adaptive intelligence in children, postformal theorists ask the question "What is *adaptive* intelligence like, qualitatively, in adulthood and old age?" (What (if anything) do the middle-aged adult and the old adult do to know reality adaptively that is different at this stage of life from what went before?)

In this chapter, when I discuss *postformal* thought, I'll discuss it as an answer to Piaget's original, basic question: What is adaptive intelligence like at different points in development? Those who do research on the stage(s) *after* formal operations (i.e., *post*formal thought) usually do address their topic in the spirit of Piaget's original question. Their tentative answer is that mature adults do demonstrate a different quality of adaptive intelligence than children or adolescents do, a sort of postformal thought.

A final intellectual ancestor of postformal studies is the study of relativity theory and quantum physics, with the associated general systems theory, self-organizing systems, and chaos/complexity theory approaches. To describe physical reality in these newer ways, one needs to frame reality adaptively in ways more complex than formal operations, learning theory, psychometric intelligence or information processing. The intelligence used by modern physicists to understand the new physics requires additional intellectual operations that seem to give us clues about how mature adults discover different ways of framing the reality of their lives.

POSTFORMAL THOUGHT: A SPECIAL FORM OF INTELLIGENCE

What characterizes postformal thought? How must an adult structure thinking, over and above the operations of formal operational adolescents, to be in touch with reality and survive? The question here is not about specific facts or processes that need to be known but rather about general intellectual operations that the knower needs to master to make sense of life and to make life work.

One key thing competent mature adults seem to need (based on their statements and on observation and task analysis) is to be able to choose one model (in other words, one formal operational structure) of the many possible models to impose on a given reality so that they can make decisions and get on with life. They also need to know that they are making necessarily (partly) subjective decisions about reality when they do this. For example, you may be considering how to interpret some information you've read on adult cognitive abilities, so you open this book. In it you find several models, each of which is an internally consistent logical system and which has some merit (i.e., may be "true"). To actually interpret the information you have in hand, you have to choose a reality (a model) you want to adopt, for now. When you select the reality (model) you want to impose, you can go on to talk about the interpretation of your data. But you *know* that no outside authority or logic could tell you which model is "true"; you had to select one, act as if it were true, and go on with life. This can be postformal operations at work in your life. As another example, consider this situation: You know your parents are coming to town tomorrow. You realize from past experience that you and your parents have had good and bad times together during various visits over the years. You can meet them expecting the best or the worst to happen. If you expect the latter and live that reality, conversations probably will lead to confrontations, and the visit probably will be bad. If you expect the former and live that reality, your welcome will be likely to lead to happier events. And you *know* this part of the future is partly up to you. You'll help decide the "truth" of your interaction with your parents. And you *know* this is how it usually works. Notice that in these two examples it certainly was important to know *content* about the subject. But something more was required, namely, the *general-operation* rule that, when confronted with many "logics" about the "truth" of an event or a relationship, one needs to select one and act as if it's true in order to go on with life. This is a kind of necessary and sophisticated subjectivity.

Knowing the general-operation rule and letting it filter your reality, consciously choosing the formal operations logical system you'll impose and living it out as "true," are the essence of postformal operations. These two elements are often referred to as "necessary subjectivity" and "ordering formal operations." Since these two elements are different from the kind of reasoning that went before in Piaget's list (i.e., formal, scientific logic), they are considered a postformal "stage." ("Stage" is in quotes here because investigators argue over the qualities which make up a true stage; see Kramer, 1983, for an example.) Since postformal thinking organizes formal thinking, giving a higher-order logic to formal operations below it, it is post*formal*. I am emphasizing the logically distinctive elements here to highlight how postformal thought is a more complex Piagetian operation than formal thought. I'm not emphasizing (yet) the social components that help it develop, the life-span developmental tasks it seems to serve, the emotional life it seems to regulate, or the interpersonal tasks it seems to facilitate or that facilitate it. But these are all an integral part of postformal operations.

Social interaction leads to greater cognitive development when the ideas of others challenge the reality of the knower. Such cognitive approaches go beyond traditional information-processing approaches; postformal thought is a complex way of solving problems, one which develops with social experience, usually not before mature adulthood. It allows a person to solve problems even in situations where conflicted formal operational belief systems and priorities overlap. These ideas are inherent in the new physics and allied approaches (Hofstadter, 1979; Sinnott, 1981; Wolf, 1981).

A new type of cognitive coordination occurs at the postformal level. This new coordination has many characteristics and outcomes, as is apparent in the data of numerous studies (see, e.g., Commons, Richards, & Armon, 1984). For example, a new coordination of perspectives occurs on an *emotional* level, taking place over developmental time (Labouvie-Vief, 1987). This coordination parallels the cognitive one and is probably engaged in a circular interaction with it. Theorists expect that postformal thought is adaptive in a social situation with emotional and social components (Sinnott, 1984) because it is hypothesized that postformal thought eases communication, reduces information overload, and permits greater flexibility and creativity of thought. The postformal thinker knows she/he is helping create the eventual *truth* of a social interaction by being a participant in it and choosing to hold a certain view of its truth. Postformal thought has an impact on one's view of self, the world, other persons, change over time, and our connections with one another over time (Sinnott, 1981, 1984, 1989b, 1991a,b, 1993b).

■ Social Impetus for the Development of Postformal Thought

Relationships are behaviors in which shared truths are essential. So relationships are likely to be fertile grounds for the logical conflicts that could nurture development and postformal thought. Two human knowers bring their personal truths with them into a relationship. To have an interaction, they must somehow match those truths in order to communicate. This presents a possibility for them to enlarge their truth to accommodate to the truth of another in order to communicate well. When marriage partners, for example, try to see each other's point of view, they may need to expand their logics to see reality through another's reality frame. If the framing were complex enough, the intelligence they would be using would be postformal. Creating a shared reality is something friends or partners seem to do frequently, nurturing their postformal thought development.

In midlife and old age the tasks of that life period are social and interpersonal, and cognitive processes must serve these ends too. I argue (Sinnott, 1994a) that creativity in midlife and old age takes on specific cognitive qualities (i.e., those of postformal thought) that are adaptive in everyday life because they regulate the integration of intellectual and emotional stimulation from events or people. This complex cognition is a bridge between affect and cognition and between a person and other persons, and is a way to make the demands and practical concerns of adult life bearable and meaningful. This complex cognition can be described in preliminary ways using research data and can be manipulated experimentally (Sinnott, 1984, 1989c; Sinnott & Cavanaugh, 1991). Its style changes during the adult life span, as is evident in cross-sectional studies. The products of this mature thought may be better reflections of the union of emotion and cognition, of heart and mind, than are products the younger person creates. Midlife issues may be the key issues which motivate creative thinking about the shifting nature of socially constructed reality in everyday cognitive events. The psychologist's awareness that the person has such postformal thought processes can help him or her explain the behavior of that person at that developmental point.

In thinking about this further, let's examine one or two typical tasks of midlife and old age that are present in various cultures and theories. At the entry point of midlife, perhaps around the age of 30, a person must make a choice of a way to go, of a life to choose, in industrial cultures of multiple possibilities (Levinson, 1978; Perry, 1975). Even as she/he sees the relativity of many truths, she/he must make a passionate commitment (Frankl, 1963; Polanyi, 1971) to live out one choice or truth. That choice also involves relinquishing several illusions, including (Gould, 1978) that there is only one correct way to proceed in life and that one's parents have the knowledge of that single way.

Erikson (1950) describes the tasks of the midlife and old individual as developing generativity and integrity, that is, a mentoring and caring for others, a creation of children and contributions which will outlast the self, and a sense of the satisfying completeness of one's life story and one's place in the overall story of life. Again the sense of meaning is in relations with others and the creation of personal truth. Many authors speak of midlife as a time to deepen commitment and to choose deliberately what one's life will mean. One must choose when (and why!) to deploy one's resources, newly aware of their limits. This choice of meaning, if it is truly adaptive, also incorporates one's emotional side, allowing for a conscious orchestration of emotional and cognitive life leading to emotional self-regulation (Jung, 1971; Labouvie-Vief, 1987) in a way that leads (we hope) to maturity and wisdom (Chinen, 1992). The midlife adult begins to see a bigger picture that involves time and persons existing before and after him or her. As Riegel (1975) suggests, discord or disharmony, whether from other people, a rapidly shortening lifetime, or the pressure of multiple social roles, demands a new adaptive stance.

These midlife tasks involve bridging realities, entering the reality of another person, and developing complex concepts of the self, of success, of personal continuity. By this time in life a person has gathered the skills and the experience to make this leap in thinking structures. Spurred by everyday social encounters, fresh from the everyday problem-solving tasks of creating a marriage, a long-term friendship, a parent–child relationship, an organization, a social role, a self, the adaptive midlife adult is primed to create new realities. Like the developing child in Piagetian theory, the midlife adult seems to use assimilation and accommodation to reach new ways of filtering life with a new postformal subjective/objective logic.

■ Postformal Thought as Wisdom

We can see a tendency in adult development in these theories to include "wisdom," more sophisticated interpersonal skills, concern for the group (over and above the self), a deepening spirituality, and the ability to deal with paradoxes whether they are within the self, among persons, or in life itself. Troll (1985) has reviewed the major theories of adult development. These theories all hypothesize that developed, mature adults have a tendency to tie things together, to give overall meaning to emotions and events, to find an overall purpose in one's feelings, life, and death. Adult development, including postformal development, seems to mean increasing maturity, by all the definitions of maturity set out by Whitbourne and Weinstock (1979). The goal of later development seems to be to tie the individual's life to the group and anchor both in a meaningful story that makes the struggle of existence worthwhile.

We are thinking beings. When we develop, when we feel, when we yearn, we think about those changes, feelings, and yearnings. And we are beings who love sharing good stories (Chinen, 1992). When we think, we want it to make sense, to us and to others, too, as shared cognition.

We are beings that seem to have, and to think about, spiritual and transcendent experiences. We point to our saints and mystics, and some of us struggle to find union with God or universal consciousness. But some of us are "psychologist" beings, who have historically found it very difficult to integrate their psychologist selves with their spiritual, yearning selves or the spiritual, yearning selves of those they see. Some of us secretly admire Mother Teresa, Buddha, Christ, and Meister Eckhard but fear these represent irrational dreams. Are we less or more rational than the normal person? Are we less as psychologists because we dare ask? It may be time now, at this point in the history of our profession, to try to make that integration.

The task of integrating the reality of wise spirituality and the reality of life-span cognitive development reflects the very process we are trying to understand: How can two disparate frames for reality coexist in a coordinated way in the human mind? How can humans function on a day-to-day, practical level with conflicting basic frameworks underlying cognitive processes? We know that individuals do this in many ways from our own experience and from descriptions by others. We know these multiple realities occur in both simple and complex cognitive developmental stages (i.e., Piaget's mechanisms of assimilation and accommodation handle multiple realities at even the sensorimotor stage). Physicists have to operate in both "big-picture" and "local" realities; clinicians and people in love simultaneously see the person they are with as real and as potential; mystics report being "in this world" at the same time as the world itself is seen both as real and as "maya" (illusion). Millions of adults have been intrigued by books like Richard Bach's *Illusions* (1977), even when they find little meaning in standard psychology. What is the cognitive logical process that allows this transcending of multiple realities and even of "self" to arrive at a *healthy* unitative state? When Jean Valjean asks, in *Les Misérables* (Hugo, 1938), who he is, convict and criminal, a pillar of the community, or one whose life has been "purchased" by God for good works, he must develop to the point where his "self" is part of the larger, unitative postformal "self" that is more than those lesser selves.

METHODS USED TO STUDY POSTFORMAL THOUGHT

The study of postformal thought does not require the use of a single methodology. Investigators have made good use of them all. However, some methods or approaches seem more congenial to postformal studies because of the traditions from which this field has emerged (see Figure 11.1). For example, although postformal thinking is a form of verbal, logical intelligence, and although studies of intelligence have usually employed paper-and-pencil tests, there are few paper-and-pencil postformal tests because the postformal traditions did not arise from the intelligence traditions. Some "paper-and-pencil" tests do exist, though (see, e.g., Kramer, 1990; Richards & Commons, 1984; Sinnott, 1993a). The discussion below describes how some approaches have been used *so far,* keeping open the possibility of adopting or adapting others.

Keep in mind that the researcher trying to understand postformal thought is trying to learn about a higher-level coordination of lower-level processes. This gives such a researcher a wide latitude of research problems, ranging from the macroscopic to the microscopic and crossing several philosophical divides. The postformal researcher finds it harder than most to just *claim* a method and keep using it; the questions are too complex for that approach. At some point, to prove his or her case, the researcher will have to go to another level of inquiry.

The usual progress in science is from description to rudimentary theory formation to correlational studies to experimental studies to multifactorial studies to cross-sequential analyses to process-oriented studies of living systems (either orderly or chaotic and possibly composed of many interacting systems). Considered within this progression, postformal studies, on average, are at the level of rudimentary theory formation and description. Only a few investigators have carried their theory through several rounds of investigation and have reached experimental or multifactorial data collection and process-oriented theorizing.

■ Qualitative and Experimental Approaches

To date, the most popular approach to the study of postformal intelligence has been a qualitative one. This is a natural choice for a new field trying to get its footing in a new area. One popular way of obtaining data is to pose an open-ended question to a respondent, then analyze what he or she produces for structure, elements, and content. For example, Armon (1984) asked respondents "What is good work?" followed by "Why is that good?" The text of the respondents' answers was analyzed, as was the text of their responses to follow-up questions. This kind of research best captures the phenomenological research preferences of those who would give the research participant a greater voice in scientific research. It is congenial for those promoting cultural diversity in the voices of psychology.

Experimental approaches are becoming more popular as the postformal field matures. Deriving cause–effect relationships with as great an objectivity as possible and highly controlled stimuli is important if postformal investigations are ever to bridge to the fields in Figure 11.1 that rest in experimental traditions. Let's look at two examples of postformal experiments. In one experiment, Sinnott (1991a) manipulated goal clarity and heuristic availability to determine whether these affect postformal thought during problem solving. In other words, were participants influenced by manipulating how well structured or ill structured the problem was or by having (or not having) a technique available to solve problems? In that study, no clear effects for the manipulation occurred; respondents were consistently postformal or not, in spite of manipulations. But in another experiment in that series, mood was manipulated to determine whether a more positive mood would increase postformal operations. That hypothesis was supported. Studies such as these will both help us understand the phenomenon in question and allow us to maximize the chance that postformal thought can be facilitated for thinkers.

Methods to enrich postformal studies can be borrowed from other traditions. For example (space considerations prevent more elaborate discussion), we have borrowed from information-processing studies to use signal detection theory (Richards & Commons, 1990), everyday problem solving (Sinnott, 1993d), thinking aloud methodology (Sinnott, 1989b,c), task-unrelated-thought-intrusions concepts (Sinnott, 1991a), and artificial intelligence goals (Sinnott, 1991a,b). A long series of studies has been derived from Kohlberg's concepts of moral development (see Commons, Armon, Kohlberg, Richards, Grotzer, & Sinnott, 1989). All these crossovers in methods allow us to communicate with other fields.

Factor-analytic approaches and multivariate approaches have proven to be useful analytic and design techniques for a number of investigators. For example, Kitchener and King (1989) analyzed 10 years of their reflective judgment model research to examine longitudinal changes in the reflective judgment mean scores of seven samples. Commons, Armon, et al. (1989) factor-analyzed data from several postformal measures to search for commonalities among them. Sinnott (1991a) employed analyses of covariance to control for age in experimental studies of postformal thought as wisdom.

Applications of process-oriented theories and computer models have only recently been introduced to postformal studies. Investigators are considering ways to apply general systems theory (Sinnott, 1989a, 1993b), quantum physics approaches (Sinnott, 1981, 1994b), and chaos and complexity theory (Sinnott, 1993c, 1994c) to studies of complex thinking. The applications of these sophisticated models are at the level of theory. Data are not yet available to test such models, and some of the models are more like metaphoric interpretation than precise sources for hypotheses.

Postformal theories lend themselves conceptually to the use of new technologies like video (especially interactive video), virtual reality devices, computer games, hypertext, and multimedia presentations because these postformal theories and technologies all center on shifts in realities. Alternative representational styles (visual versus kinesthetic representation or haptic versus auditory representation of reality) complicate a problem space, making problems potentially ill structured for many learners. New technologies such as interactive video, virtual reality, and Internet communication represent alternative realities, creating a potentially postformal knowing situation. Much of what makes cross-cultural understanding difficult is the differences in style of representation. Those studying postformal thought will find a rich supply of testing possibilities and new questions within these new communication devices. For example, is a postformal thinker postformal in visually *and* auditorially represented problems or just in his or her "home" modality?

If the answer to that last research question is that respondents are postformal in their own representational style but not in another, we might make use of interventions to try to enrich respondents' styles. Sometimes all that seems necessary for participants to produce complex postformal thought is to make it clear that the researcher is open to their complex thinking. Some of Sinnott's (1989–1991) work with follow-up probe questions demonstrates this. Respondents may need to work on something like the "learning stories" of Paula Spencer (1991) to come to an awareness of multiple realities/logic and necessary self-reference (i.e., postformal thought). Standardized tests of postformal complex intelligence which are now being created and computerized (Sinnott, 1993a) should help make more research and a wider range of research feasible.

■ Implications of Postformal Thought

For "Cognitive Aging"

The existence of postformal thought as a process emerging in middle and old age provides a challenge to standard models and stereotypes of intellectual decline (or, at least, lack of growth) at that period of life. Without arguing against the literature detailing how various cognitive processes change or decline in the laboratory or in life, the proponents of postformal theories still manage to argue that positive *development* occurs and that it has numerous implications for thinking and living. This may be a case of moving the research game to a new playing field rather than concentrating on fighting over old cognition/intelligence/wisdom "turf." It is a useful game since it opens up new research questions and new ways of conceptualizing old problems. Considering the existence of the development of postformal thought in mature years also expands implicit research models from intrapersonal to interpersonal domains, given that postformal thought is interpersonally and socially coconstructed. This is a model that by its very nature is a synthesis and a bridge since it must admit intention, life history, meaning, and individuality to cognitive science without moving as far from cognitive science as investigators in areas such as wisdom often do. Although there are many other implications, the last to be mentioned here is this: postformal thought suggests that middle-aged and older adults have a unique cognitive resource that is a way of thinking which by definition does not make sense to many younger adults or younger researchers. It therefore *demands* the involvement of mature researchers and the dialogue with (not tolerance of or condescension toward) the group which is the object of study.

For Everyday Living

There is some evidence that the individual who can use postformal thought has a powerful and useful cognitive tool. This tool permits the user to expand the views of reality available for conscious consideration and to temporarily and consciously adopt the worldviews of others without experiencing cognitive overload, contradiction, or threat. The awareness of the postformal process of coconstructing truth lets the everyday user of postformal operations apply that process to other spheres such as group dynamics, couple relations, politics, communications, and other self-regulating processes. The postformal thinker has more useful coping strategies for incorporating sides of the self, emotions, and the life of the spirit with less need for control or anxiety. Although many more advantages could be discussed, perhaps the farthest-reaching result of postformal thought in the everyday realm is the real sense of power experienced by the thinker who can understand this "bigger picture" as well as the process by which it is constructed.

IS THERE EVIDENCE FOR POSTFORMAL THOUGHT?

Do we see any signs that mature adults reason in a qualitatively different way than Piaget's formal operational adolescents? In my own research and that of other leading investigators, we do see reliable evidence that a different sort of reasoning does occur. None of these investigators argue that such reasoning occurs all the time or even predominates in the intelligent behavior of mature adults, just that it does occur and serves a useful purpose. The aspect of postformal thought that a particular investigator chooses to attend to differs from investigator to investigator, yet the overall picture is consistent.

The study of postformal thought is entering the correlational/experimental phase of scientific inquiry. It is important that we now do correlational studies and experiments rather than simply spending more time theorizing. Theories already exist (Commons et al., 1984) and to some extent have empirical support (Commons, Sinnott, Richards, & Armon, 1989; Commons, et al., 1990). My own research has indicated that postformal thought does occur in midlife and old age. In 1981 I first reported on applications of new physics theory to theories of development and on the existence of postformal operations (see Table 11.1 for a list of operations) and later examined them in the context of problem solving (Sinnott, 1984). This initial study was followed by further examinations of that existence, of the operations themselves, of the pattern of thinking during thinking-aloud studies of postformal thought, and of other aspects of context in which the use of the operations might be facilitated or hindered, namely, health, emotion, intention, problem goal clarity, and heuristic availability (Sinnott, 1989b,c, 1991a). The initial studies in a large sample were followed by more specialized investigations of the existence of the operations in special samples, for example, in family members deciding about the placement of a psychotic family member (Sinnott, 1991b), in expert teachers (Lee, 1991, 1994), and in long-term married couples (K. Rogers, 1992; Rogers, Sinnott, & Van Dusen, 1991). Let's look at some of these results to assess the presence of postformal operations.

■ Subjects and General Procedure: Sinnott's Primary Experiments

Respondents were volunteers in the Baltimore Longitudinal Study of Aging (BLSA) (Shock et al., 1985). They were well-educated, highly motivated men and women in good enough health to come to the Gerontology Research Center for 2 to 3 days of testing. Two hundred ten respondents participated in the "standard administration" of problem solving which fol-

---

TABLE 11.1 Operations in Piagetian Postformal Self-referential Thought

Metatheory shift: Shifting beliefs about reality or an a priori underlying problem

Problem definition: Naming what the problem is, within underlying a priori or any reality

Process/product shift: Looking at a problem as both "finding a good answer" and "finding a good general way to get answers to problems of this type"

Parameter setting: Deciding on the key variables in this problem

Pragmatism: Evaluating the comparative worth of several good solutions

Multiple solutions: Generating several solutions to a defined problem within a certain metatheory and parameters

Multiple causality: Evaluating the several causal paths leading to a goal

Paradox: Reaching an awareness of inherent conflicts in reality within a problem

Self-referential thought: Realizing that Truth is a commitment to one of several versions of reality that seem equally correct and that we construct with other individuals in societies or relationships on an ongoing basis

---

Source: Sinnott, 1984.

lowed the clinical interview of Piaget (Sinnott, 1984). Forty respondents took part in the "thinking aloud administration," in which respondents spoke without interruption and then answered standard questions (Sinnott, 1989c). The number of respondents in any analysis sometimes differed from the total number of subjects, however, since not every protocol was complete and some other variables of interest in some analysis (variables already on record) had not been given to all the problem solvers.

Respondents received many psychological and physical tests during each visit (every 2 years) to the BLSA. These data are on file for 30 years of visits and are the source of data for some analyses using memory or blood pressure measures (Shock et al., 1985). In each case they were given six of Sinnott's logical problems. When a respondent was scheduled to be tested with Sinnott's own tests, he or she first took problem solving, either the standard administration or the thinking aloud administration form. Standard administration subjects went on to an Everyday Memory Test (Sinnott, 1986) and a laboratory memory–response time test. Thinking aloud subjects only sometimes went on to the same laboratory memory test. All respondents had blood pressure taken in a seated position during a physical at each visit. Additional details about measures and procedures are given in the context of each section below.

■ Is There Evidence for Postformal Operations?

Data from both the standard administration and the thinking aloud administration of six logical problems were used. Protocols were scored by two raters for reliability purposes. For the standard administration, a large proportion of respondents (26%–85%, depending on the problem) displayed a crucial operation, that of creating more than one complete logical solution. For the thinking aloud sample, the proportion of respondents expressing self-referential thought aloud (i.e., making the statement that "truth" is, of necessity, based on one's choice of a standard or a logic such that two mutually contradictory solutions may both be "true" solutions) ranged from 2 percent to 27 percent, depending on the problem. Looking at evidence for self-referential thought, multiple goals, and multiple solutions, 2 percent to 85.3 percent of adult subjects showed some evidence of postformal thought and 2 percent to 60 percent showed formal operational thought.

Individual problem-solving protocols, which were analyzed after respondents thought aloud, were analyzed for processes apparent in problem solving of the six problems, including the processes of postformal thought (Sinnott, 1989b,c). Figure 11.2 shows the process of one respondent's solution. Respondents did manifest postformal intelligence, especially in solution of unstructured problems (or, richer, more "wicked" problems) with unclear goals and heuristics (Churchman, 1971).

Looking at the more specialized studies, colleagues and I have been finding postformal operations there, too. Let's first look at the (true) story of a woman trying with her family to solve the problem of care for an acutely psychotic brother. Her story is in Table 11.2, based on her journal. A flowchart showing her problem-solving process is in Figure 11.2. If she used a postformal operation, a number appears in the process entry. She obviously used postformal thought, and this allowed her to cope adaptively. To summarize, the respondent gained advantages through postformal thought: the ability to "speak" in "others' languages" or belief systems; better communication; the ability to argue within others' logics; a flexible view of what is possible for a family; more effective interventions, based on others' psychological realities; awareness of one's own biases and filtered worldviews; the ability to limit over-stimulation without limiting information flow; more creative problem solving; more flexible interpersonal relations; the ability to get a perspective on family problems; the ability to be more effective in emotion-laden interpersonal situations; a flexible view of who the other "is"; the ability to reach the best solution in view of all realities; a lessened need for control and defenses; a lower anxiety level; and the ability to interact with all the other group members at their level.

Other samples from which data is already analyzed, and other samples from studies under way, all mentioned above, have also yielded postformal thought. Lee's expert teachers, for example, showed postformal thought related to curriculum in posing problems and in solving them. Overall, these processes of intelligent cognition are found in mature adult thought samples. Do investigators using other concepts of postformal thought also find them in real life? There are numerous examples that they do, as shown by Basseches (1984), Commons et al. (1984), Commons et al. (1990), Commons, Sinnott, et al. (1989), Sinnott (1989c), and Sinnott and Cavanaugh (1991), in contexts as diverse as musical compositions (Funk, 1989), unitative consciousness (Koplowitz, 1984, 1989), emotional self-regulation (Kramer & Bacelar, 1994; Labouvie-Vief, 1987), and abstract, general stage logic models (Richards & Commons, 1984). Some of these will be discussed in greater depth later in the chapter.

■ What Are Some Factors That Facilitate Postformal Performance?

Few systematic studies have been done to test the parameters of postformal performance. Investigators always expect that there *are* limits, since not all adults demonstrate postformal thought, no matter how select the sample or promising the context. We may speculate that if every adult thought postformally most of the time, new skills that demanded simpler processing could never be learned, nor would extremely rapid "knee-jerk" responses that help in crises be accessed quickly enough. We also know that respondents' performance seldom reaches their level of competence; so what factors might give a better, truer reading of a respondent's skills?

Most of the investigators in the summary volumes cited earlier have chosen to do their theorizing, data collection, or case analyses in a setting where *complex* decisions or solutions are demanded. So *complexity of situation* seems necessary, whether that complexity is about emotional life or an individual's personal struggles. Some investigators have correlated their types of postformal scores with some other variable that postformal cognition is hypothesized to predict, if it is a valid concept, but more will be said of these applications later.

Five sets of investigators, including the author, have gathered data on factors facilitating postformal thought. Blanchard-Fields (1989) examined the effects of the emotional saliency of a problem and respondents' age on postformal thought. Adults were better able to produce postformal responses than adolescents were. Age did not matter to performance or interpretation of the nonemotionally salient stories, but, when the emotional saliency of the story increased, adults performed more postformally than adolescents did. Brabeck and Wood (1989) found that critical thinking, as measured by the Watson-Glaser Critical Thinking Appraisal, did not relate to reflective judgment, a postformal skill involving the complexity of how one justifies one's beliefs. Commons, Armon, et al. (1989) examined the ef-

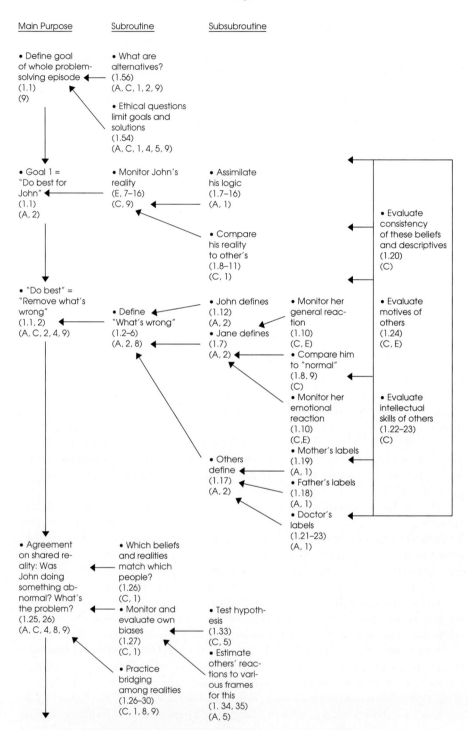

Main Purpose | Subroutine | Subsubroutine

FIGURE 11.2 Summary of processes used by key informant based on her notes alone. *Key to symbols: Letters* = problem-solving elements: A = construct problem space; B = generate and choose solutions; C = monitor; D = access memories; E = utilize "noncognitive" elements. *Numbers* = postformal operations: Operations are 1 through 9. (*Source:* Sinnott, 1991b.)

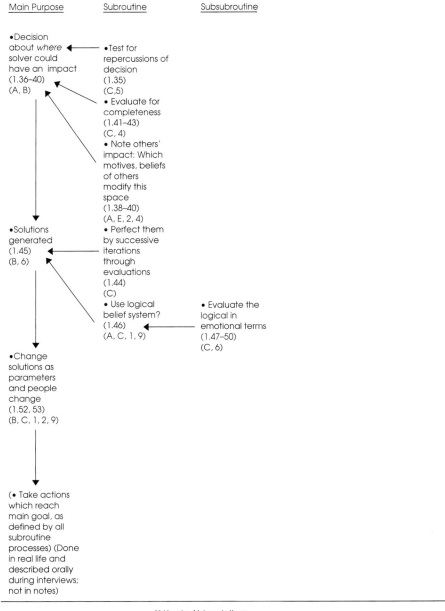

Main Purpose	Subroutine	Subsubroutine
•Decision about *where* solver could have an impact (1.36–40) (A, B)	•Test for repercussions of decision (1.35) (C,5)	
	• Evaluate for completeness (1.41–43) (C, 4)	
	• Note others' impact: Which motives, beliefs of others modify this space (1.38–40) (A, E, 2, 4)	
•Solutions generated (1.45) (B, 6)	• Perfect them by successive iterations through evaluations (1.44) (C)	
	• Use logical belief system? (1.46) (A, C, 1, 9)	• Evaluate the logical in emotional terms (1.47–50) (C, 6)
•Change solutions as parameters and people change (1.52, 53) (B, C, 1, 2, 9)		
(• Take actions which reach main goal, as defined by all subroutine processes) (Done in real life and described orally during interviews; not in notes)		

** Key to Abbreviations

Letters = Problem-solving elements   Numbers = Postformal operations

A = Construct problem space
B = Generate and choose solutions
C = Monitor
D = Memories
E = "Noncognitive" elements

TABLE 11.2 Summary of Some Concrete Facts about the Case

One peaceful afternoon, the main informant ("Jane") received a telephone call from her father, who lives hundreds of miles away. According to her father, her brother ("John"), who lived in the father's city, had been behaving very strangely. John was accusing family members of trying to get rid of him, making him sick, and plotting against him. Others were against him too, trying to control him, John said. The situation was at a crisis point.

This was very upsetting news for Jane for more than one reason. It was the first she'd heard of this problem, as communication was not a strong skill for her family. Two weeks ago, for the first time, it had appeared that John was examining familial relationships, trying to piece together family motives. John wanted to see Jane very much. Also, Jane and John had always been very close, although she was nearly a decade older than he. They were each other's emotionally closest relatives. For the better part of 30 years John had experienced problems with drugs, alcohol, and dependence on his father but had never experienced a psychotic break.

John's life always seemed to get worse. As a teen, John had been intensely hurt by his parents' destructive divorce and later had been a troubled participant in his father's second marriage. Jane and an older brother had distanced themselves. Over and over again, John would be involved in some problem and his father would try to "handle" the situation while his mother complained about them both and his stepmother complained about John. Jane felt very lucky to have escaped the family situation, but she felt helpless. She grieved over her brother's and family's pain.

Jane had planned a short visit with her father in a few days to keep family ties intact and to take her children to see their grandfather. She had hoped for a peaceful visit, but that hope was rapidly fading with the phone call. Instead of being at peace, she was going into the eye of the hurricane. But Jane had always known she was the "invulnerable child" (Garmezy, 1976) who could cope and love, and now it was time to be that again. With children in tow she headed for the plane, unsure of the reality of the situation or the state of her brother.

Upon her arrival she found that her father had already hospitalized John and was in a state of great anxiety himself. John's behavior had seriously frightened their father when John had sought refuge at the father's house, although John had not threatened others or himself. Since John had refused to take the medication prescribed by a "well-renowned" psychiatrist, the father, acting on the psychiatrist's advice, was certain that commitment was the only solution. John valued his freedom and was angry at his father's unilateral decision to hospitalize him and to commit him involuntarily. Even worse, John would be under control of a private psychiatrist who John felt was not listening to him or sympathetic with him. John had seen the psychiatrist several years before but had refused treatment from him at that time and felt antagonistic toward him. John's stepmother was glad he was out of the house. John's mother was distancing herself from the problems. The father pleaded with Jane to avoid John, the hospital, and the whole problem and to pretend to her children that nothing was happening so they could "have a good time." Jane was too upset about her brother to pretend everything was normal and intended to communicate with him unless the doctors disapproved. When they told her they had no objection, she at once drove to the hospital to visit and to find out some facts, determined to offer love and support to John.

When she arrived, she found out that John was refusing to take the prescribed antipsychotic medication because he "needed to keep his mind clear." Clarity was needed, John said, because his father (with the private psychiatrist chosen by their father) had decided to try to commit him involuntarily. As a prelude to that action, the police were due to arrive momentarily to transfer John to a locked ward in a private hospital. His agitation was increasing. No one paid attention to what he said! Why wouldn't anyone listen to him? Even his family seemed to be plotting against him! Jane listened and talked and tried to

TABLE 11.2 Summary of Some Concrete Facts about the Case

describe his options to him. She told him she loved him and he could count on her support. They discussed their "crazy family," and John became more calm and rational. Hours passed, and the police they feared would arrive did not appear.

When night came, the staff made it known that a family member needed to stay overnight with John to ensure that he would not leave the psychiatric ward. Jane said she'd stay (she saw no other option) and drove 40 minutes to her father's house, informed her children and her father, argued with her father against involuntary commitment, and drove back to the hospital. She urged John to take his medication to avoid commitment. John agreed to do so but was concerned that he would not have a "clear head" to defend himself at the hearing in the morning.

In the morning she prompted her brother to tell the judge he would take the medication, and immediately before the hearing she negotiated with her father to delay the commitment proceedings. At the hearing, however, neither occurred and John was involuntarily committed for a week.

Jane spent the next 3 days trying to understand when (and if) a second commitment hearing was to be held (which would extend the commitment to a possible 90 days), trying to find a new psychiatrist, talking with John's current and prospective psychiatrist and therapists, and talking with John. She was unsure about which of John's stories were true and the extent of his paranoia. She feared that involuntary commitment would destroy John's remaining threads of trust and self-esteem, but also that her father couldn't cope with John's release. She was looking for an ethical and practical solution to John's situation within the continually shifting demands and expectations of both her brother and father. She was concerned for her children and their anxiety in the middle of this chaos and the lack of time she was spending with them. During this time she sustained herself through journal writing, meditation, and the support of a couple of close friends. John took the medication, established a relationship with a therapist, and seemed better, but no one would call off the second commitment hearing. Everyone else in the family seemed worse, more changeable, angry, confused. The father and stepmother were frightened by the idea that if John were released he would want to stay with them. John lapsed into paranoia as the commitment hearing was on, then off, then on again, no matter how he behaved as a patient. It appeared that Jane was unable to comfort John, find another doctor acceptable to her father, penetrate the legal system, or shift her father's perspective from involuntary commitment to voluntary commitment. She grew depressed. Everyone grew more confused and unable to cope. In this highly charged emotional atmosphere, it became hard to say whose reality was "real" and whose goals merited attention.

Finally the second hearing took place and John was voluntarily committed. John's father now opposed the psychiatrist he had originally picked, and John then chose the very psychiatrist he had once vehemently rejected. No one in the family really accepted the commitment as necessary or useful, though they seemed to think there was no other alternative.

John continued contact with Jane, with whom he had a good relationship, and broke contact with their father. He was soon able to discontinue medication and entered a halfway house. Jane, exhausted, returned home with her children and a new awareness of the dynamics of her family of origin. The mother and stepmother seemed unchanged, but the father had shed some illusions and began to communicate with Jane in a new way. However, John remained convinced he was fine, the father decided to blame the psychiatrist for the chaos, and, as things calmed down and they needed her less, no one kept in touch with Jane.

Source: Sinnott, 1991b.

fects of background variables and interests on postformal thought. They found little effect for background and interest variables, except for the positive effects of investigator interest. Kitchener and King (1989) examined the longitudinal effects of age and education on reflective judgment, their postformal area. They also examined the relationship between reflective judgment and intellectual domain constructs such as verbal ability, scholastic aptitude, formal operations, and critical thinking. The intellectual constructs could not account for the age and education effects on reflective judgment, and the age and education effects are difficult to interpret so far.

Finally, Sinnott (1984, 1989c, 1991a) investigated the influence of problem context, respondent age and gender, type of problem administration, use of question probes, goal clarity, heuristic availability, one dimension of health (here, represented by blood pressure), naturalistic and laboratory memory ability, memory for designs, vocabulary, and manipulation of emotion, intention, and mind wandering on postformal intelligence performance. We also looked at whether experience with that sort of problem and verbal/visual/kinesthetic representational style mattered. The sample and method described earlier in this chapter were tested on the various tasks and the health, demographic, and experimental factors. Problems having a more social/interpersonal context and ill-structured problems more often elicited postformal thought. Mature adults in midlife produced more postformal responses and age groups had different styles of responding, but gender made no difference. Thinking aloud versus interview administration had little effect on results, but the use of probe questions increased the likelihood respondents would articulate postformal thought. The manipulation of goal clarity and heuristic availability led to mixed results (Sinnott, 1991a). The effect of blood pressure could not be interpreted clearly. High vocabulary scores and many memory elements such as memory for designs, action memory, and word recall were positively related to postformal performance. Respondents usually used mind wandering, personal experience, emotional reactions, and evaluative judgments in their solutions, but neither those nor representational style was consistently related to postformal thought. Problems judged "most interesting" were least likely to elicit postformal responses. The manipulation of mood, intention to be productive, and encouragement of mind wandering suggested that postformal performance might be enhanced slightly by upbeat mood, permission to mind wander, and low, not high, demands to "produce as many solutions as you possibly can." Overall, these studies leave us with many more hypotheses to test and some hope that postformal performance can be enhanced. Many biological, interpersonal, problem context, and intentional factors influence scores on even these relatively abstract postformal problems.

WHAT ARE THE APPLICATIONS OF THIS THEORY?

A theory need not have immediate applications to be useful in the future or provocative now. Most of the thinkers interested in postformal thought, including the author, were led there by compelling logic and curiosity, rather than by a pressing applied problem. But we usually arrived at a postformal theory with a context for our questions, and that context now leads to applications. For example, some of the contexts of those writing about postformal thought have included clinical psychology (Koplowitz, 1984), youth development (Gruber,

1984), creativity (Arlin, 1975), aging (Sinnott, 1984), education (Lee, 1991), cross-cultural development (Tannon, 1991), interpersonal relations (Powell, 1984), spiritual development (Sinnott, 1994b), corporate development (Sinnott, 1993b), women's ways of knowing (Orr & Luscz, 1994), emotional development (Labouvie-Vief, 1987), conflict resolution (Sinnott, 1984, 1993b), moral development (Armon, 1984), international development projects (Johnson, 1991), musical composition (Funk, 1989), and couple relationships (Rogers, 1992)—quite a variety! Although many of these authors did much of their writing about postformal thought at the level of theory, some of them, as well as other *non*-theorists, moved on to clear applications as well.

It's easy to see why theories of postformal thought would have applications. The theory rests on *adaptive* intelligence; it seems to develop through *interpersonal* interactions or dialogues; postformal thought *organizes* and *consolidates* lots of lower-level concepts and logic to *allow choice* and *avoid overstimulation;* and it *thrives on conflicts* between worldviews or philosophies. These sound like the tasks adults try to face every day of their mature lives in a world of ill-structured problems and fuzzy logic.

In Rogers' work, for example, 40 couples between the ages of 35 and 50, who had been married between 5 and 30 years, were prescreened for verbal intelligence and marital adjustment. They were then randomly administered five formal operational problems, two of which were formal logical or mathematical in nature while three contained both mathematical and interpersonal, or social, elements. Each dyad was videotaped during the problem-solving process.

Analyses of variance were performed on marital adjustment as related to formal and relativistic cognitions. There were no marital adjustment differences in the overall ability to use formal operations. However, maritally well-adjusted dyads evidenced significantly more relativistic cognitions, particularly on problems involving a social/everyday element, than poorly adjusted dyads did. Multivariate analyses were performed on four separate social behavior scales as related to formal and relativistic cognitions, as well as marital adjustment. Again, formal operations did not distinguish between the differing social behaviors; however, the social behavior scales, particularly avoidant versus cooperative behaviors, were strongly related to marital adjustment and relativistic thinking. If this study's results can be replicated, it would make sense to use them to help couples strengthen their interactions by stretching their cognitive style to facilitate its becoming postformal.

FUTURE DIRECTIONS

Evaluation of postformal theories is difficult at this early stage of their development. Postformal theories of intelligence have generated considerable excitement and seem to address questions about thinking in maturity that are new and important. The specifics of the genesis of postformal thought, its dynamics, and outcomes in real life (whether it is present or absent) remain to be investigated further.

Investigators have reliably found postformal thought in many types of persons in many contexts. Some of its operations and processes are becoming clearer. We now know some correlates of its occurrence and have some models (on micro and macro levels) for it. We can see its antecedents and the links between postformal theory and research traditions. We can also see more aspects of its predicted utility or adaptivity. We have done work with theory in descriptive, correlational, measurement, experimental, and applied domains and have developed the theory further. The fact that we can make so much progress with the concept of postformal intelligence shows its strength. Its *numerous* practical, everyday applications show an even greater strength.

But the concept also has weaknesses that need to be resolved. For example, the large number of theories of postformal thought that exist to some extent in selected content areas can be seen as either a strength (e.g., broad utility, stimulation to researchers) or a weakness (e.g., too many measures with no absolute "winner"). Another potential weakness is disagreement over whether postformal thought represents a clear *stage* of development. Kramer's (1983) discussion of this issue includes arguments that have never been fully addressed or resolved. Although several investigators would like to declare their subtheory *the* general theory of postformal thought, many versions are still being explored in this vibrant field. While this situation of abundance may make it harder for graduate students trying to finish a quick, "no-conflicts" dissertation, most see it as a healthy sign of intellectual life.

One inherent (and unresolvable) difficulty in the field is that complex thinking, by definition, is probably rare. Therefore fewer individuals understand the theories, can score the complicated assessments, or can see uses for such cognitive skills. Our field is not alone in this dilemma. We have company in fields like physics, space science, and artificial intelligence, where the public (and occasionally members of Congress) doze off while scientists passionately try to explain the importance of it all. We do have the virtue of being cheap—no supercollider costs for postformal research! But we also have the curse of being more frightening than physicists (the "What if they see how stupid I really am?" fear). While research should be done for its own sake, postformal research will be most welcome when it stresses basic *and* applied aspects and shows the many ways in which it is a common human trait to be postformally intelligent to some degree.

Additional research should concentrate on these three priorities: continuing the work described in this chapter; bridging to other fields, contexts, and applications; and articulating the ways in which this adaptive intelligence can be made available to more adults. We need to flesh out the skeleton of research around "postformal" theories. This will involve creating more "user-friendly" measures (e.g., Kramer's paper-and-pencil version, Sinnott's computerized test); doing more "contexted" studies; testing a variety of test takers; and studying wise or expert persons in various fields. This also involves studies that use dynamic systems approaches (see, e.g., Smith & Thelen, 1993) to bridge among thinkers or among disciplines using shared cognition. Biological factors (e.g., EEG on-line brain mapping) and postformal thought might be studied together. We might examine how the complex thinking of some individuals in a group of thinkers influences noncomplex members of the group to move toward complex thought. Is a complex, postformal thinker equally complex at home and at work? Does having family (a developmental task) influence complexity of thought over time? For whom? Do postformal thinkers use postformal thought in contexts that are emotionally charged? Is there a postformal psychopathology style or learning style? Does memory decline in advanced old age change postformal processes over time, or does postformal thought make compensatory cognitive strategies easier to use? How can we let psychotherapists and negotiators in training get a better awareness of their ability to use postformal thought? Clearly there are many projects that would address the three research priorities in interesting ways!

In conclusion, it is fair to say that concepts of postformal cognitive development (development of adult postformal intelligence) are well on their way to offering real explanatory power for life-span developmentalists. It may prove possible to use postformal concepts to examine basic and applied aspects of lifetime growth in holistic, synthetic, and dynamic ways. Important factors in development—body, mind, emotion, life stages, intention, interpersonal relation—can be joined within this theory and research, as they are in the lives of real adults.

ACKNOWLEDGMENTS

This work was supported in part by a sabbatical grant from Towson State University, Baltimore. The critical review of this chapter by Lynn Johnson and by other anonymous peer reviewers, as well as by the editors, is greatly appreciated. Thank you to the support staff in the Psychology Department who helped prepare this manuscript.

SUPPLEMENTAL READINGS

Augros, R., & Stanciu, G. (1987). *The new biology.* Boston: New Science Library.

Capra, F. (1982). *The turning point: Science, society, and the rising culture.* Toronto: Bantam.

Waldrop, M. M. (1992). *Complexity: The emerging science at the edge of order and chaos.* New York: Simon and Schuster.

REFERENCES

Arlin, P. K. (1975). Cognitive development in adulthood: A fifth stage? *Developmental Psychology, 11,* 602–606.

Armon, C. (1984). Ideals of the good life and moral judgment: Ethical reasoning across the lifespan. In M. Commons, F. Richards, & C. Armon (Eds.), *Beyond formal operations: Late adolescent and adult cognitive development* (pp. 357–380). New York: Praeger.

Bach, R. (1977). *Illusions: Adventures of a reluctant messiah.* New York: Dell.

Basseches, M. (1984). *Dialectical thinking and adult development.* Norwood, NJ: Ablex.

Blanchard-Fields, F. (1989). Postformal reasoning in a socioemotional context. In M. Commons, J. Sinnott, F. Richards, & C. Armon (Eds.), *Adult development: Comparisons and applications of developmental models* (vol. 1, pp. 73–94). New York: Praeger.

Drabeck, M., & Wood, P. (1989). Cross sectional and longitudinal evidence for differences between well-structured and ill-structured problem solving abilities. In M. Commons, C.

Armon, L. Kohlberg, F. Richards, T. Grotzer, & J. Sinnott (Eds.), *Adult development: Models and methods in the study of adolescent and adult thought* (pp. 133–146). New York: Praeger.

Chinen, A. (1992). *Once upon a midlife.* Los Angeles, CA: Tarcher.

Churchman, C. (1971). *The design of inquiring systems: Basic concepts of systems and organizations.* New York: Basic.

Commons, M., Armon, C., Kohlberg, L., Richards, R., Grotzer, T., & Sinnott, J. (Eds.) (1990). *Adult development: Models and methods in the study of adolescent and adult thought.* New York: Praeger.

Commons, M., Armon, C., Richards, F., Schrader, D., Farrell, E., Tappan, M., & Bauer, N. (1989). A multidomain study of adult development. In M. Commons, J. Sinnott, F. Richards, & C. Armon (Eds.), *Adult development: Comparison and applications of developmental models* (vol. 1, pp. 33–56). New York: Praeger.

Commons, M., Richards, F., & Armon, C. (Eds.) (1984). *Beyond formal operations: Late adolescent and adult cognitive development.* New York: Praeger.

Commons, M., Sinnott, J. D., Richards, R., & Armon, C. (Eds.) (1989). *Adult development: Comparisons and applications of adolescent and adult development models* (vol. 1). New York: Praeger.

Erikson, E. (1950). *Childhood and society.* New York: Norton.

Frankl, V. (1963). *Man's search for meaning.* New York: Washington Square Press.

Funk, J. (1989). Postformal cognitive theory and developmental stages of musical composition. In M. Commons, J. Sinnott, F. Richards, & C. Armon (Eds.), *Adult development: Comparisons and applications of developmental models* (vol. 1, pp. 3–32). New York: Praeger.

Gould, R. (1978). *Transformation.* New York: Simon and Schuster.

Gruber, H. E. (1984). The emergence of a sense of purpose: A cognitive case study of young Darwin. In M. Commons, F. Richards, & C. Armon (Eds.), *Beyond formal operations: Late adolescent and adult cognitive development* (pp. 3–27). New York: Praeger.

Hofstadter, D. R. (1979). *Gödel, Escher, Bach: An eternal golden braid.* New York: Basic.

Hugo, V. (1938). *Les misérables* (L. Wraxall, trans.). New York: Heritage.

Johnson, L. (1991). Bridging paradigms: The role of a change agent in an international technical transfer project. In J. D. Sinnott and J. Cavanaugh (Eds.), *Bridging paradigms: Positive development in adulthood and cognitive aging* (pp. 59–72). New York: Praeger.

Jung, C. (1971). The stages of life. In J. Campbell (Ed.), *The portable Jung.* New York: Viking (originally published in 1930).

Kitchener, K., & King, P. (1989). The reflective judgment model: Ten years of research. In M. Commons, C. Armon, L. Kohlberg, F. Richards, T. Grotzer, & J. Sinnott (Eds.), *Adult development: Models and methods in the study of adolescent and adult thought* (pp. 63–78). New York: Praeger.

Koplowitz, H. (1984). A projection beyond Piaget's formal operational stage: A general system stage and a unitary stage. In M. Commons, F. Richards, & C. Armon (Eds.), *Beyond formal operations: Late adolescent and adult cognitive development* (pp. 272–296). New York: Praeger.

Koplowitz, H. (1989). Unitary consciousness and the highest development of mind: The relation between spiritual development and cognitive development. In M. Commons, C. Armon, L.

Kohlberg, F. Richards, T. Grotzer, & J. Sinnott (Eds.), *Adult development: Models and methods in the study of adolescent and adult thought* (pp. 105–112). New York: Praeger.

Kramer, D. (1983). Postformal operations? A need for further conceptualization. *Human Development, 44,* 45–55.

Kramer, D. (1990). *The measurement of absolute, relativistic, and dialectical thinking.* Unpublished scoring manual, Rutgers University, New Brunswick, NJ.

Kramer, D., & Bacelar, W. T. (1994). The educated adult in today's world: Wisdom and the mature learner. In J. Sinnott (Ed.), *Interdisciplinary handbook of adult lifespan learning* (pp. 31–50). Westport, CT: Greenwood.

Labouvie-Vief, G. (1987, July). Speaking about feelings: Symbolization and self regulation through the lifespan. Paper presented at the Third Beyond Formal Operations Symposium at Harvard University, Cambridge, MA.

Lee, D. M. (1991). Relativistic operations: A framework for conceptualizing teachers' everyday problem solving. In J. Sinnott & J. Cavanaugh (Eds.), *Bridging paradigms: Positive development in adulthood and cognitive aging* (pp. 73–86). New York: Praeger.

Lee, D. M. (1994). Becoming an expert: Reconsidering the place of wisdom in teaching adults. In J. D. Sinnott (Ed.), *Interdisciplinary handbook of adult lifespan learning* (pp. 234–238). Westport, CT: Greenwood.

Levinson, D. (1978). *The seasons of a man's life.* New York: Knopf.

Orr, R., & Luscz, M. (1994). Rethinking womens' ways of knowing: Gender commonalities and intersections with postformal thought. *Journal of Adult Development, 1,* 225–234.

Perry, W. B. (1975). *Forms of intellectual and ethical development in the college years: A scheme.* New York: Holt, Rinehart and Winston.

Polyani, M. (1971). *Personal knowledge: Toward a postcritical philosophy.* Chicago: Univ. of Chicago Press.

Powell, P. M. (1984). Stage 4A: Category operations and interactive empathy. In M. Commons, F. Richards, and C. Armon (Eds.), *Beyond formal operations: Late adolescent and adult cognitive development* (pp. 326–339). New York: Praeger.

Richards, F., & Commons, M. (1984). Systematic, metasystematic, and cross-paradigm reasoning: A case for stages of reasoning beyond formal operations. In M. Commons, F. Richards, & C. Armon (Eds.), *Beyond formal operations: Late adolescent and adult cognitive development* (pp. 92–119). New York: Praeger.

Richards, F. A., & Commons, M. L. (1990). Applying signal detection theory to measure subject sensitivity to metasystemic, systemic, and lower-developmental-stage signals. In M. Commons, C. Armon, L. Kohlberg, F. Richards, T. Grotzer, & J. Sinnott (Eds.), *Adult development: Models and methods in the study of adolescent and adult thought* (pp. 175–188). New York: Praeger.

Riegel, K. (1975). Toward a dialectical theory of development. *Human Development, 19,* 50–64.

Rogers, D. R. B. (1992). *The effect of dyad interaction and marital adjustment on cognitive performance in everyday logical problem solving.* Logan: Utah State Univ. Press.

Rogers, D. R. B., Sinnott, J. D., & Van Dusen, L. (1991, July). Marital adjustment and social cognitive performance in everyday logical problem solving. Paper presented at the Sixth Adult Development Symposium, Boston.

Shock, N., Andres, R., Arenberg, D., Costa, P., Greulich, R., Lakatta, E., & Tobin, J. (1985). *Normal human aging: The Baltimore Longitudinal Study of Aging.* Washington, DC: U.S. Government Printing Office.

Sinnott, J. D. (1981). The theory of relativity: A metatheory for development? *Human Development, 24,* 293–311.

Sinnott, J. D. (1984). Postformal reasoning: The relativistic stage. In M. Commons, F. Richards, & C. Armon (Eds.), *Beyond formal operations: Late adolescent and adult cognitive development* (pp. 288–315). New York: Praeger.

Sinnott, J. D. (1986). Prospective/intentional everyday memory: Effects of age and passage of time. *Psychology and Aging, 1,* 110–116.

Sinnott, J. D. (1989a). Changing the known, knowing the changing. In D. Kramer and M. Bopp (Eds.), *Transformation in clinical and developmental psychology* (pp. 51–69). New York: Springer.

Sinnott, J. D. (Ed.) (1989b). *Everyday problem solving: Theory and application.* New York: Praeger.

Sinnott, J. D. (1989c). Lifespan relativistic postformal thought. In M. Commons, J. Sinnott, F. Richards, & C. Armon (Eds.), *Beyond formal operations* Vol. 2, *Comparisons and applications of adolescent and adult development models* (pp. 239–278). New York: Praeger.

Sinnott, J. D. (1991a). Limits to problem solving: Emotion, intention, goal clarity, health, and other factors in postformal thought. In J. D. Sinnott & J. Cavanaugh (Eds.), *Bridging paradigms: Positive development in adulthood and cognitive aging* (pp. 169–202). New York: Praeger.

Sinnott, J. D. (1991b). What do we do to help John? A case study of postformal problem solving in a family making decisions about an acutely psychotic member. In J. D. Sinnott & J. Cavanaugh (Eds.), *Bridging paradigms: Positive development in adulthood and cognitive aging* (pp. 203–220). New York: Praeger.

Sinnott, J. D. (1993a). A computerized assessment of postformal complex thought. Available from the author, Psychology department, Towson State University.

Sinnott, J. D. (1993b). The use of complex thought and resolving intragroup conflicts: A means of conscious adult development in the workplace. In J. Demick & P. Miller (Eds.), *Adult development in the workplace* (pp. 155–175). Hillsdale, NJ: Erlbaum.

Sinnott, J. D. (1993c). Teaching in a chaotic new physics world: Teaching as a dialogue with reality. In P. Kahaney, L. A. M. Perry, and J. Janangelo (Eds.), *Theoretical and critical perspectives on teacher change* (pp. 91–112). Norwood, NJ: Ablex.

Sinnott, J. D. (1993d). Yes, it's worth the trouble! Unique contributions from everyday cognition studies. In H. Reese & J. Puckett (Eds.), *Lifespan developmental psychology: Mechanisms of everyday cognition* (pp. 73–94). Hillsdale, NJ: Erlbaum.

Sinnott, J. D. (in press). Creativity and postformal thought: Why the last stage is the creative stage. In C. Adams-Price (Ed.), *Creativity and aging: Theoretical and empirical approaches.* New York: Springer.

Sinnott, J. D. (1994b). Development and yearning: Cognitive aspects of spiritual development. *Journal of Adult Development, 1,* 91–100.

Sinnott, J. D. (Ed.) (1994c). *Interdisciplinary handbook of adult lifespan learning.* Westport, CT: Greenwood.

Sinnott, J. D., & Cavanaugh, J. (Eds.) (1991). *Bridging paradigms: Positive development in adulthood and cognitive aging.* New York: Praeger.

Smith, L. B., & Thelen, E. (Eds.) (1993). *A dynamic systems approach to development: Applications.* Cambridge, MA: MIT Press.

Spencer, P. U. (1991). *Three strands in the braid: A guide for enablers of learning.* San Anselmo, CA: A Tribe of Two Press.

Sternberg, R. J. (Ed.) (1990). *Wisdom: Its nature, origins and development.* Cambridge: Cambridge Univ. Press.

Tannon, F. (1991). The influence of formal *vs.* informal education on planning skills: A cultural perspective. In J. D. Sinnott and J. Cavanaugh (Eds.), *Bridging paradigms: Positive development in adulthood and cognitive aging* (pp. 221–236). New York: Praeger.

Troll, L. (1985). *Early and middle adulthood* (2d ed.). Monterey, CA: Brooks-Cole.

Whitbourne, S., & Weinstock, C. (1979). *Adult development.* New York: Holt, Rinehart & Winston.

Wolf, F. A. (1981). *Taking the quantum leap.* New York: Harper and Row.

4

COGNITION IN CONTEXT

C H A P T E R

12

MEMORY IN CONTEXT

Thomas M. Hess and Sharon M. Pullen
North Carolina State University

A common stereotype and complaint of old age is that memory functioning is no longer what it was earlier in adulthood. Older people are perceived to have more memory problems than younger adults (see, e.g., Ryan, 1992), and their problems are more likely to be attributed to age-related, uncontrollable factors than are those of younger adults (see, e.g., Erber, 1989). Many older adults buy into this stereotype and report a greater decrement in their intellectual skills than may actually exist (McFarland, Ross, & Giltrow, 1992; Sunderland, Watts, Baddeley, & Harris, 1986). Older adults also often report having more problems than younger individuals, both anecdotally and in more systematic investigations. An interesting and important question for research on aging and cognition concerns the extent to which these perceptions have a foundation in reality. Certainly, much of the research derived from traditional laboratory studies of memory supports these claims. As reported in Chapter 6, increasing age is associated with decrements in performance on many memory tasks, and the explanations that have been proposed for these differences typically rely on models of cognitive functioning that either explicitly or implicitly have their foundation in a deterioration of physiological structures.

Whereas it would be foolhardy to overlook the overwhelming evidence for aging-related decrement from this research, such studies may not tell the whole story regarding age differences in memory. In contrast to expectations that might be derived from this work, the great majority of older adults continue to do quite well in everyday life, maintaining a high level of functioning and independence. This fact, among others, has led to increased questioning of the external validity (i.e., generalizability) of findings from traditional laboratory-based studies of aging and memory as well as increased concern about the ecological representatives (i.e., the degree to which tasks used in research are similar to the cognitive activities of everyday life) of the models and methods used in such studies, particularly as they apply to understanding changes in functioning in everyday contexts. Specifically, many laboratory tasks used by experimental psychologists (e.g., word list recall) may have less relevance to the everyday lives of middle-aged and older adults than to those of younger adults, whose proximity to the formal education process may make them particularly adept at the acquisition of new knowledge. Later in adulthood, less emphasis may be placed on verbatim memory and more on meaning derivation and knowledge utilization (see, e.g., Labouvie-Vief &

Schell, 1982). A failure to take into account the functional significance of the memory processes under investigation to the individual's life context is a major shortcoming of many studies in terms of both the identification and explanation of age differences in performance.

The usefulness of traditional laboratory-based methods and models for understanding memory and everyday functioning is currently a focus of much debate, pitting those from a more traditional experimental approach (see, e.g., Banaji & Crowder, 1989) against those with a more ecological orientation (see, e.g., Neisser, 1982). Mook (1989) has argued that much of this debate centers around the goals of memory research and the methods appropriate for achieving them. If one examines the goals underlying these two traditions, it can be seen that both approaches are important and can contribute to our understanding of aging and memory. If our goal is prediction and control, then traditional laboratory-based experimental studies built upon theoretical notions of memory can be quite beneficial in helping to isolate specific processes (e.g., strategy use) and examine their impact on performance. In this tradition, it is not so important to demonstrate that a particular variable controls performance in everyday contexts as it is to demonstrate the possibility of control. If in turn it can be determined that such processes have practical significance or predictive validity, in terms of, say, predicting the ability to perform a specific job or indicating cognitive dysfunction, such studies can be very useful.

Alternatively, if our goal is to understand development in context, a more functional approach to the study of aging and memory is needed. By examining the importance of particular skills in everyday life, not only can we identify the abilities associated with functioning, we also may develop a better understanding of the factors underlying age-related variation. For example, an observed age-related "deficit" in a particular skill might be explained by a change in the practical significance of that skill with age rather than by a decline in physiological systems. Even if a skill is discovered to exhibit normative decline with aging, examination of skills within an everyday context may provide us with a more developmentally based understanding of the phenomenon by showing how individuals adapt to the change. This in turn might benefit the development of intervention or training programs. For example, if we find that older adults compensate for a specific loss in some fashion, and this compensation allows them to maintain an adequate level of functioning, we might use this information as a model of successful aging in designing intervention programs for those who have not adapted as well.

The concern about ecological validity in aging research is being addressed quite visibly in studies of memory. Research is increasingly focusing on potential age-related mediators of performance that are context specific, such as the functional relevance of the tasks and materials to the individual's life context. In fact, one needs only to study the changes in the content of the two edited volumes from the Talland Memorial Conferences on memory to examine this trend. In the first (Poon, Fozard, Cermak, Arenberg, & Thompson, 1980), there are a few chapters relating to memory in context, such as those on knowledge actualization and the assessment of memory problems. For the most part, however, the chapters focus on traditional laboratory tasks and findings relating to, for example, attention, depth of processing, and sensory memory. In contrast, the volume from the most recent conference (Poon, Rubin, & Wilson, 1989) reflects a dramatic shift in emphasis from traditional laboratory-based work to contextually relevant studies of memory, with chapters addressing such issues as prose learning, prospective memory, spatial cognition, world knowledge, motivation, compensation, practice, and metamemory.

The goal of the present chapter is to highlight memory research that is representative of this trend toward a concern with function and context. Much of the work was stimulated by two forces: (1) the everyday memory movement, as espoused most forcefully by Neisser (1982), with an emphasis on formulating research questions within a functional context rather than letting existing models and methods drive design, and (2) the growing contextual perspective that is characteristic of the life-span movement in developmental psychology (Baltes, 1987). The aims of both approaches are often consistent with each other, and in fact the everyday movement can be reasonably classified as a contextual approach. We will begin by presenting a brief overview of the contextual perspective as it has been manifested in research on aging and memory. This will be followed by a selective review and critique of research that can be seen as relevant to this perspective and suggestions for future directions.

THE CONTEXTUAL PERSPECTIVE IN MEMORY RESEARCH: GOALS AND METHODS

As a beginning point, it is useful to discuss the assumptions behind a contextual view of memory change in adulthood. Consistent with Chapter 2, we view contextualism not so much as a specific set of models or theories, but as an approach to the study of human development that encompasses a number of core beliefs or assumptions. Briefly, contextual approaches emphasize that development is not a unitary phenomenon. Change takes place across multiple dimensions and in multiple directions, with multiple levels of influence interacting with one another and shaping the nature of change. These influences include biological, individual, cultural, and historical factors. Changes across dimensions are also viewed as interrelated, with variations in one skill influencing or reacting to variations in another (see, e.g., Meacham, 1977). A good example of this is the selective optimization with compensation model developed by Baltes, Dittmann-Kohli, and Dixon (1984). This model assumes that, due to demands on time and resources, individuals may choose to selectively optimize some skills at the expense of others, which may be seen as part of the narrowing of focus inherent in many developmental theories of adulthood (see also Labouvie-Vief & Schell, 1982). Along with this optimization comes compensation for skills that are lost, with the individual developing other means for coping with everyday problems using his or her available skills. Such compensatory mechanisms are a reflection of adaptive behavior that is present throughout the life span and help to maintain overall functioning at a reasonably high level in spite of inevitable losses. This conceptualization provides a means for understanding adult cognitive change that goes beyond a simple decrement model.

Another major characteristic of contextual approaches is an emphasis on practical or functional activity. Note that "functional" here is used in a somewhat different manner than that used by many memory researchers, who are interested in finding functional relationships in memory. In this latter case, the functional relationship refers to the predictable impact that a specific variable has on memory performance (e.g., organization facilitates free recall). Functional in a contextual perspective, however, refers to the importance and use of specific memory skills in everyday contexts (Bruce, 1989). The assumption is that development takes place within specific contexts and that the form and functions of change can be understood only by considering context. Our interest here is in examining how these assumptions have influenced work on and understanding of memory and aging.

There are few coherent research programs that proceed from a strict contextual perspective. In addition, as noted in Chapter 2, there is no single methodology that characterizes contextual studies. There are, however, several types of memory studies that inform this perspective. One type has to do with the examination of the experience of memory. Rather than proceeding from a specific memory model with a preexisting set of assumptions regarding the impact of aging, this research focuses on self-reports of memory functioning in an effort to identify age-related variations in (1) the frequency and severity of memory problems, (2) the types of memory problems, (3) the relationship of reported memory problems to traditional tests of ability, and (4) the relationship of reported memory to other contextual factors. Studies of this type assist us in identifying skills that have some practical significance to everyday functioning, in terms of both external (e.g., performance) and internal (e.g., subjective well-being) criteria, and in assessing the ecological representatives of existing conceptions of memory.

Another approach that informs a contextual perspective involves the use of materials and tasks that are presumably reflective of everyday functioning. One goal of such research is to increase the ecological validity of the assessment procedures by tapping into materials, tasks, or settings that are familiar or have high levels of functional significance in everyday life. A specific example of this type of study is that in which the congruence between the characteristics of the subject and those of the task are manipulated (e.g., studies of expertise). Such studies allow us to examine age differences in memory performance under optimal conditions (e.g., testing skills that have been optimized by the subject through selection and practice). They also allow us to examine how individuals may compensate for declining abilities in areas involving high degrees of practice and/or familiarity.

One of the positive outcomes of research focusing on problems of practical significance is the identification and investigation of interesting memory phenomena, such as prospective memory and autobiographical memory. These are clear manifestations of everyday memory functioning but have received little attention or are difficult to study in the lab using traditional methods. The identification of such phenomena is important to our understanding of aging and memory because, as will be seen, the age effects observed in these tasks are often at variance with those observed in more traditional tasks.

It is important to note that the adoption of a contextual position does not imply that all research must be done in naturalistic or everyday settings. In our view, analogues of everyday tasks used in the laboratory are perfectly reasonable ways of examining memory functioning as long as they tap into the targeted memory processes or components and the associated contextual factors surrounding performance can be approximated. Ideally, the appropriateness of laboratory methods should also be demonstrated beyond face validity by relating task performance to functioning in everyday contexts, which would allow us to examine the adaptive significance of the tested skills (Bruce, 1985, 1989).

RESEARCH REVIEW

In this section, we review research that has relevance to understanding aging and memory in context. In reviewing the literature, it is clear that some topics (e.g., spatial memory) have received substantial interest whereas other relevant areas (e.g., memory for conversations, telephone numbers, television programs) have received only limited attention. This review concentrates on the former while acknowledging the importance of other areas of inquiry. Consistent with the previous discussion, we begin our review by examining the subjective experience of memory. This is followed by a more extensive review of studies of memory performance. Consistent with an everyday approach, the organization of this review has a problem focus rather than a process focus, concentrating on specific memory skills that have functional relevance to everyday life rather than on specific models of memory. Many of the studies to be reported used extreme age groups research designs in which young adults, often college students, aged 18 to 35, were compared to older adults, who were typically in their 60s and 70s. For ease of description, we use the terms "younger" and "older" adults to refer to these age groups. We use "middle-aged" to refer to subjects whose ages fall between these two groups. Specific ages are mentioned only when circumstances warrant.

■ Everyday Memory Complaints

The importance of a contextual approach to the study of aging and memory is evident when we examine memory complaints. We would be surprised to hear a group of older adults complaining that they could no longer free-recall as many words as they could when they were younger or that their digit spans just weren't what they used to be. It would not seem unusual, however, to hear a group of older adults expressing frustration over their declining ability to recall the names of new acquaintances or their failure to remember to pick up an item at the store. Such information could provide valuable clues regarding the prevalence, nature, and importance of memory problems associated with everyday functioning.

When older adults are asked to report if and how their everyday memory skills have changed with age, they almost always report declines in memory functioning (Cavanaugh, 1987; Sunderland et al., 1986; Taylor, Miller, & Tinklenberg, 1992). In comparisons of different age groups' ratings of current memory functioning, the findings are less clear. Most researchers still find an age-related increase in the frequency of self-reported memory problems (Cavanaugh, Grady, & Perlmutter, 1983; Erber, Szuchman, & Rothberg, 1992; Hultsch, Hertzog, & Dixon, 1987), but some have found few age differences in current ratings (Crook & Larrabee, 1990; McMillan, 1984). Cavanaugh (1987) found that older adults believed that, in general, their memory had declined, but no age differences were observed for items assessing beliefs about current ability on specific memory tasks. The discrepancies across studies may have to do with the types of problems emphasized in the assessment instruments, with those studies finding substantial age differences being more likely to use questionnaires that contain a larger proportion of problems representative of the aged. Studies emphasizing problems common to all groups find fewer differences.

Some research has suggested that age differences in memory complaints are partly due to age-related differences in health factors. For example, Cutler and Grams (1988) found that health, vision, and hearing problems were all positively correlated with the reported frequency of memory problems, and Herzog and Rodgers (1989) found that the age-related increase in reported memory problems is considerably reduced when physical health status is controlled. Depression also appears to have some relationship to memory complaints in that depressed older adults report having more memory problems than nondepressed older adults, and this association between depression and memory is stronger than that observed for younger adults

(Scogin, 1985). For example, Erber et al. (1992) asked young and old respondents to rate the frequency of 24 everyday memory failures (e.g., forgetting a phone number after starting to dial; forgetting to buy an item at the supermarket; forgetting why one has come into a room) on 7-point Likert scales (1 = never; 7 = always). Respondents also completed a self-report measure of depressive symptoms. These researchers found that frequency of forgetting and self-reported depression were positively correlated in the older group but not in the younger group.

The types of everyday memory failures, the contexts in which they occur, and affective and coping responses to those failures may also show age-related differences. Cavanaugh et al. (1983) had younger and older subjects keep diaries on their memory failures and found that older adults reported that most of their memory failures occurred during activities outside their normal routine, whereas younger adults' memory failures seemed to occur mostly when they were under stress. Consistent with these results is Lovelace and Twohig's (1990) finding that, whereas 70 percent of the older adults in their sample reported having experienced increases in forgetting, only 18 percent reported these increases with respect to routine events (e.g., finding keys, taking medication).

Both younger and older adults expect to experience some intellectual decline as they age (Heckhausen & Baltes, 1991; Heckhausen, Dixon, & Bates, 1989), particularly with respect to memory functioning (Ryan, 1992). Perhaps this is why older adults are less likely than younger adults to report feeling anxiety or discomfort over the everyday memory failures they experience (see, e.g., Erber et al., 1992). In fact, few older adults complain that their memory problems in routine situations are a nuisance or that they disrupt everyday activities (Lovelace & Twohig, 1990; Sunderland et al., 1986). Not surprisingly, older adults are slightly more likely than younger adults to report using memory aids in general (Cavanaugh et al., 1983) and external aids in particular (e.g., clocks, calendars) to help solve the problem of everyday memory failures (Jackson, Bogers, & Kerstholt, 1988; Lovelace & Twohig, 1990).

Interestingly, the relationship between self-reports about everyday memory and actual memory performance is relatively weak. In a 4-year longitudinal study, Taylor et al. (1992) demonstrated that a group of older subjects showed a significant increase in memory complaints and a significant decline in performance on a word-recall task; however, there was no relationship between reports of frequency of forgetting and actual performance on the recall task at the individual level. In fact, most researchers have found virtually no relationship between self-reported memory failures and objective performance (Herzog & Rodgers, 1989; Sunderland et al., 1986; West, Boatwright, & Schleser, 1984). Herzog and Rodgers (1989) conducted extensive interviews with 1,491 adults aged 20 to 80 concerning many of the content areas of interest to gerontologists, including physical and mental health, work and retirement, and economic resources, as well as subjective memory performance. Objective memory performance was assessed at the end of the interview by both a recall and a recognition test of questions asked during the interview. In the recall measure, subjects were asked to name six mental and physical functions they had rated during the interview. In the recognition measure, questions included "Did I ask you if you had a valid driver's license [yes]?" and "Did I ask you whether you voted in the recent primary election [no]?" The sample showed a clear age-related decline in memory performance as well as a decline in subjective memory functioning across age groups, but subjective memory was not a significant predictor of objective memory.

The correlation between self-reported memory failures and objective memory performance is even weaker for depressed than for nondepressed older adults (Scogin, 1985). Self-assessments of memory are negatively associated with depression and positively associated with self-confidence, but neither depression nor self-confidence is a strong predictor of actual performance (Rabbit & Abson, 1990). West et al. (1984), in their investigation of the relationship between memory performance, self-assessment of memory, and affective status in older females, found that, while affective status and self-assessments of memory were related (depressed individuals gave lower self-assessments), performance scores were not related to self-assessments or affective status.

Why do most studies find little relationship between complaints and performance? A primary reason may have to do with the way in which performance is assessed. In most studies examining the relationship between memory complaints and actual performance, objective memory functioning is assessed using traditional laboratory tasks. A criticism of these studies is that rating and performance measures may not be assessing the same concept. West et al. (1984) propose that laboratory tests may not reflect everyday memory and that the inconsistency between self-assessment and performance on memory tasks may be due to subjects' assessing their memory performance on the basis of their everyday experience. Similarly, Herzog and Rodgers (1989) suggest that many performance measures assess relatively short-term memory for a specific set of information, whereas rating measures are subjective assessments of a subject's general ability to remember all types of information. Alternatively, Rabbit and Abson (1990) argue that self-reports tell us very little about objective everyday performance because they reflect an individual's success at adapting to the complexity of his or her environment. These researchers demonstrated that, in early old age, adults tend to overestimate their memory failures, presumably because they are still functioning in complex environments where memory lapses are noticeable. In contrast, once adults retire to a simpler environment in late old age, when memory lapses are relatively inconsequential, they tend to underestimate their memory problems. These findings emphasize the need to study the memory performance of all age groups in a variety of contexts.

In sum, older adults tend to report more memory problems than do younger adults. This difference may be in part a reflection of the belief that memory functioning declines with age, since several studies have found no age differences in self-assessments of current ability on specific everyday tasks. Importantly, only a small percentage of older adults say they experience memory problems with routine tasks. When they do have such problems, they are less likely than younger adults to feel anxiety and more likely than younger adults to employ memory aids to compensate for the problems. The relationship between memory complaints and actual memory performance is weak, but such relationships may increase in strength if more representative measures of everyday memory are used.

■ Research on Specific Memory Skills

In this section, we review research examining a wide variety of memory skills and phenomena. Although they may appear to be unrelated, there is an underlying organizational theme. Specifically, each relates to a memory function that has direct relevance to everyday functioning and/or has been investigated in such a way as to highlight a contextual focus (e.g., examined within the context of everyday activities).

Spatial Memory

Much everyday activity involves the use of nonverbal, spatial information. Such information allows us, for example, to both navigate about familiar territory (e.g., walk from one's house to a friend's) and locate objects in our environment (e.g., find a scissors in one's house). The functional significance associated with spatial memory skills may be particularly important for older adults in maintaining their independence. For example, neighborhood knowledge has been found to be related to neighborhood use in an older population (Simon, Walsh, Regnier, & Krauss, 1992). What happens to our spatial memory as we get older? This question has been addressed in several ways using methodologies that range from simple extensions of standard laboratory tasks (e.g., remembering the locations of words on cards) to examining performance using real towns and buildings. Some of the research addresses specific theory-based hypotheses, such as Hasher and Zack's (1979) assertion that the encoding of spatial location (e.g., remembering the location of a picture on a magazine page) is an automatic process that should be unaffected by variations in attentional capacity associated with age. Other research focuses on examining specific components associated with performance, such as the importance of familiarity in supporting spatial memory.

One way in which spatial memory has been investigated is by testing location recall of verbal materials, pictures, or objects that are visually or tactually presented in specific positions on a display surface, such as a computer screen or index card. Although some studies report no between-group differences (see, e.g., McCormack, 1982), the majority of the research (Denney, Dew, & Kihlstrom, 1993; Moore, Richards, & Hood, 1984; Pezdek, 1983; Schear & Nebes, 1980) has found that younger adults are superior to both middle-aged and older adults in remembering the location of a wide variety of stimulus items. Part of the age effect observed in these studies may be due to the greater use of organizational strategies by younger adults to support recall (see, e.g., Pezdek, 1983). Older adults do increase their strategy use when provided with specific instructions, and this results in a benefit to memory; however, this benefit is typically no greater than that observed for younger adults given similar instructions (see, e.g., Denney et al., 1993). Importantly, the fact that both age and instructions are related to performance is inconsistent with Hasher and Zacks' (1979) automaticity criteria, suggesting that location memory is affected by variations in the attentional resources allocated to learning.

Some studies have attempted to use more meaningful materials, such as structures depicted on a city map (Light & Zelinski, 1983; Thomas, 1985; Zelinski & Light, 1988), but older adults still exhibit poorer memory for location than younger adults do, even when age differences in structure recognition are controlled. Thomas (1985) found that the type of strategy used to learn landmarks varied with age, with the majority of younger adults using a verbal labeling strategy whereas most middle-aged and older subjects relied on strategies that emphasized specific landmarks or relative locations. Surprisingly, however, the type of strategy employed had little relationship to memory performance.

Interestingly, Zelinski and Light (1988) found that older adults benefited no more than younger adults when the structures were presented on a map versus a blank piece of paper. This result goes against the hypothesis that older adults may be especially dependent on distinctive contextual cues in remembering spatial information due to their being less likely to encode information in a distinctive manner. Other research has been mixed with respect to this hypothesis (see, e.g., Park, Cherry, Smith, & Lafronza, 1990; Sharps & Gollin, 1987), with the reasons for the inconsistencies being unclear at present (Cherry & Park, 1993; Sharps, 1991).

Other studies have examined spatial memory using techniques that vary in their consistency with the individual's knowledge base. Waddell and Rogoff (1981, 1987) presented middle-aged and older women with spatial arrays of 30 common objects that were either placed randomly in a bank of cubicles or meaningfully in a panorama depicting a landscape (see Figure 12.1). They found that middle-aged women had better location memory than the older women in the cubicle condition, apparently due to subjects in the latter group using ineffective strategies. The age difference in performance was eliminated, however, in the panorama condition, where the older women were more likely to use strategies that were correlated with location memory, such as the generation of a narrative to link objects spatially.

In related research, Hess and Slaughter (1990) found that the supports provided by consistency of the stimuli with the subject's knowledge base were more important for the old

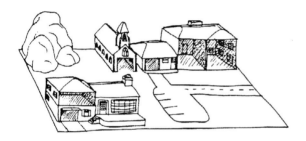

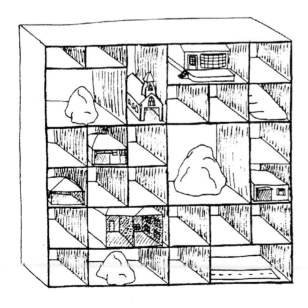

FIGURE 12.1. Examples of meaningful and nonmeaningful test displays. (*Source:* Waddell and Rogoff, 1981. Used by permission.)

than for the young in determining location memory. Specifically, age differences in the ability to remember object locations in a scene were greatest with unexpected objects (e.g., a birdcage in a kitchen) and for unorganized scenes. In these latter types of scenes, some of the problems that older adults experienced appeared to be directly related to the conflict between knowledge-based expectancies and the observed placement of expected objects in novel spatial relationships (e.g., a coffee table behind a sofa). Older adults were more likely than younger adults to alter their recall to be consistent with their experience (e.g., they placed the coffee table in front of the sofa), perhaps due to difficulty in inhibiting relevant prior knowledge or to difficulty in monitoring the source of information (e.g., schema based versus episodic) activated at retrieval. More recently, Arbuckle, Cooney, Milne, and Melchior (1994) have also provided evidence suggesting that older adults are more susceptible to schema-based interference effects in a spatial memory task (i.e., remembering spatial layouts of homes). Taken together, these results suggest that older adults benefit more from meaningfulness than do younger subjects, perhaps due to the organization provided by existing knowledge structures activated during encoding and retrieval and the lack of conflict with past experience. It should be noted, however, that aging-related factors may still limit the ability of older adults to encode information within a restricted time frame (Charness, 1981), even when relevant knowledge is easily accessible.

Several studies have taken spatial memory research a step further by examining performance in more complex environments taken from real life, including familiar and unfamiliar grocery stores (Kirasic, 1991), a museum exhibit and secretary's office (Uttl & Graf, 1993), and familiar sections of cities (Evans, Brennan, Skorpanich, & Held, 1984; Rabbitt, 1989). In comparing the results across studies, it is evident that testing involving real-world contexts is not sufficient to eliminate age differences in spatial memory. There are, however, test conditions that affect the size of the observed age differences. Specifically, older adults receive a disproportionate benefit to performance when the context is a familiar one (Kirasic, 1991), when the memory test occurs in context rather than through use of a map (Uttl & Graf, 1993), when specific instructions are given to remember the location of objects (Uttl & Graf, 1993), and when memory cues are associated with function rather than spatial location (Rabbitt, 1989). The benefits associated with familiarity appear to be similar to those observed elsewhere (see, e.g., Waddell & Rogoff, 1981), in that older adults are less likely to use effective strategies in unfamiliar situations. In addition, older adults are more likely than middle-aged and younger adults to organize and recall spatial information using cues associated with function and symbolic significance (Evans et al., 1984; Rabbitt, 1989). This may suggest that different-aged adults use different means of organizing information in memory or, alternatively, that older adults have a more difficult time encoding, retrieving, or reasoning in spatial terms.

Finally, research examining adult age differences in the ability to learn new route information in a complex environment (Kirasic, Allen, & Haggerty, 1992; Lipman, 1991; Lipman & Caplan, 1992) has obtained results consistent with those above. Specifically, older adults have a more difficult time than younger and middle-aged adults in integrating spatial and temporal information to form an abstract route representation, with the inefficiency of older adults being at least partly due to their employing learning strategies that do not focus on relevant task information. For example, Lipman (1991) observed that adolescent through middle-aged subjects organized information in memory in a sequential fashion, whereas older adults organized mostly by salience of landmarks. When instructions to pay attention to sequential information were provided, the performance of older adults was facilitated to a greater degree than that of younger subjects.

In sum, age differences are seen in spatial tasks in both laboratory and everyday settings, with increasing age being associated with lower levels of performance. Neither the specific context in which testing is done nor the distinctiveness of materials appears to have a consistent impact on the extent to which age differences are observed. Age effects in performance tend to be smallest, however, when meaningful or familiar contexts are used. It appears that older adults have well-developed and effective strategies that they can use in familiar settings, but they have problems formulating effective strategies in less familiar settings, perhaps due to lack of practice or the cognitive demands of the test situation. Their performance can be boosted, however, when they are given appropriate guidance (e.g., task-specific instructions).

Memory for Faces

Learning about and recognizing faces is an important skill necessary for effective functioning in social contexts. Given the everyday relevance of this task plus the fact that recognition memory is often associated with less age-related impairment than other direct memory tasks (see, e.g., Craik & McDowd, 1987), we might expect few age differences in the ability to recognize faces. It is somewhat surprising, therefore, that several studies have found age-related deficits in the accuracy of face recognition (Bäckman, 1991; Bartlett & Leslie, 1986; Bartlett, Leslie, Tubbs, & Fulton, 1989; Maylor, 1990b; Measso, Romaini, Martini, & Zappala, 1990). In cross-sectional studies, the onset of decline in face recognition seems to begin as early as age 50 to 59 and continues gradually until age 70, but the most accelerated decline occurs after age 70 (Crook & Larrabee, 1992).

Most studies examining face recognition assess accuracy using measures of discrimination which take into account accurate recognition (hits) as well as inaccurate recognition (false alarms). The observed age differences in discrimination between previously studied and new faces can usually be explained by an elevated false-alarm rate (i.e., incorrectly identifying new faces as old) for older subjects (Bartlett et al., 1989; Bartlett, Strater, & Fulton, 1991; Crook & Larrabee, 1992). Few age differences have been found in overall hit rates, although Wahlin, Bäckman, Mäntylä, Herlitz, Viitanen, and Winblad (1993) found that very old adults (aged 85–96) exhibited both a higher false-alarm rate and a significantly lower hit rate in recognition memory than did somewhat younger adults (aged 75–84).

Flicker, Ferris, Crook, and Bartus (1989) demonstrated that the increase in false alarms among older subjects usually occurs during the last half of the task and concluded that older adults may be more sensitive than younger adults to proactive interference. Bartlett and Fulton (1991) provided an alternative explanation for the high false-alarm rate among older adults by suggesting that older adults rely more heavily on resemblance to other faces they have seen than do younger adults. They asked subjects to rate the subjective familiarity of each face in the stimulus set (whether it was similar to a face they had seen in everyday life) and found that the false-alarm ratings of older subjects, but not younger subjects, were positively correlated with their familiarity ratings. This result is consistent with Jennings and Jacoby's (1993) suggestion that both younger and older adults use familiarity to make recognition judgments but that older adults have a more difficult time discriminating between the sources of familiarity. Older adults may sense that a face looks familiar but have trouble attributing this feeling of familiarity to a specific source or context (e.g., a face seen in the experimental session versus one from their past experience). Presumably, younger adults are better at encoding and/or accessing contextual information in memory associated with a specific face (e.g., time and place in which the person was encountered, nature of interaction), which facilitates their ability to identify the source of their feeling of familiarity when viewing a face. This makes it less likely that younger adults will falsely identify a face that seems familiar but was not actually studied.

The nature of age differences in face recognition accuracy also varies as a function of the characteristics of the stimuli. For example, Fulton and Bartlett (1991) examined the possibility that memory performance may differ for young and old faces and found that age-related deficits in accuracy were reduced when old faces were used as stimuli because younger adults showed poorer discrimination for old than for young faces. The typical age-related increase in false-alarm rates was unaffected by face age, however, since older subjects showed no difference in their discrimination for young and old faces.

Bäckman (1991) manipulated the age and familiarity of the stimulus faces to support his hypothesis that knowledge about faces changes throughout the life span. Young, young-old (62–69 years), and old-old (76–85 years) subjects studied pictures of young and old famous and nonfamous people in a standard recognition task. For the famous faces, younger adults correctly recognized more younger faces than did the older adults, whereas both groups of older adults correctly recognized more older faces than did the younger adults. For the nonfamous faces, the younger adults were best at recognizing young faces, whereas the young-old adults were best at recognizing old faces, a result in contradiction to Fulton and Bartlett (1991). The old-old adults' recognition was not affected by face age.

Bartlett and Leslie (1986) explored the effects of changing the positions and expressions of stimulus faces on recognition and found that older adults had more difficulty than younger adults distinguishing between the original stimulus faces and the same faces with either new expressions or new poses. When each face was studied in a variety of poses and expressions, no age differences in recognition accuracy were found. Older adults were also less able than younger adults to determine *how* changed faces were different from original views (Bartlett et al., 1989). These researchers propose that, perhaps because of general limitations on speed and efficiency of processing, older adults encode only face-specific information at the expense of view-specific information so that smaller age differences are found in a task for which face-specific information is the basis of recognition.

In sum, older adults perform more poorly on face recognition tasks than do younger adults because they tend to have higher rates of false recognition, perhaps due to age-related differences in encoding strategies. Older adults also remember less distinctive information regarding the positions or expressions of studied faces than do younger adults, suggesting that they are less likely to encode such information. This in turn may increase older adults' confusion regarding the context in which a specific face was encountered, forcing them to rely more on general familiarity in making memory judgments. Finally, there is some evidence that all subjects (except the very old) benefit when the faces to be learned are drawn from their own age group, suggesting that familiarity enhances performance.

Memory for Activities and Actions

Another type of nonverbal information that is commonly dealt with in everyday life involves one's own behavior. We are often asked, by others and ourselves, about behaviors that we may or may not have performed at earlier points in time. Often, recall of such information has adaptive significance because of its importance in everyday life. For example, remembering if you have or have not taken your medication has very obvious health consequences. Similarly, being able to retrace your prior activities during the day could facilitate the process of searching for your lost car keys. Because of its adaptive significance, there has been a recent interest in investigating age differences in memory for one's own behavior with the expectation that age effects might be smaller than those observed in other memory tasks. Kausler and Lichty (1988) also suggest that the encoding of one's own behaviors typically occurs in a relatively incidental fashion, with little involvement of the types of elaborative strategies that are thought to differentiate younger and older subjects in intentional learning situations.

Most of the research in this area has focused on two categories of behavior: activities and actions. Activities involve concerted behavior associated with a specific task that occurs over an extended period of time, such as completing a questionnaire. In contrast, actions are typically brief, discrete behaviors, such as writing a number or raising your hand. Note that activities may subsume a number of different actions. Some initial research suggested that memory for these two types of information might have different age functions associated with them, but, as we will see, the discrepancy is not always apparent.

Kausler and his colleagues have conducted an extensive, systematic series of studies involving memory for activities. Their prototypical research design involves having subjects perform a sequence of activities, such as taking assorted tests of ability and then taking tests of memory for the activities under varying instructional sets, test conditions, and retention intervals. As already noted in Chapter 6, this research has shown that younger adults remember more about both the activities and their temporal order than do older adults (see, e.g., Kausler & Hakami, 1983; Kausler, Lichty, & Davis, 1985) but that performance is largely unaffected by task manipulation, such as intentional versus incidental learning conditions (Kausler, Lichty, & Davis, 1985; Kausler, Lichty, Hakami, & Freund, 1986). Kausler has hypothesized that this pattern of results indicates that memory for activities is a rehearsal-independent process, with activities being encoded in a fairly automatic fashion. Further support for this hypothesis is provided by the facts that the amount of time spent performing the activity has little impact on memory (Kausler et al., 1986) and that there is no recall advantage for the first-performed activities (i.e., primacy effect) in the sequence (see, e.g., Kausler & Hakami, 1983). Primacy effects are typically thought to reflect the use of deliberate organizational strategies. The fact that they do not occur, even when subjects are instructed to remember the activities, suggests that the encoding of these events in memory is relatively unaffected by strategic behaviors on the part of the individual.

Whereas activity memory appears to be unaffected by strategic behaviors, age differences still exist, a fact that is inconsistent with Hasher and Zacks' (1979) definition of automaticity. How do we deal with this discrepancy? One way is to assume that even automatic processes might be affected by age. Thus, even though encoding mechanisms may still be automatic, slowing in processing (Earles & Coon, 1994) or other changes in nervous system functions might limit the amount of information registered. Another possible explanation is that the observed age differences reflect retrieval rather than encoding (Kausler & Lichty, 1988). That is, a performed activity may be registered in memory in a more or less automatic fashion, but retrieval of this memory may require attentional capacity. The evidence for this explanation has been equivocal (Kausler & Wiley, 1990; Kausler, Wiley, & Phillips, 1990).

In contrast to these findings, some initial research by Bäckman and Nilsson (1984, 1985) on memory for actions suggested that age differences are nonexistent. In these studies, subjects studied lists of words, read sentences describing actions, or performed a series of actions. Bäckman and Nilsson observed that the age differences in recall were greater for the verbal materials than for the performed actions and that older adults experienced a disproportionate benefit relative to the other groups when recall involved performed actions. These researchers hypothesized that the benefit was associated with the multimodal nature of actions. Since older adults are assumed to be less likely than younger adults to engage in elaborative encoding, the richer information provided by actions may serve to focus older adults' attention by guiding their encoding activity, thereby facilitating the formation of a richly elaborated memory code and enhancing recall.

Subsequent research has not always observed these age-related patterns of performance, however, with similar age effects being found for both action and activity memory (see, e.g., Cohen, Sandler, & Schroeder, 1987; Kausler et al., 1990; Knopf & Neidhardt, 1989). Norris and West (1991) did observe that older adults had better memory for actions than activities whereas younger adults exhibited equivalent levels of recall for the two, suggesting that actions do disproportionately boost memory in old age. However, the young adults still exhibited superior performance to the old for both types of events.

What might account for the disproportionate benefit associated with action memory that is occasionally observed for older adults? Research suggests that action-related factors such as duration, involvement of objects, or familiarity do not systematically interact with age in determining memory (Knopf & Neidhardt, 1989; Norris & West, 1991). Rather, it appears that there is some specific benefit for older adults that has to do with the motor component associated with performing actions. Kausler, Lichty, and Freund (1985) found that repetitions of activities enhanced recognition memory for those activities for older adults but not for younger adults. Other research has shown that participation in a complex event (e.g., making clay) or performance of actions results in fewer age differences in action memory than passive observation does (Bäckman & Nilsson, 1985; Padgett & Ratner, 1987; Ratner, Padgett, & Bushey, 1988). Similarly, Norris and West (1993) observed that motor involvement, either at encoding or retrieval, improved recall and that older adults benefited more than younger adults from motor involvement, particularly at retrieval and in conjunction with an organized set of stimulus materials (with organization based upon the part of the body involved in the action).

In sum, although age differences do exist in memory for behaviors, these differences tend to be stable across conditions and are not affected by the same sort of strategic factors that are thought to discriminate between younger and older adults in other memory situations.

In addition, motor involvement does appear to have some specific benefit in action memory for older adults that is perhaps due to the multimodal nature of behaviors. Note that activities also may have a motor component, but the associated benefits may be less systematic since activity recall depends on the subject supplying and retrieving a label which may subsume many different actions, whereas action recall involves the identity of discrete behaviors. Note also, however, that the age-related benefits of motor involvement are not consistent across studies and appear to be affected by as-yet-undetermined task variables.

Memory for the Source of Information

As can be seen in the previous two sections, being able to identify the source of a specific memory event can have important mnemonic consequences. Where have I seen that face before? Did I remember to take my medication or did I only think to do it? The answers to such questions require being able to retrieve information about the context in which the event in question was originally encountered. This enables us, for example, to identify whether a familiar face belongs to someone we know or someone we simply passed on the street. Likewise, being able to reconstruct the original encoding context enables us to remember if we actually did something (e.g., took medication) rather than just thought about it. In both cases, the ability to determine the source of the event has important behavioral consequences (Do we greet the other person? Do we take the medication?).

The ability to make such discriminations has been a focus of recent investigation in the field of aging under the headings of source memory and reality monitoring. Source memory is the more general term, referring to the ability to remember the source of a familiar event (Schacter, Harbluk, & McLachlan, 1984). Reality monitoring refers to the more specific case where you must discriminate between imagined versus experienced events (Johnson & Raye, 1981). Source memory is of interest not only because of its importance to everyday remembering but also because of the connection with laboratory-based models of aging and memory. For example, one popular view suggests that age differences occur due to older adults being less likely to encode the specific contextual information that makes an event distinctive in memory, subsequently making the event more difficult to retrieve (see Light, 1991). If this is true, we would expect older adults to exhibit poorer source memory and age differences in source memory should be correlated with other measures of memory performance (e.g., free recall).

The existing evidence does indicate that age is negatively correlated with source memory in adulthood but that the strength of the effect is related to the test conditions. For example, older adults are worse than younger adults at determining if they have performed or imagined performing an action (Guttentag & Hunt, 1988) or if they have read or generated a word (Rabinowitz, 1989). Kausler, Lichty, and Freund (1985) observed a similar effect, with older adults being more likely than younger adults to say that they performed an activity that they had only planned. In an apparent contradiction to this last result, older adults have also been observed to have more difficulty than younger adults in monitoring their own activities, resulting in them being more likely to repeat previously performed actions (Koriat, Ben-Zur, & Sheffer, 1988).

The common thread running through these results is that subjects in these studies were required to distinguish between events from the same source: all activities were self-performed. Hashtroudi, Johnson, and Chrosniak (1989) found that older adults are particularly poor at making source discriminations when the potential sources of origin fall within the same class of events (e.g., all events are performed by self). For example, older adults had a disproportionately more difficult time than younger adults in determining whether a self-generated item was said or simply thought, whereas age differences were much smaller when subjects had to determine whether they or someone else had said something. An argument could be made that within-class discriminations require more distinctive contextual information to differentiate between sources because of a greater overlap in possible cues. Such information may be less important in making discriminations between classes, where it is assumed that information about the number and types of cognitive operations used may be sufficient to distinguish between classes of events (Johnson & Raye, 1981). Research suggests that such information is equally available to younger and older adults (see, e.g., Rabinowitz, 1989).

Subsequent research (Ferguson, Hashtroudi, & Johnson, 1992; Hashtroudi, Johnson, & Chrosniak, 1990) has demonstrated that older adults are less likely than younger adults both to have distinctive perceptual information available and to be able to take advantage of such information when it is provided. Interestingly, in subjective reports of the attributes associated with their memories, older adults reported more thoughts, feelings, and evaluative comments than did younger adults, who reported the presence of more perceptual attributes (Hashtroudi et al., 1990). It is possible that these observed differences in reported attributes reflect age-related difficulties either in encoding/retrieving perceptual cues or in the ability to inhibit task-extraneous thoughts. Alternatively, these results might highlight potential differences in the types of information that younger and older adults attend to while experiencing an event, perhaps reflecting differences in motives and interests rather than deficits. Older adults may be more likely than younger adults to focus on the affective aspects of an event, which in turn has been shown to be associated with poorer source memory (Suengas & Johnson, 1988). In fact, Hashtroudi, Johnson, Vnek, and Ferguson (1994) have provided some indirect evidence for this last explanation by showing that age differences in source monitoring are reduced (for *said-versus-thought* discriminations) or eliminated (for *self-versus-other* discriminations) when subjects focus on the factual content of the to-be-remembered information rather than on the affective content.

The evidence for a relationship between source memory and other aspects of memory performance is less compelling. For example, Guttentag and Hunt (1988) found no difference in source memory for recalled versus nonrecalled actions. Similarly, Schacter, Kaszniak, Kihlstrom, and Valdiserri (1991) found that age differences in source memory for specific facts sometimes occurred in situations where no between-group differences existed in memory for these facts (also see Ferguson et al., 1992). Thus, there is no consistent evidence at present that source memory reflects a general age-related factor that can account for between-group differences in memory performance.

Given the importance of source memory in everyday life, what is the potential impact of age differences in this factor in context? Cohen and Faulkner (1989) speculated that age-related difficulties in distinguishing between something watched versus imagined might make older adults less reliable eyewitnesses than younger adults in the sense that they would be more influenced by misleading information. To test this hypothesis, younger and older adults watched a videotape of a kidnapping and then, 10 minutes later, read an accurate or inaccurate description of the events in the videotape. Older adults were found to be more likely than younger adults to falsely recognize the subsequently presented misleading information as accurate, and they were also more confident of these false recognitions.

In another study with less serious implications, Dywan and Jacoby (1990; see also Jennings & Jacoby, 1993) investigated the "false-fame" effect, which refers to the common finding that previous exposure to a nonfamous face or name will result in higher fame ratings at some later point in time. The accuracy of fame judgments relies on the ability of subjects to identify the source of memory for the person. Dywan and Jacoby found that older adults were more susceptible to this false-fame effect than were younger adults, suggesting that older subjects were less likely than younger ones to associate the previously observed nonfamous names with the context in which they occurred. They hypothesized that older adults were relying primarily on familiarity in making fame judgments, whereas younger adults were more likely to base their judgments on context information.

In sum, age differences do exist in source memory, primarily in those cases where the individual must discriminate between sources from within the same class of events. These age differences are not systematically related to performance in other episodic memory tasks, however, suggesting a dissociation between source memory and other types of memory skills. At present, the age effects appear to be due to variations in the types of source information encoded by the individual, which could be affected by motivational or, as suggested by some researchers (Craik, Morris, Morris, & Loewen, 1990; Schacter et al., 1984), aging-related physiological changes (e.g., a decline in frontal lobe functioning). It is important to note that, whereas each of these hypothesized explanatory frameworks would predict more problems for older adults in source monitoring, the nature of the underlying causal mechanisms leads to very different views of aging-related cognitive change in each case. In contrast to the deficit-oriented view associated with the physiological explanation, the results of Hashtroudi et al. (1994) support a more contextual view in which between-group differences may be attributable to age-related variations in the approach to processing information.

Long-Term Retention Processes

The typical memory study examines retention of information that was learned within the past hour under specific control conditions. Much of everyday life, however, involves the retrieval and use of information learned days, months, or years before. Obviously, the examination of such long-term retention processes creates special problems for researchers, primarily in terms of controlling for extraneous influences on performance. For example, the researcher may have little control over the initial exposure time to the to-be-remembered information or the activities engaged in by the subject during the retention interval. To the extent that these factors are associated with age, such problems complicate the interpretation of obtained age effects in memory performance. Many researchers believe, however, that these limitations should not force us to abandon the study of long-term memory phenomena and that such studies, even without traditional controls, can allow us to make reasonable inferences about memory processes that are not amenable to laboratory research. We will review two types of studies of long-term retention processes in adulthood, both of which examine retention for information acquired prior to participation in the study.

Autobiographical memory Studies of autobiographical memory examine subject-generated memories in response to different types of cues, such as individual words or judgments of importance. Two primary goals of this type of research are to describe both the characteristics of and the relative accessibility of memories from different points in the life span. The information gained from this research should give us some insight into the organization of autobiographical memory and possible age differences therein. Due to the personal nature of the memories retrieved in such studies, it is difficult to verify their accuracy. It has been argued, however, that it is the subject's perception of veridicality that is important. If the subject believes the memories to be accurate (and most often we do), he or she will treat them as such and they then become a reasonable focus of inquiry.

Initial research (see, e.g., Fitzgerald & Lawrence, 1984; Franklin & Holding, 1977; Rubin, Wetzler, & Nebes, 1986) in this area used a method based on one developed by Galton (1911) in which subjects produce autobiographical events from memory in response to individual word cues. The results of these studies are quite consistent and are typically described in terms of the distribution of the retrieved memories across the life span, which might be conceptualized as being similar to traditional forgetting curves. Rubin et al. (1986) argued that there is a basic similarity in these curves across age groups (Figure 12.2) and that the retention functions associated with these studies have three characteristic components: (1) a recency component, with most memories coming from the last year; (2) a reminiscence component in subjects over 30, reflecting unexpectedly high levels of retrieval for memories from the second and third decades of life; and (3) a childhood amnesia component, reflecting minimal recall from the first 5 years of life.

The overall retrieval function is reasonably well described as a nonmonotonically decreasing power function of age of the memories and is very similar to traditional forgetting curves in which loss is an exponential function of time since study. The fact that age differ-

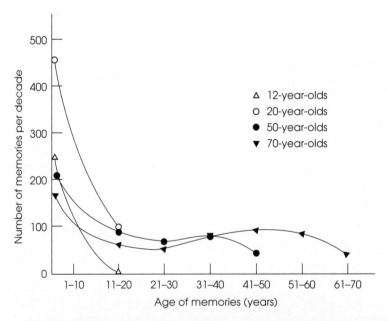

FIGURE 12.2. Retrieval functions for four different age groups from Fitzgerald and Lawrence (1984). (*Source:* Adapted from Rubin, Wetzler, & Nebes, 1986. Used by permission.)

ences in this function are minimal suggests that different-aged adults sample autobiographical memories in a similar fashion and that they acquire and retain memories at a similar rate, a finding that goes against common stereotypes.

The reminiscence component is particularly interesting because it is difficult to predict from traditional theories of forgetting in which retention is described as a simple function of time. The fact that it occurs for all age groups also suggests that it is not simply related to old age (e.g., older adults engaging in life review). Fitzgerald (1988, 1996) has argued that it may reflect the fact that the events and transitions that occur during this period of life are important for defining self and constructing a personal narrative, and that this narrative may be an organizational device for autobiographical memories that would subsequently influence their retrieval. The retrieval functions from these studies may not, however, be good indicators of relative accessibility or importance. Subsequent research has indicated that the large recency component of the function may be related to the types of retrieval cues and dating methods used in these studies. The use of different types of cues (see, e.g., Fitzgerald, 1988; Fromholt & Larsen, 1991; MacKavey, Malley, & Stewart, 1991; Rabbitt & Winthorpe, 1988) or dating procedures (Holding, Noonan, Pfau, & Holding, 1986) has resulted in less of a recency effect and a greater reminiscence component, further emphasizing the importance of this period of life in organizing personal memories, although some prompts will also exaggerate the recency effect (Fitzgerald & Lawrence, 1984).

In addition to having similar retrieval functions, there also seem to be only minor variations across age groups in the attributes of autobiographical memories, as reflected in vividness and affective qualities (Cohen & Faulkner, 1988; Hyland & Ackerman, 1988). There do seem to be differences, however, in the factors associated with vividness. Vividness for younger adults tends to be more associated with emotion (e.g., the individual's feelings surrounding a specific autobiographical event) whereas frequency of rehearsal (e.g., how many times the event has been discussed) is a stronger predictor for older adults (Cohen, Conway, & Maylor, 1994; Cohen & Faulkner, 1988). In addition, Holland and Rabbitt (1990) observed that the amount of detail in autobiographical memories was negatively correlated with age and that the content of autobiographical memories was related to performance in a text-recall task. Specifically, confabulation in text recall was related to production of irrelevant details in autobiographical recall, and there was a positive correlation between the amounts of detail produced in each situation.

Very-long-term memory As already noted, one criticism of studies of autobiographical memory is that we have no way of verifying the accuracy of the memory that subjects retrieve. Thus, it is difficult to determine whether these memories are actual events from the person's past versus reconstructions or confabulations. Obviously, such issues are important if we would like to make inferences about the ability of different-aged adults to recall remote memories in real-world settings (e.g., providing eyewitness testimony). An alternative approach to examining long-term retention involves examining memory for verifiable aspects of cultural or personal experience, such as historical events, famous people, or material learned in school. Although such studies still have little control over learning conditions and retention interval activities, systematic examination of performance as a function of time, subject age, and level of initial learning allows us to make reasonable inferences about memory processes.

The initial approach taken in this line of research was to study memory for common cultural experience. Warrington (Warrington & Sanders, 1971; Warrington & Silberstein,

1970) was one of the first to do this, using a questionnaire that tested memory for historical events occurring between the years 1930 and 1968. Forgetting was observed to occur at similar rates across all age groups, with the steepest part of the retention curve occurring during the most recent 8 years. Warrington also found that both recall and recognition declined from middle to older adulthood at all points studied.

One concern about studies such as these relates to the assumption that the memories being examined were acquired directly through personal experience rather than indirectly (e.g., learning about events in history class). This assumption is difficult to verify since we have no control over the subject's experience prior to the test. Some research (see, e.g., Perlmutter, Metzger, Miller, & Nezworski, 1980; Poon, Fozard, Paulshock, & Thomas, 1979; Warrington & Sanders, 1971) has provided indirect support for this assumption by showing that, regardless of age, memory is better for events that subjects lived through than for those they did not and that peaks in memory associated with specific historical periods tend to be greatest for those age groups who experienced the periods during their 20s and 30s. Other studies have attempted to control for exposure by testing memory for public events with limited subsequent fame, such as short-lived television programs (Squire, 1989; Squire & Slater, 1975), or by excluding test items that were answered equally well by subjects who had and had not lived through the event (Howes & Katz, 1988). The results of these studies are consistent with those of Warrington in demonstrating similar rates of forgetting across age groups.

Another way to control for exposure effects is by assessing memory for which some record exists regarding direct exposure. Researchers have examined long-term retention for high school classmates (Bahrick, Bahrick, & Wittlinger, 1975), a college campus and town (Bahrick, 1979), Spanish learned in school (Bahrick, 1984a), and material learned in a standardized cognitive psychology course given through an open university (Cohen, Stanhope, & Conway, 1992). In order to obtain less contaminated results, researchers have statistically controlled for factors that might have affected retention, such as the number and recency of visits to the college campus since graduation. Two main findings are of note. First, forgetting follows the familiar curvilinear pattern observed in lab situations, but only for the first 3 to 4 years following exposure. After that, subjects exhibit relative stability over a 45-year period. Bahrick (1984a) hypothesized that this stability reflects a relatively permanent memory and dubbed it "permastore." Interestingly, when initial acquisition levels are not very high, there is little evidence of this permanent memory record after 8 years (Bahrick, 1984b). Second, age differences in retention functions were minimal, with the greatest impact of age appearing relatively late in life. Retention interval was a stronger predictor of memory than age when initial levels of learning were controlled. In those few tests where age was a significant predictor, performance required recall of highly specific conceptual details (Cohen et al., 1992). This suggests that once information enters the permastore, it is relatively immune to the negative effects associated with aging.

In sum, studies of long-term retention have identified few age differences in forgetting and in the accessibility of memories over extended periods of time. Factors such as length of time since learning and initial level of exposure appear to be more important predictors of performance than age. The minimal aging effects that have been found appear to be related to memory for details and forgetting in very late life. This research has also suggested that retrieval of personal memories cannot be described simply in terms of forgetting functions obtained from more traditional laboratory research. In contrast to such research, recall of memories appears to be less related to time and more to personal importance (which may influence rehearsal frequency), as indicated by the fact that retrieval is best for both autobiographical and verifiable memories acquired during late adolescence and early adulthood. This may reflect the importance of this period of life in developing a sense of self, thus providing us with important clues regarding the organization of memory for personal events.

Prospective Memory

Most memory research involves retrospective reports of events for the sole purpose of examining their veracity. One important function of memory, however, involves its use in reminding and directing future action. Remembering to do things when they are supposed to be done (e.g., picking the kids up at school, taking medication) has obvious functional and adaptive significance in everyday life. Because of its importance, it has been speculated that prospective memory may have an important motivational component that encourages people to develop and use strategies that will maintain high levels of performance throughout adulthood (Sinnott, 1989).

The study of prospective memory in adulthood provides a good example of the benefits of pairing real-world and laboratory observations in order to understand more specifically the nature of the age-related mechanisms underlying performance and the means by which older adults adapt to changes in abilities. Several studies had initially examined prospective memory outside of the laboratory by asking research participants to mail in a card or telephone a certain number at a specific date and time (Moscovitch, 1982; Patton & Meit, 1993; West, 1988) or to recall information dealing with future research involvement (Sinnott, 1986). Contrary to most of the extant retrospective memory work, this research found that older adults were equivalent or superior to younger adults in their performance. Because of these types of results, the study of prospective memory was transported into the lab to increase control and to better understand the factors that resulted in these unanticipated age effects.

One factor that appears to have an important influence on the results is the extent to which subjects used memory aids to benefit their performance. Moscovitch (1982) observed that older adults relied more on external memory aids (e.g., putting a note by the phone) than younger adults, who were more likely to "trust their memory." Both Moscovitch (1982) and Maylor (1990a) found that this latter strategy was negatively correlated with performance in older adults, whereas reliance on external aids was associated with fewer memory failures.

Age differences in the reported use of external aids are not consistently observed, however, suggesting that other factors may underlie the obtained age effects. For example, West (1988) found that the older subjects in her study were less likely than younger adults to report the use of external aids but were just as likely to comply with a request to send in postcards at an appointed time. When West tested subjects in a laboratory situation where they were not allowed to use external cues, young adults outperformed the old. It may be that the situational cues in the home are more supportive to prospective memory than those in the lab. For example, the presence of a familiar telephone might act as a cue for the subject to make a phone call, whereas a typical lab situation may not have such functional cues available. Dobbs and Rule (1987) obtained similar findings and also found that perceptions of one's own skills were not correlated with performance in the lab, perhaps suggesting that subjects had developed adaptive strategies in everyday life.

One important issue in prospective memory research concerns the extent to which the age differences observed in everyday settings were due to memory or compliance failures. Younger adults may remember to perform the tasks just as well as or better than older adults, but they may not actually perform them as frequently. Patton and Meit (1993) tested this hypothesis using a postcard mail-in task and found no age differences in memory. Older adults did, however, rate the task of sending in the postcards as being more important than did younger adults, suggesting that the superior performance of older adults in such contexts may be partly due to compliance.

Recently, prospective memory skills have been examined in a more systematic way in the laboratory. Einstein and McDaniel (1990; Einstein, McDaniel, Richardson, Guynn, & Confer, 1995) have argued that there are two types of prospective memory tasks, each of which may be associated with different age effects (see also Chapter 6). One type is event-based in that prospective memory is spontaneously cued by the occurrence of a specific event (e.g., seeing a friend reminds you to ask a favor). Einstein, McDaniel, and colleagues hypothesize that such tasks may be similar in nature to indirect memory tasks (see Chapter 7), and therefore, age differences in performance in these situations should be minimal. The other type of task is time-based, in that memory is cued following the passage of time (e.g., remembering to check the roast after 2 hours). This type of task may require more self-initiated processing (checking the clock) than event-based tasks and thus may be more susceptible to aging effects.

To test their hypotheses, subjects studied several lists of words presented on a computer screen for later recall. In the event-based task, the lists contained several "cue" words and subjects were instructed to perform a specific action (e.g., depress a response key) whenever these cues appeared in the lists. In the time-based task, subjects were presented with an identical list-learning task, but they were required to press a key after 10-minute periods rather than respond to specific cue words embedded in the lists. Consistent with expectations, no age differences were observed in event-based tasks, with younger and older adults being equally successful at remembering to respond to the cue words with the appropriate actions. This was true even when subjects were not allowed to use external aids to support performance. In contrast, significant age effects were observed for the time-based tasks, with older adults taking longer than younger adults to respond after the 10-minute period had ended. This was apparently due to more efficient time monitoring on the part of younger adults.

Einstein and McDaniel (1990) found that event-based prospective memory was uncorrelated with performance on the retrospective memory tasks, perhaps suggesting that these two situations require two different sets of skills. Einstein, Holland, McDaniel, and Guynn (1992) argue, however, that event-based tasks have both a prospective component (i.e., spontaneous reminding) *and* a retrospective component (i.e., remembering what to do) and that age differences may emerge if the retrospective component is manipulated. Einstein et al. altered the complexity of the retrospective memory component by varying the number of cue words that needed to be remembered and found age differences in performance when the retrospective component was relatively complex (four cue words) but not when it was simple (one cue word). The age difference in the complex condition was attributed to the difficulties that older subjects had in remembering the cue words and not in their ability to remember to do something. In fact, when between-group differences in memory for the specific cue words were controlled, the age differences in performance disappeared. In a related study, Mäntylä (1994) also found that age differences in event-based prospective memory increased with the demands that the task placed on the subject's cognitive resources.

Maylor (1993) also observed age differences in an event-based prospective memory task. She found that age differences in performance were initially nonexistent but increased over trials as middle-aged subjects (aged 51–62) improved their performance whereas older adults (aged 70–83) remained stable. The age difference in her study appeared to be due to the older adults being more likely than the younger adults to forget to perform an action on one trial after they had correctly performed that action on a previous trial. Maylor noted that this pattern is different than that observed on retrospective tasks, where younger adults typically outperform older adults initially but forgetting rates are equivalent. This suggests once more that the two types of skills may involve different components.

In sum, age differences in prospective memory are minimal in everyday situations, apparently due to the opportunity to utilize external cues and to the motivational factors associated with the task of remembering to do something. When prospective memory is taken out of an everyday context, age differences in performance emerge, but laboratory work still suggests that some components of prospective memory are relatively age insensitive. Thus, the extent to which age differences emerge in prospective memory tasks depends on both the extent to which they tap into age-sensitive components and the opportunity for the subject to utilize compensatory strategies.

Memory for Meaningful Verbal Materials

As we have seen in the previous sections, one factor that moderates age differences in memory is the familiarity or meaningfulness of the material being remembered. One criticism of past research on verbal memory is that it often involved the use of tasks and materials that have little meaningfulness to the individual (e.g., memorizing lists of unrelated words). It could be reasonably argued that young adults have an advantage in such tasks because of their close proximity to schooling and, consequently, their being well practiced in the use of strategies that facilitate the acquisition of materials that are, at least initially, low in meaningfulness. Some of these materials may even involve lists (e.g., foreign alphabets, U.S. presidents, bones in the body). In support of this argument, student status has been found to be associated with the use of strategies that correlate with recall performance (Ratner, Schell, Crimmins, Mittelman, & Baldinelli, 1987; Zivian & Darjes, 1983).

What if the to-be-remembered verbal materials are meaningful? Is the advantage typically displayed by younger adults attenuated because older adults can benefit from the use of existing, well-developed organized schemes (as was observed to be the case with spatial memory)? One approach to the study of meaningfulness effects involves examining the impact of organizational rules associated with language and its use. If random lists of words deprive older adults of the opportunity to use language-based semantic, syntactic, and prosodic cues, then, relative to younger adults, they should exhibit a disproportionate benefit in memory when such cues are present (e.g., spoken sentences). Contrary to these predictions, some initial work indicated similar levels of benefits associated with approximation to normal grammatical structure, at least for subjects of average or better verbal skills (Craik & Masani, 1967, 1969). More recent research (Wingfield, Lahar, & Stine, 1989; Wingfield, Poon, Lombardi, & Lowe, 1985), however, has found that the presence of syntactic and prosodic language cues disproportionately benefits older adults' recall of word strings, particularly in conditions of rapid speech. This suggests that older adults may be able to compensate for aging-related reductions in processing speed through reliance on language-based organizational cues (see Chapter 8).

The impact of organization can also be examined by varying the nature of the text. Certain types of discourse have a high level of cohesiveness brought about through use of a culture-specific narrative or story structure that organizes text elements in terms of familiar temporal and causal relations. In contrast, expository text provides no such familiar structure, requiring the use of subject-determined organizational schemes to facilitate comprehension and memory. Several studies have examined these factors either by directly comparing memory for narratives versus expository text (Adams, Labouvie-Vief, Hobart, & Dorosz, 1990; Hartley, 1986; Petros, Norgaard, Olson, & Tabor, 1989; Tun, 1989) or by examining the impact of cohesiveness among story elements (Mandel & Johnson, 1984; Ratner et al., 1987; Smith, Rebok, Smith, Hall, & Alvin, 1983). Once again, the results are inconsistent, but when age-related interactions are found they do support the idea that older adults benefit more from text cohesiveness than younger ones do (but see also Zelinski & Gilewski, 1988).

A second major approach to studying age-related meaningfulness effects in memory has been to examine the impact of content familiarity on performance. As stated above, older subjects may be at a disadvantage in remembering relative to young adults when they cannot use their past experience as an organizational tool, and thus familiarity may disproportionately benefit performance in older adults. Research examining recall of words (Barrett & Watkins, 1986; Worden & Sherman-Brown, 1983), names (Hanley-Dunn & McIntosh, 1984), and text (Hultsch & Dixon, 1983) has found that the differences in memory performance between age groups favored those subjects for whom the to-be-remembered materials were most meaningful. It should be noted, however, that younger subjects typically displayed better performance than older subjects when the to-be-remembered materials were equally familiar across age groups.

Familiarity effects can also be examined by controlling for knowledge across age groups and then manipulating the content of the to-be-remembered materials in the passage with respect to this knowledge (Arbuckle, Vanderleck, Harsany, & Lapidus, 1990; Hartley, 1993; Morrow, Leirer, & Altieri, 1992). For example, Arbuckle et al. (1990) identified groups of young and older adults who did or did not have formal training in music and then tested their memory for passages that were related or unrelated (e.g., about dogs) to this knowledge. This type of research has generally found that the impact of familiarity is similar across age groups.

Taken together, these results suggest that familiarity does benefit the performance of older adults and that when studies fail to control for age differences in task-relevant knowledge, normative age differences might be artificially inflated or deflated. By the same token, however, there is little evidence that familiarity has a disproportionate benefit on the performance of older adults. As suggested in Chapter 8, younger and older adults may both depend on similar types of contextual factors in comprehension, but age-related limitations in basic processing functions that affect construction of the memory representation may still result in superior performance by younger adults.

Another set of studies, however, has identified certain circumstances under which familiarity may have different benefits across age groups. Specifically, this research has examined the representation of information about people and events in memory and age differences in the role of knowledge in organizing this information. In the typical study, subjects read and attempt to recall either a verbal description of someone engaged in a routine activity (e.g., grocery shopping, eating at a restaurant) or a behavioral description of a person. In such situations, it has been shown that our past experience—in the form of memory scripts or person/trait schemas—facilitates the creation of a representation for a specific event or person by providing a basis for relating actions to one another (Wyer & Srull, 1989). For example, when reading about someone going to a restaurant, we know that ordering from the menu precedes eating, and we use this knowledge of temporal and causal relations to integrate these actions within our memory representation of this specific event. Several studies (Hess, 1985; Hess, Donley, & Vandermaas, 1989; Hess & Tate, 1991, 1992) have demonstrated, however, that age differences still exist in memory for specific scripted events and person descriptions, especially for information that is inconsistent with expectations. Thus, relative to younger adults, older adults would have a harder time remembering "He took a pen from his pocket" than "He ordered lasagna from the waiter" when reading a story about eating at a restaurant.

Hess and Tate (1991, 1992) argue that unexpected information is difficult to integrate within the memory representation using preexisting mechanisms (e.g., temporal relations, variable slots in scripts) and thus individuals must generate their own linkages, for example, by explaining away unexpected information (e.g., he was using the pen to sign a credit card slip). Hess and Tate provide evidence that suggests that older subjects are less likely than younger adults to generate such linkages, thereby impairing retrieval of unexpected information. This makes older adults especially dependent on the supports provided by existing knowledge and puts them at some risk in situations (e.g., learning to cope with a health ailment) where adaptation is dependent upon their replacing incorrect existing beliefs with correct but contradictory beliefs (Rice & Okun, 1994). Note, however, that this type of effect is not always obtained (see, e.g., Hess & Pullen, 1994; Hess, Vandermaas, Donley, & Snyder, 1987; Light & Anderson, 1983), suggesting that variations in subject or task characteristics may alter this age-related consistency effect.

For example, Hess and Pullen (1994) examined memory for behavioral information that was either consistent or inconsistent with a previously provided description of a target person. As is often observed in studies of person memory, they found that young adults remembered inconsistent behaviors better than consistent ones, presumably due to the more extensive processing accorded to inconsistencies (see Wyer & Srull, 1989). In contrast, older adults exhibited a recall advantage not only for inconsistent information but also for behaviors that were negative in nature (e.g., taking money from someone's desk). Hess and Pullen (1994) argued that, relative to younger adults, the greater attention allocated to processing negative information by older adults is consistent with their greater belief in the immutability of negative characteristics (Heckhausen & Baltes, 1991). Such findings suggest that age effects in text memory may occur not only because of differential dependence on knowledge to support memory but also because of differences in processing goals associated with age-related variations in knowledge systems (e.g., beliefs, schemas).

Another way to think about meaningfulness is in terms of what subjects are asked to do with the materials. Adults are rarely required to remember for the sake of remembering but rather remember in the context of specific goals or tasks. The subject's motivations and goals may have a strong impact on memory, which in turn may affect the form and extent of any age differences (Hess, 1994; Labouvie-Vief & Schell, 1982). Adams (1991; Adams et al., 1990) has argued that the criterial task in many memory studies (i.e., verbatim reproduction or recognition) may be inconsistent with the typical mode of remembering in adulthood, which emphasizes the integration of the memory event within the context of the individual's personal experience (see also Hashtroudi et al., 1994). Thus, the mature adult's goal is rarely to remember verbatim but rather to understand the importance of an event and how it relates to existing personal concerns. Consistent with this perspective, Adams has shown that adults of all ages include more integrations and interpretations in their recall of discourse than do adolescents, who are more literal in their reproductions, and that such integrative processing reaches a peak in middle age. Similarly, Walsh and Baldwin (1977; Walsh, Baldwin, & Finkle, 1980) found that older adults were just as adept at integrating ideas across units of text as were younger adults in spite of the superiority of the latter subjects in standard tests of free recall. In a related study, Morrow, Leirer, Fitzsimmons, and Altieri (1994) found that age differences in memory performance by pilots depended upon the nature of the task. When air traffic controller communications were presented and recalled in a format similar to that used in actual flights, age differences in memory were minimal. When an unfamiliar procedure was used, however, age differences increased, thus highlighting the importance of familiarity and practice in maintaining performance.

■ Summary and Implications for Everyday Functioning

In this section, we have reviewed research having to do with skills and situations that have at least face validity with respect to everyday functioning in order to explore a contextual perspective of age-related change in memory. Based on this review, several observations can be made about age-differences in memory skills and their implications for everyday functioning. First, contextual variables, such as setting, materials, task, and subject characteristics, are all important determinants of age differences in performance. Consistent with a contextual perspective, age differences tend to be smallest in familiar situations (e.g., familiar grocery stores, faces from one's age group, grammatical word strings spoken with normal inflection) in which subjects can draw upon their wealth of knowledge to guide their behavior and formulate effective strategies. Adults of all ages benefit from the familiarity of a real-life task, but the advantage of familiarity is often greatest for the older adult. When subjects are tested in less familiar contexts or those of limited relevance, age differences in performance are greater, apparently due to older adults adopting ineffective (but perhaps familiar) strategies. Interestingly, when given instructions in strategy use, older adults often benefit to a greater degree than younger adults, suggesting that experience may be an important determinant of the observed age differences.

Note, however, that familiarity is not always sufficient to eliminate age differences and that the benefits of familiarity are not universal across domains. At present, it is unclear why this is the case. It may have to do with aging-related information-processing decrements which limit the degree to which past experience can be used to benefit performance. For example, Charness (1981) hypothesized that the availability of task-relevant knowledge may not enable older adults to overcome more basic age-related processing speed decrements in situations where stimulus presentation is brief and externally paced. It is also most likely the case that familiarity is a multidimensional concept and that its benefits may depend upon which task components are familiar. For example, research on spatial memory has suggested that apparently familiar forms of organization (e.g., maps, panoramas) will result in age-related benefits only when such organization taps into available knowledge that allows the older adult to make meaningful connections among stimuli (e.g., compare Light & Zelinski, 1983, to Waddell & Rogoff, 1981).

Consistent with the selective optimization with compensation notion, we also noted instances of age-related compensation in subjects' attempts to counteract real or perceived declines in memory efficiency. For example, older adults appear to develop quite effective external memory aids, and the development of such aids may be selective based upon the importance of the specific skill to the individual's life (e.g., prompting their recall of important information necessary for future action).

These familiarity and compensation effects have important implications for understanding everyday functioning. In essence, these results are consistent with the selective optimization with compensation notion of adult development, in which memory performance is optimized in important contexts through the development and practice of effective strategies. These strategies can be viewed either as optimizations of existing knowledge and past experience or as compensations for changes in ability. Both processes serve to maintain or enhance current functioning. Thus, even though we may see increasing differences in memory performance with age in the laboratory with the use of unfamiliar tasks or the examination of isolated processes, such differences may not be seen in more familiar, everyday contexts. This research also suggests, however, that older adults may have a more difficult, though not impossible, time than younger adults in adapting to new situations in which they cannot utilize previously established knowledge (e.g., health beliefs) or skills associated with specific contexts (e.g., relocation from their home to another community; transfer to a new job). Ease of adaptation may depend upon similarity of the new situation to the old.

Our review also suggests that qualitative differences may exist in the manner in which subjects approach a specific memory task. When left to their own devices, different-aged adults may vary in their interpretation of the task and/or materials and may encode different types of information (e.g., meaning in texts, evaluative and affective information in actions), resulting in variations in the nature of the representation in memory (Hess & Pullen, 1994). An important question is whether such effects are due to differences in motivations or interests, to changes in ability which limit the type of information that can be processed, or to some interaction between the two as older adults develop new interests or approaches to problems as a type of adaptive or compensatory mechanism (Adams, 1991). Regardless of the source, such findings suggest that memory differences in everyday situations may not necessarily be due to age-related deficits but in some cases to variations in knowledge, interests, and motivation which may affect how different-aged adults approach the same problem.

Another important observation from this review is that many memory skills remain relatively stable throughout life. For example, long-term retention functions do not vary considerably across adulthood and, except for the very old, different-aged adults exhibit similar levels of retention for relatively permanent memories. A great deal of similarity also exists in the organization of autobiographical memories, reflecting factors that appear to be unrelated to age (i.e., importance to development of self-concept). Such findings are important because they contradict popular stereotypes about the aged.

Lest the reader go away with an overly optimistic view of aging effects on memory, it should be noted that age differences do exist even in functionally relevant types of memory and these differences often appear to be due to factors that are similar to those identified in more traditional models of memory and aging. In many cases, older adults appear to have trouble remembering details and distinctive or context-specific information (e.g., face memory, source memory). This may limit their ability to effectively retrieve information from memory even in situations where manipulations associated with attentional capacity have no impact (e.g., activity memory). Situations requiring self-initiated processing (e.g., time-based prospective memory tasks) also result in declines in performance with age (Craik, 1986). Such findings validate many of the models and hypotheses drawn from more traditional memory research. At the same time, however, less traditional work has given us information that might not be available from the laboratory and that leads to reconceptualizations of our views of aging and memory as well as to novel phenomena that can be studied more closely in the laboratory.

One final implication of the research on memory in context concerns the impact of beliefs about the aging process on everyday performance and perceptions of everyday performance. While there is little evidence to support a relationship between beliefs about how one's memory functioning has changed and actual change in performance on memory tasks, beliefs about memory in old age do affect perceptions of one's own development as well as predictions concerning memory performance (see Chapter 15). These perceptions may ultimately influence the types of contexts in which individuals choose to live and work in late adulthood. For example, increasing age appears to be related to a greater belief in the uncontrollability of negative characteristics, such as forgetfulness. Because of this belief, older adults may choose not to participate in activities that "strain" memory skills, which in turn may eventually have a negative impact on functioning by removing the individual from social situations and opportunities for self-growth. Participation in such cognitively demanding activities, however, may be important in maintaining high levels of functioning, as suggested by recent work linking environmental complexity with intelligence (Schooler, 1987). Thus, we must consider the value of educating older adults about memory skills and factors influencing their maintenance.

THE FINAL ANALYSIS: WHERE DO WE STAND, AND WHERE DO WE GO?

Our goal in the present chapter was to take a slightly different approach to the examination of aging and memory. Much of the research in this area can be characterized as being driven by existing theories and methods derived from work with young adults. Whereas the use of such methods can be valuable in isolating the impact of age on important processes, the extent to which this work helps us to understand everyday functioning can be legitimately questioned due to lack of information regarding the generalizability of such research and to the limited scope of the phenomena investigated. It is our contention that a research approach motivated by a contextual perspective, with an emphasis on problem-driven research and on skills and contexts of performance of real-world relevance, can expand our understanding in many ways. This can be seen in the research we have reviewed in this chapter.

A problem-driven approach is consistent with the contextual perspective because it is not limited by existing methods or models. Rather, specific memory skills are investigated because of their perceived relevance to everyday life. Thus, interesting phenomena that are not easily studied using traditional laboratory procedures come under scrutiny. A good example of this is the work on long-term retention, which has provided valuable insights regarding age differences in forgetting functions and the structure of autobiographical memory.

The examination of behavior outside traditional research contexts also allows us to better understand how people adapt to new contexts and compensate for age-related loss. For example, Kirasic's (1991) research on spatial memory in grocery stores indicates how skills and strategies might become contextualized with experience. Likewise, research on prospective memory has indicated how older adults alter their everyday behavioral strategies to compensate for perceived losses. Such findings both facilitate our understanding of aging and memory by examining performance within a broader context and suggest alternatives (or modifications) to overly simplistic biologically oriented decrement models.

Another important aspect of a contextually oriented approach concerns its role in validating more traditional studies of memory. Several studies have indicated the limited external validity of traditional laboratory-based research by demonstrating that age-related deficits in the laboratory do not necessarily predict age-related deficits in real life (e.g., prospective memory). Such findings suggest the importance of examining the context surrounding everyday performance in order to better understand the source of the discrepancy across testing situations. One should not get the impression, however, that we believe that the traditional laboratory approach to research is useless. As has been demonstrated here, the importance of more traditional research approaches can be seen in their use in better understanding the factors underlying contextual facilitation in performance. Likewise, certain hypotheses derived from traditional work have received support in more everyday-oriented research. Our argument is simply that traditional and nontraditional approaches should work hand in hand in order to better describe aging and memory from a contextual perspective. Studying behavior in context allows one to identify important determinants of performance which can then be investigated in a more systemative fashion in the laboratory, with research on prospective memory being a good example of this approach.

The research reviewed in this chapter also has many weaknesses when it comes to informing a contextual perspective. In spite of identifying factors such as familiarity and meaningfulness as important predictors of age effects, we still do not fully understand the mechanisms underlying such effects. For example, West (1986) has suggested that familiarity may have benefits in terms of motivation, knowledge activation, processing speed, metamemorial knowledge, and/or anxiety levels. Future studies should attempt to identify the causal components associated with such factors and their relationship to age, perhaps using methods similar to the molar equivalence–molecular decomposition strategies used in studies of expertise (see Chapter 13).

At the same time, more systematic examinations of everyday contexts of performance should be carried out in order to understand both the types of skills that adults use in real life and the contextual supports for performance. For example, Gould and Dixon (1993; Gould, Trevithick, & Dixon, 1991) have recently begun to explore age differences in collaborative memory, recognizing the fact that remembering is often a socially shared cognitive activity in which two or more people may assist one another in recalling events. This type of recall activity, which may be particularly salient in older adults who have been married for a long time, may have an impact on the development and use of specific types of retrieval strategies across adulthood. Research in such contexts may be fruitful in helping us to understand variations in age effects across contexts.

Although some attempt has been made at examining important contextual factors, it is also clear from the reviewed research that even some of the studies that have face validity may be lacking in terms of their prediction of real-world behavior. For example, studying face memory rather than memory for nonmeaningful visual patterns seems to be a more ecologically valid approach to studying everyday skills. However, it is rare in everyday life that someone is asked to remember 20 new faces after a brief exposure to each. Thus, the age differences in such studies may still not indicate the probability that an older adult will forget one face in context. A more complete picture of age differences in memory functioning will be obtained by examining performance under a variety of conditions, at least some of which closely approximate the typical memory demands observed in everyday life.

Another weakness of current research is the lack of systematic attempts to relate memory to contextual variables and to relate age-related change to changes in life context. Longitudinal research that examines changes in memory skills, ability systems, and life circumstances would enable us to better understand the interplay among these factors in determining performance. Such studies would allow us to examine, for example, the Baltes et al. (1984) notion of selective optimization with compensation by noting the extent to which certain types of skills are used and practiced and the development of compensatory behaviors as abilities or demands change. Some promising work on contextual influences and longitudinal change is currently being done by Hultsch and his colleagues (Hultsch, Hammer, & Small, 1993; Hultsch, Hertzog, Small, McDonald-Miszczak, & Dixon, 1992).

In summary, a contextual perspective can add to our understanding of memory in adulthood by providing information about the factors determining and supporting performance across different age groups. Research from such a perspective can help toward achieving the goal of understanding behavior in context. Though systematic contextual research is only beginning to be done, much existing work informs this perspective and has provided insights that might not have been achieved from more traditional approaches to the study of memory. More programmatic contextual research is needed in the future; this, when taken in combination with traditional research, should provide us with a more complete picture of the mechanisms underlying existing and potential performance across the adult life span.

SUPPLEMENTAL READINGS

Two recent edited volumes specifically address the topic of memory in context. Each contains chapters that focus on specific theoretical and conceptual issues as well as on specific content:

Poon, L. W., Rubin, D. C., & Wilson, B. A. (Eds.) (1989). *Everyday cognition in adulthood and late life.* New York: Cambridge Univ. Press.

West, R. L., & Sinnott, J. D. (Eds.) (1991). *Everyday memory and aging: Current research and methodology.* New York: Springer.

Those interested in arguments regarding laboratory versus everyday approaches to the study of memory are encouraged to read the articles surrounding this debate that were published in *American Psychologist:*

Banaji, M. R., & Crowder, R. G. (1989). The bankruptcy of everyday memory. *American Psychologist, 44,* 1185–1193.

A series of reaction articles by prominent memory researchers was published in 1991 in *American Psychologist* (vol. 46, no. 1, pp. 16–48).

ACKNOWLEDGMENTS

Preparation of this chapter was provided by grant AG05552, awarded to Thomas M. Hess by the National Institute on Aging.

REFERENCES

Adams, C. (1991). Qualitative age differences in memory for text: A life-span developmental perspective. *Psychology and Aging, 6,* 323–336.

Adams, C., Labouvie-Vief, G., Hobart, C. J., and Dorosz, M. (1990). Adult age group differences in story recall style. *Journal of Gerontology: Psychological Sciences, 45,* P17–P27.

Arbuckle, T. Y., Cooney, R., Milne, J., & Melchior, A. (1994). Memory for spatial layouts in relation to age and schema typicality. *Psychology and Aging, 9,* 467–480.

Arbuckle, T. Y., Vanderleck, V. F., Harsany, M., & Lapidus, S. (1990). Adult age differences in memory in relation to availability and accessibility of knowledge-based schemas. *Journal of Experimental Psychology: Learning, Memory, and Cognition, 16,* 305–315.

Bäckman, L. (1991). Recognition memory across the adult lifespan: The role of prior knowledge. *Memory and Cognition, 19,* 63–71.

Bäckman, L., & Nilsson, L. G. (1984). Aging effects in free recall: An exception to the rule. *Human Learning, 3,* 53–69.

Bäckman, L., & Nilsson, L. G. (1985). Prerequisites for lack of age differences in memory performance. *Experimental Aging Research, 11,* 67–73.

Bahrick, H. P. (1979). Maintenance of knowledge: Questions about memory we forgot to ask. *Journal of Experimental Psychology: General, 108,* 296–308.

Bahrick, H. P. (1984a). Semantic memory content in permastore: Fifty years of memory for Spanish learned in school. *Journal of Experimental Psychology: General, 113,* 1–29.

Bahrick, H. P. (1984b). Memory for people. In J. E. Harris & P. E. Morris (Eds.), *Everyday memory, actions, and absent-mindedness* (pp. 19–34). London: Academic Press.

Bahrick, H. P., Bahrick, P. O., & Wittlinger, R. P. (1975). Fifty years of memory for names and faces: A cross-sectional approach. *Journal of Experimental Psychology: General, 104,* 54–75.

Baltes, P. B. (1987). Theoretical propositions of life-span developmental psychology: On the dynamics between growth and decline. *Developmental Psychology, 23,* 611–626.

Baltes, P. B., Dittmann-Kohli, F., & Dixon, R. A. (1984). New perspectives on the development of intelligence in adulthood: Toward a dual-process conception and a model of selective optimization with compensation. In P. B. Baltes and O. G. Brim, Jr., (Eds.), *Life-span development and behavior* (vol. 6, pp. 33–76). New York: Academic Press.

Banaji, M., & Crowder, R. (1989). The bankruptcy of everyday memory. *American Psychologist, 44,* 1185–1193.

Barrett, T. R., & Watkins, S. K. (1986). Word familiarity and cardiovascular health as determinants of age-related recall differences. *Journal of Gerontology, 41,* 222–224.

Bartlett, J. C., & Fulton, A. (1991). Familiarity and recognition of faces in old age. *Memory and Cognition, 19,* 229–238.

Bartlett, J. C., & Leslie, J. E. (1986). Aging and memory for faces versus single views of faces. *Memory and Cognition, 14,* 371–381.

Bartlett, J. C., Leslie, J. E., Tubbs, A., & Fulton, A. (1989). Aging and memory for pictures of faces. *Psychology and Aging, 4,* 276–283.

Bartlett, J. C., Strater, L., & Fulton, A. (1991). False recency and false fame of faces in young adulthood and old age. *Memory and Cognition, 19,* 177–188.

Bruce, D. (1985). The how and why of ecological memory. *Journal of Experimental Psychology: General, 114,* 78–90.

Bruce, D. (1989). Functional explanations of memory. In L. W. Poon, D. C. Rubin, & B. A. Wilson (Eds.), *Everyday cognition in adulthood and late life* (pp. 44–58). New York: Cambridge Univ. Press.

Cavanaugh, J. C. (1987). Age differences in adults' self-reports of memory ability: It depends on what you ask. *International Journal of Aging and Human Development, 24,* 271–277.

Cavanaugh, J. C., Grady, J. G., & Perlmutter, M. (1983). Forgetting and use of memory aids in 20- to 70-year-olds' everyday life. *International Journal of Aging and Human Development, 17,* 113–122.

Charness, N. (1981). Visual short-term memory and aging in chess players. *Journal of Gerontology, 36,* 615–619.

Cherry, K. E., & Park, D. C. (1993). Individual differences and contextual variables influence spatial memory in younger and older adults. *Psychology and Aging, 8,* 517–526.

Cohen, G., Conway, M. A., & Maylor, E. A. (1994). Flashbulb memories in older adults. *Psychology and Aging, 9,* 454–463.

Cohen, G., & Faulkner, D. (1988). Life span changes in autobiographical memory. In M. M. Gruneburg, P. E. Morris, & R. N. Sykes (Eds.), *Practical aspects of memory: Current research and issues* (vol. 1, pp. 277–282). New York: Wiley.

Cohen, G., & Faulkner, D. (1989). Age differences in source forgetting: Effects on reality monitoring and on eyewitness testimony. *Psychology and Aging, 4,* 10–17.

Cohen, G., Sandler, S. P., & Schroeder, K. (1987). Aging and memory for words and action events: Effects of item repetition and list length. *Psychology and Aging, 3,* 280–285.

Cohen, G., Stanhope, N., & Conway, M. A. (1992). Age differences in the retention of knowledge by young and elderly students. *British Journal of Developmental Psychology, 10,* 153–164.

Craik, F. I. M. (1986). A functional account of age differences in memory. In F. Klix & H. Hagendorf (Eds.), *Human memory and cognitive capabilities, mechanisms and performances* (pp. 409–422). Amsterdam: North-Holland.

Craik, F., & Masani, P. (1967). Age differences in the temporal integration of language. *British Journal of Psychology, 58*, 291–295.

Craik, F., & Masani, P. (1969). Age and intelligence differences in coding and retrieval of word lists. *Canadian Journal of Psychology, 60*, 315–319.

Craik, F., & McDowd, J. M. (1987). Age differences in recall and recognition. *Journal of Experimental Psychology: Learning, Memory, and Cognition, 13*, 474–479.

Craik, F. I. M., Morris, L. W., Morris, R. G., & Loewen, E. R. (1990). Aging, source amnesia, and frontal lobe functioning. *Psychology and Aging, 5*, 148–151.

Crook, T. H., III, & Larrabee, G. J. (1990). A self-rating scale for evaluating memory in everyday life. *Psychology and Aging, 5*, 48–57.

Crook, T. H., & Larrabee, G. S. (1992). Changes in facial recognition memory across the adult life span. *Journal of Gerontology: Psychological Sciences, 47*, P138–P141.

Cutler, S. J., & Grams, A. E. (1988). Correlates of self-reported everyday memory problems. *Journal of Gerontology: Social Sciences, 43*, S82–S90.

Denney, N. W., Dew, J. R., & Kihlstrom, J. F. (1992). An adult developmental study of the encoding of spatial location. *Experimental Aging Research, 18*, 25–32.

Dobbs, A. R., & Rule, B. G. (1987). Prospective memory and self-reports of memory abilities in older adults. *Canadian Journal of Psychology, 41*, 209–222.

Dywan, J., & Jacoby, L. (1990). Effects of aging on source monitoring: Differences in susceptibility to false fame. *Psychology and Aging, 5*, 379–387.

Earles, J. L., & Coon, V. E. (1994). Adult age differences in long-term memory for performed activities. *Journal of Gerontology: Psychological Sciences, 49*, P32–P34.

Einstein, G. O., Holland, L. J., McDaniel, M. A., & Gwynn, M. J. (1992). Age-related deficits in prospective memory: The influence of task complexity. *Psychology and Aging, 7*, 471–478.

Einstein, G. O., & McDaniel, M. A. (1990). Normal aging and prospective memory. *Journal of Experimental Psychology: Learning, Memory and Cognition, 16*, 717–726.

Einstein, G. O., McDaniel, M. A., Richardson, S. L., Guynn, M. J., & Cunfer, A. R. (1995). Aging and prospective memory: Examining the influences of self-initiated retrieval processes. *Journal of Experimental Psychology: Learning, Memory, and Cognition, 21*, 996–1007.

Erber, J. T. (1989). Young and older adults' appraisal of memory failures in young and older adult target persons. *Journal of Gerontology: Psychological Sciences, 44*, P170–P174.

Erber, J. T., Szuchman, L. T., & Rothberg, S. T. (1992). Dimensions of self-report about everyday memory in young and older adults. *International Journal of Aging and Human Development, 34*, 311–323.

Evans, G. W., Brennan, P. L., Skorpanich, M. A., & Held, D. (1984). Cognitive mapping and elderly adults: Verbal and location memory for urban landmarks. *Journal of Gerontology, 39*, 452–457.

Ferguson, S. A., Hashtroudi, S., & Johnson, M. K. (1992). Age differences in using source-relevant cues. *Psychology and Aging, 7*, 443–452.

Fitzgerald, J. M. (1988). Vivid memories and the reminiscence phenomenon: The role of a self-narrative. *Human Development, 31*, 261–270.

Fitzgerald, J. M. (in press). Intersecting meanings of reminiscence in adult development and aging. In D. C. Rubin (Ed.), *Remembering our past: Studies in autobiographical memory.* New York: Cambridge Univ. Press.

Fitzgerald, J. M., & Lawrence, R. (1984). Autobiographical memory across the life-span. *Journal of Gerontology, 39,* 692–698.

Flicker, C., Ferris, S. H., Crook, T. H., & Bartus, R. T. (1989). Age differences in the vulnerability of facial recognition memory to proactive interference. *Experimental Aging Research, 15,* 189–194.

Franklin, H. C., & Holding, D. H. (1977). Personal memories at different ages. *Quarterly Journal of Experimental Psychology, 29,* 527–532.

Fromholt, P., & Larsen, S. F. (1991). Autobiographical memory in normal aging and primary degenerative dementia (dementia of Alzheimer type). *Journal of Gerontology: Psychological Sciences, 46,* P85–P91.

Fulton, A., & Bartlett, J. C. (1991). Young and old faces in young and old heads: The factor of age in face recognition. *Psychology and Aging, 6,* 623–630.

Galton, F. (1911). *Inquiries into human faculty and its development.* New York: Dutton.

Gould, O. N., & Dixon, R. A. (1993). How we spent our vacation: Collaborative storytelling by young and old adults. *Psychology and Aging, 8,* 10–17.

Gould, O. N., Trevithick, L., & Dixon, R. A. (1991). Adult age differences in elaborations produced during prose recall. *Psychology and Aging, 6,* 93–99.

Guttentag, R. E., & Hunt, R. R. (1988). Adult age differences in memory for imagined and performed actions. *Journal of Gerontology: Psychological Sciences, 43,* P107–P108.

Hanley-Dunn, P., & McIntosh, J. C. (1984). Meaningfulness and recall of names by young and old adults. *Journal of Gerontology, 39,* 583–585.

Hartley, J. T. (1986). Reader and text variables as determinants of discourse memory in adulthood. *Psychology and Aging, 1,* 150–158.

Hartley, J. T. (1993). Aging and prose memory: Tests of the resource-deficit hypothesis. *Psychology and Aging, 8,* 538–551.

Hasher, L., & Zacks, R. T. (1979). Automatic and effortful processes in memory. *Journal of Experimental Psychology: General, 108,* 356–388.

Hashtroudi, S., Johnson, M. K., & Chrosniak, L. D. (1989). Aging and source monitoring. *Psychology and Aging, 4,* 106–112.

Hashtroudi, S., Johnson, M. K., & Chrosniak, L. D. (1990). Aging and qualitative characteristics of memories for perceived and imagined complex events. *Psychology and Aging, 5,* 119–126.

Hashtroudi, S., Johnson, M. K., Vnek, N., & Ferguson, S. A. (1994). Aging and the effects of affective and factual focus on source monitoring and recall. *Psychology and Aging, 9,* 160–170.

Heckhausen, J., & Baltes, P. B. (1991). Perceived controllability of expected psychological change across adulthood and old age. *Journal of Gerontology: Psychological Sciences, 46,* P165–P173.

Heckhausen, J., Dixon, R. A., & Baltes, P. B. (1989). Gains and losses in development as perceived by different age groups. *Developmental Psychology, 25,* 109–121.

Herzog, A. R., & Rodgers, W. L. (1989). Age differences in memory performance and memory ratings as measured in a sample survey. *Psychology and Aging, 4,* 173–182.

Hess, T. M. (1985). Aging and context influences on recognition memory for typical and atypical script actions. *Developmental Psychology, 21,* 1139–1151.

Hess, T. M. (1994). Social cognition in adulthood: Aging-related changes in knowledge and processing mechanisms. *Developmental Review, 14,* 373–412.

Hess, T. M., Donley, J., & Vandermaas, M. O. (1989). Aging-related changes in the processing and retention of script information. *Experimental Aging Research, 15,* 89–96.

Hess, T. M., & Pullen, S. M. (1994). Adult age differences in impression change processes. *Psychology and Aging, 9,* 237–250.

Hess, T. M., & Slaughter, S. J. (1990). Schematic knowledge influences on memory for scene information in young and older adults. *Developmental Psychology, 26,* 855–865.

Hess, T. M., & Tate, C. S. (1991). Adult age differences in explanations and memory for behavioral information. *Psychology and Aging, 6,* 86–92.

Hess, T. M., & Tate, C. S. (1992). Direct and indirect assessments of memory for script-based narratives in young and older adults. *Cognitive Development, 7,* 467–484.

Hess, T. M., Vandermaas, M. O., Donley, J., & Snyder, S. S. (1987). Memory for sex-role consistent and inconsistent actions in young and old adults. *Journal of Gerontology, 42,* 505–511.

Holding, D. H., Noonan, T. K., Pfau, H. D., & Holding, C. S. (1986). Date attribution, age, and the distribution of lifetime memories. *Journal of Gerontology, 41,* 481–485.

Holland, C. A., & Rabbitt, P. M. A. (1990). Autobiographical and text recall in the elderly: An investigation of a processing resource deficit. *Quarterly Journal of Experimental Psychology, 42A,* 441–470.

Howes, J. L., & Katz, A. N. (1988). Assessing remote memory with an improved public events questionnaire. *Psychology and Aging, 3,* 142–150.

Hultsch, D. F., & Dixon, R. A. (1983). The role of pre-experimental knowledge in text processing in adulthood. *Experimental Aging Research, 9,* 17–22.

Hultsch, D. F., Hammer, M., & Small, B. J. (1993). Age differences in cognitive performance in later life: Relationships to self-reported health and activity life style. *Journal of Gerontology: Psychological Sciences, 48,* P1–P11.

Hultsch, D. F., Hertzog, C., & Dixon, R. (1987). Age differences in metamemory: Resolving the inconsistencies. *Canadian Journal of Psychology, 41,* 193–208.

Hultsch, D. F., Hertzog, C., Small, B. J., McDonald-Miszczak, L., & Dixon, R. A. (1992). Short-term longitudinal change in cognitive performance in later life. *Psychology and Aging, 7,* 571–584.

Hyland, D. T., & Ackerman, A. M. (1988). Reminiscence and autobiographical memory in the study of the personal past. *Journal of Gerontology: Psychological Sciences, 43,* P35–39.

Jackson, J. C., Bogers, H., & Kernthaler, J. (1990). Do memory aids aid the elderly in their day-to-day remembering? In M. M. Gruneberg, P. E. Morris, & R. N. Sykes (Eds.) *Practical aspects of memory: Current research and issues* (vol. 2, pp. 137–142). New York: Wiley.

Jennings, J. M., & Jacoby, L. L. (1993). Automatic versus intentional uses of memory: Aging, attention, and control. *Psychology and Aging, 8,* 283–293.

Johnson, M. K., & Raye, C. L. (1981). Reality monitoring. *Psychological Review, 85,* 67–85.

Kausler, D. H., & Hakami, M. K. (1983). Memory for activities: Adult age differences and intentionality. *Developmental Psychology, 19,* 889–894.

Kausler, D. H., & Lichty, W. (1988). Memory for activities: Rehearsal-independence and aging. In M. L. Howe and C. J. Brainerd (Eds.), *Cognitive development in adulthood: Progress in cognitive developmental research* (pp. 93–131). New York: Springer.

Kausler, D. H., Lichty, W., and Davis, R. T. (1985). Temporal memory for performed activities: Intentionality and adult age differences. *Developmental Psychology, 21,* 1132–1138.

Kausler, D. H., Lichty, W., & Freund, J. S. (1985). Adult age differences in recognition memory and frequency judgments for planned versus performed activities. *Developmental Psychology, 21,* 647–654.

Kausler, D. H., Lichty, W., Hakami, M. K., and Freund, J. S. (1986). Activity duration and adult age differences in memory for activity performance. *Psychology and Aging, 1,* 80–81.

Kausler, D. H., & Wiley, J. C. (1990). Effects of prior retrieval on adult age differences in long-term recall of activities. *Experimental Aging Research, 16,* 185–190.

Kausler, D. H., Wiley, J. C., and Phillips, P. L. (1990). Adult age differences in memory for massed and distributed repeated actions. *Psychology and Aging, 5,* 530–534.

Kirasic, K. C. (1991). Spatial cognition and behavior in young and elderly adults: Implications for learning new environments. *Psychology and Aging, 6,* 10–18.

Kirasic, K. C., Allen, G. L., & Haggerty, D. (1992). Age-related differences in adults' macrospatial cognitive processes. *Experimental Aging Research, 18,* 33–39.

Knopf, M., & Neidhardt, E. (1989). Aging and memory for action events: The role of familiarity. *Developmental Psychology, 25,* 780–786.

Koriat, A., Ben-Zur, H., & Scheffer, D. (1988). Telling the same story twice: Output monitoring and age. *Journal of Memory and Language, 27,* 23–39.

Labouvie-Vief, G., & Schell, D. A. (1982). Learning and memory in later life. In B. Wolman (Ed.), *Handbook of developmental psychology* (pp. 828–846). Englewood Cliffs, NJ: Prentice-Hall.

Light, L. L. (1991). Memory and aging: Four hypotheses in search of data. *Annual Review of Psychology, 43,* 333–376.

Light, L. L., & Anderson, P. A. (1983). Memory for scripts in young and older adults. *Memory & Cognition, 11,* 435–444.

Light, L. L., & Zelinski, E. M. (1983). Memory for spatial information in young and old adults. *Developmental Psychology, 19,* 901–906.

Lipman, P. D. (1991). Age and exposure differences in acquisition of route information. *Psychology and Aging, 6,* 128–133.

Lipman, P. D., & Caplan, L. J. (1992). Adult age differences in memory for routes: Effects of instruction and spatial diagrams. *Psychology and Aging, 7,* 435–442.

Lovelace, E. A., & Twohig, P. T. (1990). Healthy older adults' perceptions of their memory functioning and use of mnemonics. *Bulletin of the Psychonomic Society, 28,* 115–118.

MacKavey, W. R., Malley, J. E., & Stewart, A. J. (1991). Remembering autobiographically consequential experiences: Content analysis of psychologists' accounts of their lives. *Psychology and Aging, 6,* 50–59.

Mandel, R. G., & Johnson, N. S. (1984). A developmental analysis of story recall and comprehension in adulthood. *Journal of Verbal Learning and Verbal Behavior, 23,* 643–659.

Mäntylä, T. (1994). Remembering to remember: Adult age differences in prospective memory. *Journal of Gerontology: Psychological Sciences, 49,* P276–P282.

Maylor, E. A. (1990a). Age and prospective memory. *Quarterly Journal of Experimental Psychology, 42A,* 471–493.

Maylor, E. A. (1990b). Recognizing and naming faces: Aging, memory retrieval, and the tip of the tongue state. *Journal of Gerontology: Psychological Sciences, 45,* P215–P226.

Maylor, E. A. (1993). Aging and forgetting in prospective and retrospective memory tasks. *Psychology and Aging, 8,* 420–428.

McCormack, P. D. (1982). Coding of spatial information by young and elderly adults. *Journal of Gerontology, 37,* 80–86.

McFarland, C., Ross, M., & Giltrow, M. (1992). Biased recollections in older adults: The role of implicit theories of aging. *Journal of Personality and Social Psychology, 62,* 837–850.

McMillan, T. M. (1984). Investigation of everyday memory in normal subjects using the Subjective Memory Questionnaire (SMQ). *Cortex, 20,* 333–347.

Meacham, J. A. (1977). A transactional model of remembering. In N. Datan & H. W. Reese (Eds.), *Life-span developmental psychology: Dialectical perspectives on experimental research* (pp. 261–285). New York: Academic Press.

Measso, G., Romani, L., Martini, E., & Zappala, G. (1990). Preliminary analysis of effects of "normal" aging on different memory processes and abilities. *Perceptual and Motor Skills, 71,* 395–401.

Mook, D. G. (1989). The myth of external validity. In L. W. Poon, D. C. Rubin, & B. A. Wilson (Eds.), *Everyday cognition in adulthood and late life* (pp. 25–43). New York: Cambridge Univ. Press.

Moore, T. E., Richards, B., & Hood, J. (1984). Aging and the coding of spatial information. *Journal of Gerontology, 39,* 210–212.

Morrow, D. G., Leirer, V. O., & Altieri, P. A. (1992). Aging, expertise, and narrative processing. *Psychology and Aging, 7,* 376–388.

Morrow, D. G., Leirer, V. O., Fitzsimmons, C., & Altieri, P. A. (1994). When expertise reduces age differences in performance. *Psychology and Aging, 9,* 134–148.

Moscovitch, M. (1982). A neuropsychological approach to perception and memory in normal and pathological aging. In F. I. M. Craik & S. Trehub (Eds.), *Aging and cognitive processes* (pp. 55–78). New York: Plenum.

Neisser, V. (1982). Memory: What are the important questions? In U. Neisser (Ed.), *Memory observed* (pp. 3–19). San Francisco: Freeman.

Norris, M. P., & West, R. L. (1991). Age differences in the recall of actions and cognitive activities. *Psychological Research, 53,* 188–194.

Norris, M. P., & West, R. L. (1993). Activity memory and aging: The role of motor retrieval and strategic processing. *Psychology and Aging, 8,* 81–86.

Padgett, R. J., & Ratner, H. H. (1987). Older and younger adults' memory for structured and unstructured events. *Experimental Aging Research, 13,* 133–139.

Park, D. C., Cherry, K. E., Smith, A. A., & Lafronza, V. N. (1990). Effects of distinctive context on memory for objects and their locations in young and elderly adults. *Psychology and Aging, 5,* 250–255.

Patton, G. W. R., & Meit, M. (1993). Effect of aging on prospective and incidental memory. *Experimental Aging Research, 19,* 165–176.

Perlmutter, M., Metzger, R., Miller, K., & Nezworski, T. (1980). Memory of historical events. *Experimental Aging Research, 6,* 47–60.

Petros, T. V., Norgaard, L., Olson, K., & Tabor, L. (1989). Effects of text genre and verbal ability on adult age differences in sensitivity to text structure. *Psychology and Aging, 4,* 247–250.

Pezdek, K. (1993). Memory for items in their spatial locations by young and elderly adults. *Developmental Psychology, 19,* 895–900.

Poon, L. W., Fozard, J. L., Cermak, L. S., Arenberg, D., & Thompson, L. W. (Eds.) (1980). *New directions in memory and aging.* Hillsdale, NJ: Erlbaum.

Poon, L. W., Fozard, J. L., Paulshock, D. R., & Thomas, J. C. (1979). A questionnaire assessment of age differences in retention of recent and remote events. *Experimental Aging Research, 5,* 401–411.

Poon, L. W., Rubin, D. C., & Wilson, B. A. (Eds.) (1989). *Everyday cognition in adulthood and late life.* New York: Cambridge Univ. Press.

Rabbitt, P. (1989). Inner-city decay? Age changes in structure and process in recall of familiar topographical information. In L. W. Poon, D. C. Rubin, & B. A. Wilson (Eds.), *Everyday cognition in adulthood and late life* (pp. 284–299). New York: Cambridge Univ. Press.

Rabbitt, P., & Abson, V. (1990). "Lost and found": Some logical and methodological limitations of self-report questionnaires as tools to study cognitive aging. *British Journal of Psychology, 81,* 1–16.

Rabbitt, P., & Winthorpe, C. (1988). What do old people remember? The Galton paradigm reconsidered. In M. M. Gruenberg, P. E. Morris, & R. N. Sykes (Eds.), *Practical aspects of memory: Current research and issues* (vol. 1, pp. 301–307). New York: Wiley.

Rabinowitz, J. C. (1989). Judgments of origin and generation effects: Comparisons between young and elderly adults. *Psychology and Aging, 4,* 259–268.

Ratner, H. H., Padgett, R. J., & Bushey, N. (1988). Old and young adults' recall of events. *Developmental Psychology, 24,* 664–671.

Ratner, H. H., Schell, D. A., Crimmins, A., Mittelman, D., & Baldinelli, L. (1987). Changes in adults' prose recall: Aging or cognitive demands? *Developmental Psychology, 23,* 521–525.

Rice, G. E., & Okun, M. A. (1994). Older readers' processing of medical information that contradicts their beliefs. *Journal of Gerontology: Psychological Sciences, 49,* P119–P128.

Rubin, D. C., Wetzler, S. E., & Nebes, R. D. (1986). Autobiographical memory across the lifespan. In D. C. Rubin (Ed.), *Autobiographical memory* (pp. 202–221). New York: Cambridge Univ. Press.

Ryan, E. B. (1992). Beliefs about memory changes across the adult life span. *Journal of Gerontology: Psychological Sciences, 47,* P41–P46.

Schachter, D. C., Harbluck, J. L., & McLachlan, D. (1984). Retrieval without recollection: An experimental analysis of source amnesia. *Journal of Verbal Learning and Verbal Behavior, 23,* 593–611.

Schacter, D. L., Kaszniak, A. W., Kihlstrom, J. F., & Valdiserri, M. (1991). The relation between source memory and aging. *Psychology and Aging, 6,* 557–568.

Schear, J. M., & Nebes, R. D. (1980). Memory for verbal and spatial information as a function of age. *Experimental Aging Research, 6,* 271–281.

Schooler, C. (1987). Cognitive effects of complex environments during the life span: A review and theory. In C. Schooler & K. W. Schaie (Eds.), *Cognitive functioning and social structure over the life course* (pp. 24–49). New York: Able.

Scogin, F. (1985). Memory complaints and memory performance: The relationship re-examined. *Journal of Applied Gerontology, 4,* 79–89.

Sharps, M. J. (1991). Spatial memory in young and elderly adults: Category structure of stimulus sets. *Psychology and Aging, 6,* 309–312.

Sharps, M. J., & Gollin, E. S. (1987). Memory for object locations in young and elderly adults. *Journal of Gerontology, 42,* 336–341.

Simon, S. L., Walsh, D. A., Regnier, V. A., & Krauss, I. K. (1992). Spatial cognition and neighborhood use: The relationship in older adults. *Psychology and Aging, 7,* 389–394.

Sinnott, J. D. (1986). Prospective/intentional and incidental everyday memory: Effects of age and passage of time. *Psychology and Aging, 1,* 110–116.

Sinnott, J. D. (1989). Prospective/intentional memory and aging: Memory as adaptive action. In L. W. Poon, D. C. Rubin, & B. A. Wilson (Eds.), *Everyday cognition in adulthood and late life.* New York: Cambridge Univ. Press.

Smith, S. W., Rebok, G. W., Smith, W. R., Hall, S. E., & Alvin, M. (1983). Adult age differences in the use of story structure in delayed free recall. *Experimental Aging Research, 9,* 191–195.

Squire, L. R. (1989). On the course of forgetting in very long-term memory. *Journal of Experimental Psychology: Learning, Memory and Cognition, 15,* 241–245.

Squire, L. R., & Slater, P. C. (1975). Forgetting in very long-term memory as assessed by an improved questionnaire technique. *Journal of Experimental Psychology: Human Learning and Memory, 1,* 50–54.

Suengas, A. G., & Johnson, M. K. (1988). Qualitative effects on rehearsal of memories for perceived and imagined complex events. *Journal of Experimental Psychology: General, 117,* 377–389.

Sunderland, A., Watts, K., Baddeley, A. D., & Harris, J. E. (1986). Subjective memory assessment and test performance in elderly adults. *Journal of Gerontology, 41,* 376–384.

Taylor, J. L., Miller, T. P., & Tinklenberg, J. R. (1992). Correlates of memory decline: A 4-year longitudinal study of older adults with memory complaints. *Psychology and Aging, 7,* 185–193.

Thomas, J. L. (1985). Visual memory: Adult age differences in map recall and learning strategies. *Experimental Aging Research, 11,* 93–95.

Tun, P. A. (1989). Age differences in processing expository and narrative text. *Journal of Gerontology: Psychological Sciences, 44,* P9–P15.

Uhl, B., & Graf, P. (1993). Episodic spatial memory in adulthood. *Psychology and Aging, 8,* 257–273.

Waddell, K. J., & Rogoff, B. (1981). Effect of contextual organization on spatial memory of middle-aged and older women. *Developmental Psychology, 17,* 878–885.

Waddell, K. J., & Rogoff, B. (1987). Contextual organization and intentionality in adults' spatial memory. *Developmental Psychology, 23,* 514–520.

Wahlin, A., Backman, L., Mäntylä, T., Herlitz, A., Viitanen, M., & Winblad, B. (1993). Prior knowledge and face recognition in a community-based sample of healthy, very old adults. *Journal of Gerontology: Psychological Sciences, 48,* P54–P61.

Walsh, D. A., & Baldwin, M. (1977). Age difference in integrated semantic memory. *Developmental Psychology, 13,* 509–514.

Walsh, D. A., Baldwin, M., & Finkle, T. J. (1980). Age difference in integrated semantic memory for abstract sentences. *Experimental Aging Research, 6,* 431–444.

Warrington, E. K., & Sanders, H. I. (1971). The fate of old memories. *Quarterly Journal of Experimental Psychology, 23,* 432–442.

Warrington, E. K., & Silberstein, E. K. (1970). A questionnaire technique for investigating very long-term memory. *Quarterly Journal of Experimental Psychology, 22,* 508–512.

West, R. L. (1986). Everyday memory and aging. *Developmental Neuropsychology, 2,* 323–344.

West, R. L. (1988). Prospective memory and aging. In M. M. Gruneberg, P. E. Morris, & R. N. Sykes (Eds.), *Practical aspects of memory: Current research and issues* (vol. 1, pp. 119–125). New York: Wiley.

West, R. L., Boatwright, L. K., & Schleser, R. (1984). The link between memory performance, self-assessment, and affective status. *Experimental Aging Research, 10,* 197–200.

Wingfield, A., Lahar, C. J., & Stine, E. A. L. (1989). Age and decision strategies in running memory for speech: Effects of prosody and linguistic structure. *Journal of Gerontology: Psychological Sciences, 44,* P106–P113.

Wingfield, A., Poon, L. W., Lombardi, L., & Lowe, D. (1985). Speed of processing in normal aging: Effects of speech rate, linguistic structure, and processing time. *Journal of Gerontology, 40,* 579–585.

Worden, P. E., & Sherman-Brown, S. (1983). A word-frequency cohort effect in young versus elderly adults' memory for words. *Developmental Psychology, 19,* 521–530.

Wyer, R. S., Jr., & Srull, T. K. (1989). *Memory and cognition in its social context.* Hillsdale, NJ: Erlbaum.

Zelinski, E. M., & Gilewski, M. J. (1988). Memory for prose and aging: A meta-analysis. In M. L. Howe & C. J. Brainerd (Eds.), *Cognitive development in adulthood* (pp. 133–160). New York: Springer.

Zelinski, E. M., & Light, L. L. (1988). Young and older adults' use of context in spatial memory. *Psychology and Aging, 3,* 99–101.

Zivian, M. T., & Darjes, R. W. (1983). Free recall by in-school and out-of-school adults: Performances and metamemory. *Developmental Psychology, 19,* 513–520.

13

AGE-RELATED DIFFERENCES IN SKILLED PERFORMANCE AND SKILL ACQUISITION

Elizabeth A. Bosman
University of Toronto

Neil Charness
Florida State University

Skilled performance is an integral part of everyday life. Most of our time is spent in activities that are highly practiced, such as our professional occupation, and activities of daily living, such as driving and shopping. Much of the training and education children and young adults receive is intended to help them develop the skills they will require to function as adults. The ability to acquire new skills continuously throughout life is also important. The rapid rate of technological advance means that many jobs and everyday activities change frequently, and new ways of doing familiar tasks must be learned. Rapid change also means that new activities are continuously being created. For example, 30 years ago no one had heard of word processing, programming a VCR, or using an automated teller machine, yet these activities are now commonplace.

Acquiring skill within a specific domain typically requires many years of study, as well as considerable experience, or practice. For example, doctors must spend many years at university and then complete several years of internship before they can be licensed to practice on their own. Skilled tasks thus differ fundamentally from the tasks described in previous chapters. The tasks typically employed by experimental psychologists are unskilled tasks, that is, novel tasks with which the study participants have had no prior experience. This difference is critical because tremendous changes occur in performance as a result of practice. In fact, it has often been suggested that the amount of experience with a task is a better predictor of performance than age per se (see, e.g., Charness & Campbell, 1988). This does not, however, imply that all age-related differences could be eliminated through the provision of extensive practice. Nor does this imply that the results of experimental studies employing novel tasks should be disregarded. The goal of many studies is to examine age-related differences in perceptual, motor, and cognitive abilities independently of the effects of experience. Clearly, in order to achieve this goal novel tasks must be used. However, such studies obviously do not provide information regarding the nature of age-related differences for highly practiced tasks or age-related differences in the effect of practice.

The goal of this chapter is to review empirical studies examining age-related differences in skilled performance and skill acquisition. The chapter is divided into three sections. The first describes the characteristics of skilled performance and outlines a theory of skill acquisition. The second and third sections discuss age-related differences in effects associated with acquired skill (i.e., skills acquired prior to participation in an experimental study) and skill acquisition, respectively.

THE NATURE OF SKILL AND SKILL ACQUISITION

The differences in the performance of a novice and an expert are quite striking. Consider, for example, the differences in performance in someone just learning to skate and in a champion figure skater, or the wobbly motion of a novice cyclist and an expert who glides smoothly through narrow spaces. More generally, the performance of a novice is slow, error prone, and awkward, whereas the performance of the expert is fast, virtually errorless, and extremely smooth and fluid. The novice often cannot perform the simplest of tasks, while the expert can perform the most difficult tasks with ease. These novice/expert differences exist because the expert has over the course of many years of study and practice developed extensive knowledge within his or her domain of expertise. During performance experts draw upon this domain-specific knowledge, and it is this knowledge, at least in part, that underlies their skilled, or expert, performance. In contrast, novices have not yet developed domain-specific knowledge, and thus their performance lacks the hallmarks of expertise.

Following from Fitts and Posner (1967), Anderson (1983) proposed that skill acquisition is characterized by three stages.[1] The initial, declarative stage is one in which the individual learns basic information and facts about the skill he or she is trying to master. This basic information is termed declarative knowledge. When the individual attempts to perform the skill, declarative knowledge is retrieved from long-term memory and held in working memory. The information held in working memory is then used to infer the means of accomplishing the desired goal. During the second stage, termed knowledge compilation, active reliance upon the interpretation of declarative knowledge retrieved from memory is reduced. Instead, the individual develops methods for performing the task, called procedures, that directly apply his or her knowledge of the task. Procedures thus represent knowledge about how to perform the task and correspond to what is termed procedural knowledge. During the final procedural stage, the individual continues to refine the procedures developed during knowledge compilation. In general, during this stage performance becomes much faster. This speedup in performance is well described by the power law of practice illustrated in Figure 13.1. This figure, which illustrates data drawn from Charness and Campbell (1988), indicates the effect of practice on the time required to mentally square a two-digit number for young, middle-aged, and elderly adults. As can be seen in the figure, speed of

---

[1]For a different theory of skill acquisition, see Logan (1988).

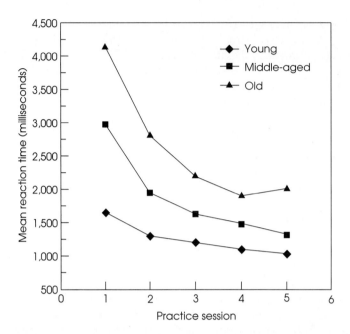

FIGURE 13.1 Changes in time to mentally square a two-digit number as a function of practice session and age group. Data are for the Class 1 problems reported in the study. (*Source:* Charness & Campbell, 1988.)

performance increased with practice for all three groups. However, the increase in speed was greatest during the initial stages of practice and smallest during the later stages of practice. Specifically, the most dramatic increases in speed occurred during the first three sessions of practice. During the last two sessions of practice there was very little increase in speed. This finding of minimal improvements in speed during later practice sessions is quite typical of studies examining the relationship between speed and practice and is taken to indicate that the later stages of skill acquisition have been reached. Further, once the final stages of skill acquisition have been reached, further improvements in performance are unlikely. Finally, in addition to increased speed of performance, during the procedural stage performance becomes more finely tuned; fewer errors are made, and the individual becomes more skilled at making decisions about how to respond to different aspects of the task environment.

These stages of skill acquisition can be illustrated by considering the process of learning to touch-type. During the initial declarative stage the individual learns information such as how to position his or her hands, where different characters are located on the keyboard, and which finger is associated with each key. When attempting to type, the individual spends a lot of time trying to remember where different characters are located and which finger is supposed to strike each key. In general, performance is extremely slow and error prone and is characterized by many long pauses while the individual searches the keyboard for a particular key. During knowledge compilation the individual spends less time actively trying to remember where keys are located and which finger strikes each key. Instead, procedures are developed that enable the individual to strike directly the appropriate key. Performance becomes faster and less error prone, and the keyboard is consulted less often. Finally, during the procedural stage, typing speed continues to increase while the number of errors decreases. The individual also becomes more skilled at typing characters that occur infrequently, such as numbers.

The amount of practice required to develop expertise depends upon the complexity of the task. Very simple tasks can be mastered in a matter of a few hours, while more complex tasks may require hundreds or thousands of hours of practice and years of study. For example, it has been estimated that approximately 600 hours of practice are required to achieve a typing speed of 60 net words per minute (Gentner, 1988). For more complex domains such as chess, music, and mathematics, it appears that at least 10 years of intensive study and practice are required to achieve the highest levels of performance (Ericsson & Charness, 1994; Ericsson, Krampe, & Tesch-Römer, 1993).

AGE-RELATED DIFFERENCES IN ACQUIRED SKILLS

It is often noted that, although experimental studies consistently demonstrate age-related declines on the vast majority of laboratory tasks, older adults perform as well as, if not better than, younger adults on a wide range of skills and occupations. For example, no relationship has been found between job productivity and age (McEvoy & Cascio, 1989). One potential explanation for this paradox is that experimental studies typically examine unskilled performance, whereas everyday performance usually involves tasks that are highly familiar and well practiced (Salthouse, 1990). Given that, relative to their performance on experimental tasks, older adults perform quite well on everyday tasks, it has been suggested that skill may enable older adults to perform at levels comparable to younger adults despite age-related declines in basic cognitive processes (Bosman, 1993; Charness, 1981a,b; Charness & Bosman, 1990; Rybash, Hoyer, & Roodin, 1986; Salthouse, 1987, 1989, 1990). Consequently, an important goal of research examining age-related differences in skilled performance is to identify the means by which older adults may be able to perform at levels comparable to younger adults'. As part of this objective, four conceptual frameworks—accommodation, compensation, maintenance, and encapsulation—have been proposed as outlining the means by which older adults may be able to perform at levels comparable to younger adults (Salthouse, 1990).

According to the accommodation perspective, older adults have acquired metacognitive knowledge related to their domain of expertise that enables them to continue to perform well. Specifically, within their domain of expertise, older adults have learned to identify the conditions under which their performance is adversely affected by age-related declines and to selectively avoid these conditions (Salthouse, 1990). For example, elderly individuals may give up driving at night because under these conditions their driving performance becomes unsafe. However, these same individuals may continue to drive during the day because under these conditions their driving performance is unaffected by age-related declines. They have thus accommodated to an age-related decrease in their driving skill, specifically, unsafe driving at night, by restricting their driving to daytime conditions. Although it may appear to the casual observer that an individual's driving performance has been unaffected by age-related declines, this appearance is the result of the individual selectively avoiding conditions under which he or she can no longer continue to perform well. The essence of accomodation is an ability to maintain high levels of performance by selectively avoiding conditions under which it is impossible to perform well. Thus, to the extent that older adults can identify these conditions and avoid them, older adults will continue to exhibit high levels of skilled performance.

In contrast, the compensation perspective suggests that the negative impact of age-related changes is offset by the development of compensatory mechanisms that enable older adults to perform at levels comparable to younger adults'. According to such a proposal, aging is characterized as consisting of two interacting processes—a decline in perceptual, motor, and cognitive processing capabilities and an accumulation of specialized knowledge (i.e., procedural and declarative knowledge; Anderson, 1983)—that offset these declines in the domain of expertise (Charness & Bosman, 1990; Salthouse, 1987, 1989, 1990). More specifically, according to this perspective, older adults develop a compensatory mechanism, or strategy, which enables them to achieve comparable levels of performance in a qualitatively different manner relative to younger adults of equivalent skill. For example, elderly persons may find that their driving performance is adversely affected by age-related slowing. However, they may compensate for these age-related declines by increasing the skill with which they evaluate traffic and road conditions. Thus, although an individual may react more slowly to events on the road, an increased ability to evaluate traffic and road conditions may compensate for this age-related slowing. It should be noted that compensation is not restricted to strategies that are consciously employed by the older adult. Compensatory mechanisms may develop unconsciously over time as an individual attempts to maintain performance in the presence of age-related declines.

Unlike the compensation perspective, which suggests that skill enables older adults to compensate for age-related declines, the maintenance, or selective sparing, perspective argues that skill prevents age-related declines from occurring. More specifically, the maintenance perspective suggests that older adults are able to maintain skilled performance because extensive practice has prevented age-related declines from occurring in the component processes underlying skill (Charness & Bosman, 1990; Salthouse, 1987, 1989, 1990). For example, according to this perspective, decades of experience driving would prevent an older person from experiencing age-related declines in driving skill.

The final perspective, encapsulation (also referred to as compilation), argues that once a skill has been acquired, it is not affected by age-related declines in the efficiency of the underlying component processes. An analogy that has been used to describe the encapsulation perspective is that of a computer program that has been compiled from several subroutines. Once the program is compiled, changes to the subroutines will not affect the compiled program (Salthouse, 1989, 1990). Similarly, during the initial stages of skill acquisition different component processes may contribute to skilled performance. However, once a skill is established, it may become independent of these component processes, and thus age-related declines in the efficiency of the underlying component processes should not affect performance because the skill has become independent of these component processes. The skill can thus be said to incorporate, or encapsulate, a more efficient form of functioning (Rybash et al., 1986; Salthouse, 1989, 1990). For example, according to this perspective, elderly individuals should not exhibit declines in their driving performance because of the encapsulation of their driving skill.

An interesting implication of the encapsulation perspective is that whether or not an individual exhibits age-related declines in the performance of a particular skill may depend upon the age at which the skill was learned. Specifically, if a skill was learned at a young age, before age-related declines began to affect performance, the encapsulated skill would presumably reflect the level of performance the individual was capable of when young. However, if the skill was learned during middle or old age, when the influences of age-related declines upon performance were becoming apparent, presumably the encapsulated skill would reflect a lower level of performance.

Currently, there is very little empirical evidence regarding the relative importance of accommodation, compensation, maintenance, and encapsulation in enabling older adults to perform at levels comparable to younger adults'. No research has been found that has examined the importance of accommodation and encapsulation. However, some research has examined the roles of compensation and maintenance in the skilled performance of older adults. Following is a discussion of this research.

■ Evidence for Compensation

Evidence suggesting that older adults may compensate for age-related declines comes from quasi-experimental studies examining age- and skill-related differences in chess (Charness, 1981a,b,c), bridge (Charness, 1979, 1983, 1987), and transcription typing (Bosman, 1993; Salthouse, 1984; Salthouse & Saults, 1987). Before providing a more detailed description of the results of these studies, it is useful to examine in some detail the methodological approach underlying most of them. The basic feature of the approach is the selection of a sample that varies widely in terms of both age and skill level but in which age and skill are uncorrelated (see, e.g., Bosman, 1993; Charness, 1981a,b, 1983, 1987; Salthouse, 1984; Salthouse & Saults, 1987). The rationale is that such a sample makes it possible to assess the effects of age and skill independently. It is also possible to assess whether there are qualitative differences in the means by which individuals of different ages achieve the same overall level of performance. Specifically, an examination of age effects on descriptors of skill other than overall performance may reveal differences that indicate how older adults are able to perform as well as younger adults.

A potential disadvantage of using a sample in which age and skill are uncorrelated is that the lack of correlation may be achieved by selecting the fittest old and the least fit young, resulting in an unrepresentative sample. That is, the elderly adults in such a sample may be more elite than the younger adults. For example, when young, the elderly adults may have exhibited higher overall ability relative to the younger adults. Such a sample makes it difficult to determine how skill enables older adults to perform at levels comparable to younger adults' because the pattern of results could be attributable to the biased sample rather than the effect of skill (for a discussion, see Charness & Bosman, 1990; Salthouse, 1989). Consequently, in addition to establishing a lack of correlation between skill and age, it is important to demonstrate that the sample is representative of normal aging. This issue can be addressed by demonstrating that within the sample there are the typical age-related patterns on domain-unrelated measures (Charness & Bosman, 1990). Examples of measures that can be employed for this purpose are measures of crystallized intelligence, such as vocabulary tests, which typically show little, if any decline, with age, and measures of processing speed, such as reaction time, which show significant slowing with age (Kausler, 1982; Salthouse, 1982). Finally, a limitation of this approach is that it does not address the issue of whether or not the overall level of performance declines with age. The requirement of obtaining a sample in which skill and age are uncorrelated precludes this possibility. For example, the sample may consist of elderly individuals who have consistently performed at a high level throughout their adult life, as well as of elderly individuals whose performance level has declined during their adult years but who still perform at a higher level than novices.

Chess and Bridge

Several studies specifically designed to examine age-related differences in chess skill, and in which the correlation between age and skill was not significant, were conducted by Charness (1981a,b). The measure used to determine chess skill was competitive chess rating, which is an index that varies as a function of the individual's performance in chess competitions. Age- and skill-related differences were assessed for two tasks. In the first, the select-a-move task, players were asked to select the best move for their side for each of four chess positions. In another task, players were shown 20 end-game positions (i.e., a configuration of chess pieces that occurs near the end of the game) and asked to categorize each position as win, lose, or draw. Both of these activities—move selection and evaluating a board position—are integral parts of a chess game. Thus, not surprisingly, the accuracy of performance in both tasks increased with skill. More important, no age effects were observed for the value of the chosen moves or for the number of correct evaluations.

Although there were no age-related differences in chess rating and in performance on these skill-related tasks, older chess players exhibited the expected memory deficits on a skill-related memory task. Memory performance was assessed by unexpectedly asking players to recall the four chess positions that had been employed in the select-a-move task. There was the expected effect of skill, indicating that more skilled players exhibited better recall. More important, there was an effect of age, indicating that older players recalled less than comparably skilled younger players. A similar age-related decline in memory performance was documented in a study not specifically designed to examine the effects of age on chess skill (Charness, 1981c). When asked to recall briefly presented (1, 2, or 5 seconds) chess positions, older players recalled significantly less than younger players of equivalent skill.

Generally, studies examining age-related differences in bridge skill have produced a similar pattern of results, indicating no age-related differences in skilled performance accompanied by age-related deficits on skill-related memory or speeded performance measures (Charness, 1979, 1983, 1987). One obstacle to research examining bridge skill is the absence of a valid measure of skill that is not confounded with age. Specifically, the commonly used index of bridge skill, master points, is cumulative across the life span. Master points can only be gained, not lost, and thus this measure may not accurately reflect a player's current skill level independently of age. Nonetheless, despite this problem, the logarithm of master point total proved to be sensitive to variations in performance on experimental tasks. Skill- and age-related differences were assessed for a task in which players were shown a bridge hand and required to produce an opening bid as quickly as possible, and for a task that examined performance on a component of the bidding task, namely, summing the number of honor card points. For both tasks there was an effect of skill indicating superior performance by more skilled players. There was also no effect of age for either task, indicating that older adults performed as well as comparably skilled younger players. However, the results did indicate that older players bid more slowly than younger ones. The latter finding is consistent with the usual findings of age-related slowing on speeded tasks. In tournament bridge, however, you are not permitted to bid quickly! All oral bids must be made in an even tempo when it is your turn to announce your bid.

Despite the absence of age-related effects for this aspect of bridge skill, there were age-related declines on a skill-related memory measure. When players were asked to recall previously presented bridge hands, there was the expected effect of skill, indicating better recall performance by more skilled players. More important, there was an effect of age, indicating that older players recalled less than comparably skilled younger players (Charness, 1979).

Thus, a consistent pattern of empirical results emerges from studies examining age-related differences in chess and bridge skill. The results of these studies document a situation in which there were no age-related differences in overall skill, or on skill-related tasks, despite the presence of age-related memory deficits for skill-related memory tasks. If these memory tasks truly reflect a component of chess and bridge skill, then, in an indirect way, these studies suggest that the older players were able to compensate for memory deficits, although the means by which they were able to do so were not identified.

There is also some intriguing, though weak, evidence for selective preservation of the cognitive activities practiced in bridge. Clarkson-Smith and Hartley (1990) showed that older bridge players who were comparable in age and activity levels to a control group of non-bridge-playing older adults had greater working memory and reasoning capacity but were not superior on other tasks such as reaction time or vocabulary. Clarkson-Smith and Hartley noted that this might be due either to bridge playing demanding working memory engagement and reasoning, hence preserving those practiced abilities, or to selective recruitment to bridge. That is, in the latter case, only those with better-than-average working memory and reasoning ability take up the game in the first place; even if there are declines with age, bridge players would, on average, retain their superiority. (The work on spatial ability in architects, to be discussed later, is consonant with the latter interpretation.) Longitudinal research would be required to distinguish between these two interpretations.

Transcription Typing

Among the skills that have been examined by investigators interested in age-related differences in skilled performance, transcription typing is unique because it is the only skill for which there is more direct evidence suggesting how older adults may compensate for age-related declines. Typing skill is typically indexed by net words per minute, a combined speed–accuracy measure commonly employed in educational and professional settings. Previous research has indicated that typing skill as indexed by net words per minute does not decline with age. That is, older typists perform just as well as younger typists. However, despite the absence of age-related declines in overall typing skill, older typists exhibit deficits on the motoric processes underlying typing (Bosman, 1993; Salthouse, 1984). Thus, similar to the results of studies examining age-related differences in chess and bridge skill, older typists exhibited no declines in overall skill but declines on the processes underlying the skill. The implication is that somehow the older typists were able to compensate for their motoric deficits.

The motoric aspects of transcription typing are thought to involve at least two classes of processes: translation, or motor programming, and execution. Translation processes function to convert characters in the text into motor programs. Execution refers to those processes involved in implementing motor programs so that the appropriate keys are struck (see Salt-house, 1986, for discussion). Evidence for age-related deficits in the motoric processes of typing was obtained from a digraph typing task (Bosman, 1993, 1994). During this task, two letters (i.e., a digraph such as *di* or *si*) were displayed on the computer screen, and the typist had to type the two letters as quickly as possible. Performance on this task yielded two measures: initial latency, which reflected the time required to hit the first key, and interkeystroke latency, which reflected the latency between the two keystrokes. The advantage of using these two measures is that they are differentially sensitive to the translation and execution components of motor performance. Specifically, initial latency primarily reflects the time associated with translation processes, whereas interkeystroke latency primarily reflects the time associated with execution processes. The results of the digraph typing task were consistent with the interpretation that low-skill older typists exhibit a deficit for both the translation and execution processes underlying transcription typing, whereas high-skill older typists exhibit a deficit for translation processes only. Specifically, the results for initial latency indicated age-related slowing at all levels of typing skill. Thus, this result is consistent with an age-related deficit in translation, regardless of skill level. The results for interkeystroke latency revealed an age × skill interaction, indicating that at low skill levels the usual age-related slowing was observed, whereas at high skill levels no age-related slowing was apparent. The implication of this pattern of findings is that low-skill older typists exhibit an execution deficit, whereas high-skill older typists do not. Why the high-skill older typists did not exhibit an execution deficit is unclear, but it may represent an instance in which expertise enables older adults to perform at levels comparable to younger adults despite age-related declines. However, while the nature of age-related deficits varied as a function of skill, older typists exhibited motoric deficits.

Given these results, an important issue is how the older typists were able to maintain overall typing performance despite their motoric deficits. The available evidence suggests that older typists may be compensating for motoric slowing by beginning keystroke preparation sooner than younger typists. Evidence for this compensatory mechanism comes from research examining age-related differences in the size of the preview span. The preview span is defined as follows: A typist always looks a few characters ahead of the character currently being executed. For example, when typing the sentence "The black dog chewed a bone," while typing the *b* in "black" the typist will be looking ahead in the text at other letters, such as the *d* in "dog." This gap between the character being fixated by the eye and the character being typed by the hand is referred to as the preview span (see, e.g., Bosman, 1993; Salthouse, 1984, 1985, 1986; Salthouse & Saults, 1987). The size of the preview span varies with skill, with more skilled typists having a larger preview span than less skilled typists. Also, if preview is restricted so that the amount the typist can read ahead in the text is less than his or her preview span, there is a dramatic decrease in typing speed. For example, if a typist has a preview span of six characters but text preview is restricted so that he or she can read only three characters ahead in the text, typing speed is slowed considerably. This relationship between typing speed and preview span has been interpreted as indicating that the preview span represents the point at which keystroke preparation begins (Bosman, 1993; Salthouse, 1984, 1985, 1986). Research examining age-related differences in the size of the preview span has found that preview span size increases with age (Bosman, 1993; Salthouse, 1984). Figure 13.2 illustrates the age-related increase in preview span. As can be seen in the figure, preview span size increases with skill. However, more importantly, preview span size

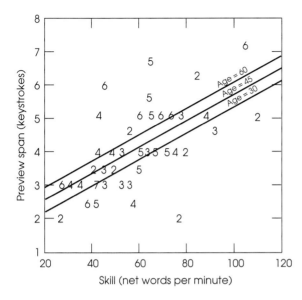

FIGURE 13.2 Scatterplot of preview span size by skill. The number representing each subject corresponds to the first number of the subject's age. The regression lines represent the predicted preview span for individuals aged 30, 45, and 60 years. (*Source:* Bosman, 1993.)

increases with age. This is indicated by the regression lines indicating the predicted preview span size for individuals aged 30, 45, and 60 years.

Given that the preview span is thought to indicate the point at which keystroke preparation begins, the implication of the age-related increase in preview span is that older typists may compensate for age-related slowing of motor performance by beginning keystroke preparation sooner (Bosman, 1993; Salthouse, 1984). Support for this interpretation has been obtained by manipulating the amount of text preview during typing and examining the impact of this manipulation upon the relationship between typing speed and age. Given that there is no age-related decrease in typing speed under normal typing conditions when text preview is unrestricted, it would be expected that when the amount of text preview is equal to or greater than the average preview span (i.e., 7–10 characters), there should be no correlation between typing speed and age. However, when text preview is restricted so that it is smaller than the average preview span (i.e., 1–3 characters), if older adults do rely upon greater advance preparation to compensate for age-related motoric deficits, it should be the case that there is a correlation between age and typing speed, indicating that the older typists are slower. In general, it has been found that when text preview is large and therefore advance preparation of keystrokes is possible, there is no correlation between age and typing speed. However, when text preview is small, there is a significant correlation between age and typing speed, indicating that the older adults are slower (Bosman, 1993; Salthouse, 1984). This pattern of results is illustrated in Figure 13.3. Thus, the age-related increase in preview span size coupled with the age-related slowing of typing speed under conditions of restricted preview suggests that a reliance on greater advance preparation may be a compensatory mechanism used by older typists.

However, a limitation of the above research examining age-related differences in preview span size is that the research is cross-sectional in nature. Consequently, it is possible that the age-related increase in preview span reflects cohort differences. That is, preview span

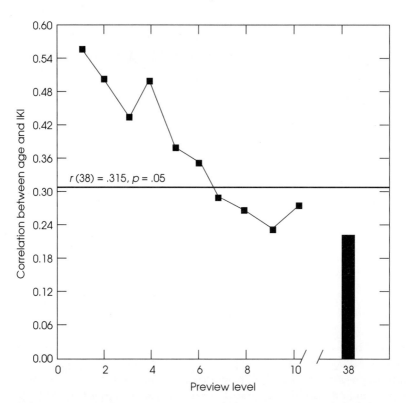

FIGURE 13.3 Correlation between age and interkeystroke interval (IKI) by preview level. (*Source:* Data from Bosman, 1993.)

size may not increase with age; rather, relative to the younger adults, the older adults may have had larger preview spans to begin with. Longitudinal research tracking the size of the preview span across the adult life span would be required to document that preview span size does increase with age and that such an increase functions as a compensatory mechanism.

■ Evidence Regarding Maintenance

Only one study has been found that examined whether or not increased experience is associated with the maintenance of cognitive abilities with age. The relevant study examined the effects of age and experience on spatial visualization ability for architects (Salthouse, Babcock, Mitchell, Skovronek, & Palmon, 1990). Before considering the results of this study, however, it is useful to examine certain relevant methodological issues. First, because the goal of such a study is to determine if extensive experience is associated with the maintenance of general cognitive abilities, specific measures of overall performance in the relevant domain are typically not obtained. Consequently, studies of this type do not address the issue of whether or not performance on skilled tasks declines with age. Another critical issue is that the underlying cognitive ability assessed must be shown to be an important determinant of performance in the skill domain of interest. Further, the measure of the underlying ability must have construct validity; that is, it must measure the ability of interest and not something else. Finally, age-related differences for the ability measure should be compared for groups of individuals who are both skilled and unskilled in the domain of interest. To demonstrate that maintenance has occurred, it must be shown that age-related declines do not occur for individuals with the relevant experience and do occur for those without the relevant experience.

In the study of interest, Salthouse et al. (1990) defined spatial visualization as the ability to interpret two-dimensional drawings of three-dimensional objects. Spatial visualization ability has been found to be predictive of success in domains such as drafting and geometry and, more important, was rated by the architects participating in the study as highly relevant to their occupational activities. Equally important, the measures used to assess spatial visualization were rated by the architects as requiring the same type of cognitive processes as did their professional activities. The relationship between age and spatial visualization abilities was compared for two groups of individuals, one of architects and one of nonarchitects. The results indicated that there were age-related declines in spatial visualization for both groups and that the rate of decline was roughly comparable. The implication is that extensive experience with spatial visualization is not associated with the maintenance of this cognitive ability. However, the results also indicated that older architects performed better on measures of spatial visualization than did older adults who were not architects. These results were interpreted as indicating preserved differentiation of cognitive abilities with age. That is, relative to the nonarchitects, the architects had probably had superior spatial visualization abilities as young adults, and this initial difference was preserved with increased age.

■ Summary and Conclusions

At the beginning of this section it was noted that older adults often perform comparably to younger adults in a variety of domains, and four conceptual frameworks that could account for this observation—accommodation, compensation, maintenance, and encapsulation—were outlined. Currently, much of the available evidence supports the compensation perspective. The results from studies examining age-related differences in chess, bridge, and typing skill suggest either indirectly or directly that older adults perform at levels comparable to younger adults' by compensating for age-related declines. Thus, this research provides some support for the argument advanced by the compensation perspective, which suggests that aging can be characterized as consisting of two interacting processes: a decline in perceptual, motor, and cognitive processing capabilities and an accumulation of specialized knowledge that offsets these declines in the domain of expertise. However, the results of these studies should not be regarded as conclusive. In the case of studies examining chess and bridge skill, only indirect evidence suggesting compensation was found. Similarly, findings suggesting that older typists compensate for age-related slowing through a greater reliance upon advance preparation of keystrokes are open to alternative interpretations such as cohort differences. No evidence was found to support the maintenance perspective, although the results of a single study cannot be definitive. Similarly, no evidence is currently available regarding the accommodation and encapsulation perspectives. A more complete understanding of age-related differences in the performance of acquired skills will require additional research to investigate the validity of the compensation, maintenance, accommodation, and encapsulation perspectives. It is unlikely that elderly adults employ compensatory mechanisms in every skill that they perform; there are undoubtedly many ways in which skilled performance changes during adulthood.

AGE-RELATED DIFFERENCES IN SKILL ACQUISITION

As indicated by the saying "You can't teach an old dog new tricks," it is often assumed that older adults have difficulty acquiring new skills. However, despite this assumption there is considerable empirical evidence indicating that older adults are able to learn new skills. Numerous studies have indicated that the performance of older adults on a variety of tasks improves considerably with training (Willis, 1985, 1987). Accordingly, the focus of this section will not be on demonstrating that older adults can acquire new skills but rather on examining age-related differences in skill acquisition. One important issue is whether or not age-related differences are reduced or eliminated during skill acquisition. Given the dramatic improvements in performance resulting from extensive practice, it might be expected that age-related differences will be minimal once young and elderly adults become practiced at a task. In contrast, it has also been argued that age-related differences will increase with extensive practice (Kliegl & Baltes, 1987; Kliegl, Smith, & Baltes, 1989). The rationale for this prediction is as follows: Extensive practice enables both young and elderly adults to optimize their performance, and thus after practice both groups will be performing close to their potential. However, despite this optimization, age-related declines in perceptual, motor, and cognitive abilities will still adversely affect the performance of older adults. Further, the optimization of performance means that the differences between the age groups will increase because both groups will be performing close to their maximum.

Another important issue is whether or not certain aspects of skill acquisition pose particular difficulty for older adults. For example, using Anderson's (1983) theory of skill acquisition as a framework, age-related deficits in working memory may cause the initial declarative stage of skill acquisition to be particularly difficult for older adults. This may further lead to an age-related difficulty in knowledge compilation and the proceduralization of skill. These issues will be considered in the following discussion of selected studies examining age-related differences in skill acquisition for mental arithmetic, memory and visual search tasks, and serial recall of word lists. However, before reviewing these studies we will examine certain methodological issues.

■ Methodological Issues

Given the importance of practice in skill acquisition, a critical methodological criterion for experimental studies of skills acquisition is to provide sufficient practice for a skill to develop. Generally, this is established by demonstrating that additional practice is unlikely to result in further marked increases in performance. Typically, performance as a function of practice is examined to determine if the later stages of skill acquisition have been reached and if further improvements in performance are unlikely. Specifically, referring back to Figure 13.1, which illustrates the power law of practice, it is important to obtain a function such as the ones illustrated in this figure in which improvements in performance during the later stages of practice are quite minimal. Such a finding would suggest that performance has reached asymptotic levels and that additional practice is unlikely to result in additional marked improvements in performance. The need to provide extensive practice is further complicated by the fact that within the context of an experimental study it is not feasible to provide hundreds, let alone thousands, of hours of practice. Thus, it is not possible to teach study participants how to type or play chess. Instead, the tasks employed in skill acquisition studies must be of modest complexity so that they can be mastered in a comparatively short period of time.

■ Mental Arithmetic

The first study to be considered is one in which subjects were taught to mentally square two-digit numbers such as 64 or 85 using the algorithm illustrated in Figure 13.4 (Charness & Campbell, 1988). The logic behind the algorithm is that it provides a method for breaking the computation down into simpler components that can be easily computed and then combined to produce the answer. Another feature of the algorithm is that it makes heavy demands upon working memory because the components must be maintained in memory while simultaneously implementing the squaring algorithm. Young, middle-aged, and elderly adults practiced mentally squaring two-digit numbers using the above algorithm for six 1-hour sessions. In addition, performance in calculating the different components of the algorithm in isolation was also measured.

From the perspective of assessing age-related differences in skill acquisition, the mental squaring task provides an opportunity to examine age-related differences in speedup and knowledge compilation. More specifically, performance on the squaring task depends in part on the speed and accuracy with which the components can be computed. However, performance also depends upon how efficiently the squaring algorithm can be implemented. Thus, the total time required to square a number is determined by the amount of time required to compute the components and the time required to implement the squaring algorithm. Reductions in the amount of time required to compute the components are indicative of the

To square a number, N, find a constant, C, to add to or subtract from N to bring it to the nearest multiple of ten, NMT. Then subtract or add C from N to produce the other number, OTN. Multiply OTN by NMT by first multiplying the decade of OTN by NMT to get the first product, P1. Then, multiply the right digit of OTN by NMT to get the second product, P2. Now add P1 and P2 to get the SUM. Square the constant, C, to get C^2. Finally, add C^2 and SUM to get the answer.

For example, the procedure for squaring 59 is as follows:

Step 1: 59 + 1(C) = 60, NMT
Step 2: 59 – 1 (C) = 58, OTN
Step 3: 50 (decade of OTN) x 60 (NMT) = 3,000, P1
Step 4: 8 (right digit of OTN) x 60 (NMT) = 480, P2
Step 5: 3,000 (P1) 1 + 480 (P2) = 3,480, SUM
Step 6: 1 (C) X 1 (C) = 1, C^2
Step 7: 3,480 (SUM) + 1 (C^2) = 3481

FIGURE 13.4 Algorithm for mental squaring. (*Source:* Charness and Campbell, 1988.)

extent to which practice has led to an increase in speed. Reductions in the amount of time required to implement the algorithm are also indicative of increases in speed but, more important, are indicative of the extent to which the squaring algorithm has been efficiently compiled into procedures.

An index of how much time is required to implement the squaring procedure can be obtained by determining the ratio of the time required to compute the components to the total time required to compute the answer. If there was no cost associated with implementing the algorithm, the total time required to compute the solution would be equal to the time required to compute the components. That is, the ratio of the summed components time to total algorithm time would equal one.[2] To the extent that the ratio drops below 1 (and approaches 0), it indicates that relatively more time is spent implementing the algorithm and less time is spent computing the components. Of course, it should be noted that using the ratio of component time to total time to draw conclusions about the role of knowledge compilation is based on certain assumptions. First, it assumes that the different components are computed independently of one another when implementing the algorithm. If this is not the case, it is not valid to estimate the time spent computing the components of the algorithm by summing the time required to compute each component. The ratio also assumes that computation of the components and implementation of the algorithm are independent. If both are performed in parallel, the ratio is not a good indicator of the relative amount of time devoted to either. Currently it is not possible to assess whether or not these assumptions are correct. However, despite this, we still believe that it is instructive to examine the change in the ratio of component time to total time as a function of practice and age in order to assess age-related differences in knowledge compilation. Although the ratio may not precisely reflect the relative amount of time devoted to computing the components versus implementing the algorithm, it seems likely that it will provide at least a rough estimate.

The results indicated that, for all three age groups, performance improved significantly with practice and that by the end of the sixth practice session performance had reached asymptotic levels, suggesting that the subjects had reached the final stages of skill acquisition. Specifically, during practice the time required to square a number decreased dramatically. Part of this speedup was attributable to increased speed in computing the components. However, the greatest increase in speed was associated with greater efficiency in implementing the squaring algorithm. Specifically, at the beginning of practice, the ratio of component time to total time was significantly less than 1, suggesting that the subjects spent most of their time implementing the algorithm. At the end of practice the ratio had increased substantially, suggesting that the subjects had become more efficient at implementing the algorithm. Thus, skill acquisition for this task was primarily attributable to knowledge compilation that resulted in the efficient implementation of the squaring algorithm.

An examination of age-related differences for time to compute the components and time to compute the answer indicated that in general the rate of speedup was greater for the older adults but that age-related differences still remained at the end of practice. For time to compute the components, at the beginning of practice both the middle-aged and elderly were

---

[2]Technically, because subjects have to execute a response for each component task and only one response for the algorithm as a whole, the sum of independent component estimates overestimates total time when you assume no overhead for implementing the algorithm. The ratio might therefore be greater than 1.

significantly slower than the young adults. The middle-aged showed the greatest improvement with practice, and by the end of the practice they were not significantly slower than the young adults. Although the elderly improved with practice, they were still slower than the young adults at the end of practice. The results for total time required to square a number produced a similar pattern of results. At the beginning of practice the elderly were slower than the middle-aged, who in turn were slower than the young. There were age-related differences in the rate of improvement, with the performance of the middle-aged adults increasing at a faster rate than that of either the young or elderly adults. At the end of practice, time to square a number did not differ for young and middle-aged adults, but the elderly were still slower. Thus, the results for time to compute the components and time to compute the final answer indicated that practice had the greatest impact upon age-related slowing for the middle-aged and less impact upon age-related slowing for the elderly, although the latter did improve substantially.

Results examining the ratio of time to compute components to total time to compute the answer indicated that, at the beginning of practice, the ratio for the elderly was significantly smaller than for the young. The middle-aged were intermediate between the young and elderly; their ratio did not differ significantly from either of the other groups'. The implication is that at the start of practice the older adults spent significantly more time implementing the algorithm. With practice there was a significant increase in the ratio for all three groups, suggesting knowledge compilation was occurring for all three groups. However, age-related differences did not change as a function of practice. That is, the ratios for the elderly and middle-aged adults were still significantly smaller than for the young adults. The implication is that the older adults were less efficient at implementing the squaring algorithm, even after considerable practice. This suggests that increased age may be associated with increased difficulty in knowledge compilation and the proceduralization of skill.

■ Memory and Visual Search

Memory and visual search tasks have frequently been used to examine age-related differences in knowledge compilation (for a discussion, see Fisk and Rogers, 1991). Age-related differences in skill acquisition will be considered first for memory search tasks and then for visual search tasks. In a typical memory search task, at the beginning of each trial the subject is shown the memory set (or targets), which usually consists of one to four symbols or letters. The subject studies the memory set for several seconds, and then the memory set is replaced with a single probe item. The subject's task is to indicate if the probe item is one of the target items or a distractor item. The task is termed "memory search" because subjects must presumably search the contents of their memory in order to determine whether or not the probe was part of the memory set.

Another critical feature of memory search tasks is whether or not the relationship between target and distractor items is consistent or variable. When consistent mapping is employed, some stimulus items are used only as targets (i.e., they are always part of the memory set and never distractors), while others are used only as distractors (i.e., they are never part of the memory set). For example, if the stimulus set consists of A, E, G, L, K, M, and P, under consistent mapping these stimuli would be divided into two groups, targets and distractors. When variable mapping is employed, the stimulus set is not divided into target and distractor groups; a stimulus can be used as both a target and a distractor. This difference between consistent and variable mapping is important because the development of skill at detecting targets as a consequence of extensive practice is greatest when consistent mapping is used. When variable mapping is used, subjects do not develop as much skill at detecting targets. The reasons for this are as follows: Under consistent mapping, subjects eventually learn which stimuli are targets and which are distractors. Subjects can then use this information during knowledge compilation to develop procedures for automatically detecting targets. In contrast, when variable mapping is employed, stimulus identity cannot be used to determine if a stimulus is a target or a distractor. Consequently, even with extensive practice, it is not possible for subjects to develop procedures for automatically detecting targets (for a discussion, see Fisk & Rogers, 1991). Given that only practice with consistent mapping has been shown to lead to skill acquisition, we will focus on studies that employed consistent mapping when examining age-related differences in skill acquisition for memory search tasks.

Performance on memory search tasks can be summarized by two measures, mean reaction time as a function of memory set size and the slope of the function relating reaction time to set size. Figure 13.5 illustrates the changes in performance in this task as a result of practice. Before extensive practice it is typically found that reaction time increases with set size. The reason for this is that on each trial subjects must search their memory and compare each item in the memory set to the probe item. The slope of the function relating reaction time to set size is thought to indicate the amount of time required to evaluate one item in memory. The more items in the memory set, the more time required to decide if the probe is part of the memory set. However, after extensive practice, in addition to decreasing dramatically, reaction time no longer varies as a function of set size and the slope of the function relating reaction time to set size approaches zero. This reduction in slope is thought to reflect the de-

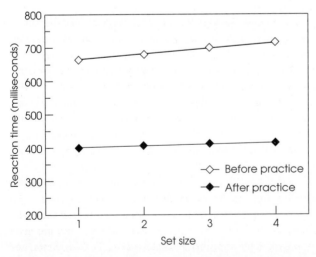

FIGURE 13.5 Hypothetical data indicating changes in performance on a memory search task as a function of practice.

velopment of procedures during knowledge compilation for the automatic detection of targets. Such procedures eliminate the need to search memory in order to determine if the probe is part of the memory set, and consequently the slope of the function relating memory set size to reaction time is greatly reduced. From the perspective of assessing age-related differences in skill acquisition for this task, there are two important issues. First, does reaction time decrease at the same rate for young and elderly adults, or is the rate of decrease faster or slower for the elderly? Second, does knowledge compilation, as indexed by decreases in slope, vary with age?

Salthouse and Somberg (1982) conducted an extensive study in which young and elderly adults practiced a consistently mapped memory search task for 50 1-hour sessions. At the beginning of practice, relative to young adults, the elderly had significantly slower reaction times. The slope relating reaction time to set size was also larger for the elderly, suggesting that they searched memory at a slower rate. During the initial stages of practice, the results indicated that reaction time decreased at a faster rate for the elderly adults. However, after the initial stages of practice, the rate of decrease in reaction time was equivalent for young and elderly adults. After 50 hours of practice, the elderly adults were still significantly slower than the young. Further, an examination of reaction time as a function of practice indicated that performance had reached asymptotic levels, suggesting that marked improvements in performance as a function of additional practice were unlikely. Thus, practice reduced but did not eliminate age-related differences in reaction time. A different pattern of results emerged for the slope measure. Although initially the slope for the elderly was larger, by the end of practice there were no age-related differences in slope, and the slope for both young and elderly approached 0. A similar pattern of results for both reaction time and slope was reported by Fisk and Rogers (1991), who also examined age-related differences in skill acquisition for a memory search task under consistent mapping. The implication is that, for this type of task, extensive practice reduces but does not eliminate age-related slowing of reaction time. However, in contrast to the results obtained for the mental squaring task, knowledge compilation was equally effective for the young and elderly.

Research examining the effect of extensive practice upon age-related differences in visual search reveals a different pattern of results. In a typical visual search task, at the beginning of each trial the subject is shown a single target item, usually a symbol or letter. After the subject has studied the target, it is replaced with a display set that usually varies in size between one and four items. The display set may contain the target item, or it may consist only of distractor items. The subject's task is to indicate if the target item shown at the beginning of the trial appears in the display set. This task is termed visual search because the subject must visually scan the display in order to determine if the target is present. Visual search tasks are also presented using either consistent or varied mapping, and, as is the case with memory search, consistent mapping leads to the greatest development of skill at detecting targets (for a discussion, see Fisk & Rogers, 1991).

Performance on visual search tasks is also summarized by the two measures used to describe memory search performance, mean reaction time as a function of display set size, and the slope of the function relating reaction time to set size. The effect of practice upon these two measures is the same as that observed for memory search. Before extensive practice, reaction time increases as a function of display set size, presumably because the subject must search the display comparing each display item to the target. However, after extensive practice, reaction time is significantly reduced, and the slope of the function relating reaction time to set size approaches 0. As was the case with memory search, this reduction in slope is thought to reflect the development of procedures during knowledge compilation for the automatic detection of targets. From the perspective of assessing age-related differences in skill acquisition for this task, again there are two important issues: Does reaction time decrease at the same rate for young and elderly adults, or does the rate of decrease vary with age? Second, does knowledge compilation, as indexed by decreases in slope, vary with age?

Fisk and Rogers (1991) had young and elderly subjects practice a visual search task under consistent mapping for either 6 (Experiment 1) or 12 (Experiment 2) hours. Their results indicated that reaction time decreased significantly as a function of practice for both the young and elderly but that the rate of decrease was greater for the elderly. However, at the end of practice the elderly were still significantly slower than the young. The results also indicated that by the end of practice reaction time performance had reached asymptotic levels, suggesting that further improvements in performance were unlikely. With regard to the slope relating reaction time to set size, again the results indicated that slope decreased with practice for both the young and elderly adults, suggesting that both groups were able to develop procedures for automatically detecting the targets. However, the decrease in slope was much less for the elderly, and at the end of practice the elderly had a significantly larger slope than the young. Thus, similar to the results obtained for the mental squaring task, for visual search tasks it appears that knowledge compilation is less effective for older adults (for a discussion, see Fisk & Rogers, 1991).

■ Memory Performance

The next study to be considered is one in which young and elderly adults were given extensive training using a mnemonic technique known as the Method of Loci (Kliegl et al., 1989). The Method of Loci involves the use of a highly familiar and ordered sequence of locations as a structure for encoding and retrieving new information. Each item to be remembered is associated with one of the locations in the sequence through the formation of a visual image. The first item to be remembered is associated with the first location, the second item with the second location, and so on. The rationale behind the Method of Loci is that having a well-known sequence of locations with which to associate new information facilitates remembering because the sequence of locations provides a means of organizing new information. Successful use of the Method of Loci depends upon two things. First, the sequence of locations must be memorized. The individual must also become skilled at creating images associating the to-be-remembered item and the appropriate location. Previous research suggests that spatial visualization is an important component of successful use of the Method of Loci (see Lindenberger, Kliegl, & Baltes, 1992, for a discussion). Thus, acquiring skill with this mnemonic may require the development during knowledge compilation of procedures for generating and remembering visual images.

In the study of interest (Kliegl et al., 1989, Experiment 2), the sequence of locations consisted of 40 well-known landmarks in West Berlin whose order the subjects memorized at the beginning of the experiment. After the Method of Loci technique was explained, subjects practiced using the mnemonic for 20 sessions. The information to be remembered consisted of lists of 30 words, and each word was presented for 20, 15, 10, 5, 3, or 1 second. At the beginning of practice, all subjects began with a 20-second presentation rate. The next fastest presentation rate was introduced when the subject was able to recall 50 percent of two consecutive word lists at a given presentation rate. At the start of practice, the young adults recalled more words than the elderly at all presentation rates except 1 second. After practice, performance improved substantially for both young and elderly; however, there was still a significant age-related difference, indicating that young adults recalled more at all presentation rates except 1 second. If, as suggested previously, skill acquisition for this task is associated with the development of procedures for generating visual images associating the to-be-remembered item and the location, these results may indicate an age-related deficit in knowledge compilation. Further, the difference in performance between young and old was larger after practice. That is, practice had increased, not reduced, age-related differences. These results are in marked contrast to previously discussed studies, which indicated that practice reduced, and in some instances eliminated, age-related differences in performance.

Benefits of Previously Acquired Expertise

In the study just discussed, the participants did not possess any skills or abilities that might have facilitated skill acquisition. An interesting question, and one that has generally been ignored, is whether or not existing expertise and abilities facilitate the acquisition of new, but related, skills. This question was addressed in a study that also employed the Method of Loci but whose subjects included young and elderly adults who were graphic designers in addition to typical young and elderly adults (Lindenberger et al., 1992). The rationale for selecting graphic designers is that their profession requires them to generate and work with visual images. Given that the Method of Loci also requires the generation of images, it might be expected that elderly graphic designers would achieve higher levels of performance using this technique than elderly adults lacking their specialized experience. More specifically, the elderly graphic designers could be advantaged in learning the Method of Loci for two reasons. Their professional experience could mean that they have acquired a body of factual and procedural knowledge for generating visual images. Another possibility is that they are superior in spatial visualization and other task-relevant abilities.

Prior to training in the use of the Method of Loci, subjects completed several psychometric tests assessing visual creativity and spatial visualization. The rationale for including these measures was to determine if memory performance, and differences in performance between graphic designers and normal adults, would be predicted by these measures. Subjects then completed seven training sessions that were approximately one hour in length. An examination of age-related differences at the end of training indicated that the performance of the younger normal and younger graphic designers did not differ and that young adults performed better than both groups of older adults. However, although the older graphic designers performed more poorly than the young adults, their performance was superior to that of the normal older adults. The implication is that the older graphic designers' professional experience in generating visual images enhanced their ability to acquire skill using the Method of Loci. An examination of memory performance as a function of performance on the criterion-related tests supported this conclusion. First, memory performance was significantly correlated with measures of spatial visualization even after the effects of age and expertise were controlled for. Second, the difference in performance between the normal elderly and the elderly graphic designers was not significant when group differences in visual creativity and spatial visualization were controlled for. The implication is that the recall advantage of the older graphic designers relative to normal older adults was attributable to the image generation required by the Method of Loci. Thus, it is possible that the elderly graphic designers' professional experience enabled them to outperform the normal elderly.

■ Summary and Conclusions

At the beginning of this section it was suggested that two issues are particularly important when examining age-related differences in skill acquisition: the impact of practice upon the magnitude of age-related differences and whether or not different stages of skill acquisition pose particular problems for older adults. With regard to the effect of practice, given the dramatic impact of practice upon performance, it might be expected that, after extensive practice, age-related differences in performance would be minimized, if not eliminated. However, it has also been suggested that once performance has been optimized via extended practice, age-related declines in performance would result in even larger age-related differences. In general, in the majority of studies, age-related differences were reduced, but not eliminated, by the end of practice. However, in the minority of studies age-related differences either were eliminated or were larger at the end of practice. Thus, the results are mixed, and it is possible that practice interacts with other factors, such as task difficulty, to influence the magnitude of age-related differences after practice. However, a limitation of all of these studies is that the amount of practice they provided is quite small compared to the amount of practice obtained in everyday activities. Many everyday activities have been practiced for thousands of hours. It may be the case that such extreme levels of practice are required to eliminate age-related differences (for a discussion, see Bosman, 1993, 1994). It is also unclear from the studies discussed if any particular aspect of skill acquisition is especially difficult for older adults. Some studies suggested that the knowledge compilation stage may be problematic for older adults, while others did not. Again, it may be the case that factors such as task difficulty influence which stages of skill acquisition are particularly problematic for older adults.

FUTURE DIRECTIONS

As the previous discussion suggests, only a small body of research focusing upon a limited number of domains has investigated age-related differences in acquired skills and skill acquisition. Clearly, there are many unresolved issues regarding the nature of age-related differences in skilled performance. For example, the research investigating age-related differences in acquired skills suggests that older adults maintain their performance level by employing compensatory mechanisms. However, it seems unlikely that older adults always employ compensatory mechanisms, and other mechanisms for maintaining performance level should be investigated. The maintenance perspective suggests that sustained practice over the course of adulthood will prevent age-related declines from occurring. Currently, there are no systematic investigations of the effect of practice upon the preservation of skilled performance with age. Likewise, the accommodation perspective suggests that older adults may possess metacognitive knowledge that enables them to avoid conditions under which they can no longer perform well. Research examining the extent to which older adults do and do not accommodate to age-related declines in this manner is required to address this issue.

Research investigating age-related differences in skill acquisition has so far not produced a consistent pattern of results that holds across all tasks. For example, in most of the research the magnitude of age-related differences is reduced, but not eliminated, by practice. In some instances age-related differences are eliminated after extensive practice, although this is rare, and in other instances age-related differences are actually greater at the end of practice. It may be the case that one of the factors influencing the effect of practice is the age sensitivity of the underlying processes. Specifically, if a process is not particularly age sensitive, practice may be successful in reducing or eliminating age-related differences. However, if a process is particularly age sensitive, practice may lead to an increase in the level of performance but not eliminate the negative impact of aging upon performance. Similarly, research investigating which stage of skills acquisition is most difficult for older adults seems to suggest that knowledge compilation is particularly difficult for older adults, though again this result is not always found. Again, whether or not a particular stage of skills acquisition is problematic for older adults may depend upon the age sensitivity of the underlying processes. Future research should attempt to address this issue.

A somewhat different picture of age-related differences in skilled performance emerges from research examining age-related differences in acquired skills, on the one hand, and age-related differences in skill acquisition, on the other. The research examining acquired skills suggests that older adults are able to compensate for age-related declines and thus achieve a level of performance comparable to that of younger adults. In contrast, the research examining skill acquisition suggests that older adults are typically not able to achieve the same level of performance as younger adults when learning new skills. A challenge for future research will be to account for these differing patterns of results. Currently, there are several factors that could account for the differences between the two types of studies. First, it should be recalled that studies examining age-related differences in acquired skills have generally not attempted to identify whether overall performance declines with age. Thus, the results of these studies should not be interpreted as indicating that the level of skilled performance does not decline with age. It may be the case that skilled performance does decline with age but that the development of compensatory mechanisms minimizes the magnitude of decline. In fact, chess skill, as indicated by competitive rating, does decline with age, although the decline is modest (Charness & Bosman, 1990).

Another difference between studies examining acquired skills and studies examining skill acquisition is the amount of practice participants have had with the task of interest. Subjects in studies of acquired skills have typically had hundreds, if not thousands, of hours of practice at the relevant task prior to participation in an experimental study. Although by the standards of the experimental literature the participants in studies of skill acquisition have received considerable practice, the amount is quite minimal when compared to the amount of practice everyday tasks and activities receive. Practice has a profound impact upon performance, and it may be the case that thousands of hours of practice are required to reduce or eliminate age-related differences. A final difference between studies examining acquired skills and studies of skill acquisition is the age at which the task is first learned. Participants in studies examining acquired skills typically learned the task of interest at a comparatively young age, while this is obviously not true of the older participants in skill acquisition studies. It may be the case that the impact of aging on skilled performance varies as a function of age of acquisition. Specifically, skills acquired while young may be more robust with regard to the effects of aging, while skills acquired when older are not. Certainly, the encapsulation perspective would suggest that this may be the case.

IMPLICATIONS FOR EVERYDAY FUNCTIONING

The results of the research reviewed in this chapter have very positive implications for the everyday functioning of older adults. The research examining age differences in acquired skills indicates that older adults are able to perform at levels comparable to younger adults, possibly by compensating for age-related declines. Further it is worth noting that the skills examined in this context—chess, bridge, and transcription typing—are representative of skills performed in everyday life. Certainly, typing is a skill performed by numerous individuals, and one that is likely to become increasingly important as the use of computers continues to spread. While chess and bridge represent recreational activities for the majority of their practitioners, the complexity of both games is comparable to that of many professional activities. The implication of this research is that older adults can probably be expected to continue to function very well in domains in which they have acquired expertise.

The research examining age-related differences in skills acquisition also indicated that older adults are capable of acquiring new skills and that practice results in dramatic increases in performance. While it might be argued that the tasks examined in this research—mental squaring, memory and visual search, and memory for word lists—have little relevance to most daily activities, we suggest that these tasks correspond to the components of many common activities. We have probably all had the experience of standing in the grocery store attempting to calculate which brand of dishwashing liquid represents the best buy. Although such a calculation is much simpler than mentally squaring two digits, it still takes some time to perform. Similarly, every day most of us are confronted by a seemingly endless list of things that we have to do, and we frequently have the experience of remembering that we forgot to do something. Visual search is also a part of many tasks. For example, during driving we have to continuously scan the environment to detect relevant stimuli, such as a traffic light turning red or a pedestrian stepping out onto the street. Memory scanning is also part of many activities, such as deciding which of several different medications is the one we are currently supposed to take. Thus, the results of research examining age-related differences in skills acquisition have more relevance to everyday functioning than might be immediately apparent. Clearly, this research suggests that older adults can successfully acquire new skills.

SUPPLEMENTAL READINGS

Chi, M. T. H., Glaser, R., & Farr, M. J. (Eds.) (1989). *The nature of expertise*. Hillsdale, NJ: Erlbaum.

Ericsson, K. A., & Smith. J. (Eds.) (1991). *Toward a general theory of expertise: Prospects and limits*. Cambridge: Cambridge Univ. Press.

Proctor, R. W., & Dutta, A. (1995). *Skill acquisition and human performance.* Thousand Oaks, CA: Sage.

ACKNOWLEDGMENTS

Preparation of this chapter was supported by a postdoctoral fellowship awarded to Elizabeth A. Bosman by CARNET: The Canadian Aging Research Network, one of 15 National Centres of Excellence established by the Centres of Excellence program, and by an NSERC grant awarded to Neil Charness. We thank Reinhold Kliegl and Ralf Krampe for their thoughful comments on a previous version of this chapter.

REFERENCES

Anderson, J. R. (1983). *The architecture of cognition.* Cambridge, MA: Harvard Univ. Press.

Bosman, E. A. (1993) Age-related differences in the motoric aspects of transcription typing skill. *Psychology and Aging, 8,* 87–102.

Bosman, E. A. (1994). Age and skill differences in typing related and unrelated reaction time tasks. *Aging and Cognition, 1,* 310–322.

Charness, N. (1979). Components of skill in bridge. *Canadian Journal of Psychology, 33,* 1–16.

Charness, N. (1981a). Aging and skilled problem solving. *Journal of Experimental Psychology: General, 110,* 21–38.

Charness, N. (1981b). Search in chess: Age and skill differences. *Journal of Experimental Psychology: Human Perception and Performance, 7,* 467–476.

Charness, N. (1981c). Visual short-term memory and aging in chess players. *Journal of Gerontology, 36,* 615–619.

Charness, N. (1983). Age, skill, and bridge bidding: A chronometric analysis. *Journal of Verbal Learning and Verbal Behavior, 22,* 406–416.

Charness, N. (1987). Component processes in bridge bidding and novel problem-solving tasks. *Canadian Journal of Psychology, 41,* 223–243.

Charness, N., & Bosman, E. A. (1990). Expertise and aging: Life in the lab. In T. M. Hess (Ed.), *Aging and cognition: Knowledge organization and utilization* (pp. 343–385). Amsterdam: North-Holland.

Charness, N., & Campbell, J. I. D. (1988). Acquiring skill at mental calculation in adulthood: A task decomposition. *Journal of Experimental Psychology: General, 117,* 115–129.

Clarkson-Smith, L., & Hartley, A. A. (1990). The game of bridge as an exercise in working memory and reasoning. *Journal of Gerontology: Psychological Sciences, 45,* P233–238.

Ericsson, K. A., & Charness, N. (1994). Expert performance: Its structure and acquisition. *American Psychologist, 49,* 725–747.

Ericsson, K. A., Krampe, R. T., & Tesch-Römer, C. (1993). The role of deliberate practice in the acquisition of expert performance. *Psychological Review, 3,* 363–406.

Fisk, A., & Rogers, W. (1991). Toward an understanding of age-related memory and visual search effects. *Journal of Experimental Psychology: General, 120,* 131–149.

Fitts, P. M., & Posner, M. I. (1967). *Human performance.* Belmont, CA: Brooks-Cole.

Gentner, D. R. (1988). Expertise in typewriting. In M. T. H. Chi, R. Glaser, & M. J. Farr (Eds.), *The nature of expertise* (pp. 1–21). Hillsdale, NJ: Erlbaum.

Kausler, D. H. (1982). *Experimental psychology and human aging.* New York: Wiley.

Kliegl, R., & Baltes, P. B. (1987). Theory-guided analysis of mechanisms of development and aging through testing-the-limits and research on expertise. In C. Schooler & K. Schaie (Eds.), *Cognitive functioning and social structure over the life course* (pp. 95–119). Norwood, NJ: Ablex.

Kliegl, R., Smith, J., & Baltes, P. B. (1989). Testing-the-limits and the study of adult age differences in cognitive plasticity of a mnemonic skill. *Developmental Psychology, 25,* 247–256.

Lindenberger, U., Kliegl, R., & Baltes, P. B. (1992). Professional expertise does not eliminate age differences in imagery-based memory performance during adulthood. *Psychology and Aging, 7,* 585–593.

Logan, G. D. (1988). Toward an instance theory of automatization. *Psychological Review, 95,* 492–527.

McEvoy, G. M., & Cascio, W. F. (1989). Cumulative evidence of the relationship between employee age and job performance. *Journal of Applied Psychology, 74,* 11–17.

Rybash, J. M., Hoyer, W. J., & Roodin, P. A. (1986). *Adult cognition and aging: Developmental changes in processing, knowing and thinking.* New York: Pergamon.

Salthouse, T. A. (1982). *Adult cognition.* New York: Springer.

Salthouse, T. A. (1984). Effects of age and skill in typing. *Journal of Experimental Psychology: General, 113,* 345–371.

Salthouse, T. A. (1985). Anticipatory processing in transcription typing. *Journal of Applied Psychology, 70,* 264–271.

Salthouse, T. A. (1986). Perceptual, cognitive, and motoric aspects of transcription typing. *Psychological Bulletin, 99,* 303–319.

Salthouse, T. A. (1987). Age, experience, and compensation. In C. Schooler & K. W. Schaie (Eds.), *Cognitive functioning and social structure over the life course* (pp. 142–157). Norwood, NJ.: Ablex.

Salthouse, T. A. (1989). Ageing and skilled performance. In A. Colley & J. Beech (Eds.), *The acquisition and performance of cognitive skills* (pp. 247–264). New York: Wiley.

Salthouse, T. A. (1990). Cognitive competence and expertise in aging. In J. E. Birren & K. W. Schaie (Eds.), *Handbook of the psychology of aging* (3d ed., pp. 310–319). San Diego: Academic Press.

Salthouse, T. A., Babcock, R. L., Mitchell, D. R., Skovronek, E., & Palmon, R. (1990). Age and experience effects in spatial visualization. *Developmental Psychology, 26,* 128–136.

Salthouse, T. A., & Saults, J. S. (1987). Multiple spans in transcription typing. *Journal of Applied Psychology, 72,* 187–196.

Salthouse, T. A., & Somberg, B. L. (1982). Skilled performance: Effects of adult age and experience on elementary processes. *Journal of Experimental Psychology: General, 111,* 176–207.

Willis, S. L. (1985). Towards an educational psychology of the adult learner: Cognitive and intellectual bases. In J. E. Birren & K. W. Schaie (Eds.), *Handbook of the psychology of aging* (2d ed., pp. 818–847). New York: Van Nostrand Reinhold.

Willis, S. L. (1987). Cognitive training and everyday competence. In K. W. Schaie (Ed.), *Annual Review of Gerontology and Geriatrics* (vol. 7, pp. 159–188). New York: Springer.

14

SOCIAL COGNITIVE DEVELOPMENT IN ADULTHOOD AND AGING

Fredda Blanchard-Fields
Georgia Institute of Technology

Current theorizing and research on cognitive change in adulthood and aging have moved away from an exclusive focus on decline to an emphasis on the multidimensionality and multidirectionality of cognitive change (see P. Baltes, 1987; Labouvie-Vief, 1992; Rybash, Hoyer, & Roodin, 1986; Chapter 2). From this perspective, both gains and losses are observed in cognitive abilities across the life span. In particular, research has demonstrated that aspects of cognition in social contexts reflect increasing competence (i.e., gains) in contrast to other cognitive mechanisms known to show decline (Salthouse, 1991; Chapter 12). As illustrated in Chapters 10 and 11, this is most evident in areas such as practical and social problem solving, postformal development, and wisdom (see also P. Baltes & Smith, 1990; Blanchard-Fields & Camp, 1990; Cornelius, 1990).

This form of adaptive cognition is also aptly defined in the social cognition literature. For example, Cantor and Kihlstrom (1989) define an intelligent person as one who employs social knowledge flexibly and adaptively to meet his or her personal goals and create good feelings. Social cognitive functioning from this perspective focuses on the interrelationship between an individual's (1) life tasks and goals, (2) representation of social reality, and (3) cognitive strategies used to adapt to everyday social dilemmas. These facets of social cognition form the foundation for research on social cognitive changes with advancing age. The goal of this chapter is to discuss (1) theoretical and methodological approaches to social cognition research, in general, and social cognition from an adult developmental perspective, in particular; (2) relevant empirical work examining adult developmental differences in social cognitive functioning; and (3) how current approaches to social cognitive research add to our understanding of cognitive changes in adulthood and aging, including avenues for future research.

MAJOR ISSUES IN SOCIAL COGNITION AND AGING RESEARCH

Before reviewing theories and the extant empirical literature on social cognition and aging, we need to further explore the definition of social cognition as discussed in the personality and social psychology literature and how it relates to an adult developmental perspective. First, traditional social cognition theory and research has focused largely on mental representations of self and other, examining either social knowledge (the content and structure of representations) or process (e.g., how such content is accessed). From an adult developmental perspective, are there age-related differences in the content and structure of self- and other representations? Do well-documented age-related changes in cognitive processes (see Chapters 5, 6, and 7) adequately explain age differences in social cognitive processing? In addition, how do these representations differentially influence the processing of social information, behavior, and adjustment outcomes such as psychological well-being in older adults? Overall, does social cognition change with advancing age, in terms of either content or process or both?

Second, research on social cognition cannot ignore the multifaceted, multilayered aspects of the sociocultural context on behavior and its development (see, e.g., Bronfenbrenner, 1979; Chapter 2). In particular, the content of representations of self, other, or social situations should, in principle, be heavily influenced by period-specific and culture-specific values, beliefs, and events. For example, beliefs concerning "the right time to get married" and "whether marriage should come before a career" have evolved considerably as a function of the women's movement of the 1960s and the increase in dual-career marriages.

Third, research on many aspects of social cognition requires a commitment to studying cognition from a functional perspective—that is, to inquiring about the functional importance of self-representations (and other variables) for actual behaviors in context. Many questions of central interest do not necessarily focus on normative changes in information-processing mechanisms, per se, but on how individuals access and use information under particular kinds of situational demands. For example, one's beliefs about whether marriage should come before a career will influence a person's interpretation of everyday marital problems (e.g., attributions as to who or what caused a problem) and the subsequent strategies used to solve those problems.

The above issues combine to emphasize the importance of research explicitly emphasizing the study of social cognition in actual everyday situations. Is there a match between the social cognitive demands of the situation-specific task (as defined by the researcher) and the social cognitive goals of the older adult (i.e., life stage–related goals, tasks perceived by older adults as integral to their everyday functioning)? For example, researchers suggest that a prototypic cognitive task for mature adults is the transmission of sociocultural knowledge and information to younger generations (Adams, Smith, Gaden, & Perlmutter, 1994; Chinen, 1989; Mergler & Goldstein, 1983). In this context, an important goal for an older adult would be to communicate effectively. This requires an adaptive interplay between producing language representing the ideas to be communicated and monitoring the comprehension of the listeners so that ideas can be reexpressed, elaborated, and illustrated whenever necessary. Expository or narrative storytelling in this context is therefore a qualitatively different task than in the traditional laboratory context, in which the explicit demand is to reproduce as much of the content of a text as possible (Adams et al., 1994). Therefore, the social cognitive processing requirements of nominally identical cognitive tasks (narrative recall) may vary as a function of both context and age-related social roles.

Finally, a particularly interesting area of social cognitive belief systems concerns the domain of emotion. Emotion is often viewed as clouding judgment or as inhibiting dispassionate, objective thought. Social cognitive research incorporating both emotion and aging examines such societally held beliefs, as well as the extent to which alternative models of emotion/cognition relationships (e.g., the dynamic interaction between the two) either provide alternative models for understanding psychological reality or represent new belief systems which could influence adults' perceptions and behaviors. For example, to what extent are current cohorts of older persons more likely to suppress negative emotions, and what impact does that have on behavior (e.g., the selection of coping strategies)?

THEORETICAL PERSPECTIVES AND METHODOLOGICAL APPROACHES

Although research has been conducted on the multifaceted aspects of social cognition in general, only recently has there been a growth in empirical research examining changes in social cognition and aging. Before reviewing this literature, let us turn our attention to current theoretical approaches to the study of social cognition and aging. These approaches have drawn heavily from traditional social cognition theory as it interfaces with contextualist views of adaptive cognitive functioning in adulthood and aging. Each of these two perspectives will be discussed.

■ Social Cognition Theory and Cognitive Processes

Traditional theory and research on social cognition are heavily influenced by cognitive psychology and the role information processing plays in social cognitive functioning. A number of researchers point out that the representation and accessibility of social knowledge are highly dependent upon fundamental cognitive processes: the activation of appropriate knowledge, attentional processes, encoding efficiency, and so on (see Hess, 1994, for a recent review). For example, Fiske and Neuberg (1990), among others (see, e.g., Gilbert, Pelham, & Krull, 1988), discuss the importance of time and effort in processing as a determinant of how and what social information is processed about people. Fiske and Neuberg make a distinction between category-based and attribute-based (or individuation) processing of social information. Category-based processing is much like schematic processing in that an individual identifies an actor or event as belonging to a particular group (e.g., career women) and possessing characteristics common to that group (e.g., assertive, intelligent, ambitious). Individuation, or attribute-based processing, occurs when an individual considers each observed characteristic of an actor or event and consciously and effortfully integrates them into a social representation of that person or circumstance. Gilbert (1989) would identify individuation as a correction procedure in which situational information (such as extenuating circumstances) is used to adjust for the initial, automatic categorization of a person or event. Category-based processing requires less resources and thus takes less effort and time than individuation or the correction procedure (Fiske & Neuberg, 1990; Gilbert et al., 1988).

Both types of processes result in an initial impression of an individual or self in a social situation. This impression can subsequently prime judgments (Fiske, 1993; Moskowitz & Roman, 1992; Newman, 1991). For example, a relationship dilemma that results in a negative outcome (e.g., a husband leaving a wife) may trigger category-based trait schemas relevant to the male character in the problem situation (e.g., stereotypes about how men behave in such situations) over and above the systematic and individuated processing of all the information regarding the male character. The activated schema may exert an influence on the judgmental process (e.g., attributing sole blame for the relationship breakup to the man). In fact, as we will see later, this indeed occurs and is influenced by a host of variables including the gender of the individual making the judgments as well as that individual's age, generation, life tasks, and goals.

Social cognition researchers specify a number of variables that determine when category-based or attribute-based processing will be activated. A primary determinant of the processing strategy of choice is motivation and/or goals. For example, Fiske (1993) argues that motivational goals determine whether people are more concerned with feeling accurate (i.e., engaging in individuation) or needing to make fast decisions and act quickly (i.e., engaging in category-based processing). Other motivational determinants of category-based processing include communication mind-sets (e.g., a need to be less complex in communication or pressure to shape the communication to fit the audience); cognitive overload (i.e., engaging in multiple tasks that prevent the consideration of more time-consuming situational information); insecurity and anxiety; or time pressure to make a decision. In contrast, individuation, or attribute-based processing, is fostered when a person (1) is made accountable for the accuracy of her or his social judgment (i.e., she or he must justify judgments to a third party, resulting in a need for more accurate impressions), (2) has the goal of predicting the behavior of another person, (3) is motivated to control the outcome of a social situation, or (4) has personally relevant values primed to motivate her/him to make less stereotypic impressions. Finally, individual difference variables such as a need for structure, intolerance for ambiguity, and expertise in the domain in question also affect strategy choice.

Each of these motivational variables has implications for social cognitive change in adulthood and aging. For example, do decreases in cognitive resource capacity in older adults lead to more reliance on category-based processing? Alternatively, perhaps the changing life tasks and goals of older adults influence whether they engage in category-based or attribute-based processing of a social situation. This latter alternative suggests a second major perspective that has influenced both social cognition research and its application to aging, the contextualist perspective.

■ The Contextualist Perspective and Social Cognition

Both the social cognition tradition and the life-span perspective emphasize the importance of paying explicit attention to context at multiple levels, from the specific situational environment of the individual to the larger cultural context in which the individual lives and develops. For example, Fiske and her colleagues (Fiske, 1993; Fiske & Neuberg, 1990) emphasize the immediate context in their discussion of motivational influences on impression formation. They argue that an individual will engage in attribute-based processing (or individuation) depending on the situational context. Other social cognitive researchers have placed even greater emphasis on motivational influences from the perspective of the individual. An individual brings a motivational framework into the task situation defined by his or her goals and what she or he deems relevant to the task situation. Subsequently, individual performance will reflect the match between these motivational goals, the situational context, and the experimenter-defined task.

A developmental approach incorporates context at multiple levels, including the larger sociohistorical context. Thus, researchers are interested in age-related differences in context factors, such as social roles and life circumstances, associated with adulthood and aging. An individual's life tasks (e.g., goals, social roles) and social knowledge are shaped by one's life experience, generational values, and cultural expectations. In turn, social knowledge and goals influence social information processing (i.e., perceptions of situations and others, past memories for events) and determine which cognitive strategies that are most effective when one encounters different problem situations (Bargh, 1989; Cantor & Fleeson, 1991; Fiske & Taylor, 1991). Overall, contextual variables play a significant role, not only in the content of social knowledge and life tasks but in their accessibility to and influence on cognitive strategies implemented in one's everyday context.

Developmental researchers also take this perspective and suggest that changes in life experiences and demands can result in different and adaptive styles of functioning for adults across the latter half of the life span (Blanchard-Fields & Camp, 1990; Cornelius & Caspi, 1987). In this case, successful or adaptive cognitive functioning involves cognitive, affective, and physical characteristics that interact or are embedded in cultural values, attitudes, and sociocultural institutions (Labouvie-Vief, 1992; Sebby & Papini, 1989). A number of developmentalists have attempted to specify life tasks unique to adult cognitive functioning in multiple contexts. For example, Schaie (1978) suggests that problem solving for youth is embedded in an academic context and typically involves a well-structured problem space with a single correct solution as the criterion of successful performance. However, situations involving a less defined problem space with multiple criteria and/or solutions for effective performance are more prominent in the problems of everyday living faced by older adults.

A common theme running through the contextual approach suggests that the cognitive functioning of older adults (whether it be logical thinking, problem solving, or problem appraisal) must be examined in the sociocultural context of everyday living. A number of criteria relevant to adaptive, everyday cognition have emerged. First, the everyday thinker is aware that the veracity of a solution to a problem is relative to the differing perspectives and goals of an individual (Dittmann-Kohli & Baltes, 1992; Labouvie-Vief, 1992; Sinnott, 1989). Second, the everyday thinker is aware of the uncertain and ambiguous nature of how effective a solution to an everyday problem will be (Dittmann-Kohli & Baltes, 1992; Labouvie-Vief, 1992). Finally, Sinnott (1989) calls attention to the importance of emotions and other psychosocial factors involved in cognitive functioning. This involves an "openness" to perspectives and solutions in order to meet the adaptive demands of one's environment.

The developmental perspective is also concerned with social contextual influences on cognition in interpreting what are gains and what are losses in cognitive functioning. With respect to gains and losses, Hess (1994) suggests that in some cases deficits in cognitive skills may be a function of age-related motivational differences (i.e., perceiving a task as personally irrelevant and therefore not engaging in extensive integrative operations).

Let's go back to the example of older adults transmitting sociocultural knowledge to younger adults. As you will recall, in this type of situation there appears to be more of an implicit social cognitive demand for older adults to communicate effectively (Mergler & Goldstein, 1983). In a recent study, Adams et al. (1994) found that when such demand characteristics of the cognitive task were relevant to the social cognitive goals and tasks of later adulthood, memory performance was facilitated in older adults. More specifically, young and older women were asked to learn and retell a story to a young child from memory. In this context, older adults' retellings of the story contained more detail (in the form of propositions from the text) and were more fluent than young adults' retellings. In contrast to past research, older adults' memory performance actually exceeded that of younger adults. The authors interpret this finding as a function of increased motivation on the part of the older adults to remember the details of the story. In other words, they were motivated to produce not only an interesting and coherent account of the story for the child but as complete a representation of the original story as possible. It would be interesting, of course, to contrast this with a "less" motivating memory context for older adults. But overall, this study illustrates the importance of taking into consideration contextual factors such as multiple levels of the social context of a task situation when investigating changes in cognitive functioning with age.

In sum, social cognitive research emphasizes the importance of considering how changing contextual demands influence how the individual processes social information. Contextual factors include (1) the social knowledge an individual brings to a situation, (2) the goals and demands of a particular context that reflect an accumulation of experience, (3) changing life circumstances, and (4) historicocultural influences. All of these factors combine to influence an adult's interpretation of a situation and motivation to employ specific strategies in that situation. As Hess (1994) points out, these factors may be even more important than the effects of processing skill. As we shall see, much of the work on social cognition and aging has focused on examining age-related differences in context factors such as the social roles and life circumstances associated with adulthood and aging and how these impact on cognitive functioning in a social context (e.g., content and accessibility of knowledge structures, perceptions of others, causal attributions).

■ Methodological Issues

There are a number of salient methodological issues that need to be addressed when studying cognition in a social context. First, the literature is replete with studies manipulating experimenter-imposed variables that are assumed to affect cognitive competence in older adults. However, recent research has questioned the sensitivity of the dependent measures used to capture developmental differences in adulthood. Often, the measures used in previous research were primarily quantitative in nature, such as the number of solutions generated in problem-solving tasks, the amount of text recalled in memory tasks, or scores on questionnaires designed to assess belief systems (e.g., stereotypes, attitudes, internal or external locus of control). Along the same line, both the responses and the criteria for efficacy of cognitive functioning generated by experimenters or questionnaires have been validated exclusively on youthful samples. These types of measures may obscure the qualitative differences that are inherent in the responses themselves. Whether or not it involves how adults transform text (Adams, 1991), expand the problem space in problem-solving situations (Arlin, 1984), or resolve interpretive discrepancies in interpersonal dilemmas (Blanchard-Fields, 1986a), adaptive cognitive functioning needs to be defined in terms of the problem solver or information processor rather than by experimenter-imposed manipulations of the task itself. In order to accomplish this, the methodology of choice needs to consider an individual's role in structuring reality or experience, that is, the way she or he approaches problem-solving situations, decision making, interpersonal dilemmas, and so on.

Second, there are concerns about the validity of questionnaire responses for measuring certain types of belief systems (e.g., attitudes, stereotypes), as well as the concerns articulated above as to the sensitivity of the dependent variable. Thus, there is a need for more qualitative and unobtrusive methods of data collection in order to identify the social cognitive functioning of older adults in context. Given that there is relatively little research examining social cognitive processes from an adult developmental perspective, traditional quantitative methods may not adequately demonstrate the richness and meaning involved in social cognitive processing. For example, how an individual structures reality—that is, adopting the stance that different realities are inherent in the same outcome—could not be explored.

A third methodological issue relates to sample distribution. Given a developmental perspective, it is important to chart differences in social cognitive functioning across a wide enough age range to ensure that, if responses of older adults are different from those of younger age groups, it can be demonstrated. In this way, differentiation between preadult maturity as well as "regressive" patterns and progressive adult responses can be demonstrated with greater precision. By contrast, previous research looked only at adolescence through middle-aged adulthood or young adulthood through older adulthood. (This is discussed more fully in Chapter 3.)

Fourth, individual difference variables such as reasoning ability, emotional maturity, personality characteristics, and so on, may better index social cognitive differences than does age alone. The current literature suggests that age may not serve as the best marker of developmental differences, given the increased interindividual variability found in adulthood. A number of researchers have found other candidates that are better predictors of developmental differences, such as ego development (Blanchard-Fields, 1986a; Blanchard-Fields & Norris, 1994; Labouvie-Vief, Hakim-Larson, & Hobart, 1987), social cognitive level (Blanchard-Fields & Irion, 1988), moral development (King, Kitchener, Wood, & Davison, 1989), and cognitive personality style (Adams, 1991). Therefore, it is important to include global and specific individual difference measures (e.g., openness to experience, locus of control, ego level) as possible mediators and/or indices of variability in social cognitive performance.

REVIEW OF THE EMPIRICAL LITERATURE

Earlier in this chapter, major issues in social cognition and aging research were discussed. These included an emphasis on the changes in the content of and processes involved in social knowledge, the influence of social context on performance, the functional importance of social cognition, and the interface between cognition and emotion. The following empirical review will incorporate the major issues along with the theoretical perspectives discussed above in four domains of research. These include the role of self in cognitive functioning, perceptions of control, attributions and appraisals of others and social situations, and attitudes toward aging. It should be noted that other areas of research, including memory in a social context, real-world problem solving, the impact of self-efficacy on cognition, and wisdom, also fall under the category of cognition in a social context. Coverage of these specific areas can be found in other chapters in this book.

■ The Role of Self in Cognition

Classically, self-conceptions are seen as being embedded within a social context (Erikson, 1968; Swann, 1987). An individual is continually attempting to render experience meaningful through social interaction, or "the looking-glass self" (Cooley, 1902; Mead, 1934). In other words, the self is built upon how others treat one and upon the social situations and roles in which one is placed over the life span. Moreover, individuals function within a structure of meaning (e.g., personal beliefs, norms, and expectations) derived from the sociocultural context (Mezirow, 1991). Experience is filtered through this self-related structure of meaning. Similarly, from a social cognitive perspective, self-knowledge serves as an organizing influence on processes such as interpretation of information (e.g., events, tasks, others) and self-regulation.

As discussed earlier, social cognition, in general, has placed great emphasis on representations of self and how such representations influence social judgments, memory, decision making, and so on. Similarly, the role of self in cognition and aging has received a considerable amount of attention. The majority of work in this area has come from either a life-span developmental framework (i.e., qualitative transformations in the understanding of self) or an application of life-span principles within social psychology (i.e., changing self-schemas and their effects on social cognitive processes).

The Life-Span Developmental Framework

The work of Labouvie-Vief and her colleagues (Labouvie-Vief, DeVoe, & Bulka, 1989; Labouvie-Vief, Hakim-Larson, DeVoe, & Schoeberlein, 1989) provides a good illustration of the life-span perspective on qualitative changes in understanding self. They examined adult age differences in the developmental complexity of self-representation in the form of emotional understanding. Labouvie-Vief contends that we are socialized as children to disassociate two modes of knowing: our emotional system (a personal, context-sensitive understanding of the world and self) and our cognitive or rational system (an impersonal, abstract understanding of the world and self). Furthermore, the socialization process teaches us that the "emotional" self should be subordinated under the "more important" rational self. She further proposes that cognitive achievement in mature adulthood is the ability to integrate these two systems, thus experiencing them as equal rather than as disproportionate in importance. For example, concrete sensations and feelings interact with, rather than being subordinate to, logical, rational thinking to produce more mature and flexible coping.

Labouvie-Vief has found evidence for this developmental progression in terms of (1) emotional regulation and (2) the relationship between emotional understanding and coping. Whereas youths placed more importance on consciously controlling their environment through logical problem solving, older adults placed more importance on integrating inner expression (how one feels) with outer presentation (how one acts) (Labouvie-Vief, DeVoe, et al., 1989). In more recent work, she and her colleagues (Murphey, Labouvie-Vief, Orwoll, & Chiodo, 1992) have worked on applying a similar developmental analysis to representations of self. Their preliminary findings suggest that self-representations vary in complexity from adolescence to later life. This continuum of developmental complexity proceeds from undifferentiated, conventional, and institutional conceptions of self (i.e., self-traits representing normative ideals and standards of self) to more dynamic conceptions of self (i.e., an emphasis on change and transformation rather than static descriptions of self). This corresponds well with other researchers' findings that, with increasing age, adults engage in the process of transforming self-definition to incorporate more meaning into life (see, e.g., Dittmann-Kohli, 1990; Levinson, Darrow, Klein, Levinson, & McKee, 1978); attempt to resolve the dynamic tension between "good" for the self and "good" for society (Armon, 1984); are more effective in regulating their emotions (Carstensen, 1992; Lawton, Kleban, Rajagopal, & Dean, 1992); and experience their affect in undefended and open ways, thus fostering self-awareness (Kramer, 1990; Orwoll & Perlmutter, 1990).

These studies on self and emotional understanding have only begun to demonstrate the ways in which individuals represent and take account of emotions of self. In general, these studies administered affectively laden tasks which asked individuals to reflect on their understanding of both emotional and cognitive components of self. There is a need to move beyond the simple manipulation of emotional tasks in order to assess emotional "understanding" of the individual toward a more experiential, process-oriented approach to the study of the emotion–cognition interface. In other words, more research is needed to examine the individual's phenomenological experience of emotion, that is, an analysis of the current level or on-line functioning of emotional self-experience from early to later adulthood.

The Social Psychological Framework

The social psychological and personality literature on self-representation has focused on changes in self by examining self-schemas or self-knowledge structures in adulthood. Without going into too much detail in this vast area of research, some pertinent theoretical perspectives and findings will be reviewed that relate directly to changes in self with advancing age.

Recent theoretical discussions by Cantor provide an example of research and perspectives on changing self-schemas with aging. Cantor (1990) suggests that although broad, dispositional self-constructs (e.g., temperament) may remain relatively constant across the life span (see, e.g., McCrae & Costa, 1988), other self-constructs such as emotional regulation or the content of self-schemas may change with changing demands in one's life context. In other words, Cantor argues that mastering one's sociocultural context requires focusing on the dynamic process of how tasks take on new meaning in different life periods.

A number of researchers (Markus & Herzog, 1991; Markus & Nurius, 1986; Ryff, 1991) have translated this perspective into the concept of positive and negative possible selves (personalized representations of future self states) as guides to future behavior and an interpretive context for current behavior. For example, Markus and Herzog (1991) argue that a positive self-concept in aging is achieved because there is little tension among one's possible selves. Similarly, changes in possible selves with age, such as lowered aspirations, may be responsible for the higher life satisfaction found among older adults (Campbell, Converse, & Rodgers, 1976). In studies comparing possible selves in younger, middle-aged, and older adults, not only did older adults report a more limited range of self-categories along with fewer hoped- and feared-for possible selves, they reported engaging in a greater number of actions to accomplish the goals defined by their possible selves (Cross & Markus, 1991). Older adults' possible selves are tied more closely to ongoing experience, whereas the self-goals of younger adults are situated more in the future and are more idealistic in nature (Cross & Markus, 1991; Ryff, 1991). Age variations in the content of possible selves reflect a greater emphasis on family and occupation for younger adults and physical and personal goals for older adults (Cross & Markus, 1991). Along the same lines, Hooker (1992) found that older adults were more likely to report possible selves in the health domain than college students were.

Another area of research on self-representation and adult development can be found in gender-role identity studies. There has been a recent increase in the literature on changes in gender-role orientation in adults and the elderly (Feldman, Biringen, & Nash, 1981; Hyde, Krajnik, & Skuldt-Niederberger, 1991; Hyde & Phillis, 1979; Sinnott, 1986). For example, Hyde and Phillis (1979) found more androgynous women (using a self-rated gender-role inventory, the Bem Sex Role Inventory) in younger age groups and more androgynous men in older age groups (ages ranging from 13 to 85) using the BSRI. More recently, Hyde et al. (1991) replicated this finding cross-sectionally, yet found longitudinal evidence for consistency in gender role categories with age.

Blanchard-Fields, Suhrer-Roussel, and Hertzog (1994) found a positive association of chronological age with interpersonal sensitivity—older persons report themselves to be more sensitive than younger persons. With respect to the conclusions of Hyde and her colleagues (age-related increases in androgyny), an alternative interpretation is that adult development may be associated with modest increases in interpersonal sensitivity, perhaps as a function of social-role transitions (e.g., grandparenting; see Feldman et al., 1981).

Summary

Whether from a traditional life-span perspective or a traditional social psychological perspective, there is evidence that age-related differences do exist in self-knowledge structures and self-understanding. These differences are reflected in variations in the content of self-knowledge structures (e.g., family focus versus health focus) as well as in the ability to integrate both emotional and rational selves into one's understanding of the total self. One of the major implications of these variations in self-structure is its functional significance. In other words, representations of self will impact self-regulatory strategies, memory, decision making, coping, and psychological adjustment. However, the majority of this research is conducted at a global level of defining self (e.g., global categories such as family or health). There is a need for more empirical work on (1) developing more tightly defined domain-specific assessments of social schemas and, most important, (2) the relationship between operationally defined social schemas and various performance outcomes.

■ Perceived Controllability

Another area related to the role of self in cognition that has received a considerable amount of attention in the adult development and aging literature is how an individual's sense of control changes across the latter half of the life span. First, let us define what is meant by a "sense of control." Lachman and Burack (1993) refer to sense of control as the perception that one governs what happens in one's life. In this light, research on controllability issues has examined the extent to which individuals believe that the outcomes of events can be attributed to internal (contingent upon one's efforts) or external (determined by outside forces) sources (Levenson, 1974; Rotter, 1966), controllability of the cause of an event (Seligman, Abramson, Semmel, & von Baeyer, 1979), self-efficacy (see Chapter 15), and the predictability of events (Rodin, 1987).

The majority of research on perceptions of control and aging has treated controllability as a generalized "style" (i.e., internal or external orientation) in which individuals report the manner in which they would bring about change in the environment through differential responding (i.e., passive acceptance versus instrumental behaviors). Accordingly, there appears to be a general consensus that internality is the more desirable of the two styles and is associated with greater education, health, wealth, and youth (Heckhausen & Schulz, 1993). Using age as the primary developmental marker of change, there is a considerable amount of research examining age differences and changes in the internal locus of control. In Lachman's (1986) review of these findings, she found the results to be less than consistent. Whereas some studies find older adults to be more internally oriented than younger adults (Gatz & Karel, 1993; Lachman, 1986; Siegler & Gatz, 1985), other studies find older adults to be less internally oriented (Cicirelli, 1980; Lachman, 1983). Finally, a comparable number of studies find no age differences in internal control (Blanchard-Fields & Irion, 1988; Nehrke, Hulicka, & Morganti, 1980; Reker, Peacock, & Wong, 1987). The discrepancy in findings has been attributed to methodological inconsistencies (Lachman, 1986), the particular dimension of control assessed (Abeles, 1987; Blanchard-Fields & Irion, 1988; Rodin, 1987), and the content domain in which controllability is assessed (Blanchard-Fields & Robinson, 1987; Lachman, 1986).

Given the inconsistent developmental findings, an important issue is to consider the treatment of the concept of controllability. Treating a sense of control as a "style" that is applied across all behavioral domains may provide a limited view of controllability changes across the life span. Such studies have relied on well-established psychometric instruments used in the social psychology literature on control (see, e.g., Levenson, 1974; Rotter, 1966). Current work on controllability and aging has moved beyond simply examining a global, overall sense of control to examining (1) beliefs in how much control we retain within specific domains of behavior, including intelligence, health, and social situations (see, e.g., Cornelius & Caspi, 1986; Lachman, 1986); (2) different types (dimensions) of internal and external control; (3) control beliefs as a function of specific situations (Blanchard-Fields & Irion, 1988); and (4) one's sense of control as it relates to cognitive development in adulthood (Blanchard-Fields, 1989; Labouvie-Vief et al., 1987).

Domain Specificity

In a recent study, Lachman (1991) examined age differences in control beliefs. She compared both general and domain-specific control beliefs in men and women ranging in age from 20 to 89 years. The domain-specific scales focused on control of intellectual, health, interpersonal, and political circumstances. In addition, the domain-specific measures of control for intellectual and health realms, as well as generalized control, included a three-dimensional conceptualization of control. One dimension is *internality*, e.g., things happen due to one's effort. The other two dimensions are external: (1) things are beyond personal control and due to *chance* and (2) things are beyond personal control and due to *powerful others*.

For the general control scales there were no age differences on internality and powerful others, but older adults were more externally oriented than younger adults with respect to the chance dimension. In comparison with younger adults in the intellectual domain, older adults held higher chance and powerful others beliefs and lower internal control beliefs. This finding is supported in other studies as well (Cornelius & Caspi, 1986; Grover & Hertzog, 1991; Lachman & Leff, 1989) Similarly, older adults believed they were less in control of their health as measured by the three dimensions. However, no age differences were found for control beliefs in the interpersonal and political domains. Overall, changes in control beliefs appear to be specialized, occurring in some domains and not in others. This is further exemplified in a study suggesting that older adults find uncontrollable issues more salient and endorse more beliefs in external control than do younger adults (Nurmi, Pullianen, & Salmela-Aro, 1992). In this case, it appeared to be a function of the domain of issues most often selected by older adults: problems encountered with their adult children.

Further Dimensionalization of Control

Although the domain-specific research on controllability employed measures which further dimensionalized external control into chance and powerful others factors, other researchers argue that there is a need to further dimensionalize internality (Blanchard-Fields & Robinson, 1987; Heckhausen & Schulz, 1993). For example, Blanchard-Fields and Robinson (1987) found that in stressful relationship situations, younger individuals were more internal in their orientation than older adults with respect to the *cause* of the stressful situation. There were no age differences in internal control over the *outcome* of the stressor. Blanchard-Fields and Irion (1988) corroborate this finding in their examination of the relationship between perceived controllability and coping. They suggest that youths may equate internal control with self-blame in response to a stressor. Consequently, they deal with this blame by avoidance of the situation or by reacting hostilely toward the situation. On the other hand, an older adult's conception of internal control involves perceiving the source of stress as located within the self, resulting in conscious, reflective appraisal. Again, the construct of internality appears to be multidimensional and related to adult developmental conceptions of maturity. Consistent with this finding, Aldwin (1991) found that older adults perceived themselves to be less responsible for the *occurrence* of a stressful event; however, no age differences were evident in perceived responsibility for the *management* of the stressful event.

Heckhausen and Schulz (1993) advance a life-span theory of control based on Rothbaum, Weisz, and Snyder's (1982) dimensionalization of primary and secondary control. Primary control is associated with direct, instrumental action on the environment that influences outcomes. Secondary control is defined as the acceptance of existing realities which cannot be changed, while at the same time control is exerted over the psychological consequences of the event. Heckhausen and Schulz (1993) argue for the primacy of primary control over secondary control. The function of secondary control is to minimize losses in, maintain, and expand the existing levels of primary control. In other words, secondary control allows the individual to cope with the need to be more selective and deal with failures in primary control over one's environment and self. They suggest that optimal aging involves striking a balance between primary and secondary control to optimize the long-term potential of primary control. They apply this adaptive process in older adulthood in terms of past research on internal and external control. Although personal control is perceived to decline with age (Heckhausen & Baltes, 1991), older adults demonstrate no negative affect or distress, which should accompany such losses. Heckhausen and Schulz (1993) suggest that the use of secondary control in older adults may account for this. For example, an individual may lower her or his goal aspirations through the use of secondary compensation. In this case, secondary control allows the individual to accept age-related losses in ability and translate them into newer, more realistic goals. Another example involves the use of secondary control in making downward social comparisons (Heckhausen & Schulz, 1993). In this case, one's own well-being is seen as better than most others (e.g., frailer peers or negative stereotypes of the elderly). Similarly, Branstadter, Wentura, and Greve (1993) suggest that older adults have the flexibility and adaptive ability to accommodate to loss of control with advancing age. In order to manage age-related change in functioning, older adults either act instrumentally to prevent or alleviate loss or shift self-goal aspirations to be more consistent with their actual loss in functioning.

Situation Specificity of Control Beliefs

The research reviewed above examines control beliefs in different domains yet does not consider the immediate and specific context in which an individual is operating. For example, control beliefs assessed by Lachman's (1986) measures of control within specific domains of intellectual/cognitive functioning and health (Wallston & Wallston, 1981) do not address the issue of how individuals' control beliefs are applied in different situations within or across domains. Situation-specific control beliefs reflect an individual's perception of controllability (i.e., as to the cause or one's ability to manage the outcome) of a specific event she or he is currently reporting or experiencing. Studies have reported differential findings for situation-specific and global measures of control beliefs. For example, Blanchard-Fields and Robinson (1987) found no significant relation between generalized and situation-specific measures of internality, indicating that they measured relatively independent control dimensions. Blanchard-Fields and Irion (1988) reported age differences on a global measure of control yet no significant age differences on ratings of control for recently experienced stressful encounters.

It is apparent that the nature of the situation (i.e., the immediate context) influences the appraisal of perceived control. This is further supported by a number of studies that have examined the extent to which an impoverished or complex immediate social environment influences one's sense of control. For example, Langer and Rodin (1976; Rodin & Langer,

1977) found that enhancing older adults' control over their environment in a nursing home setting (e.g., caring for a plant, selecting meals from a menu) improved morale, created a personal sense of control, and reduced debilitation. Similarly, M. Baltes' (1988; Baltes & Reisenzein, 1986) research on dependent behaviors in long-term care institutions demonstrated that nursing home staff rewarded dependent care behaviors by engaging in social interaction, such as conversation or complying with requests of older residents. Independent self-care behaviors were not reinforced in that the staff ignored the behaviors by not responding or continuing with other behaviors. Over time, dependent care behaviors increased.

Developmental Complexity and Control

Finally, some researchers suggest that controllability represents a process that varies with developmental changes in cognitive complexity. In this case, youthful thinkers are depicted as quite vulnerable to the influence of external sources which define reality for them (i.e., they are expected to be more externally regulated) (Labouvie-Vief, 1992; Labouvie-Vief et al., 1987; Perry, 1970). For example, youths attribute the cause of a stressful situation to external sources or allocate blame for a stressful outcome to others or circumstances in the environment (e.g., external locus of control). They do not take personal responsibility for the role they played in a stressful conflict. On the other hand, with maturity comes the ability to consciously reflect and appraise each stressful situation and make a decision or evaluation on the basis of autonomous standards and values (Labouvie-Vief et al., 1987). Mature adults take personal responsibility for their role in a stressful encounter, reflecting an internal control orientation. This orientation is similar to that taken in the literature on attributional processing from an adult developmental perspective described below.

Summary

A clearer understanding of the role controllability plays in the social cognitive functioning of older adults can be gained by addressing issues of domain and situation specificity as well as developmental implications in the following ways. First, the extent to which an adult holds internal and external control beliefs is multidimensional in nature and must be examined in the context of specific and varying situations. Second, individual and developmental factors such as motivation to optimize primary control and increased cognitive complexity may index the different control-enhancing strategies older adults use to attain optimal adaptation. Third, adaptive mechanisms of secondary control (e.g., accepting the uncontrollability of a situation) may optimize older adults' primary (direct) control over their environment. Fourth, in some circumstances, enhancing control has a demonstrated positive effect on the cognitive and social functioning of the frail elderly. In sum, examination of personal styles of control over life circumstances in general, in specific domains, and in specific situations will give us a more complete picture of changes in the sense of control across the latter half of the life span.

■ Impression Formation, Problem Appraisal, and Attributional Processing

In addition to representations of self, social cognitive research has focused a considerable amount of attention on representations and interpretations of others and social situations.

Such research has focused on the content of scripted knowledge structures regarding everyday activities (e.g., going to a restaurant, going to the doctor's office), schema- or knowledge-driven interpretations of social situations, person perception, impression formation, problem appraisal, and causal attributions individuals make about an event outcome, to name a few. Variations in knowledge structures about events or problems have implications for the pattern of strategies an individual selects for problem solving, coping, or making social judgments. This review includes research domains investigating age-related differences in the interpretation of events and others and their effect on subsequent behavior.

Impression Formation and Processing Mechanisms

In a recent review, Hess (1994) delineates a number of aging-related changes in processing mechanisms relevant to social cognitive functioning. Decreases in capacity limitations (e.g., working memory, processing resources, etc.) with advancing age are addressed extensively in the cognitive aging literature (see Chapters 6 and 7). Given that these processing changes are thoroughly examined in earlier chapters, including a contextual interpretation of these findings (see Chapter 12), only a brief overview of the implications of these changes for social cognitive functioning in adulthood will be discussed. (For a more extensive review, see Hess, 1994.)

Variations in the structure of common scripts (e.g., going to a restaurant) and knowledge activation seem to be invariant across age groups (Hess, 1994). However, decline in working memory and inhibition processes has been shown to have an impact on social cognitive performance. For example, both young and older adults read script-relevant actions faster than script-irrelevant actions, yet older adults' social knowledge activation can be disrupted if cues are not specific to the activation of knowledge relevant to the specific task (Hess, Donley, & Vandermaas, 1989). Hess and Tate (1991) found that, in comparison to young adults, older adults did not exhibit the usual consistency effect in recall of behaviors attributed to a target person. Young adults were more likely to try to explain inconsistent information with the previously attributed trait and thus were better able to integrate the new information into a more coherent memory representation. A processing interpretation as to why older adults produce more category-based impressions and less attribute-based processing than younger adults is that they have more difficulty excluding nonrelevant information during social information processing (lack of inhibition) and do not get far into the impression formation process due to a slowing in processing speed (Hess, 1994).

Another interpretation of these findings suggested by Hess and Pullen (1994) is that these age-related differences in the consistency effect on memory may be a function of information salience. They used an impression formation task in which individuals were to form negative or positive impressions of a target person and were then given additional negative or positive information. They found that age differences in impression formation were related to differential weightings given to behavioral information. In contrast to younger adults, new negative information presented about a positively portrayed target person had more of an impact on changing older adults' impressions about that person. This was not true for new positive behavioral information. They conclude that rather than attributing this difference to a processing deficit, older adults simply held stronger beliefs in the invariance of negative characteristics, which in turn, determined their judgments about people. From this perspective, age differences in making social judgments may be a function of both processing and knowledge-based (e.g., information salience) mechanisms. In contrast to social cognition research, which focuses on memory and impression formation, studies concerning problem appraisal and attributional processing concentrate on knowledge-based influences on more complex social cognitive functioning.

Problem Appraisal

A number of researchers suggest that age differences in strategy use for coping with stress or everyday problem solving can be explained by age differences in the underlying interpretations of the problem or coping situation (see, e.g., Berg, Klaczynski, Calderone, & Strough, 1994; Blanchard-Fields & Norris, 1994; Lazarus & Folkman, 1984). In fact, Lazarus and Folkman (1984) argue that effective coping depends on a realistic appraisal of the situation that matches or approximates the unfolding of events. Furthermore, Berg et al. (1994) suggest that we need to examine differences in problem appraisal between younger and older adults in order to better understand strategy use and the potential adaptive nature of such age differences.

In a recent study, younger and older adults were presented with two scripted situations familiar to both age groups: a visit to the doctor's office and problems arising at a dinner party (Berg et al., 1994). Participants were asked to describe what the "real" problem was in the situation. Interpretations were coded as (1) external social (i.e., problem caused by behavior of others), (2) internal affective (i.e., problem caused by an emotional state), (3) internal cognitive (i.e., problem caused by a mental operation such as decision making), and (4) internal social (i.e., problem caused by behavior of self and reactions of others). Age differences were found in both types of situations. Older adults tended to interpret the doctor's office problems as external social, that is, having to do with the social circumstances rather than themselves. For the dinner party problems, older adults interpreted the problem more as internal cognitive (e.g., having to do with their decision making in the context of others), whereas younger adults interpreted the problems as internal affective (e.g., having to do with their personal emotions). Berg et al. suggest that their younger and older adults had different interpretations of various problems as a function of the degree of relevance to their everyday functioning. It appears that adults employ different problem-solving strategies as a function of their distinct life and developmental contexts.

Other researchers have also revealed age differences in problem interpretation. Sinnott (1989) found that older adults interpret everyday problems differently than younger adults in that they focus on the interpersonal concerns of the problem. Arlin (1984) proposed that mature thinking involves the redefinition of the problem space by accepting and resolving inherent uncertainties. Similarly, other researchers suggest that this interpretive process in adulthood is characterized by an increased awareness of self as interpreter (Labouvie-Vief, 1984) or the ability to consider multiple perspectives in reasoning tasks of an interpersonal nature (Berg et al., 1994; Blanchard-Fields, 1986a; Kramer, Kahlbaugh, & Goldston, 1992). A number of developmental changes in how individuals structure reality and approach a problem situation (e.g., awareness of self as interpreter, cognitive representations of events, cognitive appraisal) have been identified. However, more research is needed to link these changes in problem appraisal to the subsequent selection of problem-solving strategies.

Attributional Processing

Another approach to examining the ways in which individuals attend to multiple factors in constructing a problem space is assessing their causal attributions. The area of causal attributions also provides an assessment of how an individual structures socially ambiguous everyday problem situations. This area of research has garnered recent attention in the adult developmental literature. For example, Blank (1987) asserts that attributions are developmental in nature in that they are defined by life experiences, social context, and the changing perspectives and needs of varying cohorts. Such a developmental approach to attributions has been addressed by a number of studies conducted by Blanchard-Fields and her colleagues (Blanchard-Fields, 1994; Blanchard-Fields & Norris, 1994).

Blanchard-Fields (1986b) discusses the fact that research in social psychology is replete with studies demonstrating college-aged students' tendencies to produce informational distortions when making causal attributions about problem situations. In particular, social psychologists have examined dispositional and situational loci of explanations. For example, in assessing causal relations, individuals tend to (1) make the general assumption that the outcome of an event is caused by internal personal dispositions of the actor as opposed to powerful situational determinants (the fundamental attribution error) (Jones & Harris, 1967; Kelley & Michela, 1980; Nisbett & Ross, 1980) or (2) blame the "observed" person in a hypothetical situation for the outcome if it was negative and/or high in intensity (Nogami & Streufert, 1983; Shultz & Wright, 1985; Shaw & Skolnick, 1971). Attributional biases are particularly evident when the information given about the action situation is ambiguous as to the relative contribution of the primary character and environment in producing the final outcome (Fishbein & Ajzen, 1973; Georgoudi, 1985; Shaw & Skolnick, 1971).

A limitation apparent in the social psychology literature is that these informational biases and distortions have been documented primarily with college-aged samples. Blanchard-Fields (1986b) suggests that such distortions and biases might well decrease if older adults were sampled. From a postformal developmental perspective, these attributional biases or distortions of information (i.e., attributing cause to either dispositional or situational factors) may reflect a youthful thinker's tendency to accept a dualistic, right-versus-wrong structure of reality and knowledge (see Chapter 11; also Blanchard-Fields, 1986a; Labouvie-Vief, 1992; Perry, 1970). More mature thinking, defined as a relativistic orientation—the ability to perceive and coordinate multiple perspectives—would result in more interactive attributions (i.e., viewing the cause of an event as a combination of external and internal causes). If there are developmental gains, you would expect older adults to adopt a more relativistic orientation than younger adults. This was partially supported by Blanchard-Fields' research. Forty vignettes depicting relationship and achievement event sequences with either positive or negative outcomes were presented to younger, midlife, and older adults. They were asked to rate the degree to which the final outcome of each vignette was caused by something about the main character (dispositional attribution), something external to the main character (situational attribution), and a combination of dispositional and situational factors (interactive attribution). When the vignettes were ambiguous with respect to the causal factors of an event outcome and reflected negative relationship situations, older adults made more interactive attributions than younger adults did (Blanchard-Fields, 1994). However, it was noted that older adults also made more dispositional attributions than younger age groups, particularly in negative relationship situations.

Postformal researchers also suggest that a more advanced level of reasoning in adulthood involves dialectical thinking (see Chapter 11; also Armon, 1984; Kramer et al., 1992). In the case of attributional processes, a dialectical thinker would view dispositional and situational causal factors in relation to each other, mutually determined and codefined. Georgoudi (1985) demonstrated that individuals who ranked high in dialectical reasoning did not dichotomize personal dispositions and environmental contingencies in assigning causal attributions. Instead, they viewed them as interactions within a situational context. Blanchard-Fields and Norris (1994) also examined dialectical attributional processing in adolescence through older adulthood. They used 10 of the 40 vignettes used by Blanchard-Fields (1994). The participants not only made the same three attributional ratings discussed above (dispositional, situational, and interactive) but were also asked to give explanations for their attribution ratings in a written essay. Blanchard-Fields and Norris found that middle-aged adults scored higher on dialectical attributional reasoning than did adolescents, youth, younger, and older adults. Dialectical attributional reasoning was characterized by generating multiple causes for the situation and indicating how these factors were codefined and mutually determined (the interrelationships among causal factors). However, older adults (in particular, older women) and adolescents scored lowest on dialectical reasoning.

Why were older adults more predisposed to making dispositional attributions and engaged in less dialectical reasoning in negative relationship situations? Perhaps this pattern of responding on the part of older adults is driven by schemas evoked by the particular vignettes' content. A number of researchers suggest that schemas representing past situational experiences and general knowledge structures influence the causal analysis of and inferences made about a new situation, event, or narrative (Bargh, 1989; Fiske & Pavelchak, 1986; Graesser & Clark, 1985). For example, understanding the social knowledge driving causal reasoning allows us to determine which type of dispositional or situational attribution is appropriate to a particular situation (Abelson & Lalljee, 1988; Clark, 1985). Over time, life experiences and social knowledge are accumulated and provide well-instantiated heuristics whereby problem interpretations are invoked. Perhaps these social schemas or knowledge structures were operating in the above studies. Social schemas may have been evoked as a function of the value-laden content of several of the vignettes. These social schemas may have been particularly salient and emotional for older adults, given their years of accumulated experience, life stage, and the particular generation in which they were socialized.

Emotion and Cognitive Appraisal

As suggested by the above research, emotional responses may play an important role in how the individual construes a problem space. There is another body of research exploring the interface between cognitive appraisal and emotion in relation to effective functioning in older adults. This area of research examines cognition as an antecedent (in the form of cognitive appraisals, attributions, and belief systems) in relationship to both emotion and such outcomes as everyday problem solving, coping, helping behavior, and decision making, among others.

Let us first consider the research examining the relationship between cognitive appraisal and emotion. Spearheaded by the seminal work of Weiner (see, e.g., Weiner, 1986) on attributions about achievement situations, current research suggests that emotions are associated with distinctive patterns of cognitive appraisal (Folkman & Lazarus, 1988; Manstead & Tetlock, 1989; Smith & Ellsworth, 1985). Smith and Ellsworth (1985) found that there were characteristic patterns of appraisal along six dimensions (pleasantness, anticipated effort, certainty, attentional activity, self–other responsibility/control, and situational control) associated with different emotions (e.g., shame, pity, guilt, fear, frustration). For example, fear was found to be associated with maximal uncertainty about the situation, strong attributions of situational control, and appraisals of self–other responsibility/control. Other researchers have extended these findings by including other dimensions of appraisal such as unexpectedness, benefit, and inconsistency with behavioral standards (Manstead & Tetlock, 1989).

The majority of work has focused on the relationships between these variables in college-aged students. There is limited work examining whether or not changes in the relations between cognitive appraisal and emotion occur in adulthood and aging. Weiner and his colleagues (Weiner, 1986; Weiner & Graham, 1989) elaborate on the cognition–emotion–action linkage and suggest that emotions play a mediating role in the relationship between causal attributions and specific types of action.

In a fairly recent study, Weiner & Graham (1989) presented participants ranging in age from 5 to 95 years with one of two stories designed to elicit feelings of pity or anger. They measured respondents' ratings of the degree of controllability of the cause of the outcome, the degree (i.e., intensity) of pity and anger felt toward the main character, and the likelihood of helping this person. Overall, they found that elicited affect (the degree of pity or anger) mediated the relationship between ratings of causal control and the intended helping behavior (i.e., when affect was parceled out of the control–behavior correlation, the correlation was reduced to 0). In other words, emotions rather than thoughts were the more direct determinants of action. They did not find that the magnitude of this mediating relationship differed among age groups. However, they did find that the elderly reported less anger (and more pity) than younger participants, yet were more willing to help a person in need regardless of the cause of the need. Weiner and Graham (1989) concluded that the linkages among emotion, thinking, and behavior remain stable in healthy older adults and are accompanied by an increase in social concern and tolerance.

This study further supports the notion that we need to investigate specific emotions in specific contexts and their relationship to cognitive and behavioral functioning from an adult developmental perspective. Whereas global measures of affect intensity (e.g., the Affective Intensity Measure; Larsen & Diener, 1987) may show a decline in relationship to age, more situation-specific measures may present a more individualistic picture. This situation-specific conceptualization of affective expression is further exemplified in the work on cognitive appraisal, emotion, and coping.

Lazarus and his colleagues have generated a considerable amount of research examining the cognition–emotion–action relationship with respect to coping with stress, a highly emotionally salient event (see, e.g., Folkman & Lazarus, 1988; Lazarus & Smith, 1988). Folkman and Lazarus (1988) do not simply conceptualize coping as a response to emotions; they contend that cognitive appraisal of a stressful situation generates emotions which influence coping and in turn change the stressful person–environment relationship. The person–environment relationship is then cognitively reappraised, resulting in a changed emotion. They found that four different styles of coping (planful problem solving, positive reappraisal, confrontive coping, and distancing) were associated with changes in four types of emotions (disgust/anger, pleasure/happiness, confidence, and worry/fear). Their research exemplifies the complex interplay among cognition, emotion, and action in that there is no one unidirectional relationship among them. In their model, emotion and cognition (i.e., cognitive appraisal), as well as action, can simultaneously serve as both cause and effect.

In addition, Folkman and Lazarus found age differences in the relationship between emotion and coping. Whereas younger adults' use of positive reappraisal was related to a decrease in feelings of disgust and anger and an increase in pleasure and confidence, older adults' use of positive reappraisal was associated with an increase in worry and fear. Younger adults' use of confrontive coping was associated with an increase in disgust and anger, whereas older adults' use of confrontive coping was not related to any positive or negative emotion. Folkman and Lazarus concluded that these results could be explained in terms of young and old having different methods of coping or in terms of developmental changes in coping efficacy. With respect to the latter alternative explanation, they argued that older adults might be more temperate with respect to negative emotional affect and/or might have developed their interpersonal skills in such a way that social support is more effective for them. There is some support for the notion that cognitive developmental differences are more apparent in areas that are high in emotional saliency, such as coping with stress and interpersonal reasoning (Blanchard-Fields, 1986a; Labouvie-Vief, 1990).

Blanchard-Fields and Norris (1994) also examined how relativistic causal attributions are influenced by the emotional saliency of situations. For example, do individuals confronted with an emotionally laden context display more or less interactive (relativistic) causal attributions (i.e., considering a combination of dispositional and situational information in making the causal judgment), and is this related to age differences? In order to examine the issue of emotional saliency more directly, they had respondents ranging in age from adolescents to older adulthood rate each vignette in terms of how emotionally salient the situation was for them (in addition to the rating scales described earlier). Vignettes were separated into three levels of emotional saliency (aggregated across age groups): high, medium, and low. They then examined age group differences on the relativistic rating measures as a function of level of emotional saliency. Although adolescents were lower on relativistic ratings overall, these differences were primarily a function of the level of emotional saliency; that is, adolescents scored lower on interactive attributions only for medium and high levels of emotional salience.

Summary

A number of social cognitive issues are addressed in the domain of causal attributions and problem appraisal. Not only are age-related differences in representations of self, others, and events (e.g., social schemas) important influences on social reasoning, but the domain of emotion plays a particularly salient role in social cognitive reasoning. The literature suggests that emotional salience plays an important role when examining ill-structured problems such as those found in social reasoning situations, for example, cognitive and affective appraisal of a problem space. Future research on developmental changes in emotional intensity as well as emotional understanding is needed given that these changes result in differences in problem-solving interpretation and strategy preferences. The existing evidence for adulthood changes in affect intensity, the use of affective appraisal, the social knowledge base, and emotional regulation stress the importance for future research to examine everyday problem solving within an emotional context.

■ Attitudes toward Aging

The idea that sociocultural factors play a salient role in social cognitive reasoning, such as forming social schemas about others, is most evident in research on the negative stereotypes possessed about older adults. A number of studies have compared younger and older adults' perceptions of target adults ranging in age from younger to middle-aged to older adulthood. Overall, younger adults tend to evaluate older adults and the aging process more negatively than older adults do (Heckhausen, Dixon, & Baltes, 1989; Hummert, 1990; Kite, Deaux, & Miele, 1991). However, research indicates that a number of factors determine whether or not negative evaluations of older adults are observed. Luszcz and Fitzgerald (1986) demonstrated that younger adults have more positive views of the elderly when they have greater knowledge about aging and more social contact with older adults. A number of researchers find that older adults are not negatively evaluated on all dimensions. Most people hold more differentiated views concerning changes with age than they do generalized stereotypic beliefs. For example, older adults may be thought of as grouchy, critical, and hard of hearing while at the same time viewed as likable, intelligent, and experienced (Kite et al., 1991); older adults may be viewed as less competent in skills involving psychomotor speed and memory but equally as competent as younger adults in general knowledge and logical thought (Hendrick, Knox, Gekoski, & Dyne, 1991); or older adults' memory recall is expected to decline with increasing age, whereas inferential reasoning is expected to remain stable or increase with age (Camp & Pignatiello, 1988).

Heckhausen et al. (1989) found that younger, middle-aged, and older adults' belief systems about adult development were multidirectional in nature. In other words, desirable and undesirable changes are represented across all segments of the latter half of the life span. However, older adults were more differentiated in their expectations of such changes in that they viewed a greater number of attributes associated with adult development and aging as well as more potential for change throughout adulthood. Heckhausen and Baltes (1991) expanded upon this research in a study examining the perceived controllability of developmental changes in adulthood. Although younger, middle-aged, and older adults agreed that changes in later life are less desirable, younger adults perceived less desirable changes as being more controllable than did middle-aged and older adults.

All of the above studies rely primarily on ratings of personality attributes. In a recent series of studies, Erber and her colleagues (Erber, 1989; Erber, Etheart, & Szuchman, 1992; Erber, Szuchman, & Etheart, 1993) employed a person perception procedure to assess evaluations of older adults in a specific domain, memory competence. In contrast to a trait-based rating questionnaire, Erber presented participants with various scenarios in which a target person experiences an everyday memory failure. She primarily assessed the competence appraisals of young and old targets made by younger and older adults, using written vignettes depicting older and younger targets experiencing low to moderate to high memory failure. A general finding across all studies suggested that there was an age-based double standard. Young adults rated everyday memory failure as more serious if experienced by an older target than by a younger target, whereas older adults rated young and old targets more equally.

The general negative bias toward the elderly was characterized by attributions of greater mental difficulty, a need for memory training, and a need for evaluation for older targets. Younger targets' memory failures were attributed to a lack of effort or attention. However, when participants were asked to rate the targets' capabilities (e.g., by assigning them to easy or difficult tasks) after listening to a taped interview characterized by varying degrees of memory failures, different results emerged (Erber et al., 1992). Forgetful older targets were no more likely to be affected by less task assignment than forgetful younger targets were. In other words, both younger and older adults assigned tasks equally to younger and older targets irrespective of the target's level of forgetfulness. With the more individualized information provided by the taped interviews, age played less of a focal role.

Erber extended these findings by employing a more contextualist perspective, that is, by placing the memory appraisals in a social context of "neighborly interactions" (Erber et al., 1993). Young adults were asked to rate how likely they would be to choose a certain type of neighbor (described in a vignette) to perform a memory task and to rate the young and old target neighbors on desirable and relevant traits specific to performing memory tasks. Young adult raters chose unforgetful over forgetful "neighbors" and older over younger "neighbors" regardless of their forgetfulness. In addition, older "neighbors" were rated more highly on positive traits (e.g., dependability) than younger "neighbors" were. These results speak not only to the importance of providing individuating information but to the importance of the social aspects (not simply cognitive competence) involved in person perception within a specific context (e.g., neighborly interactions).

Summary

Research on attitudes toward the elderly represents a strong movement away from simple personality trait-based ratings of an individual to an understanding of how we evaluate the elderly in specific everyday contexts. From this research it becomes clear that a multidimensional and contextual model of perceived controllability and evaluations is critical. When the "evaluation" is placed in an everyday context and includes multiple rating dimensions (e.g., competence and social desirability), a more complete understanding of the nature of the evaluation is revealed. Although competency may be rated low, other factors (e.g., ratings of responsibility) may override these concerns or simply interact with these concerns in an individual's evaluation of and decision to work with, associate with, or depend upon older adults.

SUMMARY

How has a social cognitive approach added to our understanding of cognitive changes in adulthood and aging? This domain of research has expanded our understanding of two of the major theoretical and methodological approaches to the study of cognitive aging described in Chapter 2: the experimental approach and the contextual approach. The traditional social cognition approach, which focuses on the cognitive processes involved in social understanding, addresses theoretical assumptions posited by the experimental approach to cognitive aging. Processing difficulties found in older adults on more traditional cognitive tasks can also impact their social cognitive performance. For example, the above review described the influence of working memory limitations or lack of inhibition on the process of memory for personality characteristics of a target person and impression formation (Hess, 1994). However, Hess (1994) also suggests that we can improve our understanding of age differences in cognitive performance by giving equal attention to processing and knowledge-based (e.g., social schema) mechanisms. Thus, the findings demonstrating an "integration deficit" (i.e., not integrating inconsistent information into one's memory representation leads to poor recall of that information) can also be interpreted in terms of a knowledge-based mechanism (Hess & Pullen, 1994). In this case, older adults found negative information (as opposed to inconsistent positive information) more salient and relevant and thus processed it more extensively. This alternative explanation is elaborated in the contextual approach embodied in social cognitive research and aging.

Given that age-related changes in memory were discussed in several other chapters, the majority of research reviewed in this chapter focused on a contextual approach by examining higher-level cognitive processes (e.g., attributions, social judgments) in a social context. This perspective on social cognition and aging has centered our attention on real-world social issues and the consequences of cognition (e.g., the relationship between emotion and cognition, sociocultural influences, attitudes, social behavior). Let us go back and reexamine the four major issues in social cognitive research—changes in the content of social knowledge, the functional importance of the social cognitive perspective, the influence of multiple levels of social context on performance, and the interface between cognition and emotion—in light of the empirical review.

As noted earlier, the literature suggests that there are age-related changes in both the understanding of self and other, and the content of knowledge structures about self, others, and social situations. Through the identification of qualitatively different developmental levels of understanding from adolescence through older adulthood, there appear to be gains in the understanding of the emotional self. In addition, there are developmental variations in (1) the focus of one's goals and concerns in relation to self (i.e., shifts from more family-oriented goals in young adulthood to more health-related goals in older adulthood) and (2) how one appraises a problem situation as a function of its relevance to such goals (i.e., a focus on more of the interpersonal issues involved in a problem with advancing age). The research in this area suggests that there are notable qualitative changes in the content and structure of people's social knowledge structures.

Research on social knowledge representations has been primarily descriptive in nature. Not only is it important to understand what kinds of social concepts people hold, we must also demonstrate how such knowledge structures serve as mechanisms for influencing performance, in other words, the functional significance of social representations on behavior. The literature examining age-related variations in social knowledge–based mechanisms and their impact on performance is also limited. However, the studies reviewed above do suggest that social schemas influence memory, attributional judgments, selection of problem-solving strategies, judgments of cognitive competence, and perceptions of control. Older adults appear to rely more heavily on well-instantiated knowledge structures and schemas in memory performance (Hess, 1990) and in making social judgments or attributions (Blanchard-Fields & Norris, 1994). Is this reliance on schemas a compensatory mechanism due to an inability to process more information extensively or to an adaptive mechanism for effective cognitive functioning in a social context? We cannot adequately answer this question without conducting further research on (1) the universality of such changes across individuals and within individuals across contexts, (2) in which contexts age-related deficits are likely to occur and in which contexts they are not, and (3) the ways in which social knowledge structures may change qualitatively and adaptively across the life span. Clearly, more research is needed to directly address these concerns.

From this contextual perspective, we know that performance and behavior are multiply determined. Important contextual variables include both those external to an individual, such as the task context (e.g., laboratory versus everyday context) and the sociocultural-historical context, and those internal to an individual (those provided by the social knowledge structures, goals, and motivational characteristics an individual brings to the task situation). A number of studies discussed above indicated that the type of context (e.g., threat, challenge, nursing home situation) or domain of functioning (e.g., health, intellectual) influenced the appraised controllability of a situation. Age differences in perceived controllability varied as a function of the nature of the context. Other studies demonstrated the influence of the sociocultural context on schemas for marriage and relationships (i.e., cohort-related differences), age-related stereotypes on judgments of competency of older adults, and "life stage" on the perception of possible selves. These examples demonstrate how research in social cognition and aging provides a link between societal-level processes and individual-level, psychological processes.

Finally, the research reviewed above suggests that affect plays an important role in social cognition and aging research. It was shown that affect directs and is affected by interpretation and representation of the task situation. In turn, the nature of this process affects behavior such as problem-solving strategy selection. This underscores the need to examine both the emotional and cognitive repertoires of individuals in constructing interpretations of themselves, other individuals, social situations, or a problem space. The social cognition literature suggests that adaptive social cognitive functioning involves the ability to construct multiple alternatives of a situation as well as to use affective appraisal and emotional regulation as coping mechanisms, thus allowing flexibility in adapting old strategies and learning new ones (Cantor & Kihlstrom, 1989).

IMPLICATIONS FOR EVERYDAY FUNCTIONING

The study of social cognitive processes is an important avenue in assessing everyday cognition. Much of the activity involved in everyday cognition involves understanding the causes of outcomes and/or evaluating the controllability of managing outcomes. Whether it be life tasks, self-schemata, or autobiographical memory, there is a need to link social or everyday functioning to individual differences in emotional and motivational appraisal. An area of research that takes this functional perspective on self-schemas involves self-perception and actual health behavior (as opposed to perceptions of health). Leventhal and his colleagues (E. Leventhal, Leventhal, Schaefer, & Easterling, 1993; H. Leventhal, Diefenbach, & Leventhal, 1992), for example, demonstrate how self appraisals of growing older in the form of reduced resources in physical and psychological energy affect the way an individual appraises illness risks and the need for care. Older adults tended to seek rapid care and adhered better to medical treatment in order to reduce uncertainty and conserve energy reserves. Middle-aged adults tended to avoid seeking medical help and preferred to "wait out and watch" their symptoms. These studies suggest that numerous health behaviors are influenced by varying self-schemas. This line of research provides a good illustration of how current research is linking self-schemas to functional outcomes. However, there is still a great need to more fully explore not only a wider range of health behaviors but the influence of self-schemas on other domains of functional significance in older adults.

Adaptive changes in the developing adult are likely to be documented when examining cognitive functioning in a social context. These changes seem to be related to qualitative differences in the way in which an individual perceives and structures everyday situations. For example, Carstensen (1992) finds that older adults construct their environment to maximize social and emotional gains and minimize social and emotional risks. The primary goal for young adults is to seek social contact for information gain and future contacts, whereas older adults are more concerned with affective gain and intimacy (Frederickson & Carstensen, 1990). Carstensen suggests that a number of rewards for social interactions (e.g., responsivity, attention, arousal) decrease in their reinforcing value, making the quality rather than quantity of social interactions more important.

Social cognitive research and aging have potential significance for a more applied understanding of effective interpersonal relationships for adults at different stages of the life course. For example, identifying individual differences in social schemas and their impact on causal attributions may help to differentiate adaptive from dysfunctional cognitions in dealing with everyday problem situations, in general, and relationship situations, in particular. The literature demonstrates that dysfunctional attributional processes lead to marital problems (Bradbury & Fincham, 1992). Further research on schematicity factors may help us better understand the mechanisms related to these dysfunctional attributions and has further implications for marital and relationship counseling. Furthermore, the examination of age/cohort differences in social schemas and expectations and their relationship to social reasoning has implications for understanding the nature of dysfunctional attributions and counseling couples of different age/cohort groups. Perhaps we need a more systematic assessment of functional and dysfunctional attributions as they relate to instantiated social schemas. This should have predictive utility for other variables of adaptive significance and provide diagnostic tools for healthy functioning in adulthood and aging (i.e., maintenance of mental and physical health).

CONCLUSION

The goal of this chapter was to explore research that has moved beyond the study of basic information-processing skills to examine cognition within a social context. In this way, perspectives about age-related changes in cognitive abilities are broadened by considering the reciprocal relationship between cognition and changing environments, social knowledge systems, goals, and emotional responses. The research reviewed attests to a recent proliferation in studies addressing social cognitive variables and their functional significance for behavior in context. Such complex cognitive functioning not only involves basic cognitive mechanisms but is influenced by the content and organization of knowledge and the ability to regulate emotions.

Despite the growing research in this area, there are a number of limitations that still need to be addressed. First, there are few strong conceptual foundations explaining the interrelationship among social cognitive processes within an adult developmental/aging context. The recent discussions of the role of self, life tasks, and goals in cognitive change reviewed above (see, e.g., Cantor, 1990; Markus & Herzog, 1991) are examples of promising conceptual foundations, yet there is still a need for new research agendas with new empirical paradigms in order to move research on social cognition and aging forward.

Second, including an individual differences approach to the study of social cognitive processes promises to advance the field in several important ways. First, much of the tension between so-called mechanistic and developmental views of adult cognitive functioning can be resolved by accepting the premise that, in addition to the domain specificity of gains and losses (Baltes, 1987; see above), individuals differ in their level of developmental progression in social reasoning. This point is implicit in much of the theorizing in the postformal literature (Commons, Sinnott, Richards, & Armon, 1989; Staudinger, Smith, & Baltes, 1992; Chapter 11). The individual differences approach makes the point explicit by acknowledging that (1) age is only probabilistically associated with other aspects of social cognitive functioning and (2) this association can in fact be influenced and even moderated by a host of relevant variables (e.g., beliefs, attitudes, ego level). For example, an individual differences model could make it possible to evaluate the conditions under which adults of varying ages and of different personological and developmental characteristics are likely to engage in qualitatively different strategies of social cognitive functioning.

Third, social cognition cannot merely be studied as the representations of self and others that individuals overtly produce, or indirectly manifest, during psychological tasks in laboratory experiments. It also needs to be studied as a social process. Therefore, social cognition could be studied in the context of group processes, dyadic interactions, and so on, as in the communication transmission research example given earlier.

Finally, future research on developmental changes in emotional intensity as well as emotional understanding is needed, given that these changes result in differences in the interpretation of social situations and problems and strategy preferences. In other words, the existing evidence for adulthood changes in affect intensity, the use of affective appraisal, the social knowledge base, and emotional regulation stress the importance for future research to examine everyday cognition within an emotional context.

SUPPLEMENTAL READINGS

Fiske, S. T. (1993). Social cognition and social perception. *Annual Review of Psychology, 44,* 155–194.

Fiske, S. T., & Taylor, S. E. (1991). *Social cognition.* New York: McGraw-Hill.

Hess, T. M. (1994). Social cognition in adulthood: Aging-related changes in knowledge and processing mechanisms. *Developmental Review, 14,* 373–412.

Markus, H., & Herzog, A. R. (1991). The role of the self-concept in aging. In K. W. Schaie (Ed.), *Annual review of gerontology and geriatrics* (vol. 11, pp. 110–143). New York: Springer.

ACKNOWLEDGMENT

Some of the research reported in this chapter was supported by National Institute on Aging Research Grant No. AG-7607 awarded to Fredda Blanchard-Fields.

REFERENCES

Abeles, R. (1987). *Life-span perspectives and social psychology.* Hillsdale, NJ: Erlbaum.

Abelson, R. P., & Lalljee, M. (1988). Knowledge structures and causal explanation. In D. Hilton (Ed.), *Contemporary science and natural explanation* (pp. 175–203). New York: New York Univ. Press.

Adams, C. (1991). Qualitative age differences in memory for text: A life-span developmental perspective. *Psychology and Aging, 6,* 323–336.

Adams, C., Smith, M. C., Gaden, C. P., & Perlmutter, M. (1994). Memory in a storytelling context: A story recalled by young and old adults. Unpublished manuscript.

Aldwin, C. (1991). Does age affect the stress and coping process? Implications of age differences in perceived control. *Journal of Gerontology, 46,* 174–180.

Arlin, P. (1984). Adolescent and adult thought: A structural interpretation. In M. L. Commons, F. A. Richards, and C. Armon (Eds.), *Beyond formal operations* (pp. 258–271). New York: Praeger.

Armon, C. (1984). Ideals of the good life and moral judgment: Ethical reasoning across the lifespan. In M. L. Commons, F. A. Richards, & C. Armon (Eds.), *Beyond formal operations* (pp. 357–380). New York: Praeger.

Baltes, M. M. (1988). The etiology and maintenance of dependency in the elderly: Three phases of operant research. *Behavior Therapy, 19,* 301–319.

Baltes, M. M., & Reisenzein, R. (1986). The social world in long-term care institutions: Psychological control toward dependency. In M. M. Baltes & P. B. Baltes (Eds.), *The psychology of control and aging* (pp. 315–343). Hillsdale, NJ: Erlbaum.

Baltes, P. (1987). Theoretical propositions of life-span developmental psychology: On the dynamics between growth and decline. *Developmental Psychology, 23,* 611–626.

Baltes, P. B. & Smith, J. (1990). Toward a psychology of wisdom and its ontogenesis. In R. J. Sternberg (Ed.), *Wisdom: Its nature, origins, and development* (pp. 87–120). New York: Cambridge Univ. Press.

Bargh, J. A. (1989). Conditional automaticity: Varieties of automatic influence in social perception and cognition. In J. S. Uleman & J. A. Bargh (Eds.), *Unintended thought: Causes and consequences for judgment, emotion, and behavior* (pp. 3–51). New York: Guilford.

Berg, C., Klaczynski, P., Calderone, K., & Strough, J. (1994). Adult age differences in cognitive strategies: Adaptive or deficient? In J. Sinnott (Ed.), *Handbook of adult lifespan learning* (pp. 371–388). Westport, CT: Greenwood.

Blanchard-Fields, F. (1986a). Reasoning on social dilemmas varying in emotional saliency: An adult developmental perspective. *Psychology and Aging, 1,* 325–333.

Blanchard-Fields, F. (1986b). Attributional processes in adult development. *Educational Gerontology, 12,* 291–300.

Blanchard-Fields, F. (1989). Controllability and adaptive coping in the elderly: An adult developmental perspective. In P. S. Fry (Ed.), *Advances in Psychology: Psychology of helplessness and control in the aged* (pp. 43–62). New York: North-Holland.

Blanchard-Fields, F. (1994). Age differences in causal attributions from an adult developmental perspective. *Journal of Gerontology: Psychological Sciences, 49,* P43–P51.

Blanchard-Fields, F., & Camp, C. J. (1990). Affect, individual differences, and real world problem solving across the adult life span. In T. M. Hess (Ed.), *Aging and cognition: Knowledge organization and utilization* (pp. 461–497). Amsterdam: North-Holland.

Blanchard-Fields, F., & Irion, J. (1988). The relation between locus of control and coping in two contexts: Age as a moderator variable. *Psychology and Aging, 3,* 197–203.

Blanchard-Fields, F., & Norris, L. (1994). Causal attributions from adolescence through adulthood: Age differences, ego level, and generalized response style. *Aging and Cognition, 1,* 67–86.

Blanchard-Fields, F., & Robinson, S. (1987). Age differences in the relation between controllability and coping. *Journal of Gerontology, 42,* 497–501.

Blanchard-Fields, F., Suhrer-Roussel, L., & Hertzog, C. (1994). A confirmatory factor analysis of the Bem Sex Role Inventory: Old questions, new answers. *Sex Roles, 30,* 423–457.

Blank, T. O. (1987). Attributions as dynamic elements in a lifespan social psychology. In R. P. Abeles (Ed.), *Life-span perspectives and social psychology* (pp. 61–84). Hillsdale, NJ: Erlbaum.

Bradbury, T. N., & Fincham, F. D. (1992). Attributions and behavior in marital interaction. *Journal of Personality and Social Psychology, 63,* 613–628.

Brandstadter, J., Wentura, D., & Greve, W. (1993). Adaptive resources of the aging self: Outlines of an emergent perspective. *International Journal of Behavioral Development, 16,* 323–349.

Bronfenbrenner, U. (1979). *The ecology of human development.* Cambridge, MA: Harvard Univ. Press.

Camp, C. J., & Pignatiello, M. F. (1988). Beliefs about fact retrieval and inferential reasoning across the adult lifespan. *Experimental Aging Research, 14,* 89–97.

Campbell, A., Converse, P. E., & Rodgers, W. L. (1976). *The quality of American life: Perceptions, evaluations, and satisfactions.* New York: Sage.

Cantor, N. (1990). From thought to behavior: "Having" and "doing" in the study of personality and cognition. *American Psychologist, 45,* 735–750.

Cantor, N., & Fleeson, W. (1991). Life tasks and self-regulatory processes. *Advances in Motivation and Achievement, 7,* 327–369.

Cantor, N., & Kihlstrom, J. F. (1989). Social intelligence and cognitive assessments of personality. In R. Wyer & T. Srull (Eds.), *Advances in social cognition* (vol. 2, pp. 1–60). Hillsdale, NJ: Erlbaum.

Carstensen, L. L. (1992). Selectivity theory: Social activity in life-span context. *Annual Review of Gerontology and Geriatrics, 11,* 195–217.

Chinen, A. B. (1989). *In the ever after: Fairy tales and the second half of life.* Wilmette, IL: Chiron.

Cicirelli, V. G. (1980). Relationship of family background variables to locus of control in the elderly. *Journal of Gerontology, 35,* 108–114.

Clark, L. (1985). Social knowledge and inference processing in text comprehension. In G. Rickheit & H. Strohner (Eds.), *Inferences in text processing* (pp. 95–114). New York: North-Holland.

Cooley, C. H. (1902). *Human nature and the social order.* New York: Scribner's.

Commons, M., Sinnott, J., Richards, F., & Armon, C. (1989). *Adult development.* Vol. 1: Comparisons and applications of developmental models. New York: Praeger.

Cornelius, S. W. (1990). Aging and everyday cognitive abilities. In T. Hess (Ed.), *Aging and cognition: Knowledge organization and utilization.* (pp. 411–460). New York: North-Holland.

Cornelius, S. W., & Caspi, A. (1986). Self-perceptions of intellectual control and aging. *Educational Gerontology, 12,* 345–357.

Cornelius, S. W., & Caspi, A. (1987). Everyday problem solving in adulthood and old age. *Psychology and Aging, 2,* 144–153.

Cross, S., & Markus, H. (1991). Possible selves across the lifespan. *Human Development, 34,* 230–255.

Dittmann-Kohli, F. (1990). The construction of meaning in old age: Possibilities and constraints. *Ageing and Society, 10,* 279–291.

Dittmann-Kohli, F., & Baltes, P. B. (1992). Towards a neo-functionalist conception of adult intellectual development: Wisdom as a prototypical case of intellectual growth. In C. Alexander & E. Langer (Eds.), *Beyond formal operations: Alternative endpoints to human development* (pp. 54–78). New York: Oxford Univ. Press.

Erber, J. T. (1989). Young and older adults' appraisal of memory failures in young and older adult target persons. *Journal of Gerontology: Psychological Sciences, 44,* P170–P175.

Erber, J. T., Etheart, M. E., & Szuchman, L. T. (1992). Age and forgetfulness: Perceivers' impressions of targets' capability. *Psychology and Aging, 7,* 479–483.

Erber, J. T., Szuchman, L. T., & Etheart, M. E. (1993). Age and forgetfulness: Young perceivers' impressions of young and old neighbors. *International Journal of Aging and Human Development, 37,* 91–103.

Erikson, E. H. (1968). *Identity: Youth and crisis.* New York: Norton.

Feldman, S. S., Biringen, Z. C., & Nash, S. C. (1981). Fluctuations of sex-related self-attributions as a function of stage of family life cycle. *Developmental Psychology, 17,* 24–35.

Fishbein, M., & Ajzen, I. (1973). Attribution of responsibility: A theoretical note. *Journal of Experimental Social Psychology, 9,* 148–153.

Fiske, S. (1993). Social cognition and social perception. *Annual Review of Psychology, 44,* 155–194.

Fiske, S. T., & Neuberg, S. L. (1990). A continuum of impression formation, from category-based to individuating processes: Influences of information and motivation on attention and interpretation. In M. P. Zanna (Ed.), *Advances in experimental social psychology* (vol. 23, pp. 1–74). New York: Academic Press.

Fiske, S. T., & Pavelchak, M. A. (1986). Category-based versus piecemeal-based affective responses: Developments in schema-triggered affect. In R. M. Sorrentino & E. T. Higgins (Eds.), *Handbook of motivation and cognition: Foundations of social behavior* (pp. 167–203). New York: Guilford.

Fiske, S. T., & Taylor, S. E. (1991). *Social cognition.* New York: McGraw-Hill.

Folkman, S., & Lazarus, R. (1988). Coping as a mediator of emotion. *Journal of Personality and Social Psychology, 54,* 466–475.

Frederickson, B. L., & Carstensen, L. L. (1990). Choosing social partners: How old age and anticipated endings make people more selective. *Psychology and Aging, 5,* 163–171.

Gatz, M., & Karel, M. (1993). Individual change in perceived control over 20 years. *International Journal of Behavioral Development, 16,* 305–322.

Georgoudi, M. (1985). Dialectics in attribution research: A reevaluation of the dispositional-situational causal dichotomy. *Journal of Personality and Social Psychology, 49,* 1678–1691.

Gilbert, D. T. (1989). Thinking lightly about others: Automatic components of the social inference process. In J. S. Uleman and J. A. Bargh (Eds.), *Unintended thought* (pp. 189–211). New York: Guilford.

Gilbert, D. T., Pelham, B. W., & Krull, D. S. (1988). On cognitive busyness: When person perceivers meet person perceived. *Journal of Personality and Social Psychology, 54,* 733–739.

Graesser, A. & Clark, L. (1985). *Structures and procedures of implicit knowledge.* Norwood, NJ: Ablex.

Grover, D., & Hertzog, C. (1991). Relationships between intellectual control beliefs and psychometric intelligence in adulthood. *Journal of Gerontology: Psychological Sciences, 46,* P109–P115.

Heckhausen, J., & Baltes, P. (1991). Perceived controllability of expected psychological change across adulthood and old age. *Journal of Gerontology: Psychological Sciences, 46,* P165–P173.

Heckhausen, J., Dixon, R. A., & Baltes, P. B. (1989). Gains and losses in development throughout adulthood as perceived by different age groups. *Developmental Psychology, 25,* 109–121.

Heckhausen, J., & Schulz, R. (1993). Optimization by selection and compensation: Balancing primary and secondary control in life span development. *International Journal of Behavioral Development, 16,* 287–304.

Hendrick, J. J., Gekoski, W. L., & Knox, V. J. (1991). Accuracy of young adults' perceptions of cognitive ability across adulthood. *Canadian Journal on Aging, 10,* 165–176.

Hess, T. M. (1990). Aging and schematic influences on memory. In T. Hess (Ed.), *Aging and cognition: Knowledge organization and utilization* (pp. 93–160). Amsterdam: North-Holland.

Hess, T. M. (1994). Social cognition in adulthood: Aging-related changes in knowledge and processing mechanisms, *Developmental Review, 14,* 373–412.

Hess, T. M., Donley, J., & Vandermaas, M. O. (1989). Aging-related changes in the processing and retention of script information. *Experimental Aging Research, 15,* 89–96.

Hess, T. M., & Pullen, S. M. (1994). Adult age differences in impression change processes. *Psychology and Aging, 9,* 237–250.

Hess, T. M., & Tate, C. S. (1991). Adult age differences in explanations and memory for behavioral information. *Psychology and Aging, 6,* 86–92.

Hooker, K. (1992). Possible selves and perceived health in older adults and college students. *Journal of Gerontology: Psychological Sciences, 47,* P85–P95.

Hummert, M. L. (1990). Multiple stereotypes of elderly and young adults: A comparison of structure and evaluations. *Psychology and Aging, 5,* 182–193.

Hyde, J. S., Krajnik, M., & Skuldt-Niederberger, K. (1991). Androgyny across the life-span: A replication and longitudinal follow-up. *Developmental Psychology, 27,* 516–519.

Hyde, J. S., & Phillis, D. E. (1979). Androgyny across the lifespan. *Developmental Psychology, 15,* 334–336.

Jones, E. E., & Harris, V. A. (1967). The attribution of attitudes. *Journal of Experimental Social Psychology, 3,* 1–24.

Kelley, H. H., & Michela, J. L. (1980). Attribution theory and research. *Annual Review of Psychology, 31,* 457–501.

King, P. M., Kitchener, K. S., Wood, P. K., & Davison, M. L. (1989). Relationships across developmental domains: A longitudinal study of intellectual, moral, and ego development. In M. Commons, J. Sinnott, F. Richards, & C. Armon (Eds.), *Adult development: Comparisons and applications of developmental models* (pp. 57–72). New York: Praeger.

Kite, M. E., Deaux, K., & Miele, M. (1991). Stereotypes of young and old: Does age outweigh gender? *Psychology and Aging, 6,* 19–27.

Kramer, D. A. (1990). Conceptualizing wisdom: The primacy of affect-cognition relations. In R. Sternberg (Ed.), *Wisdom: Its nature, origins, and development* (pp. 279–316). Cambridge: Cambridge Univ. Press.

Kramer, D. A., Kahlbaugh, P. E., & Goldston, R. B. (1992). A measure of paradigm beliefs about the social world. *Journal of Gerontology, 47,* 180–189.

Labouvie-Vief, G. (1984). Logic and self-regulation from youth to maturity: Model. In M. Commons, F. Richards, and C. Armon (Eds.) *Beyond formal operations* (pp. 158–180). New York: Praeger.

Labouvie-Vief, G. (1990). Wisdom as integrated thought: Historical and developmental perspectives. In R.J. Steinberg (Ed.), *Wisdom: Its nature, origin, and development* (pp. 52–86). New York: Cambridge Univ. Press.

Labouvie-Vief, G. (1992). A neo-Piagetian perspective on adult cognitive development. In R. J. Sternberg and C. A. Berg (Eds.), *Intellectual development.* (pp. 197–228). New York: Cambridge Univ. Press.

Labouvie-Vief, G., DeVoe, M., & Bulka, D. (1989). Speaking about feelings: Conceptions of emotion across the life span. *Psychology and Aging, 4,* 425–437.

Labouvie-Vief, G., Hakim-Larson, J., DeVoe, M., & Schoeberlein, S. (1989). Emotions and self-regulation: A life span view. *Human Development, 32,* 279–299.

Labouvie-Vief, G., Hakim-Larson, J., & Hobart, C. J. (1987). Age, ego level, and the life-span development of coping and defense processes. *Psychology and Aging, 3,* 286–293.

Lachman, M. (1983). Perceptions of intellectual aging: Antecedent or consequence of intellectual functioning? *Developmental Psychology, 19,* 482–498.

Lachman, M. E. (1986). Locus of control in aging research: A case for multidimensional and domain-specific assessment. *Psychology and Aging, 1,* 34–40.

Lachman, M. E. (1991). Personal control over memory aging: Developmental and intervention perspectives. *Journal of Social Issues, 47,* 159–175.

Lachman, M. E., & Burack, O. R. (1993). Planning and control processes across the life span: An overview. *International Journal of Behavioral Development, 16,* 131–143.

Lachman, M., & Leff, R. (1989). Perceived control and intellectual functioning in the elderly: A 5-year longitudinal study. *Developmental Psychology, 25,* 722–728.

Langer, E. J., & Rodin, J. (1976). The effects of choice and enhanced personal responsibility for the aged: A field experiment in an institutional setting. *Journal of Personality and Social Psychology, 34,* 191–198.

Larsen, R., & Diener, E. (1987). Affect intensity as an individual difference characteristic: A review. *Journal of Research in Personality, 21,* 1–39.

Lawton, M. P., Kleban, M. H., Rajagopal, D., & Dean, J. (1992). Dimensions of affective experience in three age groups. *Psychology and Aging, 7,* 171–184.

Lazarus, R. S., & Folkman, S. (1984). *Stress, appraisal, and coping.* New York: Springer.

Lazarus, R. S. & Smith, C. A. (1988). Knowledge and appraisal in the cognition-emotion relationship. *Cognition and Emotion, 2,* 281–300.

Levenson, H. (1974). Activism and powerful others: Distinctions within the concept of internal-external control. *Journal of Personality Assessment, 38,* 377–383.

Leventhal, E. A., Leventhal, H., Schaefer, P., & Easterling, D. (1993). Conservation of energy, uncertainty reduction, and swift utilization of medical care among the elderly. *Journal of Gerontology: Psychological Sciences, 48,* P78–P86.

Leventhal, H., Diefenbach, M., & Leventhal, E. A. (1992). Illness cognition: Using common sense to understand treatment adherence and affect cognition interaction. *Cognitive Therapy and Research, 16,* 143–163.

Levinson, D. J., with Darrow, C. N., Klein, E. B., Levinson, M. H., & McKee, B. (1978). *The seasons of a man's life.* New York: Ballantine.

Luszcz, M. A., & Fitzgerald, K. M. (1986). Understanding cohort differences in cross-generational, self, and peer perceptions. *Journal of Gerontology, 41,* 234–240.

Manstead, A. S. R., & Tetlock, P. E. (1989). Cognitive appraisals and emotional experience: Further evidence. *Cognition and Emotion, 3,* 225–240.

Markus, H., & Herzog, R. (1991). The role of self-concept in aging. In K. W. Schaie (Ed.), *Annual review of gerontology and geriatrics* (vol. 11, pp. 110–143). New York: Springer.

Markus, H., & Nurius, P. (1986). Possible selves. *American Psychologist, 41,* 954–969.

McCrae, R. R., & Costa, P. T. (1988). Age, personality, and the spontaneous self-concept. *Journal of Gerontology: Social Sciences, 43,* S177–S185.

Mead, G. H. (1934). *Mind, self, and society.* Chicago: Univ. of Chicago Press.

Mergler, N., & Goldstein, M. D. (1983). Why are there old people? Senescence as biological and cultural preparedness for the transmission of information. *Human Development, 26,* 72–90.

Mezirow, J. (1991). *Transformative dimensions of adult learning.* San Francisco: Jossey-Bass.

Moskowitz, G. B., & Roman, R. J. (1992). Spontaneous trait inferences as self-generated primes: Implications for conscious social judgment. *Journal of Personality and Social Psychology, 62,* 728–738.

Murphey, D. A., Labouvie-Vief, G., Orwoll, L., & Chiodo, L. (1992). Development of a measure for self and other representation in adulthood. Paper presented at the Cognitive Aging Conference, Atlanta, April.

Nehrke, M. F., Hulicka, I. H., & Morganti, J. (1980). Age differences in life satisfaction, locus of control, and self-concept. *International Journal of Aging and Human Development, 11,* 25–33.

Newman, L. S. (1991). Why are traits inferred spontaneously? A developmental approach. *Social Cognition, 9,* 221–253.

Nisbett, R., & Ross, L. (1980). *Human inference: Strategies and shortcomings of social judgment.* Englewood Cliffs, NJ: Prentice-Hall.

Nogami, G. Y., & Streufert, S. (1983). The dimensionality of attributions of causality and responsibility for an accident. *European Journal of Social Psychology, 13,* 433–436.

Nurmi, J. E., Pullianen, H., & Salmela-Aro, K. (1992). Age differences in adults' control beliefs related to life goals and concerns. *Psychology and Aging, 7,* 194–196.

Orwoll, L., & Perlmutter, M. (1990). The study of wise persons: Integrating a personality perspective. In R. Sternberg (Ed.), *Wisdom: Its nature, origins, and development* (pp. 160–180). Cambridge: Cambridge Univ. Press.

Perry, W. (1970). *Forms of intellectual and ethical development in the college years.* New York: Holt, Rinehart and Winston.

Reker, G. T., Peacock, E. J., & Wong, P. T. (1987). Meaning and purpose in life and well-being: A life-span perspective. *Journal of Gerontology, 42,* 44–49.

Rodin, J. (1987). Personal control through the life course. In R. P. Abeles (Ed.), *Life-span perspectives and social psychology* (pp. 103–119). Hillsdale, NJ: Erlbaum.

Rodin, J., & Langer, E. J. (1977). Long-term effects of a control-relevant intervention with the institutionalized aged. *Journal of Personality and Social Psychology, 35,* 897–902.

Rothbaum, F., Weisz, J. R., & Snyder, S. S. (1982). Changing the world and changing the self: A two-process model of perceived control. *Journal of Personality and Social Psychology, 42,* 5–37.

Rotter, J. B. (1966). Generalized expectancies for internal versus external control of reinforcement. *Psychological Monographs, 81* (1, whole no. 609).

Rybash, J., Hoyer, W., & Roodin, P. (1986). *Adult cognition and aging.* New York: Pergamon.

Ryff, C. D. (1991). Possible selves in adulthood and old age: A tale of shifting horizons. *Psychology and Aging, 6,* 286–295.

Salthouse, T. (1991). *Theoretical perspectives on cognitive aging.* Hillsdale, NJ: Erlbaum.

Schaie, K. W. (1978). External validity in the assessment of intellectual development in adulthood. *Journal of Gerontology, 33,* 695–701.

Sebby, R. A., & Papini, D. R. (1989). Problems in everyday problem solving research: A framework for conceptualizing solutions to everyday problems. In J. A. Sinnott (Ed.), *Everyday problem solving: Theory and applications* (pp. 55–71). New York: Praeger.

Seligman, M. E. P., Abramson, L. Y., Semmel, A., & Von Baeyer, C. (1979). Depressive attributional style. *Journal of Abnormal Psychology, 88,* 242–247.

Shaw, J. I., & Skolnick, P. (1971). Attribution of responsibility for a happy accident. *Journal of Personality and Social Psychology, 18,* 380–383.

Shultz, T. R., & Wright, K. (1985). Concepts of negligence and intention in the assignment of moral responsibility. *Canadian Journal of Behavioral Science, 17, 2.*

Siegler, I. C., & Gatz, M. (1985). Age patterns in locus of control. In E. Palmore, E. W. Busse, G. L. Maddox, J. B. Nowlin, & I. C. Siegler (Eds.), *Normal aging* (vol. 3, pp. 259–267). Durham, NC: Duke Univ. Press.

Sinnott, J. D. (1986). *Sex roles and aging: Theory and research from a systems perspective.* New York: Karger.

Sinnott, J. D. (1989). *Everyday problem solving: Theory and applications.* New York: Praeger.

Smith, C. A., & Ellsworth, P. C. (1985). Patterns of cognitive appraisal in emotion. *Journal of Personality and Social Psychology, 48,* 813–838.

Staudinger, U. M., Smith, J., & Baltes, P. B. (1992). Wisdom-related knowledge in a life review task: Age differences and the role of professional specialization. *Psychology and Aging, 7,* 271–281.

Swann, W. B. (1987). Identity negotiation: Where two roads meet. *Journal of Personality and Social Psychology, 53,* 1038–1051.

Wallston, K. A., & Wallston, B. S. (1981). Health-related locus of control scales. In H. M. Lefcourt (Ed.), *Research with the locus of control construct: Assessment methods* (vol. 1, pp. 189–243). New York: Academic Press.

Weiner, B. (1986). *An attributional theory of motivation and emotion.* New York: Springer.

Weiner, B., & Graham, S. (1989). Understanding the motivational role of affect: Life-span research from an attributional perspective. *Cognition and Emotion, 3,* 401–419.

C H A P T E R

15

MEMORY SELF-EFFICACY AS A MODERATOR OF MEMORY CHANGE

John C. Cavanaugh
University of Delaware

How good do you think your memory is in general? Has your memory ability changed over time? How you answer these questions provides insights into beliefs you hold about your own memory. Each of us holds such beliefs, and we can articulate them when we are asked. Beliefs about memory are important because they influence how well we remember information. This relationship between belief and action is the essence of this chapter: People hold certain beliefs about their memory ability, and these beliefs play an important role in determining what people do when confronted with the task of remembering. In this chapter, we will see where these beliefs come from, how they are measured, and how they relate to performance. The key construct central to understanding the relationship between memory beliefs and memory performance is memory self-efficacy. We will discover how memory self-efficacy can serve as a model for understanding age-related changes in memory performance.

Throughout this chapter, we will be encountering concepts discussed in other parts of this book. Clearly, the ideas expressed here must be placed into the broader theoretical frameworks discussed in Chapter 2. The types and extent of normal (and, by extension, abnormal) age-related memory changes discussed in Chapters 6, 7, and 8 set the boundary conditions for the beliefs about memory described here. How memory operates and is used in context, discussed in Chapter 12, is also important, as context itself plays an important role in determining the extent of performance differences with age. Finally, beliefs about both memory and self-efficacy are examples of the broader domain of social cognition; age-related changes in these processes and how they relate to cognition are described in Chapter 14.

THE IMPORTANCE OF MEMORY SELF-EFFICACY IN ADULT DEVELOPMENT AND AGING

Belief in oneself is a pervasive theme in literature, religion, psychotherapy, and other diverse arenas (Cavanaugh & Green, 1990). Because few other psychological constructs enjoy such wide application, belief in oneself is a central and powerful variable in any comprehensive explanation of why people do the things they do. Within the psychological literature, one of the most important incarnations of this idea is Bandura's (1986) notion of self-efficacy. Briefly, self-efficacy is the extent to which one believes in his or her ability to mobilize the motivation, cognitive resources, and courses of action needed to exercise control over task demands (Bandura, 1986). Self-efficacy is not a passive belief about some hypothetical future action. Instead, it is a belief that leads a person to behave in certain ways based on the belief. Self-efficacy is a call to action concerning a future event which becomes a motivator and regulator of behavior in the present.

Self-efficacy has been studied in several contexts, but especially in the clinical (e.g., treatment of phobias) and health (e.g., beliefs about illness) domains. Although there is considerably less research on the topic, the application of the concept of self-efficacy to adult development and aging is important for two main reasons (Welch & West, 1995): (1) Self-efficacy is influenced by personal (e.g., success or failure experiences, affect) and social (e.g., stereotypes about individuals' abilities) factors. For example, as a person ages, self-efficacy may decline as a result of personal experience of failures and/or repeated societal pressure to ascribe failures to age, even though there may be equally valid alternative explanations (e.g., insufficient effort). Changes in self-efficacy accruing through these factors may result in changes in performance. (2) The environments in which people live help foster feelings of mastery or dependence depending on the circumstances. The former tend to boost self-efficacy, whereas the latter tend to reduce it (Rodin & Langer, 1980). For older adults, providing environments that increase the likelihood of mastery experiences may improve self-efficacy and improve performance.

■ Memory Self-Efficacy as a Distinct Concept

One important application of self-efficacy in adult development and aging has been in memory research, mainly because some changes in memory performance are normative (see Chapters 6, 7, and 8) and because social stereotypes of age-related decline are pervasive (see, e.g., Cavanaugh & Morton, 1988). As Welch and West (1995) point out, older adults may also find themselves in environments that are insufficiently cognitively challenging and which do not provide mastery experiences, social contexts that promote aging stereotypes, and situations that provide little motivation for good performance. This combination might result in declines in self-efficacy and performance. Because the converse (providing cognitive challenges, mastery experiences, arguments against stereotypes, and high motivation) could result in improved self-efficacy and performance, the importance of understanding the moderating role of self-efficacy in adult development and aging, especially in terms of memory, is critical.

Interest in memory self-efficacy in adult development and aging has its roots in the earlier and larger literature concerning what people know about their memory. Such knowledge, often termed *metamemory,* is accumulated over a lifetime through personal experience and (though less often) through direct instruction (Cavanaugh & Perlmutter, 1982). Metamemory itself is an interactive, dynamic process that mediates and is mediated by a host of other constructs such as personality, cognitive developmental level, and social context (Cavanaugh & Morton, 1989).

Since the mid-1980s, adult development and aging researchers have focused on identifying various components of metamemory. To date, two general categories of metamemory have theoretical and empirical support (see, e.g., Hertzog, Dixon, & Hultsch, 1990a): memory self-efficacy and generic memory knowledge. Building upon the general definition of self-efficacy provided earlier, memory self-efficacy comprises a set of beliefs about one's capability to use memory effectively in various situations (see, e.g., Berry, West, & Dennehey, 1989). Generic memory knowledge comprises a set of representations or propositions about how memory functions, such as which memory strategies are more or less effective in general in improving performance (Hertzog et al., 1990a). A key difference between memory self-efficacy and generic memory knowledge is the notion of personal agency (i.e., effective use of memory) in various contexts and situations, which forms the core of memory self-efficacy. The distinction is the difference between *knowing* that certain memory strategies can improve performance and *believing* in one's ability (or lack thereof) to use the strategy effectively. Empirical support for this distinction comes from factor-analytic studies of memory self-evaluation questionnaires (Hertzog et al., 1990a).

The advantage in adult development and aging research of differentiating generic memory knowledge and memory self-efficacy is that it allows for the possibility that people may have extensive and accurate knowledge about how memory functions but believe that their ability to perform in a given context is poor. For example, older adults may believe that they will inevitably be victims of declining memory, which will occur despite any effort on their part to maintain their memory skills (Cavanaugh & Morton, 1988).

In addition to the distinctions described so far, memory self-efficacy has been distinguished from several other concepts in the social cognition literature (see also Chapter 14). Among the most important of these concepts are self-concept, personal control and attributions, and implicit theories.

In terms of the present discussion, self-concept includes views that people have about their ability on a wide variety of topics (Markus, 1977). In this sense, self-concept is related to self-efficacy in that both refer to ability judgments in particular domains, both influence performance, and both are sources of individual differences (Cavanaugh & Green, 1990). However, self-concept is typically viewed as a holistic concept, whereas self-efficacy is not (Bandura, 1986).

Personal control is one of the most widely used constructs in social cognition (Cavanaugh & Green, 1990). The research evidence in the adult development and aging literature strongly supports the view that the extent to which a person believes that outcomes are contingent on his or her own behaviors has a considerable influence on social, cognitive, and physical functioning (see, e.g., Baltes & Baltes, 1986). Most important for the present discussion, personal control beliefs have also been shown to be important in memory performance in older adults (see, e.g., Bachrach & Best, 1994; Cavanaugh & Morton, 1988).

The primary distinction between personal control beliefs and self-efficacy is that the former focuses on the causes of behavior, whereas the latter emphasizes judgments about one's ability to perform. To illustrate this distinction, consider what happens when a person is confronted with remembering a list of items to be picked up at the grocery store. Personal control beliefs would be reflected in whether the individual believes that he or she can do something effective that will influence performance or that forces outside one's purview will determine the outcome. Self-efficacy would be reflected in whether he or she thinks that the items in the task at hand will be remembered or not.

Implicit theories concern whether people believe that ability in some domain is fixed, termed *entity-implicit theory,* or can be modified with effort, termed *skill-implicit theory* (Dweck & Leggett, 1988). Each implicit theory is associated with different goals: performance goals in the case of entity-implicit theory (i.e., doing well is the most important thing, so failure is to be avoided), mastery goals in the case of skill-implicit theory (i.e., learning something valuable is the most important thing, so challenging situations are desirable). Implicit theories are related to self-efficacy in that the ability judgments involved in self-efficacy flow from individuals' underlying worldview of ability (Cavanaugh & Green, 1990). That is, whether one thinks one can perform a task may depend in part on what one's goals are. When confronted with a difficult task, for example, a person who holds an entity-implicit theory may make a self-efficacy judgment that he or she is incapable of performing it, whereas a person holding a skill-implicit theory may believe that he or she is capable. Thus implicit theories may influence self-efficacy judgments.

The concepts to which memory self-efficacy is related provide important ingredients for a general theoretical framework of its role in memory processing in the context of adult development and aging. It is to this topic we now turn.

■ A General Theoretical Framework

The utility of memory self-efficacy resulted in the development of theoretical frameworks incorporating the concept into broader descriptions of memory processing. One of the first of these frameworks was proposed by Cavanaugh and colleagues (see, e.g., Cavanaugh & Morton, 1989) as a way to understand everyday memory performance in older adults. A more detailed discussion of how self-efficacy fits within this framework can be found in Cavanaugh and Green (1990).

In brief, Cavanaugh describes a complex network of reciprocal, dynamic interrelationships that denote the influence of underlying cognitive developmental level, personality, situational factors, knowledge, self-efficacy, and various feedback and evaluation processes. A crucial aspect of the model is that people engage in several evaluative judgments in the course of memory processing: self-efficacy, outcome expectancies, task demands, accuracy of generic memory knowledge, and performance. However, self-efficacy evaluations are considered to be central and are thought to heavily influence processing resource allocations, strategy selection, effort, and ultimately level of performance (see also Berry & West, 1993). Moreover, none of the evaluations is conducted on the basis of direct input of generic memory knowledge; rather, the influence of generic knowledge is mediated through memory beliefs. This implies that self-efficacy evaluations are undertaken in a specific situation and are constructed by using previously stored information and judgments in addition to on-line information gained from the situation at hand. The framework thereby predicts that the connection between self-efficacy and performance should vary with the type of task and with prior experience. Indeed, this prediction has been supported by West, Dennehy-Basile, and Norris (1995), who reported that the self-efficacy–performance relationship differed, especially in older adults, as a function of prior task experience with similar memory activities and actual test experience. Related support was also reported by Hertzog, Dixon, and Hultsch (1990b), who found that memory self-efficacy judgments were stronger predictors of performance on the first, but less so on subsequent, retrieval trials.

Although there has been no research designed to test this framework, related research on self-efficacy in other domains supports the model (Berry & West, 1993). For example, self-efficacy clearly influences the task-related goals people set; people with high self-efficacy set higher goals than do people with low self-efficacy (for a review, see Schunk, 1990). People with high self-efficacy also tend to choose more challenging tasks and persevere with them longer than do people with low self-efficacy (see Berry & West, 1993).

WHERE DOES MEMORY SELF-EFFICACY COME FROM?

Having established that memory self-efficacy is an important concept for understanding memory processing in adult development and aging, we must now examine the origin of memory self-efficacy judgments. One of the limits of the original explication of self-efficacy theory was a lack of explicit discussion of the sources of self-efficacy (see Cavanaugh & Green, 1990). Using Bandura's (1986) theory as a foundation, Berry and West (1993) addressed this problem by explicating four sources of information that influence self-efficacy: *mastery experiences, vicarious observations, social persuasion,* and *states of arousal.* Each of these sources relates to the underlying nature of self-efficacy judgments and emphasizes the situation specificity of these evaluations. Each of these sources also plays an important role in the framework presented earlier. As Cavanaugh and Green (1990) point out, experience and observation both accrue throughout life, social persuasion may be incorporated into one's belief system, and arousal influences one's current affective state.

The outcome of a specific self-efficacy evaluation depends on other self-evaluative judgments about memory that have been made before (in which case the previous judgment may be available in memory and could simply be repeated) and on concurrent evaluations of the situation at hand. In the latter case, a person evaluates the present task for similarities and differences between the present task and ones that the person has confronted in the past, again searching memory for recollections of previously encountered situations. Once the search for stored information (if available) and ongoing task evaluation are complete, the individual makes a judgment.

MEASURING MEMORY SELF-EFFICACY

Since the early 1980s, memory-aging researchers have developed measures that would tap memory self-evaluations (see Cavanaugh & Green, 1990, for a review). Most of this effort has been aimed at developing paper-and-pencil questionnaires, with origins in the metamemory literature. More recently, this effort has also resulted in the development of scales specifically designed to assess memory self-efficacy. In this section, we will first briefly consider the theoretical basis for self-efficacy measurement. Next, we will review several questionnaires used in various ways to assess aspects of memory self-efficacy. Once the scales have been presented, data examining interrelationships among most of them will be presented, along with a consideration of the measurement difficulties inherent in questionnaire research. The memory prediction literature will be reviewed and integrated with the questionnaire research as a way to discuss converging measures as well as serve as an introduction to the empirical literature on the relationship between memory self-efficacy and performance. Finally, a brief critique of the various measurement approaches will be presented.

■ Theoretical Issues in Measuring Self-Efficacy

Berry and West (1993) point out that the assessment of memory self-efficacy has certain methodological requirements that are grounded in Bandura's (1986) theory. Specifically, a *task hierarchy* with its associated *goal* must be identified, and the *level, strength,* and *generality* of memory self-efficacy judgments must be measured. This is typically accomplished through several steps. First, a *task hierarchy* is created by identifying a set of target behaviors, such as learning and remembering grocery lists, which is ordered hierarchically in terms of increasing difficulty level (e.g., remembering an entire list of 10 items, 15 items, or 20 items). Confidence in one's ability to perform at each level of difficulty is assessed. The *goal* of each task hierarchy is the most difficult performance level (e.g., remembering the 20-item list). Self-efficacy *level* is the total number of tasks (i.e., levels of difficulty) in the hierarchy that a person believes he or she can perform. Self-efficacy *strength* is the average confidence the individual has in his or her ability to complete these tasks. Finally, self-efficacy *generality* is the degree to which efficacy ratings in one domain (e.g., the ability to learn and remember grocery lists) predict efficacy and performance in other domains (e.g., the ability to learn and remember phone numbers).

Perhaps the most important theoretical issue pertaining to measuring memory self-efficacy is its relationship to other terms that are often used interchangeably (see Berry & West, 1993, for a more complete discussion). Most prominent in this respect is the concept of *personal control,* the degree to which one believes that what one does in a situation makes a difference or that behavior is determined by forces outside oneself. For purposes of the present discussion, the concepts of memory self-efficacy and personal control are viewed as separate but related. Specifically, personal control beliefs can be viewed as addressing the question of who is in control, whereas memory self-efficacy refers to the issue of whether one believes one can do the task at hand (see also Berry & West, 1993).

In terms of specific assessments of memory self-efficacy, a key consideration is whether the measure is a global, omnibus measure or a domain-specific measure (Bandura, 1989); the latter is the strongly preferred approach when one desires to maximize the relationship between memory self-efficacy and performance (Berry & West, 1993; Cavanaugh & Green, 1990). Domain-specific measures include questionnaires and single-item indicators of perceived self-efficacy (Cavanaugh & Green, 1990). These measures are used in several ways, primarily as correlates of unrelated tasks or as predictions or postdictions of performance on tasks that are closely related to the measures of memory self-efficacy. It should be noted that there is considerable variation in the degree to which the measures and research designs reflect Bandura's original approach (Berry & West, 1993). For example, the questionnaires we will review in the next section vary from being based on factor analytically–derived combinations of subscales from multidimensional inventories (see, e.g., Dixon, Hultsch, & Hertzog, 1988) to scales derived more directly from Bandura's approach (see, e.g., Berry et al., 1989). One would expect that measures derived from different perspectives might relate differently to performance and to one another. An important point in this discussion is that no single measure of memory self-efficacy is adequate in isolation (Berry & West, 1993; Cavanaugh & Green, 1990).

■ Questionnaire Measures of Memory Self-Efficacy

Questionnaire assessments of memory self-efficacy in the adult development and aging literature have their roots in general measures of memory beliefs. Beginning in the early 1980s, psychometrically sound, multidimensional scales were developed that have subsequently proven to be important in assessing memory self-efficacy. Later in the decade, specific memory self-efficacy scales began to emerge as well. By the mid-1990s, an emerging issue was the degree to which these scales were related, especially in terms of their connections with scales tapping related constructs such as personal control.

General Measures of Memory Beliefs

The earliest measures that could be argued to tap memory self-efficacy were multidimensional scales that assessed several different aspects of memory beliefs. These general self-rating scales were developed within two different perspectives: one that focused on the frequency of memory problems or complaints and one that focused on remembering.

Perhaps the best-validated and most widely used questionnaire that focuses on memory complaints is Gilewski and Zelinski's (1988) Memory Functioning Questionnaire (MFQ). The MFQ is a 64-item instrument in which items are rated on 7-point Likert scales, with higher scores indicating a more positive self-evaluation of memory. (Table 15.1 contains sample items.) There are seven subscales: General (a [single-item] rating of memory problems), Retrospective Functioning (memory compared to past memory ability), Frequency of Forgetting (how often specific types of information are forgotten), Frequency of Forgetting, Reading (how often specific problems of memory arise for written materials [e.g., magazines, books]), Remembering Past Events (memory for temporally remote events), Seriousness (seriousness of problems created by memory lapses), and Mnemonics (frequency of use of techniques to aid remembering). Of these six subscales, Frequency of Forgetting is the longest and most important.

The MFQ subscales all have acceptable internal consistency reliabilities, ranging from .82 to .93 (Gilewski & Zelinski, 1988). Gilewski, Zelinski, and Schaie (1990) reported a robust common factor that included Frequency of Forgetting, Remembering Past Events, Frequency of Forgetting (Reading), and the General Rating subscales. The overall four-factor solution was age invariant over 3 years in a longitudinal study in which demographic variables were not confounded with MFQ factor scores. Zelinski, Gilewski, and Anthony-Bergstone (1990) showed that MFQ factor scores significantly predicted several types of verbal memory tasks (i.e., prose recall, word list recall, word list recognition) even after controlling for self-rated health, depression, and education. Frequency of Forgetting ratings correlated significantly with depression scores, but depression scores could not account for the relationship between the MFQ and actual memory performance.

In contrast to asking people to rate how often they forget things, other questionnaires focus on getting people to make judgments about their ability to remember (e.g., "I am good at remembering names of people I have just met") or in the form of an indirect prediction of degree of success in memory-related behaviors (e.g., "I would have little difficulty remembering a telephone number without writing it down"; Dixon & Hultsch, 1983). The best-validated scale of this type is the Metamemory in Adulthood (MIA) instrument (Dixon et al., 1988). The MIA is a 108-item questionnaire made up of seven subscales: Task, Strategy, Capacity, Change, Anxiety, Achievement, and Locus. (Table 15.2 presents sample items.) Internal consistency estimates for the MIA subscales for these seven subscales range from .74 to .93 across several samples (Hultsch, Hertzog, Dixon, & Davidson, 1988).

Consistent age differences have been reported on the Capacity, Change, and Locus subscales, with the largest differences on Change (Dixon & Hultsch, 1983; Hultsch, Hertzog, & Dixon, 1987). Older adults perceive more change in memory capacity than do young adults. Using confirmatory factor analysis, Hertzog, Dixon, Schulenberg, and Hultsch (1987) identified two higher-order dimensions. One factor was defined by major loadings of Capacity, Change, Locus, and Anxiety and was identified as Memory Self-Efficacy. A second factor, labeled Memory Knowledge, included Task, Strategy, Achievement, Anxiety, and Locus. Finally, several studies have reported moderate correlations between various MIA subscales and memory performance measures (see, e.g., Hertzog, Saylor, Fleece, & Dixon, 1994; see Hertzog et al., 1990a, for a review).

Confirmatory factor analytic analyses of the MFQ and the MIA have revealed a higher-order factor labeled Memory Self-Efficacy (Hertzog, Hultsch, & Dixon, 1989). Thus, it is

TABLE 15.1 Subscales and Sample Items from the Memory Functioning Questionnaire

Subscale	Sample Item
1. General	How would you rate your memory in terms of the kinds of problems you have?
2. Retrospective Functioning	How is your memory compared to the way it was . . . one year ago?
3. Frequency of Forgetting	How often do these present a memory problem for you . . . names?
4. Frequency of Forgetting, Reading	As you are reading a novel, how often do you have trouble remembering what you have read . . . in the opening chapters once you have read the book?
5. Remembering Past Events	How well do you remember things which occurred . . . last month?
6. Seriousness	When you actually forget in these situations, how serious of a problem do you consider the memory failure to be . . . names?
7. Mnemonics	How often do you use these techniques to remind yourself about things . . . keep an appointment book?

Source: Adapted from the appendix in Zelinski, E., Gilewski, M., & Thompson, L. W. (1980). D. laboratory tests relate to self-assessment of memory ability in the young and old? In L.W. Poon, J.L. Fozard, L.S. Cermak, D. Arenberg, & L. W. Thompson, (Eds.), New Directions in Memory and Aging. Hillsdale, NJ: Erlbaum.

TABLE 15.2 Subscales and Sample Items from the Metamemory in Adulthood Instrument	
Subscale	Sample Item
1. Task	For most people, facts that are interesting are easier to remember than facts that are not.
2. Strategy	Do you write appointments on a calendar to help you remember them?
3. Capacity	I am good at remembering names.
4. Change	The older I get the harder it is to remember things clearly.
5. Anxiety	I find it harder to remember things when I'm upset.
6. Achievement	It is important that I am very accurate when remembering names of people.
7. Locus	Even if I work on it my memory ability will go downhill.

Source: Adapted from Dixon and Hultsch, 1983. Copyright 1983 by the Gerontological Society of America. Adapted by permission.

possible to calculate a derived index of memory self-efficacy from these general scales of memory beliefs. It should be noted that this approach does not correspond to the steps proposed by Bandura (1986). Nevertheless, this derived index does provide a significant predictor of performance under certain conditions. We will examine this issue more a bit later.

The Memory Self-Efficacy Questionnaire

By the late 1980s it had become clear that general memory self-rating scales reflected, at least in part, some aspect of memory self-efficacy. However, a strong case was made that a better approach would be to develop a scale specifically designed to tap memory self-efficacy. First, memory self-efficacy was apparently reflected only in higher-order factors on general memory self-rating scales. Arguably, it is preferable to have a more direct measure. Second, the assessment approach used in general memory self-rating questionnaires (i.e., item stems with Likert-type response scales) did not conform to the approach advocated by Bandura (1986). Again, it would be preferable to have a measure that is constructed within the same analytic approach as other measures of self-efficacy.

To address these shortcomings, Berry et al. (1989) developed the Memory Self-Efficacy Questionnaire (MSEQ), which was based on Bandura's measurement approach described earlier. The MSEQ presents respondents with 10 different memory tasks at five different difficulty levels each (i.e., remembering 12, 10, 8, 5, and 2 items of each type). The first and last tasks on the scale are filler tasks and are not scored. Respondents indicate whether they think they would be able to perform a specific task at a particular level of difficulty by circling "yes" or "no." If they circle "yes," they are also asked to indicate the degree of confidence (ranging from 10% to 100%) they have in completing it successfully. (Examples of items are presented in Table 15.3.)

TABLE 15.3 Sample Task Scale from the Memory Self-Efficacy Questionnaire

Phone Task

(5)	If I looked up 3 phone numbers in the phone book at the same time, I could remember 3 complete phone numbers.												
	NO	YES	10%	20%	30%	40%	50%	60%	70%	80%	90%	100%	
(4)	If I looked up 3 phone numbers in the phone book at the same time, I could remember 2 complete phone numbers.												
	NO	YES	10%	20%	30%	40%	50%	60%	70%	80%	90%	100%	
(3)	If I looked up 3 phone numbers in the phone book at the same time, I could remember 1 complete number plus the first 3 digits in 1 other phone number.												
	NO	YES	10%	20%	30%	40%	50%	60%	70%	80%	90%	100%	
(2)	If I looked up 3 phone numbers in the phone book at the same time, I could remember 1 complete number.												
	NO	YES	10%	20%	30%	40%	50%	60%	70%	80%	90%	100%	
(1)	If I looked up 3 phone numbers in the phone book at the same time, I could remember the first 3 digits of 1 phone number.												
	NO	YES	10%	20%	30%	40%	50%	60%	70%	80%	90%	100%	

Note: The number in parentheses indicates the difficulty level represented by each item, with (5) as the highest level. The numbers are not present on the actual questionnaire.

Source: Berry, West, and Dennehey, 1989. Copyright 1989 by the American Psychological Association. Reprinted with permission.

Several scores can be derived from the scale (West & Berry, 1994). The two most commonly used are Self-Efficacy Level (SEL), which is the number of "yes" responses with at least 20 percent confidence ratings, and Self-Efficacy Strength Test (SEST), which is the average level of confidence (where "no" responses are scored as 0). Confidence ratings can also be used to compute two other indices: CONF1, which refers to the confidence level indicated by the most difficult level of a task to which a person responds "yes"; and CONF-YES, which corresponds to the average confidence level for all "yes" responses. Additionally, the degree to which there is correspondence, termed congruence (COG), between memory self-efficacy judgments and performance on a specific task can be computed. Congruence is defined as judging oneself capable of performing a task at a specific difficulty level and subsequently performing it successfully, or judging oneself incapable of performing a task and then failing to do it (Bandura, Reese, & Adams, 1982). COG scores are computed by counting the number of congruent responses across the different tasks. The MSEQ has good internal consistency, as demonstrated across several studies.

Age differences in scores on the MSEQ have been reported (West & Berry, 1994). Specifically, older adults do not believe they can perform as many difficult memory tasks as young adults do. Interestingly, however, age differences in confidence levels are generally absent. When people think they can perform a task of a given difficulty level, they are confident about it regardless of age. Additionally, scores on the MSEQ correlate with memory performance.

Relationship between Questionnaire Data and Performance

Numerous studies have examined the relationships between questionnaire assessments of memory self-efficacy and performance (for reviews, see Cavanaugh & Green, 1990; Hertzog et al., 1990a; West & Berry, 1994). These investigations have often been interpreted as indicators of the predictive validity of the questionnaires, and high correlations were argued to be necessary for self-efficacy to be an important component in understanding memory processes in adult development and aging (Cavanaugh & Green, 1990).

In general, the literature indicates that the zero-order correlations between questionnaire measures of self-efficacy and performance on memory tasks are modest. These correlations tend to be higher as the criterion task becomes more tightly related to the questionnaire. For example, some research using the MSEQ uses exact matches between the criterion memory tasks and the tasks referenced on the scales (see, e.g., West & Berry, 1994).

Measurement Issues in Questionnaire Research

Although the various approaches to assessing memory self-efficacy through questionnaires have greatly advanced our understanding of adults' beliefs about their abilities, there are several problems with this research. Among the most important is the lack of consistency across different measures, both within and across scales.

West and Berry (1994) report inconsistent findings across indicators of memory self-efficacy within the MSEQ. Specifically, compared to younger adults, older adults showed lower Self-Efficacy Level (SEL) and Self-Efficacy Strength Test (SEST), but their confidence ratings (CONF1 and CONF-YES) were largely equivalent. The latter findings support related research in the feeling-of-knowing paradigm (see, e.g., Perlmutter, 1978). The overall pattern suggests that researchers should avoid choosing a single indicator of memory self-efficacy. Moreover, it may be the case that these various measures derived from the MSEQ tap different aspects of memory self-efficacy or possibly even different constructs (e.g., standards of judgment).

A related issue concerns the degree to which various measures of memory self-efficacy interrelate. In one of the few studies to date on this issue, Cavanaugh and Baskind (in press) had 209 undergraduates complete the MIA, MSEQ, and Memory Controllability Inventory (a scale measuring personal control beliefs pertaining to memory; Lachman, Weaver, Bandura, Elliott, & Lewkowicz, 1992). In general, the correlations were low to modest and never exceeded .50.

The Cavanaugh and Baskind (in press) results indicate that three scales that purportedly tap related constructs do not intercorrelate highly, indicating that the scales may not be indexing the same latent construct. These modest correlations support the view expressed earlier that memory self-efficacy and personal control are not the same thing and the point that how one measures self-efficacy (i.e., a Likert-type scale on a general memory survey versus a specially designed self-efficacy scale) makes a difference.

A third issue relates to the magnitude of the relationship between questionnaire indicators of memory self-efficacy and performance. There are several issues involved, each of which can be understood in light of Cavanaugh and Morton's (1989) general theoretical framework presented earlier (see also Cavanaugh & Green, 1990). First, the various scales pose different types of questions, which is known to result in different patterns of self-evaluation

(Cavanaugh, 1987). To the extent different types of questions tap different aspects of the memory self-evaluation process, the magnitudes of the correlations between these ratings and performance should be expected to vary. Second, recall from the theoretical framework that there are several steps between memory self-efficacy judgments and performance, including outcome expectations, effort-level determination, and strategy selection. Thus, because each of these other steps makes direct and/or indirect contributions to performance, and because the link between memory self-efficacy and performance is indirect (i.e., is mediated by these subsequent steps), there is undoubtedly a limit to the amount of variance in performance accounted for by memory self-efficacy. However, what this limit is is unknown and is likely to vary with age, task, and experience. Third, the cognitive processes which underlie responding to self-evaluation questionnaires reflect a combination of the use of stored prior judgments of ability with on-line processing in each situation, which are used to construct a rating judgment (Cavanaugh, Feldman, & Hertzog, 1995). Thus, there may be some inconsistency from situation to situation in memory self-efficacy ratings as experience accrues, which would also affect the strength of the relationship between memory self-efficacy and performance. This appears to be especially true for older adults (Cavanaugh et al., 1995; West et al., 1995).

Unfortunately, little is known about how these issues play out with different measures. Very little research has included multiple measures of memory self-efficacy and multiple memory tasks in the same study. In order for the measurement issues raised here to be addressed adequately, such comparisons must be made.

■ Performance Predictions and Postdictions in Memory Self-Efficacy Research

Prediction and postdiction of memory task performance has been viewed over the years as one alternative to questionnaires in examining the relationship between memory beliefs and memory performance (see, e.g., Cavanaugh, 1989). More recently, this argument has been extended to viewing predictions and postdictions as indices of memory self-efficacy (see, e.g., Cavanaugh et al., 1995; West et al., 1995). In the typical prediction study, for example, people are asked to make global predictions by indicating how many items they will remember from a list of X items (see, e.g., Hertzog et al., 1994), or to indicate for each item whether they think they will remember it on a subsequent test (see, e.g., Rabinowitz, Ackerman, Craik, & Hinchley, 1982). These questions are conceptually similar to those on the MSEQ and are task specific. Thus, they could be considered as alternative measures to the extent that each prompts individuals to make judgments about their memory abilities. In terms of the theoretical framework presented earlier, performance predictions arise from the same sources as do memory self-efficacy judgments.

The research literature is fairly clear in showing that no age differences are observed for global predictions made prior to study (see, e.g., Hertzog et al., 1994), or for item-by-item predictions made either after study but prior to testing or after testing (see, e.g., Lovelace, 1990). Accuracy of prediction (usually defined as prediction minus performance) is typically greater for younger adults (see, e.g., Cavanaugh, 1989). Postdiction accuracy is greater for all ages, and these estimates correlate more strongly with performance than do predictions (see, e.g., Hertzog et al., 1990a, 1994). However, there is considerable variation in findings across studies when comparing prediction and postdiction accuracy (see, e.g., Devolder, Brigham, & Pressley, 1990; Hertzog et al., 1990a, 1994).

The most recent variation on the prediction–postdiction paradigm is the use of the MSEQ as the way to index judgments of performance (West et al., 1995). This pairing of a questionnaire and the prediction–postdiction paradigm represents an interesting approach, as long as the limitations of questionnaire research discussed above are kept in mind.

■ Issues in Prediction and Postdiction Research

The methodological issues surrounding prediction and postdiction research are more complex than those discussed above pertaining to questionnaire research for two main reasons. First, the assessment of predictions and postdictions varies a great deal across studies. For example, Rebok and Balcerak (1989) adopted the technique used in several studies of asking participants the single question of how many items they thought they could remember from the list. In contrast, West et al. (1995) used the MSEQ as a more comprehensive measure of predictions and postdictions. There is disagreement over which approach is better. On the one hand, some authors argue that single-item indicators should be avoided (see Cavanaugh & Green, 1990). For example, Bandura (1989) argues that single-item indicators do not tap all of the aspects of memory self-efficacy sufficiently to provide a good assessment; he would most likely prefer the West et al. (1995) approach. In contrast, other authors argue that the single-item approach can provide valuable insights into self-evaluations (see Cavanaugh, 1989, for a review). For example, they provide one way of indexing highly task-specific judgments of one's ability. Given the importance of assessing one's level of confidence in the self-evaluation judgment, however, single-item assessments would provide even more valuable information if they were coupled with confidence judgments.

A second complex issue pertains to the accuracy of predictions and postdictions. As noted earlier, younger adults tend to be more accurate than older adults. Upon closer inspection, though, these data reveal important methodological and developmental points. Most of the research on prediction and postdiction accuracy has included only one test trial, resulting in crucial differences between prediction and results (see Cavanaugh, 1989). More recently, researchers have begun examining changes in accuracy as a function of repeated testing. Indications are that people upgrade their accuracy as they gain experience with the task (see, e.g., Hertzog et al., 1990b). Specifically, it appears that global memory self-efficacy is a reasonably good predictor of initial performance but that subsequent accuracy depends more on incorporating knowledge of one's performance on the immediately preceding trial into the current prediction. However, important age differences may remain even after gaining experience, at least on some tasks. For example, West et al. (1995) found that, even after experience with the task, younger adults were still more accurate than older adults, especially on tasks that were initially unfamiliar to them. These findings may mean that upgrading of accuracy is itself a task-specific phenomenon.

Clearly, more research is needed in order to delineate the developmental course of the accuracy of memory predictions and postdictions. Additionally, more studies are needed that directly compare single-item indicators (augmented by confidence ratings) with more elaborate assessments (such as with the MSEQ). Such research will not only address the issues raised here but also provide important information relevant to further refinements of the theoretical framework presented earlier.

APPLICATIONS OF MEMORY SELF-EFFICACY TO ADULT DEVELOPMENT AND AGING

To this point, we have considered what memory self-efficacy means and how it is measured. We now turn our attention to its importance in the broader arena of memory across adulthood. Several authors have pointed to the utility of memory self-efficacy (see, e.g., Cavanaugh & Green, 1990; Welch & West, in press). For example, Welch and West (1995) point out that there are important links provided by self-efficacy between environmental mastery (i.e., the degree to which one feels in control in one's environment and experiences success) and memory performance. The idea is that, based on the sources of self-efficacy reviewed earlier, there is a direct relationship between memory self-efficacy and various environments that provide efficacy-changing mastery experiences.

Welch and West (1995) present a model of the processes underlying the connection between environmental mastery and memory self-efficacy as it applies to adult development and aging. Briefly, they propose that some older adults hold the assumption that memory inevitably declines with age and have experienced some age-related decrease in performance themselves. Although the causal nature of the link between memory self-efficacy and performance decline has yet to be firmly established, this view fits with the Cavanaugh and Morton (1988) framework, as do several studies establishing the causal impact of mastery experiences for increasing efficacy and failure experiences at lowering it (see, e.g., Bandura, 1986). As people experience environments across adulthood that provide success experiences, their memory self-efficacy should remain strong; those who experience environments resulting in failure experiences should show decrements in memory self-efficacy. Changes in self-efficacy in turn influence people's decisions about how to behave in the future; those with strong memory self-efficacy would be expected to seek out more challenging cognitive environments compared to those whose memory self-efficacy is declining (see also Cavanaugh et al., 1995). Additionally, people with higher environmental mastery and memory self-efficacy would be expected to perform better than those with low mastery and self-efficacy.

This dynamic relationship between memory self-efficacy and environmental mastery can be observed in many settings. For example, a more general connection between self-efficacy and environmental mastery has been reported in research examining nursing home placements (see, e.g., Atchley, 1988), mortality of nursing home residents (see, e.g., Langer & Rodin, 1976), family caregiving (see, e.g., Timko & Rodin, 1985), and psychotherapy (see, e.g., Bandura, 1986). In the cognitive domain, the most important application of memory self-efficacy is in the area of memory training.

■ Memory Self-Efficacy and Memory Training

Bandura (1986) argues that self-efficacy is a critical element in training and intervention programs and should show strong connections with subsequent performance. Research in many areas, such as the treatment of phobias (Bandura, Adams, Hardy, & Howells, 1980), bowling (Mathieu, Martineau, & Tannenbaum, 1993), physical defense (Ozer & Bandura, 1990), rappelling (Brody, Hatfield, & Spalding, 1988), and business management (Wood & Bandura, 1989), has shown such connections. As one might expect, based on our earlier discussions, a key ingredient in the success of these interventions is providing mastery experiences with less difficult tasks, with subsequent and gradual increases in task difficulty (Bandura et al., 1982).

Although memory intervention programs have existed for centuries (Yates, 1966), only recently have researchers begun incorporating self-efficacy in memory training, especially with older adults. Because the overall success of memory intervention programs with older adults has been established (Verhaeghen, Marcoen, & Goossens, 1992), it is important to begin identifying which components of intervention programs are essential. Arguably, belief in one's ability (or inability) to learn new remembering techniques should make learning such aids easier (or more difficult) and subsequently improve (or hinder) task performance. Numerous studies have shown that older adults spontaneously use fewer memory strategies than younger adults, and even when they do they tend to use them less effectively (for a review, see West, 1995). One possible reason for this developmental difference is decreases in self-efficacy, which are reflected in lower rates of strategy usage and performance.

Traditionally, memory training involves the acquisition of effective and efficient strategies with the goal of improving performance (Borkowski & Cavanaugh, 1979). Interventions involving self-efficacy would not abandon these goals but would simply create an environment that fosters mastery, as discussed above. To date, the literature on the role of self-efficacy in memory interventions is sparse in relation to the broader arena of strategy training in older adults (West, 1995). Nevertheless, a few investigations have been conducted. In a series of investigations, Lachman and her colleagues (see, e.g., Elliott & Lachman, 1989; Lachman & Dick, 1987; Weaver & Lachman, 1989) found mixed results which indicated a complex relationship between self-efficacy and memory performance. In some cases both performance and self-efficacy tended to improve over time irrespective of whether the individuals were in training groups or not. Lachman and colleagues concluded that these findings were not supportive of strong ties between self-efficacy and performance.

Based on our earlier discussion, though, this conclusion may not be entirely accurate. Recall that mastery experiences are central not only to self-efficacy beliefs but also to performance improvement. It is possible that the increase in performance observed in some of the participants in Lachman and colleagues' research resulted from such experiences. However, because mastery experiences were not directly assessed in their research, this explanation remains speculative.

Other investigators have examined the issue more directly by emphasizing change in self-efficacy beliefs in the intervention program itself. For example, West, Bramblett, Welch, and Bellott (1992) combined mastery-oriented training with discussion of memory beliefs. Memory self-efficacy increased as a result, as did performance on one of the criterion tests. Most important, the increased level of memory self-efficacy in the older adult trainees was maintained in a 1-month follow-up test. These results support the view that including memory self-efficacy as a focus of the intervention program can result in self-efficacy and performance gains that are sustainable.

Unfortunately, too little research has been conducted on this topic for any firm conclusions to be drawn. Clearly, there is considerable need for additional research on the issue, especially in terms of how best to incorporate memory self-efficacy into intervention programs. Additionally, there has yet to be a comprehensive investigation of memory interventions that include adequate assessment of memory self-efficacy and multiple-criterion tasks with tests of maintenance in everyday situations.

THE UNDISCOVERED COUNTRY: THE FUTURE OF MEMORY SELF-EFFICACY RESEARCH

We have seen that memory self-efficacy is an important emerging concept in adult development and aging. Based on the ideas set forth in this chapter and the research we have considered, much remains to be done in understanding self-efficacy and its relationship to performance across adulthood. Three areas need special attention: conceptual clarification, measurement, and model building.

At the conceptual level, the most pressing need is to figure out what is meant when self-efficacy is referred to as a "domain-specific" construct. Bandura (1986) argues strongly for domain-specific assessment of self-efficacy. But what does "domain-specific" mean? Is memory just one domain? Or is memory made up of many domains, each of which corresponds to a particular type of task (list learning, prose retention, autobiographical memory, etc.)? Indeed, some authors (see, e.g., Berry et al., 1989) use the term "task-specific" rather than "domain-specific," especially when referring to assessments of memory self-efficacy (such as the MSEQ).

How this issue is resolved will have major effects on the directions taken by self-efficacy researchers. If memory is one domain, it will be much easier at one level to develop measures and models. For example, from this perspective scales such as the MSEQ could be used to assess memory self-efficacy for any criterion task. In contrast, if memory is not a unitary domain, the job of assessing memory self-efficacy becomes much more difficult. In this case, assessments would have to be developed separately for each criterion task, or at least for each general class of memory test (e.g., paired associates, remembering phone numbers). Clearly, this would be a formidable task. More conceptual discussions of the implications of these views must occur. These discussions in turn are closely related to the need for additional research on measures of memory self-efficacy.

We need to continue exploring the measurement properties of self-efficacy scales and establish why various current approaches to measuring memory self-efficacy do not intercorrelate very well. In part, this is likely due to the different histories of existing measures (i.e., whether they were created expressly to measure memory self-efficacy). However, if indeed there is an underlying construct of memory self-efficacy, we need to ensure that alternative measurement approaches should all tap this construct. This argues strongly for continued work on establishing the construct, convergent, and discriminant validities of memory self-efficacy measures and less emphasis on their predictive validity (Cavanaugh & Green, 1990). Such psychometric research would reflect the current theoretical frameworks describing the role of memory self-efficacy as a moderating variable in memory processing.

Research aimed at testing aspects of models incorporating memory self-efficacy needs to be designed and conducted. Despite several studies supporting current concepts of how memory self-efficacy may operate across adulthood (see, e.g., Hertzog et al., 1990a), there has been virtually no research to date designed to provide direct tests of theoretical models in the adult development and aging literature. The framework presented earlier in this chapter could form the basis for proposing such a study using a structural equation model that could be tested directly. Only through such carefully designed research will we be able to establish the nature of the relationship between memory self-efficacy and memory behaviors (e.g., strategy selection, performance).

All these issues converge in the area of intervention. Programs need to be developed that flow explicitly from models of memory self-efficacy in adulthood and aging. Indeed, designing such programs will force researchers to address the conceptual, measurement, and theoretical issues discussed above. Because similar issues have been confronted in the clinical literature (see, e.g., Bandura, 1986; Beck, Rush, Shaw, & Emery, 1979), it may be possible to incorporate aspects of that literature into memory in adulthood. For example, the importance of focusing on underlying beliefs in cognitive therapy (see, e.g., Beck et al., 1979) could be included as an emphasis on underlying beliefs about changes in memory with age (Cavanaugh & Green, 1990). The important point is that carefully designed intervention programs require attention to all the issues discussed here, as well as providing a way of identifying the key elements responsible for change (Borkowski & Cavanaugh, 1979). In this way, the role of memory self-efficacy in adulthood and aging will be better understood.

None of this work will be easy. Ironically, it may even serve as a type of self-efficacy test in a way—only researchers with high self-efficacy for cracking difficult problems are likely to accept the challenge. However, the payoff for success could be high. Understanding the role of memory self-efficacy could enable us to provide ways for older adults to compensate for normative memory changes and to minimize changes that result from one's underlying beliefs rather than processes due to aging.

REFERENCES

Atchley, R. C. (1988). *Social forces and aging* (5th ed.). Belmont, CA: Wadsworth.

Bachrach, P. S., & Best, D. L. (1994). Causal attribution and memory performance in the elderly. Paper presented at the Third Practical Aspects of Memory Conference, College Park, MD, August.

Baltes, M. M., & Baltes, P. B. (Eds.) (1986). *The psychology of control and aging.* Hillsdale, NJ: Erlbaum.

Bandura, A. (1986). *Social foundations of thought and action: A social cognitive theory.* Englewood Cliffs, NJ: Prentice-Hall.

Bandura, A. (1989). Regulation of cognitive processes through perceived self-efficacy. *Developmental Psychology, 25,* 729–735.

Bandura, A., Adams, N. E., Hardy, A. B., & Howells, G. N. (1980). Tests of the generality of self-efficacy. *Cognitive Therapy and Research, 4,* 39–66.

Bandura, A., Reese, L., & Adams, N. E. (1982). Microanalysis of action and fear arousal as a function of differential levels of perceived self-efficacy. *Journal of Personality and Social Psychology, 43,* 5–21.

Beck, A. T., Rush, A. J., Shaw, B. F., & Emery, G. (1979). *Cognitive therapy of depression.* New York: Guilford.

Berry, J. M., & West, R. L. (1993). Cognitive self-efficacy in relation to personal mastery and goal setting across the life span. *International Journal of Behavioral Development, 16,* 351–379.

Berry, J. M., West, R. L., & Dennehey, D. M. (1989). Reliability and validity of the Memory Self-Efficacy Questionnaire. *Developmental Psychology, 25,* 701–713.

Borkowski, J. G., & Cavanaugh, J. C. (1979). Maintenance and generalization of skills and strategies by the retarded. In N. R. Ellis (Ed.), *Handbook of mental deficiency: Psychological theory and research* (2d ed., pp. 569–617). Hillsdale, NJ: Erlbaum.

Brody, E. B., Hatfield, B. D., & Spalding, T. W. (1988). Generalization of self-efficacy to a continuum of stressors upon mastery of a high-risk sport skill. *Journal of Sport and Exercise Psychology, 10,* 32–44.

Cavanaugh, J. C. (1987). Age differences in adults' self-reports of memory ability. *International Journal of Aging and Human Development, 24,* 271–277.

Cavanaugh, J. C. (1989). The importance of awareness in memory aging. In L. W. Poon, D. Rubin, & B. Wilson (Eds.), *Everyday cognition in adulthood and late life* (pp. 416–436). New York: Cambridge Univ. Press.

Cavanaugh, J. C., & Baskind, D. (in press). Relations among basic processes, beliefs, and performance: A lifespan perspective. In D. Herrmann, M. Johnson, C. McEvoy, C. Hertzog, & P. Hertel (Eds.), *Basic and applied memory: Research on practical aspects of memory.* Hillsdale, NJ: Erlbaum.

Cavanaugh, J. C., Feldman, J. M., & Hertzog, C. (1995). Memory beliefs as social cognition: A reconceptualization of what memory questionnaires assess. Unpublished manuscript, University of Delaware, Newark.

Cavanaugh, J. C., & Green, E. E. (1990). I believe, therefore I can: Personal beliefs and memory aging. In E. A. Lovelace (Ed.), *Aging and cognition: Mental processes, self-awareness, and interventions* (pp. 189–230). Amsterdam: North-Holland.

Cavanaugh, J. C., & Morton, K. R. (1988). Older adults' attributions about everyday memory. In M. M. Gruneberg & P. Morris (Eds.), *Practical aspects of memory: Current research and issues* (vol. 1, pp. 209–214). Chichester, U.K.: Wiley.

Cavanaugh, J. C., & Morton, K. R. (1989). Contextualism, naturalistic inquiry, and the need for new science: A rethinking of childhood sexual abuse and everyday memory aging. In D. A. Kramer & M. Bopp (Eds.), *Transformation in clinical and developmental psychology* (pp. 89–114). New York: Springer.

Cavanaugh, J. C., & Perlmutter, M. (1982). Metamemory: A critical examination. *Child Development, 53,* 11–28.

Devolder, P. A., Brigham, M. C., & Pressley, M. (1990). Memory performance awareness in younger and older adults. *Psychology and Aging, 5,* 291–303.

Dixon, R. A., & Hultsch, D. F. (1983). Structure and development of metamemory in adulthood. *Journal of Gerontology, 38,* 682–688.

Dixon, R. A., Hultsch, D. F., & Hertzog, C. (1988). The Metamemory in Adulthood (MIA) questionnaire. *Psychopharmacology Bulletin, 24,* 671–688.

Dweck, C. S., & Leggett, E. L. (1988). A social-cognitive approach to motivation and personality. *Psychological Review, 95,* 256–273.

Elliott, E., & Lachman, M. E. (1989). Enhancing memory by modifying control beliefs, attributions, and performance goals in the elderly. In P. S. Fry (Ed.), *Psychological perspectives of helplessness and control in the elderly* (pp. 339–367). Amsterdam: North-Holland.

Gilewski, M. J., & Zelinski, E. M. (1988). Memory Functioning Questionnaire (MFQ). *Psychopharmacology Bulletin, 24,* 665–670.

Gilewski, M. J., Zelinski, E. M., & Schaie, K. W. (1990). The Memory Functioning Questionnaire for assessment of memory complaints in adulthood and old age. *Psychology and Aging, 5,* 482–490.

Hertzog, C., Dixon, R. A., & Hultsch, D. F. (1990a). Metamemory in adulthood: Differentiating knowledge, belief, and behavior. In T. M. Hess (Ed.), *Aging and cognition: Knowledge organization and utilization* (pp. 161–212). Amsterdam: North-Holland.

Hertzog, C., Dixon, R. A., & Hultsch, D. F. (1990b). Relationships between metamemory, memory predictions, and memory task performance. *Psychology and Aging, 5,* 215–233.

Hertzog, C., Dixon, R. A., Schulenberg, J., & Hultsch, D. F. (1987). On the differentiation of memory beliefs from memory knowledge: The factor structure of the Metamemory in Adulthood scale. *Experimental Aging Research, 13,* 101–107.

Hertzog, C., Hultsch, D. F., & Dixon, R. A. (1989). Evidence for the convergent validity of two self-report metamemory questionnaires. *Developmental Psychology, 25,* 687–700.

Hertzog, C., Saylor, L. L., Fleece, A. M., & Dixon, R. A. (1994). Metamemory and aging: Relations between predicted, actual, and perceived memory task performance. *Aging and Cognition, 1,* 203–237.

Hultsch, D. F., Hertzog, C., & Dixon, R. A. (1987). Age differences in metamemory: Resolving the inconsistencies. *Canadian Journal of Psychology, 41,* 193–208.

Hultsch, D. F., Hertzog, C., Dixon, R. A., & Davidson, H. (1988). Memory self-knowledge and self-efficacy in the aged. In M. L. Howe & C. J. Brainerd (Eds.), *Cognitive development in adulthood: Progress in cognitive development research* (pp. 65–92). New York: Springer.

Lachman, M. E., & Dick, L. (1987). Does memory training influence self-conceptions of memory aging? Paper presented at the meeting of the Gerontological Society of America, Washington, DC, November.

Lachman, M. E., Weaver, S. L., Bandura, M., Elliott, E., & Lewkowicz, C. J. (1992). Improving memory and control beliefs through cognitive restructuring and self-generated strategies. *Journal of Gerontology: Psychological Sciences, 47,* P293–P299.

Langer, E. J., & Rodin, J. (1976). The effects of choice and enhanced personal responsibility for the aged: A field experiment in an institutional setting. *Journal of Personality and Social Psychology, 34,* 191–198.

Lovelace, E. A. (1990). Aging and metacognitions concerning memory function. In E. A. Lovelace (Ed.), *Aging and cognition: Mental process, self-awareness and interventions* (pp. 157–188). Amsterdam: North-Holland.

Markus, H. (1977). Self-schemata and processing information about the self. *Journal of Personality and Social Psychology, 35,* 63–78.

Mathieu, J. E., Martineau, J. W., & Tannenbaum, S. I. (1993). Individual and situational influences on the development of self-efficacy: Implications for training effectiveness. *Personnel Psychology, 46,* 125–147.

Ozer, E. M., & Bandura, A. (1990). Mechanisms governing empowerment effects: A self-efficacy analysis. *Journal of Personality and Social Psychology, 58,* 472–486.

Perlmutter, M. (1978). What is memory aging the aging of? *Developmental Psychology, 14,* 330–345.

Rabinowitz, J. C., Ackerman, B, P., Craik, F. I. M., & Hinchley, J. L. (1982). Aging and metamemory: The roles of relatedness and imagery. *Journal of Gerontology, 37,* 688–695.

Rebok, G. W., & Balcerak, L. J. (1989). Memory self-efficacy and performance differences in young and old adults: The effect of mnemonic training. *Developmental Psychology, 25,* 714–721.

Rodin, J., & Langer, E. J. (1980). Aging labels: The decline of control and the fall of self-esteem. *Journal of Social Issues, 36,* 12–29.

Schunk, D. H. (1990). Goal setting and self-efficacy during self-regulated learning. *Educational Psychologist, 25,* 71–86.

Timko, C., & Rodin, J. (1985). Staff-patient relationships in nursing homes: Sources of conflict and rehabilitation potential. *Rehabilitation Psychology, 30,* 93–108.

Verhaeghen, P., Marcoen, A., & Goossens, L. (1992). Improving memory performance in the aged through mnemonic training: A meta-analytic study. *Psychology and Aging, 7,* 242–251.

Weaver, S. L., & Lachman, M. E. (1989). Enhancing memory self-conceptions and strategies in young and old adults. Paper presented at the meeting of the American Psychological Association, New Orleans, August.

Welch, D. C., & West, R. L. (1995). Self-efficacy and mastery: Its application to issues of environmental control, cognition, and aging. *Developmental Review, 15,* 150–171.

West, R. L. (1995). Compensatory strategies for age-associated memory impairment. In A. D. Baddeley, B. A. Wilson, & F. Watts (Eds.), *Handbook of memory disorders* (pp. 481–500). London: Wiley.

West, R. L., & Berry, J. M. (1994). Age declines in memory self-efficacy: General or limited to particular tasks and measures? In J. D. Sinnott (Ed.), *Handbook of adult lifespan learning* (pp. 426–445) Westport, CT: Greenwood.

West, R. L., Bramblett, J. P., Welch, D. C., & Bellott, B. (1992). Memory training for the elderly: An intervention designed to improve memory skills and memory self-evaluation. Paper presented at the Fourth Biennial Cognitive Aging Conference, Atlanta, April.

West, R. L., Dennehy-Basile, D., & Norris, M. P. (1995). Memory self-evaluation: The effects of age and experience. Unpublished manuscript, University of Florida, Gainesville.

Wood, R., & Bandura, A. (1989). Impact of conceptions of ability on self-regulatory mechanisms and complex decision making. *Journal of Personality and Social Psychology, 56,* 407–415.

Yates, F. A. (1966). *The art of memory.* London: Routledge and Kegan Paul.

Zelinski, E. M., Gilewski, M. J., & Anthony-Bergstone, C. R. (1990). Memory Functioning Questionnaire: Concurrent validity with memory performance and self-reported memory failures. *Psychology and Aging, 5,* 388–399.

526

Subject Index

Cancer, 112

Candidate variables, 110, 112

CANS (central auditory nervous system) hypothesis, 141

Cardiovascular disease (CVD), 110, 112, 307

Casual attributions, 468, 470, 472, 473, 478

Category-based processing, 456–457, 468

Cause-and-effect constructs, 74

Central auditory nervous system (CANS) hypothesis, 141

Central auditory pathway, 139, 145

Central nervous system (CNS), 103, 104, 109, 110, 112

  information processing in, 171

Central vision (*see* Foveal vision)

Cerebral cortex, 139

CFF (critical flicker frequency), 133

Chaos and complexity theory, 361, 367

Chess, 433–435, 439, 450

Chronic illness, 110, 112, 306, 308, 310, 315

Chronological age, 80, 83–84, 103, 105, 108, 109, 113

Cluster analysis, 78, 101, 113

CNS (*see* Central nervous system)

Cochlea, 137, 138

Cochlear membrane, 138

COG (congruence), 497

Cognitive aging, 3–4, 10, 27, 33, 35, 36

  and attention (*see* Attention)

  auditory acuity and, 109, 153

  contextual approach to, 49–53, 387–416

  critical approach to, 17–20

  cross-sectional studies of (*see* Cross-sectional studies)

  dependency with, 5, 7

  depiction of, 3

    (*See also* Stereotypes)

  differential approach to, 29–32, 44–46, 54

  distinguishing reliability from stability, 93–94

  environment and (*see* Environment)

  experience and (*see* Experience; Expertise)

  experimental approaches to, 46–49, 94–101

  explanations of, 103–114

  extrinsic causes of, 104, 110–111

  health and (*see* Health)

  identifying average differences in, 83–88

  identifying intraindividual change in, 89

  individual differences in, 4, 13–14, 18, 102–103, 479

  intelligence and, 4, 8

    (*See also* Intelligence)

  intrinsic causes of, 104–110

  job productivity with, 5

  longitudinal studies of (*see* Longitudinal studies)

  measurement of change with, 90–91

  memory and, 4–9, 36, 192–214

    (*See also* Memory)

  method and theory interdependence in, 40–44

  multidimensional/multidirectional perspective of, 9, 11–13, 16, 33–34, 45, 52–53, 168, 454

  organismic approach to, 29, 30, 44, 53–54

  performance and, 72, 85, 94

  phenomena of, 27

    (*See also* Attention; Reasoning, Remembering)

  postformal thought for, implications of, 367–368

  problem solving and, 4, 6, 9

    (*See also* Problem solving)

  psychometric intelligence (*see* Psychometric intelligence)

  research on, 40, 66–115

  research design for (*see* Research design, principles of)

  retirement and, 4, 5, 12, 80, 396

  self-concept in, 463

  as social issue, 4–7

  stereotypes of (*see* Stereotypes)

  studies of, 7–11

    issues in, 12–14

    (*See also* Cross-sectional studies; Longitudinal studies)

  theories of, 44–54, 262–264

    implications for, 241–243

  types of changes with, 89–90

  unidimensional perspective of, 8, 9, 12, 13

  visual acuity and (*see* Visual acuity)

  (*See also* Cognitive development, adult)

Cognitive aging literature, 36, 165, 167, 168, 170, 172, 175, 177, 182, 229, 280–281, 468, 490

  review of, 231–248

Cognitive appraisal, emotion and, 471–473

Cognitive development:

  differential approaches to, 68, 78, 101–103

  normative influences on, 30–31

  Piagetian theory of (*see* Piagetian theory of cognitive development)

  research on, 4, 11–12, 66–115

  skill acquisition with (*see* Skill acquisition)

  theoretical issues in, 4, 25–55

    consistency vs. variability, 39–40

    directionality and dimensionality, 32–34

    gains vs. losses vs. maintenance, 36–39, 46

    plasticity and reversibility, 34–36

    universal vs. differential, 30–32

    variability vs. uniformity, 34, 39–40

  universality of, 30–35, 49, 53

  variables in, 31

Cognitive mechanisms, 94–101